Microsoft® FrontPage
Version 2002
INSIDE OUT

D0127940

The CD that helps you put your software to work!

Dig in—for the work-ready tools and resources that help you go way beyond just using FrontPage. You'll conquer it! Just like the INSIDE OUT book, we've designed your INSIDE OUT CD to be both comprehensive and supremely easy to use. You'll find FrontPage-focused bonus content and sample chapters that take your learning experience even deeper. The dozens of must-have tools, utilities, and add-ins have all been tested against final FrontPage 2002 code—not beta. You get essential links to online software updates, product support, and more—direct from the Microsoft Office team. And, with the CD's intuitive HTML interface, you'll always know exactly where you are and what else you can do!

Your Inside Out CD features:

- **Bonus Content**—focused reference and learning material to help you drill even deeper into FrontPage features and capabilities

- **Microsoft and Third-Party Add-ins**—dozens of must-have tools, utilities, demos, and trial software

- **Office Tools on the Web**—complete descriptions and links to official Microsoft Office resources on line

- **Author Extras**—sample Web site, source code, and other valuable resources

- **More INSIDE OUT Books**—sample chapters from INSIDE OUT books for other Office XP applications

- **Complete Microsoft Press eBook**—the complete MICROSOFT FRONTPAGE VERSION 2002 INSIDE OUT book in easy-search electronic format

Want to learn more? Read on for full details, including System Requirements (last page of this section).

Microsoft
FrontPage
Version 2002
INSIDE
OUT

Bonus Content

Get nearly 300 pages of additional content for FrontPage—more learning than we could pack between the book's two covers! Here's what you'll find on the CD; you can also see these topics in the book's table of contents or either of its indexes.

Includes:

Part XIII Bonus Application Topics
Ch. 39: Discussion Sites and Self-Registration
Ch. 40: Processing Databases with Active Server Pages

Part XIV Working Directly with Code
Ch. 41: Working with HTML Code
Ch. 42: Working with Script Code
Ch. 43: Visual Basic® for Applications

Part XV Customizing Your Copy of FrontPage
Ch. 44: Configuring FrontPage Options
Ch. 45: Configuring Page Creation Options
Ch. 46: Configuring Web Options

Appendixes
Appendix A: Toolbar reference
Appendix B: Introducing Active Server Page Objects
Appendix C: Introducing ActiveX® Data Objects
Appendix D: Configuring ODBC Data Sources

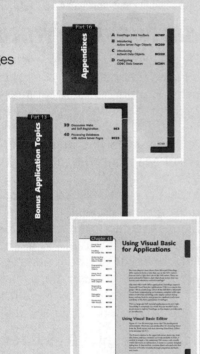

NOTE

For your convenience, you can access the bonus content in two formats:

■ **eBook**—Install the content in Microsoft Press electronic book format to perform rapid full-text searches.

■ **PDF**—Want to print out pages, or find a topic using the printed book's table of contents or index? Use PDF format.

Microsoft Add-Ins

Get Microsoft add-ins and tools for FrontPage—straight from the source—including several developed specifically for Version 2002.

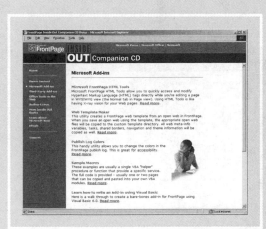

Includes:

- **HTML Tool Kit**—quickly access and modify HTML tags directly in page view
- **Web Template Maker**—copy any open site as a reusable template
- **Code Snippets**—get loads of VBA "helpers" to copy and paste into your own VBA modules
- **Microsoft Office Visual Keyboard**—type in multiple languages on the same computer by using an on-screen keyboard for other languages
- **Microsoft Visio® Auto-Demos**—use customizable auto-demos to see how to put Visio diagramming software to work on your next project

Third-Party Utilities, Demos, and Trials

All the third-party add-ins on this CD have been developed for and tested against FrontPage 2002. In this section, you'll find all the details you need about each tool—including a full description, application size, system requirements, and installation instructions.

Includes:

- **HiSoftware's metaPackager™**—encapsulate your files in *pure* XML so they're easy to index and manage
- **Com City's SalesCart**—add shopping cart capabilities to your site the easy way
- **HiSoftware's Hi-Visibility™**—this tool reads the meta tags from FrontPage files, analyzes their content, makes suggestions for better search-engine placement, and then submits your site to the selected engines
- **DPA Chameleon**—change the color, saturation, and brightness of your theme graphics in seconds
- **Pineapplesoft GraphicsButton**—Java applet works like a Submit push button but displays an image instead of text on the face of the button

Office Tools on the Web

Here you'll find ready links to the most helpful and informative online resources for Office XP, direct from Microsoft. Find out exactly how each site can help you get your work done—then click and go!

Office Assistance Center

Get help using Office products with articles, tips, and monthly spotlights. Learn more about working with documents, data, and graphics; using e-mail and collaboration features; creating presentations and Web pages; and using everyday time savers.

Office eServices

Use these Web services to get the most from Office. Learn how to store and share files on the Web; build and host Web sites; find communication services, language translation, learning and reference, and online postage resources; tune up your computer; and much more!

Office Product Updates

Obtain recommended and critical updates to enhance your Office XP experience.

Office Download Center

Download updates, add-ins, viewers, and more from the Office Download Center. Use the online search tool to find the utilities to help you work faster and smarter.

Design Gallery Live

Pick out clip art or photos for your Office project from this huge royalty-free selection. New items are constantly added to meet your needs. The advanced search facility makes finding the right artwork quick and easy.

Microsoft Office Template Gallery

Instead of starting from scratch, download a template from Template Gallery. From calendars to business cards, marketing material, and legal documents, Template Gallery offers hundreds of professionally authored and formatted documents for Microsoft Office.

Online Troubleshooters

Microsoft has developed Office XP online troubleshooters to help you solve problems on the fly. Access them using the links on the CD—and get the diagnostic and problem-solving information you need.

Microsoft
FrontPage®
Version 2002
INSIDE
OUT

Author Extras

Here's where your INSIDE OUT author went the extra mile: great sample Web pages on CD for you to take apart and study! It's an excellent way to make the examples used inside the book come to life on your PC. The Web samples illustrate a number of FrontPage features in action, allow you to tinker with them, and can help jump-start your own projects.

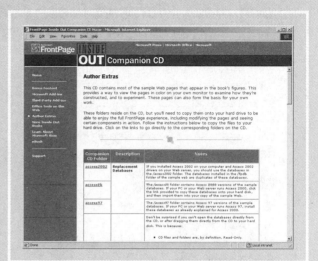

Includes:

- All the sample Web pages that appear in the book, including associated files
- Sample Microsoft Access databases
- A collection of FrontPage macros, source code, and custom components to use in your own Web sites

More Inside Out Books

The INSIDE OUT series from Microsoft Press delivers comprehensive reference on the Office XP suite of applications. On this CD, you'll find sample chapters from the companion titles listed below, along with details about the entire line of books:

- Microsoft Office XP Inside Out
- Microsoft Outlook® Version 2002 Inside Out
- Microsoft Excel Version 2002 Inside Out
- Microsoft Word Version 2002 Inside Out

Microsoft
FrontPage®
Version 2002
INSIDE
OUT

Complete Microsoft Press eBook

You get the entire MICROSOFT FRONTPAGE VERSION 2002 INSIDE OUT book on CD—along with the bonus content and sample chapters from other INSIDE OUT books—as searchable electronic books. These eBooks install quickly and easily on your computer (see System Requirements for details) and enable rapid full-text search.

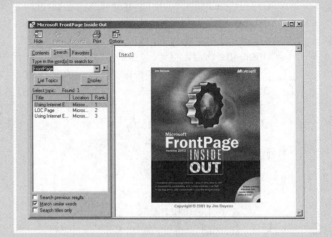

Features:

- Super-fast HTML full-text search
- Full-size graphics and screen shots
- Copy, paste, and *print* functions
- Bookmarking capabilities
- A saved history of every file viewed during a session

CD Minimum System Requirements

- Microsoft Windows® 95 or higher operating system (including Windows 98, Windows Millennium Edition, Windows NT® 4.0 with Service Pack 3, Windows 2000, and Windows XP)
- 266-MHz or higher Pentium-compatible CPU
- 64 megabytes (MB) RAM
- 8X CD-ROM drive or faster
- 31 MB of free hard disk space (to install the eBook)
- 800 x 600 with high color (16-bit) display settings
- Microsoft Windows compatible sound card and speakers (for Visio demos only)
- Microsoft Internet Explorer 4.0 or higher
- Microsoft Mouse or compatible pointing device

NOTE

System Requirements may be higher for the add-ins available on the CD. Individual add-in system requirements are specified on the CD. An Internet connection is necessary to access the hyperlinks in the Office Tools on the Web section. Connect time charges may apply.

Jim Buyens
Popular author and Microsoft FrontPage expert

Microsoft

Microsoft®
FrontPage®
Version 2002

INSIDE
OUT

- **Hundreds of timesaving solutions—easy to find, easy to use!**

- **Get tips, tricks, and workarounds, plus the straight scoop**

- **Work smarter—and take your FrontPage experience to the next level**

PUBLISHED BY
Microsoft Press
A Division of Microsoft Corporation
One Microsoft Way
Redmond, Washington 98052-6399

Library of Congress Cataloging-in-Publication Data
Buyens, Jim.
    Microsoft FrontPage Version 2002 Inside Out / Jim Buyens.
        p. cm.
    Includes index.
    ISBN 0-7356-1284-6
    1. Microsoft FrontPage.   2. Web site development--Computer programs.   I. Title.

    TK5105.8885.M53 B87   2001
    005.7'2--dc21   2001030325

Printed and bound in the United States of America.

1 2 3 4 5 6 7 8 9   QWT   6 5 4 3 2 1

Distributed in Canada by Penguin Books Canada Limited.

A CIP catalogue record for this book is available from the British Library.

Microsoft Press books are available through booksellers and distributors worldwide. For further information about international editions, contact your local Microsoft Corporation office or contact Microsoft
Press International directly at fax (425) 936-7329. Visit our Web site at mspress.microsoft.com. Send
comments to *mspinput@microsoft.com*.

Active Directory, ActiveMovie, ActiveX, bCentral, FoxPro, FrontPage, JScript, Microsoft, Microsoft Press,
MoneyCentral, MS-DOS, MSDN, MSN, Outlook, PhotoDraw, PivotTable, PowerPoint, SharePoint,
SourceSafe, Verdana, Visio, Visual Basic, Visual InterDev, Visual SourceSafe, Visual Studio, WebBot,
Webdings, WebTV, Win32, Windows, Windows Media, and Windows NT are either registered trade-
marks or trademarks of Microsoft Corporation in the United States and/or other countries. Other product
and company names mentioned herein may be the trademarks of their respective owners.

The example companies, organizations, products, domain names, e-mail addresses, logos, people, places,
and events depicted herein are fictitious. No association with any real company, organization, product,
domain name, e-mail address, logo, person, place, or event is intended or should be inferred.

Acquisitions Editor: Kong Cheung
Project Editor: Kristen Weatherby
Series Editor: Sandra Haynes

Body Part No. X08-05014

This book is dedicated to the homeless mentally ill persons of America. Why do we lavish health care dollars on victims of other, less debilitating illnesses while condemning these unfortunates to the streets and gutters?

Contents At A Glance

Contents At A Glance

Contents At A Glance

Table of Contents

Chapter 3

Managing Web Sites

61

Part 3
Creating Web Sites Automatically   179

Chapter 7
Managing
Web Structure with Navigation View   181

newfeature!

Chapter 8
Creating Web Sites
with Templates and Wizards   215

Chapter 11
Adding and Formatting Pictures   305

Chapter 12
Building Hyperlinks   355

Part 5
Publishing and Maintaining Web Sites
385

Chapter 13
Publishing Your FrontPage-Based Web
387

newfeature!

Chapter 14
Keeping Your Web Up-to-Date
409

Chapter 33

Accessing Databases with FrontPage 915

Part 11

Collaborating with Teams and Workgroups 961

Chapter 34

Managing Design Teams 963

Chapter 37
Installing and Configuring a Web Server   1049

Chapter 38
Understanding the FrontPage Server Extensions   1081

newfeature!

on the CD Part 13

Bonus Application Topics BC1

Chapter 39

Discussion Webs and Self-Registration BC3

Chapter 40

Processing Databases
with Active Server Pages BC25

on the CD Part 14

Working Directly with Code   BC53

Chapter 41

Working with HTML Code   BC55

Chapter 42

Working with Script Code   BC67

on the CD Part 15
Customizing Your Copy of FrontPage   BC135

Appendix B

Introducing Active Server Page Objects   BC209

Appendix C

Introducing ActiveX Data Objects   BC223

Appendix D

Configuring ODBC Data Sources   BC261

Acknowledgments

Many thanks to my wife, Connie, and my children, Lorrill, Justin, and Lynessa, for their support and for putting up with all the time I spent writing this book. Thanks as well to my parents, my brothers, and their families: Harold, Marcella, Ruth, Dave, Connie, Michael, Steven, Rick, Jenny, Matt, and Claire. What a bunch we are.

At Microsoft Press, thanks to Kong Cheung, who set up the business details, Laura Sackerman, the managing editor, and Kristen Weatherby, the project editor, for their ceaseless confidence, encouragement, and assistance.

Thanks to the team at Online Training Solutions, Inc., without whose tireless efforts and attention to detail a book such as this would be impossible. Through copy edit, technical review, page composition, and final packaging, working with these professionals has been as much a joy as such an effort can be.

For his assistance on various chapters throughout the book, sincere thanks to Brett Polonsky. His efforts were key in finishing the book on schedule.

Thanks to Interland, Inc., and in particular to Ken Gavranovic and Jason Peoples, for their assistance in providing the *www.interlacken.com* Web site.

Most of all, thanks to you, the readers, who make an effort such as this both possible and worthwhile. I hope the book meets your expectations and that we meet again.

We'd Like to Hear from You!

Our goal at Microsoft Press is to create books that help you find the information you need to get the most out of your software.

The INSIDE OUT series was created with you in mind. As part of an effort to ensure that we're creating the best, most useful books we can, we talked to our customers and asked them to tell us what they need from a Microsoft Press series. Help us continue to help you. Let us know what you like about this book and what we can do to make it better. When you write, please include the title and author of this book in your e-mail, as well as your name and contact information. We look forward to hearing from you.

How to Reach Us

E-mail: nsideout@microsoft.com
Mail: Inside Out Series Editor
            Microsoft Press
            One Microsoft Way
            Redmond, WA 98052

Note: Unfortunately, we can't provide support for any software problems you might experience. Please go to http://support.microsoft.com *for help with any software issues.*

Conventions and Features Used in This Book

This book uses special text and design conventions to make it easier for you to find the information you need.

Text Conventions

Convention	Meaning
Abbreviated menu commands	For your convenience, this book uses abbreviated menu commands. For example, "Choose Tools, Track Changes, Highlight Changes" means that you should click the Tools menu, point to Track Changes, and select the Highlight Changes command.
Boldface type	**Boldface** type is used to indicate text that you enter or type.
Initial Capital Letters	The first letters of the names of menus, dialog boxes, dialog box elements, and commands are capitalized. Example: the Save As dialog box.
Italicized type	*Italicized* type is used to indicate new terms.
Plus sign (+) in text	Keyboard shortcuts are indicated by a plus sign (+) separating two key names. For example, Ctrl+Alt+Delete means that you press the Ctrl, Alt, and Delete keys at the same time.

Design Conventions

newfeature!

This text identifies a new or significantly updated feature in this version of the software.

InsideOut

These are the book's signature tips. In these tips, you'll find get the straight scoop on what's going on with the software—inside information on why a feature works the way it does. You'll also find handy workarounds to deal with some of these software problems.

tip Tips provide helpful hints, timesaving tricks, or alternative procedures related to the task being discussed.

Troubleshooting

Look for these sidebars to find solutions to common problems you might encounter. Troubleshooting sidebars appear next to related information in the chapters. You can also use the Troubleshooting Topics index at the back of the book to look up problems by topic.

Cross-references point you to other locations in the book that offer additional information on the topic being discussed.

 This icon indicates sample files or text found on the companion CD.

caution Cautions identify potential problems that you should look out for when you're completing a task or problems that you must address before you can complete a task.

note Notes offer additional information related to the task being discussed.

Sidebar

The sidebars sprinkled throughout these chapters provide ancillary information on the topic being discussed. Go to sidebars to learn more about the technology or a feature.

Part 1

Introducing Microsoft FrontPage 2002

Chapter 1

Presenting Microsoft FrontPage 2002

The World Wide Web has become the predominant electronic publishing medium on the planet. Once considered an obscure technical resource, the Internet now receives prominent publicity at sporting events, in presidential debates, in television commercials, and in print advertising and marketing materials everywhere. Without the Web, most people don't consider themselves well connected.

Although people generally start out as consumers of the Web, many of them eventually want to be contributors as well. People and organizations of every type are using Web technology to represent themselves, attract others, disseminate information, and conduct business of all kinds.

The creators of Web pages and entire Web sites are as diverse as the Web itself. Some have never used a computer before, whereas others are long-time computer experts. Some lean toward the artistic side of Web design, and some tend toward details of implementation. Some have no idea of what constitutes a computer network, and some are experienced Internet specialists.

This book is aimed at intermediate to advanced computer users with an interest in creating individual Web pages and entire Web sites. These readers might need a brief introduction to the mindset of a new program or feature, but seldom need detailed help with fundamentals. They often learn to use software very quickly by trial and error. When it comes to learning basic operations, they find detailed step-by-step instructions simplistic, time-consuming, and frustrating. Questions and

3

problems arise randomly as they explore more and more features of the software and need an accurate reference to explain details and resolve problems. This book provides those introductions and references.

Using This Book

You can, of course, be a proficient computer user and still be new to Microsoft FrontPage. The first few chapters, therefore, present a whirlwind tour of basic FrontPage features that will get you started with the proper mindset. After that, you'll probably read the book randomly on a sort of "need to know" basis. The index and table of contents will guide you to the specific information you need.

Wherever possible, multiple ways of doing the same thing appear consecutively in the text. This should make it easier to contrast, compare, and pick the right tool for the job at hand.

If you're not an intermediate or advanced computer user, or if you just prefer a bit of hand holding, a book such as *Microsoft FrontPage Version 2002 Step by Step* might better suit your needs. Then, when you start needing help with those pesky details, *Microsoft FrontPage Version 2002 Inside Out* will be waiting for you. The porch light is always on.

FrontPage Overview

As the Web itself has moved from obscurity into the mainstream, so has its authoring community. Many new Web designers have neither interest nor aptitude for coding Hypertext Markup Language (HTML)—the stuff of which Web pages are actually made—but expect to create Web pages with high-level tools as sophisticated and easy to use as their favorite word-processing, spreadsheet, or desktop-publishing applications. This facility is exactly what Microsoft FrontPage provides.

The Web's basic operating approach is quite simple. It involves the exchange of information between a computer that requests information, often called a *client*, and one that delivers the information, usually called a *server*. The client's software, called a *browser*, requests Web pages from a server located somewhere on a network, whether it's a corporate intranet or the global World Wide Web. The browser identifies the requested file by its name in the server's file system and requests that the server send it. After receiving the requested file, the browser displays it to the Web visitor. If the Web page calls for additional files as components—graphics, sound, and video files, for example—the browser requests them using the same mechanism.

The designer of a Web page can designate areas of text, pictures, and other objects as *hyperlinks*. Each hyperlink specifies the network address and file name of another Web page. Clicking a hyperlink instructs the browser to retrieve and display the associated page or file.

Chapter 1: Presenting Microsoft FrontPage 2002

At the most fundamental level, browsers expect Web pages to be coded in HTML. HTML consists of plain text "marked up" with tags such as *<p>* for new paragraph, *<ul>* for unnumbered list, and *<li>* for list item. This is a format anyone can produce using a simple text editor, such as the Microsoft Notepad accessory that comes with Microsoft Windows.

The ability to produce Web pages using only simple, universally available tools has been a key factor in the growth of the Web itself and remains a common practice. For many people, though, coding Web pages by hand presents serious obstacles, such as the following:

- Coding Web pages manually requires intimate knowledge of a variety of markup commands.

- Lack of a graphical interface provides no visual feedback of what the Web page will look like to the Web visitor and offers no visual cues regarding commands and options.

- The relationships among text, pictures, and other kinds of files in a typical collection of Web pages are highly detailed and complex. Errors result if a single file is misnamed or misplaced. Initially creating such a structure is difficult, but maintaining it over time can be daunting.

FrontPage 2002 provides a rich variety of features to relieve Web page creators of these problems and others. In short, FrontPage is a tool that provides everything you need to create and manage your Web site, whether you're designing a personal Web page or a corporate Internet or intranet site.

Editing Web Pages

At some fundamental level, word-processed documents, spreadsheets, slide-show presentations, and database reports are all documents. Nevertheless, each of these types represents a different mind-set and requires a different program to handle its unique requirements. So it is with Web pages.

The basic unit of Web content is the *Web page*. Physically, Web pages consist of plain ASCII text interspersed with *markup tags* that control structure and format. Most Web pages use no more than twenty or thirty HTML tags. Because these tags are fairly easy to memorize, many Web designers create pages using nothing more than a text editor. If this works for you, great—FrontPage will support you every step of the way. If you'd rather bypass the mechanics of HTML and just create pages visually on your screen, FrontPage provides a great What You See Is What You Get (WYSIWYG) editor.

The next three figures illustrate these points visually. Figure 1-1 shows FrontPage editing a Web page in WYSIWYG view, Figure 1-2 shows FrontPage editing the same page in HTML view, and Figure 1-3 shows Microsoft Internet Explorer displaying the same page.

note FrontPage will either format HTML the way you like it or preserve the HTML formatting of any page you open. The choice is yours.

 on the CD For more information about editing HTML code directly, refer to Chapter 41, "Working with HTML Code," in the Bonus Content on the Companion CD.

Figure 1-2 shows FrontPage displaying the HTML code that actually creates the Web page shown in Figure 1-1. As you can see, for the vast majority of Web page creators, editing with FrontPage offers tremendous advantages over editing raw HTML code with an ordinary text editor.

If you compare Figure 1-1 and Figure 1-3, it's apparent that FrontPage also displays certain structural elements that the browser doesn't. FrontPage, by design, displays invisible table borders, invisible line breaks, and in some cases even invisible colors, all as aids to editing. Even though the Web visitor won't see these elements, *you* need to, in order to edit them.

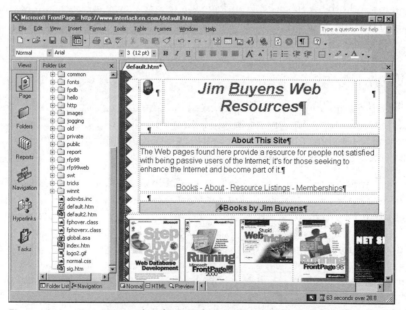

Figure 1-1. FrontPage closely matches Internet Explorer's display of a Web page (see Figure 1-3) and also provides a great assortment of editing commands and tools. Note that the Normal view tab is selected at the bottom of the screen.

Chapter 1: Presenting Microsoft FrontPage 2002

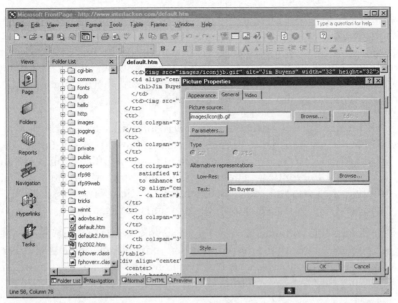

Figure 1-2. Select the HTML tab at the bottom of the Editor screen to view the HTML behind the current page. You can edit the code directly and then return to Normal view to see the results.

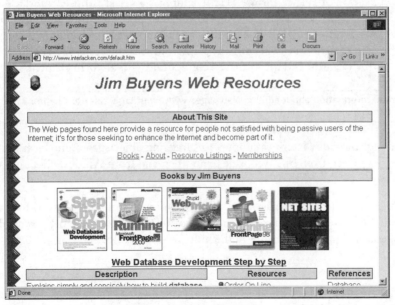

Figure 1-3. Internet Explorer displays the Web page edited in Figure 1-1.

The FrontPage 2002 user interface follows all the style and organizational conventions of other Microsoft Office XP applications. If you're familiar with other Office applications, most of the commands and toolbar icons in FrontPage 2002 are just as you expect them to be. In addition to similarities such as overall appearance, menu organization, icon assignment, dialog box similarity, keyboard shortcuts, and drag-and-drop operations, FrontPage also supports the following:

- **File format conversion to and from Microsoft Office formats and HTML.** These capabilities include inserting entire Microsoft Office files into Web pages as well as copying content from an Office application and pasting it into FrontPage. For example, if you copy a Microsoft Word table, a range of Microsoft Excel cells, or a block of Microsoft Access table records, FrontPage pastes any of them as an HTML table.

- **Uniform table commands.** The FrontPage procedures for creating and editing tables are, to the maximum extent possible, the same as in other Office applications. This single feature alone provides an order of magnitude improvement over editing HTML with a text editor.

- **Uniform layout commands.** Wherever possible, FrontPage uses familiar Office commands and dialog boxes for aligning objects, setting fonts, and controlling bullets and other paragraph properties.

- **Creation of HTML forms.** HTML supports a variety of user interface objects such as text boxes, drop-down lists, option buttons, and push buttons. A grouping of such elements is called an *HTML form*. FrontPage provides a WYSIWYG, drag and drop environment for designing HTML forms, form Wizards, and menu-driven configuration of all form elements.

> For more information about editing Web pages with FrontPage, refer to Chapter 2, "Editing Web Pages."

FrontPage provides extensive support for dragging objects from one location on a page to another, from one Web page to another, and from Windows Explorer onto Web pages.

All in all, producing Web pages is a task with unique requirements and challenges. As you'll discover from this book, FrontPage 2002 provides the most powerful and most compelling set of features in the industry for creating not only Web pages but entire sites.

Managing Web Sites

Each Web page contains a relatively small amount of content. Hyperlinks provide easy navigation from one page to another and unify groups of pages into a cohesive whole. Nevertheless, the information that most applications would keep in a single file—such

Chapter 1: Presenting Microsoft FrontPage 2002

as a Word document, Microsoft PowerPoint presentation, or Access database—
generally resides in dozens or hundreds of Web pages. Keeping all these pages
properly arranged can be a real challenge. Keeping all the hyperlinks up-to-date
can be even worse.

> **note** Short Web pages minimize transmission time and maximize the amount of information
> the Web visitor can see without scrolling up and down the browser window.

Just to complicate the situation, most Web pages have several constituent parts, and
each of these parts is a separate file. To load a Web page, the browser first requests the
file name that appears in the URL, then any files (such as frames and pictures) specified within that file, then any files specified within those files, and so forth. As a result,
representing a single technical manual, presentation, or sales catalog on the Web might
require dozens, hundreds, or thousands of files.

> **note** A *Uniform Resource Locator* (URL) identifies each page on the World Wide Web. In
> the URL *http://www.interlacken.com/fp-iso/default.htm*, *http* identifies the retrieval
> method (Hypertext Transfer Protocol), *www.interlacken.com* identifies the Web
> server, *fp-iso* identifies a folder path on that server, and *default.htm* identifies a file
> in that folder.

Dealing with all the files that make up a Web site presents three kinds of challenges:

- The first challenge relates to changing linked objects. Changes you make to
  one file might require changes to other files that refer to it. If you change a
  file's name or location, for example, you must correspondingly change
  every hyperlink that refers to it. If you have half a dozen files that link
  to the file */common/contacts.htm*, and then you rename *contacts.htm* to
  email.htm, you must locate all six files and change the hyperlinks. The same
  is true for the names of pictures. In addition, changing the size of a picture
  often requires changing the height and width attributes in every file that
  uses that picture.

- The second challenge relates to uniformity. In virtually every case, all Web
  pages in the same body of content should share a common appearance.
  They should use the same general page layout, the same fonts, the same
  colors, the same hyperlink conventions, and so forth. Even the most
  fastidious Web designers find maintaining this level of consistency
  extremely difficult, especially if the work spans a long period of time.

- The third challenge relates to changes that should apply to more than one
  page. All sites change their appearance from time to time and when this
  happens, updating dozens, hundreds, or thousands of pages all at once can
  be a daunting task.

Fortunately, all these challenges involve repetitive work on computer files and are therefore amenable to software solutions. However, this is only possible if all the files to be processed are somehow grouped into a common area. In the case of FrontPage, this common area is called a *FrontPage-based Web*. Physically, a FrontPage-based Web is a designated folder tree in your computer's file system or on a Web server.

A FrontPage-based Web that resides on your local disk or a network location you access by file sharing is said to be *disk-based*. To open such a Web in FrontPage, you'd specify a file location such as *C:\My Documents\My Webs\testweb*. Disk-based Webs are very easy to use and are sufficient for many kinds of Web development. However, you can't use a disk-based Web to test—and in some case develop—Web pages containing features that require active participation of a Web server.

If your Web server has SharePoint Team Services or the FrontPage Server Extensions installed, and if you have the required security permissions, you can create and manage FrontPage-based Webs without using any kind of ordinary file access at all. Instead, FrontPage reads data from the server in the same way that browsers do, and writes data in the same way that HTML forms do. To open such a Web in FrontPage, you specify a file location such as *http://myserver.mydomain.com/testweb/*. FrontPage-based Webs accessed this way are said to be *server-based*. Because server-based Webs, by definition, involve the active presence of a Web server, they support development and testing of Web pages that use all FrontPage features.

FrontPage-based Webs can be *nested*. This means that one Web can physically reside within the folder tree of another Web. When this occurs, a *parent-child relationship* exists. If the */groceries* Web contains a Web called */groceries/produce*:

- The */groceries* Web is the *parent* of the */groceries/produce* Web.

- The */groceries/produce* Web is a *child* of the */groceries* Web.

A Web that has no parent is a *root Web*. The first Web you create in a given file area or Web server must, by definition, be a root Web. Any Webs you create within a given root Web are, by definition, *child Webs* or *subwebs*.

No Web page or, for that matter, any other file can belong to two Webs. This means that any operations you perform on a parent Web have no effect on any subwebs it contains. To apply changes to a parent Web and all its children, you must open and change each Web individually.

If all of this seems a bit abstract or vague, rest assured you have plenty of company. Most new FrontPage users think immediately about creating or editing individual Web

Chapter 1: Presenting Microsoft FrontPage 2002

pages, and not about creating Webs to organize entire sites. That's OK; if you want to start out editing individual pages, FrontPage can do that very well. Sooner or later, however, you'll want to start working on groups of Web pages as a unit, and that's when you'll start to appreciate Webs.

Supporting FrontPage on Your Web Server

Any general-purpose Web server can deliver Web pages you create in FrontPage. This includes Windows-based Web servers, UNIX servers running Netscape, and Apache Web server software. The universal nature of HTML and other file formats guarantees this. Nevertheless, in terms of capabilities related to FrontPage, Web servers fall into three categories:

- **Non-extended Web servers.** These have no special FrontPage software installed. FrontPage can upload files to such a server using the Internet File Transfer Protocol (FTP) or Windows file sharing, and the server can deliver your Web pages, multimedia files, and other kinds of content to any and all Web visitors. Because non-extended Web servers lack FrontPage software, features such as counting and displaying page hits, collecting data from HTML forms, sending e-mail, and processing databases won't work.

- **FrontPage-extended Web servers.** These have a collection of software called the FrontPage Server Extensions installed. These extensions support hit counters, data collection, e-mailing, database processing, and other FrontPage features that non-extended servers don't. They also support advanced file upload software and the ability to open and save Web files using Internet protocols only.

  Versions of the FrontPage Server Extensions are available for Windows NT, Windows 2000, and many UNIX operating systems.

- **SharePoint Team Services servers.** These provide all the features of FrontPage-Extended Web servers plus an exciting array of features and applications that support collaboration among members of a project or workgroup. The next section will describe these features and applications in more detail. SharePoint Team Services is available only for Windows 2000 servers.

When you install the FrontPage desktop software, you don't need to know what category of Web server you'll be using. You'll need this information when you start

11

creating pages so you can take full advantage of the features available on your Web server and avoid those that aren't. And of course, the features you need should guide the requirements given to your company's IT department or Internet service provider (ISP).

Introducing SharePoint Team Services

This new Microsoft technology provides all the capability of the FrontPage Server Extensions plus the following additional features:

- **Lists.** These include announcements, event listings, member lists, to-do lists, contact lists, and so forth. SharePoint Team Services includes an initial collection of lists that you can use without changing, or that you can modify to your heart's content. You can also create entire lists that contain whatever data you want.

- **Discussion lists.** Team members can post new comments and respond to existing ones.

- **Surveys.** These are used to collect information from anyone you authorize.

- **Document libraries.** Team members can deposit, categorize, and retrieve files of any kind.

- **Annotation features.** These allow collaboration, as follows:

  - One member can post a document for review.

  - Other members can view the document using only a Web browser and post annotations at the document or paragraph levels.

  - The document creator can open the annotated document and view all comments made to date.

- **Subscription features.** Authorized users can ask SharePoint Team Services to send them e-mail whenever someone updates given lists or document libraries.

In general, the decision to install SharePoint Team Services on a given Web server won't be yours. Instead, a system administrator, a Webmaster, or someone else in your IT department, or your service provider will probably have this prerogative. If you fulfill one of these roles, you can make your own decision. Otherwise, if the SharePoint Team Services feature set appears valuable, you can certainly ask those people to install SharePoint Team Services for you or find someone else who will.

Choosing the Best Operating System for FrontPage

If you don't need to run a personal Web server, almost any Windows operating system will do. Just remember that none of the Office XP programs, including FrontPage, will run on Windows 95.

If you *do* need to run a personal Web server, your operating system must be Windows NT 4.0 or Windows 2000. No personal Web server is available for Windows Me, and no FrontPage Server Extensions 2002 are available for Windows 98.

If you plan to customize Web database pages, develop Active Server Pages, or develop other server-side processes, you should probably use either Windows NT Workstation 4.0 or Windows 2000 Professional—whichever matches your production Web server—for development.

SharePoint Team Services runs only on Windows 2000 Professional and Windows 2000 Server. If you plan to use any features listed in Table 1-1 and need to isolate development from production, you'll need a Windows 2000 machine in your environment.

Table 1-1. **Components That Need SharePoint Team Services**

Component	Function
Document Libraries	Provides Web-based storage where visitors can save and retrieve specific kinds of documents.
Lists	Tracks any kind of repeating information.
Surveys	Collects information from the site's viewers.

Installing FrontPage

In its most complete form, FrontPage follows a client-server software model. The FrontPage editing and Web management software that runs on your desktop is the client. The FrontPage Server Extensions provide the server functions.

To install the FrontPage desktop software, first make sure you're running Windows 98, Windows Me, Windows NT 4.0, or Windows 2000. None of the Office XP applications run on Windows 95, so if you haven't upgraded your operating system in the past five or six years, now is probably the time.

Setup will start automatically after you put the FrontPage 2002 CD or Office XP Premium CD into your compact disc drive. Enter your name and Product Key, accept the license agreement, choose Install Now, click Next, and wait. When Setup is complete, FrontPage 2002 is installed on your system.

Deciding When to Install Your Own Web Server

Many beginning Web developers test their Web pages by loading them into their browser directly from disk. This process is fine for many kinds of Web pages, but it doesn't work for pages that expect special programs to run on the Web server every time a Web visitor requests them. Pages that use the Web components listed in Table 1-2 fall into this category. If you want to see these features in action before you publish the pages to your production Web server, you'll need a separate Web server for testing.

If you decide, based on these criteria, that you need a FrontPage-enabled Web server for development, the first place to look is your ISP or IT department. It's quite possible they have Web servers ready and waiting for this kind of work.

If neither your ISP nor your IT department can provide a suitable test server—or if your bandwidth to that server is insufficient—then you'll need to configure your computer as a Web server. Here are some guidelines for doing this based on different operating systems:

- In Windows NT 4.0 install the Windows NT Server 4.0 Option Pack.

- In Windows 2000, go to Control Panel, double-click Add/Remove Programs, click Add/Remove Windows Components, and select Install Internet Information Server.

- Neither the FrontPage Server Extensions 2002 nor SharePoint Team Services is available for Windows 95, Windows 98, or Windows Me. In addition, note the following restrictions that apply to these operating systems:

  - Windows 95 can't run any Office XP applications.

  - Windows 98 SE can run the Personal Web Server supplied on its setup disk, but not the FrontPage Server Extensions 2002. If you run the FrontPage Server Extensions 2000 on this Web server, some FrontPage 2002 features won't work.

  - Windows Me can't support any available Microsoft Web servers.

  If you must run one of these operating systems, your choices are to use disk-based Webs, to access a Windows NT or Windows 2000 Web server elsewhere on the network, or to upgrade your computer to Windows NT or Windows 2000.

Because Windows NT and Windows 2000 predate FrontPage 2002, their Web servers don't come with the FrontPage Server Extensions 2002. Therefore, don't install the server extensions that come with the Web server. First get the Windows Web server up and running without extensions, and then install the FrontPage Server Extensions 2002 from the FrontPage 2002 or Office XP CD.

Chapter 1

Table 1-2. **Components That Need a Web Server Running the FrontPage Server Extensions or SharePoint Team Services**

Component	Function	Precaution
Hit Counter	Displays the number of visits a Web page has received.	
Web Search	Searches a FrontPage-based Web for text that Web visitors specify on an HTML form.	Operates differently depending on presence or absence of Microsoft Indexing Service.
Save Results To File	Saves data from an HTML form into a file.	
Save Results To E-mail	Sends data from an HTML form as e-mail.	
Registration	Requires Web visitors to supply sign-up information before viewing a given Web.	Is not supported on Web servers supplied by Microsoft.
File Upload	Copies a file from the Web visitor's computer onto the Web server.	Requires proper security configuration.
Discussion Web	Accumulates messages Web visitors submit through an HTML form.	Doesn't include built-in features to manage the discussion over a period of time. SharePoint Team Services discussion lists are much better.
Top 10 List	Displays 10 most popular pages, 10 most common browsers, and other statistics summarized from Web server logs.	Requires FrontPage Server Extensions or SharePoint Team Services.
Save Results To Database	Saves data from an HTML form into a file or a database.	Requires development and production Web servers to have compatible database drivers.
Database Results	Displays information from a database in tabular format.	Requires development and production Web servers to have compatible database drivers.

newfeature!

If you want more control over the setup process, choose Custom instead of Install
Now. Click Next, make sure FrontPage is selected, click Next again, and review the
options shown in Figure 1-4. To expand and contract the headings, click the plus and
minus icons. To change installation options, click the down arrow icon following any
disk icon, and choose the option you want from the drop-down menu.

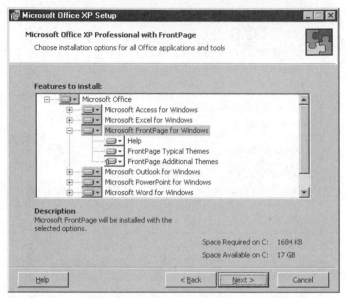

Figure 1-4. Be sure to include FrontPage when you install Microsoft Office.

Table 1-3 explains all the possibilities. The actual options available will vary depending
on the circumstances. The following choices are significant:

- **Microsoft FrontPage For Windows.** You should almost certainly choose
  Run From My Computer for this installation option. If you choose Not
  Available, FrontPage won't be installed.

- **Help.** Again, you should almost certainly choose Run From My Computer,
  or no online help will be installed.

- **FrontPage Additional Themes.** Choose Run From My Computer if you'd
  like to expand the normal selection of FrontPage themes. A FrontPage
  theme is a prefabricated set of color and graphic designs you can apply
  to Web pages.

Chapter 1: Presenting Microsoft FrontPage 2002

Table 1-3. **Custom Installation States**

State	Description
Run From My Computer	Setup installs the feature on your hard disk.
Run All From My Computer	Setup installs the feature and all components on your hard disk.
Run From Network	Setup configures the selected feature to use program files located on a network file server. If the file server isn't available when you use the feature, the feature won't work.
Run All From Network	Setup configures all components of the selected feature to use program files located on a network file server. If the file server isn't available when you use the feature, the feature won't work.
Run From CD	Setup configures the selected feature to use program files located on the product's compact disc. If the CD isn't available when you use the feature, the feature won't work.
Run All From CD	Setup configures all components of the selected feature to use program files located on the product's compact disc. If the CD isn't available when you use the feature, the feature won't work.
Installed On First Use	Setup doesn't install the feature, but instead installs a placeholder. The first time you use the feature, the application installs it from the original setup location (compact disc or file server).
Not Available	Setup doesn't install the feature. You can run Setup again to install it later.

Chapter 1

For more options that affect your use of FrontPage, scroll down to the heading "Office Shared Features." Figure 1-5 shows these options.

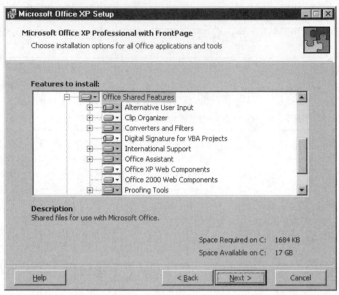

Figure 1-5.   Many Office Shared Features affect the capabilities available in FrontPage.

Expand this heading by clicking its plus icon, and then review the following options:

- **Alternative User Input.** This option controls the availability of speech recognition and handwriting as alternatives to keyboard input. Install these options as you wish.

- **Clip Organizer.** This is the new name for clip art. Most Web designers want all the clip art they can get and thus choose Run All From My Computer.

- **Converters And Filters.** This option determines which file format converters Setup installs on your system. FrontPage uses these converters for importing and exporting files used by other programs. If any file formats you're likely to use are marked Not Available, change them to Run From My Computer or Install On First Use.

- **Digital Signature For VBA Projects.** This option installs software that digitally signs Microsoft Visual Basic for Applications (VBA) modules so that other users can detect possible tampering. This option is irrelevant to FrontPage because FrontPage makes no use of VBA Projects.

Chapter 1: Presenting Microsoft FrontPage 2002

> **note** VBA is the language most often used to write macros for Office applications. VBA Projects are modules users can distribute among themselves to add features to most Office applications. Although FrontPage supports VBA, it doesn't support distribution by means of VBA Projects.

- **International Support.** If you need to have fonts installed for languages other than your primary Office language, expand this option and mark those languages Run From My Computer.

- **Office Assistant.** This option refers to the animated Clippit that appears when you start Office Help. Office XP displays this animation less frequently than Office 2000, but if you specify Not Available, it won't pop up at all.

- **Office XP Web Components.** This feature installs subsets of the Excel Spreadsheet, Chart, and PivotTable features that you can use as components in Web pages. They work only if the Web visitor is running Microsoft Internet Explorer 5 or later on a Windows computer, and they have reduced functionality if the Web visitor doesn't have Excel 2002 installed.

- **Office 2000 Web Components.** This feature installs another set of Office Web Components. These, however, are based on Excel 2000.

- **Proofing Tools.** Use this option to choose the dictionaries you want to use for translation and spelling.

Using VBA and Avoiding Viruses

In today's world of global connectivity, transmission of malicious computer programs (viruses) is a constant concern. Any facility that runs code can run malicious code, and VBA is no exception. Several high-profile e-mail viruses have, in fact, been VBA-based.

Having VBA on your system can be safe if the following are true:

- You never execute VBA code automatically, even if it arrives as an e-mail attachment or as part of an ordinary Office document.

- When asked whether to run a VBA macro, you reply No if the macro arrived from an untrusted or unknown source.

- You keep up-to-date on the names of any VBA-based macros that are currently circulating.

Not having VBA on your system means you won't execute any VBA viruses. It also means you won't execute any Office XP application macros. The choice is yours.

- **Themes.** This option controls how many themes are installed for use by the Office suite in general.

- **Visual Basic For Applications.** This option installs the files necessary to run Office XP macros. Select Not Available if you're sure you'll never want to create or run any FrontPage macros and you want to minimize the risk of viruses.

Installing and configuring the server-based part of FrontPage is a two-step process:

1 Obtain and install Web server software. This can run on any computer that's accessible to your PC, and that runs an operating system for which FrontPage Server Extensions are available.

If you're working in a home or small office environment, or if your support staff can't provide a development SharePoint Team Services or FrontPage Web server, you might need to install the Web server software on your own computer or find an ISP who supports the FrontPage Server Extensions.

> For more information about installing Web server software, refer to Chapter 37, "Installing and Configuring a Web Server."

2 Obtain and install the FrontPage Server Extensions or SharePoint Team Services on the Web server you installed in step 1. In general, you should run the most recent version of the server extensions. For example, the version that comes with FrontPage 2002 is newer than the versions that come with Windows 98, Windows NT, and Windows 2000. Microsoft's Web site (*http://www.microsoft.com/frontpage/fpse*) provides the latest version of the server extensions for FrontPage.

> For more information about installing FrontPage and Office server extensions, refer to Chapter 38, "Understanding the FrontPage Server Extensions."

Checking Out What's New in Office XP

The features described in this section are not only new to FrontPage, but also to the entire Microsoft Office XP suite.

User Interface Features

Office XP has a new, streamlined, flatter look. It's designed to decrease the amount of onscreen clutter and take advantage of high-color displays and new Windows 2000 technologies. This group of features improves the graphical interface between FrontPage and you, the Web designer:

Chapter 1: Presenting Microsoft FrontPage 2002

- **Floating toolbars.** Floating toolbars will begin to fade out after several seconds on Windows 2000 systems.

- **Task panes.** These new user interface features of Office XP perform common tasks quickly and don't interfere with ongoing edits. The first of these features you're likely to encounter in FrontPage is the New Page Or Web task pane.

> For more information about creating new FrontPage-based Webs, refer to Chapter 6, "Creating and Using FrontPage-Based Webs." For more information about creating new Web pages, refer to "Creating a New Web Page" on page 255.

- **Speech command and control.** FrontPage incorporates Microsoft's speech recognition technology. Using this feature, you can speak the names of menus, menu items, and toolbar buttons in Office. Using the Language toolbar, you can quickly switch between Dictation and Voice Command modes. The Language toolbar also provides the Speech Balloon, which displays the vocal equivalent of keyboard and mouse commands.

 For more information about speech recognition, refer to "Customizing Speech and Handwriting Options" in the Bonus Content on the Companion CD.

tip To access the Speech feature, click Speech on the Tools menu in any Office application. The first time you start Speech, it will take you through a training wizard that improves speech recognition accuracy.

note Speech recognition requires a high-quality microphone and a relatively fast computer. The preferred type of microphone is a "close-talk" microphone positioned about a thumb's width from the corner of your mouth. Microsoft recommends at least a 300 MHz Pentium II computer with 128 MB of RAM. Running speech recognition on a machine with 32 MB or less of RAM might cause Office applications to crash on startup.

Paste Options

- **Paste Options button.** Whenever you paste text into FrontPage, this button appears near the pasted text. This tells FrontPage whether to format the pasted text as it was in the source, in accordance with styles in the destination, or as plain text.

> For more information about the Paste Options button, refer to "Copying and Pasting Text" on page 270.

Part 1: Introducing Microsoft FrontPage 2002

- **Office Clipboard.** The expanded clipboard holds up to 24 items and appears in a task pane with thumbnail previews of each item. An icon in the Windows status bar controls the Office Clipboard even when it's not visible, and notifies you when items are being copied to the Office Clipboard, even from non-Office applications.

> For more information about the Office Clipboard, refer to "Copying and Pasting Text" on page 270.

- **Office Assistant.** The animated figure (for example, Clippit) no longer appears by default when Office starts. It appears only when you request help or when it has specific information to present.

> For more information about the Office Assistant, refer to "Installing FrontPage" earlier in this chapter.

- **Ask A Question box.** This element appears on the menu bar of every Office application. To ask for help, type a question into this box and press Enter.

> For more information about the Ask A Question box, refer to "Understanding the Main FrontPage Window" on page 32.

Auto Tile

- **Auto Tile button.** This addition to the Help window tiles the Help and FrontPage windows so they're both completely visible. This is one of several changes that make the Help window faster and easier to manage alongside Office applications.

Web Services

Office XP includes these new features for making it easier to save information on servers located anywhere on the Internet:

- **Add Network Place Wizard.** Using this feature, you can easily connect to Web Folders on an intranet or on the Internet. Using a step-by-step interface, the Add Network Place Wizard easily connects to existing folders and creates new folders on multiple types of servers, including Web servers extended with the FrontPage Server Extensions or SharePoint Team Services. On older operating systems, this wizard appears under the name Add Web Folder.

Chapter 1: Presenting Microsoft FrontPage 2002

- **Web Drives/Passport.** Using MSN Communities, you can save documents to a private or public file cabinet on the Internet. This means you can easily share files on the Internet without ever leaving Microsoft Office. MSN Communities use Microsoft Passport as their authentication mechanism.

File Operations

Office XP includes new collaboration features that help you track, review, and merge changes made to documents, spreadsheets, and presentations shared by multiple people:

- **New File Task pane.** All Office applications feature a New File task pane that consolidates common document functions such as opening recently used documents and creating new documents. This task pane appears by default the first time you start FrontPage. You can also display it by choosing New from the File menu.

> For more information about creating new FrontPage-based Webs, refer to Chapter 6, "Creating and Using FrontPage-BasedWebs." For more information about creating new Web pages, refer to "Creating a New Web Page" on page 255.

- **File templates.** Office can save templates to Web servers, and create new documents based on these templates. You can save a template to a Web server running server extensions for either FrontPage 2000 or FrontPage 2002.

> For more information about templates, refer to "Working with Web Templates" on page 82.

Open and Save Dialog Boxes

The Open and Save dialog boxes are some of the most universal and most used dialog boxes of any program. Information would be fleeting indeed if there were no way to save and retrieve it. These features make the job even easier than before:

- **Resizable dialog boxes.** You can now resize the Open and Save dialog boxes. Just move the mouse pointer over the bottom right corner until you see a two-headed arrow, and then drag the corner until the box is the size you want.

> For more information about the Open and Save dialog boxes, refer to Chapter 9, "Creating, Opening, Saving, and Deleting Web Pages."

- **Customizable My Places bar.** You can add a custom folder location as a shortcut on the My Places bar. To do this, choose Open or Save As from the File menu, select the folder you want to appear in the My Places bar, and then click Add To "My Places" on the Tools drop-down menu.

> For more information about the Open File and Save As dialog boxes, refer to Chapter 9, "Creating, Opening, Saving, and Deleting Web Pages."

- **Web Archive file format.** When Office applications other than FrontPage save documents as HTML, they normally create a "base" HTML file and an entire folder full of pictures, style sheets, and other components that re-create the appearance of the original document. Web Archive format avoids this nuisance by saving the base HTML file and all support files in a single compressed archive that Internet Explorer 4.0 or later can display directly. To save a non-FrontPage file in Web Archive format, set the Save As type to Web Archive (*.mht;*.mhtml).

Search Feature

FrontPage 2002 shares with Office an updated searching facility that locates files on your local computer, other networked computers, and Outlook. Results appear within the Office application that initiated the search.

> **tip** To search for text in a FrontPage-based Web, open the Web in FrontPage and then choose Find from the Edit menu. To provide a facility Web visitors can use to search your Web, open the page that will contain the Web Search, choose Web Component from the Insert menu, and then choose Web Search.

Reliability and Robustness Features

Office XP applications include a variety of robustness features that minimize the impact of crashes, hangs, and data corruption for you and your support staff. These features aren't infallible, but they do protect against and recover from a broad range of failures:

- **Office Safe Mode.** Like the Windows operating system, all Office XP applications include Office-specific tools designed to fix and trouble-shoot (if necessary) when an application fails to start. These tools provide increased resiliency for loading persistent application settings and add-ins. If an Office application fails to start, you should see a prompt regarding the problem the next time you boot.

Of course, in the long term, you need a system that tracks failures and optionally reports them to Microsoft for resolution. The next set of features provide for this need:

- **Client logging.** Key information about crashes and safe-mode actions is entered on the event log so that each machine has a persistent record of observed failures. On Windows 98, Office logs this information to a text file and the Microsoft System Info tool provides consistent access to the logged data.

- **Crash reporting.** When a crash occurs, a button appears to "report this problem to Microsoft" over a dial-up or permanent Internet connection. After a workaround or fix is determined, this reporting tool has provisions to automatically provide this data to a user for future crash reports—so keep reporting!

- **Hang manager.** If an Office XP application hangs, you can crash it by running the Microsoft Office Application Recovery program installed in the Microsoft Office Tools portion of your Start menu. This has two advantages over the Windows Task Manager's ways of ending hung applications:

  - In Word, Excel, and PowerPoint, it invokes a Save On Crash feature that recovers work in progress the next time you start the application.

  - It optionally sends a crash report to Microsoft, as described under "Crash reporting."

- **Corporate tracking.** Corporations can set a policy key to redirect all crash reporting to a corporate file server. A separate tool then provides analysis and subsequent batch reporting to Microsoft.

- **Setup failure reporting.** If Office setup encounters an unrecoverable error, it also provides the opportunity to tell Microsoft about the problem. With your consent, setup logs can be automatically sent to Microsoft for further analysis.

Checking Out What's New in FrontPage 2002

Of course, FrontPage 2002 includes many improvements beyond those that pervade the Office XP suite as a whole. Here are the highlights.

SharePoint Team Web Site Features

This group of features works only on Web servers that have SharePoint Team Services installed:

- **Document libraries.** Establish special folders on your Web site where visitors can save specific kinds of documents. You can set up required information that will be collected for each document and establish rules (similar to the ones in your e-mail inbox) for dealing with documents saved into the library. As your site grows, you can add new document libraries and customize them to meet your needs.

For more information about document libraries, lists, and surveys, refer to Chapter 35, "Using SharePoint Team Web Sites."

- **Lists.** Use a list to keep track of anything that's important for your Web site. People with permissions to use your Web site will be able to view the list information, create new items, or edit the existing ones. You can insert information from a list (or a document library) into any page on your Web site, and this information will always remain up-to-date. SharePoint Team Services comes with built-in lists for team announcements, events, links, contacts, tasks, and discussions. You can create additional lists as required.

- **Surveys.** Add a survey to your Web site to collect information from the site's viewers. You can ask many questions in a single survey and view the results of the survey graphically.

Web Components

At the touch of a button, these new components add sophisticated new features to your Web pages:

- **Link Bar.** This component replaces the Navigation Bar component included with earlier versions of FrontPage. Like the Navigation bar, a Link bar can obtain its hyperlinks from a structure you diagram in Navigation view. Unlike the Navigation bar, a Link bar can ignore Navigation view and accept manually configured links instead.

For more information about Link bars, refer to "Using Link Bars with Navigation View" on page 201 or "Using the Link Bars Component" on page 371.

- **List View.** This component displays a clickable list of items available on a server running SharePoint Team Services. When a page contains a List View component, you must save it to a SharePoint Team Services-based Web.

For more information about the Lists View component, refer to "Using Lists" on page 998.

- **Document Library View.** In a similar manner to List View, this component displays a clickable list of items available in a SharePoint Team Services-based Web. As with the List View component, you must save any page containing a Document Library View component to a SharePoint Team Services-based Web.

For more information about the Document Library View component, refer to "Using Document Libraries" on page 982.

● **Photo Gallery.** Displaying groups of pictures indexed by smaller versions is one of the most common applications on the Web. The Photo Gallery component automatically sets up just such a collection; all you have to provide are the full-sized pictures. FrontPage creates the tables, indexes, and thumbnails, and then you can add captions to each picture.

> For more information about the Photo Gallery component, refer to Chapter 22, "Using FrontPage Photo Galleries."

● **File Upload.** When a Web visitor submits an HTML form that contains this component, the browser uploads a specified file to the Web server. The component has two visible elements: a text box and a Browse button. The text box contains the name of the file to upload. The Browse button displays an Open dialog box that fills in the text box by point and click.

> For more information about the File Upload component, refer to "Configuring File Upload Options" on page 904.

● **Top 10 List.** This component displays the 10 most popular pages in your Web, the 10 most common referring sites, the 10 most popular browsers used, and so forth. These statistics come from Web server activity logs.

> For more information about the Top 10 List component, refer to "Creating Top 10 Lists" on page 843.

HTML 4 Tags

This group of features enhances the visual Web page editing process by supporting more aspects of HTML:

● **Inline frame.** This is a special type of frame that embeds a Web page within an area that's part of another Web page.

> For more information about inline frames, refer to "Using Inline Frames" on page 529.

● **Advanced button.** This object works like a standard form button, but you can customize its height, width, and caption font.

> For more information about Advanced buttons, refer to "Setting Advanced Button Properties" on page 877.

● **Group box.** This object creates a captioned rectangle that surrounds one or more form field objects. The result is a group box similar to those that appear in Windows dialog boxes.

> For more information about group boxes, refer to "Setting Group Box Properties" on page 879.

Editing Features

Using a technology called Vector Markup Language (VML), FrontPage 2002 now supports line graphics drawn within Web pages. For some kinds of graphics, this produces a considerable decrease in download time. The tools for editing tables are also improved. Here are the specifics:

- **Drawings.** This feature draws lines, arrows, rectangles, and other shapes on your Web page. FrontPage adds these objects to your Web page using VML.

> For more information about drawings, refer to "Inserting Drawings" on page 331.

- **AutoShapes.** This feature adds geometric shapes, block arrows, flowchart symbols, stars, and other predrawn objects to your Web page. It's another feature that uses VML.

> For more information about AutoShapes, refer to "Inserting AutoShapes" on page 334.

- **WordArt.** This component provides extremely rich formatting of text, using techniques such as progressive sizing, shadowing, and fitting baselines to a curve. Word, Excel, and PowerPoint users have seen this object in several past releases, but it's new to FrontPage 2002. Like Drawings and Auto-Shapes, this component creates VML output.

> For more information about the WordArt component, refer to "Inserting WordArt" on page 335.

- **Tables.** You can now edit table borders by clicking a Border button on the Borders toolbar. A new Split Table command creates two tables from one. The Fill Right and Fill Down commands complete tables with repetitive information.

> For more information about editing tables, refer to "Creating and Editing Tables" on page 475.

- **Shared borders.** This feature can now set a background (color or picture) on the shared border that is different from the page background.

> For more information about shared borders, refer to "Using Shared Borders" on page 765.

Vector Markup Language (VML)

VML is a standards-based format for delivering high-quality vector graphics on the Web. VML consists of plain text tags that describe lines, curves, and *x-y* coordinates. A line drawing expressed in VML is usually much smaller than the same drawing saved as a GIF or JPEG file.

VML is standards-based (well, sort of) because its syntax conforms to Extensible Markup Language (XML) and because Microsoft has proposed it to the World Wide Web Consortium as a standard for vector graphics on the Web. Windows versions of Internet Explorer 5.0 and later support VML. Other browsers ignore it. When FrontPage creates VML code, it also saves a GIF version of the same picture. It then mixes an *<img>* tag into the VML code. Browsers that understand VML code will bypass the *<img>* tag and display the VML. Browsers that ignore VML code will detect the *<img>* tag and display the GIF image.

Site Management Features

Publishing—the process of transferring content from one Web site to another—is now more flexible than ever before. FrontPage also provides valuable new features for gathering and reporting Web site activity statistics. Here are the specific features:

● **Publishing.** The new Publish Web dialog box shows you exactly which files will be published. Every time you publish (after the first time), the dialog box also indicates any files that might cause a conflict during the file copying process. You can view the contents of your destination Web site and perform basic file management tasks such as renaming, deleting, or moving files. In addition to publishing your entire Web site by clicking a single button, you can also move individual files in either direction between the source and the destination. Publish will run in the background and will notify you when it's done. After Publish is finished, you can view either the newly published site or a log file telling you which files were copied.

> For more information about publishing Webs, refer to Chapter 13, "Publishing Your FrontPage-Based Web."

● **Usage reports.** These reports provide statistical information such as how many people are visiting your Web site and how much activity originates inside and outside your enterprise. This helps identify potential customers, their locations, and other sites that refer visitors to yours. You can see how visitors are using your site and get information about their computers such as the browser, the operating system, and the color and display settings.

> For more information about usage reporting, refer to Chapter 30, "Monitoring and Reporting Site Activity."

- **Custom reporting.** Using the Reports view and built-in workflow features in FrontPage, you can assign files for review and keep a project flowing. You can also determine which files have not been assigned by using the (Blanks) AutoFilter. The Custom AutoFilter view can be set to display only a particular file type—for example, all the GIF files in your Web site. Each of these reports can then be assigned to someone on a team for review.

> For more information about custom reporting, refer to Chapter 34, "Managing Design Teams."

Multi-Language Handling Feature

FrontPage accommodates multiple languages in the same Web page, as follows:

- You can select the default language for any Web page from a list of over 100 languages and dialects.

- Based on the keyboard setting in Windows Control Panel, FrontPage automatically remembers the language of any text you enter.

- To change the language for any part of a Web page, select it and then choose Set Language from the Tools menu.

- Language settings affect both the character set used for display and the dictionary used for checking spelling.

> For more information about multi-language handling, refer to "Language Page Properties" on page 545.

In Summary...

FrontPage 2002 provides not only a powerful, visual Web page editor, but also a myriad of features for managing the hundreds or thousands of cross-related files that comprise a typical Web site. The latest release includes a multitude of new features that make creating Web pages easier and more productive than ever.

The next chapter provides a rapid introduction to the process of creating Web pages with FrontPage.

Chapter 2

Editing Web Pages

This chapter and the next introduce the major components of Microsoft FrontPage 2002, explain their purpose, and provide an overview of how they work. Chapter 2 is primarily about creating individual Web pages, and Chapter 3 addresses the management of multi-page sites. Together, these chapters provide not only an overview of the software but of the book as well. After you understand FrontPage conceptually, you'll be ready for the details—presented in later chapters—that will give you mastery over Web development.

As you review each feature, consider how much more difficult it would be to achieve the same results with only a simple text editor.

HTML and Text Editors

Early versions of HTML were designed for publishing scholarly and technical papers—and simple ones at that. There was no way to know what size of screen or what fonts each Web visitor would have, so these details were left to the discretion of each visitor's browser and system configuration, not to the page designer. Text would flow within whatever document window the visitor chose. The designer could, for example, assign style codes such as *<h1>* through *<h6>* for progressively smaller headings, but each computer could theoretically display these styles in a different font, size, and color. There was no provision for publishing equations, charts, or tables. Today, of course, style and appearance have become at least as important as content—no one wants to look at ugly pages—and the idea that certain kinds of content can't be displayed seems ridiculous.

The HTML specification developed in those early days still provides the basis for the most complicated Web pages we see today. In fact, plain text editors remain among the most common tools for creating Web pages, no matter how complex the page or how cryptic the HTML codes might be.

Objectively, HTML is one of the worst page description languages around. Its greatest strength and its greatest weakness are one and the same: simplicity. Its simplicity lets anyone with a plain text editor (such as Notepad) create Web pages, and lets anyone with a browser on any computer system read those pages. But at the same time, it constrains page designers so harshly that designers can spend huge amounts of time trying to overcome its limitations. Page designers should be designers, stylists, and artists, not technicians who are required to create intricate program code.

Designing effective Web pages today requires a two-pronged approach: First, use tools that simplify the coding of complex Web pages; and second, accept the fact that every Web visitor's browser is going to display your work a little differently.

WYSIWYG Editing in FrontPage

Web designers working with a text editor typically keep a browser running in the background to display the page they're working on. To preview the appearance of a page, the author saves it from the editor to disk and then clicks the browser's Refresh button to reload the file into the browser. "But this is crazy," you say. "Why doesn't someone invent a Web page editor that displays what the visitor will see—in true WYSIWYG fashion—and not a bunch of HTML gibberish?" FrontPage 2002 has done just that.

With FrontPage 2002, you can quickly create Web pages with all the familiarity and ease of use found in other Office applications, such as Microsoft Word and Microsoft PowerPoint. To the maximum extent possible, FrontPage's menu structure, toolbar icons, dialog boxes, and working conventions strongly resemble these other applications. You can look at the HTML if you want to—and even modify it—but you can also create great-looking Web pages without seeing a scrap of HTML. As a result, you can concentrate fully on your message and let FrontPage handle the mechanics.

Understanding the Main FrontPage Window

The first time you start FrontPage, it displays an application window much like the one shown in Figure 2-1.

Here are the functions of each element:

- **Menu bar.** The FrontPage menu bar is typical of those found in all Microsoft Windows programs since the advent of the WIMP (Windows, Icons, Mouse, Pointer) interface. File, Edit, and View are on the left; Help is on the right. You can customize the menu bar by choosing Customize from the Tools menu.

Chapter 2: Editing Web Pages

Ask A Question
box

Menu bar

Standard
toolbar

Formatting
toolbar

Views bar

Page
view
editing
window

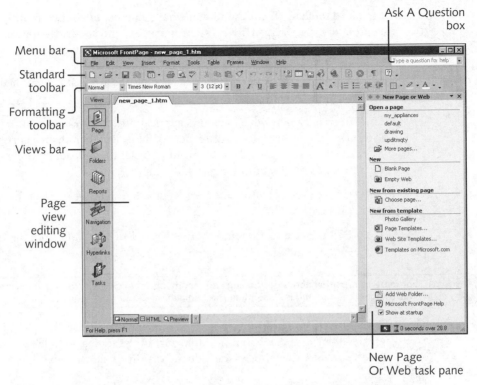

New Page
Or Web task pane

Figure 2-1. By default, the main FrontPage window contains these elements on startup.

By default, FrontPage 2002 displays personalized menus. This means the commands you use most appear when you first display a menu, and the rest appear after you leave the menu open for a few seconds or click the double arrow at the bottom of the menu. If you find personalized menus more distracting than useful:

1 Choose Customize from the Tools menu.

2 Display the Options tab.

3 To see full menus all the time, select the Always Show Full Menus option.

4 To see full menus only when you click the double arrows, clear the Show Full Menus After A Short Delay option.

For more information about customizing FrontPage menus and toolbars, refer to "Customizing Menus and Toolbars" in the Bonus Content on the Companion CD.

- **Standard toolbar.** The most fundamental and most often used FrontPage commands—New, Open, Save, Cut, Copy, Paste, and so forth—appear on this toolbar.

 For more information about the Standard toolbar, refer to "The Standard Toolbar" in the Bonus Content on the Companion CD.

FrontPage, like many other Windows applications, features dockable toolbars. This means you can rearrange toolbars, lengthen them, shorten them, dock them at any side of the window or let them float anywhere on the screen. To display or hide a particular toolbar:

- Choose Toolbars from the View menu, and select or deselect the appropriate toolbar.

- Right-click a toolbar, and choose the toolbar you want from the shortcut menu.

 For more information about positioning and modifying toolbars, refer to "Customizing Menus and Toolbars" in the Bonus Content on the Companion CD.

Be alert to down arrows in any toolbar. A down arrow beneath a pair of greater-than symbols (>>) means that part of the toolbar is hidden. Clicking the down arrow displays the hidden portion, as shown here:

- **Formatting toolbar.** This toolbar contains buttons for the most often used formatting commands: Style, Font, Font Size, Bold, Italic, and so forth. This toolbar is one of the easiest to use because it provides the same buttons and functions in most other Office applications.

 For more information about the Formatting toolbar, refer to "The Formatting Toolbar" in the Bonus Content on the Companion CD.

- **Views bar.** This bar controls what kind of information appears in the main FrontPage window. Table 2-1 describes the available views.

Chapter 2: Editing Web Pages

Table 2-1. **FrontPage Views**

View name	Description
Page	The WYSIWYG FrontPage editor.
Folders	An Explorer-like view of the files and folders in a Web.
Reports	Various listings and statistics regarding the contents of a Web.
Navigation	An area for drawing the structure of a Web. After you draw such a structure, FrontPage can automatically create Link bars that connect all your pages.
Hyperlinks	A graphic display of the relationships among files in a Web (for example, "uses" and "where used").
Tasks	A "to do" list pertaining to a Web. You can open a Web page directly from any relevant task. When you save a Web page that has open tasks, FrontPage asks whether those tasks are now complete.

newfeature!

- **Ask A Question box.** At any time, you can type a plain-English question in this box, and FrontPage will try to answer it.

newfeature!

- **New Page Or Web task pane.** This element provides the options listed in Table 2-2 on the next page. It appears by default whenever you start FrontPage, depending on the following conditions:

  - If you clear the Show At Startup check box at the bottom of the pane, the pane no longer appears when FrontPage starts. This check box is synonymous with the Startup Task Pane check box that appears on the General tab of the Options dialog box. (Choose Options from the Tools menu to display this dialog box.)

tip If the Show At Startup check box isn't visible in the New Page Or Web task pane, scroll down using the arrow that appears at the bottom of the pane.

  - The New Page Or Web task pane doesn't appear if a Web was open the last time you closed FrontPage and the check box titled Open Last Web Automatically When FrontPage Starts is selected on the General tab of the Options dialog box.

  You can display the New Page Or Web task pane at any time by choosing New from the File menu, and then choosing Page Or Web.

Chapter 2

Table 2-2. **Options on the New Page Or Web Task Pane**

Section	Description
Open A Page	Opens a Web page from the FrontPage Most Recently Used (MRU) files list. This is the same list of files that appears when you choose Recent Files from the File menu.
New	Opens a new, blank Web page or empty Web.
New From Existing Page	Opens a new copy of an existing Web page. Saving this copy doesn't overwrite the original file.
New From Template	Opens a new Web page based on a template installed with your copy of FrontPage, saved on a Web site, or provided on Microsoft's Web site.
Add Web Folder (Windows 98) or Add Network Place (Windows 2000)	Adds a Web folder to your Web Folders or My Network Places list.
Microsoft FrontPage Help	Opens the online help installed with FrontPage.

note Task panes are one of the new user interface elements in FrontPage 2002. They display useful selections and commands you might expect to find in a dialog box, but without restricting access to open document windows. In addition to the New Page Or Web task pane, FrontPage provides Clipboard and Insert Clip Art task panes.

- **Page view editing window.** This is where the most important work occurs—the work of actually creating Web pages. By default, the window displays an editable preview of what your Web visitors will see. Most of the FrontPage menu commands are dedicated to creating, configuring, and formatting elements in this window.

  The tabs at the bottom of the editing window control how the current Web page appears: in editable WYSIWYG view (Normal), editable HTML view, or display-only Preview mode. The tabs at the top of the editing window identify each currently open page by name. To edit a particular open page, click the tab for its file name.

Initializing a New Web Page

The next few sections step through the process of creating a simple Web page. The purpose of this exercise is to describe the FrontPage editor, and not to produce a stunning, award-winning, real-world page. Here's how to begin:

1 Start FrontPage.

2 If FrontPage automatically opens a Web, close it by choosing Close Web from the File menu.

> **tip** To determine whether a FrontPage-based Web is currently open, click the File menu, and inspect the Close Web option. If it's enabled, a Web is currently open. If it's dimmed, no FrontPage-based Web is open.

3 If the New Page Or Web task pane isn't visible, display it by choosing New from the File menu and selecting Page Or Web.

4 If a new Web page isn't already open and ready for editing, go to the New Page Or Web task pane, locate the section titled New, and click the Blank Page option.

> **tip** In Figure 2-1, a new, blank Web page named *new_page_1.htm* is ready for editing. This file name appears in the tab along the top left edge of the editing window. If the editing window is empty (that is, it displays a background color and no file tabs), click Blank Page in the New Page Or Web task pane.

5 If the New Page Or Web task pane is still open, close it by clicking the Close button in its top right corner.

Entering and Formatting Text

FrontPage should display a blinking insertion point in the top left corner of the editing window. Because Web pages "grow" from the top left corner, this point is "ground zero" for adding content. In this respect, creating Web pages is more like entering text in a word processor, such as Word, than arranging objects in a graphics program such as PowerPoint or Microsoft Visio. Here are the familiar steps for entering text:

1 To create some heading text, type *My Appliances*.

2 Press Enter to start a new paragraph.

3 To create some body text, type *Here are a few of my favorite things*.

4 To format the heading, set the insertion point anywhere within the My Appliances heading, and then choose Heading 1 from the Style box on the Formatting toolbar.

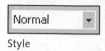

Style

The Web page should now resemble Figure 2-2.

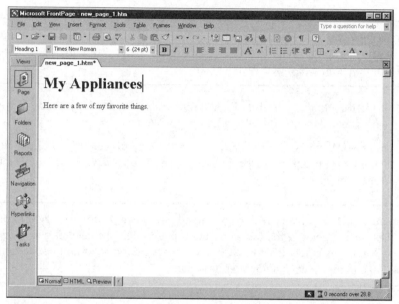

Figure 2-2. In Page view, adding text to a Web page is as simple as typing in a word processor.

For more information about entering and formatting text, refer to Chapter 10, "Adding and Formatting Text."

Drawing Tables

The rest of the Web page will contain three pictures arranged vertically with a caption to the right of each one. The best way to arrange these elements is with an HTML table. Here are the steps required to insert such a table:

1 Move the insertion point to the end of the Web page. (Press Ctrl+End, or click the mouse anywhere below and to the right of the last existing content.)

Chapter 2: Editing Web Pages

Insert Table

2 Click the Insert Table button on the Standard toolbar. A drop-down grid appears. Move the mouse over the grid until an area two cells wide and three cells high is darkened, and then click the last darkened cell.

tip There are two ways to use the Insert Table button. The first method is to click the button, move the pointer to the last desired cell in the drop-down grid, and then click again. The second method is to click the button, point to the first cell, hold down the mouse button, drag the pointer to the last desired cell, and then release the mouse button. The difference is that the first method can't expand the drop-down grid, and the second can.

3 By default, FrontPage creates a table that fills the entire width of the Web page. It also tries to make each table cell equal in size (that is, for a table of two columns, it specifies that each cell should occupy 50 percent of the table width). To override this behavior, set the insertion point anywhere within the table, and then choose AutoFit To Contents from the Table menu.

4 Also by default, FrontPage creates a table with no space between cells, no space between cell contents and cell edges, and a visible border. To override these settings, right-click anywhere in the table, and choose Table Properties from the shortcut menu. The Table Properties dialog box shown in Figure 2-3 appears.

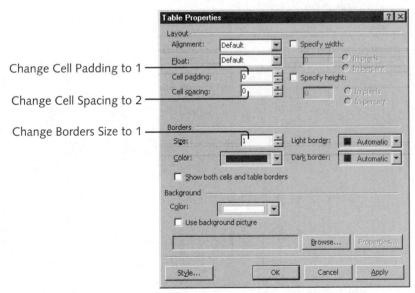

Figure 2-3. This intuitive dialog box controls table properties in both Page view and HTML view. There's no need to memorize and manually enter cryptic HTML codes.

5 In the Table Properties dialog box, do the following:

a Change the Cell Padding value to 1.

b Change the Cell Spacing value to 2.

c Change the Size setting (under Borders) to 1.

d Select the Show Both Cells And Table Borders check box. Click OK.

> **For more information about working with HTML tables, refer to "Creating and Editing Tables"
> on page 475.**

Inserting Pictures

This example uses three clip art pictures provided with Office. Follow this procedure to insert the first picture:

1 Click in the top left cell—column 1 of row 1—of the HTML table.

2 Choose Picture from the Insert menu, and then choose Clip Art.

3 The Insert Clip Art task pane appears in the FrontPage window. Under the Search For heading, type *appliance* in the Search Text box, and then click Search. Your screen should now resemble Figure 2-4.

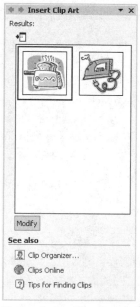

Figure 2-4. The Insert Clip Art task pane makes finding and inserting clip art a breeze.

Chapter 2: Editing Web Pages

4 Do one of the following:

■ Right-click the picture of the toaster; or

■ Click the down arrow that appears on the right of the toaster picture, and then choose Insert from the shortcut menu.

A very large toaster picture appears in the table cell where you set the insertion point in step 1.

5 To reduce the size of the toaster picture, right-click the large, newly pasted version, and choose Picture Properties from the shortcut menu. This displays the dialog box shown in Figure 2-5.

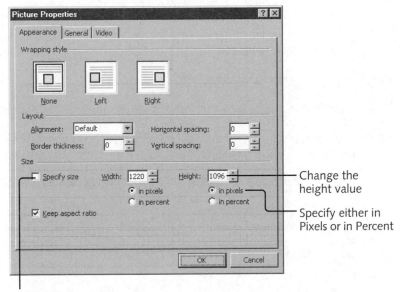

Select this box to
override picture size

Change the
height value

Specify either in
Pixels or in Percent

Figure 2-5. With this dialog box, you can easily modify the characteristics of a picture.

6 Under the Size heading, select the Specify Size check box, and then change the Height value to 75 In Pixels.

7 Click the General tab, and then, under Type, choose GIF. Click OK.

> For more information about working with pictures, refer to Chapter 11, "Adding and Formatting Pictures."

Follow these steps to insert the second picture (the iron):

1   Click in column 1 of row 2 of the table.

2   In the Insert Clip Art task pane, right-click the iron, and choose Insert from the shortcut menu.

3   Repeat steps 5 through 8 from the previous procedure to resize the picture to 75 pixels high and select the format.

To insert the last picture:

1   Click the Modify button in the Insert Clip Art task pane, type *computer* in the Search Text box, and then click Search.

2   Insert one of the computer pictures into the cell below the iron, and resize it as you did the toaster and iron.

To add captions for the graphics:

1   Click column 2 of row 1 of the table, and type *Tommy the Toaster*.

2   Add the captions *Irene the Iron* and *Conrad the Computer* in the same manner for the remaining pictures. Your page should look similar to Figure 2-6.

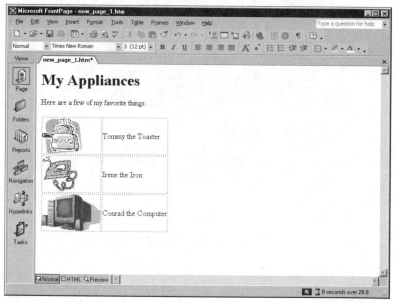

Figure 2-6.   HTML tables are a great way to align elements spatially on a page. Using a text editor to create even simple compositions like this can be difficult. Using Page View makes it a snap.

Chapter 2: Editing Web Pages

Adding a Hyperlink

FrontPage makes it easy to add hyperlinks. To see how this process works, follow this procedure:

1 Double-click the word *Computer* in the *Conrad the Computer* caption. This selects the entire word.

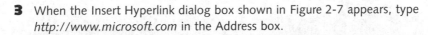

Insert
Hyperlink

2 Right-click the selected word, and choose Hyperlink from the shortcut menu. (Clicking the Insert Hyperlink button on the Standard toolbar has the same effect.)

3 When the Insert Hyperlink dialog box shown in Figure 2-7 appears, type *http://www.microsoft.com* in the Address box.

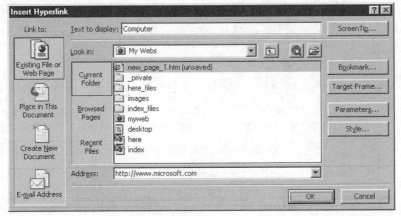

Figure 2-7.   This FrontPage dialog box provides a rich array of tools for locating Web locations with point-and-click methods. If you prefer, you can also fill in the Address box by hand.

4 Click OK.

For more information about working with hyperlinks, refer to Chapter 12, "Building Hyperlinks."

Saving the Web Page

Saving this page on disk requires more steps than you might suspect. This is because there are actually four files to save: the Web page itself and three picture files. Here's the procedure:

Save

1 Click the Save button on the Standard toolbar.

2 When the Save As dialog box shown in Figure 2-8 on the next page appears, click the My Documents icon on the My Places bar.

Part 1: Introducing Microsoft FrontPage 2002

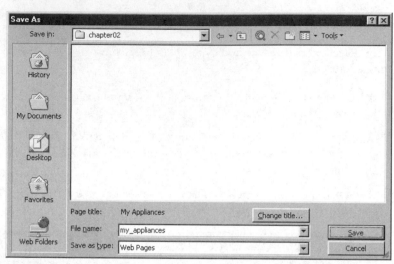

Figure 2-8. The My Places bar at the left of the Save As dialog box sets the Save In location to one of several common starting points.

3 Click the Create New Folder button.

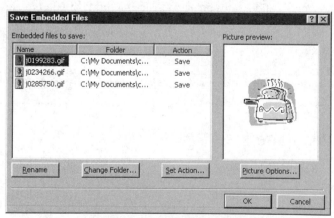

Create New
Folder

4 When the New Folder dialog box appears, type a memorable name, such as *chapter02*, for the location of this Web, and then click OK.

5 Type *my_appliances.htm* in the File Name box, and click the Save button.

6 The Save Embedded Files dialog box shown in Figure 2-9 appears next. This box suggests you save the three converted clip art files in the same folder as the *my_appliances.htm* page with the names listed in the Name column of the dialog box.

Figure 2-9. Saving a Web page can require saving any number of components as well as the main HTML file. FrontPage displays this dialog box when you save a Web page that contains unsaved components.

Chapter 2: Editing Web Pages

To rename a file, select it, and click the Rename button. To save it in a different folder, select the file, and click the Change Folder button. To change a file's action from Save to Don't Save (or back again), click the Set Action button. To change a picture's format from GIF to JPEG or to change other format properties, click the Picture Options button. Click the OK button when all these options are set the way you want them.

For more information about saving Web pages, refer to "Saving Pages" on page 264.

Checking Your Work

To preview the Web page as Microsoft Internet Explorer would display it, click the Preview tab at the bottom of the editing window. This saves the current Web page as a temporary file on disk, loads Internet Explorer into the main FrontPage window, and tells Internet Explorer to display the temporary file. Figure 2-10 shows a preview of the current page. To resume editing, click the Normal button at the bottom of the display window.

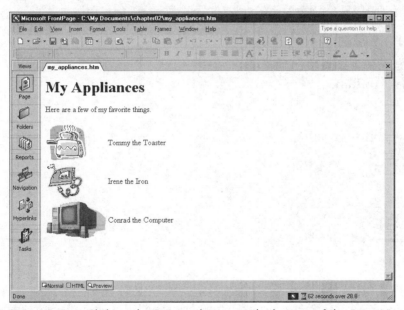

Figure 2-10. Clicking the Preview button at the bottom of the Page View window displays a temporary copy of the current page as Internet Explorer would present it.

Preview in
Browser

To view your Web page in a browser outside of FrontPage, choose Preview In Browser from the File menu or click the Preview In Browser button. This displays the Preview In Browser dialog box shown in Figure 2-11 on the next page. Choose the browser you want to run, select a window size, and click Preview.

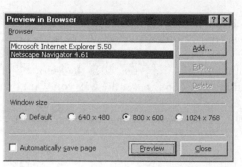

Figure 2-11. If you have several browsers installed on your computer, FrontPage can display the current Web page in any of them.

FrontPage checks to see whether you've made any changes since you last saved the page, prompts you to save the page if necessary, starts the selected browser if it isn't already running, and then tells the browser to display the page. Figure 2-12 shows the sample page developed in this chapter displayed in Netscape Navigator.

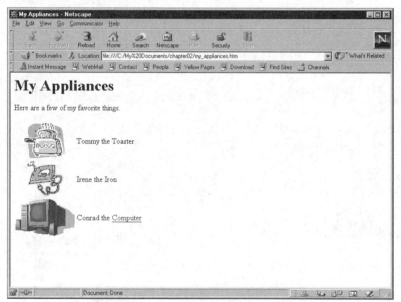

Figure 2-12. FrontPage is quite capable of creating Web pages that are compatible with Netscape Navigator.

There are, of course, limits to the extent that any HTML editor can provide a WYSIWYG view. Your Web visitor's system still controls the screen resolution, color depth, page width, font, font size, and other visual aspects, according to its operating system, browser software, installed fonts, and so forth. No HTML editor can predict what these settings will be at display time, so no HTML editor can preview them 100 percent accurately. FrontPage does, however, provide a reasonable preview of what a visitor with browser settings similar to yours would see.

Chapter 2

Chapter 2: Editing Web Pages

The fastest way to end an editing session is simply to close its editing window (that is, to click the Close button in the window's top right corner). However, you can also choose Close from the File menu.

Opening an Existing Web Page

The New Page Or Web task pane provides a convenient way to open a new or recently used page. The Recent Files choice on the File menu also provides access to the list of recently used pages. The most flexible way to open pages, however, is by using the Open File dialog box shown in Figure 2-13. (To open this dialog box, choose Open from the File menu.)

For more information about opening Web pages, see "Editing an Existing Web Page" on page 259.

My Places bar   Toolbar

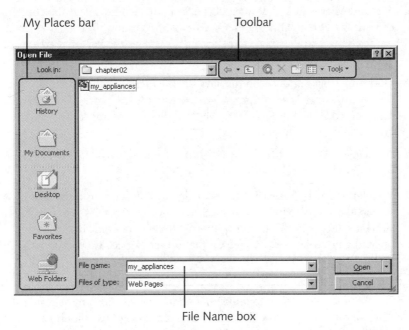

File Name box

Figure 2-13. The FrontPage Open File dialog box provides a My Places bar and enhanced toolbar controls, just like those in the Save As dialog box.

This dialog box can open any sort of Web page located on your computer, on a file server, or on the World Wide Web. If you type a file name in the File Name box, FrontPage opens that file via the Windows file system. If you type a Web address, such as *http://www.interlacken.com/fp-iso/default.htm*, FrontPage retrieves all the files from that location just as a browser would and then loads them into the editing window.

> **note** Just because you can load a page from the Web into the FrontPage editing window doesn't mean you can save changes back to the same location. For you to do that, the Web server needs software capable of receiving file updates, and the server's administrator must grant you permission to use it.

The remaining controls in the Open File dialog box save you from having to type file names in the File Name box; in other words, you can use them to specify file names by pointing and clicking. For the most part, these controls work like those in any other Windows application, but the five icons in the My Places bar (at the left of the dialog box) deserve special mention:

- **History.** Clicking this icon displays a list of the URLs you recently accessed with Internet Explorer.

- **My Documents (Personal).** On Microsoft Windows 98, Microsoft Windows Me, and Microsoft Windows 2000, clicking this icon displays the contents of your My Documents folder. On Microsoft Windows NT 4.0, the icon's name changes to Personal, and clicking it displays the Personal area of your Windows NT user profile.

- **Desktop.** Clicking this icon displays the file locations that normally appear on your desktop: My Computer, My Documents, Network Neighborhood, and so forth. On Windows 2000, My Network Places appears instead of Network Neighborhood.

- **Favorites.** Clicking this icon displays the same Internet shortcuts that appear on the Favorites menu in Internet Explorer.

- **Web Folders (My Network Places).** Clicking this icon displays a list of Web servers that have SharePoint Team Services or the FrontPage Server Extensions installed. Servers appear in this list for two reasons: because you opened a FrontPage-based Web on that server or because you used the Add Web Folder or Add Network Place Wizard to add the server manually.

> **tip** You can tell the My Places bar to remember additional locations by selecting the location in the main file list window in any file-oriented dialog box, clicking the Tools toolbar button, and clicking Add To "My Places" in the drop-down menu.

 For more information about the Open File toolbar, refer to "The File Dialog Box Toolbar" in the Bonus Content on the Companion CD.

When you open several pages at the same time, they all normally appear within the same FrontPage window. To edit a particular page, click its tab at the top of the editing window, choose its name from the Window menu, or press Ctrl+Tab until the page you want appears.

Chapter 2: Editing Web Pages

If you want two editing sessions to be visible at the same time, first open an additional FrontPage window by choosing New Window from the Window menu, and then open one page in each window. Repeat this process to open as many windows as you want. To switch between windows, press Alt+Tab until the window you want appears.

FrontPage Web Components

To help you produce sophisticated Web pages quickly, FrontPage includes a powerful collection of intelligent Web components. FrontPage inserts these components wherever you specify, prompts you for any variable information, and then generates the corresponding HTML code when it saves the page. Along with the HTML, FrontPage saves the dialog box values you specified so that it can redisplay them in future editing sessions or re-create the HTML if some other factor changes.

In almost every case, Web components provide active output (that is, their content or appearance changes automatically based on events beyond the Web page that contains the components). These changes may occur for any of the following reasons:

- The generated HTML includes a browser-side or server-side script that produces variable output.

- The generated HTML runs a program on the server, such as a database query or full text search.

- The generated HTML reflects information located elsewhere within the FrontPage-based Web. If you change the information located elsewhere, FrontPage automatically corrects all the Web pages that reference it.

  FrontPage 2002 provides a plethora of Web components, some of which appear prominently in the user interface and some of which are more subtle. This chapter will provide a brief introduction to the most commonly used components.

  The following components operate totally within either the FrontPage authoring environment or the Web visitor's browser and don't require that any FrontPage software be installed on the Web server.

note Unless stated otherwise, you can insert these components by choosing Web Components from the Insert menu and then selecting the appropriate component.

- **Comment.** This component displays text that's visible only in FrontPage. The same text doesn't appear when the Web page is viewed with a browser. To insert a Comment component, choose Comment from the Insert menu.

For more information about the Comment component, refer to "Inserting Comments" on page 282.

● **Date And Time.** FrontPage replaces this component with the date and time of the last update to the page. To insert a Date And Time component, choose Date And Time from the Insert menu.

For more information about the Date And Time component, refer to "Using the Date and Time Component" on page 769.

● **File Upload.** If a page contains this component, Web visitors can upload files along with other HTML form input. To insert this component, choose Form from the Insert menu and then choose File Upload.

For more information about the File Upload component, refer to "Configuring File Upload Options" on page 904.

● **Hover Button.** HTML provides a built-in button object that's commonly used to submit forms or trigger actions. FrontPage provides a more interesting type of button called a hover button. Hover buttons provide much more flexibility because you can customize their appearance and even change their appearance in various ways when the Web visitor passes the mouse pointer over them.

For more information about the Hover Button component, refer to "Using Hover Buttons" on page 695.

● **Marquee.** This component creates an area of text that moves across the Web page. FrontPage provides a rich assortment of colors, effects, and timing options that control the marquee's appearance at browse time.

Some browsers, such as Netscape Navigator, don't display marquees actively. In these cases, the marquee text appears but remains stationary.

For more information about the Marquee component, refer to "Displaying a Marquee" on page 711.

● **Banner Ad Manager.** This component displays a series of pictures, each for a specified number of seconds. When Web visitors load the page, their browsers load a FrontPage Java applet that continuously retrieves and displays the specified pictures.

For more information about Java applets, refer to "Java Applets" later in this chapter.

- **Photo Gallery.** This component organizes groups of pictures by creating and displaying miniature versions (thumbnails) of each one. Web visitors scan the thumbnails until one catches their interest, and then click the thumbnail to display the full-sized picture.

For more information about the Photo Gallery component, refer to "Creating Photo Galleries" on page 349.

- **Substitution.** This component replaces itself with a page-level or Web-level configuration variable.

For more information about the Substitution component, refer to "Using Web Parameters and the Substitution Component" on page 762.

- **Include Page.** FrontPage replaces this component with the contents of another page in the same site. When the same features appear in many Web pages and you might need to change them in the future, you should consider using the Include Page component.

For more information about the Include Page component, refer to "Using the Include Page Component" on page 750.

- **Scheduled Include Page.** FrontPage replaces this component with the contents of another Web page (or page segment) every time the page is saved during a specified time period. After the time expires, FrontPage no longer displays the included page.

For more information about the Scheduled Include Page component, refer to "Using the Scheduled Include Page Component" on page 755.

- **Scheduled Picture.** This component works like the scheduled Include Page component except that the Scheduled Picture component replaces itself with a picture rather than a Web page. Figure 2-14 on the next page shows the dialog box that controls the Scheduled Picture component. In this example, the component labels an element on the Web page as *New!* for a period of a year.

For more information about the Scheduled Picture component, refer to "Using the Scheduled Picture Component" on page 758.

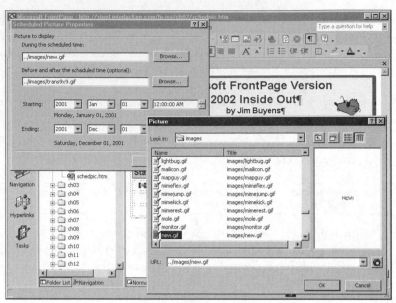

Figure 2-14. The Scheduled Picture component starts and stops displaying a picture based on date.

● **Page Banner.** This component inserts a text or graphic object containing the current page's title, as specified in various Page Properties dialog boxes. The Page Banner component is particularly useful when constructing page templates or standard page headings. Each time the template or heading is used, the Page Banner component displays the title of the current page.

For more information about the Page Banner component, refer to "Using Page Banners" on page 212.

● **Link Bars.** This component builds a set of text or graphic hyperlinks and inserts them wherever you want on the current Web page. A single Web page may contain any number of Link bars.

In earlier versions of FrontPage, Link bars (then called Navigation bars) always got their links from the structure coded in Navigation view. The Link bar contained the Navigation view names and link locations for the current page's children, parents, left and right siblings, and home page, as drawn in Navigation view. Changing the structure in FrontPage's Navigation view updated the Link bars—automatically—in any relevant pages. This mode of operation is valuable, and FrontPage 2002 still supports it.

For more information about Navigation view, refer to Chapter 7, "Managing Web Structure with Navigation View."

Chapter 2: Editing Web Pages

newfeature!

FrontPage 2002 also supports a second way of using Link bars—you can now configure a Link bar entirely by hand. Configuring by hand provides the look and feel of Link bars without forcing the designer to diagram the site.

> For more information about Link bars, refer to "Using Link Bars with Navigation View" on page 201 and "Using the Link Bars Component" on page 371.

- **Table of Contents Relative To A Web Page.** This component creates an outline with hyperlinks to each page in your Web. It also updates the outline whenever the Web changes.

> For more information about the Table Of Contents For This Web Site component, refer to "Using the Table Of Contents For This Web Site Component" on page 771.

- **Table of Contents Based On Page Category.** Given one or more category codes, this component builds a list of hyperlinks to pages in those categories. You can categorize Web pages either as you edit them or from the Folder List in Folders view. (Right-click the file, choose Properties, and then choose Workgroup.)

> For more information about the Table of Contents Based On Page Category component, refer to "Using the Table of Contents Based On Page Category Component" on page 776.

- **Insert HTML.** If you know how to code HTML and want to insert some special code into a Web page, this component provides the method. FrontPage inserts any HTML you provide directly into the Web page without interpretation, validation, or correction.

> **tip**   To fully integrate your HTML with the HTML generated by FrontPage, insert the new HTML lines after switching FrontPage to HTML view. This technique permits subsequent WYSIWYG viewing and editing. Use the Insert HTML component only for HTML that you don't want FrontPage to process in any way.

> For more information about the Insert HTML component, refer to "Using the Insert HTML Component" in the Bonus Content on the Companion CD.

Five Web components operate at least partially on the Web server, and you need to be sure your Web server has SharePoint Team Services or the FrontPage Server Extensions installed before using these components:

- **Confirmation Field.** When providing feedback to a Web visitor who has submitted an HTML form, FrontPage replaces this component with the submitted contents of a form field. For example, if a Web visitor fills out a name-and-address form, this component can redisplay the information for the Web visitor to verify what's been stored on the server.

> For more information about the Confirmation Field component, refer to "Using the Confirmation Field Component" on page 906.

- **Hit Counter.** This component increments and displays a counter every time a Web visitor accesses the page that contains it.

> For more information about the Hit Counter component, refer to "Using the Hit Counter Component" on page 827.

- **Save Results.** You won't find this component on any of the standard FrontPage toolbars; it's an option in the Properties dialog box for an HTML form. The Save Results component processes data submitted from an HTML form by writing it to a new or existing file on the server, sending it to a designated e-mail address, or adding it to an existing database on the server.

> For more information about the Save Results component, refer to "Saving Form Results as Files or E-Mail" on page 896 or "Saving Form Results to a Database" on page 917.

newfeature!

- **Top 10 List.** This component summarizes and displays activity statistics from your Web server. These statistics can include the ten most popular pages in your Web, the ten browsers most frequently used to access your Web, and so forth.

> For more information about the Top 10 List component, refer to "Creating Top 10 Lists" on page 843.

- **Web Search.** This component creates a form for full-text searching of a Web. The Web visitor submits a form containing words to locate, and the component returns a list of hyperlinks to relevant pages.

> For more information about the Web Search component, refer to Chapter 28, "Providing a Text Search Capability."

All Web components depend on FrontPage to run them whenever a page is saved. If you make changes to your Web with *another* editor, the Web component won't be invoked at save time and might not function correctly. Scheduled Web components take effect only if you save the affected pages on or after the specified start and stop dates.

Advanced Components

The fact that computers deliver Web pages on demand and display them interactively means that computer programming instructions can be inserted at any step of the process: when storing pages to the server, when processing Web visitor requests, when delivering requested pages, or when displaying the pages. This flexibility is one of the significant differences between the Web and other mass media. Newspapers, magazines, books, radio, and television all provide very little interactivity or opportunities for customization.

Developers have invented a wide range of technologies for adding programmed intelligence to the Web experience. These include the following:

- Server-side scripting
- Script languages
- Java applets
- ActiveX controls
- Plug-ins
- Design-Time controls

Server-Side Scripting

Common Gateway Interface (CGI), Netscape Server Application Programming Interface (NSAPI), and Internet Server Application Programming Interface (ISAPI) are three interfaces that programs running on a Web server can use to receive data from Web visitors and produce Web pages as output. A Web visitor starts such programs by submitting a special Web page request, and the Web server returns the generated page to that Web visitor. Creating such programs is beyond the objectives of FrontPage, but FrontPage does provide a useful, prewritten set of them—the FrontPage Server Extensions.

> For more information about the FrontPage Server Extensions, see Chapter 38, "Understanding the FrontPage Server Extensions."

Active Server Pages (ASP) is a higher-level technology for creating special Web pages containing both HTML code and script code that runs on a Web server. FrontPage supports the development of ASP in three scenarios:

- If you create a Web page that contains a database results region, FrontPage generates ASP code and saves the Web page with an *.asp* filename extension.

> For more information about database results regions, refer to "Using the Database Results Wizard" on page 922.

- If you open the Web Site Templates dialog box and run the Database Interface Wizard, FrontPage creates a group of ASP pages collectively called a *database editor*. A database editor can display, add, change, and delete database records at will.

> For more information about the Database Interface Wizard, refer to "Using the Database Interface Wizard" on page 240.

- By switching to HTML view, you can add ASP code to any Web page. This code won't prevent you from returning to Normal view and resuming WYSIWYG editing for any fixed portions of the page.

> For more information about Active Server Pages, refer to "Processing Form Data with ASP Pages" on page 910 and "Sending Custom E-Mail" on page 912.

 More information about Active Server Pages is also available in Chapter 40, "Processing Databases with Active Server Pages," and Appendix B, "Introducing Active Server Page Objects," in the Bonus Content on the Companion CD.

Script Languages

Scripts are short sections of program code inserted directly into Web pages and set off by special tags so that the source code doesn't appear on the displayed page. Scripts can run on either a browser or a Web server, subject to the design of the script and the capabilities of the environment.

Two common uses for scripts are inserting variable information, such as the current date or the date a page was last saved, and responding to Web visitor events, such as resizing the browser window or clicking a button. Script languages can also interact with ActiveX controls and Java applets on the same page, and with the browser or server itself.

 For more information about using scripts, refer to Chapter 42, "Working with Script Code," in the Bonus Content on the Companion CD.

Chapter 2: Editing Web Pages

FrontPage supports script languages by providing a way to insert developer-written scripts into Web pages and by automatically generating script code for common functions, such as field validation. FrontPage supports both Microsoft Visual Basic Scripting Edition (VBScript) and JavaScript, the two most popular browser script languages. Figure 2-15 shows a line of JavaScript inserted into a Web page.

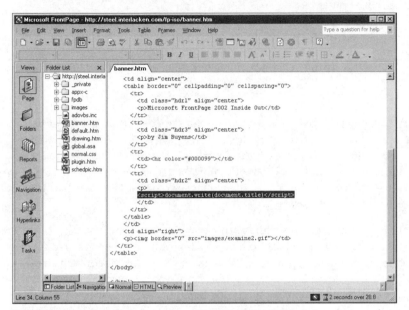

Figure 2-15. FrontPage can insert JavaScript or VBScript code anywhere on a Web page.

Java Applets

Java applets are small programs written in the Java programming language. Programmers convert their Java programs to a format called *bytecode*. The bytecode files can run on any computer on which a piece of software called a *Java bytecode interpreter* is installed. The interpreter creates an environment called the *Java Virtual Machine*, which at least in theory, can run any Java program. This approach frees programmers from having to write different versions of their programs for each type of computer. The interpreter must be matched to the type of computer, but the Java program need not be matched.

Java applets are designed to run as part of a Web page. An applet usually occupies a portion of the browser window, controls its contents, and responds to any Web visitor

events that occur there. For security reasons, applets can't access files and other resources on the local computer, and they can initiate network connections only to the
server from which the applet was downloaded. (These restrictions are frequently compared to a "sandbox," in which Java applets must play.) FrontPage isn't a development
environment for Java applets, but it can add existing applets to a page and display them
in their initial state.

> **For more information about using Java applets, refer to "Incorporating Java Applets" on
> page 739.**

ActiveX Controls

Like Java applets, ActiveX controls are programmed objects capable of providing a
given function in a variety of contexts. Unlike Java applets, however, ActiveX controls
are based on the OLE approach developed for Microsoft Windows. ActiveX is a very
flexible specification that defines not only Web page objects but objects that run in all
sorts of Windows environments. In fact, most ActiveX objects are background components with no visible display.

Controls designed to run within a browser window occupy a portion of the Web page
and accept input from HTML code, the Web visitor, or other controls. In response, the
controls change their appearance and make results available for transmission back to
the Web server. ActiveX controls running on a Web server don't create visual output
directly, but instead perform server-side functions such as writing and retrieving data
in files and databases. They typically get their input from requests originating from a
browser client or from a script that invokes them. As output, they might return values
to the script that invoked them or write HTML for transmission to the Web visitor.

ActiveX controls are compiled for a specific type of computer and a specific class of
operating system. A separate version is therefore required for each environment. Currently, almost all ActiveX controls run on X86 processors and Win32 operating systems.

There's no "sandbox" limiting what an ActiveX control can do, but each control is
digitally signed so that the Web visitor can verify that it arrived both intact and from
a trusted source. Although FrontPage isn't a development environment for ActiveX
controls, it supports placing such controls on a page and displaying them in their
initial state.

> **For more information about using ActiveX controls, refer to "Incorporating ActiveX Controls"
> on page 716.**

Plug-Ins

This is another category of software modules, first developed by Netscape Communications Corporation, that integrate into the display of a Web browser. Plug-ins typically provide interactive and multimedia capability. Here's how the process of displaying content with a plug-in works:

1 The Web page contains special HTML coding that tells the browser to retrieve a file and display it with a plug-in. However, the HTML coding doesn't tell the browser which plug-in to use.

2 The browser requests the specified file from the Web server.

3 The Web server sends the requested file and identifies it with a MIME type.

> **note** MIME stands for Multipurpose Internet Mail Extensions, and a MIME type is a text string such as *audio/wav*. Windows-based Web servers usually derive the MIME type from the filename extension.

4 The browser looks up the MIME type in a table and determines whether any available plug-ins can display that MIME type.

5 The browser loads the first suitable plug-in and tells it to display the downloaded file.

The fact that the HTML coding doesn't tell the browser what plug-in to use is very disturbing to many Web designers. It means that designers have much less control with plug-ins than they have with Java applets and ActiveX controls. With applets and ActiveX controls, designers can specify—and the browser can download—all the software needed to display the object. With plug-ins, designers can only tell the Web visitor what plug-in the page requires and provide a manual link to the plug-in vendor's download site.

For more information about using plug-ins, refer to "Incorporating Plug-Ins" on page 736.

Design-Time Controls

The purpose of Design-Time Controls is to preview Web functions and create the required HTML. As such, Design-Time Controls run only in the authoring environment. The HTML or other created objects can run either on the Web server when a request is received, or in the browser when it receives a response. However, servers and browsers use the output of a Design-Time Control and not the control itself.

Eventually, Design-Time Controls might permit designers to seamlessly add new functions at will to Web editors like FrontPage. For now, FrontPage accommodates them—but not seamlessly.

For more information about using Design-Time Controls, refer to "Incorporating Design-Time Controls" on page 743.

In Summary...

This chapter explained the essentials of creating a Web page with FrontPage. FrontPage provides a rich array of powerful tools that make it easy for both beginners and experts to create Web pages that look the way they want. For more detail on these techniques and others, please refer to the book's later chapters.

The next chapter explains how FrontPage works not only with individual Web pages, but also with entire Web sites.

Managing Web Sites

Creating Web pages one-by-one is certainly a useful task, but realistically, you can't present much content on a single page. All but the simplest projects require interrelated Web pages numbering in the dozens, hundreds, or more. Additionally, because each Web page typically uses several constituent files, the total number of files to create, interconnect, and maintain over time can be intimidating.

Site management is an area that many beginning Web designers fail to appreciate. Hard experience is frequently the best teacher in this regard, and if you want to try this approach, go ahead. But if you'd rather learn from the experience of experts, please consider the approaches described in this chapter.

Microsoft FrontPage 2002 comes equipped with a broad collection of highly useful tools that can help you create a well-organized site and keep it organized over time. As your expertise grows, you'll probably come to appreciate these features even more than the WYSIWYG editor that possibly drew you to FrontPage in the first place.

Planning Your Web Environment

For most projects, it makes perfect sense to have two FrontPage environments: a development environment where you develop and test new or updated pages, and a production environment that delivers finished pages to Web visitors. When new content is ready for world consumption, you transfer it from your development environment server to your production environment server.

Initially, your development environment could be a small collection of freestanding Web pages and associated pictures located in a folder on your hard disk. For sites consisting of more than just a few pages, however, you'll benefit greatly from using a FrontPage-based Web. This could be a disk-based Web not involving a Web server, a server-based Web administered by someone else, or a personal Web server administered by you.

In general, the more alike your development and production environments, the more effective your testing will be and the fewer problems you'll encounter. This situation argues strongly for two Web servers, both running the FrontPage Server Extensions or SharePoint Team Services. At the same time, other configurations are certainly possible, workable, and in many cases preferable, depending on your circumstances. The remainder of this section will describe some of these scenarios.

If your needs are simple and formal control over content changes isn't critical, a single server might suffice. If your needs are complex, a battery of servers might be needed. Your development environment might be disk-based or Web-server-based. Your production server might be Microsoft Windows 2000 or UNIX, and in either case it might or might not have the FrontPage Server Extensions installed. If your production server doesn't have the server extensions, publishing your Web won't be quite as smooth, and FrontPage services that run at browse time—such as Search, Save Results, and Database Access—won't be available. This might or might not present a crisis, depending on your requirements. All in all, these are decisions only you, your organization, or your client can make.

Here are some common scenarios:

● You create Web pages in your home or small office, and connect only periodically to the network where your production Web server resides. Your development Web is disk-based.

An Internet service provider, a Web presence provider, or your corporate IT department operates the production server. Your service provider doesn't have the FrontPage Server Extensions installed, and so you have to publish using either an external FTP program or FrontPage's built-in FTP. Neither your development nor production environment supports server-based Web components such as Hit Counter, Web Search, and Save Results.

- You create Web pages in an office or campus having a permanent network connection. Your development and production Webs both reside on Windows 2000 servers running the FrontPage Server Extensions. To get a FrontPage-based Web created on either machine, you submit paperwork to a system administrator. All FrontPage functions work on both machines.

- Your development environment consists of a personal Web server running on your home computer. The FrontPage Server Extensions are installed on your personal Web server.

- Your production environment is a UNIX server operated by your ISP, and the server doesn't have the FrontPage Server Extensions. This means that although all Web components work perfectly in your development environment, they fail in production. However, if your ISP supplies sample HTML for hit counters, forms processors, or other components supported on the UNIX Web server, you can paste it onto FrontPage's HTML view.

> For more information about installing a personal Web server, refer to Chapter 37, "Installing and Configuring a Web Server."

If you've decided you need a personal Web server and you're working remotely, or if you're cursed and have to *be* the network administrator, you'll need to learn how to install a Web server yourself. Later chapters explain in detail how to choose the proper Web server for your platform and how to coordinate installation of the Web server, the FrontPage Server Extensions, and the FrontPage client.

> For more information about installing the FrontPage Server Extensions, refer to Chapter 38, "Understanding the FrontPage Server Extensions."

Creating a FrontPage-Based Web

Many of the most powerful features in FrontPage work not just on single Web pages, but on all Web pages in a given set. This invites the question of what constitutes a set, and the answer is, a FrontPage-based Web.

A FrontPage-based Web consists of all the individual pages and folders that reside within a specially designated folder tree on your hard disk or Web server. The only exception is that no one file or folder can be a member of two Webs. You can physically locate one Web inside another, but operations on the "outer" Web won't affect the "inner" Web (as they would if the "inner" Web were an ordinary folder.)

> For more information about FrontPage-based Webs, refer to Chapter 6, "Creating and Using FrontPage-Based Webs."

As you start to work with groups of Web pages, you'll almost certainly find it worthwhile to set up your groups in such a way that FrontPage will understand the boundaries of each group. To do this, create a different Web for each group of Web pages.

Here's the procedure for creating a Web:

1 Start the FrontPage desktop software.

2 If the New Page Or Web task pane isn't visible, choose New from the File menu, and then choose Page Or Web.

3 Click the Empty Web option listed under New; or

Click the Web Site Templates option listed under New From Template. FrontPage displays the Web Site Templates dialog box shown in Figure 3-1.

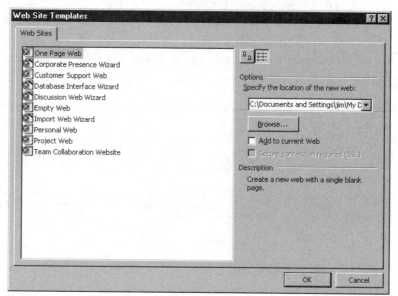

Figure 3-1. The Web Site Templates dialog box lists templates containing good starting points for your new Web.

The templates listed on the left side of the Web Sites tab offer various kinds of initial content for your new Web:

■ If you chose the Empty Web option in step 3, the Empty Web template is selected. This template creates a Web with no initial content.

■ If you chose the Web Site Templates option in step 3, the One Page Web template is selected. This template creates a Web with a blank home page.

To create a new Web with initial content other than these defaults, click the icon for the type of content you want.

Chapter 3: Managing Web Sites

The options on the right side specify the location of the new Web and other options. In the box titled Specify The Location Of The New Web, type the full path to the location where you want the Web to reside:

■ If you enter a file location, such as *C:\My Documents\My Webs\fp-iso* or *\\spike\webshare\fp-iso*, FrontPage creates a disk-based Web.

■ If you enter a Web address, such as *http://www.interlacken.com /fp-iso*, FrontPage creates a server-based Web.

> **note** You can create server-based Webs only on a Web server that has the FrontPage Server Extensions or SharePoint Team Services installed. In addition, you must have the necessary security permissions to access the Web server.

By default, the first Web that FrontPage creates is called *myweb* and is located in *C:\My Documents\My Webs*. (If you're running Windows 2000, the default location is *C:\Documents and Settings\<username>\My Documents\My Webs.*) If you create additional Webs, their default names will be *my web2*, *myweb3*, and so on, and their paths will be

> *C:\My Documents\My Webs\myweb2*
> *C:\My Documents\My Webs\myweb3*

and so forth. However, if you create a Web somewhere else, such as *http:// www.interlacken.com/fp-iso*, subsequently clicking the New, Empty Web option will create a Web at *http://www.interlacken.com/fp-iso2*.

4 If you prefer to specify the Web location by pointing and clicking rather than by typing, click the Browse button. Clicking this displays the New Web Location dialog box. (This box looks much like the Open File dialog box mentioned in Chapter 2.) Navigate to the location you want, and then click Open.

5 Select the Secure Connection Required (SSL) option if you're creating a server-based Web and that server's security policy requires the use of Secure Sockets Layer (SSL) communication.

6 Click OK to create the new Web.

> For more information about creating and managing FrontPage-based Webs, refer to Chapter 6, "Creating and Using FrontPage-Based Webs."

Chapter 6 presents much more information about creating and managing Webs, but here are some quick tips to get you started:

● If the file or network path to a new FrontPage-based Web contains an existing Web, the new Web will be a subweb. Suppose, for example, that you create a new Web at *C:\My Documents\My Webs\Statues\Grecian* and

Chapter 3

C:*My Documents**My Webs**Statues* is already a FrontPage Web. The Grecian Web becomes a subweb of the Statues Web.

● Another—even easier—way to create subwebs is to follow these steps:

   1 Use FrontPage to open the Web that will contain the new subweb.

   2 If necessary, display the Folder List by choosing Folder List from the View menu.

   3 Create a folder where you want the subweb to reside (that is, right-click the parent folder, choose New from the shortcut menu, and name the new folder as you want).

   4 Right-click the new folder in the Folder List, and choose Convert To Web from the shortcut menu. Click Yes when prompted.

● The more files a Web contains, the longer certain Web operations take. Web publishing is particularly affected by file quantity. Try to keep the size of your Webs down to a few hundred files if possible, or a few thousand files at most.

● You should update FrontPage-based Webs only by using Web Folders in Microsoft Windows 98 or Microsoft Windows NT, a Web location in My Network Places in Windows 2000, or FrontPage itself. Updating a Web by any other means doesn't update all the file indexes and cross-references that FrontPage needs for proper operation and doesn't maintain consistency among files the way FrontPage can.

> **tip** If you must update a Web by means other than FrontPage, you need to take corrective action by opening the Web in FrontPage and choosing Recalculate Hyperlinks from the Tools menu.

● FrontPage security operates at the Web level; one part of a Web can't have different security—whether for authoring or for browsing—than another part of the same Web. Security needs are therefore an issue to consider when planning your Webs. Each different security requirement necessitates its own Web or subweb.

● The Import Web Wizard (available when you choose Import from the File menu) works by importing another Web's home page, followed by all the files the home page refers to, all the files those files refer to, and so forth. Unfortunately, this process usually retrieves less than 100 percent of the files in the source Web and none of the configuration settings. By far, the best way to copy a FrontPage-based Web from place to place is to follow these steps:

Chapter 3: Managing Web Sites

1 Open the source Web in FrontPage.

2 Choose Publish Web from the File menu.

3 In the Publish Destination dialog box, specify the address of the destination Web in the box titled Enter Publish Destination. This can be a
file location, an HTTP location, or an FTP location.

4 Click OK, and then click Publish.

> **For more information about publishing FrontPage-based Webs, refer to Chapter 13, "Publish-
> ing Your FrontPage-Based Web."**

Opening a FrontPage-Based Web

The first step in working with a FrontPage-based Web is to open it. Here's one way to
do this:

1 Choose Open Web from the File menu. The Open Web dialog box shown in
Figure 3-2 appears.

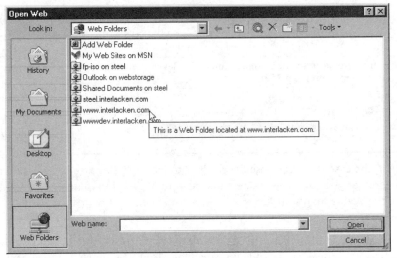

Figure 3-2. The Open Web dialog box is very similar to the Open File dialog box shown in Figure 2-13. Rather than opening a single file, however,
this box opens a group view of many files.

2 Locate the Web you want using either of the following options:

■ To locate a disk-based Web, use the History, My Documents, Desktop,
or Favorites icon. (In Windows NT, a Personal icon replaces the My
Documents icon.)

■ To locate a server-based Web in Windows 2000, use the My Network
Places icon. (In Windows 98 or Windows NT 4, use the Web Folders
icon.)

---

note The first time you try to open a server-based Web, its server might not appear in
the Web Folders list. FrontPage can't display a list of Web servers in your environment, because your environment might be the entire Internet! If the folder you want
doesn't appear in the Web Folders list, just type its URL, and then click Open. This
both opens the Web and adds it to the list for next time.

By the way, in folder listings, the icon for a FrontPage-based Web looks like a folder
with a globe on it. This visually distinguishes FrontPage-based Webs from regular
folders.

---

3 Double-click the name of the Web, or select the name and click the Open
button.

Opening a Web is such a common task that FrontPage provides many ways to do it.
Here are some additional ways to open a Web:

● Open a Web page that resides in a FrontPage-based Web. FrontPage opens
both the specified file and the Web that contains it.

For information about opening individual files in FrontPage, refer to "Opening a Page from
Page View" on page 259.

● Choose Recent Webs from the File menu. If the Web you want to open
appears in the list, simply select it.

---

note In the case of server-based Webs that support user-level security, FrontPage might
prompt you for a user name and password. If you don't know what to enter, contact
the Web administrator.

● Locate the Web within the Folder List of another Web, and double-click it.
(Right-clicking and choosing Open from the shortcut menu accomplishes
the same thing as double-clicking.)

Opening a regular folder in FrontPage displays that folder's contents in the
same window. Opening a FrontPage-based Web creates a new window displaying that Web.

Figure 3-3 shows a Web open in FrontPage. Below the toolbars appear three distinct
frames:

Chapter 3: Managing Web Sites

- **Views bar.** The icons in this frame display any of six views in the document frame:

    - **Page.** Displays Web pages in WYSIWYG view for editing.

    - **Folders.** Displays a tabular list of files in the Web organized by folder.

    - **Reports.** Displays an assortment of tabular listings useful for site management.

    - **Navigation.** Graphically displays the logical hierarchy of a Web.

    - **Hyperlinks.** Graphically displays files in a Web, organized by hyperlink reference.

    - **Tasks.** Displays a list of reminders about completing or correcting pages.

- **Folder List.** This frame displays the Web contents as a folder tree.

- **Document window.** This frame displays the document, report, or work area you select in the Views bar.

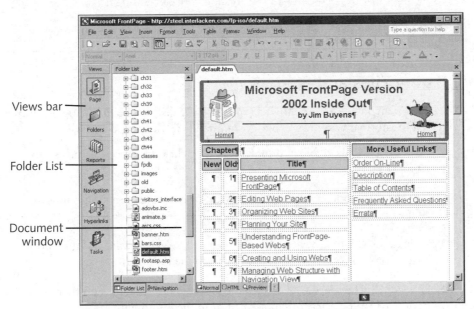

Figure 3-3. FrontPage displays an open Web in three main panes. From left to right, these are the Views bar, the Folder List, and the Document window.

To hide or display the Views bar, choose Views Bar from the View menu. To hide or display the Folder List, choose Folder List from the View menu.

The next section explains how to use the Folder List.

Chapter 3

Working with Web Folder Lists

The Folder List normally appears whenever a FrontPage-based Web is open. It occupies the middle pane of the main FrontPage window and provides access to all files and folders in the Web. In addition to providing information, the Folder List has two main uses: manipulating the files and folders in the Web, and opening files with the appropriate editor.

> **tip** The Folder List is never visible when the main FrontPage window is in Reports view or Tasks view. If the Folder List doesn't appear within any other view, choose Folder List from the View menu.

In some cases, the Navigation Pane appears in place of the Folder List. The Navigation Pane displays the same information as Navigation view but in a smaller format that FrontPage can display simultaneously with an open Web page. To display the Folder List instead of the Navigation Pane, choose Folder List from the View menu or click the Folder List tab located at the bottom of the Navigation Pane.

> For more information about Navigation view, refer to "Creating a Web Site in Navigation View" later in this chapter.

Manipulating Files and Folders

The center pane in Figure 3-3 shows a typical Folder List. As the following list illustrates, all the normal Windows Explorer commands work as expected:

- To open a collapsed folder, double-click it or click the preceding plus-sign icon.

- To collapse an open folder, double-click it or click the preceding minus-sign icon.

- To load the Clipboard with a file to be copied, select the file, and then press Ctrl+C or Ctrl+Insert or choose Copy from the Edit menu.

- To load the Clipboard with a file to be moved, select the file, and then press Ctrl+X or Shift+Delete or choose Cut from the Edit menu.

- To complete a move or copy operation, select the desired folder, and then press Ctrl+V or Shift+Insert or choose Paste from the Edit menu.

- To move a file from one folder to another, drag the file over the destination folder's icon, and then drop it.

Chapter 3: Managing Web Sites

- To copy a file from one location to another, hold down the Ctrl key while dragging the file to the new location.

- To move or copy a file or folder and control the operation from a shortcut menu, drag the file or folder with the right mouse button to the desired location, release the button, and then make a selection from the shortcut menu.

- To rename a file or folder, either select it and press F2, or right-click it and choose Rename from the shortcut menu.

- To delete a file or folder, select it and press Delete, select it and choose Delete from the Edit menu, or right-click it and choose Delete from the shortcut menu.

You can also cut, copy, and drag files to transport them between two Webs and between a disk location and a Web. However, the following special precautions apply:

- You can't move files into or out of a Web. You can only copy them.

- You can't copy or drop files or folders onto a Web folder displayed in a parent Web. To copy between Webs, you must open each Web in a separate FrontPage window.

- When you drag or copy a file out of a Web and onto your Windows desktop, Windows creates an Internet Shortcut to the file. Clicking this shortcut launches your default browser and displays the file.

Note that you can't copy a file from a FrontPage Web to a physical location on your hard disk by dragging it out of a FrontPage Folder List or view. However, there are two other ways you can do this:

- Open the file in Page view, choose Save As from the File menu, and specify a location on your hard disk.

- Drag the file from a Web folder to the desired location in Windows Explorer. There are two variations to this procedure:

  - In Windows 98 or Windows NT, first open the My Computer icon on your desktop, and then open the Web Folders icon.

  - In Windows 2000, open My Network Places, open the Web location that contains the file you want, and then open any necessary folders.

  In either case, first open the FrontPage-based Web that contains the file you want, then open any necessary folders, and then drag the file into My Computer (or Windows Explorer). To control the specifics of the dragging operation, drag with the right mouse button, and choose a command from the shortcut menu that appears when you release the button.

Chapter 3

Figure 3-4 shows the shortcut menus you see after right-clicking a file, a folder, and a subweb icon in the Folder List.

Figure 3-4. Right-clicking a Folder List file, folder, and subweb produces these shortcut menus, respectively.

Note the Convert To Web option on the Folder shortcut menu and the Convert To Folder option on the Web menu. These are reciprocal operations but, as explained in Chapter 6, both operations alter or discard Web-related data. After converting a folder to a Web, converting the same Web back to a folder might not restore all the files and FrontPage indexes back to their original condition.

> **For more information about conversion between folders and Webs, refer to "Converting a Folder to a Web" on page 164 and "Converting a Web to a Folder" on page 165.**

Whenever you move or rename files in FrontPage, FrontPage automatically corrects all hyperlinks, image tags, and other references in the same Web. Suppose, for example, that 23 pages in your Web use a picture called *boots.gif*. For some reason, you decide to rename the file from *boots.gif* to *shoes.gif*. When you rename the file from within FrontPage, FrontPage updates all 23 pages so that they reference *shoes.gif* rather than *boots.gif*. FrontPage also warns you before it deletes a file used by other files in your Web.

> **caution** FrontPage can't correct references from outside your Web to files within it. First, this would require searching the entire Internet. Second, even if FrontPage *could* locate such references, you probably wouldn't have the authority to update them. You can minimize this problem by organizing related Web pages into the same Web.

To add an external file to the current Web, select the folder where it should reside, and then choose Import from the File menu. If the Web isn't on the local machine, the Import command copies the file across the network. The Import command also updates FrontPage with appropriate file information, an operation that wouldn't occur if you simply copied the file to the Web's physical location using some other method.

Chapter 3: Managing Web Sites

The Add Task option, available from the Tasks submenu of the Edit menu, creates a Tasks entry for the selected page. The section titled "Working with Tasks View" on page 964 discusses this feature in detail.

Choosing an Editor

Double-clicking any file in the Folder List opens that file using the appropriate editor. Unfortunately, FrontPage's idea of what constitutes an appropriate editor might be different from yours, and this can lead to confusion. Here's how FrontPage chooses an editor:

- Normally, FrontPage opens Web page files—identified by filename extensions such as *.htm*, *.html*, and *.asp*—in Front Page (that is, in Page view).

- Most Office 2000 and Office XP applications can directly save their native documents as pages in a FrontPage-based Web. FrontPage opens all such files in the same application that created them, even if the filename extension is *.htm*, *.asp*, or something else that FrontPage would normally open in Page view. You can tell what application FrontPage will start by looking at each file's icon. Figure 3-5 shows examples of Folder List icons representing HTM files saved by PowerPoint, Excel, and FrontPage.

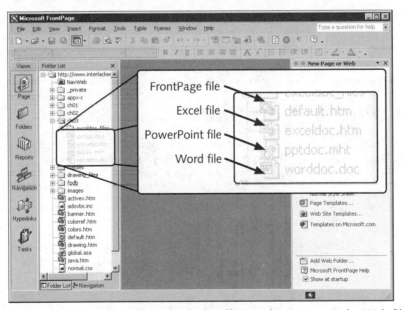

Figure 3-5. FrontPage detects which Office application created a Web file, displays a corresponding icon, and opens files in that same application.

> **tip** If you want FrontPage to open all Web pages in Page view, regardless of the application that created them, choose Options from the Tools menu in FrontPage, click the Configure Editors tab, and clear the check box titled Open Web Pages In The Office Application That Created Them.

- For other kinds of files, FrontPage first tries looking up the filename extension in a list of configured editors. To revise this list, choose Options from the Tools menu, and then click the Configure Editors tab.

on the CD For more information about the Configure Editors tab, refer to "Configuring External Editors" in the Bonus Content on the Companion CD.

- If all else fails, FrontPage chooses an editor by using Windows file associations (that is, it uses the same program Windows would use if you double-clicked the same type of file in Windows Explorer).

There are two ways to temporarily override FrontPage's normal choice of editors (that is, to use a different editor than double-clicking the same file would use):

- If the application you want to use has a Web Folders choice in its Open File dialog box, you can simply start the application and open the file you want.

- You can right-click the file in any Folder List or Folders view, and then choose Open With from the shortcut menu. If the application you want doesn't appear in the resulting dialog box, add it to the list on the Configure Editors tab just described.

Building a Web Site

FrontPage supports three primary ways of populating a new Web with content (that is, of building a Web site). The best choice of a particular job depends, of course, on the nature of the job. Here are the three ways:

- **Manual.** You create all your Web pages and the hyperlinks that connect them by hand.

- **Navigation View.** You diagram your site in Navigation view and let FrontPage create the individual Web pages automatically. Components called *Link bars* use the Navigation view structure to automatically create hyperlinks from one page to another.

- **Web Templates.** You tell FrontPage the type of content you want, and FrontPage supplies a typical collection of Web pages. This provides a starting point for developing your own pages.

Chapter 3: Managing Web Sites

Manually Building a Web Site

The time-honored, classic way of building a Web site is first to create a home page, then create pages that the home page will link to, then add the appropriate hyperlinks to the home page, and so forth, for as many levels as the site requires.

Despite the fact that it's 100 percent manual, this approach to building a Web site remains the most common. It's fast, it's flexible, and it's simple. FrontPage makes it easy to create as many pages as you want, to create hyperlinks by point and click, and to move things around without breaking links as your site changes and evolves. In return for you doing all the work, you have complete control over the results.

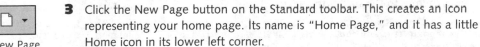

For more information about creating hyperlinks, refer to Chapter 12, "Building Hyperlinks."

Rank beginners tend to choose this method because it requires the least amount of technology to learn. Experts choose it because they want complete control over the results. If learning curves and control don't concern you, FrontPage provides two ways to build a Web site automatically. The next two sections describe these approaches.

Creating a Web Site in Navigation View

For Web sites of moderate size, you can save yourself some work, but sacrifice some flexibility, by creating the site in Navigation view. At a very surface level, here's how this works:

1 Create and open a new empty Web.

2 Click the Navigation button on the Views bar.

New Page

3 Click the New Page button on the Standard toolbar. This creates an icon representing your home page. Its name is "Home Page," and it has a little Home icon in its lower left corner.

4 To change the name of the home page, make sure it's selected, press the F2 key, type the new name, and then press Enter. This name becomes the title that appears in large type at the top of the page.

5 To add a second page to the Web, click the New Page button again. This page will appear a child of the home page. As before, press F2, give the page a meaningful name, and press Enter.

6 To add a third page, click the New Page button yet again. This page will appear as a child of whatever page was selected when you clicked the New Page button. To place any page beneath a different parent, drag it around the Navigation view window until a line connects the page you're dragging to the page you want to be its parent.

7 Repeat Step 6 to add and place more pages as you want.

At this point, your screen should look similar to the one pictured in Figure 3-6. To physically create the pages so that they appear as in the Folder List, click any Views bar button other than Navigation. This creates a new blank page for each node you diagrammed in Navigation view.

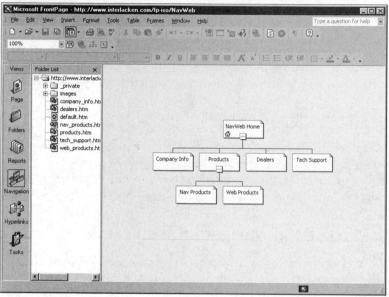

Figure 3-6.   Navigation view provides an electronic storyboard for designing Web sites.

New blank pages might be interesting—or not—but the real payback from creating your Web in Navigation view comes when you add shared borders, Web components, and themes to the site, as the next sections describe.

For more information about Navigation view, refer to Chapter 7, "Managing Web Structure with Navigation View."

Adding Shared Borders

Shared borders are a high-powered way to replicate content throughout a Web. A Web can have up to four shared borders located at the top, left, right, or bottom edge of each page in a Web. Whatever you put in, say, the top shared border appears in the top border of every page in that Web. Whatever you put in the left shared border appears at the left of every page, and so forth.

Shared borders would be boring, mundane, and downright monotonous if not for some special Web components that display different content depending on the page in which they occur. These Web components include:

● **Page Banner.** This component displays a Web page's title as entered in Navigation view. Putting a Page Banner component in a Web's top shared

Chapter 3: Managing Web Sites

border displays—in one fell swoop—each page's Navigation view title at the top of each page.

● **Link Bar.** This component is even more exciting. This component automatically displays a series of hyperlinks to pages above, below, to the left, or to the right of the current page as diagrammed in Navigation view. This saves you the work of manually building the hyperlinks that Web visitors use for traversing your site.

● **Date And Time.** This component automatically displays the date—and optionally, the time—of the last update to the page that contains it.

Here's the procedure for adding shared borders to a Web:

1 Open the Web in FrontPage.

2 Choose Shared Borders from the Format menu.

3 When the Shared Borders dialog box shown in Figure 3-7 appears, make sure that the All Pages option is selected. Otherwise, shared borders will apply only to any pages you selected before performing step 2.

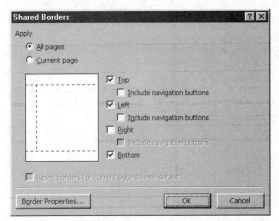

Figure 3-7. Shared borders are reserved areas of content replicated to all or selected pages in a FrontPage Web.

4 Select the check boxes for each shared border you want to use. For purposes of this example, select the Top, Left, and Bottom borders.

If you select the Include Navigation Buttons check box under Top, FrontPage adds a Page Banner component and a Link Bars component to the top shared border.

If you select the Include Navigation Buttons check box under Left or Right, FrontPage adds a Link Bars component to the respective border.

5 Click OK to apply the shared border.

For more information about shared borders, refer to "Using Shared Borders" on page 765.

Adding Shared Border Content

To add content to the shared borders you just created, open any page in the current Web and take the following actions. This example assumes you've opened the home page, *default.htm*, and that it appears as shown in Figure 3-8. To add a Page Banner component to the Top shared border, proceed as follows:

1 Set the insertion point inside the top shared border. If a comment appears within this border, click it, and then press the Delete key.

2 Choose Web Component from the Insert menu.

3 When the Insert Web Component dialog box appears, choose Included Content in the Component Type list, and then choose Page Banner in the Choose A Type Of Content list.

4 Click Finish. When the Page Banner Properties dialog box appears, accept the default property settings, and click OK.

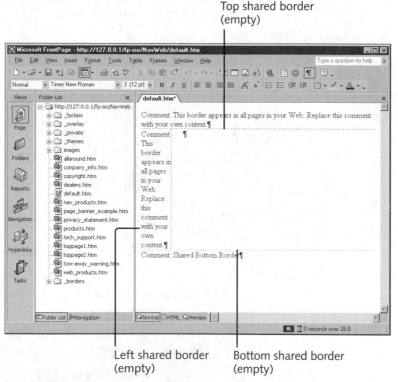

Figure 3-8. This Web page contains three shared border areas: top, left, and bottom. None as yet contain displayable content.

Chapter 3: Managing Web Sites

Follow the next procedure to add a Link Bars component to the left shared border:

1 Set the insertion point inside the left shared border. If a comment appears within this border, click it, and then press the Delete key.

2 Choose Web Component from the Insert menu. This displays the Insert Web Component dialog box.

3 Click Link Bars in the Component Type list, and then click Bar Based On Navigation Structure in the Choose A Bar Type list.

4 Click Finish.

5 When the Link Bar Properties dialog box shown in Figure 3-9 appears, make sure the General tab is visible. Select the Child Level option if necessary, and then select the Home Page and Parent Page options.

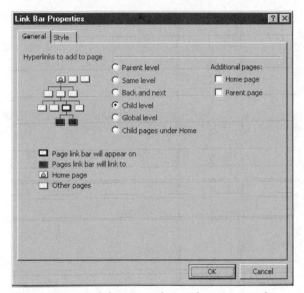

Figure 3-9. Link bars can derive their content from a structure you draw in Navigation view. If you need more than one category of hyperlinks on the same page, include two or more Link Bars components.

6 On the Style Tab, make sure Use Page's Theme is selected in the Choose A Style list. (To see this choice, you might need to scroll the list to the top.) Under Orientation And Appearance, select both the Vertical and the Use Active Graphics options.

7 Click OK.

The next procedure adds a Date And Time component to the bottom shared border.
Follow these steps:

1 Set the insertion point inside the bottom shared border. If a comment
appears within this border, click it, and then press the Delete key.

2 Type the phrase *This page last modified on* and a space.

3 Choose Date And Time from the Insert menu. Under Display, select Date
This Page Was Last Edited. For Date Format, select a format that displays
the name of the month and a four-digit year.

---

tip Because various countries specify month, day, and year in different orders, a date like
2/3/4 can be quite ambiguous. February 3, 2004 is much more specific.

---

4 Click OK.

Align Right

5 To right-align the contents of the bottom border, click the Align Right
button.

The Web page should now appear as in Figure 3-10.

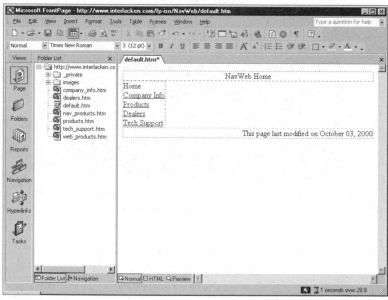

Figure 3-10.   Here the Web page pictured in Figure 3-8 has some typical
content added to it.

Chapter 3: Managing Web Sites

Applying a Theme

The sample Web is now functional but hardly attractive. FrontPage themes provide an excellent way—again with one fell swoop—to improve the appearance of all the pages in a given Web. Here's the procedure for applying a theme to a Web:

1 Open the Web in FrontPage.

2 Choose Theme from the Format menu.

3 When the Themes dialog box shown in Figure 3-11 appears, select the options you want. For example, you might select the following:

■ Under Apply Theme To, select All Pages.

■ In the list of themes, select Axis.

■ Below the list of themes, choose Vivid Colors, Active Graphics, and Background Picture.

4 Click OK. (If a warning dialog box appears, click Yes.)

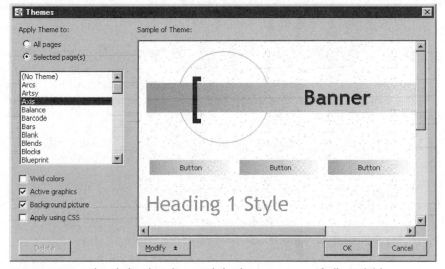

Figure 3-11. This dialog box lists and displays previews of all available FrontPage themes.

You can now preview the Web page in Internet Explorer to see the results shown in Figure 3-12 on the next page. This is quite an improvement over the spartan Web page shown in Figure 3-10. In addition, the right bracket that appears just right of the Company Info hyperlink actually slides up and down as the mouse pointer hovers over each menu choice. All that remains is adding the detail content for each page.

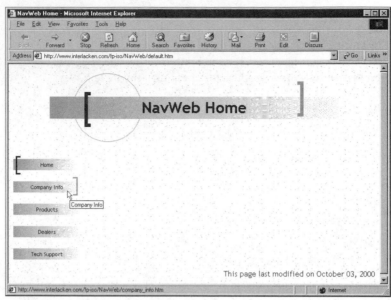

Figure 3-12. Here's how the Web page in Figure 3-10 looks with a theme applied. The improvement is striking.

Creating Web sites with Navigation view, shared borders, Web components, and themes has many advantages. You can add, rearrange, or delete pages at any time; FrontPage will update the Link bars in all your pages automatically. All page banner and Link bar choices will use consistent names for each page. All your pages will share a consistent, attractive appearance.

Of course, there are disadvantages as well. If a Web contains only a few pages, it might be quicker to lay it out by hand. If the Web consists of hundreds or thousands of pages, Navigation view can become unwieldy. If some pages need to be formatted quite differently from others, the forced uniformity of themes can become a real hindrance. And finally, if your home page, like so many today, contains dozens of tiny hyperlinks grouped by function, Link bars might not generate the appearance you need. Despite these disadvantages, an automatic FrontPage-based Web works quite well for many kinds of Web sites and is definitely an option to consider.

For more information about themes, refer to Chapter 19, "Using FrontPage Themes."

Working with Web Templates

Earlier in this chapter, the section titled "Creating a FrontPage-Based Web" briefly mentioned the Empty Web and One Page Web options that appear after you display the New Page Or Web task pane and then click Web Site Templates. The following list describes the remaining options in that dialog box. The Wizard templates prompt you for information; the remaining templates create exactly the same results every time you create a new Web site with them:

- **Corporate Presence Wizard.** Creates an archetypical site that represents your organization on the Internet.

- **Customer Support Web.** Creates a Web that provides customer support services, particularly for software companies.

- **Database Interface Wizard.** Creates a Web that contains a Database Editor. This is a group of Web pages that work together to display, modify, add, and delete records in a database.

- **Discussion Web Wizard.** Creates a discussion group with threads, a table of contents, and full-text searching.

- **Import Web Wizard.** Creates a Web filled with documents from your local computer or the Internet. Choosing this option is equivalent to creating an Empty Web, choosing Import from the File menu, and clicking From Web in the Import dialog box.

- **Personal Web.** Creates a prototype Web that describes you. It includes pages to describe your interests, show photos, and list your favorite Web sites.

- **Project Web.** Creates a Web for coordinating project members and activities. It provides a list of members, a schedule, status, an archive, and discussions.

- **SharePoint-based Team Web Site.** Creates an Office.Net team Web site. This is a prefabricated site that centralizes information for groups of people working together. It supports upload, display, and download of a shared document library; discussion groups; and lists of contacts, tasks, announcements, events, and Web links.

For more information about Web templates, refer to Chapter 8, "Creating Web Sites with Templates and Wizards."

For the most part, these templates aren't terribly exciting. The Corporate Presence, Customer Support, and Personal Webs provide basic starting points for your work but no real flashes of brilliance. You can run the Import Web Wizard just as easily after creating a new blank Web or, for that matter, on a Web with existing content. If your Web server supports it, a SharePoint team Web site provides much better features than a Discussion Web or Project Web.

tip You can create a SharePoint team Web site only on a server running SharePoint Team Services.

The SharePoint-based Web site option is the real star among this group. Figure 3-13 illustrates the home page for such a site. Here are descriptions of the major options it has to offer:

- **Document Library.** These special folders make it easy to share documents with others. Each library displays documents in a list that Web visitors can sort, filter, and possibly—depending on the file format—display.

  For documents saved as HTML—and remember that all Office applications can save their native document types as HTML with no loss of intelligence or appearance—people using only a browser can review documents, insert comments about the document in general, and insert comments inline with document text. When the originator later opens the document, comments from all reviewers appear in a single copy of the document.

- **Discussion Board.** This feature makes it easy for team members to conduct newsgroup-style discussions about any topics they like.

- **Contacts.** This list displays the names, addresses, telephone numbers, and other information for your team members and the people they work with.

- **Tasks.** This task list keeps track of work that you or your team needs to complete. You can expand a task list by adding columns relevant to your line of work.

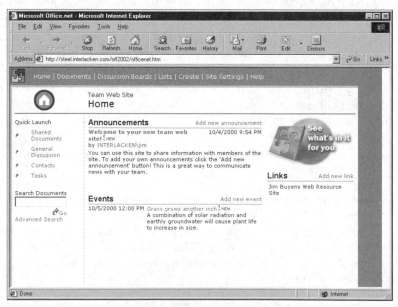

Figure 3-13. SharePoint team Web sites provide a wide assortment of features that enhance collaboration.

Chapter 3: Managing Web Sites

- **Announcements.** This feature provides a place for team members to notify each other of news and other information by posting it to a list.

- **Events.** This is a schedule of upcoming meetings, deadlines, and other events that team members need to keep in mind.

- **Links.** This section contains a list of Web sites that are interesting or useful to SharePoint team Web site members.

- **Survey.** This feature makes it easy to poll team members. Creating surveys is easy; just use the supplied Web pages to enter a list of questions and acceptable answers.

- **Custom List.** This section makes it easy to create lists with any columns, such as a list of lunch spots, a sign-up sheet, an excuse list, and so on.

- **Site Settings.** This series of Web pages configures the site name and description, the list of authorized users, the characteristics of the built-in lists, and other settings related to the SharePoint team Web site.

Team site lists are actually database tables, and team Web sites have facilities to upload and download these tables as Microsoft Excel worksheets. This makes it easy to use the data in other applications or to effect mass changes.

The information contained in a SharePoint team Web site resides in three locations:

- A Microsoft SQL Server or Microsoft Date Engine database. This database contains all the data you see in lists and surveys, plus many kinds of information about files that reside in document libraries

- A folder named *Shared Documents* that's located in the root of your Web. This contains all the Web forms that team members use for uploading, describing, locating, and viewing documents, plus the documents themselves.

- A folder named *Lists* that's located in the root of your Web. This folder contains all the Web forms that team members use for creating, managing, and using lists and surveys.

In general, it's a very bad idea to directly manipulate files in the *Shared Document* and *Lists* folders of a Web. Updating or relocating these files doesn't update the corresponding information in the database, and this can prevent the SharePoint team Web site from operating as it should.

Subscriptions are another important feature of team Web sites. Subscribing means that you receive e-mail whenever someone changes a SharePoint team Web site list. You can receive notifications when someone adds a new item, changes an existing item, or deletes an item, or any combination of the three.

For more information about SharePoint team Web sites, refer to Chapter 35, "Using SharePoint Team Web Sites."

Managing Appearance

Most, if not all, Web designers readily agree that all Web pages in the same body of content should share a common appearance. There is, however, much less agreement on how to achieve this lofty goal. The problem isn't a lack of tools or methods, but a glut of them.

FrontPage provides four methods for maintaining a common appearance among multiple Web pages. One method is sure to be right for whatever job you have in mind.

Manually Managing Appearance

Most beginning Web designers learn how to format text, assign colors, and otherwise modify page elements one element at a time. If they want a heading to be blue Arial font, they select the heading, choose Font from the Format menu, and specify that font name and color. This approach works well for small numbers of pages, but usually falls down when you want a large collection of pages to look alike. Maintaining uniformity becomes increasingly difficult if you create the pages over an extended period of time, or if several different people do the work.

If you want to format page elements manually, FrontPage supports you with a rich set of toolbar buttons, commands, and dialog boxes that implement almost every capability of HTML. These features look and behave much like those in other Office applications and are therefore very easy to learn and use.

Unfortunately, no matter how easy a command structure might be, applying it dozens, hundreds, or thousands of times to as many Web pages is tedious and error-prone. For this reason, you'll almost certainly want to learn and adopt one of the broader formatting approaches described in the next few sections.

> For more information about entering and formatting text, refer to Chapter 10, "Adding and Formatting Text."

Using Color Masters

Centrally managing the appearance of multiple Web pages obviously requires a master definition that all the managed pages can reference. The simplest way to do this, from a FrontPage point of view, is to designate one page as a color master.

To create a color master, simply create a new Web page, assign the colors and background you want to the page, and save it. This page might or might not be a page you intend Web visitors to browse, but any page you want can nevertheless inherit the properties of the color master.

To make any other Web page use colors from a color master, follow these steps:

Chapter 3: Managing Web Sites

1 Open the Web page in FrontPage.

2 Choose Properties from the File menu to open the Page Properties dialog box.

3 Click the Background tab of the Page Properties dialog box, shown in Figure 3-14.

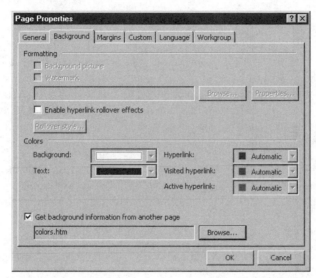

Figure 3-14. When a color master controls a page's text colors and background appearance, you can't override these settings by hand.

4 Select the Get Background Information From Another Page check box.

5 Click the Browse button at the bottom of the dialog box, and locate the page you've designated as the color master.

6 Click OK to select the color master page, and then click OK again to close the Page Properties dialog box.

Changing the colors or background on a color master automatically changes the same attributes of any page set up to inherit its colors.

Color masters control only the following six aspects of page appearance. As such, they are much less powerful than newer group formatting options available in FrontPage 2002:

● Background color

● Background picture

● Normal text color

● Hyperlink text color

Chapter 3

- Visited hyperlink text color
- Active hyperlink text color

Color masters appeared in very early versions of FrontPage and are now included mostly for compatibility. They continue to fill a certain need and might be useful in some situations.

Applying Themes

Its collection of themes is the most pervasive, all-encompassing style facility FrontPage has to offer. Themes control overall page properties such as colors, fonts, bullet styles, graphical buttons, and backgrounds. Applying a theme to a page or Web locks in a professionally designed appearance and disables any command that could override it. If you want to guarantee that your site has consistent style and colors, nothing else has the force of FrontPage themes.

The earlier section on building a Web site with Navigation view explained how to apply a theme to every page in a FrontPage-based Web. Those steps established a given theme as the Web default. To exclude a page from the Web's default theme, follow these steps:

1 Select the page in Page view, the Folder List, or Folders view.

2 Choose Theme from the Format menu.

3 When the Themes dialog box shown previously in Figure 3-11 appears, locate the Apply Theme To setting and, if necessary, choose Selected Page(s).

4 Select the theme you want the selected page to have or, if you don't want any theme applied, select (No Theme).

5 Click OK.

The greatest disadvantage of themes is their all-or-nothing nature (that is, a theme can be applied in its entirety or not at all to a given page). After you apply a theme, FrontPage deactivates most normal formatting options and blocks you from overriding any options set by the theme.

In FrontPage 2002, you can create and modify themes directly within the FrontPage application. However, don't fall into the trap of creating numerous, slightly different themes to accommodate different kinds of pages. The more different themes you use, the more difficult each theme is to manage, update, and apply as intended.

For more information about themes, refer to Chapter 19, "Using FrontPage Themes."

Chapter 3

Working with Cascading Style Sheets

To overcome the many stylistic limitations of HTML, the World Wide Web Consortium
(W3C) devised a new specification that fills in most of HTML's gaps. (The W3C is the
international standards body that controls the definition of HTML.) This specification,
as you might have guessed from the heading of this section, is called cascading style
sheets (CSS), and it consists of two levels:

● **CSS Level 1.** This level is primarily concerned with typography. Compared
to HTML, CSS provides powerful control over typefaces, colors, and paragraph formatting.

● **CSS Level 2.** This level is primarily concerned with positioning (that is, the
ability to locate elements precisely on a page).

You can apply either set of CSS features—or both—to individual Web page elements,
to portions of Web pages, to whole Web pages, or to groups of Web pages. FrontPage
supports all these options. In Figure 3-15, for example, FrontPage is modifying a CSS
style named *.hdr1*.

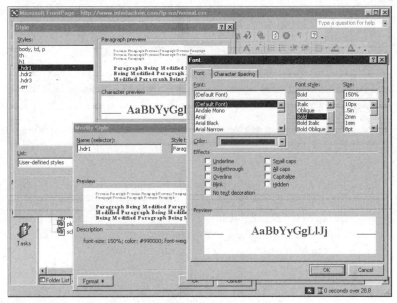

Figure 3-15. These dialog boxes are building a new style named *.hdr1*. After you
create this style, it appears in the Style list on the Formatting toolbar.

After this style exists, it'll appear in the Style list on the Formatting toolbar, and you can
apply it to anything on the Web page.

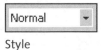

Style

There are two kinds of CSS styles: *inline* and *named*. An inline style pertains to one and only one HTML element, such as a paragraph or table. FrontPage uses inline styles to apply some of the settings available with Format-menu commands such as Font, Paragraph, and so forth. You can specify inline styles directly by right-clicking a page element, choosing Page Properties from the shortcut menu, and clicking the Style button.

Using inline styles might provide more typographical control than using HTML attributes but offers no opportunity for managing overall appearance at the page or Web level. For that, you must initialize a style sheet, define one or more named styles, and then apply those styles to the pages or page elements you want.

The official term for the name of a CSS style is a *selector*. There are three kinds of selectors:

- **Type Selectors.** These have the same names as (and control the appearance of) HTML tags. To modify the appearance of all page elements defined by a given HTML tag, simply assign properties to a type selector named after that tag. Here are two examples:

  - To change the appearance of all Heading 1 text in a page, set up an *h1* type selector and give it the properties you want.

  - To change the appearance of all normal paragraphs, set up a *p* type selector and assign it the desired properties.

  A type selector is a very powerful facility. Using type selectors, you can create Web pages that have no special formatting commands mixed into the HTML, but that nevertheless appear with rich and consistent formatting.

- **Class Selectors.** These begin with a period, and using them involves a two-step process. First you define the class, and then you apply it to each HTML element you want.

  Class selectors are very useful for styling specialized content. You might, for example, set up a class selector named *.errmsg*, and then assign this class to any part of a Web page that displays error messages. If you were publishing the script of a play, you might set up class selectors for scene headings, stage directions, character names, speech text, and so forth.

- **ID Selectors.** These begin with a pound sign, and using them involves a slightly different two-step process. First you give the desired HTML element an ID, and then you define a corresponding ID selector that specifies the CSS properties you want that element to have. In practice, this type of selector receives very little use.

For more information about controlling typography with cascading style sheets, refer to Chapter 20, "Managing Appearance with Cascading Style Sheets."

Chapter 3: Managing Web Sites

Creating Page-Level Styles

To create a style sheet for a single page, open the page in Page view, and then choose Style from the Format menu. This displays the Style dialog box shown in Figure 3-16. Here's how to use the controls on this box:

- To create or modify a type selector, make sure HTML Tags appears in the List list, select the name you want from the Styles list, and then click the Modify button.

- To modify an existing class or ID selector, select User-Defined Styles in the List list, select the name you want from the Styles list, and then click the Modify button.

- To create a new class or ID selector, click the New button, and enter the class or ID name in the Name (Selector) box.

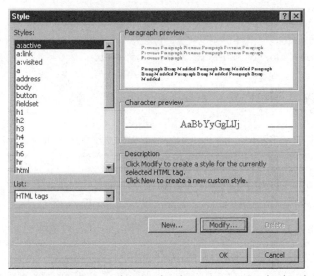

Figure 3-16. Cascading Style Sheets can override the default appearance produced by any HTML tag.

After completing any of these actions, you should see the Modify Style dialog box shown in Figure 3-17 on the next page. (The New Style dialog box, if it appears, works essentially the same way.) Click the Format button to display the list of style types, select a style type, and then use the resulting dialog box to set the properties you want.

For more information about creating page-level styles, refer to "Formatting Single Web Pages" on page 602.

Chapter 3

Part 1: Introducing Microsoft FrontPage 2002

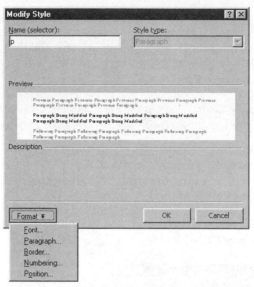

Figure 3-17. The commands that modify CSS styles aren't visible when you first display this dialog box. To see them, you must click the Format button.

Creating Shared Style Sheets

The procedure just discussed describes how to modify and create CSS styles that apply to a single Web page. The first time you create or modify a named style, FrontPage automatically adds a style sheet to the page and uses that area for any styles you define.

Styles that apply to multiple pages must reside in a file that's separate from any of them. Such files have a *.css* filename extension. To create such a file in FrontPage:

1 Open the Web that contains the pages the style sheet should affect.

2 Choose New from the File menu, and then choose Page Or Web.

3 When the New Page Or Web task pane appears, look under the New From Template heading, and click Page Templates.

4 When the Page Templates dialog box shown in Figure 3-18 appears, select the Style Sheets tab, select Normal Style Sheet, and then click OK.

5 A new, blank style sheet page appears in Page view. Save this page in the Web's root folder with a name that denotes its use. If this style sheet should apply to most pages in your Web, a good name is *normal.css*.

6 To create styles, choose Style from the Format menu and proceed as you did when creating and modifying styles for a single Web page.

Because style sheet files don't contain any content, FrontPage can't display styles in WYSIWYG view. Instead, it displays the "raw" CSS code, as illustrated in Figure 3-19.

Chapter 3: Managing Web Sites

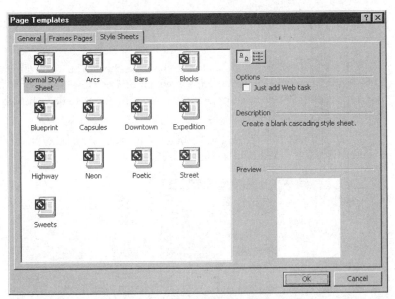

Figure 3-18. FrontPage provides this assortment of prefabricated style sheets.

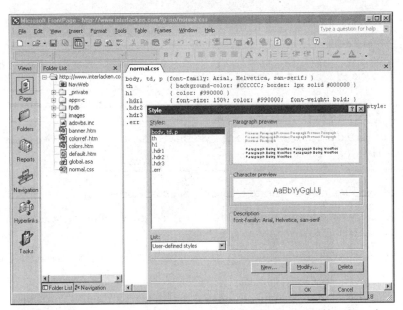

Figure 3-19. Even though FrontPage displays style sheet files as code, you can modify their styles through commands on the Format Style menu.

After a while, you might become familiar enough with CSS to modify the code directly, but until then, don't make any changes you might have difficulty undoing later.

After you create a style sheet file, the next step is designating each Web page that will use it. Here's the procedure for doing this:

1 Select the page or pages that should use the style sheet. You can do this by clicking on a page that's open in Page view, on one or more pages or folders that appear in the Folder List, or on one or more pages or folders that appear in another FrontPage view.

2 Choose Style Sheet Links from the Format menu. This will display the Link Style Sheet dialog box shown in Figure 3-20.

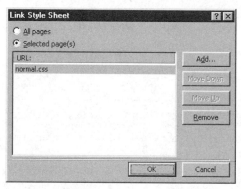

Figure 3-20. To apply a shared style sheet to a Web page, select the page, and then choose Style Sheet Links from the Format menu. The Add button browses the current Web for CSS files.

> **note** If the Style Sheet Links command on the Format menu is dimmed, this means you haven't selected any files that can use style sheets. You can't apply style sheets to picture files, for example.

3 Make sure that the Selected Page(s) option is selected.

4 Click the Add button, find the style sheet file you want in the Select Style Sheet dialog box, and then click OK.

5 To remove a style sheet, select it in the URL box and click the Remove button.

6 If a given page uses multiple style sheets and you need to change the order or precedence, select one of the style sheets, and use the Move Down and Move Up buttons to reposition it.

7 When you're satisfied with your changes, click OK to close the Link Style Sheet dialog box.

> **note** When two style sheets modify the same property for the same selector, the definition that occurs last prevails.

Chapter 3: Managing Web Sites

To apply a style sheet to every page in a Web, skip step 1 and then, in step 3, make sure that the All Pages option is selected.

Setting up shared style sheet files and applying them to Web pages might at first seem convoluted compared to just formatting each page the way you want it. The payback comes when you have many Web pages that you want to look alike. If they all use the same style sheet, they will.

Shared style sheets are both more flexible and less commanding than themes, yet they offer a similar degree of site-level control. This is the approach most experienced Web designers use for at least part of their work.

Browsers earlier than Internet Explorer 3 and Netscape Navigator 4 ignore CSS commands and therefore display Web pages using default fonts and colors. However, the number of Web visitors using these older browsers is constantly declining. What's more, although those Web visitors won't see your well-chosen fonts and colors, they'll at least see a legible version of the page.

For more information on creating shared style sheets, refer to "Formatting Multiple Pages" on page 607.

Using Page Templates

Another way FrontPage can provide a consistent Web appearance is through its *templates* feature. Creating and using a template is simple:

1 Use FrontPage to create a Web page with the color scheme, background, and other standard features you want in the template.

2 Save the page as a template, as follows:

    a Choose Save As from the File menu.

    b Select FrontPage Template in the Save As Type drop-down list.

    c Click Save.

    d When the Save As Template dialog box shown in Figure 3-21 on the next page appears, review the title, name, and description fields.

    e Click OK.

3 When creating a new Web page that should have the given template features, select that template in the Page Templates dialog box.

For more information about templates, refer to Chapter 8, "Creating Web Sites with Templates and Wizards."

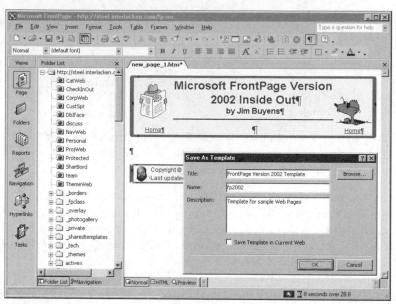

Figure 3-21. FrontPage can save draft Web pages as templates, which then serve as models for other pages.

As you can see in Figure 3-22, FrontPage also provides its own assortment of templates.

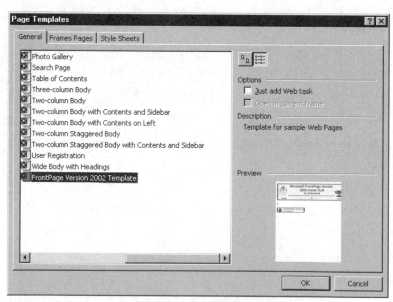

Figure 3-22. You can choose any template as the starting point for a new Web page.

For more information about using page templates, refer to Chapter 8, "Creating Web Sites with Templates and Wizards."

Laying Out Pages

FrontPage provides a full complement of intuitive dialog boxes for applying colors, fonts, alignment, and other properties to the content of your Web pages. Virtually every feature of HTML is available for making your pages look their best; you can access the features through the familiar Office XP user interface.

Despite all this flexibility, members of a group should generally be united by a common appearance—rock bands notwithstanding. FrontPage offers a number of tools that impart a unified and attractive style to all your pages. And anyway, why format Web pages one at a time when you can do them all together in bunches?

Working with Tables

Most page designers—Web or print—use grids as the basis for all page layout. A *grid*, in this sense, is a series of columns and horizontal lines—visible or invisible—that serves to line up the elements in the composition. Layout grids are most obvious in newspapers and magazines, but if you look closely, most brochures, display ads, and posters use them as well.

For Web pages, an HTML table is the closest analog to a physical layout grid. Page layout tables usually fill the entire page width, and they normally have invisible borders and backgrounds. Their only purpose is to align page elements horizontally and vertically.

Envisioning the appearance of an HTML table can be a real challenge when you're working with raw HTML code. The code is one-dimensional—top to bottom—but the table, having height and width, is two-dimensional. Fortunately, the WYSIWYG editor in FrontPage makes working with tables not only two-dimensional and intuitive, but even enjoyable.

The sample Web page developed in Chapter 2 used an HTML table to organize its elements. Another, slightly more complex example appears in Figure 3-23 on the next page. This is a hand-made page banner (not to be confused with a FrontPage Page Banner component) that will appear at the top of most examples throughout the rest of this book.

For another example of page layout using HTML tables, refer to "Drawing Tables" on page 38.

This example contains three tables nested one inside another. The outer table fills the entire page width and has three rows and three columns. The eight outside cells have a dark background. The corner cells display small pictures that produce the rounded corners. The other dark cells contain transparent GIF files for spacing.

The first table's middle cell contains the second table, which has two rows and three columns. The first and third columns contain a picture in the upper cell and a

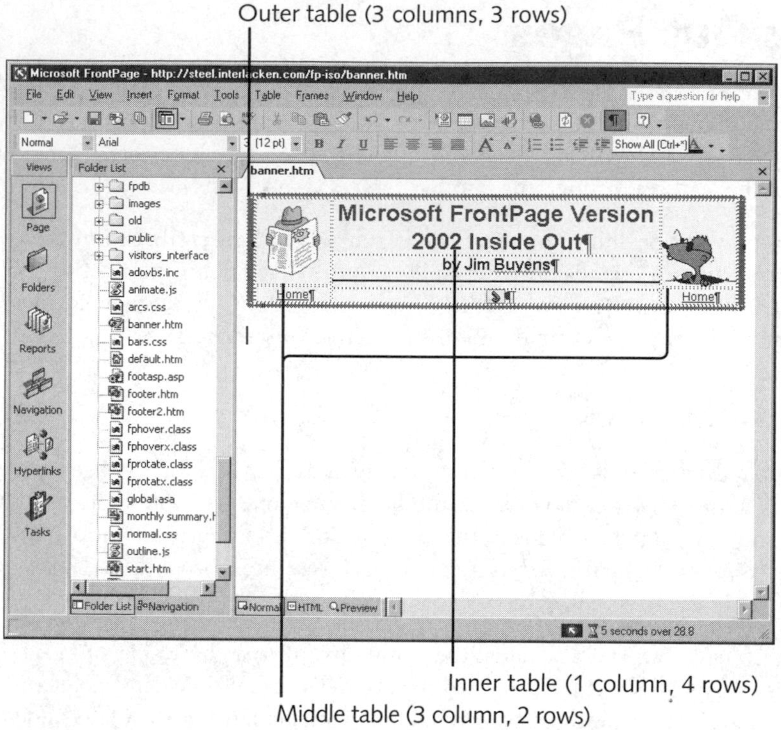

Outer table (3 columns, 3 rows)

Inner table (1 column, 4 rows)

Middle table (3 column, 2 rows)

Figure 3-23. This page layout uses two HTML tables: an inner table to organize the titles and an outer table to organize the pictures.

Previewing Browser-Side Scripting

All modern browsers have the capability of running simple programs that appear in Web pages. This can occur whenever the page loads or whenever certain actions—such as button clicks—occur.

To view the script in the *banner.htm* page shown in Figure 3-23, open the page in FrontPage, and double-click the "J" icon. The script contains this statement:

```
document.write(top.document.title)
```

The *document.write* command writes text into the Web page as if a Web designer had coded it by hand. The *top.document.title* expression supplies the title of the current page (or the frames, if any, that displays it) as specified in the Page Properties dialog box. The script also contains a function named *goHome* that jumps to the current home page.

on the CD For more information about browser-side scripting, refer to Chapter 42, "Working with Script Code," in the Bonus Content on the Companion CD.

hyperlink to Home in the lower cell. The two cells in the middle column are merged and contain the third table.

The inner table contains one column and four rows. The first two rows contain text; the third row contains an HTML horizontal line element, and the fourth row contains a small browser-side script that displays the page's title as configured in the Page Properties dialog box.

For more information about using HTML tables for page layout, refer to Chapter 16, "Using HTML Tables for Page Layout."

Working with Shared Borders

The Shared Borders feature applies any combination of top, bottom, left, and right borders—including the content within them—to selected pages or to an entire Web. Shared borders are very handy for applying standard heading styles, standard footers, and standard margin content to an entire Web. The procedure for applying a shared border to an entire Web was covered earlier in this chapter in the section "Adding Shared Borders."

When you apply shared borders to one or more pages, FrontPage surrounds the existing content of each page with an all-encompassing table. If you apply all four borders, you get a table three cells high and three cells wide, with all three columns in rows 1 and 3 merged. Figure 3-24 shows a page with four shared borders open in FrontPage.

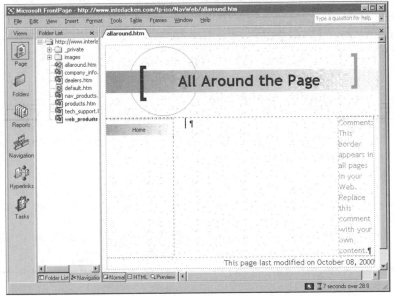

Figure 3-24. The rectangular areas at the top, bottom, left, and right of this page are shared borders and will be applied to all pages in the Web.

The most confusing thing about shared borders is that every shared border in the same Web contains *exactly the same content*. This content resides in the following four files:

- *_borders/bottom.htm*
- *_borders/left.htm*
- *_borders/right.htm*
- *_borders/top.htm*

You can edit the shared border contents by opening these files directly, or by opening any page that uses them. In all cases, however, changing the shared border contents in one page affects every page in the same Web that uses the same shared border.

Frequently Asked Question

How can FrontPage make every page in a Web display its own Navigation view title?

Adding a Page Banner component to any Web page displays that page's Navigation view title. Therefore, one solution to this question is to carry out the following procedure for each page in your Web:

1 Open each page in your Web.

2 Add a Page Banner component.

3 Save and close the page.

If you have too many pages for this answer to be practical, here's another way:

1 Choose Shared Borders from the Format menu.

2 Under Apply To, click All Pages.

3 Select the check box labeled Top.

4 Click OK.

5 Open any page in your Web, locate the top shared border area, and add a Page Banner component to it.

6 Save and close the page.

Because every page in your Web now contains the Top shared border, and because the Top shared border now contains a Page Banner component, every page in your Web now contains a Page Banner component. And the Page Banner component in each page displays *that page's* Navigation view title.

Chapter 3: Managing Web Sites

Including exactly the same content on every page would be extremely boring and mundane unless the content consists of Web components that change based on the page that contains them. Three such components are:

- **Page Banner.** This displays the Navigation view title of the page that contains it.

- **Link Bar.** This displays hyperlinks based on the Navigation position of the page that contains it.

- **Date And Time.** This displays the date and optionally the time of the last change to the pages that contains it.

Each of these components, if present in a shared border, will display differently based on the page that contains the shared border.

As discussed in the "Adding Shared Borders" section earlier in this chapter, most use of shared borders occurs in Webs managed by Navigation view. In that environment, shared borders are a great way to make sure that every page has a consistent page banner and Link bar. However, don't overlook the use of this feature for adding page footers and other repeating content to every page in a Web.

For more information about shared borders, refer to "Using Shared Borders" on page 765.

Working with Frames Pages

A frames page is a special kind of Web page whose sole purpose is dividing the browser window into several rectangular areas called *frames*. Each frame has a *name* and a *target*; the *name* identifies the frame, and the *target* identifies the Web page the frame should display.

Hyperlinks clicked in one frame can load pages into another frame. A common application of frames pages is to define a menu as the target of one frame and corresponding content as the target of another. Clicking a hyperlink in the menu frame changes the target in the content frame. This avoids the need to keep menus up to date on each content page. Of course, many other applications are possible as well. Anytime you want to replace only portions of the browser window, a frames page is an option worth considering.

Figure 3-25 on the next page shows a frames page open in FrontPage. Frames pages and default targets appear in fully editable, WYSIWYG view. Note the title frame at the top of the page, the menu bar at the lower left, and the large content frame at the lower right. This is a fairly typical arrangement.

For more information about frames, refer to Chapter 17, "Using Frames for Page Layout."

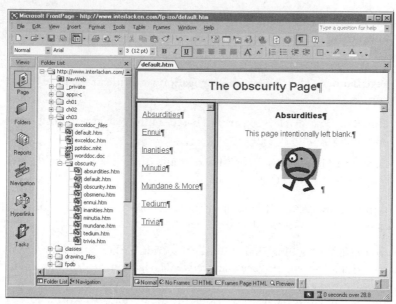

Figure 3-25. FrontPage 2002 provides full WYSIWYG editing of frames pages. Four HTML files are open in this example: the frames page itself plus an ordinary HTML page in each of its three frames.

Positioning

The "Working with Cascading Style Sheets" section earlier in this chapter introduced CSS Level 2, but this topic deserves further discussion in terms of layout. CSS Level 2 (CSS2 or CSS Positioning) is primarily concerned with positioning Web page elements.

In some of its documentation, Microsoft likes to call CSS2 pixel perfect positioning. This is because CSS2 can position Web page elements precisely on the page based on measurements in pixels or, for that matter, in inches, centimeters, percent of available space, or obscure measurements like ems and points that come from the printing industry.

CSS2 uses two positioning strategies: *absolute* and *relative*. Absolute positioning displays page content a specified distance from the upper left corner of its container. (The topic of containers is complex, but the default container is the space a document occupies in the Web visitor's browser.) Relative positioning displays content a specified distance from its normal position (that is, from where it would appear if no positioning were in effect).

The dialog box for CSS Positioning (that is, CSS2) is shown in Figure 3-26.

Absolute Positioning and the Z-Index

Absolute positioning is a feature of browsers that support the Cascading Style Sheet Level 2 specification. CSS2 provides a way to locate elements at specific locations, measured either from their normal location or from the upper left corner of their container. (The default CSS container is the space inside the document's margins. However, marked subsections of a Web page can also be containers. Table cells, divisions, and spans can all be CSS containers.)

A new CSS property called *z-index* governs the visibility of overlapping page elements. When several page elements on the same Web page overlap, the element with the highest z-index appears on top (that is, unobstructed), and those with lesser z-indexes appear in order behind it.

Normal page elements have the default z-index, which is zero. Elements with positive z-index values appear superimposed over normal page content, and those with a negative z-index appear behind it.

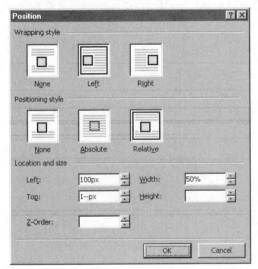

Figure 3-26. This FrontPage 2002 dialog box specifies CSS2 positioning for the currently selected content.

Positioning a block of content can be as easy as this:

1 Open the Web page in Page view.

2 Select the elements you want to position.

3 Choose Position from the Format menu.

4 Select the position settings you want.

5 Click OK.

> **For more information about CSS2 positioning, refer to "Positioning Content with Style Sheets" on page 629.**

If parts of your Web page are positioned and parts aren't, the parts that aren't might not flow properly around the ones that are.

In Summary...

This chapter introduced the wide assortment of tools that FrontPage provides for managing Web sites. It explained how to create FrontPage-based Webs, how to fill them with content, and how to avoid repetitive, manual work both when creating Web pages and when maintaining them over time.

The rest of the book presents these topics again in much greater detail, along with many additional features, tips, tricks, and advice on what to do when things go wrong.

Part 2

Planning and Organizing Your Web Site

Planning and Organizing FrontPage-Based Webs

Whatever your site's size and purpose, proper advance planning will produce a better appearance, more organized content, faster construction, and easier ongoing maintenance. More importantly, a well-planned site will attract more visitors, better meet its original goals, and be cheaper to run.

This chapter addresses the core aspects of planning and producing a Web site. These aspects are highly interrelated; you can't plan without understanding the work to be done, and without a sound plan you can't properly do the work. That's why learning to organize and produce Web sites is an iterative process that considers increasing levels of detail.

Most of all, keep in mind that design of any kind—Web, print, or other—is a human process requiring human judgment to obtain human objectives. No piece of software—not even Microsoft FrontPage—can design your site or judge it ready for public consumption. Beauty is in the eye of the beholder, and not in some machine.

Defining Your Site's Content

All successful Web sites start out with a well-defined mission. This leads to a well-organized, well-defined body of content and ultimately to effective communication. Taking the time up front to understand your mission will certainly pay off in timely, effective results later.

107

Identifying Your Message

Step one in building or maintaining a Web site is understanding the message its sponsors want to send. Whether your site describes yourself, an area of interest, your organization, your client, or a large multinational corporation, the message you want to send probably isn't "I'm just learning HTML," "I'm scatterbrained," or "I'm trying to increase ugliness and confusion in the world."

"Establishing a presence" is probably the most common reason for starting a Web site, but this is terribly vague. It usually means following a perceived trend, keeping up with competitors, or responding to requests from others. Here are more focused (and more useful) reasons for starting a Web site:

- Increasing knowledge and awareness of a person, a topic, or an organization
- Releasing information in accordance with law or an organization's charter
- Promoting a desired public image
- Advertising products and services
- Selling products or services directly to Web visitors
- Providing post-sale product support information

You'll almost certainly need to drill through several levels of detail to fully understand your site's mission. Investigating each level generally leads to questions for the next. The end result should be a mission statement, even if informal, that describes the site's purpose and objective.

Understanding the Audience

As important as knowing your site's message is knowing its audience. "Everyone on the Web" is too vague an audience to be useful; you should have some particular *kinds* of people in mind—perhaps even specific people to use as models. The following are typical audiences:

- Everyone in a certain industry
- Practitioners of a certain skill
- Purchasers of a certain type of product or service
- Users of a specific product or service

After you decide who your audience is, you should learn whatever you can about them. Are they technical, artistic, or people-oriented? What are their skills and interests? What's their level of vocabulary and education? Do they respond more to detailed text or to color, style, and visual metaphors?

108

You hope, of course, that your audience will find your site's message inherently interesting and attractive. Often, however, they'll need some other enticement. Perhaps you can entice visitors with a free clip-art library and then, while they browse, sell them your graphics program. Perhaps you can sell art supplies as people browse a library of works or techniques. If they come for information about a product they already own, perhaps you can sell them another.

The ultimate enticement, according to recent thinking, is to make your site the meeting place for a community of some kind—presumably a community with an interest in your product or message. The goal is then to make your site such a valuable resource—such a compelling place for people in your target audience to find each other and interact—that the site becomes a "must visit." This generally requires some sort of added content that's updated frequently and not readily available elsewhere. It also requires a means for visitors to enhance the site themselves and to find other visitors without invading anyone's privacy. This sort of community is more often talked about than achieved in practice, though it remains a lofty goal. It also illustrates the importance of providing a magnet to attract targeted visitors.

Identifying Content Categories

If your site is typical, the home page will be the most time-consuming of all to construct. There are several reasons for this:

- The home page presents the site's first impression; therefore, it's usually the most elaborate page in the site. Remember another old saying: "You get only one chance to make a first impression."

- Despite being the site's most elaborate page, the home page must download quickly. Otherwise, Web visitors will give up after a minute or two and go elsewhere.

- The home page often serves as the prototype for the entire site's visual appearance. It sets the tone and image for every page that follows.

- If you're new to creating Web pages, a home page will probably be your initial learning experience.

- The options on the home page intrinsically represent the site's primary structure.

The first four points usually work themselves out, but the last one is critical. If you can identify the top few options in your site, you probably have a good understanding of its message and audience. If you can't get your home page organized, your content plan probably isn't organized either.

FrontPage provides built-in templates and wizards that create typical pages for many kinds of sites, but at best they produce only starting points. No two sites are exactly alike; your site's content and organization are ultimately your unique creation.

109

Here are some terrible ways to organize a site:

- An option for each member of the design committee
- An option for each person who reports to the top executive
- An option for each category someone thought of, in chronological order
- The same options you used at a previous site

All the above share the same problem: They ignore the target visitor's likely interests and mindset. They indicate a lack of defined message, defined audience, or both.

Defining Your Site's Style

Every site should have a consistency suited to its purpose. Pages should be unified by a common theme, a common organization, and a common style. The words, pictures, colors, and layout should lead the visitor to the messages—both overt and subtle—that justify the site's existence.

Artists and computer specialists usually embody completely different mindsets. Nevertheless, both types of skills are needed to produce an effective Web site. To reduce the gap between art and science—at least in a small way—this section introduces a few topics regarding pleasing and effective visual design.

Elements of Design

Artistic design isn't an exact science, so many technically inclined people conclude that it's beyond them—or at least that it gives them a headache. Even if you lack the talent to become a professional artist, though, you can use certain principles of good design to enhance your work and communicate your message more effectively. Contrast and symmetry are two such principles, and they appear in a variety of contexts.

Contrast vs. Clash

The polar bear at the North Pole and the black cat in the coal bin figure in two old jokes involving contrast. In both cases, lack of contrast makes the key element indistinguishable from its surroundings. Graphic contrast serves two important purposes in Web pages or, for that matter, any other document:

- Contrast enhances legibility. For example, the black type and white background in this book make it easier to read than if one color were gray.

- Contrast visually communicates distinctions among various page elements. In this book, for example, contrasting typography makes it easy to distinguish headings from body type.

The contrast knob on your monitor or TV set controls the difference in brightness between the lightest and darkest parts of a picture. Contrast, however, occurs in many other dimensions as well: contrast between adjacent colors, contrast between differently sized or shaped fonts, contrast between positions on a page, and many more. The total contrast between two page elements thus involves the number of contrasting attributes as well as their individual extents.

The need for contrast is generally intuitive; document creators ordinarily realize that items like titles, headings, body text, and captions are intrinsically different and that a unique appearance should identify each such element. They run into greater problems deciding what kind of contrast to provide and how much. Too much or too little contrast can be illegible, confusing, or just irritating to the eye.

To understand the need for contrast, look at the Web page shown in Figure 4-1. Other than the contrast of black text on a white background and normal paragraph formatting, this page has no contrasting elements. There's nothing to guide the eye to various kinds of content, and certainly nothing interesting to look at.

Figure 4-1. This Web page provides no contrast among the various kinds of content it contains. Not only is it boring to look at, but it also communicates poorly.

The Web page shown in Figure 4-2 on the next page has plenty of contrast—but please, please don't try this at home, or in the office, or anywhere else. The contrast in the background image overpowers the text, despite the use of a bold font and a white-on-dark color scheme. Notice as well how white and near-white areas in the background blend into the text, making it hard to read. Use of strong backgrounds is the number one cause of ugly and illegible Web pages. (Use of blue text on black is probably number two.)

111

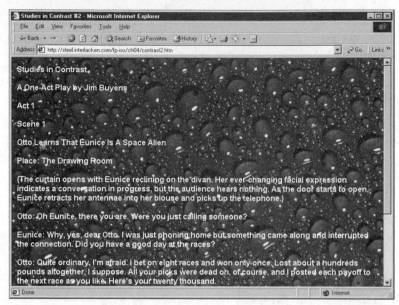

Figure 4-2. The high-contrast background in this Web page overwhelms and obscures the content. Today's expert Web designers use very soft backgrounds, if any.

Figure 4-3 shows another Web page loaded with contrast.

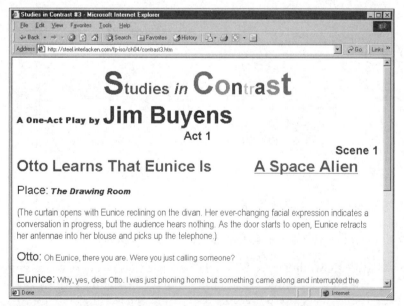

Figure 4-3. The many fonts and varied page placements in this Web page provide lots of contrast. Unfortunately, contrast this random is a distraction rather than a way to communicate.

The rampant use of fonts in this page produces an appearance experts call a "ransom note." Creating a page like this might be an interesting exercise for a Web designer who just discovered the font menu, but the use of so many different fonts, without any clear rationale, is very distracting. This page shows some effort at page design—not everything is flush left—but the alignment of page elements is essentially random.

None of the previous examples used appearance to enhance content. Even worse, the appearance of the second and third examples actually detracted from content. Figure 4-4, by contrast (sorry), shows a Web page where contrast truly enhances the content and makes it easier to understand.

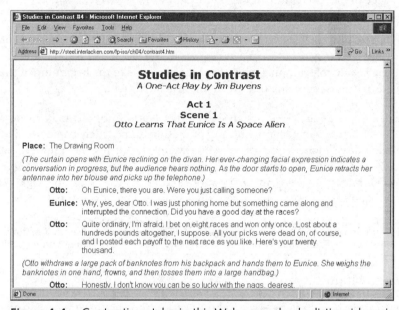

Figure 4-4. Contrasting styles in this Web page clearly distinguish various kinds of content. Consistencies in the style and alignment of similar items provide symmetry.

Note the following features:

● The fonts are interesting yet simple. Because computer monitors are low in resolution, complex fonts generally don't appear clearly.

> **tip** In print media, serif fonts are usually easier to read. The serifs, which are tiny horizontal lines at the end of each character stroke, create a horizontal "track" for the eye to follow. Because computer monitors are much less precise than a laser printer or typesetting machine, they generally do a poor job of displaying serifs. That's why most designers now believe that sans serif fonts are more legible on the Web. Just remember to provide enough line spacing whenever you use a sans serif font.

● All major titles use the same font. Smaller font sizes indicate lower-level titles and larger font sizes indicate more significant ones.

● Subtitles (some people call them "kickers") are universally indicated by italics.

● Specific formatting identifies the "place" line, stage directions, and speeches. All speeches look alike, for example, and nothing else looks like a speech.

● Note the alignment of elements along invisible gridlines. These alignments occur at the left margin, at the left edge of the speaker names, at the left edge of the speech text, at the right edge of the speech text, and at the right margin.

● Speeches occupy less than the full page width not only to give them a distinct appearance, but to make them easier to read. If text is too wide, the eye has trouble jumping from the end of one line to the beginning of the next. This is especially true when line spacing is tight.

Real life offers—as does Web design—a countless variety of potential contrasts. Contrasts of color, of size, of alignment, and of motion immediately come to mind. If something doesn't look right, consider increasing or reducing the number of contrasts as well as varying their intensities. And remember, the visual equivalent of screaming in someone's face isn't necessarily the best way to communicate your message. When contrast is required, don't be a wimp, don't be a screamer, and don't mix signals.

> For more information about choosing colors for Web pages, refer to "Design Tips for Choosing Colors" on page 558 and "Achieving Accurate Rendition—Safe Colors" on page 556.

Symmetry vs. Monotony

In any page layout, similar elements should have a similar appearance, and elements that differ should have a different appearance. Neither contrast nor uniformity should be random. This is the principle of symmetry.

All chapter headings in this book are set in the same font, color, size, and position on the page. When you encounter some text that visually resembles the other chapter headings, you assume that that text is a chapter heading as well. You also assume that any text with a different appearance is *not* a chapter heading.

Note that chapter headings are similar to each other, but not to body text. Because chapter headings and body text are quite different elements, there's a lot of contrast between them. There's essentially no contrast (other than distance) between one chapter heading and another, because all chapter headings are alike.

The same reasoning applies to this book's figures, tables, and side notes such as warnings and tips. Each element has a unique style that helps identify it and generally makes the book appear cohesive. It would be confusing if notes in this chapter and the next appeared differently.

The principle of symmetry (or parallelism) applies equally to Web pages. Make all your top-level headings look the same, for example, not just within each page but within an entire Web site or major section. Use the same color scheme, the same typography, the same alignment (left aligned, centered, right aligned, or justified), the same menu appearance, the same title conventions, and so forth. Avoid monotony by adopting (and testing on your eyes and the eyes of others) an attractive set of designs up front, not by making each page look completely different.

The same is true for pictures. If your site has a logo, use exactly the same logo file in every page that requires one. This not only ensures uniformity but minimizes download time: The browser downloads the same file (the same URL, actually) only once, no matter how many different pages use it. However, don't use the same picture to communicate different concepts, even if they're in different places. Do try to use an assortment of pictures all done in the same style, though.

An overall site design should be a guide, never a straitjacket. Certainly you'll have several different types of pages, and each page type should have unique elements that visually alert the Web visitor. The number of page types and their corresponding appearances are strictly your decision, but each page type should have the following elements:

- Symmetry that unifies it with all other pages in the same site
- Distinctive contrasts that visually identify each unique type of page or content
- Symmetry among similar types of page or content

In short, similar types of content call for fewer contrasting elements having a narrower range of contrast. Dissimilar types call for a greater variety and degree of contrast.

Choosing a Visual Concept

Visual appearance plays a critical role in the way visitors perceive your site and receive its message. No matter how interesting and well-organized your site's content may be, a drab presentation will provide a poor viewing experience for your Web visitors and indicate a lack of interest on your part. Because most Web sites devote the best visual presentation to the most important content, many Web visitors now associate drab presentation with boring, outdated information.

Visual presentation is no substitute for well-organized and useful content; both are necessary to produce an effective site. Except for a few highly specialized sites, content doesn't *consist* of presentation; instead, presentation is a means to *convey* content. HTML is such a weak page description language that the challenge of achieving visual appeal frequently overshadows that of developing content. Don't let this happen to you.

115

Your site's graphic design should complement its message and appeal to its audience. An abstract, garish design patterned after an album cover might be appropriate for a rock group, but certainly not for a bank or a brokerage house. A site's overall graphic design conveys messages just as surely as its text and pictures, and you should strive to have those messages reinforce each other rather than clash.

If it happens that you're not an experienced graphic design professional, don't despair. In many cases the site's organization will already have logos, colors, and style guidelines designed by professionals for use in other media. If so, these can be adapted for Web use as well. This might even be a requirement of the Legal department.

In the absence of other guidelines, choose a theme related to some aspect of the site's content. For a school, consider the school colors, emblem, and mascot. For an athletic league, consider the colors and textures of the playing field or equipment. For a restaurant, consider the scenes and colors related to the cuisine or locale, the style of the restaurant's menu, fixtures and objects from the restaurant's decor, or ingredients and cooking utensils.

Beyond these relatively obvious approaches, consider a theme based not on products themselves, but rather on settings where the product is used, cities or sites where it's manufactured or sold, or aspects of the organization's history or technology. Your site's theme should suggest colors, pictures, and icons you can use throughout the site or its principal sections. If a particular theme doesn't suggest a set of workable colors and pictures, move on to another. You'll probably get an "aha!" feeling when you've found it.

The default colors on most browsers are black on gray or black on white. This is every bit as interesting as black-and-white slides projected on a basement wall. Black, white, and gray aren't necessarily colors to avoid, but they *do* deserve augmentation with adjacent frames, pictures, and borders. When choosing text and background colors, choose dark text on a light background. Bright text on a dark background is harder to read, especially for small type sizes. It's usually a good idea to maintain color contrast as well as brightness contrast between text and background.

For information on choosing colors that display correctly on Web pages, refer to "Achieving Accurate Rendition—Safe Colors" on page 556.

Planning Your Pages

Given a mission, an audience, a content plan, management go-ahead, a visual concept, and knowledge of what HTML can and cannot do, you're finally ready to design pages in detail. To at least some extent, this will probably involve storyboards and sketches.

The classic storyboard consists of index cards pinned to a wall. You write up an index card for each Web page, annotate it to indicate planned content, and then arrange all the cards in some kind of hierarchy or sequence. Web visitors will traverse the site along these sequences and hierarchies. Team members and your project sponsor will review the chart, suggest revisions, and someday pronounce it worthy of prime time.

Actual storyboards of this type are rare, but the concept is sound. Your storyboard might be notes on a yellow pad, an outline in a word processor, a draft set of menu pages, or even a Navigation view in FrontPage. No matter: The key result is a well-organized set of pages, not the method used to achieve it.

> **note** FrontPage Navigation view provides an excellent means to record and modify your storyboard electronically. Navigation view has the added bonus of building and hyperlinking your pages for you.

For more information about Navigation view, refer to "Creating a Web Site in Navigation View" on page 75, or Chapter 7, "Managing Web Structure with Navigation View."

It's easy to go wild with menus. Visitors are unlikely to find pages more than two or three clicks away from the main page, however, so don't nest menus too deeply. Avoid long pages of hypertext links by using drop-down lists, option buttons, check boxes, and other HTML form elements. Together, a drop-down list of 10 product names and another with 4 kinds of information can efficiently support 40 menu choices.

You should also start sketching or drafting pages at this point. Identify each type of page you plan to use, and then make up a draft or template for each type. Identify changeable components that will exist on multiple pages—menu bars, signature blocks, contact names, and the like. Then plan site parameters and include blocks to support them. Accumulate stock pictures, too. These are logos, icons, buttons, bars, and theme pictures that, if standardized, will help the site achieve a unified appearance.

Lengthy text, either as content or HTML commands, is seldom the cause of excessive download times. Pictures, Java applets, and ActiveX controls are far more often the culprits. As you plan your pages and accumulate your pictures, keep a rough total of download bytes for each type of page. There are no hard-and-fast rules on the size of Web pages, and this is less a consideration on high-bandwidth intranets than on public Internet sites accessed by dial-in Web visitors. Pages with more than 25,000 to 30,000 download bytes are generally considered too large for dial-in Web visitors. This is equivalent to 15 to 20 pages of double-spaced plain text, or one uncompressed picture that's 170 pixels on a side.

A final bit of planning advice: You *can* have too much of a good thing. All Web sites are always under construction, so trying in advance to nail down every nit for every page is probably a futile exercise. If you try to plan too much detail, the site's rate of change will exceed the rate of planning. Don't let "paralysis by analysis" happen to you.

Achieving Effective Page Layout

The normal progression of topics on a page, whether on the Web or in your morning paper, is top to bottom and left to right. Every Web page should have both a meaningful title and a meaningful heading. As Figure 4-5 on the next page illustrates, the title appears

117

in the browser's title bar, and the heading appears somewhere near the top of the page. The title serves to identify the page externally to processes such as FrontPage and to search engines such as Yahoo!, Lycos, AltaVista, and MSN Search). The heading immediately informs the Web visitor what content appears on the page. A visitor who has chosen a wrong link can immediately jump back to the previous page. Otherwise, the heading confirms that the visitor has arrived at the correct page. If the page is long, bookmark links should provide pathways to each major subsection, to avoid extensive scrolling (at least on the home page).

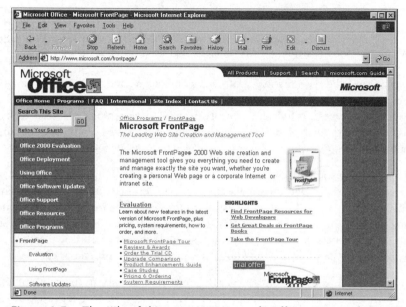

Figure 4-5. The title of this page is "Microsoft Office - Microsoft FrontPage," and its heading is "Microsoft FrontPage."

Experienced page designers often find HTML's weak page-layout features extremely frustrating. This reflects a fundamental conflict between the HTML goal of device independence and the artistic desire for precise control. This conflict isn't likely to subside any time soon, though FrontPage does support a number of recent HTML page-layout facilities:

● **Alignment tags.** The normal flow of HTML text is down the left margin, wrapping lines automatically when they reach the right margin, with a hard-coded line break and an explicit or implied paragraph ending. Pictures, Java applets, and ActiveX controls retain their relative positions within the HTML text.

Implied paragraph endings occur in several situations:

- Before and after tables
- At transitions in paragraph style
- Before and after numbered and bulleted lists

Recent versions of HTML support attributes to left-align or right-align pictures and other objects, flowing text around them. A centering attribute centers the same kinds of objects, but no text flows to the right or left of the centered picture. Additional attributes align non-text objects vertically with the surrounding text flow. FrontPage supports all of these attributes.

> For more information about using alignment attributes to control page placement, refer to "Aligning Text" on page 290.

- **HTML tables.** Originally designed to display tabular data, HTML tables have become one of the premier means to place items spatially on a page. Any time you'd like to draw an imaginary grid on a page and align items within it, an HTML table should be your choice.

> For information about using FrontPage to create HTML tables, refer to "Creating and Editing Tables" on page 475.

- **Cascading style sheet (CSS) positioning.** This technology finally gives Web designers pixel-precise positioning and layering control over their work. FrontPage provides access to CSS positioning though the Position choice on its Format menu.

> For more information about CSS positioning, refer to "Positioning Content with Style Sheets" on page 629.

- **Frames.** This feature provides a way to divide a Web page into tiled rectangles and to independently control the content of each rectangle. One Web page defines a *frames page*—an object that controls the number, sizes, and placement of the frames—while additional Web pages provide the content for each frame. Standard frames have visible borders between them and scroll bars for moving up, down, left, and right within each frame. Borderless frames have no visible borders and are simply page-layout areas that corral your text where you want it.

> For more information about frames, refer to Chapter 17, "Using Frames for Page Layout."

Chapter 4

In Summary...

This chapter described the process of Web design at a very high, human-oriented level. It also introduced some useful concepts for giving your site a uniform, attractive, and effective visual appearance.

The next chapter examines Webs, a FrontPage facility that groups Web pages together for convenience, group processing, accountability, and security.

Understanding FrontPage-Based Webs

Although most new designers understand that creating a Web site means creating and linking many Web pages, many of them intuitively look for tools that work on one Web page at a time. Such tools can make the page creation process faster, more enjoyable, and generally more successful, but they provide no help in keeping the site organized, uniform, and functional. Only when things get out of hand do beginners look for software that can manage and organize the site as a whole.

Microsoft FrontPage doesn't share this page-at-a-time mentality; its mindset is to first create a managed file area, and then index new or changed pages as you develop them. This provides much better results than any after-the-fact analysis can hope to achieve, but it does catch new FrontPage designers by surprise. Learning to think and work in terms of first creating and then populating entire Webs is probably the greatest single barrier new FrontPage designers face.

This chapter describes at a surface level what constitutes a FrontPage-based Web and what a FrontPage-based Web can do. The next chapter continues this discussion by explaining in some detail how to create and operate FrontPage-based Webs. If you're reading the book sequentially and prefer to jump directly into the details of creating individual pages, skip ahead to Part 4, "Editing Basic Page Content."

FrontPage-Based Webs

Web sites are more than the sum of their parts. When Web pages work together effectively, their organization, their cohesion, and their ability to follow each Web visitor's mindset and interest is what makes hypertext such a different experience from print.

To manage and administer your Web content, FrontPage organizes Web pages into units called FrontPage-based Webs. Physically, a Web is a folder tree located somewhere on your local hard disk, on a file server, or on a Web server. Logically, it's a file area gifted with intelligence about the files it contains and the relationships among them. FrontPage leverages this intelligence to make your job as a Web designer easier.

The next three sections compare and contrast the three ways FrontPage can store and retrieve Web pages: as individual files, in disk-based Webs, and in server-based Webs.

Creating Web Pages as Individual Files

Creating Web pages as individual files is the simplest approach for beginners because to create a page, you just start FrontPage, add the text and pictures for the page, apply formatting, and save the page just like any other Microsoft Office document (that is, you save it with the Save or Save As command and open it with the Open command). Unfortunately, as the number of pages grows, memorizing the function of each page and all its relationships to other pages becomes harder and harder.

> **note** For purposes of this discussion, files on a network file server are equivalent to files on your local hard disk.

You can partially resolve this problem by faithfully maintaining written documentation and by using tools like the Search For Files Or Folders command that comes with Microsoft Windows. Sooner or later, though, most designers end up wanting more.

Using Disk-Based Webs

The simplest kind of FrontPage-based Web is a just a designated folder on your hard disk. FrontPage calls this a *disk-based Web*. The folder itself can be almost anything: a new empty folder you create yourself, a new folder FrontPage creates and perhaps populates with sample pages, or an existing folder full of Web pages, pictures, and other files you've already created.

> For more information about the mechanics of creating FrontPage-based Webs, refer to Chapter 6, "Creating and Using FrontPage-Based Webs."

After you've defined a disk-based Web, FrontPage can perform global operations on it. These operations include things like checking spelling in the entire Web, checking all the hyperlinks within the Web, and copying the Web to another computer.

Figure 5-1 shows Windows Explorer displaying the root folder of a disk-based Web called *My Webs*. To make all the files and folders visible, the Hidden Files option is set to Show All Files.

Figure 5-1. Blue globe icons identify folders that contain FrontPage-based Webs. Each Web contains not only the content folders that Web designers use, but hidden folders that FrontPage uses.

> **note** The blue globe that designates a FrontPage-based Web might or might not appear, depending on your operating system and system settings.

Note the following details:

- The folder icon in the top left corner contains a blue globe. This indicates that the folder contains a FrontPage-based Web.

- The folder icons *myweb*, *myweb2*, *myweb3*, and *myweb4* also contain globes. This indicates that these folders contain additional Webs.

- FrontPage has added a number of special folders to this Web:

  - *_derived.* Contains pictures created by certain FrontPage components. In this case, it contains the pictures that appear in the Link bar at the left of the Web's home page. Windows displays a preview of this home page in the lower left corner of Figure 5-1. The Link Bar component generates the five text balloons visible at the left of the preview. When you display the home page in your browser, each balloon is a hyperlink to another page.

123

■ **_fpclass.** Contains any Java applets that FrontPage components will use when Web visitors display pages in this Web. FrontPage automatically puts these applets in place as required.

■ **_overlay.** Contains additional pictures created by FrontPage.

■ **_private.** Contains data files you don't want Web visitors to access. If, for example, you add a Hit Counter component to one of your Web pages, the file that stores the current count goes in the _private folder. This is also a good place to store data accumulated from HTML forms.

■ **_themes.** Contains one folder for each theme used in your Web. Each folder contains all the files and folders required to display the given theme.

■ **_vti_cnf.** This hidden folder is where FrontPage stores information about the files that make up your Web. To understand how this works, refer again to Figure 5-1. The *C:\My Documents\My Webs* folder contains two files named *drawing.htm* and *index.htm*. The _vti_cnf folder also contains two files with these names, but they aren't HTML files at all. They're special text files where FrontPage stores information about the corresponding content files. In Figure 5-2, for example, Microsoft Notepad shows the contents of the _vti__cnf/index.htm file that describes *index.htm*.

Figure 5-2. This file, located in a _vti_cnf folder, describes a Web page named *index.htm*.

FrontPage creates and maintains all the files and file contents that reside within the *_vti_cnf* folder. Disturbing this information might interfere with the proper operation of FrontPage.

- **_vti_pvt.** Another hidden folder. This is where FrontPage stores Web settings, the Navigation view structure, the Task List, and other information about the current Web.

- *drawing_files.* Contains files that FrontPage generated for use by the *drawing.htm* file.

- *images.* Contains pictures and graphics you want to use in your Web pages.

- *index_files.* Contains files that FrontPage generated for use by the *index.htm* file.

The point of presenting this information isn't because you need to work with these special files and folders yourself. The point is rather to show that FrontPage maintains a great deal of information about the pages in your Web. The term for this information is *metadata,* or data about data. If you change files manually (for example, without going through FrontPage), the metadata will be incorrect and FrontPage will malfunction in any number of major or minor ways. This situation leads to the following advice:

- After you create a FrontPage-based Web, always use FrontPage to make any changes to the Web. If you want to use an editor other than FrontPage occasionally, identify it to FrontPage by choosing Options from the Tools menu and then selecting the Configure Editors tab. Then right-click the file you want to edit, choose Open With from the shortcut menu, and select the editor you want.

 For more information about configuring FrontPage to invoke external editors, refer to "Configuring External Editors" in the Bonus Content on the Companion CD.

- If you must change a FrontPage-based Web directly, finish your changes and then open the Web in FrontPage. Next choose Recalculate Hyperlinks from the Tools menu. This will regenerate all the metadata FrontPage depends on for proper operation.

note FrontPage isn't the only program that can maintain the integrity of a FrontPage-based Web while making changes. The Web Folders feature in Microsoft Windows 98, Microsoft Windows Me, and Microsoft Windows NT is actually a front-end to parts of FrontPage that correctly update Webs, as are any HTTP locations that appear under My Network Places in Microsoft Windows 2000.

Chapter 5

Figure 5-3 shows the Web selected in Figure 5-1 open in FrontPage. With the exception of the _private_ and _images_ folders, FrontPage doesn't show any of its special folders because you, as the Web designer, should never need to modify them. FrontPage does the modification automatically, silently, and unseen.

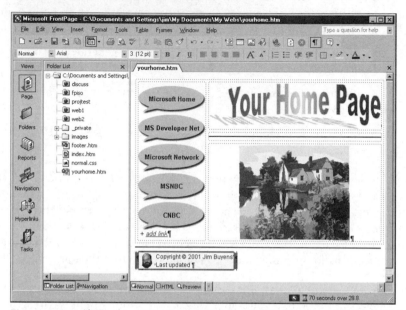

Figure 5-3. This is how FrontPage displays the Web shown in Figure 5-1. FrontPage hides its special folders because Web designers have no need to work with them directly.

One FrontPage-based Web can contain another. A Web that contains another Web is said to be a _parent_, and the Web it contains a _child_ or _subweb_. A Web that has no parent is a _root Web_.

There are no concrete rules or technical requirements that dictate how many Webs a server should have, or what they should contain. Certain principles do, however, apply:

- Pages with many hyperlinks among themselves usually belong in the same Web (that is, distinct bodies of content should generally reside in the same Web).

- Groups of pages administered by different people should generally be in different Webs.

- The larger the Web, the longer it will take to upload and update. For purposes of both performance and content management, FrontPage-based Webs generally shouldn't exceed a few thousand files.

Using Server-Based Webs

Disk-based Webs are very suitable for many kinds of work, but what they *can't* do is emulate active processes designed to run on a Web server. These processes include displaying hit counters, using an HTML form to search for content, processing data from HTML forms, and working with databases. The programs that do these things on the World Wide Web are designed to run as part of a Web server and not as part of your disk—it's as simple as that. If you want these functions to work in your development environment, that environment must include a Web server.

A FrontPage-based Web that resides on a Web server is called, logically enough, a *server-based Web*. Your Web pages and associated files reside on a real Web server, one you can access via your network connection, of course. This connection could be a dial-up network connection, a Local Area Network (LAN) at your office, or a Home Area Network that connects the computers in your house. (Have faith; this is going the be the Next Big Thing.) The FrontPage desktop software reads files from the Web server instead of from your local disk, and writes files to the Web server as well. Whenever a FrontPage client changes a file, software on the Web server updates the necessary FrontPage cross-references and indexes.

Using a FrontPage-based Web is very simple if you already have a FrontPage-enabled Web server on your network. Just ask the Webmaster for a FrontPage-based Web, specify its HTTP location in FrontPage's Open Web dialog box, and away you go. Unfortunately, not everyone is in an office with a dedicated Webmaster and so, for full functionality, you might need to become your own Webmaster.

If there's no FrontPage-enabled Web server already on your network—or even if you have no network—you can still enjoy full-bore, server-based FrontPage functionality. All you need to do is install network software, Web-server software, and the FrontPage Server Extensions all on one machine. Figure 5-4 on the next page illustrates this arrangement. Installing all of these isn't as hard as it sounds, but it does mean you need to become your own Webmaster.

> **For more information about installing a Personal Web Server, refer to Chapter 37, "Installing and Configuring a Web Server."**

If you already connect to a TCP/IP network, either on a LAN or by dialing into an Internet service provider, the network software is already installed. If not, go to Control Panel, and then Network, and add the TCP/IP protocol.

You can use any Web server software that both runs on your computer and has a version of the FrontPage Server Extensions available. For most computers running Windows, this will be the Microsoft Web server software that corresponds to your operating system.

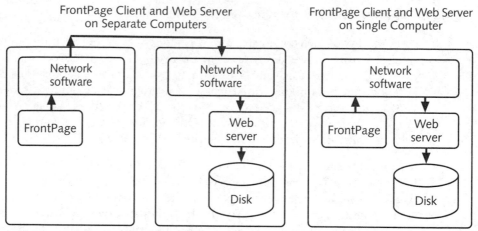

Figure 5-4. The FrontPage 2002 client and a Web server used for authoring can reside either on separate computers or on the same computer.

Microsoft provides Web servers that run on most Windows operating systems, and these are generally the best Web servers for running FrontPage. The latest and greatest version of the Web server for your operating system will of course change from time to time, but here's the most recent information available at the time Microsoft began selling FrontPage 2002:

- **Windows 2000.** Use Add/Remove Programs to install the version of Internet Information Service (IIS) that comes with the operating system, and then install the latest Windows 2000 service pack.

- **Windows Me.** No Microsoft Web servers are available for this platform. If you need to run a Web server on a Windows Me machine, you must either upgrade the machine to Windows 2000 or downgrade to Windows 98.

- **Windows NT.** Obtain and install the Windows NT Option Pack. This will install IIS 4, the most recent version supported under Windows NT.

- **Microsoft Windows 98 SE.** Run the *\add-ons\pws\setup.exe* file from the Windows 98 CD. Be aware, however, that FrontPage Server Extensions 2002 aren't available for this platform. You can run the FrontPage 2000 Server Extensions but this means some new FrontPage 2002 features won't work.

- **Microsoft Windows 95 and Windows 98.** Obtain and install the Windows NT Option Pack. This isn't a misprint; to install a personal Web server for Windows 95 or Windows 98, you install the Windows NT Option Pack. The setup program installs the proper software for your operating system. Again, however, no FrontPage Server Extensions 2002 are available for these platforms. And neither FrontPage 2002 nor any other Office XP programs will run on Windows 95.

In all cases, checking Microsoft's Web site for hot fixes and new versions is to your advantage. Also, unless the Web server's setup program specifically offers to install *FrontPage Server Extensions 2002*, you'll save time by not installing the server extensions that come with the Web server. Here are some useful URLs:

- **Windows 95**
  http://www.microsoft.com/windows95/

- **Windows 98**
  http://www.microsoft.com/windows98/

- **Windows Me**
  http://www.microsoft.com/windowsme/

- **Microsoft Windows NT Workstation 4.0**
  http://www.microsoft.com/ntworkstation/

- **Microsoft Windows NT Server 4.0**
  http://www.microsoft.com/ntserver/nts/

- **Windows 2000**
  http://www.microsoft.com/windows2000/

- **FrontPage**
  http://www.microsoft.com/frontpage/

FrontPage achieves its maximum potential when the FrontPage Server Extensions are installed on both the Web server used for developing pages and the Web server that delivers those pages worldwide. Installing the server extensions is a very good idea for these three reasons:

- Reading files from a Web server is no problem for FrontPage 2002; it just reads them in the same way any browser would read them. The tricky part comes in *writing* files to a Web server, and FrontPage does this by packing up the file and submitting it like data coming from an HTML form. This requires a program on the other end of the connection—on the Web server—that can unpack the file and write it into the server's file system. And that program is part of the FrontPage Server Extensions.

- Whenever the server extensions make changes to a Web, they update FrontPage's cross-references, its indexes, and other site-management information. These updates, in turn, can trigger server-based updates to hyperlinks and Web components.

- The server extensions provide various centralized services—such as data collection, mailing, and search capabilities—that Web visitors can use when they visit your site.

Chapter 5

The Hit Counter is among the simplest of these services. When you tell FrontPage to create the HTML for a hit counter, FrontPage generates code that tells the Web server to run the FrontPage hit counter program. And to install that program, the Webmaster needs to install the FrontPage Extensions.

Server extensions are available for a variety of popular Web servers and computing platforms including Windows 95, Windows 98, Windows NT, Windows 2000 and UNIX. If you're a server administrator planning to support Web authors running FrontPage, you should definitely install the extensions and keep them up-to-date. If you're a FrontPage Web designer, you should definitely encourage your Web server administrator to do the same. If you have a Web site hosted by an Internet service provider (ISP), check to see if the provider has installed (or will install) the latest FrontPage Server Extensions.

There are three ways to install the FrontPage Server Extensions. In general, you should choose the method that provides the most current software available:

● SharePoint Team Services includes the FrontPage Server Extensions. Thus, installing SharePoint Team Services for use by regular Office users also installs the FrontPage Server Extensions for use by Web designers.

For more information about SharePoint Team Services, refer to Chapter 35, "Using SharePoint Team Web Sites."

● Server extensions might come with—and perhaps install with—the Web server software.

● You can download the extensions from Microsoft's Web site.

For more information about installing the FrontPage Server Extensions, refer to "Installing the FrontPage Server Extensions" on page 1086.

Installing SharePoint Team Services or the FrontPage Server Extensions 2002 on a computer makes them available for installation on any Web servers running on that computer. Those Web servers, however, initially remain unaffected.

Adding the server extensions to a Web server creates a root Web that includes the server's entire existing content. The root Web's administrator will initially be the Web server's administrator. The root Web administrator can then create subwebs—either new, empty subwebs or subwebs covering existing content—and grant appropriate permissions for administration, authoring, and browsing.

Appreciating Webs

The natural FrontPage way of doing things is to first create a Web and then put pages in it. This is often confusing at first, and for two quite logical reasons. First, FrontPage-based Webs are rather abstract entities. Second, the need to manage and organize Web pages might not be obvious when you don't yet *have* any Web pages!

To resolve this dilemma, the following topics present a brief yet practical overview of the features and merits of FrontPage-based Webs.

Maintaining Hyperlink Locations

When you use FrontPage to move or rename files in an open Web, FrontPage locates and updates all hyperlinks that use the affected files. Suppose, for example, that you have a picture file named *clown.jpg* that's located in a FrontPage-based Web. If you open the Web in FrontPage and rename the file to *joker.jpg*, FrontPage changes any picture tags, hyperlinks, or other references to the *clown.jpg* file within that Web so they point to *joker.jpg* instead. Of course, this works for any type of file, not just picture files, and it also works when you move a file from one folder to another.

Figure 5-5 shows this feature in action. The Web designer has opened a Web, switched to Folder view, and renamed the first file listed from *BD18186_.gif* to *bd18186_.gif*. After consulting its indexes, FrontPage determines that three pages in the current Web have links to this file and offers to correct all three.

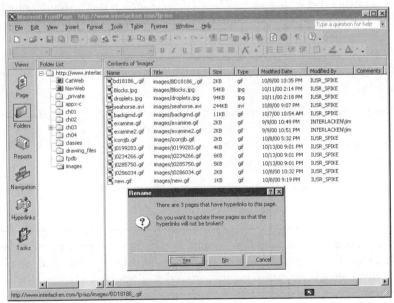

Figure 5-5. When you use FrontPage to rename or relocate a Web file, FrontPage offers to update all links in all pages that refer to that file.

Working with Web Components

Many Web components work only in the context of a FrontPage-based Web. Consider, for example, the Include Page component, which copies the content of one page into another. This is a very handy way to create content once, use it many times, and be confident that the content looks the same everywhere.

Most Web servers offer a similar capability called Server Side Include (SSI). This feature merges the included content into the surrounding page every time a visitor requests that page. This ensures that the included content is always up to date, but incurs three disadvantages as well:

- It complicates WYSIWYG display at design time.
- Many sites restrict the use of SSI because it involves extra work for the Web server.
- Many sites restrict the use of SSI for security reasons.

To avoid these problems, each page that uses an Include Page component contains a physical copy of the included content. You might think that having a copy of the included content on every page would create a problem when you change it, but not so. In fact, within the same Web, FrontPage updates all copies of an included page whenever you update it.

Suppose, for example, that you design a footer to appear in every page in your site. Suppose further that dozens or hundreds of pages incorporate this footer by means of the Include Page component. Whenever FrontPage updates the footer, it updates every included instance of the footer as well. FrontPage is able to do this because it maintains cross-references of every location that includes a given page. When you change the included content, FrontPage knows the location of each copy of that content and updates every one.

This kind of mass update isn't possible if you keep your pages as files in an ordinary disk folder. When working with individual files, FrontPage lacks the indexes and cross-reference files necessary for propagating changes. Therefore, the Include Page component isn't available unless a FrontPage-based Web is open.

Table 5-1 provides a summary of the need for FrontPage-based Webs when using Web components.

> **note** The Save Results to E-mail and Save Results To Database components mentioned on the next page don't appear as objects you can insert using the FrontPage user interface. Instead, they're options in the Properties dialog box for an HTML form.

Table 5-1. **Web Components and FrontPage-Based Webs**

Component	Requires disk-based or server-based Web for development	Requires server-based Web for testing	Requires server-based Web for development
Banner Ad Manager	No	No	No
Comment	No	No	No
Date And Time	No	No	No
Hover Button	No	No	No
Marquee	No	No	No
Spreadsheets And Charts	No	No	No
Photo Gallery	No	No	No
Insert HTML	No	No	No
Table Of Contents For This Web Site	Yes	No	No
Include Page	Yes	No	No
Scheduled Picture	Yes	No	No
Scheduled Include Page	Yes	No	No
Table Of Contents Based On Page Category	Yes	No	No
List View	Yes	No	No
Document Library View	Yes	No	No
Link Bars	Yes	No	No
Page Banner	Yes	No	No
Substitution	Yes	No	No
File Upload	No	Yes	No
Hit Counter	No	Yes	No
Top 10 List	No	Yes	No
Confirmation Field	Yes	Yes	No
Save Results To E-Mail Or File	Yes	Yes	No
Web Search	Yes	Yes	No
Save Results To Database	No	Yes	Yes
Database Results	No	Yes	Yes

Chapter 5

Creating Web Pages from Site Information

Chapter 3 explained how to record a site structure in Navigation view and thereby create a complete set of Web pages with page banners, Link bars, high-tech formatting, and so forth. This process requires FrontPage to collect and record various kinds of information about the group of pages in question—information not stored in any specific Web page. Of course, the location of that information and the bounds of that group are one and the same—a FrontPage-based Web.

The Table Of Contents component is another device that creates content automatically from information in a FrontPage-based Web. This component has two modes: a Table Of Contents For This Web Site and a Table Of Contents Based On Page Category. In the first mode, FrontPage creates an indented list of hyperlinks based on any starting point you designate. The following text discusses each of these modes in order. Figure 5-6 shows the dialog box that configures a Table Of Contents For This Web Site component.

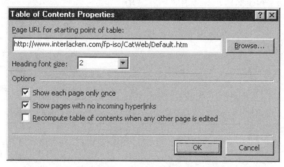

Figure 5-6. This dialog box specifies the starting location and other properties for a Table Of Contents For This Web Site component.

Here's the procedure to try this yourself:

1 Open any FrontPage-based Web.

2 Create a new blank page.

3 Choose Web Component from the Insert menu.

4 When the Insert Web Component dialog box appears, choose Table Of Contents in the Component Type list, choose For This Web Site in the Choose A Table Of Contents list, and then click Finish.

5 When the Table Of Contents Properties dialog box shown in Figure 5-6 appears, locate the Page URL For Starting Point Of Table box, and enter the location of the Web page that should head the table of contents.

When FrontPage creates the table of contents, the heading will be the title of the Web page you specify in this box. FrontPage will create one subheading for each hyperlink on that page, then additional subheadings for each hyperlink on those pages, and so forth.

6 Click the OK button to insert the Table Of Contents component. To see the results, you'll need to save the Web page and view it in your browser. Figure 5-7 shows some typical results.

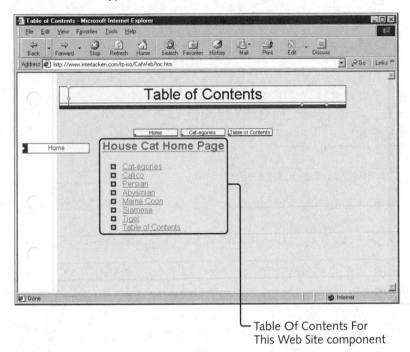

Table Of Contents For
This Web Site component

Figure 5-7. The Table Of Contents For This Web Site component in this Web page displays all hyperlinks that appear on the House Cat Home Page.

For more information about the Table Of Contents For This Web Site component, refer to "Using the Table of Contents For This Web Site Component" on page 771.

The Table Of Contents Based On Page Category component works quite differently. First you assign one or more category codes to selected pages in a Web. Then you insert a Table Of Contents Based On Page Category component that specifies one or more of these categories. When you display the page containing the component in a browser, the component will display a hyperlink to each page that matches the specified categories. Figure 5-8 on the next page illustrates the first part of this process: assigning categories to a Web page.

135

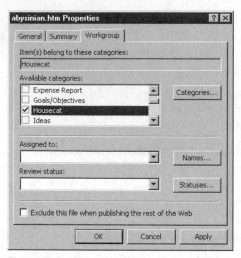

Figure 5-8. To assign category codes for a Web page, open its property sheet and click the Workgroup tab.

Here are the steps to try this yourself:

1 Right-click the page you want to categorize in the Folder List or Folders view.

2 Choose Properties from the shortcut menu, and click the Workgroup tab.

3 Check all applicable categories in the Available Categories box.

4 To add, modify, or delete categories, click the Categories button, make any desired changes, and click OK.

Proceed as follows to insert the actual Table Of Contents Based On Page Category component:

1 Open the page that will display the component and set the insertion point where you want it to appear.

2 Choose Web Component from the Insert menu.

3 When the Insert Web Component dialog box appears, choose Table Of Contents in the Component Type list, choose Based On Page Category in the Choose A Table Of Contents list, and then click Finish.

4 When the Categories Properties dialog box shown in Figure 5-9 appears, select the check box for each category the component should display. Click OK.

To see the complete results you'll need to save the page and display it in your browser. The Web page shown in Figure 5-10 contains two Table Of Contents Based On Page Category components: one for the Housecat category and one for the Wildlife category.

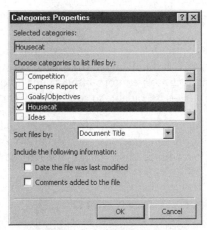

Figure 5-9. The Table Of Contents Based On Page Category component displays links to all pages in a Web that are coded with given category codes.

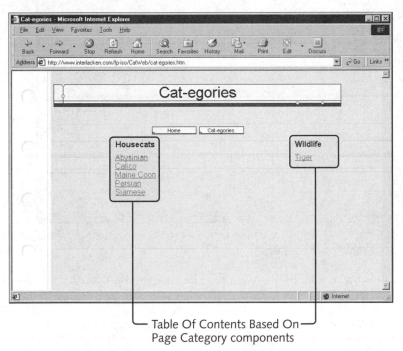

Table Of Contents Based On Page Category components

Figure 5-10. This Web page contains two Table Of Contents Based On Page Category components. Each displays Web pages with a different category of content.

The Table Of Contents components illustrate how a FrontPage-based Web collects information about its contents and uses that information to make the designer's job easier.

For more information about the Table Of Contents Based On Page Category component, refer to "Using the Table Of Contents Based On Page Category Component" on page 776.

Deriving Site Information From Web Pages

By now it should be clear that FrontPage accumulates a wealth of information about each file in a Web, and that Web components and built-in features make keen use of that information to do their jobs. Of course, the same information might hold interest for you directly, and FrontPage therefore makes it available in several different ways.

The Hyperlinks view in Figure 5-11 graphically displays a Web's hyperlink relationships. The page in the center is the current point of reference, and defaults to the home page. To make any other page the point of reference, right-click it and choose Move To Center from the shortcut menu.

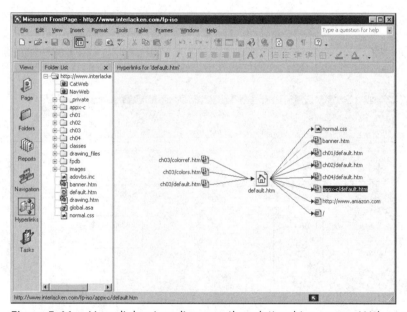

Figure 5-11. Hyperlinks view diagrams the relationships among Web pages and other files in a FrontPage-based Web.

Pages drawn to the left of the center page have hyperlinks *to* the center page. Pages drawn to the right of the center page have links *from* the center page to themselves.

To see additional levels of detail, click the plus icon on any node. Clicking the plus icon for the *banner.htm* page shown in Figure 5-11, for example, expands the diagram to the right and shows all hyperlinks from *banner.htm* to other pages. An expanded plus icon changes to a minus icon that hides the additional detail.

Right-clicking the background area displays the following shortcut menu. These shortcut menu commands toggle the display between URLs and page titles, reveal or suppress hyperlinks to pictures, reveal or suppress multiple links from one page to another, and display the Web Settings dialog box for the current Web.

Reports view displays many kinds of information about your Web in tabular format. Figure 5-12 shows the Site Summary report, which shows the highest-level statistics and provides links to all the other reports. To sort a report on any column, click the column heading. All the usual options apply to Web pages and related files that appear in the various reports: double-clicking a file or page opens the file in the default editor; right-clicking a file displays a shortcut menu that has options for opening the file with any other editor, displaying the file in your browser, renaming the file, and so forth.

Hyperlinks view and Reports view are just two features that illustrate how organizing pages into FrontPage Webs adds value for you, the designer.

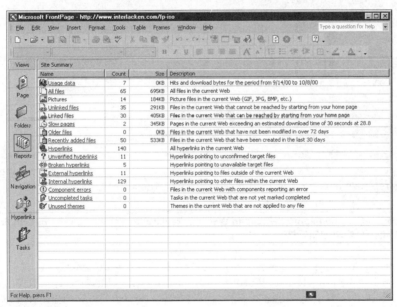

Figure 5-12. Reports view displays information about your Web in tabular format.

For more information about Reports View, refer to "Working with Reports View" on page 424.

Using Management and Monitoring Tools

FrontPage includes a number of powerful tools that keep your site in tip-top condition—provided, of course, that you keep your site in a FrontPage-based Web. Some of these tools include:

● **Find and Replace in Web.** FrontPage can search all pages in a Web for a given string of text. The result of a search is a clickable list of pages that match the search criteria. After displaying this list, FrontPage can replace the given string with any other string you want. The replacement can apply to all found pages or just the ones you designate. Figure 5-13 shows this feature in action.

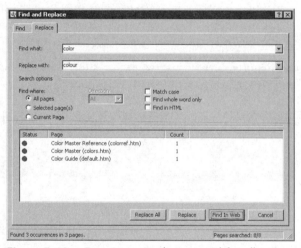

Figure 5-13. Running a Find command for all pages in a Web produces a clickable list of Web pages like this. To replace the found string, enter the replacement text and then click Replace or Replace All.

For more information about the Find in Web and Replace in Web tools, refer to "Finding and Replacing Text" on page 411.

Don't confuse this feature with the Web Search component. Designers using the FrontPage desktop software use the site-wide Find And Replace tool to help them build Web pages. The Web Search component receives search terms Web visitors enter in an HTML form and sends the browser a list of Web pages that match those terms.

For more information about the Web Search component, refer to Chapter 28, "Providing a Text Search Capability."

- **Check Spelling in Web.** FrontPage can check spelling in every page in a given Web. To use this feature, move the highlight outside the Page view window (by clicking the Folder list), choose Spelling from the Tools menu, click the Entire Web option, and then click Start.

> For more information about site-wide spelling checking, refer to "Checking Spelling in Your Web" on page 418.

- **Verify Hyperlinks.** FrontPage can check the validity of every hyperlink in a Web. For hyperlinks among pages in the same Web, FrontPage does this using its own, internal indexes. To verify hyperlinks that point outside the current Web, it attempts a physical connection. Here's how this works:

    1 Choose Reports from the View menu, then choose Problems, and then choose Broken Hyperlinks.

    2 FrontPage displays a Reports View dialog box that offers to verify all the hyperlinks in your Web:

    ◆ To check all your links immediately, click the Yes button.

    ◆ To check links at a later time, perhaps individually, click the No button.

    ◆ To avoid this prompt in the future, check the box titled Don't Ask Me This Again before you click Yes or No.

    3 The Status column shows the status of each hyperlink: OK, Broken, or Unknown:

    ◆ To correct a broken hyperlink, right-click the line that reports it and then choose Edit Hyperlink from the shortcut menu.

    ◆ To resolve a status of Unknown, right-click the line that reports it and then choose Verify Hyperlink from the shortcut menu.

> **tip** To verify any hyperlink listed in the Broken Hyperlinks report, right-click it and choose Verify Hyperlink. To correct any listed hyperlink, right-click it and choose Edit Hyperlink. Corrections can apply to a single occurrence of the bad URL, to all occurrences in all pages, or to selected occurrences.

> For more information about verifying hyperlinks, refer to "Checking Links in Your Web" on page 422.

- **Recalculating Hyperlinks.** FrontPage can regenerate all of its internal indexes and cross-reference files using this command. You should run this

141

command whenever you feel these items might be out of date, and especially after making changes to the Web other than through FrontPage. Choose Recalculate Hyperlinks from the Tools menu, and then click Yes when prompted.

> **For more information about Recalculating Hyperlinks, refer to "Re-Indexing Your Web" on page 421.**

- ● **Server Health.** This series of commands can perform various consistency checks on server-based Webs. In many cases, these commands restore a malfunctioning Web to proper operation. To run the full set of server health commands, you must be an administrator of the root Web of your server. Even if you don't have authority to use this command yourself, it's worth knowing that you can ask your administrator to run the commands for you on a one-time or scheduled basis.

> **For more information about checking server health, refer to "Checking Server Health" on page 1110.**

Using Workgroup Version Control

If your Web site is a group effort, you might occasionally run into problems when two people are working in the same page at the same time. When one person saves his or her changes, he or she wipes out the other person's changes, or vice versa. To avoid this problem:

1 Choose Web Settings from the Tools menu.

2 Click the General tab.

3 Select the Use Document Check-In And Check-Out check box, and click OK.

With Document Check-In And Check-Out in effect, you must perform a Check-Out transaction before modifying any file. Checking out the file prevents anyone else from checking out the same file—and thus from changing it—while your changes are in progress. When you're done making changes, you perform a Check-In transaction to finalize your changes and make the file available to others.

As an added benefit, you can perform an Undo Check-Out procedure any time before checking a file back in. This removes any changes you made to the file and restores the file to a version saved at the time of checkout.

To perform Check-Out, Check-In, or Undo Check-Out procedures, right-click a file in any Folder List or view and look for these commands on the shortcut menu. If they don't appear, it's probably because document check-in and check-out aren't activated for the current Web.

For more information about workgroup version control, refer to "Using Page Level Check-In/Check-Out" on page 972.

Built-In Upload/Download

While developing your Web pages, you have a choice of four ways to store them:

- As individual files on your local disk or file server.
- As a FrontPage-based Web on your local disk or file server.
- As a FrontPage-based Web on a Web server that runs on your computer. (Remember, this requires the FrontPage Server Extensions as well as the Web server itself.)
- As a FrontPage-based Web on a Web server that runs on some other computer. (Again, the FrontPage Server Extensions are required.)

In the latter two cases, it's certainly possible that the Web server is accessible to all your intended Web visitors; if so, your pages are ready and waiting for access the moment you finish them. It's more likely, though, that you'll need to copy your finished work to some other location for public consumption. FrontPage calls this function *publishing*.

For more information about the role multiple servers can play in a FrontPage environment, refer to "Planning Your Web Environment" on page 62.

If the target of your publishing operation is another FrontPage-based Web, FrontPage 2002 can intelligently upload your finished pages a page at a time, a FrontPage-based Web at a time, or an entire tree of FrontPage-based Webs at a time.

If the target of your publishing operation is a Web server that doesn't have the FrontPage Server Extensions, FrontPage 2002 can still upload your pages via the Internet's File Transfer Protocol (FTP). However, being less intelligent, such transfers might take a little longer and any FrontPage features (such as Hit Counter) that require the extensions won't work.

The Publish Web dialog box shown in the background of Figure 5-14 on the next page controls the way FrontPage publishes a Web. To display this dialog box, choose Publish Web from the File menu. Type or select the URL of the destination site's home folder, click the Publish button, and you're on your way.

Chapter 5

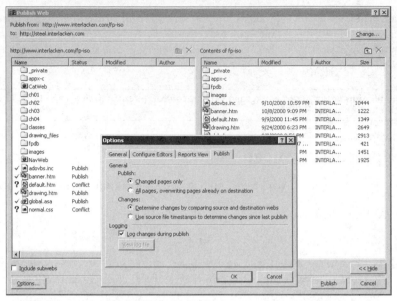

Figure 5-14. This dialog box starts FrontPage's built-in publishing feature, which copies Webs from one location to another.

newfeature!

Clicking the Options button in the lower left corner of the Publish Web dialog box displays the Options dialog box shown in the foreground of Figure 5-14. With this box you can specify:

● Whether to publish only those files in the source Web that are different from those in the destination Web.

● Whether to detect file differences by comparing directory information for the two Webs or by comparing timestamps in the current Web to its last publish date.

● Whether to retain a log of all changes that a publishing operation makes to the destination Web.

Publish
Web

You can also start publishing by clicking the Publish Web button on the Standard toolbar. However, this displays the Publish Web dialog box only if you've never before published the current Web. If you *have* previously published the current Web, clicking the Publish Web button publishes it again without prompting for new settings.

For more information about Web publishing, refer to Chapter 13, "Publishing Your FrontPage-Based Web."

Publishing, Copying, and Importing: What's the Difference?

The FrontPage Publish command is the only supported way of copying a FrontPage-based Web from one location to another without losing information. Publishing a Web ensures that the target location contains not only 100% of your content files, but a full set of well-structured cross-reference and index files as well.

Copying a Web in, say, Windows Explorer copies all the files in a Web, including cross-reference and indexes, but it doesn't adjust FrontPage's internal files to reflect the new physical location.

Creating a new Web and then importing an existing one imports the home page, then all pages and files referenced on the home page, then all pages and files on those pages, and so forth. This bypasses any files that aren't explicitly mentioned in hyperlinks. For example, it doesn't usually import database files or files mentioned in JavaScript or VBScript code. It also bypasses FrontPage files that contain information such as Web settings and the Navigation view structure. If the source Web contains any Active Server Pages or other components that execute on the Web server, you will most likely import the result of running those pages rather than the source files.

By far, the best procedure for copying a FrontPage-based Web is to open the source Web, choose Publish Web from the File menu, specify a target location, and click the Publish button.

To transport a Web on a ZIP, DirectCD, or other read-write removable media, first open the source Web and publish it as a disk-based Web on the removable media. When the removable media arrives at its destination, open the disk-based Web in FrontPage and then publish it to its permanent location.

To transport a FrontPage-based Web on CD, first publish it to a temporary disk location and then use your CD creation software to create a compact disc. At the destination site, open an MS-DOS command window and use the XCOPY command to copy the disk-based Web from the CD to a temporary hard disk location. (Using Windows Explorer to copy files from a CD marks them as Read-Only, which isn't acceptable to FrontPage.) Finally, open and publish the disk-based Web to its permanent location.

Like all Office XP applications, FrontPage also supports Web publishing through a facility called Web Folders:

- In Windows 98, Windows Me, and Windows NT, Web Folders is an icon that appears in the My Computer desktop window and on the My Places bar of all file-oriented dialog boxes in Office.

- In Windows 2000, Web Folders are HTTP locations that show up in My Network Places. This applies to the My Network Places desktop icon and the My Network Places icon on the My Places bar of Office applications.

145

Here's the procedure for using Web folders from the desktop:

1 In Windows 98, Windows Me, or Windows NT, open My Computer and double-click Web Folders.

In Windows 2000, double-click the My Network Places icon.

2 If the Web location you want is already listed, double-click it. If not, add it using either of these procedures (depending on your operating system):

■ In Windows 98, Windows Me or Windows NT, choose New from the File menu and then choose Web Folder.

■ In Windows 2000, double-click the Add Network Place icon.

> **caution** Any locations you add to Web Folders must be Web servers running the FrontPage Server Extensions. Otherwise, the Web Folders software can't communicate with the locations.

3 Add the Web site as a Network Place per the resulting wizard's instructions.

4 The Web Folders window now resembles Figure 5-15. Instead of folder locations on your local disk or file server, this window shows Internet addresses.

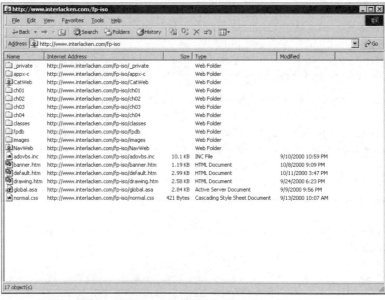

Figure 5-15. Office XP's Web Folders feature handles files on remote FrontPage Web servers as easily as those on a local disk.

5 To transfer files and folders to and from the remote Web server, drag them in and out just as you would in Windows Explorer.

Chapter 5

newfeature!
Using SharePoint Team Services Collaboration Features

All the features described so far in this chapter are available on disk-based Webs and server-based Webs running the FrontPage Server Extensions. These features are tightly integrated into FrontPage and uniquely designed for creating Web pages.

> **For more information about SharePoint Team Services, refer to Chapter 35, "Using SharePoint Team Web Sites."**

Installing SharePoint Team Services on a Web server provides all the services of a server-based FrontPage Web plus a collection of features uniquely tied to Microsoft Office. A framework called a *SharePoint team Web site* organizes these features into a cohesive unit.

SharePoint team Web sites are built around the concept of lists, which are essentially database tables you can configure with any fields you like. Some lists stand by themselves, such as lists of upcoming events and to-do lists. Other lists have associated document libraries that contain files associated with each list record. SharePoint team Web site members can add documents to a SharePoint team Web site document library through special Save options in Office applications or by using a Web page to upload the document.

Many SharePoint team Web site features key off user IDs. When someone updates a SharePoint team Web site list or document library, for example, SharePoint Team Services records who did it. For this reason, using a SharePoint team Web site generally requires that:

● You have a logon account on the server that hosts the SharePoint team Web site.

● The Administrator of the SharePoint team Web site has authorized you to use it.

If both of these conditions are true, you're a *member* of the SharePoint team Web site.

SharePoint team Web site members can view uploaded documents in their browsers and annotate them with comments. When the creator of a document opens the SharePoint team Web site copy, all comments from all reviewers will be properly interspersed.

SharePoint team Web site members can subscribe to receive, via e-mail, notifications when certain events take place. For example, they can request e-mail notification whenever someone updates a certain list, whenever someone adds a certain type of document, whenever someone annotates a given document, and so forth.

Chapter 5

147

A SharePoint team Web site can reside within a FrontPage-based Web that's also used for designing Web pages, but there are no links between the two activities. For example, you can't use a SharePoint team Web site to review and annotate Web pages stored in the normal part of a Web. Nor can you subscribe to changes that occur to the normal parts of a Web. FrontPage can add SharePoint team Web site lists to a Web and subsequently modify them, but it doesn't integrate SharePoint team Web site functions with FrontPage functions. For this reason, it's best to think of SharePoint team Web sites and server-based Webs as two products that are installed together, valuable in their own right, but not especially integrated.

In Summary...

This chapter introduced the operating concepts of FrontPage-based Webs and explained how they can be valuable to you, the Web designer. Hopefully, it convinced you that the first step in creating any group of Web pages is to create a FrontPage-based Web.

The next chapter explains in some detail the procedures for creating, configuring, and deleting FrontPage-based Webs.

Creating and Using FrontPage-Based Webs

Describing FrontPage-based Webs and justifying their existence may be very interesting—or perhaps not—but the essence of understanding Microsoft FrontPage 2002 is knowing how to create them and start using them. The use of FrontPage-based Webs permeates almost everything described in this book. This chapter therefore explains in some detail how to create FrontPage-based Webs.

When creating a new Web site, you should think in terms of first creating a FrontPage-based Web and then filling it with Web pages, pictures, and all the other files that constitute a working site. If you'd rather read about creating individual Web pages, jump ahead to Part 4, "Editing Basic Page Content."

Creating a FrontPage-Based Web for New Content

When you're ready to create a new Web site, you should first create a new Web. FrontPage can create new Webs on your computer's hard disk or on a Web server, with or without sample content. This section explains the necessary procedures.

This section doesn't explain how to create a new Web for content that already exists. For those procedures, refer to the section titled "Creating a FrontPage-Based Web for Existing Content" later in this chapter.

149

Here's how to create a FrontPage-based Web populated with no content at all, with just a home page, or with sample content designed for common situations:

newfeature!

1 Choose New from the File menu, and then choose Page Or Web. This will display the New Page Or Web task pane shown in Figure 6-1.

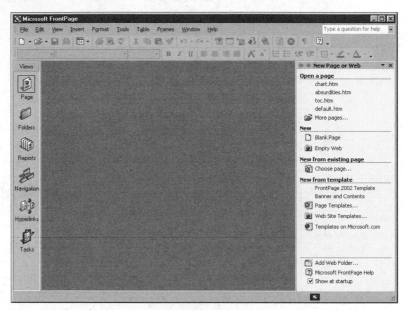

Figure 6-1. The New Page Or Web task pane provides quick access to features that create new pages or Webs.

2 If you want to create a new Web that takes all defaults, click the Empty Web option on the New Page Or Web task pane, double-click the Empty Web icon in the Web Site Templates dialog box, and then skip the rest of this procedure. The new Web has these features:

■ FrontPage supplies no initial content.

■ FrontPage chooses a location for the new Web based on the folder or server location of the last Web you created. If you've never created a Web before, FrontPage normally creates one at *My Documents \My Webs\myweb* or at *http://127.0.0.1/myweb*. FrontPage uses the HTTP location, known as a *loopback address*, only if the computer is running a Web server with the FrontPage Server Extensions installed.

> The loopback address, 127.0.0.1, is a special IP address that always means *this computer*. For more information about the loopback address, refer to the sidebar titled "Talking to Yourself—The Loopback Address" on page 1028.

■ When creating the second or any subsequent Web on a given machine, FrontPage gives the new Web the same name as the previous new Web plus 1. If the last new Web contained any digits at the right end of its name, FrontPage adds 1 to those digits. If the last new Web didn't end in a digit, FrontPage appends the digit 1.

tip To skip steps 1 and 2 and arrive directly at step 3, open the New Page button's drop-down menu on the Standard toolbar and choose Web.

3 If you want to gain more control over the new Web you're creating, click the Web Site Templates option in the New Page Or Web task pane. This displays the Web Site Templates dialog box shown in Figure 6-2.

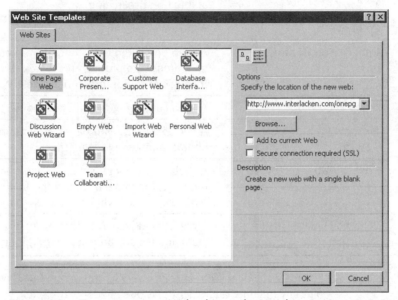

Figure 6-2. To create a new Web, choose the initial content you want, specify an HTTP or disk location, and then click OK.

4 Select the type of initial content you want in your Web. The large area at the left of Figure 6-2 lists the available types. As you select each choice on the left, FrontPage provides relevant information under the Description heading on the right. Table 6-1 on the next page summarizes these choices.

5 Under the Options heading, in the box titled Specify The Location Of The New Web, indicate where you want the new Web to reside. Two types of locations are valid:

- To create the new Web on a local disk or file server, enter a drive letter and folder name. If any of the folders you specify don't exist, FrontPage will create them. For example:

    C:\My Webs\creating\new\web

    This works even if the *creating*, *new*, and *web* folders don't exist.

151

Table 6-1. New FrontPage-Based Web Templates and Wizards

Template or wizard	Description
Corporate Presence Wizard	A comprehensive Internet presence for your organization.
Customer Support Web	A Web for providing customer support services.
Database Interface Wizard	A set of Web pages that displays, adds, modifies, and deletes information in a database.
Discussion Web Wizard	A discussion group with threads, a table of contents, and full-text searching.
Empty Web	A Web with nothing in it.
Import Web Wizard	A Web populated with content from an existing location. FrontPage prompts for the existing location, then copies its content into the new Web.
One Page Web	A Web containing only a blank home page.
Personal Web	A personal Web, with pages for your interests, photos, and favorite Web sites.
Project Web	A Web for a project team; it includes Web pages for the project members, status reports, the project schedule, an archive area, and ongoing discussions.
SharePoint-based Team Web Site	A database-driven Web that maintains lists and document libraries for project or workgroup members.

■ To create the new Web on a Web server, enter an existing Web's URL, plus any intermediate folders, plus one new or existing folder. For example:

http://www.interlacken.com/creating/new/web

This works only if the *creating* folder and the *new* folder already exist.

Naming FrontPage-Based Webs

You can name a FrontPage-based Web anything that's valid as a folder name on your disk or Web server, but the following restrictions will minimize later problems:

● Use only lowercase letters or numbers.

● Don't use any spaces or special characters.

● Create a name that's meaningful, but no longer than 8 or 10 characters.

You should choose a Web name, folder names, and file names for your Web that are valid on any server that will host it. This is one reason to avoid special characters, spaces, and uppercase letters when choosing these names.

6 Select the Add To Current Web check box if you don't want to create a new Web, but you want the new content added to the current Web. This option is dimmed unless a Web was open when you started this procedure.

7 Select the Secure Connection Required (SSL) check box if you specified a Web server location in step 5, and the server you specified requires Secure Sockets Layer (SSL) communication for authoring. This option is dimmed unless you specified an HTTP location in step 5.

FrontPage begins building your Web. If it's a server-based Web, FrontPage might prompt you for the parent Web's administrator name and password, as shown in Figure 6-3.

Figure 6-3. Enter the parent Web's administrator name and password here.

> **tip** FrontPage doesn't prompt for parent Web account information under three circumstances: first, if you're creating a disk-based Web; second, if your Web server has no security in effect; and third, if your computer automatically supplies a password from a previously successful network or HTTP logon.

If you chose a wizard in step 4, FrontPage now prompts you for additional input. Figure 6-4 on the next page, for example, shows one screen from the Corporate Presence Web Wizard. Answer the questions to the best of your ability, but don't agonize; you can always delete the new Web and start over. In fact, you *should* expect to delete the new Web and start over several times until you get the results you want.

> **note** The Corporate Presence Web Wizard produces a Web that uses more FrontPage features than any other new Web template or wizard.

When FrontPage finishes building the new Web, it displays it as shown in Figure 6-5 on the next page.

> **note** When creating a new Web on a given server, FrontPage uses that server's default-page name as the file name of the new Web's home page.

Chapter 6

153

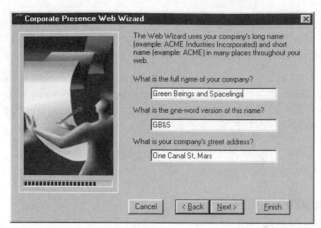

Figure 6-4. This is a prompt from the Corporate Presence Web Wizard. Your answers determine the initial content of the new Web.

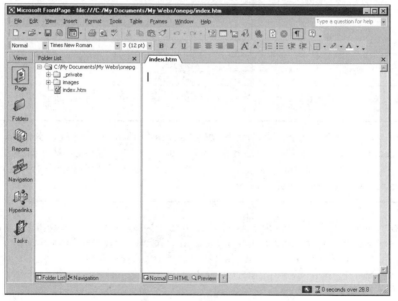

Figure 6-5. FrontPage Explorer displays a new FrontPage-based Web like this. The drive letter and folder-path location mark this as a disk-based Web. The One Page Web template produced these results.

Creating a Project Web, for example, produces the 23 generic Web pages shown in Figure 6-6. This is a server-based Web named *http://www.interlacken.com/fp-iso/ProjWeb.* Figure 6-7 shows an unmodified page from this Web: the Discussions page.

The difference between wizards and templates lies in their degree of automation. A template is relatively static and preformatted; a wizard prompts you for local information and then custom-builds your site accordingly. The Corporate Presence Web Wizard, for example, displays 15 pages of prompts for information such as company name, company address, color scheme, and background, which affect the resulting site. It also presents lists of pages you can choose to generate or not. Although detailed discussion of these wizard prompts is beyond the scope of this book, the prompts are fairly self-explanatory, and there's on-screen Help for each one.

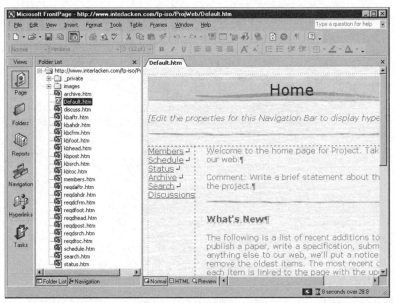

Figure 6-6. All the pages in this Web resulted from choosing the Project Web template.

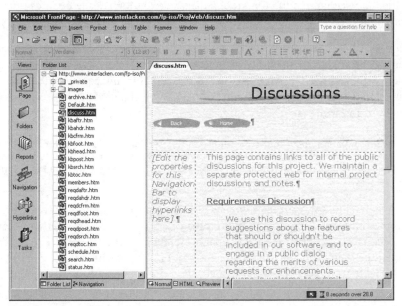

Figure 6-7. This is a typical Discussions page in a new FrontPage-based project Web.

Figure 6-8 shows that the Corporate Presence Web Wizard has created Site Parameters for changeable information and Tasks view items to remind you to finish the Web's pages.

> For more information about Tasks view, refer to "Working with Tasks View" on page 964.

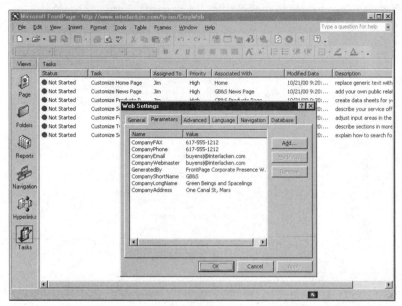

Figure 6-8. Creating a Corporate Presence Web initializes the FrontPage Tasks list (shown in the background) with a list of themes you need to complete manually. Changing the Value column in the foreground dialog box automatically updates references throughout the Corporate Presence Web.

Figure 6-9 shows FrontPage displaying the Corporate Presence home page that the wizard generated; note the boilerplate text suggesting information you should enter under each heading. This Web's appearance resulted from specifying the Value Added theme while running the wizard, but themes can be changed at will from the Themes dialog box in FrontPage.

> For more information about topics mentioned in this section, refer to Chapter 19, "Using FrontPage Themes"; "Using Link Bars with Navigation View" on page 201; "Using Web Parameters and the Substitution Component" on page 762; "Using the Include Page Component" on page 750.

Figure 6-10 shows the Navigation view of the Corporate Presence Web. The wizard prompted the Web's creator for the number of press releases, products, and services. The Feedback, Contents, and Search pages aren't actually part of the hierarchy; they're peers at the Web's top level and, by virtue of a Link bar included in a shared border, are available from every page in the Web.

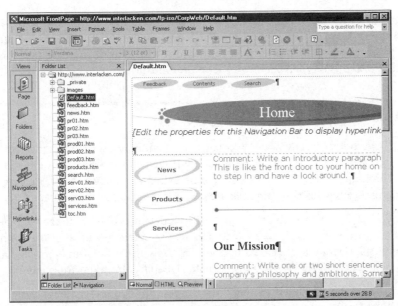

Figure 6-9. FrontPage is ready to modify the default Corporate Presence home page. Boilerplate text suggests typical content.

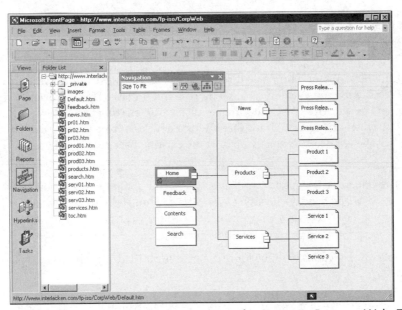

Figure 6-10. This is the Navigation view of a Corporate Presence Web. The first button on the Navigation toolbar toggles the diagram between portrait and landscape.

For more information about Navigation view, refer to Chapter 7, "Managing Web Structure with Navigation View."

FrontPage's wizards for creating a new Web can produce so many unique variations that describing them all is impossible. The best advice is simply to try them and judge the results for yourself. Create, decide, delete, and re-create until you have the starting point you want, and then begin your own modifications.

FrontPage and the File System

Within the root Web, FrontPage maintains information not only about the root Web itself, but also about each subweb. In addition, each subweb maintains indexes and other information about itself. You should be extremely cautious about moving, renaming, or otherwise updating file areas under the control of FrontPage.

After you've created a Web using FrontPage, you should use FrontPage for making changes whenever possible. If you add, change, or delete any content files without going through FrontPage, be sure to open the Web afterward with FrontPage and verify your changes by choosing Recalculate Hyperlinks from the Tools menu.

Never use Windows Explorer or any other program to update FrontPage system files or folders. This might create situations that are very difficult to recover from.

Creating a FrontPage-Based Web for Existing Content

Creating new Webs in FrontPage is relatively straightforward, but converting an existing Web site to FrontPage is perhaps a more common task. This is especially true for designers new to FrontPage, who frequently have an existing body of work. FrontPage 2002 provides an Import Wizard that builds a new Web from existing content. Its ease of use, however, depends greatly on how the existing pages are organized.

caution The Import command on FrontPage's File menu doesn't create a new Web; its purpose is to add files to an existing Web. To use FrontPage to create a new Web from an existing Web, follow the instructions on the next several pages.

The following sections describe four scenarios for initializing a new Web with existing content:

- Initializing a new Web with files from a file system folder
- Initializing a disk-based Web that's already in place
- Initializing a new Web with files from a Web server
- Converting a folder to a Web

Chapter 6

Initializing a New Web from a File System Folder

Having FrontPage create a blank or standardized Web provides a good start for new projects, but converting existing Web sites to FrontPage is equally important, especially for new users and clients. FrontPage therefore provides an Import Web Wizard that creates new Webs from existing file system folders and existing sites.

> To learn about adding individual files to a Web, refer to "Importing Web Pages" later in this chapter.

To initialize a new Web with existing content from disk:

New Page

1 Display the Web Site Templates dialog box. To do this in the most direct way, drop down the menu associated with the New Page button on the Standard toolbar, and then choose Web.

2 Select the Import Web Wizard icon.

3 Specify a folder location in the box titled Specify The Location Of The New Web (under Options). As in the previous section, this location should be either a drive letter-and-folder combination for locations on your hard disk, or an *http* URL for locations within an existing server-based Web.

4 Click OK. If you specified a location within an existing server-based Web, FrontPage might prompt you for that Web's administrator name and password.

FrontPage displays the Import Web Wizard's Choose Source dialog box shown in Figure 6-11, asking you for the location of your existing Web files.

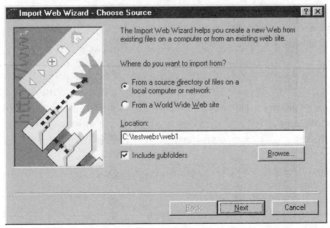

Figure 6-11. FrontPage can populate a new Web with files from a local disk or from a remote Web site.

159

5 Because this procedure assumes that you're importing files from a local computer or network, choose the first option (From A Source Directory Of Files On A Local Computer Or Network), and then do the following:

a Specify the file location by typing it in the Location text box or by using the Browse button.

b To import files in the specified source folder only, leave the Include Subfolders check box blank. To import all folders contained within the source folder, select the check box.

6 The wizard next displays the Import Web Wizard's Edit File List dialog box, shown in Figure 6-12. Here you can exclude any files from the existing Web that aren't necessary for the new Web. After making your selections, click Next. Click Finish in the final dialog box.

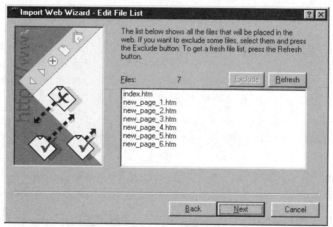

Figure 6-12. You can choose which files are imported into your new FrontPage-based Web.

When the import process is complete, you'll have a new FrontPage-based Web that contains all your former pages. You might also have a mess. Unless you've been extraordinarily meticulous in the past, you'll probably discover many cases of inconsistent file names, missing page titles, and files not residing in the most logical location. Fortunately, FrontPage makes it easy to reorganize files without breaking hyperlinks among pages.

> For more information about repairing a poorly organized Web, refer to "Planning and Managing Folders" later in this chapter.

> **note** All Web servers running the FrontPage Server Extensions contain at least one FrontPage-based Web: the *root Web*. The root Web's URL is *http://<servername>/*. You can create additional Webs—called *subwebs*—directly within the root Web or within another subweb.

Initializing a Disk-Based Web in Place

If you already have a set of Web files in a folder tree on your computer, FrontPage can directly convert it to a disk-based Web. Here's all you need to do:

1 Choose Open Web from the File menu.

2 Use the Look In drop-down list or any of the My Places bar icons to locate the folder that contains your existing files, and click Open.

3 FrontPage displays the Add FrontPage Information To The Folder dialog box shown in Figure 6-13. The information referred to in this dialog box is the information, other than content files, that makes up a FrontPage-based Web. In terms used by some documentation, this dialog box is offering to *Webify* the chosen folder.

Figure 6-13. To convert an existing disk folder to a disk-based Web, simply tell FrontPage to open it as a Web and then reply Yes to this prompt.

4 To convert the folder to a disk-based FrontPage-based Web, click Yes.

Converting a folder to a Web doesn't remove or modify any existing files. It does, however, add a great many files. If you change your mind about making this folder a disk-based Web, removing all these files can be a nuisance. If you think you might change your mind, make sure you have a good backup of the folder in question or do your work on a copy.

Initializing a New Web from Files on a Web Server

caution If the content for your new FrontPage-based Web already resides in the desired server's root Web, skip to the next section in this chapter.

The best way to copy a Web from one location to another is by using the Publish Web command. This requires that both the existing and new locations be FrontPage-based Webs. If they are, proceed as follows:

1 Open the existing FrontPage-based Web in FrontPage, and choose Publish Web from the File menu.

2 Specify the location of the destination Web and click OK. If this location doesn't exist, FrontPage will create it if possible, applying the normal rules for new Webs.

> **For more information about Web publishing, refer to Chapter 13, "Publishing Your FrontPage-Based Web."**

If the source location is a Web server that doesn't have the FrontPage Server Extensions installed, proceed as follows:

1 Start the Import Web Wizard using steps 1 through 4 in the "Initializing a New Web from a File System Folder" section.

> **caution**   When importing from a Web location that doesn't have the FrontPage Server Extensions installed, FrontPage determines what pages to retrieve based on an analysis of hyperlinks. This means it won't download orphan pages—pages never referenced in the site's HTML.

2 When FrontPage displays the Import Web Wizard's Choose Source dialog box shown in Figure 6-11, choose From A World Wide Web Site. The dialog box changes to the format shown in Figure 6-14.

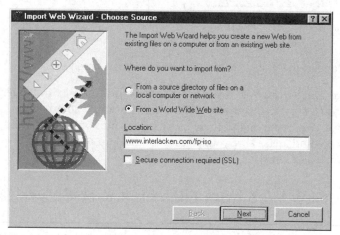

Figure 6-14.   FrontPage presents this dialog box for populating a new Web with files from a remote Web site.

3 In the Location text box, specify the URL of the site's home page.

4 Select the Secure Connection Required (SSL) check box if the source Web server requires a secure connection.

5 Click Next to display the Import Web Wizard's Choose Download Amount dialog box shown in Figure 6-15. This dialog box optionally limits the amount of material FrontPage adds to the new Web.

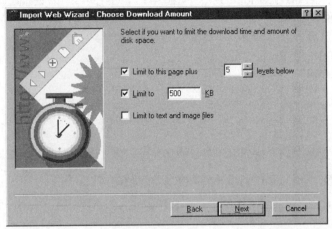

Figure 6-15. FrontPage provides three ways to avoid excessive downloading when importing an existing Web site.

6 To limit the depth of retrieval, select the Limit To This Page Plus check box, and specify the maximum number of levels between an imported page and the home page. Specifying 1, for example, means FrontPage will import the home page and any files referenced on it. Specifying 2 means FrontPage will import the home page and any files referenced on it, plus any files referenced on those pages.

note When determining which Web files to download, FrontPage ignores hyperlinks and other references external to the requested site. That is, FrontPage imports files only from the requested site, and not from other sites it may refer to.

7 To limit the number of kilobytes downloaded, select the Limit To check box, and specify the maximum number of kilobytes.

8 To download text and picture files only, select the Limit To Text And Image Files check box. This imports Web pages and pictures, but skips content such as ZIP files and executables.

caution Honor copyright restrictions whenever you import pages or pictures from the World Wide Web.

9 Click Next, and then click Finish in the final dialog box.

Converting a Folder to a Web

As Webs grow in size and complexity, it often becomes apparent that what started as an ordinary folder deserves to become a Web in its own right. This breaks your content into more manageable units, both in terms of data volume and administrative responsibility, and it sets limits on FrontPage functions that process an entire Web.

Here's the procedure for converting a folder in an existing Web to a FrontPage-based Web of its own:

1 Open the existing Web in FrontPage, and right-click the existing folder.

2 Choose Convert To Web from the shortcut menu.

3 When the confirmation prompt shown in Figure 6-16 appears, click Yes.

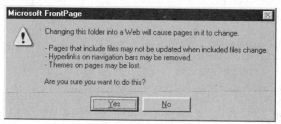

Figure 6-16.   This prompt warns you that making a new Web out of a folder in an existing Web severs ties between the converted folder and the existing Web.

Recall that no file or folder can belong to two Webs, even if one Web physically resides within another. This explains the confirmation prompt in Figure 6-16. Suppose, for example, that the Web page *default.htm* has a hyperlink to the page *birds/ducks.htm*:

- If these pages are in the same Web, renaming *birds/ducks.htm* to *birds /geese.htm* would update the hyperlink in *default.htm*.

- If you converted the *birds* folder to a subweb and *then* renamed *ducks.htm* to *geese.htm*, FrontPage *wouldn't* update the hyperlink in *default.htm*, because the two files would then be in different Webs.

The second part of the prompt reminds you that for each file included in the new Web, any references from the old Web will become *external* (that is, those references will now point to locations outside the old Web).

Converting a folder to a Web can be a relatively major change. Planning is the key. Here are some things to consider:

- Organize your content *before* creating the new Web, while FrontPage can still fix hyperlinks as you move things around. Make sure your content is clearly and logically divided between the old and new areas.

- Don't forget to organize pictures and other files as well as Web pages. Create a folder named *images* inside the folder you plan to convert, and then move or copy any required pictures into that *images* folder. Again, do this while FrontPage can still fix hyperlinks for you.

If the existing Web is server-based and uses SharePoint Team Services or the FrontPage Server Extensions 2002, you can also convert folders to subwebs using the administration Web pages.

For more information about converting folders to subwebs by means of the administration Web pages, refer to "Creating a Subweb" on page 1112.

Converting a Web to a Folder

Just as you can convert folders into Webs, you can also convert Webs back into ordinary folders. There is, however, one significant catch: Any Web you convert into a folder must already reside within another Web (that is, you can convert a subweb into a folder, but you can't convert a root Web into something dangling in space). Here's the procedure:

1 Open the Web that contains the subweb you want to convert.

2 Locate the subweb in the Folder List, right-click the subweb's folder icon, and then choose Convert To Folder from the shortcut menu.

3 When the confirmation prompt in Figure 6-17 appears, click Yes to proceed.

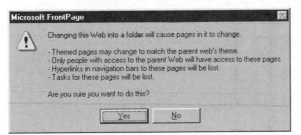

Figure 6-17. This prompt warns that converting a FrontPage-based Web to an ordinary folder discards any information unique to that Web.

The warning reminds you that when the subweb loses its identity, it also loses its unique security, its Navigation view data, and its Tasks list. Furthermore, if you've applied a theme to the entire parent Web, that theme may now apply to pages in the converted Web as well.

165

Importing Web Pages

Adding existing Web pages, pictures, and other files to a FrontPage-based Web is a common requirement. FrontPage calls this process *importing* and can perform it at the file or folder level. There are two methods: the menu method and the dragging method.

> **note** FrontPage can import pages accessible on a local disk or through Windows file sharing, but it can't import individual pages accessible only via HTTP. To import pages from an intranet or the World Wide Web, open them in Page view, and then save them to the current Web.

Importing files with menus is a two-step process. First you must build a list of files to import, and then you must actually import them. To build the list:

1 Open the receiving Web in FrontPage.

2 Select the Web folder you expect to receive the most files.

3 Choose Import from the File menu. This displays the Import dialog box shown in Figure 6-18.

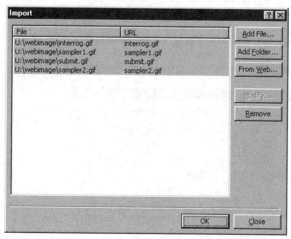

Figure 6-18. Use this dialog box to build a list of items to import.

4 Depending on what you want to import, choose any of these:

■ To add individual files, click the Add File button. When the Add File To Import List dialog box appears, find the files you want to import, and then click Open. FrontPage will add the selected files to the import list shown in Figure 6-18.

■ To add all the files in a given folder (and all its subfolders), click the Add Folder button. When the File Open dialog box opens, locate the desired folder, and click Open. FrontPage will add all the files in the selected folder, including subfolders, to the import list.

■ To add the files from an intranet or World Wide Web site, click the From Web button. The Import Web Wizard appears and prompts you for all of the import options.

5 Normally, FrontPage imports all files to the current folder in FrontPage. To change the destination of an individual file, select the file, and click Modify. (You won't have this option if you're importing a Web.) When the Edit URL dialog box shown in Figure 6-19 appears, change the displayed destination, and click OK.

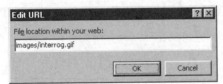

Figure 6-19. Use the Edit URL dialog box to change the planned destination of an imported Web file.

6 To remove a file you've placed on the import list, select it and click Remove.

caution Imported pages frequently contain incorrect or nonstandard HTML, especially if they were previously maintained by hand. FrontPage might interpret these questionable elements differently than a browser would. Keep the original files until you view the imported versions in FrontPage, save them, and review the results with your browser. If they need more than a minor cleanup, you might want to correct the originals and reimport them.

When you're ready to import the files in the list, click OK. To abandon or postpone importing, click Close. FrontPage will remember the import list for this session. To import the list later in the same session, choose Import from the File menu.

To import Web files by dragging:

1 Open the receiving Web with FrontPage.

2 Use Windows Explorer to locate the files or folders you want to import.

3 Drag the files or folders from Windows Explorer to the desired destination in FrontPage.

To copy content between two Webs, open both Webs in FrontPage, and then drag the desired content between the two FrontPage windows.

Of course, you can also move content into, out of, and among FrontPage-based Webs using the Web Folders feature that comes with Office XP. The default drag operation is Copy, as long as the source and target locations are on different drives, on different servers, or on one drive and one server. If both locations are on the same drive or server, the default operation is Move. You can reverse these defaults by holding down the Ctrl key while dragging, but it's often less confusing to drag with the right mouse button instead.

> **tip** After you drag something with the right mouse button, Windows displays a shortcut menu asking whether to copy, move, create a shortcut, or cancel.

Importing vs. Copying—What's the Difference?

If your Web resides on a local disk or file server, copying files into the Web file area with Windows Explorer or the command prompt might seem quicker and easier than importing them with FrontPage. The difference is this: When FrontPage imports a Web file, it copies the file into place and also updates all the necessary FrontPage indexes and cross-reference files. Externally copying the files into place doesn't perform the FrontPage updates. To restore a FrontPage-based Web to consistency after an external process has changed it:

1 Open the Web with FrontPage.

2 Choose Recalculate Hyperlinks from the Tools menu.

Planning and Managing Folders

Other than the hidden folders used by FrontPage, there are no requirements and no limits on the number of folders your Web can use. Most sites use folders to segregate and categorize their content, but the extent of such use is a matter of judgment and preference.

When a FrontPage wizard or template creates a site, it normally places all HTML files in the root folder of the current Web and all pictures in an */images* folder. There are several good reasons for having an */images* folder:

- At most sites, HTML files require more structure and management than picture files. Keeping all the pictures in one folder reduces clutter and makes it easier to manage folders of Web pages.

- Many pictures are stock items used on several pages. Keeping all pictures in one folder makes it easy to locate and use stock pictures when creating new Web pages.

● Most browsers cache Web files to eliminate unnecessary downloads. If you store the same picture in two different folders, however, the browser has no way of knowing the two pictures are identical, and it downloads them both. Keeping all pictures in one folder eliminates duplicate downloads.

It's often a good idea to put all pages for a given topic in one folder, and to name the topic's home page with the server's default page name. Subtopics can then be nested in subordinate folders to form a topical tree. This keeps individual folders small enough to be reviewed at a glance and also provides a navigational aid for Web visitors. When Web visitors see a URL such as

http://www.interlacken.com/fruit/citrus/lemons.htm

they expect that shortening it to

http://www.interlacken.com/fruit/citrus/

will bring up a Citrus Fruit home page, and that shortening this further to

http://www.interlacken.com/fruit/

will produce a Fruit home page.

This isn't to say that every page—or even every menu page—should reside in its own folder. This is poor practice. It's also poor practice, however, to locate all pages in a large site in a single folder. The organization you choose depends on the structure of your content, but there should be organization of some kind.

Folder names are again a matter of preference, but long dual-case names containing special characters usually create more problems than clarity for the following reasons:

● Users do sometimes type URLs by hand—perhaps copying them out of magazines—and long names are simply hard to type. Folder names are limited to 32 characters on UNIX Web servers, and to 8 on Windows 3.1 systems.

● Dual-case names create confusion because some systems (particularly UNIX) are case-sensitive and others (such as Windows) are not. To UNIX, */Potions* and */potions* are two completely different folders—as different as */potions* and */notions*. To a Windows Web server, however, */Potions* and */potions* mean the same thing. Always using lowercase avoids such confusion.

● Many special characters, even though acceptable as folder names, require special encoding when used in URLs. The coding consists of a percent sign followed by the hexadecimal value of the character's ASCII code. If you create a folder name containing a space, for example, you'll have to represent the space as *%20* in all URLs—ungainly and hard to fathom.

Working with FrontPage Views

Keeping all but the smallest Web-page collections organized would be difficult without a graphical organizer like FrontPage. To suit various needs, FrontPage provides six distinct views of a Web. To select a particular view, click its icon on the Views bar, or choose the desired view from the View menu.

- **Page view.** This multipurpose view actually provides three views of a Web page: an editable, WYSIWYG view, an editable view of the HTML source code, and preview of the finished page, displayed by Internet Explorer

  If a Web is open (as opposed to one or more single Web pages being open), Page view also displays a list of the folders and files in the current Web. This permits editing, creating, deleting, moving, and renaming files just as in Windows Explorer, even if the Web is located on another computer.

- **Folders view.** In this view, you can see a more complete list of a Web's files and folders than Page view's simple Folder List.

- **Reports view.** This view displays 15 reports to help you manage your site.

- **Navigation view.** In this view, you can create and display the hierarchy of the pages in your site. You create the hierarchy by dragging rectangles representing Web pages into a diagram that resembles an organization chart. Adding a Link Bars component to any Web page then creates a menu corresponding to your hierarchy.

- **Hyperlinks view.** This view is, in some ways, the reverse of Navigation view. With Navigation view, you create the structure, and the Link Bars component creates the hyperlinks. With Hyperlinks view, FrontPage analyzes your existing hyperlinks and graphically displays links to and from any page.

- **Tasks view.** This view displays a list of tasks that have been created for the current Web. In essence, it's an electronic, multi-user to-do list.

Regardless of which view is in effect, though, FrontPage's menu bar and toolbar provide rich options to:

- Create, globally modify, or delete Web sites.

- Import pages from existing sites not controlled by FrontPage.

- Check spelling and search text throughout a site.

- Copy sites from one server to another.

- Control security.

For more information about Page view, refer to "Working with Page View" on page 171. For more information about Folders view, refer to "Working with Folders View" on page 174. For more information about Reports view, refer to "Working with Reports View" on page 424. For more information about Navigation view and Link Bars components, refer to Chapter 7, "Managing Web Structure with Navigation View." For more information about Hyperlinks view, refer to "Using Hyperlinks View" on page 454. For more information about Tasks view, refer to "Working with Tasks View" on page 964. In Page, Folders, Navigation, and Hyperlinks views, you can also use the Folder List to manipulate files. For more information about using the Folder List, refer to "Working with Web Folder Lists" on page 70.

Working with Page View

In all probability, the main reason you bought FrontPage was to create Web pages visually (that is, by working through a WYSIWYG view instead of HTML code). It's therefore only logical that Page view be the first and default view FrontPage provides. Page view, shown in Figure 6-20, presents FrontPage's WYSIWYG editor.

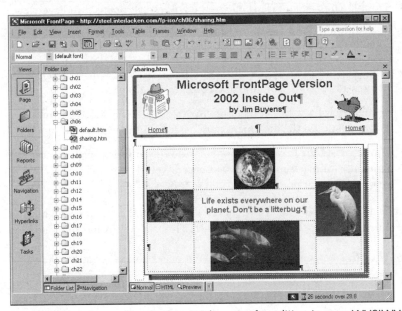

Figure 6-20. Page view displays Web pages for editing in near-WYSIWYG mode. The Folder List on the left shows the contents of the current Web.

Ignoring the usual title bar, menu bar, and toolbars at the top of the window—and the status bar at the bottom—the Page view window consists of four panes:

● The Views bar at the far left provides access to all the views in FrontPage 2002, including, of course, Page view itself.

- The Folder List, second from the left, is active only if you've opened a FrontPage-based Web. In that case, it shows the files and folders in that Web. All the usual Windows Explorer functions work here, even if the Web resides on a Web server on another computer. Double-clicking a file opens it with the default editor—FrontPage's WYSIWYG editor in the case of HTML files.

- The editing pane, which is usually the largest area in Page view, is where you edit your Web pages. Here you can enter text, import pictures, paste content from the Clipboard, and apply a rich variety of formatting options.

newfeature!

- The task pane displays four categories of shortcuts: New Page Or Web, Clipboard, Basic Search, and Insert Clip Art.

The following operations are available whenever a FrontPage-based Web is open:

- Double-clicking an HTML file in the Folder List opens it in Page view.

- Dragging a picture or other displayable file from the Folder List onto an open Web page displays the picture or file.

- Dragging any other type of file from the Folder List onto an open Web page creates a hyperlink from the open page to the dragged file.

- If Page view has no document open, dragging an HTML file from the Folder List onto the document pane's background opens that file.

- A number of FrontPage components and development features are available only for pages in a FrontPage-based Web. The remaining chapters in this book are largely devoted to these topics.

To open a Web page in Page view, choose Open from the File menu. This displays the Open File dialog box shown in Figure 6-21. This dialog box has the following features:

- The History icon displays a list of Web pages you've recently opened.

- The My Documents icon displays the contents of the same *My Documents* folder that Office XP and other applications use. (On Windows NT 4.0, a Personal icon replaces the My Documents icon.)

- The Desktop icon displays a list of items on your Windows desktop: My Computer, My Documents, Network Neighborhood, My Briefcase, and so forth.

- The Favorites icon displays the same list of Web pages as the Favorites menu in Internet Explorer.

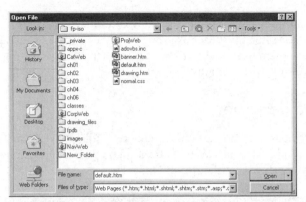

Figure 6-21. FrontPage uses the standard Office XP dialog box for opening files and Webs in Page view. It can open not only files from your local disk or file server but also, acting like a browser, files from the Web.

● The Web Folders icon displays a list of the Web locations you've used in the past. (On Windows 2000, the My Network Places icon replaces the Web Folders icon.)

To open a folder displayed by any of these icons, double-click the folder. Keep clicking through as many folders as needed to locate your file, and then double-click the file to open it.

You can also open any file or folder by typing its name in the File Name box and clicking Open. You can type either file locations, such as *C:\My Documents\Web Docs \mypage.htm,* or URLs, such as *http://www.interlacken.com.* When you enter a URL, FrontPage reads the HTML file, its pictures, and any other components from the Web, as though FrontPage were a browser.

If you open a file that's contained within a FrontPage-based Web, FrontPage opens both the Web and the file. To open a Web without opening any particular file, choose Open Web from the File menu.

If you open more than one file in the same Web, only one file at a time will be visible in Page view. To switch between open files click the file tabs at the top of the editing pane, press Ctrl+Tab, or select a file name from the Window menu.

It's also possible to open two files from the same Web in different windows. Here's the procedure:

1 Open the first file.

2 Choose New Window from the Window menu.

3 Open the second file in the new window.

You can repeat this procedure to create as many windows as you like. If you open more than one Web at the same time, each Web appears in a separate FrontPage window. You can switch among them in typical Windows fashion (that is, by clicking buttons on the Windows taskbar or by pressing Alt+Tab).

Working with Folders View

Folders view provides a representation, strongly resembling Windows Explorer, that displays the files and folders in a Web. It also displays properties such as file date and file size. Figure 6-22 shows an example of Folders view.

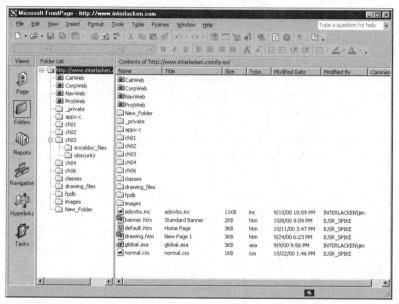

Figure 6-22. FrontPage's Folders view gives a graphical view of the files and folders that make up a FrontPage-based Web site.

This view provides a way to view or manage the physical arrangement of files and folders that make up your Web. It supports all the cut, copy, paste, and drag features described in the previous section for the Folder List. The difference is in the display: Folders view presents a tabular view of one folder at a time.

To display the contents of a specific folder, either select it in the Folder List or double-click it in the document window.

> **For more information about using the Folder List, refer to "Working with Web Folder Lists" on page 70.**

To sort the Folders view listing on any column, click its column heading. Repeatedly clicking the same column heading switches between ascending and descending sequence.

Folders view works very much like Explorer in Windows 95, Windows 98, Windows NT, and Windows 2000. Note the extra column for Title, however. As in Windows Explorer, double-clicking folders navigates through them. Double-clicking Web pages opens them in Page view, and double-clicking a picture file opens your default picture editor.

> **tip** You can maintain the list of available editors by choosing Options from the Tools menu and clicking the Configure Editors tab.

Right-clicking a file in Folders view displays a shortcut menu that contains these commands:

- **Open.** Opens the file in Page view, PhotoDraw, or another program appropriate to the type of file.

- **Open With.** Opens the file with another editor of your choice.

- **Preview In Browser.** Starts your browser if necessary and then tells it to display the file you right-clicked.

- **Cut.** Moves the clicked file to the Clipboard and adds a Paste option for storing the file elsewhere. After pasting, the original file is deleted.

- **Copy.** Like Cut, moves the clicked file to the Clipboard and adds a Paste option. However, the original file is retained after pasting.

> **tip** When you move or rename a file by any means in FrontPage, FrontPage updates references from other files in the same Web.

- **Paste.** Creates a copy of a file previously moved to the Clipboard.

newfeature!
- **Remove Filters.** Disables any restrictions that limit which files are visible.

newfeature!
- **Set As Home Page.** Designates the current page as the home page in Navigation view. (Because the home page must reside in your Web's root folder, this command is unavailable for files in subfolders.)

- **Rename.** Selects the file name for editing.

- **Delete.** Permanently removes the file. (There is no Undelete.)

newfeature!
- **Publish Selected Files.** Displays the Publish Destination dialog box shown in Figure 6-23 on the next page. You use this dialog box to publish all currently selected files and folders to another location.

Chapter 6

175

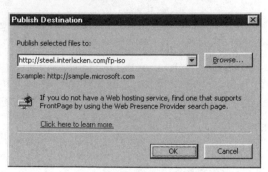

Figure 6-23. With FrontPage 2002, you can publish only the parts of a Web that you select.

newfeature!

- **Don't Publish.** Excludes the currently selected files from any future publishing operations. Use this option when you don't want files at the destination—such as data collection files—to be overlaid with files from the source.

- **Properties.** Displays a dialog box showing the object's characteristics and settings.

FrontPage's Folders view supports all the dragging operations you've grown accustomed to in Windows. The difference is that if you move or rename a file in Windows, you have to manually locate each hyperlink from other pages in your site to the moved or renamed one; and update each of these pages manually. When you move or rename a file in FrontPage, FrontPage automatically updates the other pages in your Web.

Referring again to Figure 6-22, note the Title column in the right pane. For Web pages, FrontPage obtains this title from the HTML code itself. To update the title of a Web page:

1 Open the Web page in Page view. (Double-click the file name, or right-click it and select Open.)

2 Choose Properties from the File menu, and update the Title field on the General tab.

3 Click OK, and save the file.

To update the title of any file, html or not:

1 Right-click the file name in the Folder List or Folders view, and choose Properties from the shortcut menu.

2 Update the Title field on the General tab, and click OK.

Figure 6-24 illustrates this updating process.

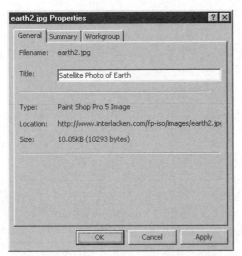

Figure 6-24. Use the Properties command to update the title of any file in your Web.

To change the comments for any type of file, right-click the file; choose Properties from the shortcut menu; and then click the Summary tab, shown in Figure 6-25. Finish by entering or updating the comments and clicking OK.

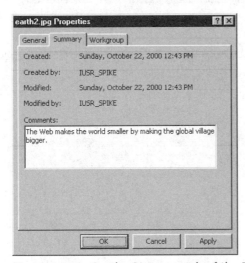

Figure 6-25. On the Summary tab of the Properties dialog box, you can modify the Comments field for a FrontPage-based Web file.

Deleting a FrontPage-Based Web

To delete a FrontPage-based Web:

1 Open the parent Web (that is, the Web that contains the Web you want to delete).

2 In the Folder List, select the Web you want to delete.

3 Choose Delete from the Edit menu (or right-click the Web you've selected and choose Delete from the shortcut menu).

4 Click Yes in the resulting Confirm Delete dialog box.

> **caution**   Deleting a FrontPage-based Web deletes absolutely everything it contains—Web pages, pictures, text files, FrontPage system files, and all folders. If you want to save the Web pages, pictures, and other content, back them up before deleting the Web.

In Summary...

This chapter explained how to create FrontPage-based Webs under various circumstances. It also introduced two of the ways of viewing FrontPage-based Webs: Page view and Folders view.

The next chapter explains how to enter a new site's structure in Navigation view so that FrontPage can create the Web pages automatically.

Part 3

Creating Web Sites Automatically

Chapter 7

Managing Web Structure with Navigation View

After you've created an empty Web, the next step is, naturally, to fill it with pages. Just as naturally, these pages should be organized and linked together in a way that presents your message effectively and that Web visitors can readily understand.

FrontPage has a feature called *Navigation view* that records the content you have in mind and then, together with certain Web components, creates a set of Web pages complete with titles and hyperlinks. What's more, as you revamp and reorganize your content over time, FrontPage updates all the page titles and hyperlinks automatically.

Appealing as Navigation view might be, it's not the best choice for every Web. As so often occurs, the price of Navigation view's automation is a certain loss of design flexibility and control. Nevertheless, using Navigation view is an excellent approach for creating many kinds of Web sites and one you should consider for sites of medium size and complexity.

Working with Navigation View

Most Web designers organize their content hierarchically (that is, much like an organization chart). As seen in Figure 7-1 on the next page, Navigation view provides a way to organize and record this structure.

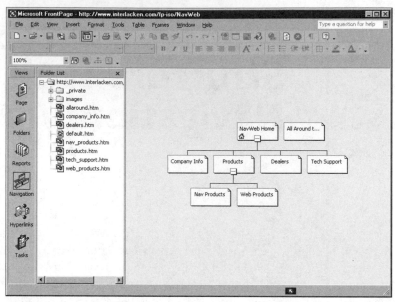

Figure 7-1. Navigation view provides a way to record and view the logical structure of a Web.

Using Navigation view has several advantages over other methods of diagramming a Web's logical structure:

- Navigation view, being electronic, is easier to revise than paper drawings.

- FrontPage automatically creates a Web page for each node you enter in the Navigation view diagram.

- If you add a Link Bar Based On Navigation Structure component to each page contained in Navigation view, FrontPage creates hyperlinks among your pages that perfectly reflect the Navigation view structure. Furthermore, if you later rearrange all or part of your Navigation view diagram, FrontPage will adjust all the Link bar hyperlinks accordingly.

For more information about Link bars, refer to "Using Link Bars with Navigation View" later in this chapter.

- If you add a Page Banner component to each page diagrammed in Navigation view, the text in every page heading and the text in every Link bar selection will agree perfectly. This is because both components incorporate the page names you assign in Navigation view.

For more information about page banners, refer to "Using Page Banners" later in this chapter.

Chapter 7: Managing Web Structure with Navigation View

● Constructing hyperlinks based on a diagram ensures that your Web's design concept, its Navigation view, and the actual hyperlinks are always in sync, and that all page titles and link titles are consistent throughout your Web.

Navigation view and the Link Bar Based On Navigation Structure component work very much hand-in-hand. After you diagram your page in Navigation view, adding a Link Bar Based On Navigation Structure component to any page creates hyperlinks that correspond to the structure you drew.

All Link bars are single FrontPage components that contain multiple links. If you choose not to configure these links yourself and instead tie them to the Navigation view structure, the result is an automatically generated, automatically maintained set of hyperlinks Web visitors can use to traverse your site. In Figure 7-2, a Link Bars component in the Products page displays hyperlinks to the Web's home page and the two children diagrammed in Figure 7-1.

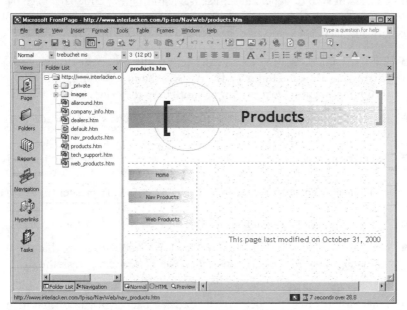

Figure 7-2. FrontPage can generate attractive Link bars like these based on the site structure you diagram in Navigation view.

Documenting the structure of your Web might at first seem like redundant work; you might think FrontPage should infer your site's structure by analyzing hyperlinks or folder structures. On reflection, however, you'll find that neither of these methods produces the same results as good human judgment. Here are the reasons:

● Hyperlink analysis fails because most Web pages contain hyperlinks that are convenient for the visitor but extraneous to the Web's primary content structure.

- Folder analysis fails because most sites become disorganized over time and because utility pages often exist separately from the Web's main structure.

- If several pages have hyperlinks to the same target page, there's no way to determine which is the target page's true parent in terms of overall structure.

For these reasons, FrontPage takes an opposite approach to eliminating double work: Rather than inducing the Web's structure from hyperlinks among its pages, FrontPage generates HTML from information you provide about your Web's structure—information you enter in Navigation view.

Deciding Whether to Use Navigation View

Many successful Web designers never use Navigation view, Link bars, page banners, or any other FrontPage features designed to organize, create, and maintain a Web automatically. Here are some guidelines to aid your decision:

- Rank beginners creating very small sites usually prefer the direct approach (that is, creating and linking a few pages by hand). Working indirectly through Navigation view might be more than they can initially absorb.

- Expert designers usually take the manual approach as well, because it give them more flexibility over the Web's design.

- Navigation view can neither organize nor create a site that uses frames.

For more information about frames, refer to Chapter 17, "Using Frames for Page Layout."

- Navigation view is probably overkill for a Web with five or fewer pages.

- Navigation view is likely to be unwieldy for a Web with more than 100 to 200 Web pages. To use Navigation view for a larger site, break the site into multiple subwebs, each having its own Navigation view diagram.

- Link bar buttons are typically rather large, especially if you format them with a graphical theme. This makes it difficult to design pages that have more than six or eight hyperlinks to child pages. If this many links seems sufficient for any page you can think of, count the number of links on the home page of any large e-commerce or Internet portal site.

Chapter 7: Managing Web Structure with Navigation View

Displaying Navigation View

Because Navigation view deals with groups of Web pages, it's applicable only to FrontPage-based Webs. A Web defines the boundaries of the Navigation view diagram and provides the file areas that store the Navigation view structure. Here's the procedure for displaying the Navigation view structure of a Web:

1 Open your Web.

2 Click the Navigation icon on the Views bar.

FrontPage 2002 can also display a condensed version of Navigation view, called the Navigation pane, while the program is actually in Page view. Here's the procedure to display the Navigation pane:

1 Switch to Page view by clicking the Page icon on the Views bar.

2 Choose Navigation Pane from the View menu; or

Click the Navigation button at the bottom of the Page view Folder List.

Figure 7-3 shows the Page view Navigation pane displaying the same Navigation structure as Figure 7-1.

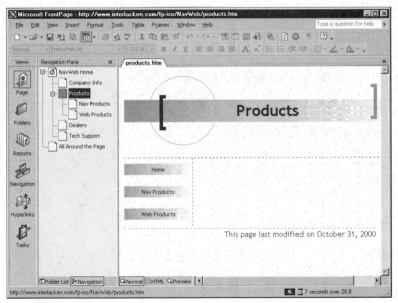

Figure 7-3. The Navigation pane displays a miniature version of Navigation view that you can look at and update while editing a page in Page view.

Chapter 7

Defining a Navigation View Home Page

A home page is the jumping off point for all the content and features your Web has to offer. The home page is the initial, default, and generally most important page in your Web. This holds equally true for your Web's logical structure and its physical implementation.

You, your Web server, and Navigation view should all agree on the identity of the home page. As to its location, the home page always resides in a Web's root folder. In a disk-based Web, the home page is always named *index.htm*. On a server-based Web, it's named in accordance with the Web server's default document name.

> **note** On Microsoft Web servers, the default document name is usually *default.htm*. On others, it's usually *index.htm*.

If your Web contains a page named in accordance with these rules, FrontPage normally makes it the home page in Navigation view as well. To verify this, display Navigation view and look for a page that appears at the top level of the hierarchy and contains a house icon like this:

If no one has ever drawn a Navigation view structure for the current Web, the home page will be the only page displayed.

If Navigation view can't identify a home page, it displays the following message:

To create a Home Page, click New Page on the toolbar.

New Page

If your Web doesn't yet contain a home page, the solution is simple: click the New Page button on the Standard toolbar. FrontPage creates a blank home page and places it at the top of your Navigation view hierarchy. Its file name is *index.htm* in a disk-based Web, or the Web server's default page name on a server-based Web.

If the Web *does* contain a home page, try the following methods, in order, of making Navigation view recognize it:

● First try using the command FrontPage provides for this purpose:

1 Locate your home page in Folder view or in any Folder List.

2 Right-click the file name.

3 When the shortcut menu appears, choose Set As Home Page.

Chapter 7: Managing Web Structure with Navigation View

4 Display Navigation view and look for the home page. If you're already in Navigation view, press F5, the Refresh key.

This method will rename your home page to the name Navigation view is looking for.

● If your home page still doesn't appear in Navigation view, proceed as follows:

1 Choose Recalculate Hyperlinks from the Tools menu.

2 Display Navigation view and look for the home page. If you're already in Navigation view, press F5.

● If a home page still doesn't appear, follow these steps:

1 Rename the existing home page file.

2 In Navigation view, create a new home page by clicking the New Page toolbar button.

3 Open both pages for editing.

4 Copy the entire contents of the old home page file.

5 Paste the contents into the new home page file.

6 Save the new home page file, and close both files.

7 Display Navigation view and look for the home page. If you're already in Navigation view, press F5, the Refresh key.

8 Delete the old, renamed file.

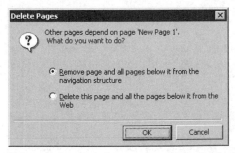

New Page

After you've identified the correct home page in Navigation view, you should probably never delete it. If you try to delete it in Navigation view, FrontPage displays the Delete Pages dialog box shown in Figure 7-4. This dialog box presents only two options: deleting the home page and all pages beneath it from Navigation view, and deleting the home page and all pages beneath it from your Web. These are both extreme actions with no possibility of being undone.

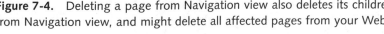

Figure 7-4. Deleting a page from Navigation view also deletes its children from Navigation view, and might delete all affected pages from your Web.

Troubleshooting

Default page names differ on development and production Web servers

Confusion can result if your authoring environment and production Web server have different default page names. Here are two such scenarios:

- You create Webs using a Microsoft Web server whose default page name is *default.htm*, but publish them on a UNIX Web server whose default page name is *index.html*.

- You create disk-based Webs with home pages named *index.htm* and publish them to a Microsoft Windows 2000 server whose default page name is *default.htm*.

The cleanest and most desirable solution is to change your authoring environment, your production Web server, or both so they use the same default document name. Unfortunately, this isn't always possible. In the case of a disk-based Web, FrontPage has no facility to change the file name that identifies the home page. In the case of a server-based Web, you might not have access to the Web server's configuration, the server's administrator might not be willing to make the change, or making a change might adversely affect other applications.

FrontPage renames the home page when it copies a Web from one location to another and all the following are true:

- You use the FrontPage Publish command to copy the Web.
- Both the source and target locations are FrontPage-based Webs.
- The default document name in the two Webs is different.

Of course, just as it always does when renaming files, FrontPage adjusts all hyperlinks so they keep working as you intend.

If you can't eliminate the discrepancy in default document names and you must publish by FTP, file sharing, or some other mechanism that doesn't rename the home page, proceed as follows:

1 Use the development server's default file name (in other words, *default.htm*) as the Navigation view home page.

2 Create a redirection file having the production server's default file name (in other words *index.htm*). This page should redirect visitors to the default file name from step 1 (*default.htm*).

For information about creating redirection pages, refer to "Configuring HTML Header Properties" on page 548.

Chapter 7: Managing Web Structure with Navigation View

Attempting to delete the home page from the Folder List or from any other view displays the Confirm Delete dialog box shown in Figure 7-5. If you click Yes in this dialog box, FrontPage deletes the home page from your Web, deletes it from Navigation view, and deletes any Navigation view references that were subordinate to the home page.

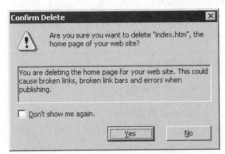

Figure 7-5. Deleting the home page from a Web that uses Navigation view deletes the main Navigation view structure in its entirety.

Keep in mind that whenever you delete entries from Navigation view, you're deleting hyperlinks from Link bars as well. This explains why, after deleting the home page and its children from Navigation view, any Link Bars components you've added might be blank or significantly diminished.

Adding Child Pages to Navigation View

After Navigation view correctly displays a home page, adding child pages is easy. From the following, choose the method that seems most suited to the task at hand:

- To create a new page and immediately define it as the child of another:

  1 Right-click the parent page in Navigation view.

  2 Point to New, and then choose Page from the shortcut menu.

  This procedure is very handy when designing the initial structure of a Web.

  New pages created this way are just Navigation view entries and not physical files. As such, they don't appear immediately in the Folder List. However, when you update the screen, FrontPage creates all the pages using file names and titles similar to their Navigation view names. You can update the screen by using any of these four methods:

  - Right-click the Navigation view background, and choose Apply Changes from the shortcut menu.

  - Switch to another view.

■ Edit a page in FrontPage.

■ Close the Web.

After FrontPage creates any new files, you can change their file names by using the normal Folder List commands.

● To designate an existing page in your Web as the child of a page in Navigation view:

1 Drag the page from the Folder List.

2 Drop the page under the appropriate parent in the document frame.

As you drag files near prospective parents, FrontPage draws shaded lines suggesting a relationship. When the shaded line connects to the correct parent, release the mouse button. FrontPage retains the left to right positioning of any nearby pages. Figure 7-6 shows this operation in progress.

● To first create a physical file and then add it to Navigation view:

1 Select anything in the Folder List.

2 Click the New Page button.

3 Switch to Navigation view, if necessary.

4 Save and rename the new page, and then drag it into position.

New Page

Organizing Your Web Content

Here are some tips for organizing Web pages in a way that presents your message clearly and simply:

● Confine each Web page to a single topic. If you put two or more topics on the same page, the combined page won't fit into the Navigation view hierarchy. Each page can appear in Navigation view only once.

● Have the choices near the top of the structure deal in broad categories. Pages at the bottom should present detailed information.

● Put the most important hyperlinks and the most important information at the top of the page. Most Web visitors decide whether or not a page is interesting long before they scroll down.

● Use clear links up and down your site's hierarchy. Most Web visitors want to drill down to specific pieces of information rather than traversing, accepting, or rejecting many pages sequentially. No one, for example, wants to locate a product or any other listing by clicking a Next button several hundred times.

Chapter 7: Managing Web Structure with Navigation View

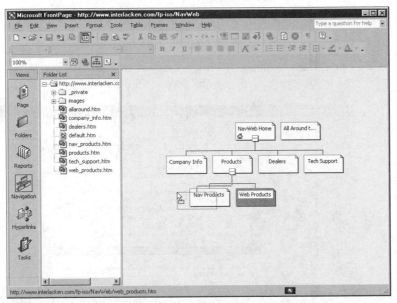

Figure 7-6. When you drag a page around in Navigation view, FrontPage draws a shaded line to the closest available parent. Drop the page when the shaded line connects it to the parent page you want.

Troubleshooting

FrontPage won't add a page to Navigation view

If FrontPage won't draw shaded lines to a page that you drag from the Folder List, it's because that file already appears beneath the home page or a top page. (For more information about top pages, refer to "Adding Top Pages to Navigation View" later in this chapter.) Attempting to add the same page to the same location using the Add Existing Page command produces the following message:

> *The page you are trying to add is already in the navigation structure. Rename this page or select a different page and then try again.*

This behavior occurs because FrontPage requires each page in Navigation view to have at most one parent. Therefore, each page in a Web can appear in the main navigation structure only once.

To avoid this restriction, add the destination page to a custom Link bar and then add a Link Bar With Custom Links component to the pages in which you want the links to appear. The section titled "Creating a Link Bar with the Custom Links Component" later in this chapter explains how to create this component.

● To add a page outside the current Web to your hierarchy:

1 Right-click the page that will be the external page's parent.

2 Choose Add Existing Page from the shortcut menu. This displays
the Insert Hyperlink dialog box seen in Figure 7-7.

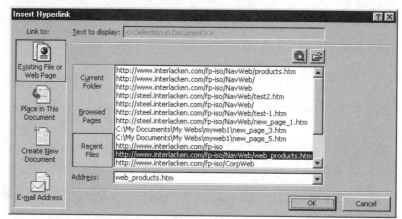

Figure 7-7. Choosing Add Existing Page in Navigation view
displays this dialog box for entering locations inside or outside
the current Web.

3 Locate or type the desired link, and then click OK.

The only nodes that can have children in Navigation view are Web pages in the current
Web. However, you *can* add external links, pictures, multimedia files, Common Gateway Interface (CGI) programs, or anything you want as the *child* of a page in the current Web. Because FrontPage can't manipulate Link bars and other components in such
files, they can't be Navigation view parents.

---

tip As the diagram becomes larger and more complex, you might want to zoom in, zoom
out, collapse branches, and then expand them. For instructions on doing this, refer to
"Controlling the Navigation View Display" later in this chapter.

Here's how FrontPage names the pages you add to Navigation view:

● When you create a new page in Navigation view, Front Page gives it a
Navigation view name of *New Page x* where *x* is a sequential number.

● When you add an existing page to Navigation view, FrontPage uses the
page's title as the Navigation view name. (This is the title you assign on

an open page's Page Properties dialog box, and not the page's file name.)
If the existing page resides outside the current Web, you'll also see a small
globe icon in the external page.

Even though a page's HTML title provides a reasonable first guess, in most cases you'll
want to shorten the Navigation view name. HTML page titles—assigned in FrontPage
from the General tab of the Page Properties dialog box—are the strings that search
engines and browsers use to identify the page. You'll probably want your HTML titles to
be fully descriptive of each page, and possibly to contain your company or site name as
well. The Navigation view name, by contrast, frequently becomes the menu text displayed in Link bars, and you'll likely want to keep this short.

In either case—new page or existing—accepting a page's default Navigation view name
is usually a bad idea. Fortunately, changing the Navigation view name of a Web page is
quite simple. Just do this:

1 Highlight the page's icon by clicking it in the main Navigation view window
or in the Page view Navigation pane.

2 Right-click the page and choose Rename, press the F2 key, or click the
name.

3 Type or revise the page's Navigation view name.

4 Press Enter or click anywhere outside the Navigation view name.

Rearranging Pages in Navigation View

Rearranging pages is even simpler than adding them. If you're working in Navigation
view, click the page you want to move, hold down the mouse button while you drag,
and then release the button when the shaded line connects the dragged page to the
desired parent.

The procedures are somewhat different if you're working in the Page view Navigation
pane. Proceed as follows:

● To move a page under a different parent, drag the child page and drop it
onto the parent page.

● To rearrange the children of a particular parent, drag one of the pages you
want to move and drop it above, below, or between its siblings. A black
horizontal line indicates the new page position, should you drop the page
with no further movement. Figure 7-8 on the next page shows this operation in progress.

Part 3: Creating Web Sites Automatically

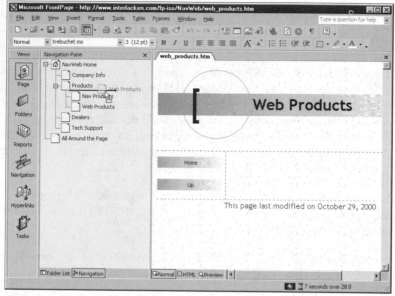

Figure 7-8. If you drop a page where a vertical bar appears, FrontPage makes the page a peer of the page above the line.

Adding Top Pages to Navigation View

Orphan pages are perfectly valid in Navigation view. These are pages that don't fall within the hierarchy beneath the home page—pages such as Search, Send Mail, and Contact Webmaster. Because these pages aren't the home page and yet have no parent, FrontPage calls them *top pages*. They appear at the top of the Navigation view diagram, adjacent but not connected to the home page. To designate an existing page as a top page:

1 Drag it from elsewhere in the Navigation view diagram or from the Folder List.

2 Drop it—just as you probably suspected—adjacent to but not beneath the home page.

You can create as many top pages as you want. Follow this next procedure to create a new top page:

1 Right-click anywhere in the Navigation view diagram.

2 Choose New from the shortcut menu, and then choose Top Page.

3 FrontPage gives new top pages names like *Top Page 1*, *Top Page 2*, and so forth. Rename the page as you would any other page in the diagram.

Top pages can have children just as the home page does. To add children, drag them under the top page just as you would under any other page.

The Link Bars component treats pages drawn beneath a top page much as it does pages drawn under the home page: that is, it honors relationships such as parent pages, child pages, and left and right pages. Link bars can also display links to all top pages in a Web. However, you can't add special top page links to all forms of Link bars as you can home page links.

> **tip** To view the file name of a page displayed in Navigation view, right-click its icon and then choose Properties from the shortcut menu.

newfeature! Adding Custom Link Bars to Navigation View

A custom Link bar is a named group of hyperlinks that's not associated with any specific page. Custom Link bars have these properties:

- Unlike most nodes in the Navigation view diagram, custom Link bars don't represent a specific page. They're simply a named list of links that you can use in as few or as many pages as you want.

- Custom Link bars have at most a two-level structure: the custom Link bar itself, and any number of direct children. However, the children can't have children.

- The links on a custom Link bar can point inside or outside the current Web.

- One page can belong to any number of custom Link bars. By contrast, one page can belong to the main Navigation view structure only once.

- Custom Link bars normally reside in the Navigation view structure as peers of the home page.

- You can drag a custom Link bar beneath a regular page in the Navigation view diagram but, because the custom Link bar isn't a page, its parent can't link to it. Instead, any Link bars in the parent page will link to the custom Link bar's first child.

To create a custom Link bar that's a peer of the home page, right-click anywhere on the Navigation view or Navigation pane background, choose New from the shortcut menu, and then choose Custom Link Bar. This creates a new custom Link bar named New Link Bar that you can modify as described in the "Creating a Link Bar with the Custom Links Component" section later in this chapter.

To create a custom Link bar that's the child of another page, right-click that page, choose New from the shortcut menu, and then (you guessed it) choose Custom Link Bar.

Chapter 7

You can drag a page out of the main Navigation view structure and drop it under a custom Link bar, but this removes the page from the main structure. The following procedures offer better alternatives:

- In Navigation view:

  1 Drag the page you want to include out of the Folder List.

  2 Drop it under the desired custom Link bar.

- In Navigation view:

  1 Select the custom Link bar.

  2 Click the Add Existing Page button on the Navigation toolbar.

  3 When the Insert Hyperlink dialog box appears, specify the page you want and click OK.

Add Existing
Page

- In either Navigation view or the Navigation pane:

  1 Right-click the page you want the custom Link bar to include.

  2 Choose Copy from the shortcut menu.

  3 Right-click the custom Link bar, and choose Paste.

- In either Navigation view or the Navigation pane:

  1 Right-click the custom Link bar.

  2 Choose the Add Existing Page option.

  3 When the Insert Hyperlink dialog box appears, specify the page you want, and click OK.

- In Page view:

  1 Open any page that uses or should use the custom Link bar.

  2 If the page doesn't already contain a Link Bar With Custom Links component, add one.

  3 In the Link Bar Properties dialog box, associate the custom Link bar defined in Navigation view with the Link Bar With Custom Links component in the Web page.

  4 While still in the Properties dialog box, configure the links you want, and click OK.

> **For more information about the Link Bar With Custom Links component, refer to "Creating a Link Bar with the Custom Links Component" later in this chapter.**

Figure 7-9 shows a Navigation view structure that contains one custom Link bar. The Link bar is named *Miscellaneous Links* and contains three children.

Chapter 7: Managing Web Structure with Navigation View

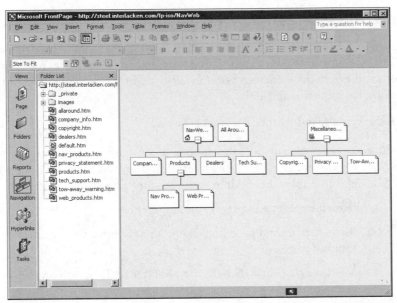

Figure 7-9. The structure at the left is a custom Link bar. Any Link Bar With Custom Links component that references this custom Link bar will display the given links.

The appearance of the following page icon differentiates custom Link bars from ordinary pages.

Deleting a Page From Navigation View

To delete a page from Navigation view or the Page view Navigation pane, do *one* of the following:

- Select the page, and choose Delete from the Edit menu.
- Select the page, and press the Delete key.
- Right-click the page, and choose Delete from the shortcut menu.

Following any of these actions, FrontPage displays the dialog box shown previously in Figure 7-4. This dialog box asks whether you want to remove the page and its children just from Navigation view or completely from your Web. Make your choice and click OK. To also delete children of a page you're deleting, click Yes when prompted.

> **caution** Deleting a file from the Folder List always removes it completely from the Web. You can't undo this action.

Controlling the Navigation View Display

As the size of your structure grows, you might find it convenient to hide the parts you aren't working on, or to view the diagram on a greater or lesser scale. You might even decide the diagram fits the screen better in left-to-right mode than in top-to-bottom. FrontPage has all these capabilities.

Collapsing and expanding the view works like this:

- To collapse (that is, to hide) the children of any page, click the minus icon on that page's lower edge. The children disappear, and the icon changes to a plus sign. To display the children again, click the plus icon.

- To collapse the parent and peers of any page, either:

  - Right-click a child page, and choose View Subtree Only from the shortcut menu; or

  - Select the page, and click the View Subtree Only button on the Navigation toolbar.

View Subtree
Only

A View All icon will appear in place of the hidden pages.

on the CD For more information about the Navigation toolbar, refer to "The Navigation Toolbar" in the Bonus Content on the Companion CD.

The same two commands toggle the display back to its former appearance, as does clicking the View All icon.

Right-clicking the background area in Navigation view displays the shortcut menu shown in Figure 7-10.

Figure 7-10. Right-clicking the Navigation view background produces this shortcut menu.

Here's a brief explanation of what the shortcut menu commands do:

- **New.** Adds a new top page or custom Link bar to the diagram.

- **Apply Changes.** Saves the current Navigation view structure to disk. In so doing, it also creates empty Web pages for any nodes (other than external hyperlinks) that don't have them.

Chapter 7: Managing Web Structure with Navigation View

- **View Subtree Only.** Collapses or expands all nodes above, to the left of, or to the right of the current selection.

- **Zoom.** Controls the degree of magnification, as a percent of normal size. The Size To Fit subcommand scales all visible pages into the main Navigation view window.

Zoom

The Zoom drop-down list on the Navigation toolbar provides essentially the same options.

Portrait/
Landscape

- **Portrait/Landscape.** Toggles Navigation view between top-to-bottom and left-to-right display mode.

The Portrait/Landscape button on the Navigation toolbar provides the same display options.

- **Expand All.** Enlarges the view so that all pages in the structure are displayed. This has the same effect as clicking all the plus icons to show all the child pages.

- **Web Settings.** Displays the same dialog box as choosing Web Settings from the Tools menu.

> For information about the Web Settings dialog box, refer to "Reviewing Web Settings" in the Bonus Content on the Companion CD.

Right-clicking a Navigation view icon produces the shortcut menu shown in Figure 7-11.

Figure 7-11. Right-clicking a Navigation view node produces this shortcut menu.

These commands work as follows:

- **New.** Creates either a new page with the selected page as its parent or a custom Link bar.

- **Add Existing Page.** Displays a dialog box for locating a new child page for the currently selected parent. The page you select needn't be part of the current Web.

Add Existing Page

  The Navigation toolbar includes an Add Existing Page button that also displays this dialog box.

- **Open.** Opens the node using the standard editor configured for its file type.

- **Open With.** Opens the node with an editor you select from a menu.

- **Preview In Browser.** Displays the current page in your browser. FrontPage starts the browser if necessary.

- **Cut.** Copies the current selection and all its children to the Clipboard, and then removes the selection from the Navigation view.

- **Copy.** Copies the current selection and all its children to the Clipboard.

- **Paste.** Adds the current Clipboard contents to Navigation view as the child of the currently selected node.

- **Rename.** Changes the Navigation view name of the currently selected node. To rename the physical file, rename it in the Folder List.

> **note** Despite the fact that one defaults to the other, a Web page's title and its Navigation view name are two separate fields. After both exist, changing one doesn't change the other.

- **Delete.** Removes the node from Navigation view. A dialog box asks whether to delete the actual file or just remove it from Navigation view (and thus from all Link bars).

- **View Subtree Only.** Collapses or expands all nodes above, to the left of, or to the right of the current selection.

View Subtree Only

  The View Subtree Only button on the Navigation toolbar provides the same function.

- **Included In Navigation Bars.** Toggles whether the current node appears in Link bars. The color of a node indicates its state: yellow if included in Link bars, gray if not.

Chapter 7: Managing Web Structure with Navigation View

Included in
Navigation
Bars

The Included In Navigation Bars button on the Navigation toolbar also
controls this option.

● **Properties.** Displays the Properties dialog box for the selected icon's Web
page. This dialog box appeared previously in Figure 6-25 and Figure 6-26.

> For more information about the Properties dialog box, refer to "Working with Folders View"
> on page 174.

To print a copy of the Navigation view structure, make sure the Navigation view structure is visible, and then choose Print from the File menu. To preview the printed appearance, choose Print Preview. You can also print the Navigation view structure when
it appears in Print Preview mode by clicking the Print button.

Using Link Bars with Navigation View

Navigation view, the Link Bars component, and the Page Banner component all work
together in the following way:

● In Navigation view, you arrange your pages and give them names.

● Link bars use the relationships and names from Navigation view to build
menus that jump among your pages.

● The Page Banner component displays a page's Navigation view name
as the heading of the page that contains it.

> For more information about the Page Banner component, refer to "Using Page Banners" later
> in this chapter.

The Link Bars component automatically creates and maintains menu bars (often called
jump bars) that connect the pages in your Web. There are three kinds of Link bars:

newfeature!

● **Link Bar With Custom Links.** Displays hyperlinks based on a Navigation
view custom Link bar.

● **Link Bar With Back And Next Links.** Displays hyperlinks to the two pages
immediately left and right of the current page, and at the same level.

● **Link Bar Based On Navigation Structure.** Displays hyperlinks based on the
Navigation view diagram. This means it can display links to all children of
the current page, to all pages at the same level as the current page's parent,
and so forth.

Creating a Link Bar with the Custom Links Component

Designers using FrontPage 2000 and earlier versions have long admired the convenience (and especially the appearance) of Link bars. But in many cases, these same designers were unwilling to diagram their site in Navigation view. What they really wanted, they said, was a Link bar they could add to a page and then configure manually.

FrontPage 2002 introduces a Link Bar With Custom Links component that not only meets this need but adds a bonus. The bonus is that when you create a Link Bar With Custom Links, FrontPage saves its list of hyperlinks as a named object in Navigation view. That way, if you have other pages that need the same collection of links, their Link Bar With Custom Links components can get them from the same named object.

Unfortunately, the following object names are both long and confusing:

- **Link Bar With Custom Links.** This is a Web component that occupies space in a Web page and displays a list of links.

- **Custom Link bar.** This is a Navigation view object that stores a list of links for use in one or more pages. It's *not* a Link bar and therein lies the confusion. A better name for this object would have been custom Link list or custom Link set, for example.

  It's worth noting that you can create Navigation view custom Link bars first, and use them later in Link Bar With Custom Links components. The "Adding Custom Link Bars to Navigation View" section earlier in this chapter described how to create custom Link bars while in Navigation view.

Here's the procedure for adding a Link Bar With Custom Links component to a Web page:

1 In Page view, open the page that should display the Link Bar With Custom Links component.

2 Set the insertion point where you want the Link Bar With Custom Links to appear.

3 Choose Navigation from the Insert menu. This displays the Insert Web Component dialog box shown in Figure 7-12.

4 Make sure that Link Bars is selected in the Component Type list.

5 Make sure Bar With Custom Links is selected in the Choose A Bar Type list.

6 Click Next to display the next dialog box, shown in Figure 7-13.

Chapter 7: Managing Web Structure with Navigation View

7 Choose any of the bar styles listed in the Choose A Bar Style list. The first
entry in the list uses the same theme as the Web page that will contain the
Link Bar With Custom Links component. Following this are options for
using any other theme available in FrontPage. Scrolling to the end of the
list reveals various text-based options.

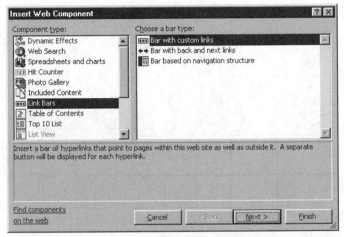

Figure 7-12. The Insert Web Component dialog box appears with
the Link Bars and Bar With Custom Links options already selected for you.

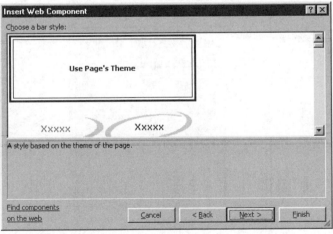

Figure 7-13. When FrontPage displays this dialog box, you can choose
to use the same theme as the rest of the current page, any other theme,
or various text formats.

8 Click Next to display the dialog box shown in Figure 7-14 on the next page.
Choose an orientation—horizontal or vertical—and then click Finish.

Part 3: Creating Web Sites Automatically

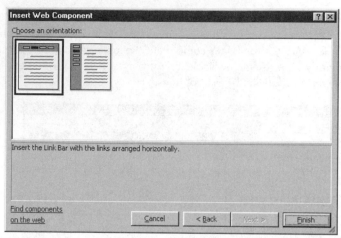

Figure 7-14. Link bars can arrange hyperlinks horizontally or vertically.

9 After you click Finish, FrontPage displays the Link Bar Properties dialog box shown in Figure 7-15.

Figure 7-15. Options in this dialog box configure a Link Bar With Custom Links. Navigation view automatically reflects any custom Link bars you create or modify with this dialog box.

This dialog box contains the following options to configure the hyperlinks that the Link Bar With Custom Links component will display:

■ To use the links from an existing Navigation view custom Link bar, select its name in the Choose Existing list.

Chapter 7: Managing Web Structure with Navigation View

◼ To create a new Navigation view custom Link bar, click the Create New button to display the Create New Link Bar dialog box. Give the new custom Link bar a name, and click OK.

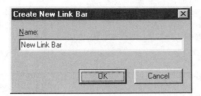

FrontPage displays this dialog box automatically if the current Web contains no Navigation view custom Link bars.

10 Use the following buttons to modify the links associated with the custom Link bar you chose in step 9. These changes will affect all Link Bar With Custom Links components—regardless of page—that use the same custom Link bar:

◼ **Add Link.** Displays the Add To Link Bar dialog box shown in Figure 7-16. In the Text To Display box near the top, type the text you want the hyperlink to display. In the Address box near the bottom, type the hyperlink location. Finally, click OK.

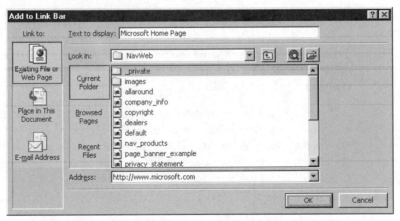

Figure 7-16. A custom Link bar can include locations within the current page, within the current Web, or anywhere in the world.

◼ **Remove Link.** Deletes the selection in the list box titled Links.

◼ **Modify Link.** Displays a Modify Link dialog box that strongly resembles the Add To Link Bar dialog box shown in Figure 7-16. Update the Text To Display and Address boxes as required, and then click OK.

- **Move Up.** Moves the selection in the Links box one position higher in the list.

- **Move Down.** Moves the selection in the Links box one position lower.

11 Use the following check boxes to add additional links to the current Link Bar With Custom Links component. These settings will affect only the current instance of the component:

- **Home Page.** Adds a link to the current Web's home page.

- **Parent Page.** Adds a link to the parent of the page that contains the Link Bar With Custom Links component.

12 Click OK.

Creating a Link Bar Based On Navigation Structure

This section describes how to create a Link Bar With Back And Next Links and a Link Bar Based On Navigation Structure. The section groups these topics together because the Back And Next variety is actually a type of Link Bar Based On Navigation Structure.

Using a Link Bar Based On Navigation Structure requires first entering structure information in Navigation view, and then inserting and configuring one or more Link bars in each Web page.

You can insert Link bars and control their appearance while editing individual Web pages, but you can't configure the number of choices on the bar, their titles, or their destinations. Instead, you diagram your site in Navigation view and then let FrontPage create the appropriate links.

A Link Bar Based On Navigation Structure component inserted in Page view reflects the current structure in Navigation view. You can change the bar's options and appearance in Page view, but not its list of hyperlinks. To change the bar's list of hyperlinks, update the Navigation view and FrontPage propagates the changes to each Link Bar Based On Navigation Structure in the same Web.

Troubleshooting

Updates to Navigation pane don't appear in Page view

After renaming or relocating pages in the Navigation pane, pages open for editing in Page view might not immediately reflect the changes. This is because the Navigation pane changes are still in a pending state.

To finalize your Navigation pane changes and update any open pages, right-click the Navigation pane background and choose Apply Changes from the shortcut menu. Closing the Navigation pane by displaying the Folder List or another FrontPage view has the same effect.

Chapter 7: Managing Web Structure with Navigation View

Assuming you've already diagramed your Web in Navigation view, add a Link Bar Based On Navigation Structure by doing the following:

1 Open a page and place the insertion point where you want the Link Bar Based On Navigation Structure to appear.

2 Choose Navigation from the Insert menu.

3 Verify that Link Bars is selected in the Component Type list

4 Choose Bar Based On Navigation Structure from the Choose A Bar Type list.

If you want to create a Link Bar With Back And Next Links, choose either:

- Bar With Back And Next Links; or

- Bar Based On Navigation Structure.

If you choose Bar Based On Navigation Structure, be sure to select Back And Next later in the Link Bar Properties dialog box.

5 Click Next to display the next wizard dialog box, shown in Figure 7-13. Choose a theme as described in the "Creating a Link Bar with the Custom Links Component" section earlier in this chapter, and then click Next.

6 Choose an orientation—horizontal or vertical—and then click Finish.

7 Make your choices in the Link Bar Properties dialog box shown in Figure 7-17. (The next section describes the options available in this dialog box.) Click OK.

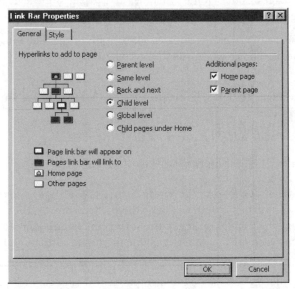

Figure 7-17. This dialog box adds a Link Bar Based On Navigation Structure to the current Web page.

Setting Link Bar Based On Navigation Structure Properties

FrontPage provides the dialog box shown in Figure 7-17 for controlling the content and appearance of Link Bars Based On Navigation Structure. The same dialog box applies for both creating new Link Bars Based On Navigation Structure and modifying existing ones. The following sections and controls appear on the General tab:

- **Hyperlinks To Add To Page.** You can apply only one of the following six options to a single Link Bar Based On Navigation Structure. However, nothing prevents you from placing several Link Bar Based On Navigation Structure components on the same page, each configured with different options:

  - **Parent Level.** Specifies that the Link Bar Based On Navigation Structure should contain hyperlinks to all pages one level higher than the current page, as positioned in Navigation view.

  - **Same Level.** Specifies that the Link Bar Based On Navigation Structure should list all pages at the same level as itself.

  - **Back And Next.** Includes the two pages immediately left and right of the current page, and at the same level.

  - **Child Level.** Includes all pages that have the current page as their parent.

  - **Global Level.** Includes the home page and any other pages drawn at the same level.

  - **Child Pages Under Home.** Includes all the pages one level below the home page.

- **Additional Pages.** You can include either or both of the following pages regardless of the choice you made in the Hyperlinks To Add To Page section:

  - **Home Page.** Adds the home page to the Link Bar Based On Navigation Structure.

  - **Parent Page.** Adds the parent of the current page.

The following controls appear on the Style tab of the Link Bar Properties dialog box:

newfeature!

- **Choose A Style.** The first option in this list tells FrontPage to format the Link bar in conformance with the same theme that controls the rest of the current page. The last few options format the Link bar as plain text. The options in between use any other available themes to format the Link bar.

> **tip** Plain text Link bars needn't be plain. You can format text Link bars with all the colors, fonts, and typographical properties available for other text on your Web page.

Chapter 7: Managing Web Structure with Navigation View

- **Orientation And Appearance.** The following options control the appearance of the Link Bar Based On Navigation Structure:

  - **Horizontal.** Arranges the choices on the Link Bar Based On Navigation Structure as a single line of text.

  - **Vertical.** Arranges the Link Bar Based On Navigation Structure choices vertically, with each choice on its own line.

    You can choose either Horizontal or Vertical, but not both.

  - **Use Vivid Colors.** If the theme you select in the Choose A Style box includes soft and vivid colors, selecting this check box selects the vivid ones.

  - **Use Active Graphics.** If the theme you select in the Choose A Style box includes optional buttons that change appearance when the mouse pointer passes over them, checking this box selects those buttons.

FrontPage labels each option on the Link Bar Based On Navigation Structure with the title of the target page as it appears in Navigation view. This provides an incentive to keep the Navigation view names short but descriptive. To change the label appearing on a Link Bar Based On Navigation Structure, change the title of the target page in Navigation view.

The Navigation tab of the Web Settings dialog box, shown in Figure 7-18, contains options for setting the labels displayed for the home, parent, previous, and next pages. The default labels are, respectively, Home, Up, Previous, and Next. To globally apply your own labels, select Web Settings from the Tools menu, select the Navigation tab, and then type the text you want Web visitors to see.

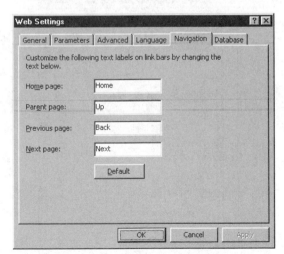

Figure 7-18. The default navigator bar names of Home, Parent, Previous, and Next can be globally customized here.

Figure 7-19 on the next page illustrates a horizontal text Link bar in Navigation view. The bar appears between the two horizontal lines.

Figure 7-20 shows a vertical Link bar built using picture buttons. FrontPage gets the button picture from the Web page's theme. (Graphic Link bar buttons are a popular feature.)

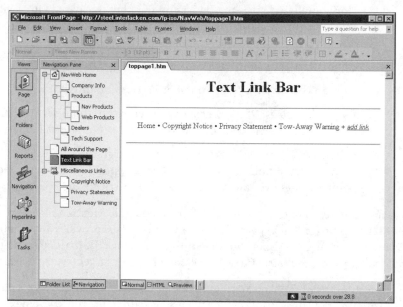

Figure 7-19. This page includes a horizontal text Link bar between two horizontal lines.

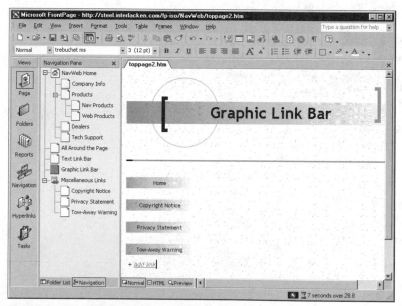

Figure 7-20. To get attractive buttons like the ones in this Web page, format your Link bars with themes.

Chapter 7: Managing Web Structure with Navigation View

Frequently Asked Questions About Link Bars

Is there any way to generate graphic Link bar buttons without applying themes to a Web page?

newfeature!

Yes. You can select any style you want from the Style tab of the Link Bar Properties dialog box.

Is there any way to set up Link bars without diagramming a site in Navigation view?

newfeature!

Yes. Create a Link Bar With Custom Links as described in the "Creating a Link Bar with the Custom Links Component" section earlier in this chapter.

After diagramming a site, is there any way to add Link Bars Based On Navigation Structure to all its pages automatically?

Yes. The Shared Border feature can do exactly that. However, lest happiness overcome you, you'll still need to manually edit each page and take out your old, hand-coded navigation menus.

For more information about shared borders, refer to "Using Shared Borders" on page 765.

Troubleshooting

Link bar appears blank or missing

If you configure a Link Bar Based On Navigation Structure with options that don't apply to the current page, the Link bar will appear blank or missing when you open the page in a Web Browser. Here are some situations where this might occur:

- The home page contains a Link Bar Based On Navigation Structure configured to display links to all parent pages. By definition, of course, the home page has no parent.

- A page contains a Link Bar Based On Navigation Structure configured to display links to all pages at the same level, but the current page is the only page at its particular level.

- A page at the bottom of the structure contains a Link Bar Based On Navigation Structure configured to display all child pages. Because the current page is at the bottom of the navigation structure, it has no children.

This behavior occurs most often when you propagate identical Link bars to many pages through such means as shared borders and templates. If the Link bar isn't in a shared border, either reconfigure the Link bar or delete it and create a new one.

Deleting or reconfiguring a Link bar in a shared border will affect other pages where the Link bar is working properly. In such a case, add a new Link bar outside the shared border and configure it to display pages at the correct level.

Using Page Banners

The Page Banner component performs a single function requiring very little configuration: It displays a page's Navigation view title.

Using the Page Banner component has two advantages compared to just typing a heading into your Web page. First, it ensures that a page's visual heading contains exactly the same text as all Link bar references to that page. This occurs because FrontPage bases both page banner text and Link bar text on the same source: the page's Navigation view title. Second, if your page uses themes, FrontPage can superimpose the page banner text over the theme's designated banner picture.

Adding a page banner is a snap when you follow these steps:

1 Open the Web page in Page view.

2 Set the insertion point where you want the banner to appear, which is most frequently at the top of the page.

3 Choose Web Component from the Insert menu. This displays the Insert Web Component dialog box shown previously in Figure 7-12.

4 In the Component Type list, choose Included Content.

5 In the Choose A Type Of Content list, choose Page Banner.

6 Click Finish to display the Page Banner Properties dialog box shown in Figure 7-21.

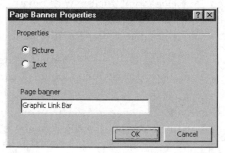

Figure 7-21. This dialog box controls the appearance of a Page Banner component. The Picture option has meaning only on pages controlled by a theme, and you can specify page banner text only for pages already entered in Navigation view.

7 Select Picture if the current page is controlled by a theme and you want the page banner text displayed over the theme's banner picture. Select Text if you want a plain-text banner (this banner overrides the default banner of any themes that you might have previously applied).

For more information about themes, refer to Chapter 19, "Using FrontPage Themes."

Chapter 7: Managing Web Structure with Navigation View

8 Review the suggested page banner text, and correct it if necessary.

Initially, the Page Banner box contains the current page's Navigation view title. Updating this text also updates Navigation view, and therefore all Link Bars Based On Navigation Structure pointing to this page. If the current page doesn't appear in Navigation view, FrontPage ignores this field and the page banner is blank.

9 Click OK.

The Page Banner component works only for pages you've diagrammed in Navigation view. You can insert Page Banner components even in Web pages not diagrammed in Navigation view, but instead of a page banner, FrontPage displays this message:

[Add this page in the Navigation view to display a page banner here.]

If your Web page uses themes, the difference between a picture banner and a text banner is quite apparent. In Figure 7-22, the upper banner is a picture whereas the lower one is text. Both banners display the title *Page Banner Example*.

---

tip Just because a page banner appears as text doesn't mean it has to be plain. You can apply any and all FrontPage text formatting commands to textual Page Banner components, as done with the bordered-text example in Figure 7-22.

Figure 7-22. The banner *Page Banner Example* appears first as a picture and then as text with borders above and below it.

If you like using themes but don't like diagramming your site in Navigation view, you might wonder if there's any other way to specify page banner text. There isn't. The only text a Page Banner component can display is the current page's Navigation view name. If you haven't added the page to Navigation view, that name will be blank.

To learn about superimposing text on graphics, refer to "Inserting Text on GIF Components" on page 330.

To insert a page banner for every page in a Web, activate shared borders and place a Page Banner component in the desired border (most likely the top one). Of course, this doesn't remove any existing page headings, and it produces the message previously noted for any page not diagrammed in Navigation view.

For more information about shared borders, refer to "Using Shared Borders" on page 765.

The true power of the Page Banner component lies not in formatting page headings one by one, but rather in centralizing control of Link bars and page headings through Navigation view. Although initially it might seem awkward to leave Page view and configure the page banner text in Navigation view, there's great power when changing a page's title once in Navigation view updates its page banner and all Link bars.

In Summary...

This chapter explained how to enter a new site's structure in Navigation view and how FrontPage—using certain Web components—automatically creates Web pages that reflect that structure.

The next chapter explains another way to create Web sites automatically: namely, through the use of Web site templates and wizards.

Creating Web Sites with Templates and Wizards

During your travels around the Web, you've undoubtedly noticed that certain kinds of Web sites occur over and over again. Some are personal Web sites where people describe themselves or their families. Others provide information about businesses, government agencies, and other large organizations, or about a particular project or task force.

Microsoft FrontPage 2002 can't create sites like these completely on its own, and even if it could, you probably wouldn't like the results. After all, your content is unique, and you probably want your site's organization and appearance to be unique as well. No one wants a site that's just one more rubber-stamp copy of thousands of others, with just the names and a few other components changed.

At the same time—regardless of the task at hand—starting from nothing can be a daunting proposition. FrontPage provides a limited collection of templates and wizards that can populate a new Web with several kinds of typical pages. Even if you never create an actual site this way, the resulting Webs provide interesting examples of a variety of FrontPage techniques.

If you'd rather start by learning how to create Web pages by hand and then learn later about creating them automatically, skip to the next chapter.

Understanding Templates and Wizards

A template is a static unit of content saved for repetitive use. Every time you use a template, the new Web will be exactly like all the other new Webs you created with the same template, until you change the template.

FrontPage provides the following templates for creating a new Web:

- **Empty Web.** Creates a Web with nothing in it. If you're one of those people who likes to talk about the null case, please do so now.

- **One Page Web.** Creates a Web with a blank home page.

- **Customer Support Web.** Creates a Web for a company offering customer support on the Internet. This template is designed particularly for computer software companies.

- **Personal Web.** Creates a Web that represents an individual, with pages for interests, favorite sites, and photos.

- **Project Web.** Creates a Web for use by members of a project team. It includes Web pages for a list of project members, status reports, the project schedule, an archive area, and ongoing discussion.

- **SharePoint-based Team Web Site.** Creates a specialized Web that coordinates the activities of a project or workgroup. Your Web server must be running SharePoint Team Services for this feature to work.

  The SharePoint-based Team Web Site option is in a class by itself. Choosing this option sets aside a dedicated part of your Web that supports database-driven lists, document libraries, surveys, document annotation, document subscription, and all the other features of an Office team Web site.

After creating a Web based on any of these templates, the next step is normally to open each page and start replacing the generic content and placeholders with your own content.

For more information about creating and modifying page content, refer to Part 4, "Editing Basic Page Content."

Wizards operate in a structured way and perform more complex operations. Each wizard first prompts you for information and preferences with a series of dialog boxes like the one shown in Figure 8-1. It then customizes its results accordingly, completing its work uninterrupted. This avoids prompts for unnecessary options and minimizes the chance of a partially completed update. Unless you give all the same answers, you'll never get the same results twice.

Chapter 8: Creating Web Sites with Templates and Wizards

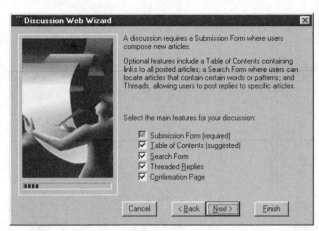

Figure 8-1. A wizard uses dialog boxes like this one to collect your preferences and then to customize its results.

FrontPage provides the following wizards for creating new Webs:

- **Corporate Presence Wizard.** Creates a typical set of Web pages for representing a company on the Internet. The wizard contains generic pages you can use as a starting point and leaves notes in purple text indicating what you should update and what kinds of information to include.

- **Database Interface Wizard.** Creates a Web that includes pages to add, view, and optionally update a new or existing database.

- **Discussion Web Wizard.** Creates a special Web designed for interactive discussions. Web visitors can submit topics by entering text in a form, review existing articles listed in a table of contents, or locate articles by word searching.

- **Import Web Wizard.** Adds an existing set of pages to a new or existing Web.

After you run a wizard and view its results, you may regret your answers to one or more prompts. The solution is simple; just delete the Web and run the wizard again. Keep doing this until you're satisfied that the wizard has done its best. Then, as with templates, start customizing pages with your own content and preferences.

For more information about deleting Webs, refer to "Deleting a FrontPage-Based Web" on page 178.

To create a new Web based on any of the templates or wizards, follow this procedure:

1 Start FrontPage.

2 Choose New from the File menu, and then choose Page Or Web.

217

3 When the New Page Or Web task pane appears, click either Empty Web or Web Site Templates. This will display the dialog box shown in Figure 8-2.

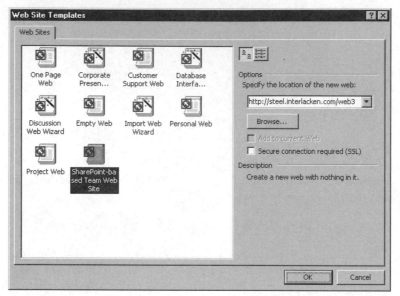

Figure 8-2. FrontPage provides this collection of templates and wizards for creating new Webs.

4 Choose the type of Web you want.

5 In the box titled Specify The Location Of The New Web, enter either the drive letter and path, the UNC path, or the Web address where you want the new Web to reside.

A UNC (Universal Naming Convention) path is a Windows file sharing location of the form \\<*servername*>\<*sharename*>\<*path*>.

If you specify a Web address (one beginning with *http://*), the Web server must have either SharePoint Team Services or the FrontPage Server Extensions installed. Unless the Web server is operating with no security in effect, you'll also need an administrator password for the new Web's parent Web.

If you're creating a SharePoint team Web site, you must enter a Web address in this box. Furthermore, the Web server at that address must be running SharePoint Team Services.

6 Click OK. FrontPage opens the new Web automatically after it's created.

For more detailed instructions on creating a new Web, refer to "Creating a FrontPage-Based Web for New Content" on page 149.

The same templates and wizards that add pages to new Webs can add pages to existing Webs as well. To do this:

1 Open the existing Web.

2 Display the New Page Or Web task pane.

3 Choose Web Site Templates, and select a template or wizard for the pages you want to add.

4 Select the option box titled Add To Current Web, and click OK.

If the template or wizard attempts to create a Web page with the same name as an existing page, FrontPage displays the Confirm Save dialog box shown in Figure 8-3. Click Yes to overwrite the existing file with the template or wizard file. Click No to discard the new file and keep the existing one.

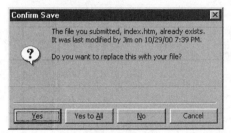

Figure 8-3. When you use a template or wizard to add pages to an existing Web, FrontPage displays this prompt before overwriting an existing page.

Using Web Site Templates

This section explains the purpose of each Web template that FrontPage provides. It also explains any special FrontPage features the resulting Web uses and how to modify them.

Using the Empty Web Template

Creating a new Web with this template provides the absolute maximum in flexibility because FrontPage provides the absolute minimum in terms of initial content: zero. There's nothing to get in your way. The world is your oyster.

The Empty Web template excels at one other task—namely, converting an existing disk folder to a disk-based Web. To do this, create a new Web as described in the previous section, specify the existing disk folder as the location for the new Web, and specify the Empty Web template. This creates a new Web that incorporates any existing content files in the specified folder. Because the Empty Web template doesn't create any new content files, it won't overwrite any existing content files.

Using the One Page Web Template

This template provides all the functionality of the empty Web template with the added benefit of creating a blank home page. This saves you from switching to Navigation view and clicking the New Page button on the Standard toolbar.

Don't laugh; the Empty Web and One Page Web templates probably account for at least 99 percent of all new Webs created in FrontPage.

Using the Customer Support Web Template

Every time you use this template to create a Web, FrontPage supplies the files and supporting elements that appear in the Folder List in Figure 8-4. Navigation view includes the home page (titled Customer Support Web), two top pages (Contact Us and Search), and seven children of the home page.

By default, top, left, and bottom shared borders are in effect for every page in this Web. As shown in Figure 8-5, the top border contains a Page Banner component and the left border contains a Link Bar Based On Navigation Structure component. The bottom border isn't visible in the figure, but it contains a second Link Bar Based On Navigation Structure component (this time formatted as text), a copyright statement, and a Date And Time component showing when someone last updated the page.

Most of the 11 pages that don't appear in the Navigation view structure override the default shared border settings to omit them. On the pages that don't override this setting, the top and left shared border areas are naturally blank.

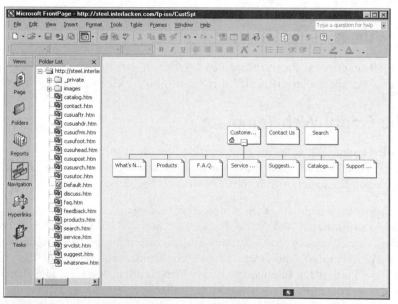

Figure 8-4. The Customer Support Web template creates this arrangement of pages.

Chapter 8: Creating Web Sites with Templates and Wizards

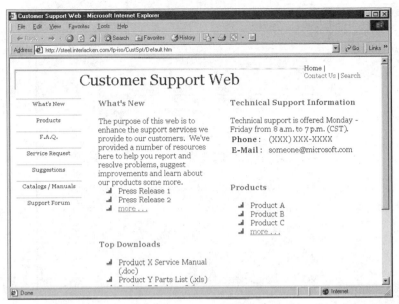

Figure 8-5. The Customer Support Web uses shared borders, page banners, Link bars, and a theme to produce an attractive and functional Web.

The Customer Support Web provides these three ways to collect information from Web visitors:

- The *service.htm* page contains an HTML form that collects service requests. Web visitors experiencing problems with the company's products or services can request assistance by filling in the form and clicking a Submit Service Request button.

- The *suggest.htm* page contains a similar HTML form that Web visitors can use to suggest new products, features, or services.

- The *discuss.htm* page leads into a Support Forum where Web visitors can post and respond to articles about any problems, solutions, tips, tricks, pitfalls, and other tidbits they encounter.

The service request and suggestion pages both use a Web component called Save Results. This component receives input from an HTML form and appends it to a text file, a Web page, or a database. To visualize how this process works, refer to Figure 8-6 on the next page. This figure shows Internet Explorer displaying the portion of the *service.htm* page that contains the HTML form. When the visitor clicks the Submit Service Request button on the *service.htm* page, the following occurs:

1 The browser transmits the data to the Web server.

2 The Save Results program, which lives on the server and comes as part of SharePoint Team Services or the FrontPage Server Extensions, saves the data in whatever location the Web designer specified.

221

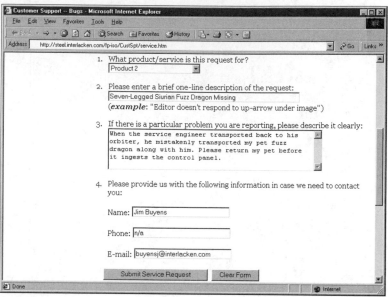

Figure 8-6.   This section of the *service.htm* page collects data from Web visitors.
Clicking the Submit Service Request button transmits the data to the Web server
for storage.

3   The Save Results program then sends the Web visitor a confirmation page
so the visitor knows that the Web server successfully received and processed
the data.

4   If the designer configured the Save Results component to save the data in
a Web page, visitors can view that Web page and see the effect of their submissions. For example, Figure 8-7 shows the results of appending the input
from Figure 8-6 to a Web page.

5   If the designer configured the Save Results component to save the data
to a text file or database, visitors can view the data only if the designer also
provided a Web page that queries and displays the text file or database.

> **For more information about the Save Results component, refer to Chapter 32, "Processing
> Data Submitted from Forms."**

To briefly review the configuration of the Save Results component in either the
service.htm or *suggest.htm* page, follow this procedure:

1   Use the Customer Support template to create a new Web, or open an
existing Web created with this template.

2   Open either the *service.htm* or *suggest.htm* page in Page view.

3   Right-click the HTML form area, and choose Form Properties from the
shortcut menu. This displays the Form Properties dialog box that appears in
the middle window shown in Figure 8-8.

Chapter 8: Creating Web Sites with Templates and Wizards

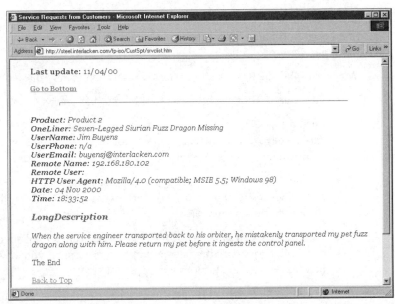

Figure 8-7. The Web server has saved the data submitted in Figure 8-6 as HTML. It also saved the data as a text file that other programs can use.

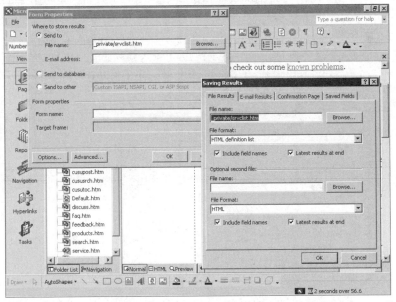

Figure 8-8. This dialog box configures the results and confirmation options of the HTML form shown in Figure 8-6.

4 Verify that the Send To option is selected under Where To Store Results and that the File Name box specifies the name of the file you want to update. (If you want to update two files, specify one of them here.)

5 To view all the Saving Results options in detail, click the Options button in the Form Properties dialog box. This displays the Saving Results dialog box shown in the foreground of Figure 8-8.

6 Make sure the File Results tab is selected, and then review these options:

- **File Name.** This text box specifies the file that receives the saved data.

- **File Format.** This drop-down list specifies the file format. Web visitors can directly view the HTML formats, but the text formats are better for subsequently adding the data to a spreadsheet or database.

- **Include Field Names.** Select this box if you want field names as well as field values to appear in each block of saved HTML or in the first record of any new text file.

- **Latest Results At End.** Select this box if you want submissions saved as HTML to appear after any existing submissions. If you leave the box blank, new submissions will appear first.

   Note that all these fields appear twice on the File Results tab. If you want to save the data in only one format, don't specify anything in the File Name field that appears under the heading Optional Second File. To save data in two formats, specify a file name in each File Name box and configure the accompanying options as you wish.

7 To control which form fields the Save Results component saves, click the Saved Fields tab. This displays the dialog box shown in Figure 8-9, where you can configure the names and the order of the fields FrontPage will save.

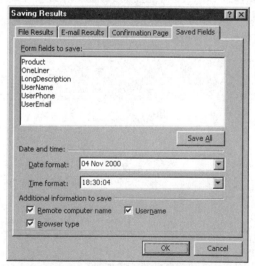

Figure 8-9. The Saved Fields tab controls which form fields and other data the Web server will record. To view or modify the name of an HTML form element, display its Properties dialog box.

224

Chapter 8: Creating Web Sites with Templates and Wizards

The Save Results component has no facilities to modify submitted data, to send submitted data to other processes, or to delete old data. If you want to perform one of these tasks, take the following actions:

- To correct or delete data saved as HTML, open the Web page in Page view, make your changes, and save.

- To correct data saved as text, right-click the file in Folders view or the Folder List, choose Open With, and open the file with Notepad. Make your changes and save.

- To download text data for use in other programs, locate the file in Folders view or the Folder List and then drag it somewhere on your local disk or file server.

- To delete a text file that contains data you no longer need, select it in Folders view or the Folder List and then press the Delete key. FrontPage will create a new file the next time a visitor submits data.

The Support Forum uses the FrontPage Discussion Web feature. Figure 8-10 shows this discussion containing, so far, three postings.

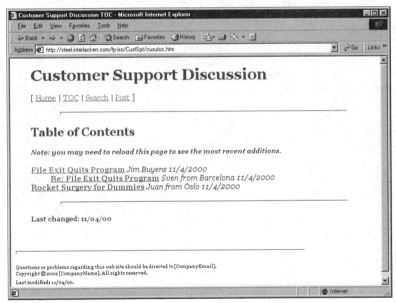

Figure 8-10. So far this discussion has three postings. Two begin new threads and one is a response.

Here are some common actions in a FrontPage Discussion Web:

- To start a new thread, a Web visitor would click the Post hyperlink.

- To read an existing posting, the visitor would click that posting.

225

Part 3: Creating Web Sites Automatically

● To respond to a posting, the visitor would click a Reply hyperlink while reading the posting.

Here's how to view or modify the configuration of a Discussion Form Handler:

1 Locate the Web page that posts new articles.

2 Right-click the HTML form that collects data for posting, and then choose Form Properties from the shortcut menu.

3 When the Form Properties dialog box shown in Figure 8-11 appears, the Send To Other option should be selected and set to Discussion Form Handler. Click the Options button to view or modify the current settings.

on the CD For more information about FrontPage discussion sites, refer to Chapter 39, "Discussion Webs and Self-Registration," in the Bonus Content on the Companion CD.

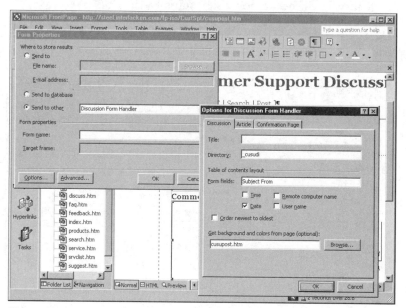

Figure 8-11. To configure a FrontPage discussion, display the properties of the HTML form that visitors use for posting.

note A SharePoint team Web site provides discussion lists that are both richer in function and easier to manage than lists managed by the Discussion Form Handler. If you have access to a Web server running SharePoint Team Services, be sure to investigate those facilities before implementing any discussions that use the Discussion Form Handler.

A Customer Support Web also includes two Web search facilities:

Chapter 8: Creating Web Sites with Templates and Wizards

● The *search.htm* page searches the entire FrontPage-based Web and displays a clickable list of pages that contain a given string.

● The *cususrch.htm* page searches only the *_cusudi* folder for a given string and again displays a clickable list of matching pages.

The *_cusudi* folder contains the table of contents and all posted articles for the Support Forum. To verify this, look at the Directory field in the Options For Discussion Form Handler dialog box, shown previously in Figure 8-11.

Because it's entirely controlled by FrontPage, the *_cusudi* folder is normally hidden. To make it visible, choose Web Settings from the Tools menu, click the Advanced tab, and make sure the option titled Show Hidden Files And Folders is selected.

You can add a Web Search facility to any Web by following this procedure:

1 Set the insertion point in any open page.

2 Choose Web Component from the Insert menu.

3 Choose Web Search from the Component Type list, and then click Finish.

4 A dialog box similar to the one shown in Figure 8-12 appears. Review the default options, and change anything that seems inappropriate.

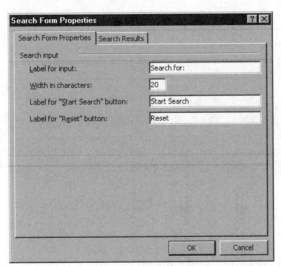

Figure 8-12.   This dialog box configures the Web Search component when Microsoft Indexing Service is available on the Web server.

5 To expand or limit the range of pages to search, click the Search Results tab. In Figure 8-13 on the next page, for example, Scope Of Search Results is set to the *_cusudi* directory.

This tab also controls the number of hits to display on each results page, the maximum number of hits to present, and the fields displayed for each page.

227

6 Click OK.

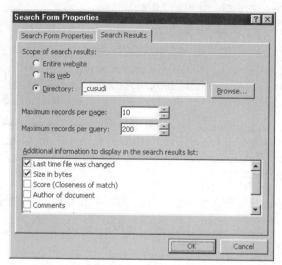

Figure 8-13. The Search Results tab controls the range of the search and the format of the results.

> For more information about the Web Search component, refer to Chapter 28, "Providing a Text Search Capability."

Troubleshooting

Search Form Properties dialog box shows fewer properties

When you display the properties of a Web Search component, you might see a dialog box that shows fewer properties than the one shown in Figure 8-12 and Figure 8-13. The versions shown appear only if all the following are true:

- You must be using a server-based Web.
- The Web server must be running the following software:
  - Windows NT Server 4.0, Internet Information Server 4.0, and Microsoft Index Server; or
  - Windows 2000, Internet Information Services 5.0, and Microsoft Indexing Service; or later versions.
- Microsoft Index Server or Microsoft Indexing Service, as applicable, must be configured to index the current Web.

If any of these conditions are false, FrontPage performs Web searches using its own indexes and cross-references. This type of search has fewer features than Microsoft Indexing Service, and its dialog box therefore displays fewer options.

Using the Personal Web Template

This template always contains the same six pages: those shown in the Navigation pane of Figure 8-14. FrontPage arranges these pages in Navigation view and formats them with a theme. Each page contains a Page Banner component, two Link Bar Based On Navigation Structure components (one at the left side and one at the bottom of the page), a Hit Counter component, a Weather component, and a Date And Time component. However, the pages don't use shared borders.

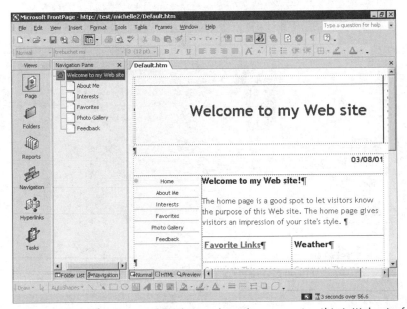

Figure 8-14. The Personal Web template always creates this initial set of pages.

The home page contains a Hit Counter component that records and reports the number of times visitors display it. The home page and, for the matter, most of the other pages also contain links to various Microsoft Web sites such as Search With MSN, Travel With Expedia, Read The Latest News With MSNBC, MSN People And Chat, CarPoint.com, and MSN Money Central.

newfeature! With two exceptions, the rest of the pages in this template consist of ordinary HTML. The first exception occurs in the Photo Gallery page, which contains, as you might suspect, a Photo Gallery component. Follow this procedure to add or delete photos:

1 Open the Web you created with the Personal Web template.

2 Open the *photo.htm* page in Page view.

3 Right-click anywhere in the Photo Gallery area (which is quite large and occupies the center of the page), and choose Photo Gallery Properties from the shortcut menu.

4 When the Photo Gallery Properties page shown in Figure 8-15 appears, use the Add, Edit, and Remove buttons to modify the list of pictures.

Figure 8-15. This dialog box adds, modifies, deletes, rearranges, and annotates pictures in a Photo Gallery.

Use of the Photo Gallery component isn't limited to Webs created with the Personal Web template. FrontPage can add Photo Galleries to any page or Web.

> **For more information about the Photo Gallery component, refer to Chapter 22, "Using FrontPage Photo Galleries".**

The page that might require special attention is the Feedback page, the top portion of which appears in Figure 8-16. This is an HTML form that saves its data, by default, to a file named *feedback.txt*, which is located in the *_private* folder of your Web. The form works by using the Save Results Web component.

Chapter 8: Creating Web Sites with Templates and Wizards

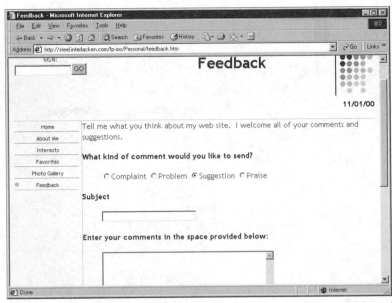

Figure 8-16. This HTML form collects comments from Web visitors and transmits them to the Web server for later viewing.

To view the comments, you'll need to download this file or display it as plain text in your browser. To clear out the file and start over, simply delete it from your Web.

Follow this procedure to change the name or location of the *_private/feedback.txt* file:

1 Open the Web you created with the Personal Web template.

2 Open the *feedback.htm* page in Page view.

3 Right-click anywhere in the HTML form, and choose Form Properties from the shortcut menu.

4 When the Form Properties dialog box shown in Figure 8-17 on the next page appears, overtype the path and file name in the Send To File Name box. Click OK.

The Form Properties dialog box can also direct form results to an e-mail address or to a database. Click the Options button to configure the details of any Save Results format. Figure 8-17 on the next page shows the options for saving form input as text.

The Save Results component works only on Web servers that have SharePoint Team Services or the FrontPage Server Extensions installed. This is because the program that writes the data to disk runs on the Web server and comes as part of the server extensions. (Remember, SharePoint Team Services includes the server extensions.)

Chapter 8

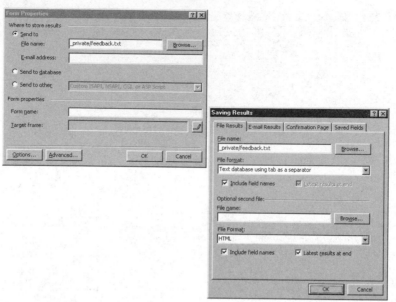

Figure 8-17. These dialog boxes configure how the Web server saves data that Web visitors submit with the HTML form shown in Figure 8-16.

The Save Results program that actually saves the data runs neither as part of the FrontPage desktop software nor on the Web visitor's browser. This explains why you can't test this component by switching FrontPage to Preview mode or by loading the Web page into your browser from a disk location.

> For more information about saving HTML form data as a disk file or sending it as mail, refer to Chapter 32, "Processing Data Submitted from Forms." For more information about saving HTML form data in a database, refer to "Saving Form Results to a Database" on page 917.

Using the Project Web Template

Creating a Web with this template creates the Web pages and supporting files visible in the Folder List shown in Figure 8-18. If you click the Navigation tab at the bottom of the Folder List, you'll see seven of these pages diagrammed in Navigation view. The home page and the six pages listed in the Link Bars component at the left of the *default.htm* Web page use shared borders, page banners, and Link Bar Based On Navigation Structure components. A theme governs the Web's appearance.

The Home, Members, Schedule, Status, and Archive pages consist of ordinary HTML. The template creates some, but not all, of the pages that these pages reference. Because this Web consists of sample pages only, you'd probably delete the missing pages anyway.

The Search and Discussions pages both use Web components that work only on Web servers that have SharePoint Team Services or the FrontPage Server Extensions installed.

Chapter 8: Creating Web Sites with Templates and Wizards

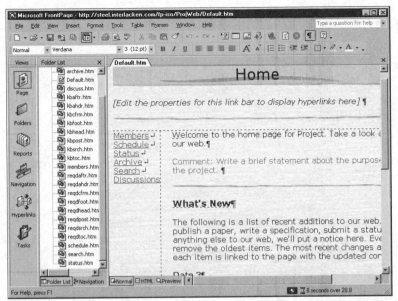

Figure 8-18. The Project Web template creates the pages shown in this Folder List.

This is because both pages call programs that run on the Web server, not within the Web visitor's browser, and not within the FrontPage desktop software.

The first of these is the Search page shown in Figure 8-19.

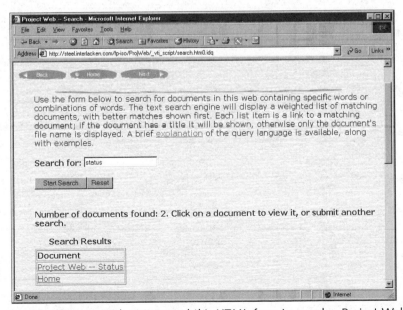

Figure 8-19. A Web visitor used this HTML form to search a Project Web for the word *status*. The Web Search component located the matching pages listed at the bottom of the window.

To obtain this display, the Web visitor entered the search term *status* and then clicked the Start Search button. The Web Search component responded with clickable hyperlinks to two Web pages that contain this word. This is the same Web Search facility described in "Using the Customer Support Web Template" earlier in this chapter.

> For more information about the Web Search component, refer to Chapter 28, "Providing a Text Search Capability."

The Discussions page has links to two threaded discussions managed by the Discussion Form Handler component. This is the same component described earlier this chapter in the section titled "Customer Support Web." The Project Web template creates two discussions controlled respectively by the *reqdpost.htm* and *kbpost.htm* pages.

SharePoint team Web sites outclass Project Webs in almost every respect. This is because a SharePoint team Web site stores any data it collects as database records and not, like a Project Web, as lines of HTML code. Information stored in a database is much easier to leverage for other purposes than data stored in HTML format.

> For more information about SharePoint team Web sites, refer to Chapter 35, "Using SharePoint Team Web Sites."

Using Web Site Wizards

The difference between wizards and templates is that wizards prompt you for information and then customize their output. Some of these wizards display quite a few prompts and thus produce quite variable results.

Reprinting these prompts and explaining the effect of each choice would produce a rather boring series of chapters with little practical use. Most of the prompts are intuitive and very well explained by the on-screen and help text. Also, you can always delete the resulting Web and try running the wizard again until you get the Web you want. Finally, it's fairly rare to use a Web that's produced by a wizard, unless you make major changes to it. As a result, there's no incentive to obsess about the exact results a wizard produces.

Using the Corporate Presence Wizard

Nowadays the rush by corporations to establish a presence on the Web is largely over. Most corporations already have a Web site—probably one with thousands or tens of thousands of pages. Even for new companies the procedure seems to be:

1 Find a domain name you can register.

2 Pick the name of the company.

3 Build a Web site.

4 Get your venture capital.

Chapter 8: Creating Web Sites with Templates and Wizards

This makes the Corporate Presence Wizard less useful than it once might have been. However, this wizard produces a Web with more FrontPage features than any other wizard or template. Chapter 6 provides a brief introduction to this Web, and the Corporate Presence Wizard and its resulting Web appear in Figure 6-4, Figure 6-8, Figure 6-9, and Figure 6-10.

> **For more information about the Corporate Presence Wizard, refer to "Creating a FrontPage-Based Web for New Content" on page 149.**

The Corporate Presence Wizard produces a variable number of pages based on how you answer its prompts. If you select all the features, a Corporate Presence Web includes these FrontPage features:

- Navigation view includes all pages in this Web.

- A theme controls the appearance of all pages in this Web.

- Shared borders add uniform content to all pages in this Web, including:

    - Page Banner components.

    - Link Bar Based On Navigation Structure components.

    - A page footer that includes Substitution components and a Date And Time component.

- A Feedback page that accumulates comments from Web visitors in a text file. This page uses the same techniques as the feedback form produced by the Personal Web Template.

- A Table of Contents page for the current Web.

- A Search page that searches the Corporate Presence Web. This uses the same technique as the search form that the Project Web template creates.

- A variable number of static Web pages for press releases, products, and services.

Substitution components are useful for displaying changeable names, addresses, titles, or other text that appears on multiple pages. Using a Substitution component is a two-step process:

1 Create a site parameter for each name, phrase, or other text string that's used in several places but subject to change. To create a site parameter:

    a Choose Web Settings from the Tools menu.

    b Click the Parameters tab. Figure 8-20 on the next page shows the Parameters tab of the Web Settings dialog box.

    c Use the Add, Modify, and Remove buttons to create, update, or delete site parameters.

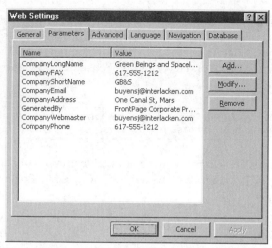

Figure 8-20. This dialog box maintains a list of site parameters that
any page in the same Web can display by name.

For more information about site parameters, refer to "Using Web Parameters and the Substitution Component" on page 762.

2 To display a site parameter value in a Web page, insert a Substitution
component as follows:

a Set the insertion point where you want the value to appear.

b Choose Web Component from the Insert menu.

c Choose Included Content from the Component Type list.

d Choose Substitution from the Choose A Type Of Content list.

e When the Substitution Properties dialog box shown in Figure 8-21
appears, select the name of the site parameter you want to display.

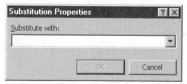

Figure 8-21. A Substitution component displays the value of a given
site parameter.

f After you click OK, FrontPage will display the site parameter's value. If
you later change the site parameter's value, FrontPage will update all
the pages in your Web that use it.

For more information about site parameters and the Substitution component, refer to "Using
Web Parameters and the Substitution Component" on page 762.

Understanding Static, Dynamic, and Data-Driven Web Pages

A *static* Web page is one that doesn't change unless you change its HTML code, one of its pictures, or some other aspect of its content. These were the earliest sort of pages used on the Web. The designer coded them, the visitors looked at them, and that was that. The WYSIWYG editor in Page view is an excellent tool for creating static pages.

A *dynamic* Web page is one that modifies itself. A dynamic Web page might, for example, change its own appearance based on the date, on the capabilities of the Web visitor's browser, or on actions taken by the visitor. Creating such pages generally requires writing scripts that modify the page while it's loading or after it's already on display. (Scripts are short blocks of program code written in languages such as JavaScript and Visual Basic.)

on the CD For more information about scripts, refer to Chapter 42, "Working with Script Code, in the Bonus Content on the Companion CD."

FrontPage includes Web components that create many dynamic effects without requiring any programming on your part. By providing full access to the HTML code, FrontPage also supports development of custom dynamic effects.

> For more information about creating dynamic Web pages, refer to Chapter 24, "Enhancing Web Pages with Animation."

A *data-driven* Web page is essentially a template for displaying information from another source. That source could be a simple text file, an XML file, or almost anything else, but the most common source is a database. Based on form values from the Web visitor, lookup values coded in hyperlinks, the date, the time, or some other factor, a program retrieves the correct data values, merges them into the data-driven Web page, and sends the resulting HTML to the visitor's browser for display and further action.

FrontPage can build Web pages that add, modify, delete, and display database information in a variety of ways. Of course, the more you want the Web page to change depending on data, the more likely it is that you'll need to work with both the HTML code and the program code yourself.

> For more information about building Web pages that interact with databases, refer to Part 10, "Using Forms and Databases."

The Table of Contents page from a typical Corporate Presence Web appears in Figure 8-22. A so-called Table Of Contents For This Web Site component derives the page names, their organization, and the hyperlink location from analysis of hyperlinks, not, as you might expect, from the Web's Navigation structure.

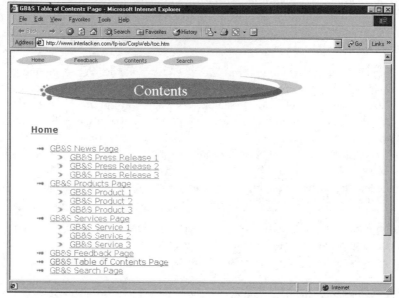

Figure 8-22. A Table Of Contents component automatically built the list of links in the center of this Web page.

Here's how to view the configuration of the Table Of Contents For This Web Site component in the Corporate Presence Web:

1 Open the Corporate Presence Web in FrontPage.

2 Open the *toc.htm* page in Page view.

3 Locate the Table Of Contents component in the center of the page. (By default, it should read "Table of Contents Heading Page.") Right-click it, and choose Table Of Contents Properties from the shortcut menu. In Figure 8-23, the Table Of Contents component is highlighted in the background window.

4 Use the Table Of Contents Properties dialog box shown in the foreground of Figure 8-23 to configure these options:

■ **Page URL For Starting Point Of Table.** In this box, type the name of the page that will furnish the top-level entries for the table of contents. Each hyperlink in the page you specify here will become a top-level entry in the table of contents, provided the hyperlink points within the current Web.

Chapter 8: Creating Web Sites with Templates and Wizards

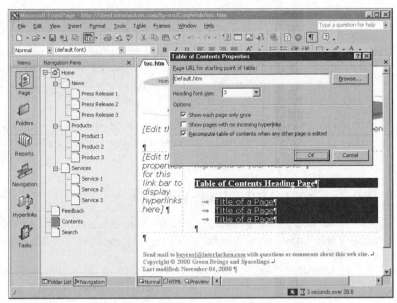

Figure 8-23. This dialog box configures the Table Of Contents component shown in Figure 8-22.

- **Heading Font Size.** To control the size of the title text, select one of the drop-down list entries provided. The choices are none (no heading) and 1 through 6 (largest through smallest).

- **Show Each Page Only Once.** Select this box if you want to suppress multiple instances of the same page. If several pages hyperlink to the same target page, the table of contents will display only the target page under the first page that links to it.

  Clear the box if you want the table of contents to display all links to all pages.

- **Show Pages With No Incoming Hyperlinks.** Select this box if you want the table of contents to include any "orphan" pages in your Web (that is, any pages that aren't the target of hyperlinks from other pages).

- **Recompute Table Of Contents When Any Other Page Is Edited.** Select this box if you want FrontPage to regenerate the table of contents whenever you edit and save any page in the current Web. This means the table of contents will always be up to date, but every Save operation will take longer to complete.

  To save time when saving pages, clear this check box. Then, whenever you think the table of contents has changed, either open and save the page that contains it or choose Recalculate Hyperlinks from the Tools menu.

For more information about Table Of Contents components, refer to Chapter 27, "Displaying Derived Content."

The Corporate Presence Wizard creates a separate Web page for each product or service. This approach offers initial simplicity, but it seldom scales very well. If your business has hundreds, thousands, or tens of thousands of salable items, you should almost certainly use a database to put your catalog on line. That way, all the pages will be uniform, and you can keep them up to date by synchronizing the catalog database with your internal business systems.

Be all that as it may, the Corporate Presence Wizard can still be useful when starting a new corporate site. It also provides several good examples of ways to use Web components.

newfeature!
Using the Database Interface Wizard

Unlike most Web templates and wizards, this one doesn't create a new sample Web. Instead, it creates up to three special Web pages that perform the following functions:

- A page named *new.asp* displays an HTML form that collects values from the Web visitor and uses them to add one record to a database.

- A page named *view.asp* displays the contents of a database as a tabular listing.

- A page named *database_editor.asp* displays a selection list of records in a database. It can also add, display, modify, and delete individual records.

Figure 8-24 shows a new Web created by the Database Interface Wizard. The *new.asp* and *view.asp* pages are in a folder named *guestbk_interface/results*. The *database_editor.asp* page and a number of support pages are buried even deeper in a folder called *guestbk_interface/results/editor*. This structure minimizes the chance that adding a database interface to an existing Web will overwrite or interfere with any existing pages. The prefix *guestbk* represents the name of the database connection, which is something you designate when running the wizard. (This convention makes it easy to accommodate multiple database interfaces in the same Web.)

In the case of Figure 8-24, FrontPage created not only the Web pages in the *guestbk_interface* folder but the database as well. The new database is named *guestbk.mdb*, it is a Microsoft Access database, and it resides in a folder named *fpdb*. The Database Interface Wizard can also connect to existing Access databases, to Microsoft SQL Server, to Oracle, and to other database systems that support Open Database Connectivity (ODBC).

The *new.asp* page is shown in Figure 8-25. To add a record to the database, the Web visitor fills in the text boxes, selects an option, and clicks OK. You can select more or fewer fields, different fields, different storage formats, and different form field types while running the wizard. The *new.asp* page uses the Save Results To Database component. Therefore, as soon as the page exists, you can add or remove form fields, replace controls with different types, change the values assigned to radio buttons and drop-down lists, and change the page's overall appearance very easily.

Chapter 8: Creating Web Sites with Templates and Wizards

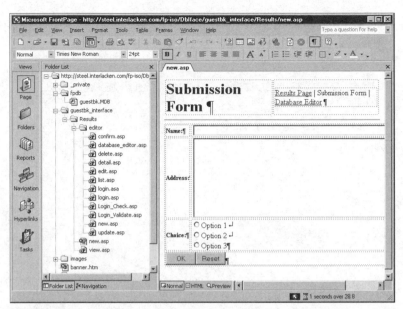

Figure 8-24. The Database Interface component creates a Web page like this one for adding records to the database.

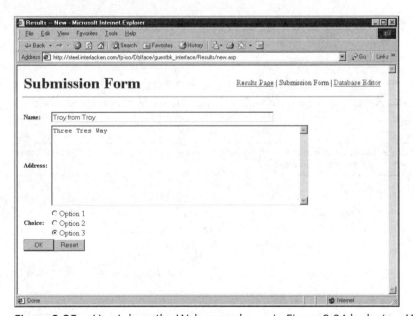

Figure 8-25. Here's how the Web page shown in Figure 8-24 looks to a Web visitor.

For more information about the Save Results To Database component, refer to "Saving Form Results to a Database" on page 917.

241

Figure 8-26 shows typical results from the *view.asp* page. This page basically lists the contents of the database. The *view.asp* page is a standard implementation of the Database Results component supplied with FrontPage.

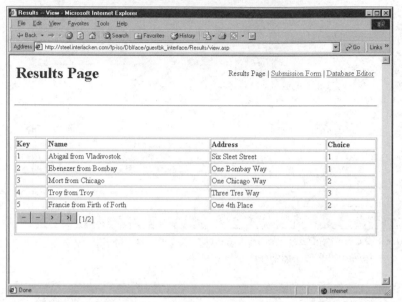

Figure 8-26. The Database Interface Wizard creates this Web page for viewing the contents of a database.

The Database Results component has a powerful wizard of its own that can add and remove fields, change the sort order, change the number of lines listed on each page, reformat the page, and so forth.

> **For more information about saving form results to a database, refer to "Saving Form Results to a Database" on page 917.**

The Database Editor page is a frames page with two frames. The upper frame provides record selection, and the lower frame provides record processing. In Figure 8-27, for example, the Web visitor clicked the hyperlink for record 4 in the upper frame and received a display of that record in the lower frame.

Here are the procedures for using the Database Editor to view, add, update, and delete records:

- To add a record, click the Add New Record button in the upper frame, fill in the resulting HTML form, and click OK.

- To view a record, locate its entry in the upper frame and click the listed Key value.

Chapter 8: Creating Web Sites with Templates and Wizards

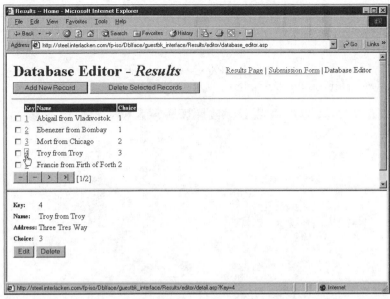

Figure 8-27. The Database Editor can locate, display, add, modify, and delete records from a database.

- To update a record, display it as just described and then click the Edit button. Overtype the fields you need to change, and then click OK.

- There are two ways to delete records:

  - Display the record as previously described, and then click the Delete button.

  - In the upper frame, select the check boxes in front of each record you want to delete, and then click the Delete Selected Records button.

Here's the procedure for running the Database Interface Wizard and adding these capabilities to a new or existing Web:

1 If you want to add a set of Database Interface pages to an existing Web, open that Web. Otherwise, just start FrontPage.

2 Choose New from the File menu, and then choose Page Or Web.

3 When the New Page Or Web task pane appears, click either Empty Web or Web Site Templates. This displays the dialog box shown earlier in Figure 8-2.

4 In the list of possible Web types, choose Database Interface Wizard.

5 If you're adding Database Interface components to the Web you opened in step 1, select the Add To Current Web check box, and click OK.

If you're creating a new Web, enter its drive letter and path, UNC path, or Web address in the box titled Specify The Location Of The New Web, and then click OK. FrontPage creates the new Web and opens it.

6 When step 5 is finished, FrontPage starts the Database Interface Wizard, which displays the dialog box shown in Figure 8-28.

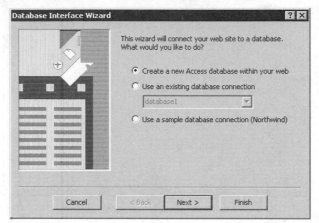

Figure 8-28. The Database Interface Wizard begins by asking what database to use.

Note the following options in this wizard dialog box:

■ **Create A New Access Database Within Your Web.** Creates a new Access database. This database will contain fields you specify in subsequent dialog boxes.

■ **Use An Existing Database Connection.** Tells the wizard to create Database Interface pages using a database connection already defined within the current Web. Select the connection from those listed in the accompanying list box. If the current Web has no database connections (as a new Web never will), this option will be dimmed.

■ **Use A Sample Database Connection (Northwind).** Adds the Northwind Traders database to the current Web and creates a connection to it. This is a sample Access database that is widely used for instructional purposes.

To follow this procedure, choose Create A New Access Database Within Your Web, and then click Next.

Chapter 8: Creating Web Sites with Templates and Wizards

7 Using the dialog box shown in Figure 8-29, the wizard next prompts for a name to give the new database connection. This name will end up being part of a directory name that appears in URLs, so a short, meaningful, lowercase name is best. To follow this procedure, enter the name *guestdb*, and then click Next.

Figure 8-29. A database connection is a named, saved pathway to a database. This prompt assigns a name to the database connection that the pages in a Database Interface will use.

8 The dialog box shown in Figure 8-30 controls what columns the new database will contain, the format of each column in the database, and the type of form element to use on input forms.

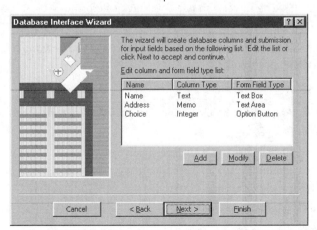

Figure 8-30. This dialog box creates or selects the fields (columns) the Database Interface pages will use.

note What most people call fields, database experts call columns. Humor them.

245

In this dialog box, you can do the following:

- To add a column, click the Add button, and specify a column name, column type, and form field type.

- To change the definition of a column, select the column you want to change, then click the Modify button, and then change the column name, column type, and form field type as required.

- To remove a column, select it, and then click the Delete button.

For this example, just take the defaults, and click Next. When the wizard alerts you that the connection has been established, click Next again.

9 At this point the wizard will create the database and then use the dialog box shown in Figure 8-31 to ask which Database Interface pages you want. Select the check box for each page you want, and then click Next. This procedure assumes that you want all three pages.

Frequently Asked Questions About the Database Interface Wizard

What operating environment do Database Interface pages require?

Because they're ASP pages, the *new.asp*, *view.asp*, and *database_editor.asp* pages work only on Microsoft Web servers that support Active Server Pages. Generally, this means Internet Information Server 4.0 or Internet Information Services 5.0 (both known as IIS). The server also needs to have Microsoft Data Access Component (MDAC) drivers compatible with the database types and version you want to access.

Why won't Database Interface pages work in FrontPage preview mode or when loaded from a disk-based Web?

Neither of these environments meets the requirements stated above.

Where does FrontPage store the username and password that provides access to the Database Editor page?

FrontPage keeps these values in a text file named *<database>_interface/results /editor/login.asa* where *<database>* is the name you entered in the dialog box of Figure 8-29. If you forget the password or need to change it, open this file.

Extraneous Link bars and page banners are showing up in Database Editor. Why?

You probably have shared borders turned on for the current Web. The Database Editor uses a frames page and, unfortunately, shared borders and frames pages don't live well together. This is because the shared borders show up in every page that's loaded into any frame. The only solution is to open each offending target page and override its default shared border settings.

Chapter 8: Creating Web Sites with Templates and Wizards

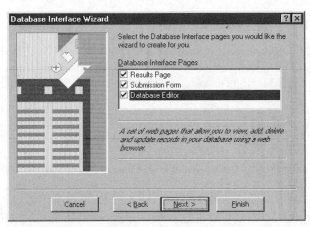

Figure 8-31. The Database Interface Wizard can create any combination of its three basic pages.

10 If you told the wizard to create a Database Editor page in step 9, the wizard displays the prompt shown in Figure 8-32. If you want to password-protect the Database Editor page, enter the username and password that the Web visitor (presumably you) will need to know. You'll need to enter the password twice and enter it the same both times.

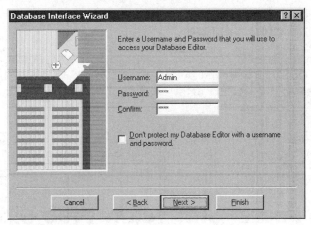

Figure 8-32. Because the Database Editor provides full access to every field in a database, the Database Interface Wizard can protect it with a password.

If you don't want to password-protect the Database Editor page, select the check box titled Don't Protect My Database Editor With A Username And Password.

11 Click Next to display a final confirmation page, and then click Finish.

> **For more information about the Database Interface Wizard, refer to the sidebar "Using the Database Interface Wizard" on page 947.**

Using the Discussion Web Wizard

This wizard adds a FrontPage discussion to a new or existing Web. The Support Forum described earlier in this chapter in connection with the Customer Support Web is typical of discussions created by the Discussion Web Wizard as well.

Like the Database Interface Wizard, the Discussion Web Wizard slips fairly easily into an existing Web. It won't overwrite your home page or replace your navigation structure, for example.

Discussions created by this wizard use the Discussion Form Handler, which handles new posts by updating a series of static Web pages. Facilities to sort, filter, and download postings are limited. There are no system-level facilities to delete old or objectionable postings, or to otherwise manage discussions. To perform such functions, you need to manually edit or delete the Web pages that the Discussion Form Handler updates.

Discussion lists in a SharePoint team Web site are more powerful, more flexible, and more manageable by far than FrontPage discussions. If your Web server runs (or could run) SharePoint Team Services, this is a strong option to consider.

 For more information about discussion sites, refer to Chapter 39, "Discussion Webs and Self-Registration," in the Bonus Content on the Companion CD.

Using the Import Web Wizard

This wizard creates a new Web and then imports pages from an existing Web. Chapter 6 has already described both of these operations and, as a consequence, there's not much more to say here. If you need to run these two functions in sequence, the Import Web Wizard will save you a step.

For more information about creating a new Web, refer to "Creating a FrontPage-Based Web for New Content" on page 149. For more information about the Import Web Wizard, refer to "Importing Web Pages" on page 166.

Creating a SharePoint Team Web Site

If your Web server has SharePoint Team Services installed, you can use FrontPage to create—and to some extent modify—SharePoint team Web sites. Chapter 1 and Chapter 5 have already introduced these features. Chapters 35 and 38 provide extensive coverage on using and administering both SharePoint Team Services itself and team Web sites.

Installing SharePoint Team Services on a Web server installs the FrontPage Server Extensions, additional SharePoint Team Services software, and a team Web site that resides in

Chapter 8: Creating Web Sites with Templates and Wizards

the server's root Web. However, it's unlikely that one SharePoint team Web site will serve the needs of all the projects, departments, teams, and task forces in your organization. More likely, each of these entities will want a site of its own. Fortunately, the process of creating a SharePoint team Web site is very simple:

1 Start FrontPage.

2 Choose New from the File menu, and then choose Page Or Web.

3 When the New Page Or Web task pane appears, click Web Site Templates.

4 When the Web Site Templates dialog box appears, choose SharePoint-based Team Web Site from the list of possible Web types.

5 In the box titled Specify The Location Of The New Web, enter the Web address the new team Web site will occupy. This must be a folder on a Web server running SharePoint Team Services. If it isn't, you'll get the error message shown in Figure 8-33.

Figure 8-33. You can create a SharePoint team Web site only on a server running SharePoint Team Services. Otherwise, this error message appears.

Figure 8-34 on the next page shows the structure of a new SharePoint team Web site. The *Lists* folder contains subfolders for each list, survey, or discussion. The *Shared Documents* folder contains the forms that process document libraries.

The Web pages that control a SharePoint team Web site are complex and contain many special elements used by SharePoint Team Services. You should therefore exercise extreme care when making changes to these pages. Change the appearance of the pages if you want, but not their underlying structure.

Web pages control most aspects of a SharePoint team Web site. Clicking the Create option on the home page, for example, displays the Web page shown in Figure 8-35, also on the next page. This page has options to create a new custom list, document library, survey, or discussion board. It can also creates these standard kinds of lists: links, announcements, contacts, events, and tasks. Finally, it can upload and import a list already created in Microsoft Excel format.

Part 3: Creating Web Sites Automatically

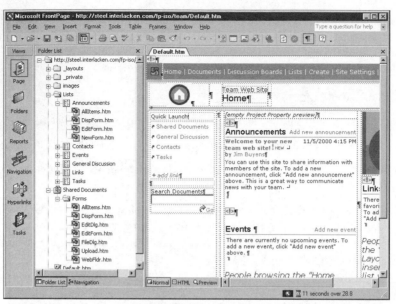

Figure 8-34. The SharePoint-based Team Web site Wizard produces this collection of rather complex pages. For the most part, you should use these pages "as is."

Figure 8-35. A SharePoint team Web site provides its own Web-based features for adding and maintaining lists and document libraries.

Clicking the Site Settings option on the home page displays the Site Settings Web page shown in Figure 8-36.

Chapter 8: Creating Web Sites with Templates and Wizards

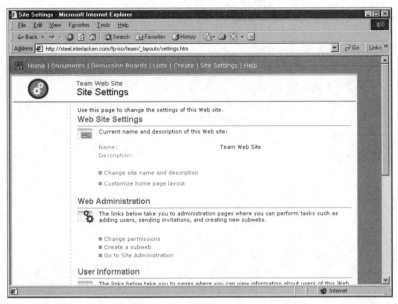

Figure 8-36. This page controls most settings that configure the daily operation of a SharePoint team Web site.

This page provides the following groups of options:

- **Web Site Settings.** These options change the current site's name, its description, and the layout of the home page.

- **Web Administration.** These options add new participants to the current site, send e-mail invitations to participate in the site, and create new subwebs.

- **User Information.** The options under this heading display information about users of the current site and provide ways for users to change information about themselves.

- **Modify Site Content.** Not visible in the figure is this group of options, which change the design of a list, document library, discussion board, or survey.

> For more information about SharePoint Team Services and team Web sites, refer to Chapter 35, "Using SharePoint Team Web Sites."

In Summary...

This chapter explained how to create FrontPage-based Webs using the templates and wizards that FrontPage supplies. Reviewing the resulting Webs also showed how many FrontPage features fit together.

The next chapter explains how to create, open, and save individual Web pages.

Part 4

Editing Basic Page Content

Creating, Opening, Saving, and Deleting Web Pages

Performing basic file operations on Web pages is a mundane but necessary task. Without the ability to save and reopen work, the value of your work would be fleeting indeed.

File operations in Microsoft FrontPage parallel those in most other Microsoft Windows applications, and especially those of other Microsoft Office applications. Still, with their ability to read and open Web pages over the Internet, to create new preformatted Web pages, to save and manipulate files in FrontPage-based Webs, and to detect and save unsaved Web page components, the basic FrontPage file features are worth a look.

This chapter doesn't address filling new Web pages with content. For that, skip forward to the next chapter.

Creating a New Web Page

New Page

If you can click an icon, you can create a new Web page. All you need to do is simply start FrontPage, click the New Page button on the Standard toolbar, and FrontPage displays a blank Web page ready to receive text, pictures, or anything else you care to toss in.

255

Figure 9-1 illustrates the default, blank Web page, ready for input.

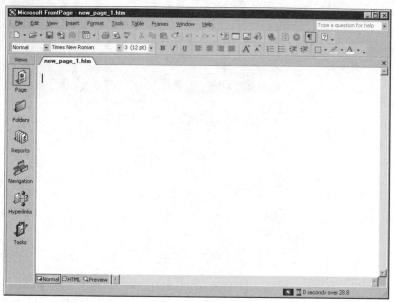

Figure 9-1. FrontPage presents a new, blank Web page, ready to receive content.

Entering text, inserting pictures, creating hyperlinks, and other tasks are the topics of subsequent chapters. If you feel the need to learn about these things right away, feel free to skip ahead and return here later. Regardless, clicking the New Page toolbar button is far from the only way to create new Web pages. Here's the complete list:

- **Use the New Page button on the Standard toolbar.** This is the method just described. It always creates an empty Web page.

- **Use the Keyboard. Press Ctrl+N.** This works exactly like pressing the New Page button on the Standard toolbar.

- **Use the Right Mouse Button.** This creates a new page in any view except Tasks or Reports view. Here are the steps:

  1 Right-click a folder icon or a blank space in any folder or file list.

  2 Choose New and then choose Page from the shortcut menu.

  This method always creates a normal, empty Web page.

newfeature! **Use the New Page Or Web task pane.** This creates a blank page or a way to choose a page template:

  1 Choose New from the File menu.

  2 Choose Page Or Web. The New Page Or Web task pane shown in Figure 9-2 appears.

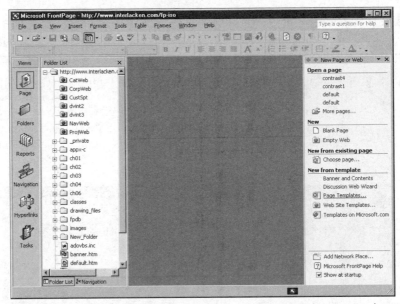

Figure 9-2. Click Blank Page to create a new empty Web page, and click Page Templates to display the Page Templates dialog box shown in Figure 9-3.

3 Do either of the following:

◆ Click Blank Page to create a new blank page; or

◆ Click Page Templates to create a page with preformatted content, a frames page, or a cascading style sheet file.

● **Display the New Page button's menu on the Standard toolbar and choose Page.** This method creates pages using a variety of page templates including standard pages with preformatted content, frames pages with various arrangements, and cascading style sheet files. Here's the procedure:

1 Click the drop-down arrow next to the New Page button on the Standard toolbar.

2 Choose Page.

---

tip To display one of several pages open in Page view, click its tab above the Page view window, choose it from the Window menu, or press Ctrl+Tab.

In all views except Page view (discussed shortly) and Tasks view (where you create new tasks rather than new Web pages), creating a new Web page means creating an HTML file in the current folder, giving the file a default name, and leaving the file name ready for renaming. FrontPage *doesn't* switch to Page view and open the new file; for that, you have to double-click or otherwise open the new file yourself.

257

> **tip** Remember, if you haven't opened a Web, the viewing options—Folders view, Reports view, Navigation view, Hyperlinks view, and Tasks view—won't be available.

In Page view, clicking the New Page toolbar icon immediately creates and displays a new blank page. The last two methods—via New on the File menu and via the New Page menu on the Standard toolbar—also display a new page ready for editing but only after presenting the opportunity (or nuisance, depending on your mood) to select a choice of templates. The dialog box showing all the available templates appears in Figure 9-3.

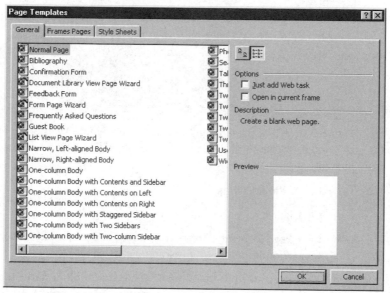

Figure 9-3. This dialog box offers a choice of types and formats for initializing new Web pages.

The tabs at the top of the left pane divide the templates into three categories:

- **General.** This tab provides a list of currently available page templates. Single-clicking any template selects it, displays its description in the Description frame at the right of the dialog box, and displays a visual preview in the Preview frame.

  If you don't know what template or wizard to choose, select Normal Page. This produces a blank page with no special features or attributes.

> For information about creating your own Web page templates, refer to "Creating Custom Templates" on page 471.

- **Frames Pages.** This tab works much like the General tab, except that the listed templates create frames pages.

Chapter 9

For information about frames pages, refer to Chapter 17, "Using Frames for Page Layout."

- **Style Sheets.** This tab initializes a Cascading Style Sheet (CSS) file. Such files have a *.css* filename extension and contain instructions for overriding the appearance of standard HTML elements such as normal paragraph, heading 1, table heading, and table cell. CSS files can also define custom styles. Any number of Web pages can reference the same CSS file and thus assume a common appearance.

For more information about style sheet files, refer to Chapter 20, "Managing Appearance with Cascading Style Sheets."

Other useful options appear on the right side of the New dialog box:

- **Large Icons and List buttons.** Located above the Description frame, these change the format of the main selection window.

- **Just Add Web Task option.** This adds a task to the Task List rather than initializing a new page in Page view.

- **Open In Current Frame option.** This is available only if the active document in Page view is a frames page. Ignore this for now.

It's important to note that creating a new page in Page view *doesn't* create an actual Web file. It creates only an unsaved file, open for editing. To create the actual file, you must save it.

caution   If you create a new page in Page view and then close it without making any changes, FrontPage won't ask whether you want to save it. To save a new empty page, choose either Save or Save As from the File menu.

Editing an Existing Web Page

There are many ways to open a Web page for editing, and they vary somewhat depending on the view you're using. The following sections detail your options for each view.

Opening a Page from Page View

If you're starting from Page view, there are six ways to open a Web page:

- Choose Recent Files from the File menu. This displays a submenu of your most recently opened files. To open a specific file, just choose it from the Recent Files submenu.

- Locate the file in Page view's Folder List, and then double-click it or press Enter.

Remember, the Folder List is available only if you've opened a FrontPage-based Web. It won't be available if you're editing individual files (that is, if no Web is open).

● Locate the file in the Navigation pane, and then double-click it.

● In the Open A Page portion of the New Page Or Web task pane, click one of the four recent files or the More Pages link.

To display the New Page Or Web task pane, choose New from the File menu and then choose Page Or Web.

caution   You can't open a Web page by dragging it out of Folders view or the Navigation pane and dropping it onto an open Web page in Page view. That operation does something else: it modifies the open page by adding a hyperlink to the page you dragged.

● Right-click a hyperlink in a page that's already open, and then choose Follow Hyperlink from the shortcut menu. This opens the hyperlinked page in Page view.

● Use the Open File dialog box shown in Figure 9-4. There are three ways to do this:

■ Choose Open from the File menu.

■ Press Ctrl+O.

■ Click the Open button on the Standard toolbar.

Open

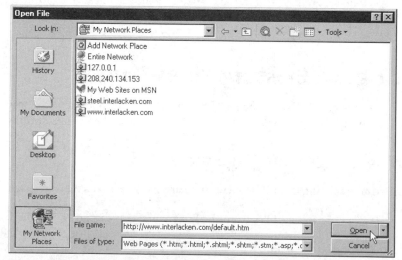

Figure 9-4.   The FrontPage Open File dialog box accepts either a local file location or the URL of a page on the Web.

The icons along the left of the Open File dialog box provide five ways to locate a Web page:

- **History.** Displays a list of recently opened Microsoft Office documents. To browse various categories of recent documents, click the drop-down arrow of the Look In list at the top of the dialog box.

- **My Documents** or **Personal.** Displays files in your computer's default File Save location. This icon is titled Personal on Microsoft Windows NT 4 computers and My Documents on all others.

- **Desktop.** Displays files visible from your Windows desktop. This includes files located within My Computer, My Documents, Network Neighborhood, My Briefcase, and so forth.

- **Favorites.** Displays the same choices you've configured Microsoft Internet Explorer's Favorites menu to display.

- **Web Folders** or **My Network Places.** Displays files located in a FrontPage-based Web. FrontPage builds up a list of server-based Webs as you access them. This icon is titled My Network Places on Microsoft Windows 2000 systems and Web Folders on all others.

No matter which place you choose to browse, selecting a file name enters it in the File Name box at the bottom center of the dialog box. The file name can be either a file location, such as *C:\My Documents\mypage.htm*, or a Web location, such as *http://www.interlacken.com/default.htm*. FrontPage opens file locations as Windows applications have been doing for years. It opens Web locations by reading the necessary files as a browser would.

> **tip** Don't forget the prefix *http://* when you enter a Web location. If you omit it, FrontPage tries to open the URL as if it were a local folder location.

If convenient, you can also enter file locations and Web locations by hand—that is, by typing or pasting them into the File Name box. In any event, when the file name is entered, the Open button becomes active, and clicking it tells FrontPage to open the file.

The Files Of Type drop-down menu works as in most Windows Open dialog boxes: it controls which filename extensions appear in the file listing. Table A-13 in Appendix A explains the remaining icons in the Open File dialog box toolbar.

 For more information about the Open File dialog box toolbar, refer to "The File Dialog Box Toolbar" in the Bonus Content on the Companion CD.

261

Opening a Page in a New Window

FrontPage normally creates one main window for each Web that you open. If you open several Web pages in the same Web, the pages are identified by tabs that appear along the top edge of the Page view document window. Figure 9-5 illustrates this arrangement.

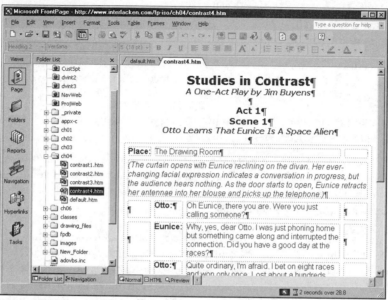

Figure 9-5. Two Web pages are open in this screen shot, but only one page is visible. To display either page, click the corresponding tab at the top of the document area.

To open multiple pages in the same Web and display them in separate main windows, follow these steps:

1 Open the Web that contains the two pages you want to open in separate windows.

2 Create a new window by choosing New Window from the Window menu.

3 Open one page in each window.

Figure 9-6 shows how this looks.

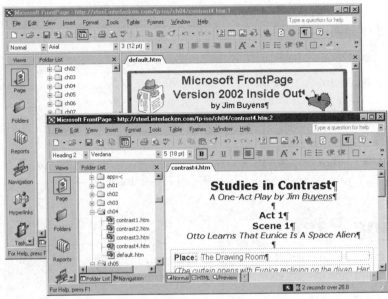

Figure 9-6. If you like, FrontPage can open pages from the same Web in different windows.

Opening a Page from Tasks View

Because Tasks view displays tasks, not Web files, the procedure for opening a file is unique. Do either of the following:

● Right-click a task that references the page, and then choose Start Task from the shortcut menu; or

● Select a task that references the page, choose Tasks from the Edit menu, and then choose Start Task.

For more information about Tasks view, refer to "Working with Tasks View" on page 964.

Opening a Page from Other Views

If you're starting from Folders view, Reports view, Navigation view, or Hyperlinks view, do any of the following to open a page:

- Double-click the file name or icon of the page you want to open.

- Right-click the file name or icon of the page you want to open, and then choose Open from the resulting shortcut menu.

- Select the file name or icon of the page you want to open, and then press Enter.

- Choose Open from the File menu or press Ctrl+O, and then open a page as you normally would in the Open File dialog box.

Saving Pages

If you fail to regularly save your files, all your hard work could be for naught. To save a file open in Page view, use one of the following methods:

- Choose Save from the File menu.

- Click the Save button on the Standard toolbar.

- Press Ctrl+S.

Save

If the Web page or any of its components weren't previously saved in the current Web, FrontPage displays Save As dialog boxes for them.

To save a page using another name, choose Save As from the File menu. The resulting dialog box is almost the same at the one that opens Web pages, with all the same options plus two:

- **Page Title.** Displays the name of the page in words. Although this is an optional field, for optimal user-friendliness, don't omit it. A page's title appears whenever a Web visitor browses the page, and in many FrontPage contexts.

- **Change Title.** Displays the page title in a Set Page Title dialog box so that you can change it. Click the Change Title button to display the dialog box. Figure 9-7 shows this facility in action.

As when opening files, the File Name location can be either on a local disk or file server, or within a FrontPage-based Web. If the specified Web isn't already open, FrontPage opens it.

Occasionally, when you save a Web page, FrontPage displays a Save Embedded Files dialog box like the one in Figure 9-8.

264

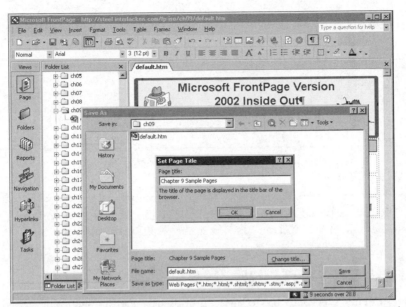

Figure 9-7. This is FrontPage's Save As dialog box with the Set Page Title dialog box also open.

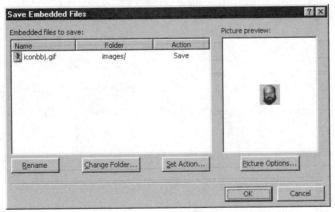

Figure 9-8. When Page view saves a Web page containing elements held only in memory, it displays this dialog box asking what to do with them.

This means Page view has an object in memory—in this case a picture pasted from the Clipboard—and FrontPage doesn't know where to save it. This also happens after using some of FrontPage's picture processing tools. The original picture might reside on disk but the modified version doesn't; FrontPage therefore has to ask where the modified version should go.

For more information about FrontPage's picture processing tools, refer to Chapter 21, "Editing Pictures in FrontPage."

To change the proposed Save properties for any file listed, first select the file, and then do any or all of the following:

- To change the name of the saved file, click the Rename button and edit the proposed name.

- To change the folder location of the saved file, click the Change Folder button and select a folder from the resulting dialog box.

> **tip** If a file's Folder column is blank, FrontPage saves the file in the same folder as the Web page itself.

- To change the action for the given file, click the Set Action button and select either Save or Don't Save from the resulting dialog box.

Deleting an Existing Web Page

Sooner or later, everybody has to carry out the garbage. Along with the successful pages you create and add to your Web site will be the inevitable failed experiments, schemes gone awry, and pages gone obsolete over time. There are three ways to delete a page. (You must be in Folders view, Reports view, Navigation view, or Hyperlinks view.) Do one of the following:

- Select the file name or icon by single-clicking it, and then press the Delete key.

- Select the file name or icon, and then choose Delete from the Edit menu.

- Right-click the file name or icon, and then select Delete from the shortcut menu.

In each case FrontPage will ask you to confirm the deletion before it permanently erases the page.

newfeature!
Saving and Opening Files in SharePoint Team Web Sites

If the current Web contains a SharePoint team Web site, you can open and save Web pages in the team Web site's shared document areas quite easily. Simply save them or look for them in the Web's *Shared Documents* folder. Figure 9-9 shows a SharePoint team Web site with one document library and three documents. The Folder List shows the contents of the *Shared Documents* folder.

> For more information about SharePoint team Web sites, refer to Chapter 35, "Using SharePoint Team Web Sites."

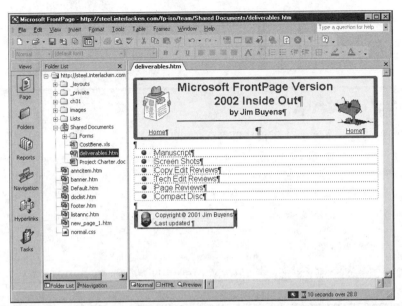

Figure 9-9. If a Web contains a SharePoint team Web site, the *Shared Documents* folder contains its shared document libraries.

The Save File and Open File dialog boxes can access SharePoint team Web sites directly. Figure 9-10, for example, shows the Open File dialog box preparing to open a file in a SharePoint team Web site. Because the *deliverables.htm* file (as indicated by its icon) was created in FrontPage, it opens in FrontPage. The other files open in the application that created them.

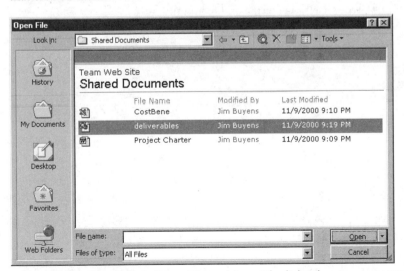

Figure 9-10. FrontPage's Open File and Save File dialog boxes can access shared documents in the familiar SharePoint team Web site manner.

267

The Save Dialog box provides a similar interface for saving files into a shared document library. In either case, be aware that you must open the library (that is, double-click it) before you can view or update its documents.

Troubleshooting

SharePoint team Web site panel appears by default

When a FrontPage-based Web contains a SharePoint team Web site, viewing that Web in an Open File or Save File dialog box might display the SharePoint team Web site interface by default. This overrides access to the Web's normal file structure.

Views

To view the normal file structure, locate the Views button on either the Open File or Save File dialog box toolbar, open the associated pull down menu, and choose any view other than WebView.

Alternatively, click the Views button repeatedly until the dialog box displays the view you want.

In Summary...

This chapter explained how to create, open, save, and delete Web pages, and explained the special features available when working with shared documents.

The next chapter is one of several concerned with adding content to Web pages. It particularly devotes itself to entering and formatting text.

Adding and Formatting Text

This chapter explains how to add text to a Web page. At one level this is a very simple task: just create a new Web page and start typing. Of course, more issues and more complexity arise when you start pasting text from other programs; formatting text with different fonts and paragraph styles; inserting symbols and special text elements; and finding, replacing, and checking the spelling of text. This chapter addresses those issues as well. Given that most Web pages consist mainly of text, this is an important chapter.

What you won't find here are instructions on page layout. For that, refer to "Defining Your Site's Style" on page 110 or Part 6, "Structuring Individual Web Pages."

Word Processing Conventions Used in FrontPage

Entering text in Microsoft FrontPage is very much like typing into a word processor. Follow these steps in Page view:

1 Set an insertion point on the page by clicking the desired spot. The insertion point will jump to the nearest location where text can appear.

2 Start typing.

> **tip** FrontPage accepts input like a word processor, and not like some picture editing and publishing programs. You can't just click in the middle of some white space and locate objects there.

To end a paragraph and start another, press the Enter key. To begin a new line within the same paragraph, press Shift+Enter.

Copying and Pasting Text

You cut, copy, paste, and delete work in standard fashion, as shown in Table 10-1. In addition, you can drag selected text anywhere on the page that text can normally appear. Simply dragging text moves it, and holding down the Ctrl key and dragging copies it.

Table 10-1. Copying, Moving, and Deleting Text

Operation	Preparation	Standard Toolbar	Menu Command	Keystroke	Dragging
Cut	Select source text		Edit/Cut	Press Ctrl+X or Shift+Delete	N/A
Move	Select source text		Edit/Cut, set insertion point, Edit/Paste	Press Crtl+X, move insertion point, press Ctrl+V	Drag to new location
Copy	Select source		Edit/Copy	Press Ctrl+C or Ctrl+Insert	Hold down the the Ctrl key and drag to additional location
Paste	Set insertion point		Edit/Paste	Press Ctrl+V or Shift+Insert	N/A
Paste Special	Set insertion point		Edit/Paste Special	N/A	N/A
Clear	Select source text		Edit/Delete	Press Del	N/A

newfeature!

When you paste text directly into FrontPage, FrontPage normally does its best to preserve all formatting that was present when you copied the same text. To override this behavior, look for a Paste Options button below newly pasted content and open its drop-down list. Figure 10-1 shows the options this reveals after pasting a highly formatted Microsoft Word table into FrontPage.

The following Paste Options are available:

● **Use Destination Styles.** Formats the pasted text with styles in effect in the destination document.

- **Keep Source Formatting.** Formats the pasted text with styles that were in effect in the source document.

- **Keep Text Only.** Removes all formatting—including table cell divisions—from the pasted text.

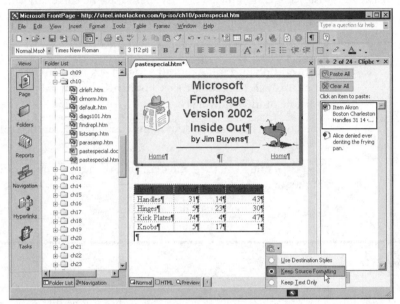

Figure 10-1. To change the format of something you've just pasted into Page view, open the drop-down menu on the Paste Options button.

Depending on the circumstances, other options might appear. If you're not sure which option to select, try them all one at a time. The Paste Options button won't disappear until you start working on another part of the Web page.

newfeature! Figure 10-1 also shows the Clipboard task pane, which displays up to 24 items copied onto the Clipboard from various applications:

- To show the Clipboard task pane, choose Office Clipboard from the Edit menu.

- To paste any item in the Clipboard, either:

  - Click it; or

  - Move the mouse pointer over its right edge, click the shaded arrow to display the drop-down list, and then choose Paste.

Chapter 10

- To delete an item from the Clipboard task pane, display the drop-down list and select Delete.

The Clipboard task pane also contains these buttons:

- **Paste All.** Pastes all items in the Office Clipboard into the current document.
- **Clear All.** Removes everything from the Office Clipboard.
- **Options.** Displays a drop-down list that controls these settings:
  - **Show Office Clipboard Automatically.** If a check mark appears in front of this selection, the Office Clipboard automatically appears whenever one of the following occurs:
    - You copy or cut two different items consecutively in the same program.
    - You copy one item, paste the item, and then copy another item in the same program.
    - You copy one item twice in succession.

InsideOut

This option and the next affect global settings for all Office programs. Unfortunately, FrontPage ignores those settings. FrontPage uses the Office Clipboard only when the Clipboard taskbar is on display or another Office program is using the Office Clipboard.

  - **Collect Without Showing Office Clipboard.** If a check mark appears in front of this selection, all cut and copy operations update the Office Clipboard even if it isn't on display. If no check mark appears, cut and copy operations don't update the Office Clipboard unless it's visible.

  - **Show Office Clipboard Icon On Taskbar.** If a check mark appears in front of this selection, displaying the Office Clipboard in FrontPage also displays the Office Clipboard icon in the tray area on the Windows taskbar.

    The icon in the Microsoft Windows tray appears whenever at least one active Microsoft Office program is displaying the Office Clipboard task pane. If another Office application occupies the foreground and isn't displaying the Office Clipboard task pane, clicking the Windows tray icon causes it to do so.

  - **Show Status Near Taskbar When Copying.** If a check mark appears in front of this selection, the message "Item collected" appears under the Clipboard counter whenever a clipboard operation is in progress.

The Office Clipboard and the normal Windows Clipboard are two separate facilities. Here's how they're related:

- When you copy multiple items to the Office Clipboard, the Windows Clipboard always contains the last item you copied.
- Clearing the Office Clipboard clears the Windows Clipboard as well.
- When you use the Paste command, the Paste button, or the shortcut keys (Ctrl+V), you paste the contents of the Windows Clipboard, not the Office Clipboard.

The FrontPage Paste Special command can paste text in the four special formats listed in Table 10-2 or as HTML. When pasting text, the Paste Special options first remove all typographical formatting such as bold, italic, underline, font name, and font size. Then they apply one of these paragraph styles:

- **Formatted.** This style displays text in a monospaced font—usually a form of Courier—and honors all white space characters present in the data.

  A white space character is any character that's invisible but occupies space. This includes spaces, tabs, carriage returns, and line feeds.

- **Normal.** This style displays text in a proportional font—usually a form of Times Roman—and displays all sequences of white space characters as if the data contained one space.

Table 10-2. **Paste Special Options**

Command	Pasted			
	Paragraph endings	Line breaks	Paragraph style	Font
One Formatted Paragraph	Line breaks	Line breaks	Formatted *<pre>*	Monospaced
Formatted Paragraphs	Paragraph endings	Paragraph endings	Formatted *<pre>*	Monospaced
Normal Paragraphs	Paragraph endings	Paragraph endings	Normal *<p>*	Proportional
Normal Paragraphs With Line Breaks	Line breaks	Line breaks	Normal *<p>*	Proportional

Because of an apparent bug, early versions of FrontPage 2002 processed the Normal Paragraphs With Line Breaks option as if the designer chose the Normal Paragraphs option. If this isn't fixed in the version you receive, watch for an Office XP update.

In addition, the Paste Special command can paste paragraph endings either as paragraph endings (no surprise there!) or as line breaks. The difference is that most browsers display a blank line after each paragraph ending, but not after a line break.

The Paste Special command can also paste HTML code directly into your page. This is quite useful if someone sends you a piece of HTML that does some special job. Follow this procedure to insert such HTML:

1 Open the file that contains the HTML code in Microsoft Notepad or another text editor.

2 Select and copy the HTML code.

3 In FrontPage, open the Web page that should contain the special HTML.

4 Set the insertion point where you want the HTML to appear.

5 Choose Paste Special from the Edit menu.

6 Choose Treat As HTML and click OK.

Selecting Text

Table 10-3 lists the commands for selecting text.

Table 10-3. Text Selection Commands

Operation	Command
Select range	Do one of the following: ● Drag mouse pointer across range. ● From insertion point, hold down Shift and click at end of range. ● Hold down Shift and use arrow keys to highlight desired selection.
Select word	Double-click word.
Select paragraph	Hold down Alt and click anywhere in paragraph.
Select entire document	Choose Select All from the Edit menu, or press Ctrl+A.

Table 10-4 lists the keyboard commands for changing the insertion point. Again, these are much the same as those in any word processor. Holding down Shift while changing the insertion point extends the current selection.

Table 10-4. **Keyboard Commands for Changing the Insertion Point**

Operation	Keystroke
Move one character right or left	Right Arrow or Left Arrow
Move one word right or left	Ctrl+Right Arrow or Ctrl+Left Arrow
Move to start of line	Home
Move to end of line	End
Move up or down one line	Up Arrow or Down Arrow
Move to beginning or end of current paragraph	Ctrl+Up Arrow or Ctrl+Down Arrow
Move up or down one paragraph	Ctrl+Up Arrow or Ctrl+Down Arrow from beginning or end of paragraph
Move to top of Web page	Ctrl+Home
Move to bottom of Web page	Ctrl+End

Importing Text

FrontPage is remarkably capable of accepting whole files or selected portions—in almost any format—and converting them to HTML. To add such content to a Web page, open the page in FrontPage and take the following steps:

● To insert an entire file by dragging it:

1 Locate the file's icon in Windows Explorer.

2 Drag the icon to the desired location in FrontPage.

● To insert an entire file using commands:

1 Place the insertion point where you want the file to appear in FrontPage.

2 Choose File from the Insert menu and locate the file you want to insert.

3 Double-click the file name, or select it and click the Open button.

● To insert less than an entire file by dragging:

1 Open the file in its normal application.

2 Select the desired content.

3 Drag the selection to the desired location in FrontPage.

- To insert part of a file using commands:

  1 Open the file in its normal application.

  2 Select the desired content.

  3 Copy the selection to the Clipboard.

  4 In FrontPage, set the insertion point where you want the content to appear.

  5 Choose Paste from the Edit menu, or press Ctrl+V.

Frequently Asked Question

How does FrontPage interpret pasted text and pictures?

When asked to incorporate content that isn't in HTML format, FrontPage first determines whether the data is character-based or pictorial.

If the data is character-based:

- FrontPage consults the table of standard file translators installed on the local computer.
- FrontPage translates the data to Rich Text Format (RTF).
- FrontPage translates the RTF to HTML.

Tabular data, such as a spreadsheet, becomes an HTML table. Other data becomes free-flowing text. FrontPage attempts to retain formatting instructions in the original data.

If the data is pictorial:

- FrontPage converts the data to a Windows bitmap for display.
- When you save your Web page, FrontPage identifies pictures that originated outside the current Web and displays a Save As dialog box for each one.
- If a picture uses transparency or contains no more than 256 colors, FrontPage saves it, by default, as a GIF file. If the picture contains more than 256 colors and no transparency, it's saved in JPEG format.

For more information on HTML tables, refer to "Creating and Editing Tables" on page 475. For more information on using pictures in Web pages, refer to Chapter 11, "Adding and Formatting Pictures."

Chapter 10

Text Conventions Unique to HTML

The preceding section might have convinced you that entering text in FrontPage is no different than using virtually any word processor. This is no accident, and in fact it's a unique strength of FrontPage. Nevertheless, the nature of HTML introduces a number of unique restrictions:

- HTML considers tab characters the same as word spaces. Outside of creating a table, there's no facility for setting "tab stops" to line up text in columns.

- HTML treats all strings of white-space characters as a single space. White-space characters are spaces, tabs, line feeds, carriage returns, and so forth. FrontPage counteracts this behavior by detecting any repeating spaces you enter and replacing all but the last with nonbreaking spaces—that is, spaces neither FrontPage nor the browser will suppress.

- HTML provides no direct control over first-line indentation, paragraph indentation, line length, or line spacing.

Inserting Special Text Elements

The Insert menu in FrontPage can add four kinds of special text elements: line breaks, horizontal lines, symbols, and comments.

Inserting a Line Break

Choosing Break from the Insert menu displays the dialog box shown in Figure 10-2. This dialog box inserts four different kinds of line breaks:

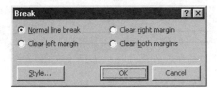

Figure 10-2. The Break dialog box inserts a line break at the current insertion point. Clearing a margin means resuming text flow just beyond any non-text objects aligned at that margin.

- **Normal Line Break.** This is an ordinary line break, just as you would create by pressing Shift+Enter. Text resumes flowing normally exactly one line below the line containing the break.

- **Clear Left Margin.** If this break occurs in text flowing around a picture or other object aligned at the left margin, text following the break will start flowing immediately below that object.

- **Clear Right Margin.** If this break occurs in text flowing around an object aligned at the right margin, text following the break will start flowing immediately below that object.

- **Clear Both Margins.** If this break occurs in text flowing around objects aligned at either or both margins, text following the break will start flowing immediately below them.

> For more information on using pictures in Web pages, refer to Chapter 11, "Adding and Formatting Pictures."

Clicking the Style button in the lower left corner of the dialog box displays FrontPage's Modify Style dialog box, discussed in Chapter 20. Any cascading style sheet (CSS) properties you specify will apply to the current line break.

> For more information about cascading style sheets, refer to Chapter 20, "Managing Appearance with Cascading Style Sheets."

Figure 10-3 shows a Normal line break.

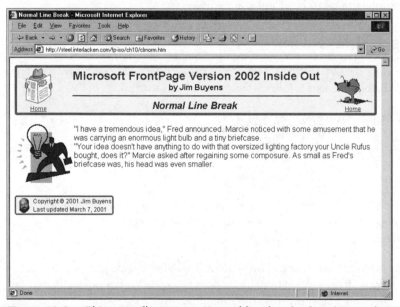

Figure 10-3. This page illustrates a Normal line break after the words "tiny briefcase."

Frequently Asked Question

Is there any way to make the browser display two or more spaces in a row?

By design, browsers compress all strings of white-space characters down to a single space before displaying them. This means there's no way, in HTML, to provide extra word spacing by adding extra spaces. If you really want to insert extra spaces—for instance, to align program code or to provide extra word spacing—you have several options:

- Use the Formatted paragraph style, which provides an exception to HTML's normal handling of white space. FrontPage uses the HTML *<pre>* tag to format paragraphs assigned this style. The *<pre>* tag displays content in an unattractive monospaced font but with all spaces and carriage returns honored, as if you were using a typewriter. You can't, however, use heading levels or other elements within a formatted paragraph; and you should avoid tabs because different browsers might assign different numbers of spaces to them. But if you don't mind the monospaced font, if you stick to using spaces rather than tabs, and if you want to control the alignment of each character on a line, the Formatted style might be acceptable.

- HTML provides a special, *nonbreaking space* character that browsers don't compress. A nonbreaking space appears in HTML code as the string * * and every time a browser sees this code, it displays a space, no matter how many appear consecutively. There are three ways to enter nonbreaking spaces in FrontPage:

  - When you type multiple spaces in FrontPage, FrontPage inserts nonbreaking spaces rather than ordinary spaces for all but the last of them.
  - When you're entering text, FrontPage treats pressing the Tab key the same as pressing the Spacebar four times.
  - When you want to insert nonbreaking spaces one at a time, press Ctrl+Shift+Spacebar.

Despite the presence of these features, spacing text or other objects by using multiple space characters still constitutes bad style. Repeating spaces will seldom produce the results you want, given HTML's use of proportional fonts, variable page width, and automatic line wrapping.

The practice of inserting two spaces between each pair of sentences is a carryover from the days of typewriters when, because of monospaced fonts, letter spacing within words tended to be wide. Nowadays, with proportional fonts, letter spacing is narrower, and one space provides plenty of separation between sentences.

Figure 10-4 shows a Clear Left Margin break for clearing an object on the left margin.

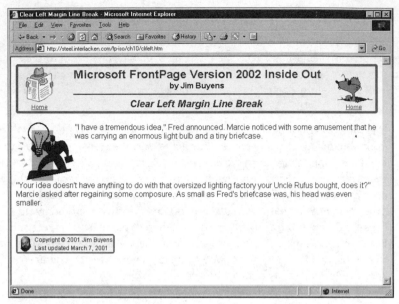

Figure 10-4. Text following a Clear Left Margin line break jumps around any object on its left and resumes flowing at the true left margin below the object.

Inserting Horizontal Lines

HTML provides a special horizontal line object that's often useful for breaking pages or other blocks of content into sections. The horizontal line forces line breaks before and after itself and normally occupies the entire width of its container (typically the browser window or a table cell). Figure 10-3 and Figure 10-4 each contain two horizontal lines just below the words "by Jim Buyens." In each case, the horizontal lines fill the width of a table cell.

For more information on HTML tables, refer to "Creating and Editing Tables" on page 475.

Here's the procedure for inserting a horizontal line:

1 Set the insertion point where you want the horizontal line to appear.

2 Choose Horizontal Line from the Insert menu.

To modify the properties of a horizontal line, right-click it and choose Horizontal Line Properties from the shortcut menu. This will display the Horizontal Line Properties dialog box shown in Figure 10-5.

Figure 10-5. This dialog box sets the properties of a horizontal line.

The options in this dialog box work as follows:

- **Width.** Specifies the width of the horizontal line in pixels or as a percentage of the available display width. The default is 100 percent.

- **Height.** Specifies the height or thickness of the line in pixels. The default is 2 pixels.

- **Alignment.** Sets the line's alignment to the left, to the right, or in the center.

- **Color.** Selects the line's color.

> For more information about using FrontPage color dialog boxes, refer to "Using FrontPage Color Dialog Boxes" on page 552.

- **Solid Line (No Shading).** Eliminates the normal three-dimensional effect along the edges of the line.

- **Style.** Opens the Modify Style dialog box where you can select any applicable CSS properties for the horizontal line.

Inserting Symbols

You can easily insert special characters—those that don't appear on your keyboard—using the Symbol dialog box shown in Figure 10-6 on the next page. To insert a special character:

1 Place the insertion point where you want to insert the symbol.

2 Choose Symbol from the Insert menu.

3 Double-click the desired character, or select the desired character and click Insert.

4 Close the dialog box.

Chapter 10

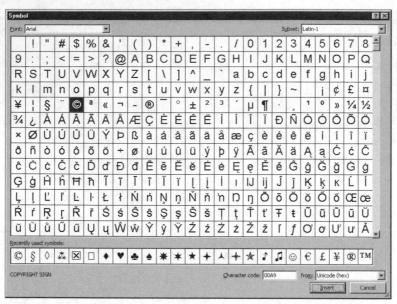

Figure 10-6. To insert characters not on the keyboard, choose Symbol from the Insert menu.

Inserting Comments

Comments include text that appears in FrontPage but that won't be seen by Web visitors. As shown in Figure 10-7, comments typically contain notes (preferably the scrutable kind) about the page for yourself or others on your team. To add comments to a Web page:

1 Set the insertion point where you want the comment to appear.

2 Choose Comment from the Insert menu.

3 Enter your comments in the Comment dialog box, and click OK.

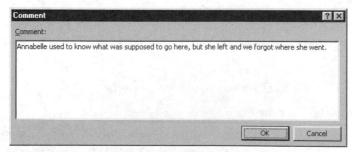

Figure 10-7. Comments inserted here won't be visible to viewers of your Web site.

In Page view, comments appear as purple text. To modify a comment, either double-click it or right-click it and select Comment Properties. To delete a comment, click it and then press the Delete key.

Searching, Replacing, and Checking Spelling

FrontPage can search for, replace, and check the spelling of text in your Web page.

Searching for Text

To search for text in an open page:

1 Set the insertion point where you want the search to begin. Pressing Ctrl+Home, for example, sets the insertion point at the start of the Web page.

2 Choose Find from the Edit menu. The dialog box shown in Figure 10-8 appears.

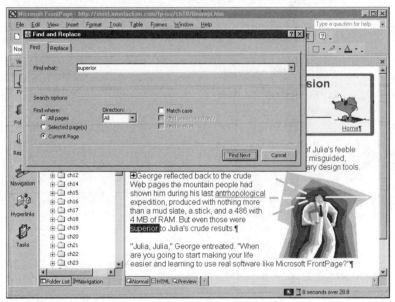

Figure 10-8. This dialog box searches your Web page for a specified text string.

3 In the box marked Find What, type the text you hope to find.

4 Review the following settings:

▪ **Find Where.** Specify where you want the search to occur:

◆ Choose All Pages to search the entire document.

◆ Choose Selected Page(s) to search only pages that are currently selected.

◆ Choose Current Page to search the current page.

▪ **Direction.** Specify the direction in which you want to search to occur:

◆ Choose All to search from the insertion point to the end of the document, and then from the top of the document down to the insertion point.

◆ Choose Up to search from the insertion point to the top of the document.

◆ Choose Down to search from the insertion point to the end of the document.

▪ **Match Case.** Select this box to make the search case sensitive. A search for *walker* wouldn't stop at *Walker*.

▪ **Find Whole Word Only.** Select this box to ignore partial word matches. A search for the word *walk*, for example, wouldn't stop at the word *walking*.

▪ **Find In HTML.** Select this box if you want FrontPage to search for your string not only in ordinary page text, but also within the HTML code. However, for this to work, you must click HTML at the bottom of the editing window before choosing Find from the Edit menu.

5 Click the Find Next button.

To search for additional occurrences of the Find text, keep clicking the Find Next button. To edit the page, you don't need to close the Find window; just move it out of the way.

For information about finding text in selected Web pages or an entire Web, refer to "Finding and Replacing Text" on page 411.

Replacing Text

Choosing Replace from the Edit menu displays the dialog box that appears in Figure 10-9. This dialog box works just the same as the Find function, except that after finding a match, you can click the Replace button to replace it (with the contents of the Replace With box, of course). Clicking Replace All replaces all occurrences of the Find What string.

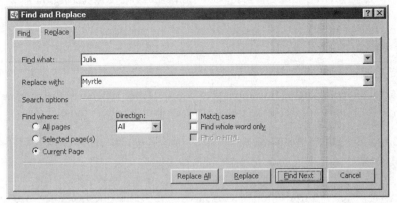

Figure 10-9. The Replace function works much like Find, except that clicking either the Replace or Replace All button modifies the original text.

Checking Spelling

FrontPage 2002 supports two kinds of spelling checking. First, it can check the spelling of words as you type them, and second, it can scan an entire Web page for errors.

Checking spelling as you type is the feature that displays squiggly lines under each misspelled word in your document. In Figure 10-8, for example, the word *anthropological* is misspelled and therefore underlined. To configure this feature, choose Page Options from the Tools menu. The following check boxes appear in the Spelling section on the General tab:

- **Check Spelling As You Type.** Controls whether or not FrontPage immediately checks the spelling of each word you type. You might elect to clear this because it slows down your system, or if your page content contains a lot of nonstandard words. This option is selected by default.

- **Hide Spelling Errors In All Documents.** Controls whether FrontPage displays squiggly lines under the misspelled words. Why check spelling as you type and not display the squiggly lines? Well, maybe you don't like squiggly lines but you do like very rapid spelling checks later.

When you right-click a misspelled word—one with a squiggly underline—FrontPage displays a shortcut menu containing suggested correct spellings, an Ignore All choice that temporarily accepts the questionable word as correct, and an Add To Dictionary choice that adds the questionable word to the spelling dictionary.

InsideOut

The misspelled word shortcut menu appears in place of any normal shortcut menus. For example, you can't change paragraph properties by right-clicking a misspelled word and choosing Paragraph, because all you'll get is the spelling correction menu. The solution is to right-click some other part of the paragraph that lacks squiggly underlining.

The actual Spelling dialog box appears in Figure 10-10. Whenever the spelling checker finds a word on your page that's not in its dictionary, it offers these choices:

- **Ignore.** Makes no change to the questionable word and continues the spelling check.

- **Ignore All.** Works the same as Ignore, except that the spelling checker won't stop if it finds more occurrences of the same questionable word during the current spelling check.

- **Change.** Replaces the questionable word with the word in the Change To box. You can accept the spelling checker's initial suggestion, select another word from the Suggestions list, or hand-type a word yourself.

- **Change All.** Works like Change, except that for the remainder of the spelling check operation, it makes the same replacement whenever it finds the same questionable word.

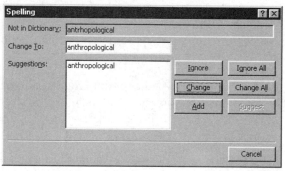

Figure 10-10. FrontPage uses the same spelling checker as the rest of the Office XP family.

- **Add.** Adds the questionable word to the spelling checker dictionary.

- **Suggest.** Checks the spelling of the word in the Change To box and, if it can't be verified, offers suggestions.

Chapter 10

Using the Thesaurus

As you're thinking great thoughts and pounding out text, finding just the right word is frequently a problem. Or perhaps you need the opposite of a word. To resolve both dilemmas, FrontPage 2002 has a built-in thesaurus. Neither prehistoric nor reptilian, a thesaurus is a dictionary of words with like and opposite meanings. FrontPage uses the same thesaurus as the rest of the Office XP suite.

To use the thesaurus:

1 Select the word you want to replace.

2 Choose Thesaurus from the Tools menu. This displays the Thesaurus dialog box that appears in Figure 10-11.

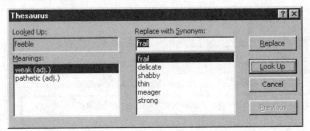

Figure 10-11. The thesaurus searches for words with like and unlike meanings.

FrontPage automatically displays the selected word's synonyms (words with like meanings) and antonyms (words with opposite meanings). When the original word has several meanings, the Meanings box will have an entry for each. In the example, clicking the *weak* meaning at the left displays a different list of synonyms at the right than clicking the *pathetic* meaning.

3 If a synonym is closer to what you want but still not exact, select it and click Look Up. This tells the thesaurus to look up the selected word and display *its* synonyms. If this takes you further from your goal rather than closer to it, click the Previous button.

4 Clicking any word in the Replace With Synonym list copies that word into the Replace With Synonym box.

5 To look up synonyms for an entirely new word, enter it in the Replace With Synonym box and then click the Look Up button.

6 When the best word appears in the Replace With Synonym box, click the Replace button. This closes the dialog box and replaces the word you selected in Step 1.

Formatting Paragraphs

The arrangement and layout of paragraphs—or any blocks of text—are key elements of page layout and visual communication. FrontPage therefore provides a rich assortment of tools that control paragraph appearance.

Using HTML's Basic Paragraph Styles

FrontPage supports the 15 basic HTML paragraph styles shown in Figure 10-12. These are paragraph styles and not font styles; they modify the appearance of an entire paragraph and not of any specific text. HTML was designed to specify the structure of a document's elements, not the explicit formatting of a given element; therefore, each browser will display these elements according to its own settings and the system configuration on which it's running.

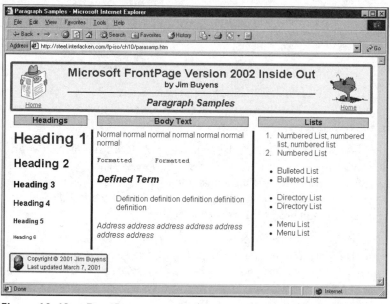

Figure 10-12. FrontPage supports these standard HTML paragraph styles.

Headings 1 through 6 are for successively lower-level titles. In practice, any page with six levels of titles is probably too long and an excellent candidate for separation into multiple pages. Nevertheless, the availability of six styles provides more flexibility in selecting sizes (you might, for example, choose to use Headings 1 through 3, or 4 through 6). Heading 1 generally uses the largest font and Heading 6 the smallest.

The Normal style is designated for most ordinary text. Like the heading styles and most of the others, it specifies no fixed line width but instead wraps within the current browser window.

The Formatted style is unique in three respects: it uses a monospaced font; it preserves and displays multiple spaces; and it doesn't wrap within the browser window. Because of these characteristics, the Formatted style is useful for applications like tabular data and program-code listings, where preservation of columns and letter spaces is vital.

The Address style is designated to identify Web addresses. Its most common use is making e-mail hyperlinks stand out from ordinary text. Web address paragraphs frequently appear in italics.

To assign one of the 15 default styles to a paragraph, set the insertion point in the paragraph or select any part of the paragraph, and then select the desired style from the Style drop-down list on the Formatting toolbar.

Style

In addition, there are two style shortcut keys:

- **Ctrl+Shift+N.** Applies the Normal style.
- **Ctrl+Shift+L.** Applies the Bulleted List style.

The following buttons on the Formatting toolbar also modify the appearance of text:

- **Align Left.** Left-aligns text in selected paragraphs.
- **Center.** Centers text in selected paragraphs.
- **Align Right.** Right-aligns text in selected paragraphs.
- **Justify.** Aligns text in selected paragraphs to both right and left margins.

Align Left   Center   Align Right   Justify

- **Numbering.** Creates a numbered list.
- **Bullets.** Creates a bulleted list.
- **Decrease Indent.** Decreases the paragraph indentation or nesting level of selected list items.
- **Increase Indent.** Increases the paragraph indentation or nesting level of selected list items.

Numbering   Bullets   Decrease Indent   Increase Indent

Chapter 10

289

Aligning Text

HTML provides only five settings for aligning paragraph text: Default, Left, Center, Right, and Justify. There are three ways to apply these settings:

- Use the Align Left, Center, Align Right, and Justify buttons on the Formatting toolbar, as described in Table A-2 on the Companion CD. When an alignment is in effect, its button will remain selected. To specify default alignment, click the selected button again to clear it.

- Choose Paragraph from the Format menu, and select the Alignment from the drop-down list. See Figure 10-13.

- Right-click the paragraph, choose Paragraph from the shortcut menu, and then select the Alignment from the drop-down list.

Align Left   Center   Align Right   Justify

> **tip**   The following keystrokes also align text: Ctrl+R toggles right alignment; Ctrl+L toggles left alignment; Ctrl+E toggles centering.

Fine-Tuning Paragraph Properties

The Paragraph dialog box appears in Figure 10-13. You can display it by right-clicking the paragraph and choosing Paragraph from the shortcut menu. Or if you prefer, select all or part of the paragraph, and then choose Paragraph from the Format menu.

Use this facility with caution. If you need to format a particular paragraph beyond HTML's defaults, you'll most likely need to format other paragraphs in your Web the same way. If you format each paragraph of a given type individually, you'll probably miss a setting or two in one or more Web pages. Changing the specialized style later will cost you even more time and leave your pages prone to further errors. For these reasons, you should always consider using themes or shared cascading style sheets to control specialized paragraph formatting.

> For more information about themes, refer to Chapter 19, "Using FrontPage Themes." For more information about cascading style sheets, refer to Chapter 20, "Managing Appearance with Cascading Style Sheets."

The Paragraph dialog box controls the following settings:

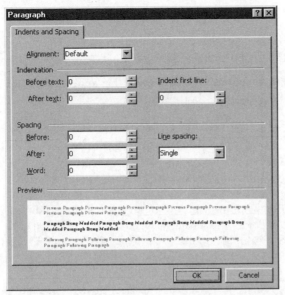

Figure 10-13. Use the Paragraph dialog box to choose paragraph styles.

- Alignment:

  - **Default.** Each line within a paragraph will butt against the default border.

  - **Left.** Each line will butt against the left border.

  - **Right.** Each line will butt against the right border.

  - **Center.** The browser will center each line between the left and right borders.

  - **Justify.** The browser will add enough word spacing so that each line butts against both the left and the right borders.

- Indentation:

  - **Before Text.** Controls the amount of blank space that appears between the left edge of a paragraph and its container. This is actually the left margin setting. (CSS)

  - **After Text.** Controls the amount of blank space that appears between the right edge of a paragraph and its container. In other words, it controls the right margin. (CSS)

  - **Indent First Line.** Specifies first-line paragraph indentation. Negative numbers produce "outdents," where the first line extends to the left of second and subsequent lines. (CSS)

- Spacing:

  - **Before.** Controls the amount of blank space that appears above a paragraph—that is, the paragraph's top margin. (CSS)

  - **After.** Controls the amount of blank space that appears below a paragraph—the paragraph's bottom margin. (CSS)

  - **Word.** Adjusts the normal spacing between words. Positive values increase spacing and negative values decrease it. (CSS)

  - **Line Spacing.** Specifies the amount of vertical space reserved for a line. A common value is the font size times 1.2. (CSS)

The effects flagged "(CSS)" appear only in browsers that support cascading style sheets; other browsers ignore them. For all the settings flagged "(CSS)," you can enter a unit of measure as well as a numeric value. The values *1* and *1px* both mean one pixel, but you can also enter measurements such as *0.5in* and *3mm*.

For more information about CSS units of measure, refer to Table 20-13, "Cascading Style Sheet Units of Measure," on page 639.

Formatting Lists

In HTML terminology, lists are collections of paragraphs the browser will format with leading bullets or numbers. Because lists inherently have a structure to them, creating and updating them is slightly trickier than working with normal paragraphs. Fortunately, FrontPage takes care of this complexity for you.

Creating Bulleted and Numbered Lists

As shown in Figures 10-14, 10-15, and 10-16, FrontPage supports three kinds of bulleted and numbered lists:

- **Picture Bullets.** FrontPage uses a picture that you select as the item identifier.

- **Plain Bullets.** FrontPage instructs the browser to display a standard bullet character.

- **Numbers.** FrontPage instructs the browser to sequentially number the list items.

To convert existing paragraphs to a list:

1 Select the desired paragraphs.

2 Do one of the following:

Bullets

Numbering

▪ Choose Numbered List or Bulleted List from the Style drop-down list on the Formatting toolbar.

▪ Click the Numbering button or Bullets button on the Formatting toolbar.

▪ Choose Bullets And Numbering from the Format menu.

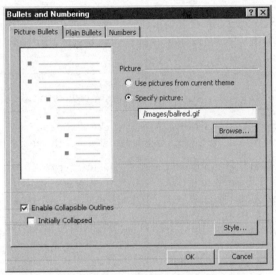

Figure 10-14. If you choose Bullets And Numbering from the Format menu, you can insert picture bullets from this dialog box.

---

note You can't create a picture bullet list from the Formatting toolbar. To create a picture bullet list, choose the Bullets And Numbering command from the Format menu, and then select the Picture Bullets tab as shown in Figure 10-14. You can also select the Picture Bullets tab by right-clicking an existing plain bullet list and then choosing List Properties from the shortcut menu.

You can create a new list in two ways. The first is to create normal paragraphs and convert them as just described. The second is this:

1 Place the insertion point where the list should begin.

2 Do one of the following:

Bullets

■ Click either the Bullets button or the Numbering button on the Formatting toolbar.

■ Choose Bullets And Numbering from the Format menu, select a style, and then click OK.

Numbering

3 Enter the text for each item in the list, and press Enter to continue to the next item.

4 To end the list and return to Normal paragraph style, press Enter twice. (If you don't want an extra blank line, press Backspace to delete it.)

> **note** Remember the convention that two consecutive paragraph endings denote the end of a list. This explains many otherwise curious behaviors that occur around the ends of lists.

From the Picture Bullets tab, you can select pictures for your bullets in two ways:

● If the current Web or page uses themes, choose the Use Pictures From Current Theme option to use the bullet pictures supplied with the theme.

● Choose the Specify Picture option if there's no theme in effect or if you don't want the standard theme bullets. Continue either by typing the picture's URL or file path, or by clicking the Browse button to display a standard Select Picture dialog box. As usual, this dialog box can browse local file locations, browse locations in server-based Webs, or receive URLs you locate using Microsoft Internet Explorer.

> **note** Picture bullet lists aren't lists in an HTML sense. Rather, they're tables that FrontPage builds and maintains, using the same commands it uses for true HTML lists.

Figure 10-15 shows the Plain Bullets tab of the Bullets And Numbering dialog box, from which you can select any one of several bullet styles that use text symbols rather than pictures. Click the style you want, and then click OK. Click the Style button to set CSS properties.

Figure 10-16 shows the Numbers tab of the Bullets And Numbering dialog box. Click the numbering style you want, verify or change the Start At value for the first paragraph in the list, and then click OK. Click the Style button to set CSS properties.

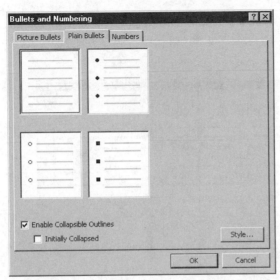

Figure 10-15. FrontPage assigns the properties of normal bulleted lists according to the settings made here.

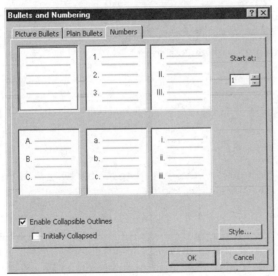

Figure 10-16. The Numbers tab of the Bullets And Numbering dialog box controls the properties of numbered lists.

Figure 10-17 shows examples of indented lists using plain bullets, numbered lists, and picture bullets. These are actually lists inside of lists; each sublist is part of the text for the item just above it.

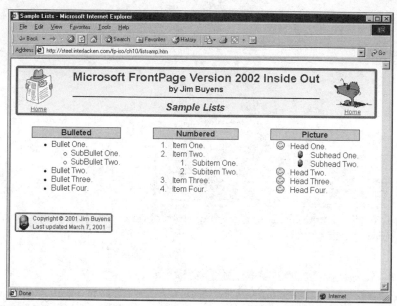

Figure 10-17. Each sublist is included within a parent list.

To begin a sublist:

1 Place the insertion point at the end of the bullet that will precede the first indented bullet.

2 Press Enter to create a new list item.

Increase
Indent

3 Click the Increase Indent button on the Formatting toolbar twice. The first click creates a Normal style paragraph, and the second click creates a sublist bullet.

> **caution** You can't add multiple items to the end of a list without entering text as you go. Placing the insertion point at the end of the list and pressing Enter once will create a new item, but pressing Enter *again* will delete the newly created item and terminate the list.

Decrease
Indent

To convert any item in a list to a normal paragraph, first select it and then click the Decrease Indent button on the Formatting toolbar. More than one click might be necessary, depending on the original indentation. If you experiment with successive clicks of the Increase Indent and Decrease Indent buttons, you'll see that you can move from level to level, passing through a Normal style level between list levels.

296

To continue adding new items at the current list level, simply press Enter at the end of each preceding item.

To change an existing list's overall style, right-click anywhere in the list and choose List Properties from the shortcut menu. Figure 10-18 shows the resulting dialog box.

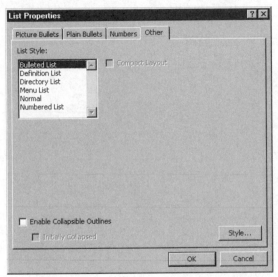

Figure 10-18. The Other tab of the List Properties dialog box contains additional list choices.

On the Other tab of the List Properties dialog box, choose from the following options:

- **List Style.** Changes the list's overall style.
- **Compact Layout.** Appears only for definition lists. For an explanation of Compact Layout, refer to the next section.

Creating Collapsible Lists

FrontPage can make multi-level lists *collapsible*. This means that sublists appear and disappear as the visitor clicks their parent list items. Figure 10-19 on the next page provides an example. FrontPage, running in the back window, displays the collapsible list in its entirety. Internet Explorer, running in the front window, displays details only for entries the visitor has clicked.

Two settings control the behavior of collapsible lists. For convenience, they appear on all four tabs of the List Properties dialog box:

- **Enable Collapsible Outlines.** If selected, means that sublists should appear and disappear as the visitor clicks their parent list items.

● **Initially Collapsed.** If selected, means that the collapsible portion of a list will initially be hidden. Otherwise, they initially appear.

caution Collapsible lists don't collapse in Netscape Navigator, at least not through version 4. For Internet Explorer, they require at least version 4. This is because collapsible lists use dynamic HTML (DHTML) features first introduced in Internet Explorer 4.

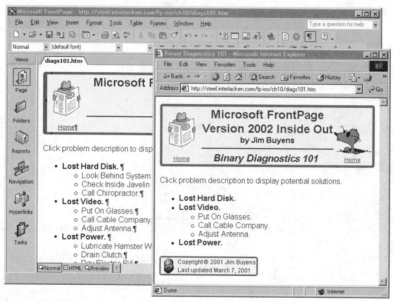

Figure 10-19. Collapsible lists expand and contract as the Web visitor clicks headings.

Using Other List Types

The Other tab of the List Properties dialog box presents some alternative options for formatting a list. Among these are directory lists and menu lists, which current browsers seem to display identically to bulleted lists. Nevertheless, you can use this tab to assign the directory or menu list types to be used if the need arises. Bulleted lists are by far the most common of the three and therefore the most universally supported.

The Definition List option on the Other tab combines two HTML styles, Defined Term and Definition, to create a special type of list. The browser displays a Defined Term paragraph flush left, followed by an indented Definition paragraph. Glance back at Figure 10-12 to see how the Definition appears in the middle window. To create a defined term and its definition:

1 Type the term you plan to define.

2 Select Defined Term from the Style drop-down list on the Formatting toolbar. This formats the paragraph as a defined term.

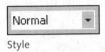

Style

3 Set the insertion point at the end of the Defined Term paragraph, and then press Enter. FrontPage starts a new line and applies the Definition style, indenting the new line.

4 Type the definition of the term and press Enter. FrontPage starts a new line and begins a new defined term so that you can type a list of terms and definitions without interruption.

5 When you're done with the entire definition list, terminate the list by pressing Enter twice at the end of the final definition line.

If you want your definition list to take up less space, select the Compact Layout check box. This displays the definition on the same line as the defined term, provided the defined term is short enough not to overlap.

Formatting Text Fonts

Controlling fonts on Web pages presents unique difficulties. For one, there's no way of knowing what fonts or font technologies a given Web visitor will have available. For another, it's unlikely that all the same fonts will be available to any two Web visitors. Finally, even fonts that appear identical down to their names might have subtle differences when obtained from different vendors or even from the same vendor when used on different platforms.

The original HTML specification tried to avoid font confusion by avoiding fonts. That is, instead of providing a way to specify fonts by name, it provided ways to flag blocks of text by their structural use in the document. Responsibility for assigning specific fonts then fell to the Web visitor's browser.

For information on how to format small amounts of text as pictures, refer to "Adding Text to Pictures" on page 649.

Some newer versions of HTML *do* support specific font name assignments, as does FrontPage. However, just because FrontPage lets you specify font names such as Estrangella Edessa and Palatino Linotype doesn't mean those fonts are available to your Web visitors. If the remote system doesn't have a font with the name you specify, it will substitute another font—usually the default browser font, which, if not stylish, will at least be legible.

Chapter 10

Recommendations for Using Fonts on the Web

Consider these five commonsense suggestions for using font attributes effectively in your Web pages:

- **Use fonts large enough to read.** Small print is for lawyers. If the text isn't important enough to present legibly, omit it.
- **Don't waste space with large fonts.** Large amounts of text in a large font slow down the reader and lead to excessive scrolling. In addition, they have far less impact than a pleasing and effective page design.
- **Stick to mainstream fonts.** If Web visitors don't have the artistic font you want, their browser will probably substitute an ugly one.
- **Avoid ransom notes.** Stick to a few well-chosen sizes and styles of type.
- **Aim for contrast, not clash.** Achieve a pleasing contrast between background and text.

note Most browsers correctly substitute a local version of Arial, Helvetica, or Times Roman for any known variation of those names. Font substitution for less common names, however, can be problematic.

There's another reason to approach font attributes with caution. If you need to use a special font in a particular situation, you should use exactly the same font settings everywhere else in the same page and the same Web where the same situation occurs. If you format all this text manually, you'll almost certainly miss some spots and make some errors. Furthermore, changing the specified font later will be difficult at best. For these reasons, always consider using global facilities like themes and shared cascading style sheets to control typography.

For more information about themes, refer to Chapter 19, "Using FrontPage Themes." For more information about cascading style sheets, refer to Chapter 20, "Managing Appearance with Cascading Style Sheets."

FrontPage provides seven font-related icons on the Formatting toolbar. Each icon applies an attribute to the selected text, or removes an attribute previously applied.

- **Font.** Applies a selected font name.
- **Font Size.** Increases or decreases font size.

Font   Font Size

- **Bold.** Toggles boldfacing on and off.

- **Italic.** Toggles italicizing on and off.

- **Underline.** Toggles underlining on and off.

- **Highlight.** Controls a text area's background color.

- **Font Color.** Controls the color in which the browser displays text.

| Bold | Italic | Underline | Highlight | Font Color |

You can also toggle boldfacing, italicizing, and underlining of selected words on and off by pressing Ctrl+B, Ctrl+I, and Ctrl+U, respectively.

Press Ctrl+Shift+> to increase the font size of selected words, and Ctrl+Shift+< to decrease it.

Ctrl+Shift+Plus formats text as a superscript and Ctrl+Equal formats it as a subscript.

For maximum control of font settings, select the text you want to modify and then choose Font from the Format menu. The resulting dialog box contains the Font tab shown in Figure 10-20 and the Character Spacing tab shown later in Figure 10-21.

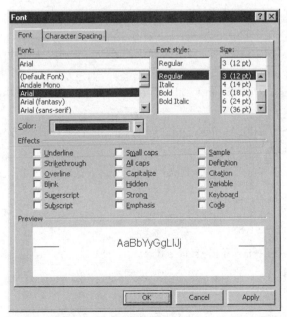

Figure 10-20. The Font tab of the Font dialog box provides controls similar to those of any word processor.

301

> **tip** You can obtain the same dialog box by right-clicking a block of text and choosing Font on the shortcut menu.

The Font tab controls the following settings:

- **Font.** Selects a specific font name.

- **Font Style.** Controls the following effects: regular, italic, bold, bold italic.

- **Size.** Specifies a code from 1 through 7, indicating the relative size of the font. The dialog box lists typical point-size equivalents for convenience, although these can vary by browser and system configuration.

- **Color.** Provides the usual FrontPage color dialog boxes, beginning with a drop-down list of 16 colors.

- **Underline.** Underlines text.

> **note** The underline setting has no effect on the underlining of hyperlinks.

- **Strikethrough.** Draws a horizontal line through the selected text.

- **Overline.** Draws a horizontal line above the selected text. (CSS)

- **Blink.** Displays flashing text. Web browsers that can't display blinking text will ignore this setting.

- **Superscript.** Reduces text in size and shifts its baseline upward, like the 2 in πr^2.

- **Subscript.** Reduces text in size and shifts its baseline downward, like the 2 in H_2O.

- **Small Caps.** Displays reduced-size capital letters in place of any lowercase letters in the actual text. (CSS)

- **All Caps.** Displays all letters in uppercase, even if the actual text is lowercase. (CSS)

- **Capitalize.** Displays the first letter of each word in uppercase, even if the actual text is lowercase. (CSS)

- **Hidden.** Suppresses display of the selected text. (CSS)

- **Strong.** Enhances text to convey a stronger meaning. Most browsers use boldface for this.

- **Emphasis.** Enhances text to convey extra emphasis. Most browsers use italics for this.

- **Sample.** Displays a sequence of literal characters in a monospaced font, usually some variation of Courier.

- **Definition.** Indicates a definition, typically in italics.

- **Citation.** Indicates a style designed to be assigned to a manual, section, or book, typically in italics.

- **Variable.** Indicates a variable name, typically in italics.

- **Keyboard.** Indicates typing by a visitor, as when following a procedure. This is usually similar to the monospaced (Courier) font.

- **Code.** Indicates a code sample. This is usually similar to the monospaced (Courier) font.

Effects flagged "(CSS)" appear only in browsers that support cascading style sheets; other browsers ignore them.

> For more information about applying fonts to an entire page or Web site, refer to Chapter 20, "Managing Appearance with Cascading Style Sheets."

 For more information on configuring FrontPage to reflect the capabilities of various browsers, refer to "Configuring Compatibility Options" in the Bonus Content on the Companion CD.

You can preview the results of setting the various Font controls in the Preview box.

Figure 10-21 shows the Character Spacing tab.

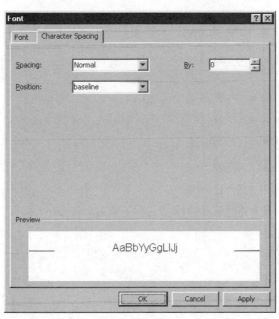

Figure 10-21. The Character Spacing tab controls space between characters, as well as character position relative to the baseline.

Chapter 10

The Character Spacing tab controls the following font settings, which require a numeric value:

- **Spacing.** Choose Normal for the default spacing, Expanded for extra space between letters, or Condensed for less than the normal spacing. (CSS)

- **By.** Enter a CSS measurement for the amount of extra or lesser spacing you want.

For more information about valid CSS measurements, refer to "Specifying Style Sheet Measurements" on page 639.

- **Position.** This setting dictates the vertical position of the text. Options include Baseline, Sub, Super, Top, Text-top, Middle, Bottom, and Text-bottom.

Effects flagged "(CSS)" appear only in browsers that support cascading style sheets; other browsers ignore them.

To preview the results of setting Character Spacing controls, see the Preview box at the bottom of the dialog box.

In Summary...

This chapter explained the basics of entering and pasting text; formatting paragraphs and fonts; and finding, replacing, and checking the spelling of text.

The next chapter explains how to add pictures to a Web page.

Adding and Formatting Pictures

Pictures (also called graphics and images) are among the most important components of any Web page—so important that it's rare to see a page without them. A Web page without pictures is like a day without sunshine—a dull and dreary prospect.

Recognizing this importance, Microsoft FrontPage includes features that easily search for existing pictures, acquire new ones from scanners or digital cameras, and in some cases, even create pictures. What's more, FrontPage can modify pictures in a variety of ways right in the Page view editing window.

This chapter provides the basic techniques of adding pictures to Webs and to Web pages. For completeness, it also introduces a plethora of advanced techniques covered more fully by individual chapters later in the book. Feel free to jump ahead to those chapters as the mood strikes you.

Adding Pictures to a Page

FrontPage can add many kinds of pictures to your Web pages in a variety of ways. One of these is almost sure to meet any requirements you encounter:

● **Picture Files.** FrontPage can insert pictures from any file location on your computer, from the clipboard, from the Web you're working in, or from any location on the World Wide Web. If the existing file format isn't one of those usually found on the World Wide Web, FrontPage will convert it automatically.

For more information about picture file types used on the World Wide Web, refer to "Choosing Picture File Formats" on page 684.

- **Clip Art.** FrontPage can use the Microsoft Clip Organizer, which is the same picture gallery that the rest of the Microsoft Office XP suite uses. If none of the thousands of pictures in the Clip Organizer meet your needs, you can search further on Microsoft's Web site.

- **Pictures from a Scanner or Camera.** FrontPage can directly accept pictures from TWAIN-compliant devices such as scanners and digital cameras. This bypasses the usual steps of first capturing the picture as a disk file, then adding the file to your Web, and finally adding it to your Web page.

note Despite reports to the contrary, TWAIN doesn't stands for Technology Without An Interesting Name. TWAIN isn't an acronym; it's simply the name of a software standard for connecting scanners and digital cameras to computers. For more information about TWAIN, browse *www.twain.org*.

- **Multimedia Files.** FrontPage can add video and sound files to a Web page as easily as it can add picture files.

- **Text on GIF.** FrontPage can superimpose text over an ordinary picture file in your Web page. FrontPage saves the original picture file, the super-imposed text, and the resulting picture file separately so you can easily change the text in the future.

newfeature!

- **Line Art.** FrontPage can add line art to a Web page. The following kinds of pictures all use Vector Markup Language (VML) to express line drawings. VML is an XML-based way to describe pictures using curves, lines, and X-Y coordinates:

  - **Drawings.** FrontPage can now draw lines, arrows, rectangles, and other objects within a Web page.

  - **AutoShapes.** FrontPage can now create geometric shapes, block arrows, flowchart symbols, stars, and other shapes selected from a library.

  - **WordArt.** FrontPage can now provide extremely rich formatting of text. This feature has been present in past releases of Microsoft Word, Microsoft Excel, and Microsoft PowerPoint. The introduction of VML makes it usable in FrontPage as well.

A line drawing expressed in VML is usually much smaller than the same drawing saved as a GIF or JPEG file. Currently, only Microsoft Internet Explorer 5 and later can display XML. Other browsers ignore the VML code and display a substitute GIF picture instead.

After a picture is present in a Web page, FrontPage provides full access to its HTML properties through easy-to-use dialog boxes. FrontPage also provides a variety of tools

306

for modifying pictures. With these tools, you can enlarge pictures, reduce them, flip them top to bottom or right to left, and change their brightness and contrast.

No matter where the picture comes from, FrontPage prompts you for a Save As location the next time you save the Web page.

Inserting Pictures by Dragging

FrontPage makes adding a picture to a Web page as easy as drag and drop. Figure 11-1 shows how you can drag pictures from Page view's Folder List to a page open for editing. As you drag over the open Web page, the insertion point shows where the picture will appear.

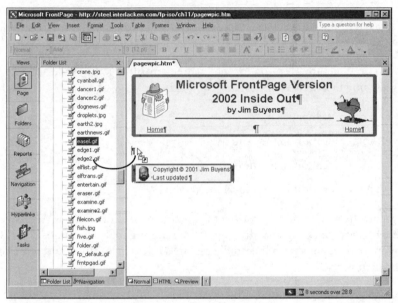

Figure 11-1. FrontPage can accept pictures dropped from the Folder List, from Windows Explorer, or from Internet Explorer.

If the picture you want to use isn't located in the current Web, there are two ways to proceed:

- Drag the file from its current location and drop it into the current Web. (If you have no reason to put the file anywhere else, the *images* folder is usually a good choice.) Then drag the file from its new location into the open Web page.

- Drag the file from its current location and drop it in the open Web page. The next time you save the open page, FrontPage displays the Save Embedded Files dialog box shown in Figure 11-2 on the next page. This dialog box asks where in the current Web you want to save the copied file.

307

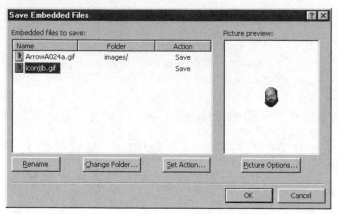

Figure 11-2. When you save a Web page that contains pictures not already saved in the current Web, this dialog box lists and suggests a save location for each picture.

You can drag picture files—or, for that matter, any other kind of file—to and from the following locations in almost any combination:

- An open Web page
- A folder location in the same Web
- A folder location in a different Web
- A folder location in your local file system

Drag-and-drop operations involving the document area of an open Web page follow different rules than drag-and-drop operations among folder locations. This is because a Web page contains only a link to the picture's physical location, and not a copy of the picture itself.

The rules governing drag-and-drop operations involving open Web pages are these:

- Dragging a picture from one spot in a Web page to another spot in the same page performs a *move* operation. In effect, the picture disappears from its old location and appears in the new one.

- Dragging a picture from one Web page to another in the same Web also performs a *move*. The picture disappears from the page that formerly displayed it.

- Dragging a picture from an open page in one Web to an open page in a different Web *copies* the picture. The picture doesn't disappear from the page that originally displayed it.

Be aware that this last operation doesn't copy the picture file into the second Web. FrontPage holds the copied picture in memory until you save the Web page, and then displays the Save Embedded Files dialog box to prompt you for a Save location inside the second Web.

Dragging a picture file from a folder location to an open Web page never copies the file physically. It creates only an instruction to display the file from its location within the same Web. If the file doesn't reside in the same Web as the open Web page, FrontPage again holds the copied picture in memory and displays the Save Embedded Files dialog box when you save the page.

Dragging files between folder locations in the same Web always moves the files. Dragging files between folder locations in different Webs always copies them, as does dragging files between FrontPage and Windows Explorer. Table 11-1 summarizes all these rules.

Table 11-1. Drag-and-Drop Results in FrontPage

Drag from	Drop on				
	Open page		Folder		
	Same Web	**Different Web**	**Same Web**	**Different Web**	**File location**
Open page	Move Link	Copy into memory	Not Allowed	Not Allowed	Not Allowed
Folder in Web	Create Link	Copy into memory	Move File	Copy File	Copy File
Folder in file location	Copy into memory	Copy into memory	Copy File	Copy File	Copy file if drive letters are different, otherwise move.

If an operation would normally move a file and you actually want to copy a file, hold down the Ctrl key while you drag.

If you have trouble remembering these rules, try dragging with the right mouse button. Whenever you drop an object after dragging it in this way, Microsoft Windows displays a shortcut menu with Move Here, Copy Here, Link Here, and Cancel options.

Using the Save Embedded Files Dialog Box

The Save Embedded Files dialog box, previously shown in Figure 11-2, appears whenever you save an open Web page that contains a picture or other object not yet saved in the current Web. This situation occurs when you drag or paste a picture from outside the current Web into an open Web page, when you insert clip art, when you use certain FrontPage picture editing tools to create a new version of a picture, and in various other situations. If there are several such files, FrontPage lists them all in one dialog box. From the Save Embedded Files dialog box, you can do the following:

- If you want to rename a file, select it and click the Rename button.

- If you want to save one or more files in a different folder, select the files and click the Change Folder button.

- If you want to change a file's action from Save to Don't Save (or back again), click the Set Action button. If a file with the same folder location and file name already exists in the current Web, clicking the Set Action button displays a Set Action dialog box with these options:

    - **Overwrite.** FrontPage replaces the existing file with the new one and makes the current Web page refer to the new file.

    - **Use Existing.** FrontPage discards the picture it has in memory, retains the existing file, and makes the current Web page refer to it.

    - **Don't Save.** FrontPage retains both the existing file and the new version in memory. The Save Embedded Files dialog box will reappear the next time you save the page.

    Unless you have strong reasons to the contrary, you should accept FrontPage's suggestion and save these files to your Web. Rename them or change the folder where they reside, if you like, but do save them. If you don't, sooner or later they're bound to come up missing from your Web page.

- If you want to change a picture's characteristics, click the Picture Options button. This displays the Picture Options dialog box shown in Figure 11-3. From this dialog box, the following options are available:

    - **JPEG.** Select this option if you want FrontPage to save the picture as a JPEG file. JPEG files are generally preferable for photographs and other pictures that contain many colors.

    - **Quality.** Specify an integer from 1 to 99. Lower numbers increase compression and decrease file size, but sacrifice picture quality. Typical values are 70 through 90.

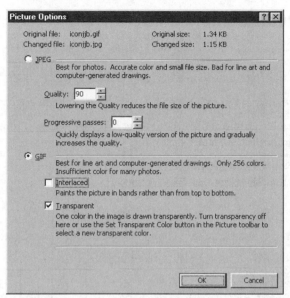

Figure 11-3. Clicking the Picture Options button in Figure 11-2 provides these options for the currently selected picture.

■ **Progressive Passes.** To display the picture first in coarse resolution and then, as more of it arrives, in finer resolution, specify a number from 1 to 100. The number you specify controls how many steps of increasing resolution there will be. To display the picture in full resolution as it arrives, specify 0.

■ **GIF.** Select this option if you want FrontPage to save the picture as a GIF file. GIF files are preferable for pictures that contain sharp lines, flat areas of color, and at most 256 colors.

■ **Interlaced.** Select this box if you want the browser to display a coarse version of the picture at first and then a full resolution version when the file is completely received.

■ **Transparent.** If a GIF picture has one color marked as transparent, clear this box to return the color to normal visibility. If no colors are currently marked as transparent, the box is unavailable (dimmed).

For more information about designating a GIF color as transparent, refer to "Setting Transparency" on page 657.

● Click OK when you've set all these options the way you want them.

Chapter 11

Inserting Pictures Using the Insert Menu

You can also insert pictures using the FrontPage Insert menu. Here's the procedure:

1 Open the page that should display the picture.

2 Set the insertion point where you want the picture to appear.

3 Choose Picture from the Insert menu, and then choose From File. This produces the Picture dialog box shown in Figure 11-4.

4 Select the picture file you want to display, or type the name of the picture file in the File Name box, and click Insert.

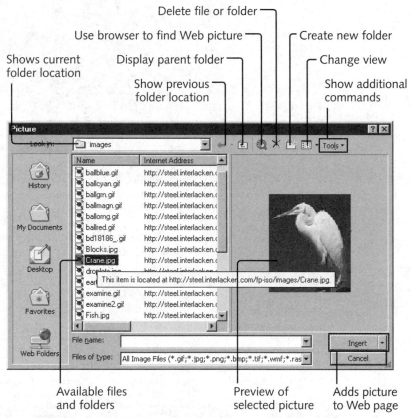

Figure 11-4. Use this FrontPage dialog box to locate a desired picture.

If the Picture dialog box shown in Figure 11-4 looks familiar, there's a reason: It's essentially a duplicate of most other file-oriented dialog boxes in FrontPage. All the toolbar buttons and other controls work as they do in other such dialog boxes.

For more information about the buttons and icons in the Picture dialog box, refer to "The File Dialog Box Toolbar" and "The My Places Bar" in the Bonus Content on the Companion CD.

Views

Shifting the file-selection list into Preview mode is particularly useful when searching for pictures. Figure 11-4 shows the dialog box in this mode previewing a picture. To select Preview mode, choose Preview from the Views button's drop-down list, or repeatedly click the Views toolbar button until Preview mode is in effect.

Search
The Web

The Search The Web toolbar button at the top of the dialog box uses your Web browser to find a picture. To find a picture in this way requires the following procedure:

1 Click the Search The Web button, and wait for the browser to appear and search for the picture you want.

2 Display the picture (and not just the Web page that contains it) in the browser window. The address in the browser's Location or Address box must end in a picture filename extension such as *.gif*, *.jpg*, or *.jpeg*. Select this address, and then copy it to the Clipboard by pressing Ctrl+C.

3 Switch back to FrontPage, redisplay the Picture dialog box, set the insertion point in the File Name box, and press Ctrl+V.

4 Finally, click Insert.

Completing step 3 is easy when the remote Web site provides direct hyperlinks to pictures, typically through thumbnail previews. Otherwise, it's usually easier to just copy the picture's URL out of the Web page and paste it into the Picture dialog box. Here are the procedures for copying and pasting a picture's URL:

● In Internet Explorer:

  1 Locate a Web page containing the picture you want.

  2 Right-click the picture and choose Properties from the shortcut menu.

  3 When the Properties dialog box appears, select the contents of the Address (URL) box by dragging the mouse pointer across it. Then copy the address by:

   ◆ Pressing Ctrl+C; or

   ◆ Right-clicking the Address box and choosing Copy from the shortcut menu.

  4 Click OK to close the dialog box.

  5 Return to FrontPage and redisplay the Picture dialog box.

  6 Click the File Name box to activate the insertion point, and then press Ctrl+V or Shift+Insert to enter the URL you copied in step 3. Click Insert.

Chapter 11

313

- In Netscape Navigator:

  1 Locate a Web page containing the picture you want.

  2 Right-click the picture and choose Copy Image Location from the shortcut menu.

  3 Return to FrontPage and redisplay the Picture dialog box.

  4 Click the Fie Name box to activate the insertion point, and then press Ctrl+V or Shift+Insert to enter the URL you copied in step 2. Click Insert.

The easiest way to insert pictures from the Web doesn't require using the Picture dialog box at all. However, it works only with Internet Explorer:

1 Open the page that needs to display a picture.

2 Use Internet Explorer to display a Web page that already contains the picture you want to display in your Web page.

3 Right-click the picture and choose Copy from the shortcut menu.

4 Switch back to FrontPage, set the insertion point where you want the picture to appear, and press Ctrl+V to paste the picture directly into the Web page. (Invoking the Paste command any other way works equally well.)

Inserting Clip Art

If you don't have an existing picture that meets your needs, it's very likely you can find one in the extensive Clip Organizer that comes with FrontPage. The Clip Organizer is a shared resource used by the entire Office XP suite of programs. This means any clip art you install for any Office application (such as Microsoft Publisher) is available to FrontPage as well. FrontPage also provides a series of clips on the Web that includes buttons, horizontal rules, backgrounds, pictures, and other figures you can use to enhance your Web pages.

Office XP provides three distinctly different ways to search for and select clip art:

- The Insert Clip Art task pane shown in Figure 11-5 provides a quick and easy way to search for clip art without leaving FrontPage and without obscuring the current Web page.

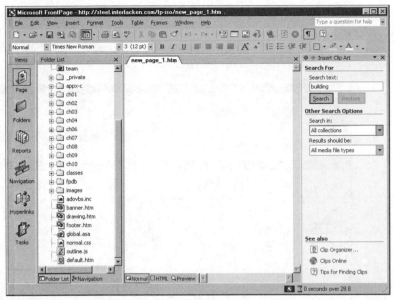

Figure 11-5. This task pane searches for clip art pictures without obscuring or disabling the main document window.

● The Clip Organizer application shown in Figure 11-6 provides more ways to search for clip art, more screen space to display search hits, and better previewing capabilities.

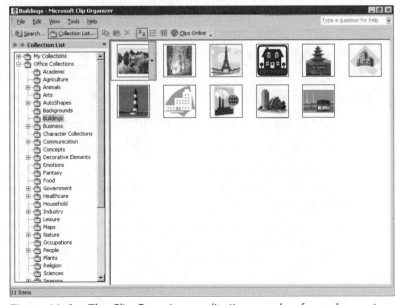

Figure 11-6. The Clip Organizer application searches for and organizes clip art.

● Design Gallery Live, shown in Figure 11-7, provides additional clip art from Microsoft and a community section where you can share images and ideas with other people. You must agree to a license agreement before accessing the Design Gallery Live clip art.

Figure 11-7. Microsoft's Design Gallery Live site provides additional Microsoft clip art and provides a way for clip art users and creators to find each other.

Here's the procedure for inserting a piece of clip art by means of the Insert Clip Art task pane:

1 Open the Web page that you want to display the clip art picture.

2 Set the insertion point where you want the picture to appear.

3 Choose Picture from the Insert menu, and then choose Clip Art.

4 When the Insert Clip Art task pane appears as shown at the right of Figure 11-5, use one or more of the following controls to describe the picture you hope to find:

■ **Search Text.** Enter one or more keywords that categorize the picture. Concrete terms like man, woman, building, and water usually produce better results than abstract terms like happy and sad.

- **Search In.** Display this drop-down list and modify the category selections to further refine your search. By default, All Collections is selected. To limit the search, clear the categories you don't want. To display subcategories, click the Plus sign that precedes each category. The example shown in the following graphic searches the entire My Collections collection and the Agriculture and Animals portions of the Office Collections collection.

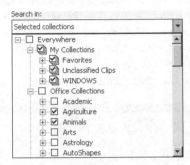

- **Results Should Be.** Display this drop-down list to specify the file formats you want: Clip Art, Photographs, Movies, or Sounds. To display subtypes, click the Plus sign that precedes each file format. This list starts with all file formats selected. Clear any file formats you don't want.

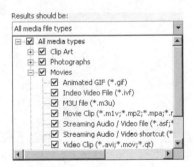

5 After you've described your criteria as completely as possible, click the Search button. This will hide your input fields and display a Results list in their place. As soon as this happens, FrontPage begins searching for matching art.

6 While searching is in progress, the message "(Searching…)" appears near the top of the Insert Clip Art task pane and a Stop button appears at the bottom. To terminate the search, click the Stop button.

> **tip** To resize the Insert Clip Art task pane (or, for that matter, any other task pane), drag its inner border to the right or left. To move any task pane to the outer side of the main window, drag its title bar. To detach a task pane, drag its title bar completely outside the main FrontPage window. To reattach it, drag the title bar over the left or right window border.

7 When the search is complete, the (Searching…) message disappears and a Modify button replaces the Stop button. The Results box displays a scrollable list of matching pictures. Holding the mouse pointer over any picture displays the pop-up information box and the drop-down arrow shown in Figure 11-8. The pop-up information shows the picture's assigned keywords, its width and height, its size, and its format.

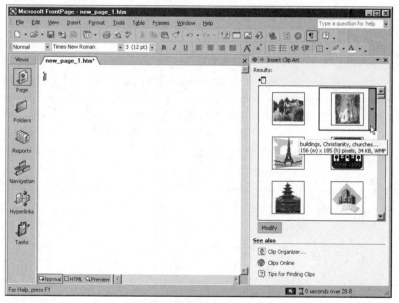

Figure 11-8. After a clip art picture appears in the Insert Clip Art task pane, clicking it adds it to the current Web page.

8 To add any displayed clip art picture to a Web page, open the page, set the insertion point, and then click the displayed picture once. For more options, click the picture's drop-down arrow. Here are the options this provides:

■ **Insert.** Adds the selected picture to the current Web page at the insertion point.

- **Copy.** Copies the selected picture to the Clipboard. This is handy if you want to paste the clip art picture into another program, modify it, and only then paste it into your Web page.

- **Delete From Clip Organizer.** Removes the selected picture from the Clip Organizer.

- **Open Clip In.** Starts an editor capable of modifying the selected picture and tells that program to open it.

- **Tools On The Web.** Displays Microsoft's Web site devoted to clip art.

- **Copy To Collection.** Copies the selected picture's catalog entry to another area of the Clip Organizer. For example, you might want to create your own collection of frequently used pictures.

- **Move To Collection.** Moves the selected picture's catalog entry to another area of the Clip Organizer.

- **Edit Keywords.** Displays a Keywords dialog box where you can add, modify, or delete the keywords assigned to the current picture. You can use this facility to associate pictures with keywords (like product departments, or project names) that are uniquely meaningful to you.

- **Find Similar Style.** Conducts a new search, this time for pictures drawn in the same style as the selected picture. Using the same clip art style throughout a Web site adds to the site's sense of unity.

- **Preview/Properties.** Displays a dialog box that shows a larger version of the selected picture and a text listing of Its properties (name, file format, size, creation date, keywords, and so forth).

9 Unless you're having the luckiest day of the year, the newly inserted clip art picture will almost certainly be too large, too small, too light, too dark, or too terrible to describe. Fortunately, FrontPage has built-in tools for correcting such problems. Even more fortunately, a later section in this chapter describes how to use them.

> For more information about modifying pictures in Web pages, refer to "Modifying Picture Properties" later in this chapter.

10 If the search results are unsatisfactory (or if you just want to start a new search), click the Modify button. This displays the clip art Search fields with all previous Search options still in effect. Modify any settings you like, click the Search button, and return to step 6.

319

Frequently Asked Questions About WMF Files

Is it true that WMF stands for World Mustache Federation?

No. Windows Metafile (WMF) is a file format that stores the Windows API commands required to draw something on your screen. WMF usually stores pictures as lines, curves, and shapes rather than as pixels. This makes WMF a great format for clip art because you can enlarge, reduce, or reshape such pictures with no loss of resolution. Microsoft supplies most clip art pictures in WMF format.

Is Windows Metafile a good format for display on the Web?

No. Because some browsers can't display WMF, it isn't a good format to use on Web pages. FrontPage therefore converts pasted WMF pictures to GIF or JPEG format the first time you save the receiving page.

Is it better to modify WMF pictures before or after FrontPage converts them to GIF or JPEG?

After FrontPage converts a WMF picture to GIF or JPEG, resizing or otherwise changing the picture will degrade the picture just as it does for any other GIF or JPEG file. Therefore, it's much better to resize, resample, or otherwise modify any new clip art pictures before you save the page that contains them. This ensures that the picture is saved with the proper size and without loss of resolution.

Is there any way to convert a WMF picture to GIF or JPEG format without saving the Web page?

Yes. After the picture is the size you want, select it and click the Resample button on the Pictures toolbar.

For more information on resizing and resampling pictures, refer to "Resampling Pictures" on page 660.

Clicking the Clip Organizer link at the bottom of the Insert Clip Art task pane starts the Clip Organizer application pictured in Figure 11-9. You can also start Clip Organizer directly from the Programs submenu of the Windows Start menu; it's under Microsoft Office Tools.

The Search task pane in Clip Organizer works exactly as it does in FrontPage. When a search yields results, however, the matching files appear in the main document window instead of a Search results task pane. The main document window has three viewing modes, which you can select by using either the View menu or the Clip Organizer Standard toolbar:

- **Thumbnails.** Displays a small preview picture of each matching file.
- **List.** Displays a compact list of each matching file name.

- **Details.** Displays the file name, size, type, caption, keywords, duration, and date of each matching file. Duration refers to the amount of time that a sound or video file will play.

Thumbnails   List   Details

 For more information about the Clip Organizer Standard toolbar, refer to "The Microsoft Clip Organizer Standard Toolbar" in the Bonus Content on the Companion CD.

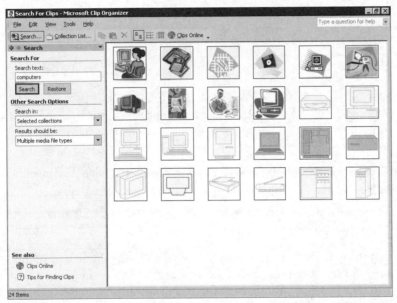

Figure 11-9. Microsoft Clip Organizer searches for pictures and other media files. It can also add, rearrange, and delete individual files or whole collections within the gallery.

To view the entire contents of a given collection:

1 Click the Collection List button on the Clip Organizer toolbar or choose Collection List from the View menu. This shows the Collection List task pane shown in Figure 11-10 on the next page.

Collection List

321

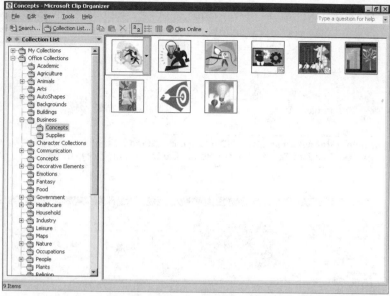

Figure 11-10. The Collection List task pane displays the names of each collection in the Clip Organizer. The main document window shows the clip art files in the current gallery.

2 Click any listed collection to display all its files in the main document window.

3 To view files in subfolders, expand the parent folder and click the subfolder you want to view.

Note that the main document window doesn't display files located in subfolders of a collection you select. For that, you must explicitly select the subfolder. Clicking a plus sign displays the subfolders of a given folder and clicking a minus icon hides them.

Use the menu commands listed below to add, reorganize, or delete Clip Organizer files or collections:

● File:

■ **New Collection.** Creates a new collection folder and specifies its location.

■ **Open Clip In.** Loads a selected picture into the default editor for its file type. If the file type has no default editor on your system, an Open With dialog box will prompt for one.

- **Add Clips To Organizer.** Enlarges the gallery with new files. This command can add all media files on all or part of your hard disk, individual files, or files from a scanner or camera.

- **Send To Mail Recipient (As Attachment).** Sends an e-mail message containing the currently selected clip files to recipients you specify.

- **Collection Properties.** Displays or modifies the physical location of the current collection and offers an option to update the Clip Organizer index with current information.

● Edit:

- **Cut, Copy,** and **Paste.** Work as they do in all other Windows programs.

- **Move To Collection.** Relocates the catalog entries of the currently selected clip files to a different collection.

- **Copy To Collection.** Duplicates the catalog entries for the currently selected clip files in a different collection.

- **Rename Collection.** Changes the name of a collection.

- **Delete From Collection.** Removes the catalog entries for the currently selected clip files from the current collection.

- **Delete From Clip Organizer.** Removes all catalog entries for the currently selected clip files from all collections where they occur.

- **Keywords.** Displays a Keywords dialog box where you can add, modify, or delete the keywords assigned to the current picture. This is the same dialog box you get by right-clicking a picture and choosing Edit Keywords from its shortcut menu.

● View:

- **Thumbnails, List, Details, Collection List,** and **Search.** Duplicate the functions of the corresponding toolbar buttons.

- **Preview/Properties.** Displays a dialog box that shows a larger version of the selected picture and a text listing of its properties. This is the same dialog box you get by right-clicking a picture and choosing Preview/Properties from its shortcut menu.

- **Refresh.** Reloads the display with current information.

● Tools:

- **Compact.** Reclaims wasted space in the Clip Organizer catalog.

Inserting Pictures from a Scanner or Camera

To record a picture directly from a scanner or digital camera to a Web page, follow this procedure:

1 Open the Web page that should contain the scanned picture.

2 Set the insertion point where you want the scanned picture to appear.

3 Choose Picture from the Insert menu, and then choose From Scanner Or Camera.

4 If FrontPage displays a dialog box like the one in the following graphic, click the Source Button, select the scanner or camera you want to use, and then click Select. Finally, click the Acquire button.

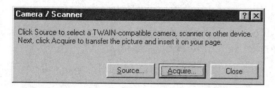

5 The software that captures pictures from your scanner or camera appears. Acquire the picture you want by following the instructions that came with that software.

6 Instead of the usual Save and Save As commands, the scanning software provides a command called Place Image, Insert Picture, or something of the like. Choose this command to terminate the scanner or camera software and add the scanned picture to your Web page.

7 The next time you save the Web page, FrontPage will display the Save Embedded Files dialog box to confirm the file name and folder location for the captured picture.

Inserting Video Files

FrontPage can add video clips to a Web page in three distinctly different ways. Here are the possibilities:

Broken
Picture

● **Display The Video As A Picture File.** This is the easiest and most direct way to add video using FrontPage, but it creates HTML that Netscape Navigator doesn't understand. Instead of the video, Netscape displays a Broken Picture icon.

Internet Explorer displays a video inserted this way, but without any playback controls such as Play, Pause, and Stop, or a Playback bar.

Troubleshooting

Unable to connect to scanner or camera

Whenever you choose the From Scanner Or Camera command, FrontPage searches the local computer's configuration for software that complies with a specification called TWAIN. If no such software is installed on the computer running FrontPage, the following message appears:

> *Unable to connect to scanner or camera. Check the connection and reinstall driver if necessary.*

The normal way to resolve this problem is to locate the COMPUTER software that came with your scanner or camera and install it on the computer running FrontPage.

This message might also appear if the software is installed but your scanner or camera is turned off or not connected to your computer. The solution in this case is to make sure the device is properly connected and turned on.

Most scanner and camera software complies with the TWAIN specification. If yours doesn't, save the picture to disk and drag the disk file from Windows Explorer to your open Web page.

- **Display The Video Using An ActiveX Control.** This method creates HTML that tells the browser to load a specific ActiveX control—usually the Windows Media Player—and have the ActiveX control display the video. This method can either display or suppress playback controls in Windows versions of Internet Explorer, but displays nothing in any other browser.

For more information about using ActiveX controls, refer to "Incorporating ActiveX Controls" on page 716.

- **Display The Video Using A Plug-In.** This method tells the browser to retrieve the video file from your Web server and then display it using whatever program the browser associates with the video's file type. This means the Web visitor controls—by configuring the browser—what program displays your video. Although you have no control over which, if any, program displays the video, this method works with all current-day browsers.

For more information about using Plug-Ins, refer to "Incorporating Plug-Ins" on page 736.

Chapter 11

Frequently Asked Questions About Video Files

What guidelines exist for distributing video on the Web?

- Exercise restraint when placing video files on Web pages. These files are extremely large by Web standards and might take several minutes to download, possibly frustrating or angering some visitors.

- Place warnings on hyperlinks that lead to such downloads so that viewers have a chance to avoid starting a lengthy download.

- If you're using a plug-in to display the video, tell your visitors which plug-in you expect them to have and provide a hyperlink to its download location.

What's the procedure for displaying an animated GIF file?

Animated GIF files don't qualify here as video. Insert animated GIFs using the Picture dialog box, as you would for any other GIF or JPG picture.

Here's the procedure for enhancing your Web page with a video that will display as a picture file:

1 If the video file doesn't reside in the current Web, drag it from its current location and drop it into the FrontPage Folder List or Folders view. The *images* folder is a good place to store such files.

2 Open the Web page that should display the video.

3 Set the insertion point where you want the video to appear.

4 Choose Picture from the Insert menu and select Video. This will display a Video dialog box that's almost identical to the Picture dialog box shown in Figure 11-4.

5 Select the video file you want to display. Normally, this will be a file with an *.avi* file name extension. Click Open.

> **tip** Dragging a video file from the Folder List and cropping it onto an open Web page accomplishes the same results as procedure steps 3 through 6.

The WYSIWYG editor in Page view doesn't display video files in full animation and sound. Instead, to avoid distractions, FrontPage displays the first video frame as a still picture. If you want to see the video file actually play, click the Preview tab at the bottom of the Page view window. Figure 11-11 shows how the page should look.

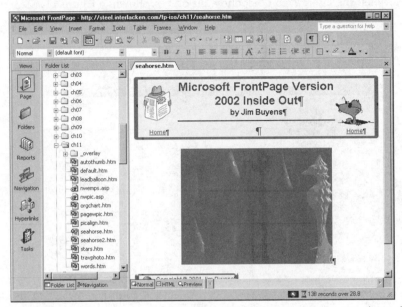

Figure 11-11. Adding a video like this to any Web page is as simple as dragging it from the Folder List and dropping it into the page.

To modify the playback properties of a video on any open Web page, first double-click it to display the Picture Properties dialog box and then select the Video tab. Right-clicking the video and then choosing Picture Properties accomplishes the same end.

> For more information about configuring video properties, refer to "Modifying Video Proper-ties" later in this chapter.

Here's the procedure for inserting an ActiveX control that displays a video:

1 If the video file doesn't reside in the current Web, drag it from its current location and drop it into the FrontPage Folder List or Folders view. The *images* folder is a good place to store such files.

2 Open the Web page that should display the video.

3 Set the insertion point where you want the video to appear.

4 Choose Web Component from the Insert menu.

5 When the Insert Web Component dialog box appears, choose Advanced Controls from the Component Type list.

6 Choose ActiveX Control from the Choose A Control list and then click Next.

7 When the Insert Web Component dialog box shown in Figure 11-12 appears, make sure ActiveMovieControl Object is selected, and then click Finish.

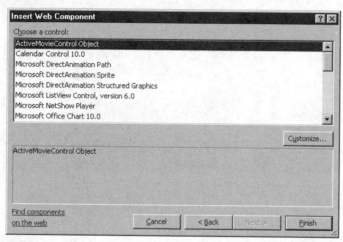

Figure 11-12. From this dialog box, select the control you want to insert.

8 You must now tell the ActiveMovieControl Object which video file to play. To do this, double-click the control (or right-click it and choose ActiveX Control Properties).

9 When the Options dialog box shown in the lower left corner of Figure 11-13 appears, click the Parameters tab and scroll down to the Filename attribute. Double-click the line that contains this property (or select it and then click the Modify button) to display the Edit Object Parameter dialog box also shown in Figure 11-13.

10 Click the Page option under Value, and then click the Browse button to locate the video file you want to display. When the associated text box shows the right file name, click Open, and then click OK twice to close both dialog boxes.

> For more information about using ActiveX controls, refer to "Incorporating ActiveX Controls" on page 716. For instructions on inserting a Plug-In that displays a video, refer to "Plug-Ins" on page 59. For general information about using Plug-Ins, refer to "Incorporating Plug-Ins" on page 736.

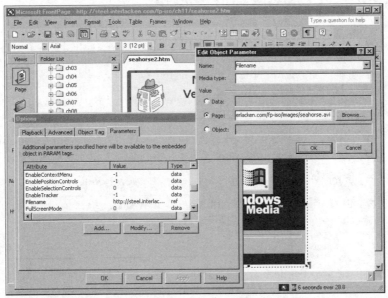

Figure 11-13. These general-purpose dialog boxes configure the properties of most ActiveX controls. Here, they're configuring an ActiveMovieControl.

Inserting Sound Files

The browser can play a background sound while Web visitors view your page. To add this feature, follow the instructions given in Chapter 18 for the Page Properties dialog box.

The procedure for setting up a hyperlink that plays a sound file is the same as that for linking to any other type of file. Chapter 12 explains how to do this.

For more information about playing a background sound, refer to "General Page Properties" on page 538. For more information about building hyperlinks of any kInd, refer to Chapter 12, "Building Hyperlinks."

Keep in mind that WAV files, although very common in Windows environments, usually aren't supported in others. Browsers on virtually all operating systems support a sound file format named AU, which was first developed on UNIX, but finding software that converts WAV files to AU format can be difficult.

Musical Instrument Digital Interface (MIDI) files (which on PCs often have the file name extension *.mid*) also enjoy wide support and tend to be small in size. However, because MIDI files essentially record the musician's actions rather than the resulting sound, creating a MIDI file generally requires playing music on a synthesizer or scoring notes in a specialized music program.

Inserting Text On GIF Components

The Text On GIF component is quite a unique feature. Any time an open Web page contains a picture, the following procedure can overlay the picture with text:

Text

1 Select the picture you want to overlay with text.

2 Click the Text button on the Pictures toolbar. If the picture you selected isn't in GIF format, a message box asks whether to convert it or exit.

3 Unless you exited the procedure in step 2, a bounding box and a second set of sizing handles appears within the picture area.

4 Enter whatever text you want inside the new bounding box.

5 To change the font properties of the new text, select the text and then choose Font from the Format menu.

Flip
Vertical

The Web page shown in Figure 11-14 includes three Text On GIF components: the text on the trailing banner and the text on the two blimps are both hand-entered. The Flip Vertical button on the Pictures toolbar inverted both the blimps and the overlaying text.

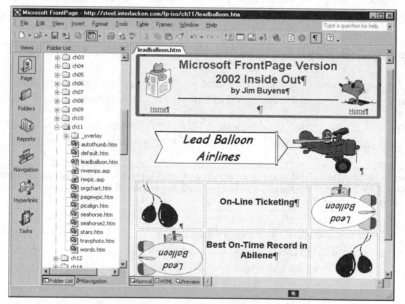

Figure 11-14. This Web page displays three Text On GIF components: the airplane banner and the two blimps. The text remains fully editable even between editing sessions.

When you overtype a graphic with text, FrontPage remembers the file name of the original picture, the text string you enter, and the font characteristics you specify. It then formats the text onto the picture, saves the results using an internally generated file name, and displays the combined text-and-graphics picture rather than the original.

This feature is useful not only for labeling pictures, but also for creating headings and titles that use special fonts or colors. To create headings and titles, you should typically choose a textured surface, solid color, or completely transparent picture as the background.

> For more information about the Text on GIF component, refer to "Adding Text to Pictures" on page 649.

Inserting Drawings

Figure 11-15 shows a drawing done entirely in FrontPage. The various boxes, lines, text fragments, and shading are all VML objects. Transmitting a VML drawing to the Web visitor uses far less bandwidth than transmitting a GIF or JPEG picture of the same size. This is because VML transmits instructions for drawing the objects rather than a picture of the entire diagram.

Chapter 21 includes detailed instructions for creating drawings such as the one shown in Figure 11-15.

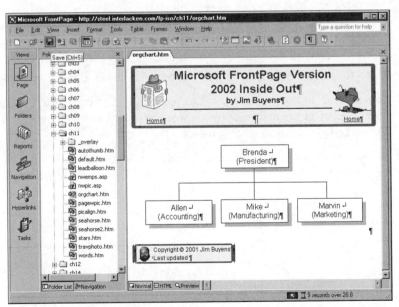

Figure 11-15. This line art drawing was drafted completely in FrontPage. If a browser supports VML, downloading the line art will be much faster than downloading an ordinary picture file of the same size.

At a surface level the procedure for creating this picture goes like this:

1 Set the insertion point where you want the drawing to appear.

2 Choose Picture from the Insert menu, and then choose New Drawing. This creates a drawing area, which appears as the large shaded rectangle shown in Figure 11-15. A Drawing Canvas toolbar also appears; this controls the size of the drawing area (that is, of the canvas). If necessary, use the side handles to change the size of the drawing.

For more information about the Drawing Canvas toolbar, refer to "The Drawing Canvas Tool-bar" in the Bonus Content on the Companion CD.

3 If the Drawing toolbar isn't visible, choose Toolbars from the View menu and then choose Drawing. The Drawing toolbar appears below the main document window in Figure 11-15.

For more information about the Drawing toolbar, refer to "The Drawing Toolbar" in the Bonus Content on the Companion CD.

Text Box

4 To create each of the four text boxes shown in Figure 11-15, first click the Text Box button on the Drawing toolbar and then drag the mouse pointer across the area where you want the text box to appear.

You can alter text boxes in the following ways:

- To resize a box, drag one of its side handles.

- To reposition a box, drag it by the edge.

- To enter text in a box, click in the center of the box and start typing.

Line

5 To draw each of the connecting lines, click the Line button on the Drawing toolbar, position the mouse pointer where you want the line to start, and then drag the pointer to where you want the line to end.

Shadow

6 To add the three-dimensional shading, click the Shadow Style button on the Drawing toolbar and then click the style of shading you want.

If you plan to start working with drawings without referring to Chapter 21, you should know that drawing areas use CSS Positioning. This technology positions objects on a Web page in a variety of ways, including pixel-precise X-Y coordinates. CSS Positioning is a powerful but frustrating tool because not all browsers support it equally.

For more information about CSS Positioning, refer to "Positioning Content with Style Sheets" on page 629.

Not all browsers support VML either, but this is less of a problem than you might expect. Every time you save a Web page that contains an object created using the Drawing tools, FrontPage creates a copy of the drawing as a GIF file. Then inside the VML code, it buries an HTML tag that displays the GIF file. Browsers that understand the VML code bypass the tag that displays the GIF file, and those that don't understand VML will ignore it and display the GIF file. This accounts for the fact that in Figure 11-16, Netscape Navigator is displaying the drawing created in Figure 11-15.

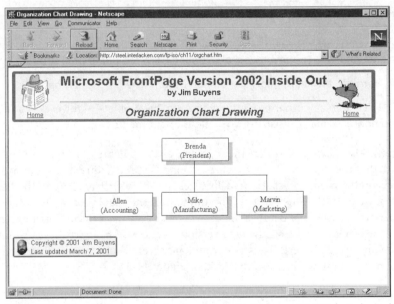

Figure 11-16. Netscape Navigator 4.x doesn't support VML but does display this drawing by downloading a substitute GIF file.

For more information about creating drawings in FrontPage, refer to "Creating Drawings" on page 662.

newfeature!
Inserting AutoShapes

Many common objects such as arrows, banners, flowchart symbols, and charts are very tedious to draw using only basic elements such as curves, lines, and boxes. FrontPage therefore includes several collections of predrawn shapes you can include in your Web page. Here's the procedure for inserting one of these shapes:

1 Set the insertion point where you want the shape to appear.

2 Choose Picture from the Insert menu, and then choose AutoShapes.

3 When the AutoShapes toolbar appears, click any of the first six buttons to display a drop-down list of available shapes. To add any shape you want to the current Web page, click it, and then drag it in the desired direction until it's the size you want.

 For more information about the AutoShapes toolbar, refer to "The WordArt Toolbar" in the Bonus Content on the Companion CD.

4 To resize the inserted shape or change its proportions, select it and drag the side handles. To move the shape around the Web page, drag it by the edge.

5 To rotate the shape, drag its rotation button (the little green handle).

6 To change any other property of an AutoShape object, right-click it and choose Format AutoShape from the shortcut menu.

Figure 11-17 shows a Web page that contains an AutoShape object: a large gray star. Notice that the star is partially transparent, and that it occupies the same space as other objects on the page. The star is actually black, but it's 95% transparent; the transparency is a feature of VML. The fact that it occupies the same space as, but lies behind, ordinary Web content is possible because the drawing uses features of CSS Positioning. Because Netscape Navigator, at least through version 4.7, doesn't support these features, it won't display this page properly. Netscape would, however, display a page that used AutoShapes along the lines, so to speak, of Figure 11-15.

You can avoid compatibility problems of this type by not overlapping drawings (or other objects) with other content. As long as Netscape can display a GIF file instead of the VML drawing, the page will look essentially the same on either browser.

For more information about CSS Positioning, refer to "Positioning Content with Style Sheets" on page 629. For more information about creating AutoShape objects, refer to "Creating AutoShapes" on page 660.

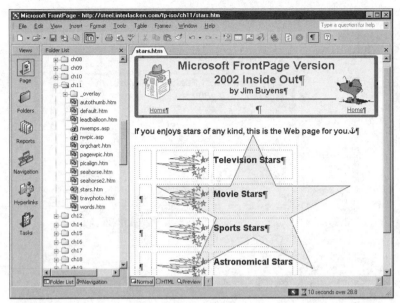

Figure 11-17. The large star in this Web page is transparent and occupies a layer behind the normal Web content.

Inserting WordArt

Applications like Word, Excel, and PowerPoint have for some time provided a feature called WordArt that transforms text into a decorative object. Now, for the first time, FrontPage's support for drawing objects makes the WordArt feature practical on Web pages as well. A WordArt object formatted the phrase "Words for Worriers" in Figure 11-18 on the next page. Here's the procedure for creating such an object:

1 Set the insertion point where you want the WordArt object to appear.

2 Choose Picture from the Insert menu, and then choose WordArt.

3 When the WordArt Gallery shown in Figure 11-19 on the next page appears, select one of the styles shown, and then click OK.

4 When the Edit WordArt Text dialog box appears, enter the text you want to display. Change the font, size, bold, and italic properties if you want, and then click OK.

5 The WordArt object now appears in your Web page. To change its size, proportions, or rotation, use the handles that appear when you select it. To make other changes, right-click it, and then choose Format WordArt from the shortcut menu.

Chapter 11

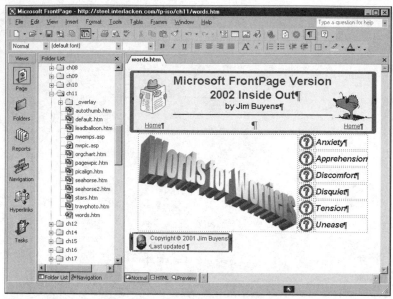

Figure 11-18. WordArt provides stylized rendition of text.

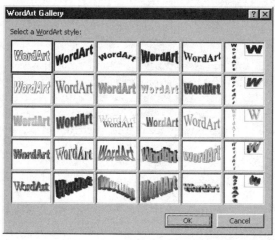

Figure 11-19. These formats are available when you create a WordArt object. You can introduce many other variations after the WordArt object exists.

As with drawing and AutoShape objects, FrontPage uses VML whenever possible to display WordArt objects. If the browser ignores the VML code, it will discover an ordinary tag that displays an equivalent (though slower to download) GIF picture.

> **For more information about creating WordArt objects, refer to "Creating WordArt Objects" on page 664.**

Chapter 11

Modifying Picture Properties

Very often, making a picture appear on a Web page is only half the job. The remainder involves details of placement and presentation. HTML, and therefore FrontPage, provides a variety of settings for this purpose.

To open the Picture Properties dialog box, do *one* of the following while in the Page view editing window:

- Click a picture and choose Properties from the Format menu.
- Right-click a picture and choose Picture Properties from the shortcut menu.
- Click a picture and press Alt+Enter.
- Double-click a picture.

The three tabs of the Picture Properties dialog box are shown in Figure 11-20, Figure 11-22, and Figure 11-25.

Modifying Size and Placement Properties

The Appearance tab of the Picture Properties dialog box, shown in Figure 11-20, controls picture layout and size.

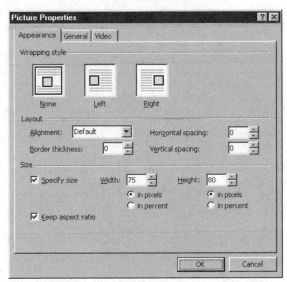

Figure 11-20. The Appearance tab on the Picture Properties dialog box controls page positioning and displayed picture size.

This tab controls the following settings:

- **Wrapping Style.** This group of controls provides a quick way to set the Alignment control in the next group to the three most frequently used choices:

  - **None.** Sets the Alignment control to None.

  - **Left.** Sets the Alignment control to Left.

  - **Right.** Sets the Alignment control to Right.

- **Layout.** This section positions the picture relative to any surrounding text:

  - **Alignment.** Controls vertical positioning of a picture and text in the same line. See Table 11-2 for a listing and description of each option.

Table 11-2. HTML Picture Alignment Settings

Alignment	Description
Default	Sends the browser no instructions as to picture alignment. Most browsers, however, default to *baseline*.
Left	Floats the picture down and left to the next spot available at the left margin; wraps subsequent text around the right side of that picture. See Figure 11-21 for illustrations of this and the following settings.
Right	Aligns the picture with the right margin; wraps subsequent text around the left side of that picture.
Top	Aligns the picture with the top of the tallest item in the line.
Texttop	Aligns the picture with the top of the tallest text in the line (this is usually, but not always, the same as top).
Middle	Aligns the baseline of the current line with the middle of the picture.
Absmiddle	Aligns the middle of the current line with the middle of the picture.
Baseline	Aligns the bottom of the picture with the baseline of the current line.
Bottom	Aligns the bottom of the picture with the baseline of the current line.
Absbottom	Aligns the bottom of the picture with the bottom of the current line.
Center	Aligns the bottom of the picture with the baseline of the current line; see Figure 11-21 for illustrations of this and the following settings.

  - **Border Thickness.** If nonzero, surrounds the picture with a border. The specified integer controls the border's thickness in pixels. Hyperlinked pictures have blue borders; others have black borders.

  - **Horizontal Spacing.** Controls the separation, in pixels, between the picture and other elements on the same line.

■ **Vertical Spacing.** Controls separation between the picture and any text or pictures in lines above or below.

● **Size.** This frame controls the displayed size of a picture:

■ **Specify Size.** If selected, indicates you want to override the natural size of the picture.

■ **Width.** Sets the amount of horizontal space the browser should reserve for the picture. Use the In Pixels or the In Percent buttons to denote the units of width.

■ **Height.** Sets the amount of vertical space the browser should reserve for the picture. Use the In Pixels or the In Percent buttons to denote the units of height.

■ **Keep Aspect Ratio.** Specifies that changing either the picture's height or its width changes the other dimension proportionally.

As Figure 11-21 illustrates, placing pictures inline with text pictures often also results in uneven, distracting line spacing. Therefore, most Web designers demand more control over picture placement than inline pictures provide.

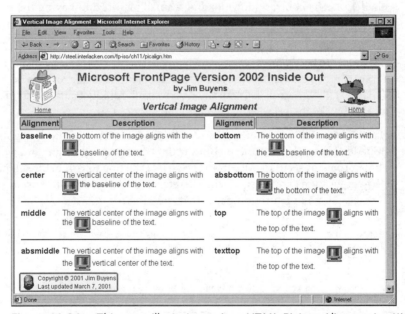

Figure 11-21. This page illustrates various HTML Picture Alignment settings.

This explains why, of the nine picture-alignment settings, Left and Right are probably the most often used. The Left and Right settings provide at least some absolute positioning—to the margins—and they also maintain uniform line spacing.

339

To center a picture by itself, put it in its own paragraph. To center the paragraph, do either of the following:

Center

● Select the paragraph and click the Center button on the Text toolbar.

● Right-click the paragraph, choose Paragraph from the shortcut menu, and set the Alignment control to Center.

By default, the browser determines the size of each picture it receives and then displays it at its natural size. Nevertheless, most experienced Web designers hard code pictures sizes into their HTML. Here are the reasons:

● Using the default behavior, the browser can't allocate window space to a picture until it's received enough of the file to determine its dimensions. Not knowing the size of a picture might also delay placement—and therefore display—of other page elements. Specifying sizes for all pictures on a page means many page elements display sooner than otherwise might be possible.

● Occasionally, you might want to display a picture larger or smaller than its natural size. This used to be rare because downloading a large picture and having the browser reduce it takes more time than downloading a smaller one. By contrast, downloading a small picture and having the browser expand it results in a loss of resolution. More recently, however, the practice of expanding small pictures has become surprisingly common.

Anywhere Web designers want some blank space on a page, they display a transparent picture. Because such pictures, being invisible, can't possibly look fuzzy, designers usually specify a very small, rapidly transmitted picture and make the browser stretch it to the required size.

● Older browsers tend to have difficulty with pages containing both scripts embedded in the HTML and pictures with no preassigned height and width. These problems seem to arise from the scripts starting to run before all page element locations are determined. Therefore, always specify dimensions—in pixels—for all pictures on pages that contain scripts.

> For more information about the use of transparent pictures to reserve white space, refer to "Using Transparent Pictures for Page Layout" on page 503.

 For more information on scripts that run when the browser receives a page, refer to "Scripting Web Pages on the Browser" in the Bonus Content on the Companion CD.

Fortunately, FrontPage automatically hard codes picture sizes in the following two cases:

● For all pictures in the current Web, even if the Specify Size box shown in Figure 11-20 isn't selected

● For all pictures, regardless of location, where you select the Specify Size box and choose a Width and Height in pixels

Chapter 11

Modifying General Picture Properties

You can use the General tab of the Picture Properties dialog box shown in Figure 11-22 to modify the properties of a picture. Certain options might be unavailable (dimmed), depending on the context.

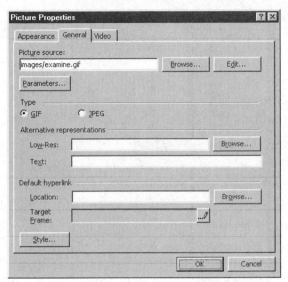

Figure 11-22. The General tab of the Picture Properties dialog box specifies the location of a picture file and other details of presentation.

The full complement of fields includes the following:

● **Picture Source.** This text box specifies the full or relative URL of the picture file being modified. It might be read-only, depending on the context.

   ▥ **Browse.** Click this button to browse the current Web or file system to locate a picture. This option will be dimmed if the Picture Source box isn't modifiable.

   ▥ **Edit.** Click this button to modify the current picture. FrontPage chooses an editor based on the picture's filename extension.

 For more information about configuring FrontPage to run the picture editor you want, refer to "Configuring External Editors" in the Bonus Content on the Companion CD.

   ▥ **Parameters.** Click this button if the browser should transmit query string parameters to the Web server whenever the browser requests the specified picture. FrontPage displays the Hyperlink Parameters dialog box shown in Figure 11-23 on the next page so you can add, modify, remove, or clear such parameters.

341

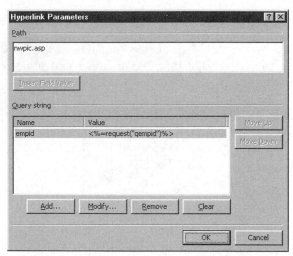

Figure 11-23. This dialog box creates, modifies, and deletes keyword=value expressions appended to a URL by means of a query string.

Here are two scenarios where this might be necessary:

◆ First, if the picture source specifies not an ordinary GIF or JPEG file, but rather a program that runs on the Web server and generates a picture file on the fly. Many such programs—and hit counters in particular—use query string parameters to control their results.

◆ Second, if you're displaying pictures (such as banner ads) provided by certain Internet advertising sites, you might need to specify parameters in order to get paid.

● **Type.** This section initially displays the current picture type—GIF or JPEG—and permits changing it:

■ **GIF.** If selected, this option instructs FrontPage to save the picture as a GIF file.

■ **JPEG.** If selected, this option instructs FrontPage to save the picture as a JPEG file.

> For more information about query strings, refer to "Coding URL Fields for Executable Programs" on page 384. For more information about programs that generate picture files, refer to the "Pictures by Programming" sidebar later in this chapter. For more information about the GIF and JPEG file formats, as well as additional file formats, refer to "Choosing Picture File Formats" on page 684.

● **Alternative Representations.** The fields in this section control alternate views of a picture:

■ **Low-Res.** This specifies a low-resolution picture the browser displays while downloading the larger picture file. You can use the Browse button to find such a picture file.

■ **Text.** This line of text appears in browsers that can't display the picture. Some browsers that *can* display pictures also display this text while the picture is downloading, or when the visitor passes the mouse pointer over the picture.

● **Default Hyperlink.** This section establishes a hyperlink to another location from any part of the current picture that has no hotspot defined. The command isn't available for background pictures:

■ **Location.** This field contains the URL the browser will retrieve when the Web visitor clicks the current picture. You can use the Browse button to locate it.

■ **Target Frame.** This field specifies the frame in which the Location page will appear.

● **Style.** This button accesses the Modify Style dialog box where you can apply cascading stylesheet properties to the current picture.

For more information on normal and hotspot hyperlinks, refer to "Creating and Managing Hyperlinks" on page 356. For more information about assigning CSS properties, refer to "Assigning Style Sheet Properties" on page 613.

Pictures by Programming

If you know anything about Active Server Pages, the dialog box shown in Figure 11-23 creates quite a dilemma. An Active Server Page (ASP) is usually a special Web page that contains not only HTML, but also special script code that runs on the Web server. The script code accesses databases, files, or other resources available on the server and uses this information to customize the HTML each Web visitor receives.

The *nwpic.asp* file referenced in the figure is a special ASP page that sends the browser a picture in bitmap (BMP) format rather than a Web page in HTML format. Specifically, the picture is a photo of an employee in the ubiquitous Northwind Traders database. The following HTML tag displays the photo for employee number 5:

```
<img src="nwpic.asp?empid=5">
```

(Microsoft distributes the Northwind Traders database in Microsoft Access format. Many Microsoft products use this database in sample exercises. A copy of this database, in Access 2002 format, is in the */fp-iso/fpdb* folder on the Companion CD.)

Interesting as this might—or might not—be, it would be even more interesting if the Web visitor could use an HTML form to select an employee, and then receive

(continued)

Pictures by Programming *(continued)*   not only the picture but also some associated database information. Figure 11-24 shows just such a page. The drop-down box appears as the Employee list to Web visitors but its name in HTML is *qempid.* It lists each employee in the database. When the Web visitor clicks the Submit button, the browser transmits the list box's name and a value associated with the current selection to the Web server. (In this case, the value associated with each selection is the employee ID.) The Web server then adds this name and value to a so-called *request* object.

Figure 11-24.   This Web page displays pictures stored as objects in an Access database. A better approach is to store only the picture name in the database.

The expression

```
<%=request("qempid")%>
```

is a small fragment of ASP code that searches for a field named *qempid* in the Web visitor's request and supplies its value.

Compare the HTML code that displays the picture for employee ID 5 with the following code which displays the picture for the employee selected in the *qempid* drop-down box when the Web visitor submitted the form:

```
<img src="nwpic.asp?empid=<%=request("qempid")%>">
```

For more information about drop-down boxes, refer to "Setting Drop-Down Box Properties" on page 872.

The Web page shown in Figure 11-24 involves quite a few advanced techniques, some of which this book touches upon only lightly. However, it does provide a somewhat realistic example of a picture location that uses query string parameters.

For more information about processing form data with Active Server Pages, refer to "Processing Form Data with ASP Pages" on page 910.

 For more information about using Active Server Pages to process databases, refer to Chapter 40, "Processing Databases with Active Server Pages" in the Bonus Content on the Companion CD.

---

on the web   For more information about sending pictures stored in an Access database to Web visitors, search for article Q175261, "Retrieving Bitmap from Access and Displaying In Web Page" on Microsoft's Web site at *http://www.microsoft.com/search*. For information about sending pictures stored in a Microsoft SQL Server database to Web visitors, search on Microsoft's Web site for article Q173308, "Displaying Images Stored in a BLOB Field."

Incidentally, the preferred method of displaying pictures associated with a database record is not to store the picture in the database, but only the picture's file name. Then when you write the ASP code that customizes the outgoing HTML, you can just insert the picture's file name into the picture tag. This way is much easier to program and much more efficient in terms of CPU usage than the method used in this example.

If you want to try running this example on your own Web server, you'll have to perform the following procedure first:

1   Log onto the Web server's console as an Administrator.

2   Copy the file named *dbpic.dll* from the *\dbpic* folder on the Companion CD into the *\WINNT\SYSTEM32* folder on the Web server's system drive.

3   Open a command window on the Web server.

4   Change to the system drive and then to the folder *\WINNT\SYSTEM32*.

5   Enter and run the following command:

```
regsrv32 dbpic.dll
```

A dialog box should appear that says, "DllRegisterServer in dbpic.dll succeeded."

6   Close the command window and log off the server.

Finally, please note that the techniques used in the *dbpic.dll* file are unsupported. Microsoft article Q175261 states this fact quite clearly. Because of this, the *dbpic.dll* file itself is unsupported as well.

Modifying Video Properties

The Video tab of the Picture Properties dialog box, shown in Figure 11-25, controls the display and playback of video files added to a Web page as a picture.

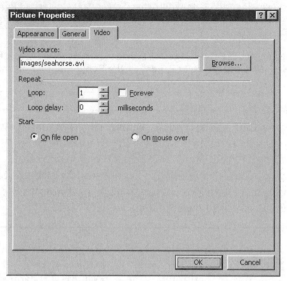

Figure 11-25. This tab controls presentation of full-motion video files.

> For more information about changing the properties of ActiveX controls or plug-ins that display video files, refer to "Incorporating ActiveX Controls" on page 716.

The options on this tab control the following:

- **Video Source.** Specify the location of the file containing digitized video. It can be in the current Web, on your local hard disk, on a file server, or on the World Wide Web. You can use the Browse button to locate the file.

> **note** If the Picture Properties dialog box contains both a Picture Source and a Video Source entry, the browser first displays the static picture and then, when possible, replaces it with the first frame of the video.

- **Repeat.** Settings in this section control the replaying of the video:

  - **Loop.** Controls the number of times the browser should replay the video.

  - **Forever.** Overrides the Loop setting and repeats the video continuously.

  - **Loop Delay.** Causes a delay between repeat playings. The default is zero; any other value is milliseconds. A five-second delay, for example, would be specified as 5000.

- **Start.** This section controls when the browser plays the video:

  - **On File Open.** Plays the video as soon as the browser opens the file.

  - **On Mouse Over.** Plays the video when the mouse pointer passes over the display area.

Organizing Pictures with Thumbnails

On the Web, a thumbnail is a small preview version of a larger picture. To view the full-sized picture, the Web visitor clicks its thumbnail equivalent. Thumbnails are very popular on Web pages that display a series of pictures the Web visitor can select because:

- The thumbnails download much faster than the full-sized pictures.

- The thumbnails present more options at a glance than are possible with full-sized pictures.

FrontPage provides two features that create thumbnails. The AutoThumbnail feature creates thumbnail pictures one at a time. The Photo Gallery feature organizes an entire set of pictures into a scrollable, clickable list of thumbnails that displays one full-sized picture at a time.

Using the AutoThumbnail Feature

The AutoThumbnail feature creates one thumbnail picture at a time. Here's the procedure for using it:

1 Open the Web page that you want to display the thumbnail.

2 Set the insertion point where you want the thumbnail to appear.

3 Insert the full-sized picture using any method.

4 If the Pictures toolbar isn't on display, choose Toolbars from the View menu, and then choose Pictures.

Auto
Thumbnail

5 Click the Auto Thumbnail button on the Pictures toolbar. FrontPage then takes these actions:

  - Removes the full-sized picture from the Web page

  - Inserts a thumbnail picture in its place

  - Creates a hyperlink from the thumbnail picture to the full-sized picture

Figure 11-26 on the next page shows typical results from using the AutoThumbnail feature. Clicking the small picture in the background page displays the large picture shown in the foreground page.

Chapter 11

Figure 11-26. Clicking the thumbnail picture in the background Web page displays the full-sized picture in the foreground.

To control the size, shape and other properties of the thumbnail picture, choose Page Options from the Tools menu, and then select the AutoThumbnail tab. This tab, shown in Figure 11-27, controls the size, border, and edge effects for any AutoThumbnail pictures you create in the future.

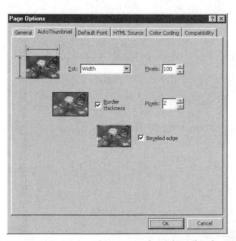

Figure 11-27. The AutoThumbnail tab controls the characteristics of all thumbnail pictures created by the Auto Thumbnail button on the Pictures toolbar.

Using the AutoThumbnail feature triggers the ubiquitous Save Embedded Files dialog box the next time you save the Web page. This confirms the save location for the new thumbnail pictures.

348

Troubleshooting

Using the Page Properties dialog box to create a thumbnail produces no improvement in download time.

You can display a large picture in a small space by opening the Picture Properties dialog box, selecting the Specify Size box on the Appearance tab, and specifying small values for height and width. This doesn't, however, create a smaller picture file. It only forces the browser to display the large picture in a small space.

If you want to create a thumbnail picture entirely by hand, set its display size as just described, close the Picture Properties dialog box, and then with the picture still selected, click the Resample button on the Pictures toolbar. The Resample button creates a new version of the picture with genuine, physically smaller dimensions.

Using the Resample button triggers the Save Embedded Files dialog box the next time you save the Web page, which in turn confirms the save location for the resampled picture. Unless you want to replace the full-sized picture, be sure to rename the thumbnail when this dialog box appears.

> For more information about the Resample feature for editing pictures, refer to "Resampling Pictures" on page 660.

Double-clicking a thumbnail picture in Page view (or right-clicking it and choosing Picture Properties from the shortcut menu) displays the properties of the thumbnail and not the properties of the original picture.

> For more information about creating thumbnail pictures, refer to "Creating Thumbnail Pictures" on page 652.

 For more information about configuring page options, refer to Chapter 45, "Configuring Page Creation Options" in the Bonus Content on the Companion CD.

newfeature!
Creating Photo Galleries

Regardless of the interest level of their audience, most people enjoy showing off their snapshot collections. This is as true in business and government institutions as it is in schools, clubs, and for individuals. To support this playful indulgence, FrontPage now includes a component designed specifically for displaying collections of photos. Its name, as you might suspect, is the Photo Gallery. Here's how to create one:

1 Open the Web page that you want to contain the Photo Gallery.

2 Set the insertion point where you want the Photo Gallery to appear.

349

Chapter 11

tip To create a new Web page and a new Photo Gallery in one fell swoop, pull down the menu associated with the New Page button on the Standard toolbar, choose Page, and then choose the Photo Gallery template.

3 Choose Web Component from the Insert menu.

4 Choose Photo Gallery from the Component Type list.

5 The right side of the Insert Web Component dialog box titles itself Choose A Photo Gallery Option and displays four thumbnail layouts: Horizontal, Vertical, Montage, and Slideshow. Choose the layout you want, and then click Finish. Don't obsess about your selection—you can change it later.

6 When the Photo Gallery Properties dialog box shown in Figure 11-28 appears, click the Add button to specify the location of each photo you want included in the gallery. This displays a drop-down menu with two choices:

■ **Pictures From Files.** This option displays the File Open dialog box. Use this dialog box just as you did the Picture dialog box shown previously in Figure 11-4. To select two or more pictures from the same folder, hold down the Shift or Ctrl key while you make your selections.

■ **Pictures From Scanner Or Cameras.** This option uses the techniques described previously in this chapter for capturing pictures directly from a scanner or camera.

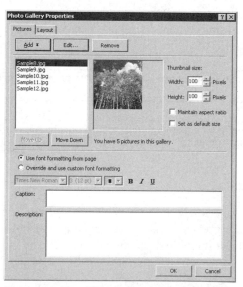

Figure 11-28. This dialog box configures the list of pictures in a Photo Gallery, the size of the thumbnails, and a caption and description for each picture. The Layout tab controls the gallery's overall appearance.

For more information about capturing pictures from a scanner or camera, refer to "Inserting Pictures from a Scanner or Camera" earlier in this chapter.

7 To move a picture up or down, select it and click the Move Up or Move Down button. To move several pictures up or down as a group, hold down the Shift or Ctrl key while selecting them.

8 To modify a picture, first select it, and then click the Edit button. This displays an Edit Picture dialog box that can resize, rotate, and crop pictures.

9 To remove a picture, select it, and then click the Remove button.

10 To enter a caption or description for any picture, select the picture, and fill in the Caption box, the Description box, or both. To change the font used for displaying these fields, use the controls above the Caption box.

11 Click the Layout tab to change the Photo Gallery's appearance. This tab provides the same four options as the Choose A Photo Gallery Option list mentioned in Step 5: Horizontal, Vertical, Montage, and Slideshow. Click OK when you're satisfied with your entries.

Figure 11-29 shows a fully configured Photo Gallery displayed in Internet Explorer. This Photo Gallery uses the Slideshow layout: clicking any thumbnail picture at the top of the page displays the corresponding full-sized picture at the bottom. The arrows at the left and right of the thumbnails move the list left and right.

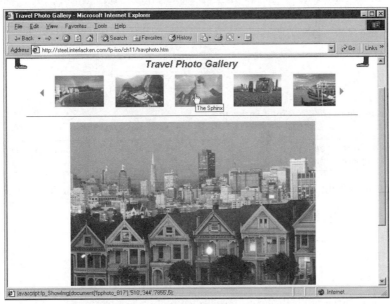

Figure 11-29.   This is how a Slideshow Photo Gallery looks to a Web visitor.

The other three Photo Gallery formats display only thumbnails in the page that contains the Photo Gallery. When you click a thumbnail, the browser displays the full-sized picture as a separate page.

For more information about Photo Galleries, refer to Chapter 22, "Using FrontPage Photo Galleries."

Editing Pictures in FrontPage

In addition to its tools for editing and managing Web pages, FrontPage provides a rich assortment of tools for directly modifying pictures. You can find these tools on the Pictures toolbar:

Insert Picture From File

- **Insert Picture From File.** Displays a dialog box for adding a new picture to your Web page. You can select pictures from your local hard disk, the Office Clip Art library, or any location on the Web.

Text

- **Text.** Provides for entry of text superimposed over a picture.

Auto Thumbnail

- **Auto Thumbnail.** Replaces a large picture with a smaller version, and creates a hyperlink so that clicking the small picture displays the original, larger one.

Position Absolutely

- **Position Absolutely.** Indicates that the currently selected picture, rather than flowing with the rest of the Web page, should appear at exact X-Y coordinates. To set the coordinates, drag the picture into place after clicking this button.

- **Bring Forward.** Increases the Z-index of a selected picture by one. When two elements with different Z-index values overlap, the one with the higher value appears in front.

- **Send Backward.** Decreases the Z-index of a selected picture by one.

Bring Forward   Send Backward

> For more information about Z-indexes, refer to the Sidebar "Absolute Positioning and the Z-Index" on page 103.

- **Rotate Left.** Rotates the selected picture 90 degrees counterclockwise.

- **Rotate Right.** Rotates the selected picture 90 degrees clockwise.

Rotate Left   Rotate Right

Flip Horizontal

- **Flip Horizontal.** Reverses the selected picture left to right.

- **Flip Vertical.** Reverses the selected picture top to bottom.

- **More Contrast.** Increases the contrast in a picture. Light colors get lighter and dark colors get darker.

Flip Vertical

- **Less Contrast.** Decreases the contrast in a picture. Light colors get darker and dark colors get lighter.

Chapter 11

- **More Brightness.** Increases the brightness of a picture. Dark colors get lighter.

- **Less Brightness.** Decreases the brightness of a picture. Light colors get darker.

More Contrast   Less Contrast   More Brightness   Less Brightness

- **Crop.** Provides a way to display only a rectangular subset of a picture. You can adjust the rectangular area using the mouse button.

- **Line Style.** Selects the style and thickness of selected lines in a drawing.

- **Format Picture.** Displays either the Format AutoShape or Format Drawing Canvas dialog box for any selected line drawing objects.

- **Set Transparent Color.** Makes any single color in a picture transparent by clicking a pixel of that color.

Crop   Line Style   Format Picture   Set Transparent Color

Color

- **Color.** Applies Automatic, Grayscale, Black & White, or Wash Out effects to a selected picture:

  - **Automatic.** Displays pictures contained within VML in the unmodified state.

  - **Grayscale.** Converts a picture to grayscale tones.

  - **Black & White.** Displays pictures contained within VML using the colors black and white only. This creates a silhouette effect.

  - **Washout.** Adds whiteness to all the colors in a picture, making it look washed out. This is frequently desirable for pictures used as backgrounds.

  The Automatic and Black & White command are available only for pictures enclosed within VML code, such as pictures copied out of Microsoft Word documents and pasted in an open Web page. They're not available for pictures, including VML pictures, that you add to a Web page using FrontPage only.

- **Bevel.** Adds a three-dimensional border around the picture. FrontPage lightens the top and left edges while darkening the bottom and right edges.

Resample

- **Resample.** Converts a picture to the desired size. Suppose, for example, you used the Picture Properties dialog box, or dragged the mouse, to display a 200x100 pixel picture at 100x50 pixels. This would download the original 200x100 picture to the browser and tell the browser to resize it. In contrast, the Resample command would create a new picture whose actual size is 100x50, and download it in 1/4 the time.

353

Select

- **Select.** Tells FrontPage that clicking a picture selects it. This is the default; all remaining tools require that a picture first be selected.

- **Rectangular Hotspot.** Marks a rectangular area within a picture as a *hotspot*. At browse time, clicking any pixel within a hotspot activates an associated hyperlink.

- **Circular Hotspot.** Marks a circular area within a picture as a hotspot.

- **Polygonal Hotspot.** Marks an irregular, straight-sided area as a hotspot.

- **Highlight Hotspots.** Displays all current hotspots within a picture.

Rectangular   Circular   Polygonal   Highlight
Hotspot   Hotspot   Hotspot   Hotspots

> **note** A *hotspot*, in FrontPage parlance, is a designated portion of a picture that's associated with a hyperlink. When a picture has hotspots, clicking different parts of the picture tells the browser to display different Web pages. In more official contexts, what FrontPage calls a hotspot is called an *image map area*. An *image map* is a block of code that defines all clickable areas (hotspots) for a given picture.

Restore

- **Restore.** Returns a picture to its original appearance. However, this might not be possible after the picture is saved.

> For more information about the Pictures toolbar, refer to "The Pictures Toolbar" in the Bonus Content on the Companion CD.

> For more information about FrontPage picture editing tools, refer to Chapter 21, "Editing Pictures in FrontPage."

In Summary...

This chapter explained the basics of adding pictures to a Web page. It also provided an introduction to a variety of picture types and picture techniques that later chapters explain in greater detail.

The next chapter explains how to construct hyperlinks, the glue that holds the World Wide Web together.

Building Hyperlinks

Hyperlinks are the essence of the Web. Without hyperlinks, there would be no point-and-click navigation among Web pages—and without point and click, the Web would be dead. Every time you click some underlined text or a picture and thereby jump to another page, you're using a hyperlink. A Web page lacking hyperlinks is truly a Web page going nowhere.

Without hyperlinks, visitors would have to manually type the URL of each page they wanted to visit. Given the length and cryptic nature of many URLs, visitors probably wouldn't visit many pages, or would get lost in a thicket of typos along the way.

This chapter describes the most common Web mechanisms for linking Web pages, and explains how to employ these mechanisms using FrontPage:

- **Hyperlinks.** These are special areas on a Web page that hold the address of another page in waiting. When a Web visitor clicks such an area, the browser retrieves the Web page at the associated address.

- **Bookmarks.** These provide a means for jumping not to the top of a Web page but to some point further within the page. Essentially, they associate a name with a spot on a Web page and provide a way of jumping to that name.

- **Hotspots.** These provide a way of jumping to a different Web location depending on which part of a picture the visitor clicks. This can be useful when a set of hyperlinks lends itself to visual selection.

The chapter concludes with a brief description of each field in a URL, along with practical guidelines on naming any URLs you create yourself.

355

Creating and Managing Hyperlinks

The most common form of hyperlink is the anchor. Clicking text or a picture that bears this type of link takes a Web visitor to another page. A simple anchor has the following HTML syntax:

```
<a href="contact.html">Click here for contact information.</a>
```

The browser would display this code as follows:

Click here for contact information.

Clicking this text would take a Web visitor to the *contact.html* page in the current server's home folder. The *a* in *<a href=…>* stands for *anchor*, and *href* means *Hypertext Reference*. Content that appears between the *<a href=…>* and *</a>* appears as a link, and clicking it jumps to the *href* location.

> **tip** Hyperlinked pictures work virtually the same as hyperlinked text. Format the anchor tags just as you would for text, but put the HTML code that displays the picture between them.

Of course, a major reason FrontPage exists is to isolate you from HTML tags such as *<a href=…>*. The next few sections will explain how to do exactly that.

Creating Hyperlinks with Drag-and-Drop

If you're working in a Web—either disk-based or server-based—creating hyperlinks within your Web is as easy as dragging. Here's the procedure:

1 Open the page that should contain the hyperlink.

2 Locate and select the target Web page in the Folder List.

3 Drag the target onto the open page.

FrontPage creates a hyperlink to the page you dragged, using that page's title as the hyperlink text. Table 12-1 shows the results of dragging or pasting objects of various kinds into an open Web page.

newfeature!

The following procedure is more flexible and easier to remember, and it offers more options for dragging files into an open Web page:

1 Open the page you want to update.

2 Locate the file you want added to the open page. The file can be in the Folder List of the FrontPage window that contains the open page, the Folder List or Folders view of any other FrontPage window, or Windows Explorer.

Table 12-1. **Effects of Dragging or Pasting a File Into an Open Web Page**

Drag or copy from	Type of file	Typical extensions	Results
Folder List	Web page	.htm, .asp	Creates hyperlink to dragged file with page title as hyperlink text.
	Picture file	.gif, .jpg, .avi	Displays dragged picture in Web page.
	Folder		Creates hyperlink to dragged folder with folder location as hyperlink text.
	Other	.doc, .pdf, .txt, .zip	Creates hyperlink to dragged file with file location as hyperlink text.
Windows Explorer	Web page	.htm, .asp	Merges HTML from dragged file into current Web page.
	Picture file	.gif, .jpg, .avi	Displays dragged picture in Web page. Displays Save Embedded Files dialog box during next page save.
	Folder		Nothing.
	Other	.doc, .txt, .zip	Translates dragged file to HTML and merges results into current Web page. Fails if the given file type has no available translator.

3 Use the right mouse button to drag the file into the open Web page. Releasing the right mouse button displays the following shortcut menu, with operations that are not allowed in the current context dimmed:

- **Create Hyperlink.** Adds a hyperlink from the open Web page to the dragged file. When you drag a file from Windows Explorer, this command is dimmed. Drag the file from Windows Explorer into the Folder List, and from there into the open Web page.

357

■ **Open File.** Loads the dragged file into the default editor for the file type. This performs the same action as double-clicking the dragged file and doesn't modify the open Web page.

■ **Insert File.** Performs two different actions depending on the type of file. For pictures, it displays the picture in the open Web page as if you'd used the Insert Picture command. For other types of files, it converts the file to HTML and merges the result into the open Web page.

■ **Auto Thumbnail.** Creates a thumbnail version of a dragged picture, adds it to the open Web page, and hyperlinks the thumbnail to the full-sized version. For types of files other than pictures, this option is dimmed.

■ **Cancel.** Cancels the dragging operation without taking any action.

Creating Hyperlinks with Menus

FrontPage also creates hyperlinks by means of menus and dialog boxes. This is the best way to create hyperlinks with special options or hyperlinks that point outside the current Web. The basic procedure is as follows:

1 Select the text or picture you want the Web visitor to click.

Insert
Hyperlink

2 Choose Hyperlink from the Insert menu, or click the Insert Hyperlink button on the Standard toolbar. The Insert Hyperlink dialog box shown in Figure 12-1 appears.

3 Specify the hyperlink's target address in the Address field, and click OK.

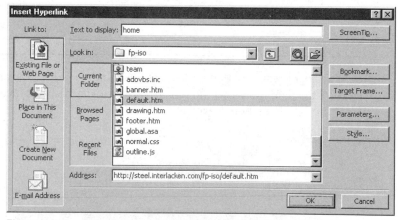

Figure 12-1. FrontPage uses this dialog box to hyperlink a selected text string or picture to another page in the current Web.

All other options in the Insert Hyperlink dialog box are variations on performing step 3. These variations fall into the following four major categories, which correspond to the icons in the Link To bar at the left of Figure 12-1:

- **Existing File Or Web Page.** Selects an address that points anywhere in the current Web, an intranet, or the World Wide Web.

- **Place In This Document.** Selects an address that points to a bookmark in the current Web page.

- **Create New Document.** Creates an address that points to a page that doesn't exist yet. You can tell FrontPage to open a new, empty Web page at this address for editing or defer creating the page completely.

- **E-Mail Address.** Creates an address that opens the Web visitor's e-mail program and addresses a new message to a given recipient.

Clicking any of these Link To options changes the rest of the Insert Hyperlink dialog box. However, the following controls apply to all four options:

- **Text To Display.** Displays and optionally modifies the clickable text the Web visitor sees. This box is dimmed if the clickable area contains a picture.

- **ScreenTip.** Opens the Set Hyperlink ScreenTip dialog box shown below. Any text you enter in this box will appear as a screen tip (that is, as text in a small yellow box) whenever the Web visitor's mouse rests over the clickable area.

This facility is subject to two restrictions:

- If the clickable area includes a picture configured with alternative representation text, that text will supersede the hyperlink's ScreenTip text when you move the mouse pointer over the picture.

For more information about alternative representation text, refer to "Modifying General Picture Properties" on page 341.

- ScreenTip text is supported only by Microsoft Internet Explorer 4 and later.

359

● **Target Frame.** Applies to two situations:

▪ It specifies which frame will display the hyperlink's target page. This applies only if the current page occupies one frame of a frameset.

For more information about framesets, refer to Chapter 17, "Using Frames for Page Layout."

▪ It can also specify that the target page should appear in a new window. To make this happen, click the Target Frame button, choose New Window when the Target Frame dialog box shown in Figure 12-2 appears, and then click OK.

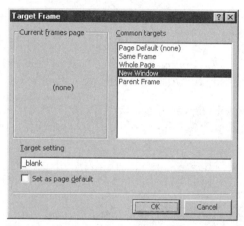

Figure 12-2. For hyperlinks that appear on pages edited within a frameset, this dialog box specifies which frame will display the target page. Even for pages that don't appear in a frameset, it can make the target page appear in a new browser window.

● **Parameters.** Displays a dialog box that creates, modifies, and deletes parameters in a URL's path information or query string.

● **Style.** Applies cascading style sheet properties to the hyperlink.

For more information about cascading style sheets, refer to Chapter 20, "Managing Appearance with Cascading Style Sheets."

Linking to an Existing File or Web Page

The following controls appear only if the Existing File Or Web Page icon is selected in the Link To box shown in Figure 12-1. What's more, they appear no matter which of the Look In bar's buttons you click (Current Folder, Browsed Pages, or Recent Files):

● **Address.** Specifies the location of the page that clicking the hyperlink will display. If you know this location and you're willing to type or paste it into this box, do so and ignore all the other controls.

tip   To paste a URL into the address box, press Ctrl+V or Shift+Ins.

Browse
The Web

● **Browse The Web.** Locates the target page with your browser. To use this feature:

     1   Click the Browse The Web button.

     2   When your browser window appears, display the page you want the hyperlink to target.

     3   Switch back to FrontPage without quitting the browser. FrontPage will get the address of the current page from the browser and paste it into the Address box.

Browse For File

● **Browse For File.** Displays the Link To File dialog box. Locate the target page you want, and then click OK.

tip   Linking directly to a file on your computer is usually a bad idea, because Web visitors don't have access to the files on your computer. It's better to first add the file to the current Web and then create a hyperlink to that location.

● **Bookmark.** Specifies not only a particular page, but a particular location within that page.

For more information about bookmarks, refer to "Setting and Using Bookmarks" later in this chapter.

The Current Folder button in the Look In bar displays files and folders in the current folder. Because this feature can also change the current folder to any available Web or file location, it's much more powerful than its name might suggest. The following controls appear only after selecting the Current Folder option:

● **The Look In box.** Displays and controls the folder that's listed in the large selection list that occupies the center of the dialog box. Open the drop-down list to display and select folder locations above and below the current folder.

● **The selection list.** Itemizes the contents of the current Web:

     ▪   Click a file or folder once to copy its location to the Address box.

     ▪   Double-click a file to copy its location to the Address box, close the dialog box, and update the hyperlink.

361

■ Double-click a folder to display its contents.

Up One
Folder

● **The Up One Folder button.** Navigates to the parent of the current folder
and display its contents in the selection list.

The Browsed Pages button displays a list of pages you recently browsed using Internet
Explorer. Figure 12-3 shows an example of this list. To use any of the listed pages as the
target of your hyperlink, either select a page and click OK, or double-click the page.

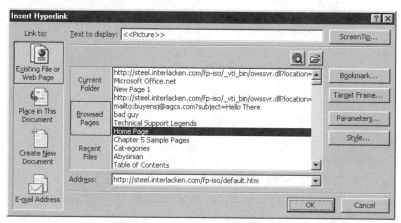

Figure 12-3. The Browsed Pages button displays a list of Web pages you recently
displayed in Internet Explorer.

The Recent Files button displays a list of files you recently opened with FrontPage.
Figure 12-4 provides an example. Selecting any file and clicking OK makes that file the
target of your hyperlink. Double-clicking any file does the same thing.

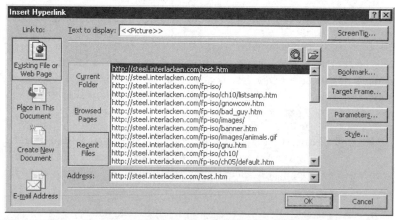

Figure 12-4. The Recent Files button displays a list of Web pages you recently opened
in FrontPage.

Clicking the Parameters button—when it's available—displays the Hyperlink Parameters dialog box shown in Figure 12-5. This dialog box modifies any values that need to appear in the path information portion or the query string portion of a URL that invokes a program on the Web server.

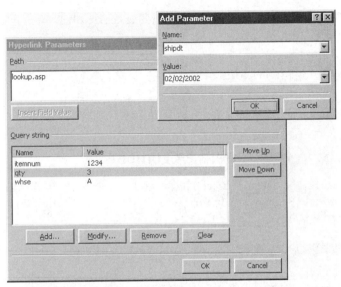

Figure 12-5. Clicking the Parameters button in the Insert Hyperlink dialog box displays the Hyperlink Parameters dialog box, which specifies parameter names and values passed to server-side programs as a query string.

> For more information about paths and query strings, refer to "Coding URL Fields for Executable Programs" later in this chapter.

The options in this dialog box are as follows:

- **Path.** Use this box to enter any data you want to appear between the name of the program that will execute on the Web server and the query string.

- **Insert Field Value.** Click this button to add an expression containing the value of a database field to the *path* string. This button is dimmed unless the hyperlink appears within a Database Results region.

> For more information about Database Results regions, refer to "Using the Database Results Wizard" on page 922.

- **Add.** Click this button to display the Add Parameter dialog box, which appends a new *keyword=value* pair to the query string. Figure 12-5 shows the Add Parameter dialog box in the foreground.

Chapter 12

- **Modify.** Click this button to change the value of the parameter currently selected in the Query String list.

- **Remove.** Click this button to remove the parameter currently selected in the Query String list.

- **Clear.** Click this button to remove all parameters currently present in the query string.

- **Move Up.** Click this button to move any parameters currently selected in the Query String list one position higher.

- **Move Down.** Click this button to move any currently selected parameters one position lower.

Linking to a Place in the Current Document

Clicking the Place In This Document icon in the Link To bar hides all the controls described in the previous section and, in their place, displays the selection list (essentially a list of bookmarks) shown in Figure 12-6.

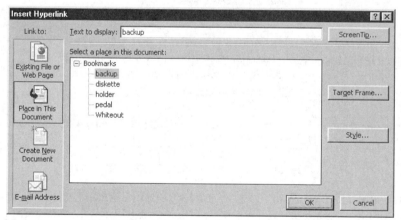

Figure 12-6. Clicking the Place In This Document icon displays a list of bookmarks in the current page.

> For more information about bookmarks, refer to "Setting and Using Bookmarks" later in this chapter.

Linking to a New Document

Clicking the Create New Document icon in the Link To bar switches the Insert Hyperlink dialog box into the mode shown in Figure 12-7. The Create New Document mode creates a hyperlink to a Web page that doesn't yet exist.

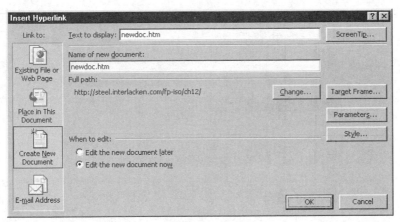

Figure 12-7. After clicking the Create New Document icon, create a new page and link to it in one operation.

The unique controls in this mode provide the following functions:

- **Name Of New Document.** This specifies the name of the Web page you want to create. If you enter this value by hand, enter a location relative to the Full Path value.

- **Full Path.** This is a read-only field that displays a path to the location where the new page will reside.

- **Change.** This displays the Create New Document dialog box. Click your way to the folder location that should contain the new Web page, enter the file name you want to create, and then click OK.

- **Edit The New Document Later.** This creates a new blank Web page at the specified location, but doesn't open it for editing.

- **Edit The New Document Now.** This creates a new blank Web page at the specified location and opens it for editing in FrontPage.

Linking to an E-Mail Address

Clicking the E-Mail Address icon in the Link To bar displays the fields shown in Figure 12-8 on the next page. This icon creates a *mailto* URL that launches the Web visitor's e-mail program and initializes a new message addressed to the specified recipient.

The input boxes listed below control this process:

- **E-Mail Address.** Specifies the e-mail address that will receive the message.

- **Subject.** Provides a subject line for the new message. Some mail programs ignore this field.

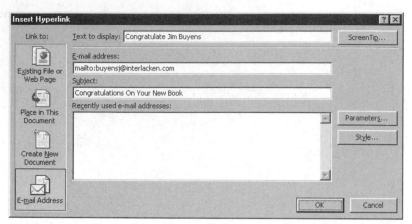

Figure 12-8. The E-Mail Address icon displays the controls necessary to create a link that starts the Web visitor's e-mail program.

● **Recently Used E-Mail Addresses.** Displays a list of e-mail addresses you've recently set up as *mailto* links in FrontPage. Clicking any of these addresses enters the name and subject line in, respectively, the E-Mail Address and Subject boxes.

> For more information about the structure of URLs, refer to "Creating URLs" later in this chapter.

Modifying Hyperlinks

Assuming that the page is already open in Page view, use any of the following procedures to modify the properties of an existing hyperlink:

● Right-click the hyperlink and choose Hyperlink Properties from the shortcut menu.

● Select the hyperlink and then:

  ■ Click the Insert Hyperlink button on the Standard toolbar; or

  ■ Choose Hyperlink from the Insert menu; or

  ■ Press Ctrl+K.

Any of these actions displays an Edit Hyperlink dialog box that is essentially identical to the Insert Hyperlink dialog box shown in its many variations earlier in this chapter. All the controls and options work the same as they do when creating a new hyperlink.

To delete a hyperlink, click the Remove Link button that appears in the lower right corner just above the Cancel button in the Edit Hyperlink dialog box.

> **tip** To follow a hyperlink in Page view, Ctrl-click it. This opens the target page in Page view.

Setting and Using Bookmarks

Sometimes, especially when a Web page is long, it's desirable for hyperlinks to point somewhere other than the top of a page. Bookmarks provide this handy function. They can jump from one location to another in the same page, or even from one page to any bookmark in another page. To define a bookmark:

1 Open the target page in FrontPage.

2 Set the cursor at the spot you want displayed in the browser's top left corner. (This is where you'll insert the bookmark.) You can either set the insertion point at this location or select some text or other content there.

3 Choose Bookmark from the Insert menu to display the Bookmark dialog box shown in Figure 12-9.

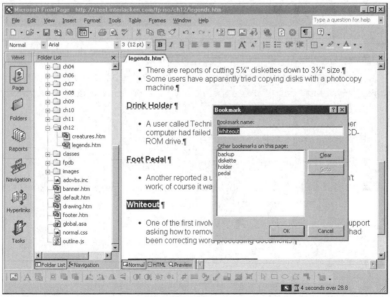

Figure 12-9. Bookmarks move viewers to specific page locations.

4 Type the name of the bookmark in the Bookmark Name box. Use a unique name for each bookmark on a page.

Flag Icon

5 Click OK. If you selected any content in step 2, dotted underlining, as pictured in the Drink Holder and Foot Pedal examples of Figure 12-9, denote the bookmark's location. Otherwise, a flag icon will indicate the bookmark.

> **note** When the browser jumps to a bookmark, it won't position the bottom of a Web page higher than the bottom of the browser window. Therefore, jumping to a bookmark near the end of the page might not position the bookmarked text at the top of the window.

The following buttons in the Bookmark dialog box perform a couple of useful functions:

- **Clear.** To delete a bookmark, double-click its name in the Other Bookmarks On This Page list. Then, after the bookmark appears in the Bookmark Name box, click the Clear button.

- **Goto.** To move the insertion point to an existing bookmark, select its name in the Other Bookmarks On This Page list, and then click the Goto button.

To set up a hyperlink that jumps to the bookmark:

1 Open the page that will contain the hyperlink.

2 To add a bookmark to an existing hyperlink, select the hyperlink. To create a new hyperlink that jumps to a bookmark, select the text, picture, or other content that will become the clickable area.

Insert Hyperlink

3 Choose Hyperlink from the Insert menu, or click the Insert Hyperlink button on the Standard toolbar. If you're linking to an existing hyperlink, the Edit Hyperlink dialog box appears; if you're creating a new link, the Insert Hyperlink dialog box appears.

To link to a bookmark in the current page:

1 Click the Place In This Document button.

2 In the Select A Place In This Document list, select the bookmark to which the hyperlink should jump, and click OK.

To link to a bookmark in a different page:

1 Click the Existing File Or Web Page button.

2 Specify the Web page you want as the target of the hyperlink. Use the procedure described earlier in the section titled "Linking to an Existing File or Web Page."

3 Click the Bookmark button.

4 When the Select Place In Document dialog box shown in Figure 12-10 appears, select the bookmark you want, and then click OK.

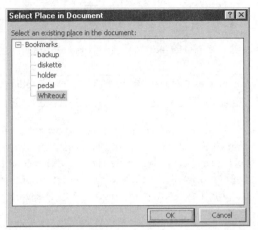

Figure 12-10. Clicking the Bookmark button displays a list of bookmarks in the current Web page.

5 Click OK a second time to apply your changes.

If the page you specify in step 2 isn't currently available, clicking the Bookmark button will produce an error message rather than the Select Place In Document dialog box. Your options at this point are as follows:

● Establish connectivity to the target Web page, and then try again.

● Enter the bookmark manually by typing a pound sign and the bookmark name at the end of the Address box. Here's an example:

http://www.interlacken.com/fp-iso/ch12/legends.htm#pedal

Creating and Using Hotspots

Hotspots provide another form of hyperlinking—one that permits assigning different URLs to different parts of a picture. Another name for hotspots is *image map areas*. The most common uses for hotspots are in menu bars and maps; however, you can use hotspots for any application that requires jumping to different locations by clicking different areas of a picture.

Here's how to add hotspots to a picture in FrontPage:

1 Open the Web page that contains the picture, and click the picture once to select it.

2 Click the Rectangular Hotspot, Circular Hotspot, or Polygonal Hotspot button on the Pictures toolbar described in Appendix A.

Rectangular Hotspot   Circular Hotspot   Polygonal Hotspot

 For more information about the Pictures toolbar, refer to "The Pictures Toolbar" in the Bonus Content on the Companion CD.

3 When using the Rectangular or Circular Hotspot tools, drag the mouse pointer over the portion of the picture that should define the hotspot. When using the Polygon tool, draw your polygon by clicking the mouse pointer at each corner of the shape you want. To close the polygon, double-click the next-to-last point, and FrontPage draws the final line to the starting point.

4 When dragging is complete, FrontPage opens the Insert Hyperlink dialog box, the same dialog box used for setting up hyperlinks for both text and pictures. Define the hyperlink as described earlier in the section titled "Linking to an Existing File or Web Page."

5 Repeat steps 3, 4, and 5 to define additional hotspots for the same picture.

6 To define a hotspot for the picture as a whole, click any portion that's not already a hotspot and specify its URL in the usual way.

When you select a picture that has hotspots, FrontPage displays the clickable areas as shown in Figure 12-11. The figure shows a single picture with eight hotspots.

With hotspots, you can do the following:

Highlight
Hotspots

● If the picture's hotspots are difficult to see, click the Highlight Hotspots button on the Picture toolbar. This toggles the picture to a solid white background.

● To modify a hotspot area, select it once, and then drag the edges or corner handles.

● To modify a hotspot hyperlink, double-click the hotspot area, or right-click it and choose Picture Hotspot Properties from the shortcut menu.

tip A frequent criticism of hotspots—and of picture hyperlinks in general—is the lack of visual clues they provide. Visitors are reduced to moving the mouse pointer over a picture and watching for the pointer to indicate a hyperlink, or to clicking pictures at random to discover what they do. If the picture you're hyperlinking lacks obvious visual clues, be sure to provide instructions in the surrounding text.

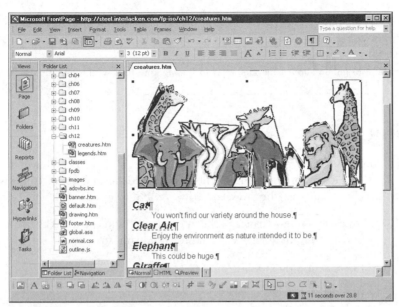

Figure 12-11. The irregular lines around each animal enclose hotspot areas. Each hotspot area jumps to a different URL.

Early implementations of hotspots (or image maps, as they were called) transmitted the *x-y* coordinates that the Web visitor clicked to a program on the Web server. That program read an *image map file*, determined which area the Web visitor clicked, identified the corresponding jump location, and sent that information back to the browser. The browser would then request the resulting page. Newer browsers can translate hotspot clicks to hyperlink locations using image maps coded into the HTML. This is a much cleaner and more efficient approach than server-side image maps and is now the only approach that FrontPage supports.

Lack of server-side image map processing means that hotspots created in FrontPage won't work in certain very early browsers. Visitors with visual disabilities will have no use for hotspots, and fully sighted visitors frequently overlook them. These are all good reasons not to rely exclusively on hotspots for navigation through your Web.

Using the Link Bars Component

Chapter 7 explained how the Link Bars component can create sets of hyperlinks automatically based on a structure you diagram in Navigation view or based on free-standing "mini-structures" called *custom Link bars*. In comparison to the manual hyperlinks described in this chapter, Link bars offer advantages of accuracy, uniformity, and attractive formatting. Manual hyperlinks, of course, are more flexible, and accommodate URL features such as bookmarks, query strings, and path information that Link bars don't.

Chapter 12

371

Whichever method you prefer, it's good to have the other method in your toolbox. You never know when it's going to come in handy.

For more information about Link bars, refer to "Using Link Bars with Navigation View" on page 201.

Creating URLs

Despite their impact, hyperlinks are extremely simple mechanisms. They mark a given string of text, picture, or Web component with the address of another Web page. When the visitor clicks that area, the browser retrieves and displays the associated page.

A URL provides, in a single string, all the information required to access a file on the Web. In its most common form, a URL has the following structure:

```
<protocol>://<computername>:<port>/<folder>/<filename>
```

For example:

http://www.microsoft.com:80/frontpage/learn.htm

Here's the breakdown of each field in this URL:

Field	Value
protocol	*http*
computername	*www.microsoft.com*
port	*80*
folder	*frontpage*
filename	*learn.htm*

The next few sections describe each URL field. They also provide guidance for naming each field for Webs you create.

Coding URL Protocols

The first and most important field in a URL specifies the protocol that the browser should use for requesting and receiving the specified file.

A protocol describes how to act in a particular situation. In the case of a URL, the protocol field specifies how the browser should process the given URL string. Here are the most common protocols that appear in URLs:

● *http.* Tells the browser to request and then receive a file by means of the hypertext transfer protocol. This is by far the most common protocol used on the Web. In its simplest form, HTTP connects to the specified computer and then transmits the word GET, a space, a folder name, a file name, a space, the protocol version, and two line endings. Here's an example:

GET /default.htm HTTP/1.0

The specified computer returns a few lines of header information, one blank line, and then the contents of the requested file:

```
HTTP/1.1 200 OK
Server: Microsoft-IIS/4.0
Date: Sun, 26 Nov 2000 03:00:00 GMT
Content-Type: text/html
Accept-Ranges: bytes
Last-Modified: Sun, 15 Oct 2000 21:08:58 GMT
ETag: "9abe7c22ec36c01:307c"
Content-Length: 23900
```

The first returned header line contains a status code such as *200 OK* or *404 File not found*. Subsequent header lines typically describe the type of server, the server's date and time, a code that denotes the type of file, the file's date last modified, and various other information.

Don't make the mistake of thinking *http* can retrieve only Web pages. It can also retrieve pictures, videos, sounds, *.zip* and *.exe* files, Adobe Acrobat files, and in fact, any type of file at all. The browser will handle these files in accordance with the type-of-file code that the Web server supplies.

● *ftp.* Tells the browser to retrieve a file by using the Internet's File Transfer Protocol.

FTP is a very powerful and flexible protocol. It can transmit or receive individual files or groups of files, it can be anonymous or restricted by username and password, and it works on almost every type of computer ever built. However, *ftp* URLs use only a fraction of these capabilities; they always retrieve single files anonymously. In addition, *ftp* URLs have the following limitations:

▪ FTP is a more complicated protocol than HTTP and usually runs more slowly.

▪ Some Internet firewalls permit FTP only among browsers and Web servers that support a feature called PASV. Unfortunately, many older browsers and older FTP servers lack this feature.

▪ *ftp* URLs support fewer features than *http* URLs. For example, *ftp* URLs can't trigger a program that runs on the Web server and produces custom output.

Because of these limitations, *ftp* URLs are becoming less and less common on the Web. Even for applications such as downloading software, it's much more common to transfer files by HTTP.

373

Chapter 12

Frequently Asked Questions

Do ftp URLs compromise a Web visitor's anonymity?

ftp URLs used to hold favor among Web site operators because of a security loophole. When browsers retrieved files by supposedly anonymous FTP, they would actually supply a username of *anonymous* and a password consisting of the Web visitor's e-mail address. Web site operators could therefore tell the browser to retrieve a picture on the home page or some other innocuous file by FTP, record all the e-mail addresses in the server's FTP activity log, and then build a database of Web visitors to pummel with e-mail advertisements.

Up-to-date browsers no longer transmit real e-mail addresses for anonymous FTP. Internet Explorer, for example, always uses an anonymous FTP password of *IE30User@*. Netscape Navigator uses *mozilla@*.

What's the PASV feature?

When a client program (such as a browser) needs to retrieve a file by FTP, the first step is to open a session for sending commands to the server. This is called a *control session,* and by definition, the client always initiates the connection.

When the client subsequently sends the FTP server a GET command to retrieve a file, the server normally initiates a second session to the client, transmits the file, and then terminates the second connection. This is called a *transfer session.*

Transfer sessions create a problem when an Internet firewall stops any machine outside the firewall from opening a connection to any machine inside the firewall. Such firewalls block all transfer sessions and thus block the use of normal FTP.

To avoid such problems, the FTP client can send the server a PASV command before it sends any GET commands. Then, instead of opening a new transfer session, the server transmits the file over the existing control session. This is an elegant solution, but it works only if both the FTP client and the FTP server support PASV.

- *mailto.* Tells the browser to start the Web visitor's default mail program and create a new blank message addressed to a given recipient. The Web visitor decides what the message will say.

  A *mailto* URL contains only the keyword *mailto* followed by a colon and an e-mail address. No computer name, folder name, file name, or other fields can be present.

  FrontPage can create Web pages that collect information from an HTML form, transmit the form contents to the Web server, and have the Web server send formatted mail to a designated recipient. It can also accommodate server-side mail tools from other vendors. However, neither of these approaches uses a *mailto* URL.

For more information about HTML forms, refer to Chapter 31, "Creating and Using Forms." For more information about sending HTML form data as mail, refer to "Configuring E-Mail Results Options" on page 900. For more information about writing scripts that send customized mail, refer to "Sending Custom E-Mail" on page 912.

- *news.* Tells the browser to start the Web visitor's news reader and display the article list for a given newsgroup.

  A *news* URL contains only the keyword *news* followed by the name of a Usenet newsgroup. No computer name, folder name, file name, or other fields can be present. Settings within the news reader—and not within the *news* URL—specify the name of the news server and other configuration details.

Coding URL Computer Names

The computer name portion of an *http* or *ftp* URL identifies the server that contains the desired content (that is, the desired Web page, picture file, or other content). This can be either an Internet Protocol (IP) address such as 207.46.230.219 or a Domain Name System (DNS) name such as *www.microsoft.com*.

An IP address consists of four numbers separated by periods. Each number represents one byte and can thus range from 0 to 255. To pronounce the address 207.46.230.219 you'd say, "Two oh seven dot forty-six dot two thirty dot two nineteen."

For more information about IP addresses, refer to "Understanding TCP/IP" on page 1026.

Because IP addresses are difficult to remember and subject to change, most server operators register their computers in DNS. This is a highly distributed database that can look up the IP address of a mnemonic name such as *www.microsoft.com*. It can also perform reverse lookups, such as finding the mnemonic name associated with an IP address such as 207.46.230.219.

Clients gain access to DNS by configuring their network software with the address of one or more DNS servers maintained by their Internet provider, hosting company, or IT department. If those servers don't know the IP address associated with a given name, they'll contact other servers to get it.

For more information about DNS, refer to "Server Names and the Domain Name System" on page 1030.

Coding URL Port Numbers

A single computer can provide many kinds of services at once: HTTP, FTP, mail, news, DNS, time, logon validation, and many others. This is possible because each service listens on a different *port number*.

Listening on a port number means that the Web, FTP, mail, DNS, or other service responds to incoming traffic coded with that number. This puts the onus on the remote client to know and specify the correct port number. Fortunately, most administrators configure their services to listen on well-known ports. Mail servers, for example, almost always listen on port 25. FTP servers listen for control sessions on port 21. Web servers usually listen for HTTP requests on port 80.

An *http* URL defaults to the well-known port number 80. Similarly, an *ftp* URL defaults to port 21. This means you seldom need to code a port number in a URL. If a particular server uses a nonstandard port, you must code the port number immediately after the computer name and, as shown below, separated from it by a colon:

> *http://fictitious.microsoft.com:8080/*

(This, by the way, is a fictitious site. Don't try browsing it unless you like imaginary Web pages.)

Coding URL Folder Names

After you've connected to a Web or FTP server, any folder in the server's file system, starting from some point, becomes a folder you can specify in a URL. The starting point is called the server's *http* root or *ftp* root. To see how this works, consider this URL:

> *http://steel.interlacken.com/fp-iso/default.htm*

The *http* root of this server is *C:\InetPub\wwwroot*, and the URL location */ftp-iso /default.htm* therefore corresponds to this physical location:

> *C:\InetPub\wwwroot\fp-iso\default.htm*

Figure 12-12 shows this file location as seen in Windows Explorer.

If you link to a page someone else created, you'll have to accept the creator's name for it. When naming Web pages and folders yourself, however, keep in mind that any folder (and file) names used in a URL are subject to restrictions of two kinds:

● First, the names must be valid on any server where a folder might physically reside. Suppose, for example, that you create and test a Web on a Windows 2000 computer and then upload it to a UNIX server that provides public access. In such a case, all your folder and file names must be valid on both Windows 2000 and on UNIX. You must consider such factors as allowable characters, allowable length, and case sensitivity of names.

UNIX file systems are case sensitive, so asking for a file named *Index.html* will fail if the actual file name is *index.html*. Windows file systems aren't case sensitive, however, so the same request would work on a Windows-based Web server.

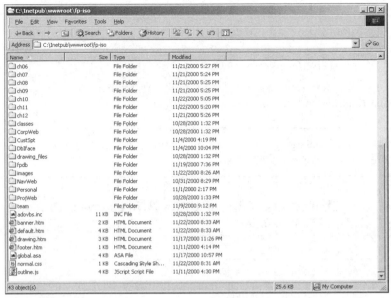

Figure 12-12. A Web server on this computer has an http root at *C:\InetPub\wwwroot*. This is the starting location for all URLs sent to this server.

tip Case-sensitive names are relatively confusing, even to hard-core UNIX visitors, and the normal solution is to use lowercase file names only. This is an excellent habit to acquire.

The maximum length of a file name or folder name under UNIX is 32 characters—certainly a practical limit for Web pages as well. Extremely long file names and folder names constitute cruel and unusual punishment for anyone who needs to hand-type a URL. Errors and frustration will result, and ultimately, perhaps, the visitor will move on to a simpler site.

The file allocation table (FAT) system used for years under MS-DOS and Windows 3.x supported an eight-character file name base plus an optional three-character extension. You should conform to these restrictions if there's any chance of moving your site or any of its files to such a platform, even temporarily. This will involve shortening *.html* and *.jpeg* filename extensions to *.htm* and *.jpg*, respectively.

● Second, just because a given character is valid in a folder or file name doesn't mean it's valid in a URL. In fact, only the characters listed in Table 12-2 on the next page are valid. If you need to include any other character as part of a computer name, folder name, file name, path expression, or

Chapter 12

query string, you must code a percent sign followed by the character's two-digit hexadecimal code in the ASCII character set. A "friendly" folder name such as *What's New?* thus becomes *What%27s%20New%3F*—decidedly less friendly than *whatsnew* or *whats-new*.

It's good practice to use only letters, numbers, hyphens, and underscores in path names and file names used on the Web.

---

on the web For official information about URL format, browse *http://www.ietf.org/rfc /rfc2396.txt* on the World Wide Web.

Table 12-2. **Characters Valid in URLs (Unreserved Characters)**

Character	Description	Character	Description
0–9	Numerals	!	Exclamation point
a–z	Lowercase letters	~	Tilde
A–Z	Uppercase letters	*	Asterisk
-	Hyphen	'	Apostrophe
_	Underscore	(	Left parenthesis
.	Period	)	Right parenthesis

Coding URL File Names

File names are generally subject to the same restrictions as folder names in terms of case sensitivity, length, and allowable characters.

There are two further considerations:

- Use the Web server's default file name where appropriate. On Microsoft Web servers, the default file name is usually *default.htm*. On others, it's usually *index.html*. In both cases, the server administrator can override these values.

- Use filename extensions that map to the proper file types as defined by the Multipurpose Internet Mail Extension (MIME) protocol. (MIME was first developed to describe the contents of an e-mail attachment.)

The subject of a Web server's default file name came up in Chapter 7. The point, in that context, was that the Navigation view home page must reside in the root folder of its Web and be named in accordance with the Web server's default file name.

For more information about use of a Web server's default file name in Navigation view, refer to "Defining a Navigation View Home Page" on page 186.

The point in this chapter is that whenever a Web visitor submits a URL that doesn't contain a file name, the Web server searches the given or implied path for the server's default file name. If the server finds a file with that name, it satisfies the visitor's request by delivering that file. If no such file exists, the Web server sends the visitor either a clickable list of subfolders and files or a *404 File not found* error message. Clickable folder lists are no substitute for a well-constructed menu page, and Web visitors much prefer successful requests to error messages. You should therefore try to put a file with the default name in every folder. This will generally be a menu page that provides links to other pages in the same folder.

note Many Web servers support multiple default file names. This means the server can search for several different file names before giving up and delivering a folder list or *404 File not found* status code. A server could, for example, search for a *default.htm* file, a *default.asp* file, an *index.htm* file, and an *index.html* file before giving up.

At the risk of belaboring a point, consider the following and totally fictitious (yet highly entertaining) URL:

http://bogus.interlacken.com/greek/statues/ancient/veggies.htm

Web visitors will expect that each of the following URLs will return a useful menu page for the applicable category:

http://bogus.interlacken.com/greek/statues/ancient/

http://bogus.interlacken.com/greek/statues/

http://bogus.interlacken.com/greek/

http://bogus.interlacken.com/

This will happen only if there's a page with the Web server's default file name in each folder.

When coding a URL that refers to an existing file you must, of course, use the correct filename extension. It also stands to reason that whenever you add new files to a Web server, you name them with the proper and customary filename extensions. Nevertheless, there's an added wrinkle to filename extensions on the Web.

Contrary to what you might suspect, most browsers don't use filename extensions when deciding how to handle a given file. Instead, they refer to a so-called *Content-Type* header that the Web server transmits as a prefix to the contents of the requested file. The Content-Type header identifies the type of file using a code called a *MIME type*. Unlike filename extensions, MIME types are independent of any operating system. Most Web servers assign these MIME types by looking up filename extensions in a table. Table 12-3 on the next page illustrates how this works for some common filename extensions.

Chapter 12

Table 12-3. **MIME Types Associated with Common Filename Extensions**

Filename extension	MIME type	Description
.htm .html	text/html	Ordinary Web page
.asp	text/html	Active Server Page
.stm	text/html	Web page containing a server-side include
.xml	text/xml	Data coded in Extensible Markup Language format
.gif	image/gif	Picture in CompuServe Graphics Interchange Format
.jpg .jpeg	image/jpeg	Picture in Joint Photographic Experts Group format
.wav	audio/wav	Sound file in Microsoft WAV format
.avi	video/x-msvideo	Video in Microsoft Media Player format
.mpg	video/mpeg	Video in Moving Picture Experts Group (MPEG) format
.pdf	application/pdf	File in Adobe Acrobat format.

Accounting for Content-Type headers and MIME types, the sequence of events for displaying a *.gif* file is as follows:

1 The browser sends the Web server a request for a file.

2 The browser verifies that the file exists.

3 The browser translates the filename extension *.gif* to the MIME type value *image/gif*. It then sends the following header line, along with any others, to the browser:

```
Content-Type: image/gif
```

4 After it has sent all the header lines, the Web server transmits a blank line and then the contents of the requested GIF file.

5 When the browser receives the file, it detects the Content-Type header and handles the subsequent content as a GIF file.

At first glance, you might surmise that this is perfectly equivalent to the Web server transmitting the GIF file with no headers and the browser responding to the filename extension *.gif*. However, this ignores the fact that steps 3 and 5 can go wrong:

- If step 3 goes wrong—usually because the Web server doesn't have a MIME type assigned to the current filename extension—it will transmit either no MIME type or a generic MIME type such as *application/octet-stream* (which basically means an arbitrary stream of bytes). This usually leads to an unexpected download prompt or an incorrect browser display.

  If you encounter this problem, you should either update the Web server's table of MIME types or switch to a type of file that's already included in that table.

> For more information about configuring the table of MIME types on both the browser and the Web server, refer to "MIME Types and Other Curiosities" on page 1039.

- If step 5 goes wrong—usually because the computer running the browser doesn't have an application that can process the given MIME type—the Web visitor either gets a download prompt or a prompt asking the visitor to identify an installed application that can process the file.

  If this problem occurs, the Web visitor should either install an application that can process the given MIME type or update the table of MIME type associations so it points to a suitable application that's already installed.

Coding URL Bookmarks

Web designers sometimes want a hyperlink to position a Web page at some spot other than the top. Bookmarks provide this capability. Using bookmarks is a two-step process:

1 Assign a bookmark to the desired spot on the Web page as previously discussed in this chapter. (For specific instructions, refer to "Setting and Using Bookmarks.")

2 Add a number sign and the name of the bookmark to the URL that jumps to the given page.

The syntax for linking to a bookmark is a number sign (#) and the name of the bookmark, appearing immediately after the file name. For example, the following URL jumps to the bookmark *space*:

http://www.foo:interlacken.com/far/out/place.html#space

Using Relative Locations

In URLs that appear within Web pages, a protocol, a computer name, a port, a path name, a file name, and a bookmark are all optional. In general, it's best to let these values default whenever possible because it minimizes changes when you move pages from one site or folder to another. Here are the rules that apply when you omit any of these subfields:

- **Protocol.** Defaults to that of the page currently on display.

- **Computer name.** Defaults to that of the current page.

- **Port.** Reverts to the default for the protocol if the URL specifies a computer name. (For HTTP, the default is 80.) If the URL takes the computer name from the current page, it also takes the default port from the current page.

- **Folder.** Defaults to that of the current page:

  - To access a child of the folder where the current page resides, code the folder name without a leading slash. For example, if the location of the current page is

    http://www.interlacken.com/fp-iso/ch12/default.htm

    then the URL

    kiddies/abner.htm

    would actually point to

    http://www.interlacken.com/fp-iso/ch12/kiddies/abner.htm

  - To access the parent of the folder where the current page resides, code two periods and a slash. Suppose again that the location of the current page is

    http://www.interlacken.com/fp-iso/ch12/default.htm

    In that case, the URL

    ../images/iconjjb.gif

    would actually point to

    http://www.interlacken.com/fp-iso/images/iconjjb.gif

> **note** In URLs, file names and folder names are always separated by a slash (/)—even if the Web server is running an operating system such as Windows that normally uses a backslash (\) separator.

- **File name.** Defaults to an empty value. The Web server responds by searching the current folder for the server's default file name. If the folder contains no such file, the server transmits either a list of files or a Not Found message, depending on its security configuration.

- **Bookmark.** Defaults to an empty value (that is, to the top of the page).

Despite the fact that the computer name, folder, file, and bookmark are all optional, you must specify at least one of them. The following are all valid URLs, but a completely blank URL is not:

www.microsoft.com

/frontpage/

learn.htm

#question5

A URL that omits the computer name and a full path name is called a *relative URL*. The is because the URL specifies its location *relative* to the current page. Experienced Web designers use relative URLs whenever possible. The reason for this is portability. A Web that uses relative URLs endures no loss of function if you move it to another folder or another Web server. Moving a Web that links to its own pages using hard-coded server names and folder names normally requires updating nearly every hyperlink in that Web.

Note that except for file names, your browser's Address or Location field doesn't support relative URLs. Suppose, for example, the browser window displays the following URL:

http://www.microsoft.com/frontpage/learn.htm

To jump to the What's New page, you'd have to change the browser's Address or Location box to

http://www.microsoft.com/frontpage/brochure/whatsnew.htm

This entire string isn't required within the definition of the *learn.htm* file, however. Within *learn.htm*, you could simply specify

brochure/whatsnew.htm

and allow the rest of the URL to default. The browser will add *http://www.microsoft.com /frontpage/* in front of *brochure/whatsnew.htm* for you.

Coding URL Fields for Executable Programs

Query strings, path information, and the POST method are three different ways of sending data from a browser to a program on a Web server. The method required by any given program depends on how that program was written. The following methods involve adding information to the URL:

- **Query strings.** In some cases, rather than the name of a file to transmit, a URL specifies the name of a program the server should run. Such programs may require command-line arguments, and the query string provides a way to transmit them. As shown in the following example, a question mark indicates the beginning of a query string:

  http://www.foo.interlacken.com/scripts/lookup.exe?cust=123&order=456

  The query string contains one or more *name=value* pairs, separated by ampersands (&).

> For more information on collecting data at the browser and processing it on the server, refer to Chapter 31, "Creating and Using Forms." For more information on storing data received from HTML forms, refer to "Saving Form Results to a Database" on page 917.

- **Path information.** Anything appearing between the name of an executable file and the beginning of a query string is passed to the executing program as path information. This URL contains the string "zilch" as path information:

  http://fictitious.microsoft.com/cgi/query.exe/zilch?cust=123&order=456

The POST method transmits data from the browser to a program on the Web server by adding lines to the HTTP request header. This avoids adding any extra information to the URL.

> For more information about HTTP request headers and the POST method, refer to "Hypertext Transfer Protocol—A Simple Concept" on page 1033.

In Summary...

This chapter explained how to create and modify hyperlinks, the mechanism that sends Web visitors from one page to another when they click on designated areas of a Web page. It also completes Part 4 of the book, which explained the fundamental processes of creating new pages, adding text, incorporating pictures, and linking pages together.

Part 5 explains how to copy your Web from its development location to a server that's accessible to its intended audience, how to check it for errors, and how to analyze its content. Subsequent parts explain how to lay out pages, how to apply typography and color on a global basis, and how to include more advanced kinds of content.

Part 5

Publishing and Maintaining Web Sites

Chapter 13

Publishing Your FrontPage-Based Web

After you've developed a Microsoft FrontPage-based Web, you'll almost certainly want to copy it at some point. The most common reason is that you need to copy the Web from your development environment to a public Web server to make it available to the intended audience. However, there are lots of other reasons for copying Webs from place to place, including delivery to a client, a change of working environment, and precautionary backups. Some people even copy Webs to compact discs for distribution with computer books!

You might think that FrontPage-based Webs are nothing more than sets of files, and that copying files is hardly cutting-edge technology. You can copy files with Windows Explorer, a tape-backup program, an FTP program, or the MS-DOS prompt, just to name a few methods. None of those approaches copies every aspect of a FrontPage-based Web, however; none of them adjusts all the FrontPage indexes and pointers so that the Web will work properly in its new location. To do this, use the FrontPage Publish command.

This chapter explains everything you need to know about publishing FrontPage-based Webs, even if the destination is a Web server that is not running the FrontPage Server Extensions or is not a Web server at all. What's more, one command does it all. What could be easier than that?

Web Publishing Fundamentals

Publishing is the only supported means of copying a FrontPage-based Web from one location to another. Publishing copies not only your content files—Web pages, pictures, programs, applets,

387

and the like—but also unique FrontPage information such as Navigation view and database connections. And finally, publishing won't copy certain data—such as security settings and hit counts—that ought to be different in the two locations.

Publishing always begins with opening the Web you want to copy. This is the *source* of the Publish operation. The *destination* is the location that receives the copied content. The destination can be a server-based Web, a disk-based Web, or any FTP location your network can reach. Table 13-1 summarizes these possibilities.

> **note** Because you can't open an FTP location as a FrontPage-based Web, FTP locations can't be the source of a Publish operation.

Table 13-1.   Acceptable Sources and Destinations for Publishing

Type of Web	As source	As destination
Disk-based	OK	OK
Server-based	OK	OK
FTP accessible	Not supported	OK, but result isn't a FrontPage-based Web

You should think of publishing as a *push* operation, and not necessarily as an *upload* operation. Although the most common use of the Publish command is uploading Webs from a development area to a production Web server, publishing can also *download* Webs from the production server to your local machine. To do this, open the Web on the production server and specify your computer as the destination.

To emphasize, the following two operations don't produce the same results:

- Opening the destination Web and importing the source Web (by choosing Import from the File menu.) Think of this as *pulling* the source Web into the destination Web.

- Opening the source Web and publishing to the destination Web. Think of this as *pushing* the source Web into the destination Web.

Importing the source Web adds its home page, all hyperlinked pages in the same folder tree, and all ancillary files such as pictures and animations to the destination Web. This might not include every file in the source Web, however. Importing an entire Web misses orphan pages, unused pictures, and other files with no hyperlinks in the source Web. In addition, importing an entire Web won't include the Navigation view structure, task list, Web settings, and other FrontPage data. To copy all aspects of a Web from place to place, always open the source Web and use the Publish command.

The next three sections describe the process of publishing Webs to three different kinds of destinations:

- Publishing to a FrontPage-based Web server
- Publishing to a non-extended Web server
- Publishing to a disk-based Web

newfeature! To learn specifics about publishing single files, refer to "Publishing Single Files" later in this chapter.

Publishing to a Server-Based Web

This section explains how to publish a server-based or disk-based Web at one location to a server-based Web at a different location. Two subsequent sections explain publishing to an FTP server or a disk-based Web.

Here's the procedure for publishing to a server-based Web:

1 In FrontPage, open the Web you want to copy.

2 To begin publishing, choose one of these actions:

> ▪ Choose Publish Web from the File menu. This choice always produces a full set of prompts.

Publish Web

> ▪ Click the Publish Web button on the Standard toolbar. If the source Web has been published before, this command publishes it again—to the same location and using the same settings as last time—with no further prompts. Skip ahead to the section later in this chapter titled "Monitoring the Publish Operation."
>
> If the source Web has never been published, clicking the Publish Web button produces a full set of prompts just as if you'd chosen Publish Web from the File menu.

3 If no one has ever published the source Web, choosing either command displays the Publish Destination dialog box shown in Figure 13-1 on the next page. Locate the Enter Publish Destination box, and type the full path of the destination server-based Web using this format:

> *http://<server name>/<web name>*

If you'd rather point and click your way to the destination location, click the Browse button. This displays the New Publish Location dialog box shown in Figure 13-2 on the next page. Navigate to the server and Web location you want, and then click the Open button.

Part 5: Publishing and Maintaining Web Sites

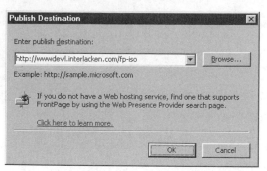

Figure 13-1. Enter the Publish destination as shown here to specify a server-based Web.

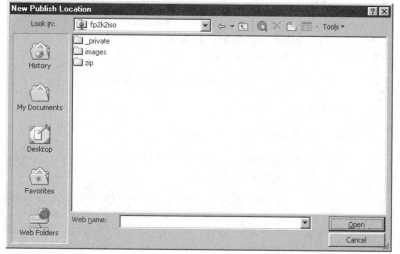

Figure 13-2. Clicking the Browse button in the Publish Destination dialog box displays this dialog box for locating a destination Web.

To create a new Web on the destination server, specify the path you want it to have. However, as when creating any new Web, all folders but the last must already exist. For example, to create a Web at

> *http://yourserver/veggies/green/broccoli/*

the path

> *http://yourserver/veggies/green/*

must already exist.

If the destination Web server requires Secure Sockets Layer (SSL) communication, specify *https* instead of *http* in the Enter Publish Destination box.

For more information about setting up Web servers to require SSL, refer to "Creating a Virtual Server" on page 1075.

Chapter 13: Publishing Your FrontPage-Based Web

Clicking the Click Here To Learn More link starts your browser and displays a page on Microsoft's Web site that lists Web Presence Providers (WPP) who sell Web space with the FrontPage Server Extensions installed.

> **on the web**   To locate a WPP who offers full support for server-based Webs, visit the Web site *http://www.microsoftwpp.com/wppsearch*.

4   Click OK in the Publish Destination dialog box. If the destination location you specify doesn't already contain a server-based Web, the prompt shown in Figure 13-3 appears.

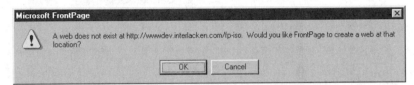

Figure 13-3.   If you specify a destination Web that doesn't exist, FrontPage displays this dialog box to ask whether FrontPage should create one.

Here you have the following options:

■   Click OK if you want to create a new server-based Web at the destination location. If your current user name and password don't have authority to create a Web at the given location, FrontPage prompts you for a user name and password that does. Given the required credentials, FrontPage creates a new blank Web at the given location.

■   Click Cancel to quit and start over.

newfeature!
5   When the Publish Web dialog box shown in Figure 13-4 on the next page appears, the Web displayed in the list box at the left is ready for publishing to the Web displayed in the list box at the right. The From and To locations appear above each list box, and again just below the title bar. From this dialog box, you can do the following:

■   To change the destination Web, click Change. This displays the Publish Destination dialog box shown in Figure 13-1.

■   To change the source Web, click Cancel, open the desired source Web, and choose Publish Web from the File menu.

To continue the publishing process, skip ahead to the section later in this chapter titled "Controlling the Publish Operation."

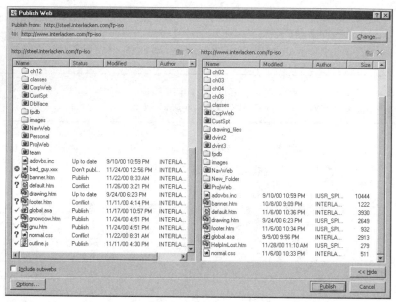

Figure 13-4. This dialog box previews the actions of a Publish operation.

Publishing to a Non-Extended Web Server

If your destination Web server doesn't have the FrontPage Server Extensions installed, attempting to publish a Web as described produces the dialog box shown in Figure 13-3. Fear not, however; with minor changes in procedure, you can publish your Web using FTP, the Internet's File Transfer Protocol.

Publishing a Web using FTP doesn't create a FrontPage-based Web on the destination server. Specifically, FrontPage doesn't upload all the private directories, indexes, and settings it would upload to a server running the FrontPage Server Extensions. This saves bandwidth and upload time, but the lack of Server Extensions means you don't have any FrontPage authoring or run-time services on the destination server.

Providers who offer Web servers lacking the FrontPage Server Extensions almost always provide designers with FTP access to their home directories. This involves four pieces of information:

- The name of the FTP server
- A user name for logging on
- A password for logging on
- A directory path that accesses your HTTP home directory.

Chapter 13: Publishing Your FrontPage-Based Web

To upload files, designers run command-line or graphical FTP programs. The following section is the start of a typical command-line session, with the four items just listed appearing in bold. The *put* command uploads the file *default.htm*.

```
ftp spike.interlacken.com
Connected to spike.interlacken.com.
220 spike Microsoft FTP Service (Version 4.0).
User (spike.interlacken.com:(none)): jim
331 Password required for jim.
Password: xxxxxx
230 User jim logged in.
ftp> cd public_html
250 CWD command successful.
ftp> put default.htm default.htm
```

Fortunately, FrontPage can upload your entire Web without exposing you to any of this gibberish. The procedure for publishing by FTP is the same as that for publishing to a FrontPage-extended Web server, with three exceptions:

1 Open the server-based Web in FrontPage, and choose Publish Web from the File menu.

2 If the Publish Destination dialog box shown in Figure 13-1 appears, skip to the next step. If the Publish Web dialog box shown in Figure 13-4 appears, click the Change button.

3 In the Enter Publish Destination box, enter an *ftp* URL like the following:

> *ftp://<server name>/<path>*

where *<server name>* identifies the FTP server, and *<path>* is the value required to access the Web's home folder. The URL corresponding to the character-mode FTP session previously shown would be:

> *ftp://spike.interlacken.com/public_html*

Figure 13-5 shows the Publish Web dialog box with this URL entered.

Figure 13-5. To publish the source Web via FTP, enter an *ftp* URL.

Part 5: Publishing and Maintaining Web Sites

Frequently Asked Questions

Why doesn't Microsoft Windows include a graphical FTP interface?

Beginning with Microsoft Windows 2000, it does. Follow the procedure described below to set up graphical connectivity to any FTP server:

1 Open My Network Places, and double-click Add Network Place.

2 When the Add Network Place Wizard appears, enter an *ftp* URL in the box titled Type The Location Of The Network Place, and click Next.

3 To log into the FTP server anonymously, select the Log On Anonymously check box.

To log in with a user account, clear the check box and enter the name of the account in the box titled User Name.

4 Click Next to display the third and final screen in the wizard. The value in the box titled Enter A Name For This Network Place will become the name of a shortcut that connects to the FTP server. The default (and an excellent choice) is the computer name in the URL you entered in step 3. Override this name if you want.

5 Click Finish to create a shortcut and connect to the FTP server. If the FTP server requires a password, Windows displays a dialog box so you can enter it.

To connect to the same FTP connection any time in the future, simply double-click its entry in My Network Places.

4 After you click OK, FrontPage connects to the FTP server and then, with the dialog box shown in Figure 13-6, prompts you for a user name and password acceptable to the FTP server.

Figure 13-6. This dialog box asks for an FTP login user name and password.

To continue the publish process, skip ahead to the section later in this chapter titled "Controlling the Publish Operation."

This shortcut will also appear in the My Network Places section of most file-oriented dialog boxes in Microsoft Office XP. And yes, this means you can read Office documents from and write them to FTP servers as easily as your local disk.

That's still too complicated. Give me something easier.

OK. Click the Start menu, choose Run, type *ftp://ftp.microsoft.com*, and press Enter.

I can't cope with that either. There must be an easier way.

Type *ftp://ftp.microsoft.com* into the Address bar of any Windows Explorer or Microsoft Internet Explorer window.

My Explorer window doesn't have an Address bar. Now what?

Choose Toolbars from the View menu, and then choose Address Bar.

Connecting though the Run menu or an Explorer window always results in an anonymous logon. Is there a way to login with an account?

Right-click the main part of the window, and choose Login As from the shortcut menu.

What if I don't have Windows 2000?

The Start, Run and Address bar methods work on any system that has Internet Explorer 5.5 installed.

Can I use these graphical FTP windows to watch my grandmother's Webcam in Zanzibar?

No.

Publishing to a Disk-Based Web

Publishing to a disk-based Web is just as easy as publishing to a server-based Web or FTP location. In the Enter Publish Destination box, simply enter the desired disk location. Figure 13-7 illustrates this. Click OK, click the Publish button, and away you go.

Figure 13-7. To publish to a disk-based Web, enter a disk location as the destination.

If the disk location you specify isn't already a FrontPage-based Web, FrontPage displays a dialog box similar to that shown in Figure 13-3. Click OK to create a Web, or Cancel to terminate the Publish operation.

Publishing to a disk-based Web is quite handy for creating backup copies of a Web, for moving a Web to a drive with more space, and for putting Webs on a removable drive (a ZIP or JAZ drive, for example) for portability.

Controlling the Publish Operation

After you've established the location of the destination Web, FrontPage displays the Publish Web dialog box shown in Figure 13-4. The contents of the source Web appear in the large box at the left, and the contents of the destination Web appear in the large box at the right. These buttons control the display of the destination Web:

- **Show>>.** Makes the contents of the destination Web visible and changes itself to a <<Hide button.

- **<<Hide.** Conceals the contents of the destination Web and changes itself to a Show>> button.

Here's how to navigate through the file and folder listings for both the source and destination Webs:

- To view the contents of a folder, double-click its entry in the list box.

Up One Level

- To view the parent of the folder that's currently displayed, click the Up One Level icon.

Delete

- To delete a file or folder from either Web, click the Delete icon.

The Name, Modified, Author, and Size fields listed for the source and destination Webs are largely self-explanatory. The Status column in the source Web's list box indicates the action FrontPage will take when you click the Publish button. This column contains one of four values:

- **Up To Date.** Indicates that the given file exists on both the source and destination Webs and that the versions are equal. During a normal Publish operation, which publishes changed pages only, FrontPage won't copy any files with this status to the destination Web.

✓

Publish

- **Publish.** Indicates that either:
    - The given file doesn't exist in the destination Web; or

    The given file exists in the destination Web, has the expected version, and that version is prior to the version in the source Web.

FrontPage always copies files with this status to the destination Web.

Chapter 13: Publishing Your FrontPage-Based Web

Don't Publish

● **Don't Publish.** Indicates that FrontPage won't publish the given file because you or someone else told it not to. Here's how this works:

■ To prevent FrontPage from publishing a given file, right-click it and
choose Don't Publish from the shortcut menu.

■ To cancel a Don't Publish instruction already in effect, right-click the
file and once again choose Don't Publish. This toggles off the Don't
Publish setting.

tip   You can also toggle the Don't Publish setting in the Folder List or Folders view.

Frequently Asked Question

What's the best way to distribute a Web on compact disc?

To put a disk-based Web on a compact disc, first publish it to your hard disk and then
use a CD creator program to copy the hard disk version to the CD. Be sure the CD
creator program copies not just ordinary files, but hidden and systems files as well.

You can't open a disk-based Web on CD because whenever FrontPage opens a Web,
it updates certain system files within that Web. This obviously fails when the Web
resides on a read-only medium like CD-ROM.

Dragging the Web from the CD to a hard disk in Windows Explorer provides no relief
because when Windows Explorer copies all the files from the CD, it copies their Read-
Only file attributes as well. FrontPage still can't open the Web because it can't open
the Read-Only files.

Fortunately, the XCOPY command can copy files from a CD to a hard disk without
copying Read-Only file attributes. Unfortunately, this is a command you must enter
and run from the command line. Here's the procedure:

1 Open a command window (that is, a C:\ prompt).

2 Enter a command like the following:

xcopy D:\<cdrom path>*.* C:\<hard disk path> /s

assuming D: is your CD-ROM drive and C: is your hard disk. Here's an
example:

xcopy D:\fp-iso*.* "C:\My Documents\My Webs\fp-iso" /s

Note that the destination path is enclosed in quotation marks. This is necessary only because the destination path contains spaces. If the source path
contained any spaces, it would require quotation marks as well.

3 Open the disk-based Web at the destination you specified in step 2. If you
want, you can now publish this Web to a server-based Web.

Chapter 13

?
Conflict

- **Conflict.** Indicates that the given file exists in both the source and the destination Web but doesn't have the expected version. To understand how this happens, consider the following scenario:

  1 On Monday you publish your working copy of a Web to its public Web server. This synchronizes the versions of all the files on the public Web server with the versions in your working copy.

  2 On Tuesday someone else in your group creates a second working copy by publishing the contents of the public Web server to another location.

  3 On Wednesday, that person publishes some changed pages back to the public Web server.

  4 On Thursday you make changes to one of the files that your coworker changed and try publishing them to the public Web server. FrontPage notices that the version on the public server isn't the same version you last synchronized with your working copy of the same Web. In short, FrontPage notices that you're about to overwrite your coworker's changes.

When you click the Publish button, FrontPage displays the Do You Want To Overwrite This File? dialog box shown in Figure 13-8. This informs you that someone else has changed the same file that you have. You can then decide whether to overwrite the file on the destination server.

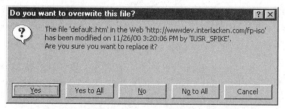

Figure 13-8. This dialog box appears when corresponding files on the source and destination Webs both get updated with no intervening synchronization.

Note that this scenario can occur even if you're the only person who updates the destination Web. If you make spot corrections to the destination Web or publish to the same Web from two different working copies, the roguish coworker might be you!

Right-clicking any file or folder in either the source or destination Web displays the shortcut menu show in the following graphic.

Chapter 13: Publishing Your FrontPage-Based Web

Here are explanations of this shortcut menu's options:

- **Cut.** Puts the selected file or folder on the Clipboard and adds a Paste option for storing it elsewhere. After you paste it, the original file or folder is deleted.

- **Copy.** Like Cut, puts the selected file or folder on the Clipboard and adds a Paste option. However, the original file or folder is retained after you paste it.

- **Paste.** Copies a file or folder marked on the Clipboard to the current destination. If a Cut command put the source file or folder on the Clipboard, a Paste command deletes it.

- **Rename.** Makes the name of a file or folder available for editing.

- **Delete.** Erases a file or folder from its current location.

- **Publish Selected Files.** Immediately copies any selected files or folders from the source Web to the destination Web.

- **Don't Publish.** Toggles the Don't Publish state of any selected files between Publish and Don't Publish.

- **Properties.** Displays the normal FrontPage property sheet for the current file or folder.

> For more information about the FrontPage property sheet for files, refer to "Working with Folders View" on page 174 and "Using the Table of Contents Based On Page Category Component" on page 776.

 For more information about the FrontPage property sheet for folders, refer to "Reviewing Folder Settings" in the Bonus Content on the Companion CD.

The following controls are also available in the Publish Web dialog box (Figure 13-4):

- **Change.** Displays the Publish Destination dialog box shown in Figure 13-1, Figure 13-5, and Figure 13-7. Use this dialog box to change the location of the destination Web.

- **Include Subwebs.** Tells FrontPage whether to publish all Webs contained within the source Web. To publish these Webs, select the check box. To take no action regarding such Webs, clear the check box.

- **Options.** Displays the Publish tab of the Options dialog box shown in Figure 13-9. You can display and update this tab any time—without starting a Publish operation—by choosing Options from the Tools menu. The dialog box controls the following options:

  - **Changed Pages Only.** Bypasses copying any file from the source Web to the destination Web if the two files appear to be identical.

  - **All Pages, Overwriting Pages Already On Destination.** Copies every file to the destination Web that exists on the source Web.

  - **Determine Changes By Comparing Source And Destination Webs.** Determines which files to copy from the source Web to the destination Webs by downloading a directory listing of the destination Web and comparing it to current directory information for the source Web.

    This provides the most accurate results but requires time to download the destination Web's directory listing. If the destination Web is large and the communications link is slow, this time can amount to several minutes.

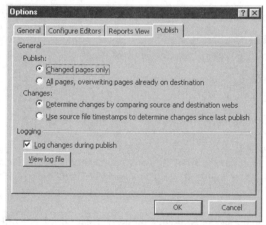

Figure 13-9. The Publish tab in the Options dialog box configures and saves various settings related to publishing a Web.

  - **Use Source File Timestamps To Determine Changes Since Last Publish.** Determines which files on the source and destination Webs are different by comparing the date of the last update of each file in the source Web with the date and time of the last Publish operation.

    This method is less accurate than comparing the source and destination Webs, because in some cases it ignores changes made by other people to the destination Web. Of course, if you're the only person who publishes to the given destination Web, this isn't an issue.

Chapter 13: Publishing Your FrontPage-Based Web

The primary advantage of this method lies in not having to download
a directory listing from the destination Web.

newfeature!

■ **Log Changes During Publish.** If selected, tells FrontPage to keep a
log of each change that publishing makes to the destination Web. If
the box isn't checked, FrontPage doesn't create a log.

■ **View Log File.** Displays the log for the most recent Publish operation. Figure 13-10 shows a typical display.

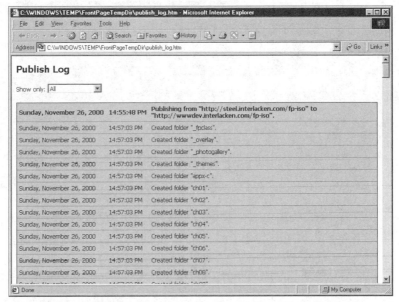

Figure 13-10. FrontPage can create a log file like this to show you
the results of a Publish command.

Click the Publish button on the Publish Web dialog box when you're satisfied all entries
are correct.

Monitoring the Publish Operation

If the destination Web server has security controls in effect, FrontPage might prompt
you for an authorized user name and password. For updating an existing server-based
Web, this must be a user name with authoring privileges. For creating a new server-
based Web, the user name must be an administrator of the new Web's parent.

Part 5: Publishing and Maintaining Web Sites

Troubleshooting

Unable to open destination Web during publish operation

Clicking the Publish button might result in the dialog box shown in Figure 13-11. The appearance of this dialog box indicates that your copy of FrontPage was unable to establish communications with the FrontPage Server Extensions on the destination Web server.

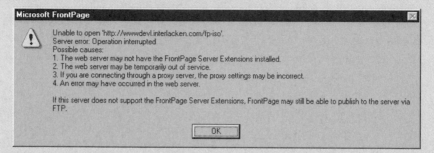

Figure 13-11. This dialog box indicates a failure to connect with the FrontPage Server Extensions at the destination Web.

Here are the four most likely causes of this problem and the most likely solutions:

● The Web server might not have the FrontPage Server Extensions installed.

If you believe the FrontPage Server Extensions are installed on the destination Web server, contact the server administrator and ask to have the Server Health jobs run against the destination Web. If that fails, ask to have the server extensions reinstalled.

> **For more information about the checking server health, refer to "Checking Server Health" on page 1110.**

If you believe the FrontPage Server Extensions aren't installed, you can:

■ Contact the server administrator and ask to have the server extensions installed.

■ Contact your Web provider or IT department and ask for space on a Web server that runs the server extensions.

■ Find a new Web provider that supports the FrontPage Server Extensions.

■ Publish your Web by FTP as described in the "Publishing to a Non-Extended Web Server" section earlier in this chapter.

- The Web server might be temporarily out of service. If so:
  - Wait to see if the connectivity problem goes away.
  - If you have an intermittent Internet connection (such as a dial-up line), make sure it's active.
  - Check connectivity to the destination server by pointing your browser to one of its pages. Here are two options for this situation:
    - If you can't access the destination server and also can't access any other sites on the same network, contact your network provider.
    - If you can access sites almost anywhere but the destination server, contact whoever administers the destination server.
- If your connection is through a proxy server, the proxy server settings might be incorrect.

  FrontPage uses the same Internet settings as Internet Explorer. This means you can resolve FrontPage proxy server problems by resolving Internet Explorer proxy server problems. The location of these settings tends to change with each version of Internet Explorer, but to see the settings in Internet Explorer 5.5, choose Internet Options from the Tools menu, click the Connections tab, and click LAN Settings. Contact whoever administers the proxy server for the correct settings. If Internet Explorer can browse the destination server, any inability to publish in FrontPage isn't a proxy server problem.

  A proxy server is a special network device that isolates a private network from the Internet. It lets computers on the private network browse Internet sites, but blocks computers on the Internet from connecting to those on the internal network.

- An error might have occurred in the Web server.

  This is an explanation of last resort. If all else fails, contact the folks who operate the destination Web server and ask them to check it for proper operation. Some actions they might take include checking the Event Log for unusual errors, running Check And Fix on the destination Web, reinstalling the server extensions, stopping and restarting the Web server, and rebooting the entire server.

newfeature!
Publishing Single Files

Sometimes it's very handy to publish just a single file or folder. For example, you might know exactly which files you changed recently and want to avoid the time required to determine changes by comparing the source and destination Webs over a slow link. Another scenario occurs when your working copy of a Web contains both finished and unfinished changes, and you want to publish only the finished ones. FrontPage provides three ways of doing this:

- Open both Webs in FrontPage and drag the files or folders you want to publish from one Folder List or Folders view to the other.

newfeature!
- Publish individual files or folders to the destination Web you used during the last full Publish operation. Here are the steps:

  1 Right-click the file or folder in the Folder List or in Folders view.

  2 Choose Publish Selected Files from the shortcut menu.

newfeature!
- Publish individual files or folders to a destination Web that you explicitly select. Here are the steps:

  1 Choose Publish Web from the File menu.

  2 Proceed until the Publish Web dialog box shown in Figure 13-4 appears.

  3 Verify the location of the destination Web. If necessary, click the Change button to change the location.

  4 Right-click the file or folder in the source Web listing.

  5 Choose Publish Selected Files from the shortcut menu.

How Web Publishing Works

Regardless of the type of source Web and the type of destination Web, Web publishing basically occurs in four phases:

1 Determining which files need to be added, replaced, or deleted on the destination Web.

2 Copying all the files that need to be added or replaced, plus instructions to delete those that are no longer needed, plus any changes to Navigation view, database connections, or any other Web settings.

3 Processing all the updates on the destination Web server. This includes both normal file updates, Web settings, and recalculation of hyperlinks.

4 Reporting completion of the publishing process.

Chapter 13: Publishing Your FrontPage-Based Web

Figure 13-12 shows the status display for each of these steps. Cancel buttons in the lower-right corner of the first two boxes are hidden, but they look much like Cancel buttons anywhere. Clicking Cancel terminates the Publish operation.

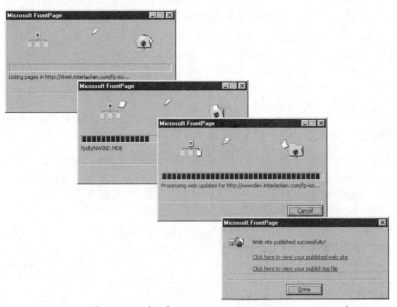

Figure 13-12. These are the four status messages you receive during a successful FrontPage Publish operation.

If a message like one of those shown in Figure 13-13 appears, it means that the Web you're publishing uses features that the destination Web can't support. This can occur if, for example, the FrontPage Server Extensions on the destination server are outdated or absent. However, despite the error messages, FrontPage still copies the listed pages to the given destination. Subsequent Publish operations then depend on the type of destination.

Figure 13-13. This dialog box warns you of any pages that won't work properly after being published to a disk-based Web.

FrontPage works with destination types in these ways:

● If the destination is a disk-based Web, subsequently publishing from that location to a FrontPage 2002 server-based Web restores full functionality. Be sure to use FrontPage 2002 for any such publishing, however.

● If the destination is a FrontPage 2000 or earlier server-based Web, subsequently publishing from that location to a FrontPage 2002 server-based Web might or might not restore the Web to full operation. This depends on the exact features you used and the exact outdated version of the server extensions that was installed. The same considerations apply if you publish a FrontPage 2002 Web to a server with outdated extensions and subsequently upgrade the server.

After you have access to a server running the FrontPage Server Extensions 2002, the best approach is to republish the original FrontPage 2002 source Web to the new destination. That is, don't try to migrate the copy you published from the obsolete or the non-extended Web server.

● If the destination is an FTP server, you can't subsequently open the FTP location as a FrontPage-based Web, nor can you publish it to another location. This is because FrontPage strips all unique FrontPage information out of any Web it publishes to an FTP location. (The logic is that a non-extended Web server you have reached by FTP can't make use of this information anyway.)

Again, the best way to republish the Web to a more capable location is to publish it from the original FrontPage 2002 location and not from the non-extended Web server.

Frequently Asked Question

Can I publish my FrontPage 2002 Web to a server running older server extensions?

FrontPage 2002 can publish to any Web server running any earlier version of the FrontPage Server Extensions. To this extent, FrontPage 2002 is fully compatible with earlier versions of the server extensions.

Any features that are new to FrontPage 2002 and involve server-side pro-cessing, however, do require the FrontPage Server Extensions 2002. These features won't work properly (or at all) on earlier versions of the extensions.

For a list of features that require the later server extensions, please see article Q232524 in the Microsoft Knowledge Base.

Chapter 13: Publishing Your FrontPage-Based Web

The Do You Want To Overwrite This File? dialog box shown in Figure 13-9 appears when a Publish operation detects that any file version on the destination server has changed since the source Web was last published to it. You have five options:

- **Yes.** Replaces the existing file on the destination Web with the corresponding file in the source Web.

- **Yes To All.** Works the same as Yes. Additionally, it applies the Yes answer to all future prompts of this type, for the duration of the current Publish operation.

- **No.** Bypasses the update of the questionable file, but continues the Publish operation.

- **No To All.** Works the same as No. Additionally, it applies the No answer to all future prompts of this type, for the duration of the current Publish operation.

- **Cancel.** Bypasses the update of the questionable file and terminates the Publish operation.

A similar message might appear if the destination Web contains files not present in the source Web. FrontPage offers you the choice of keeping or deleting such files.

If the prompt shown in Figure 13-14 appears during a Publish operation, it means there's a version conflict between the Navigation view structures of the source and destination Webs.

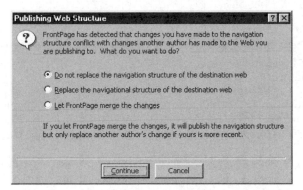

Figure 13-14. The Publishing Web Structure dialog box appears if the destination Web's Navigation view changes between successive publications from the same-source Web.

To understand how this can happen, consider the following series of events:

1 You create a new Web, enter a Navigation view structure, and publish the Web to your production server.

2 You create some new pages, enter them in Navigation view, and publish your Web once more to the same production server.

No error or warning message occurs from this pattern of working, no matter how often you repeat step 2. Imagine, however, that events continue this way:

3 You publish the Web to the production server.

4 Someone else downloads the Web, changes its Navigation view structure, and then publishes it to the production server.

5 You update your copy of the Web, change its Navigation view structure, and then try publishing in to the production server.

Step 5 will produce the dialog box shown in Figure 13-13 because FrontPage knows the destination Web contains Navigation view changes not reflected in your copy of the Web. Here are your choices:

■ **Do Not Replace The Navigation Structure Of The Destination Web.** This option publishes your revised content, but not the revised Navigation view.

This is probably the safest choice because it leaves both versions of the Navigation view intact. After publishing is completed, you can open both Webs, compare the two Navigation view structures, and decide what to do.

■ **Replace The Navigational Structure Of The Destination Web.** This option replaces the destination Web's Navigation view with the source Web's Navigation view, based on revision dates for each Navigation view entry. As to any other Navigation view changes made to the destination Web, they'll be lost.

■ **Let FrontPage Merge The Changes.** This option tells FrontPage to reconcile the two Navigation view structures. This is a somewhat risky choice, because the assumptions coded in FrontPage might be contrary to your wishes.

If you choose either the first or third options, the two Navigation structures will still be different after the Publish operation ends. To resolve such a conflict, correct the Navigation view in either the source or the destination Web, and then publish that Web to the other location.

In Summary...

This chapter explained how to publish a FrontPage-based Web from one location to another. This is the only supported way of copying a Web from place to place without losing any information.

The next chapter explains how to summarize, analyze, and validate the content of a Web.

Chapter 14

Keeping Your Web Up-to-Date

As time passes, your Web will likely grow in size and complexity. Pages will evolve, gaining and losing text, pictures, and hyperlinks along the way. As this process continues, the difficulty of maintaining technical and visual continuity will grow as well. Microsoft FrontPage provides a number of features to assist in ongoing maintenance. These include:

- A way to update hyperlinks automatically when you move or rename a page.

- A way to find or replace text anywhere in your Web.

- A command for updating all cross-references and indexes for your Web.

This chapter also explains how to use Reports view and Hyperlinks view. Reports view displays information and statistics about your Web, locates apparent problems, and displays usage statistics. Hyperlinks view displays a graphical diagram of the hyperlinks among your pages. All these facilities help you analyze, check, and correct your Web.

Moving, Renaming, and Reorganizing Pages

As the number of files in your Web grows, organizing them into folders and establishing naming conventions will become increasingly important. The need to reorganize or rename pages isn't necessarily a sign of poor planning; more often it's simply a sign that your Web has grown. A topic that began

409

Part 5: Publishing and Maintaining Web Sites

as a single Web page might, over time, become a dozen pages and warrant its own folder. And a small collection of picture files will likely become difficult to search after growing to a hundred or so pictures.

If you have local or file-sharing access to your Web's file area, you can move, copy, rename, or delete files with Windows Explorer, the command prompt, or any number of utility programs. Even if you don't have such access, you can make changes with an FTP program. Unfortunately, these approaches do nothing to adjust hyperlinks from other pages to the moved or renamed files. Unless you locate and correct these links manually, your Web won't function properly.

> For more information about the mechanics of moving, copying, and deleting files in FrontPage, refer to "Manipulating Files and Folders" on page 70.

Changing file names and locations from within FrontPage avoids the problem of broken hyperlinks because FrontPage corrects links automatically. FrontPage maintains indexes of all links within a Web and uses these to find and update the necessary Web pages. To keep these indexes accurate, it's best to always use FrontPage for organizing Web pages.

> For more information about using other programs to update FrontPage-based Webs, refer to the Frequently Asked Question sidebar titled "How Can Programs Other than FrontPage Safely Update a FrontPage-Based Web?" later in this chapter.

Here are several cautions:

- FrontPage corrects hyperlink and picture references only within the current Web. When you reorganize pages or pictures, whoever maintains other Webs will need to manually correct their links to your site.

- If you have reason to suspect that FrontPage's indexes are out of date, run the Recalculate Hyperlinks command before reorganizing the files. The procedure is described later in this chapter. FrontPage can't update your Web correctly if its indexes are incorrect.

- Changing a Web by any means other than FrontPage is the number one cause of incorrect indexes.

- FrontPage can't reliably identify picture tags and hyperlinks coded as values within script code. Thus, FrontPage doesn't always update hyperlinks and picture references located within scripts.

- Close any Web Pages open in FrontPage before reorganizing files. FrontPage doesn't update hyperlinks located within open pages.

> For more information about what to do if you suspect that your Web already has broken hyperlinks or picture locations, refer to "Checking Links in Your Web" later in this chapter.

Chapter 14

Finding and Replacing Text

From time to time you'll no doubt find it valuable to search your Web for all instances of a certain word or phrase. You might need to locate all instances of a person's name, a product name, an address, or some other text expression and check those pages for accuracy. The Find In Web feature in FrontPage provides an excellent facility for such searches.

Find In Web differs from the Web Search component in the following respects:

● Find In Web operates in the FrontPage environment. When you find a matching page, a single mouse click opens it in Page view. Find In Web is always available.

● The Web Search component operates at run time, using a browser, and has no direct links to authoring tools. Also, it must be activated in advance as part of your Web.

For more information about the Web Search component, refer to "Using the Web Search Component" on page 785.

Find In Web differs from file system search utilities as well:

● Find In Web offers one-click access to editing Web pages in FrontPage.

● A file system search locates word or phrase instances in FrontPage index and cross-reference files, as well as in Web pages.

● A file-system search misses phrase instances that contain carriage returns, line feeds, tabs, or extra spaces.

Both All Pages operations—Find and Replace—are two-phase processes. Phase one creates a list of Web pages containing a specified string, and phase two opens each found page for editing. To run Find In Web on your Web:

1 Open your Web in FrontPage.

2 To ensure accurate results, close any pages that are open for editing.

3 Choose Find from the Edit menu.

4 When the Find And Replace dialog box shown in Figure 14-1 on the next page appears, configure the following settings:

■ **Find What.** Specifies the word or phrase you want to find.

■ **Find Where.** Controls the pages searched as follows:

◆ **All Pages.** Searches all pages in the current Web. Always choose this option for searching an entire Web.

411

Part 5: Publishing and Maintaining Web Sites

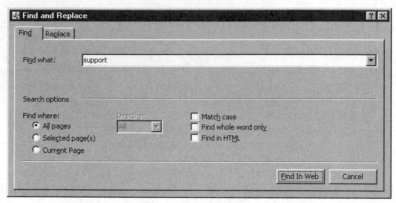

Figure 14-1. This dialog box begins a Find In Web operation in FrontPage.

◆ **Selected Page(s).** Searches any files or folders currently selected in the active window. The active window, in this sense, is the Folder List, Folder view, or the Page view editing window, whichever you clicked last.

◆ **Current Page.** Searches the current page open for editing. This is the form of Search and Replace FrontPage uses when editing single pages.

■ **Direction.** Controls the order of searching within a Web page (available only when you open a page for editing and select Current Page). Choose from:

◆ **All.** Searches from the insertion point to the end of the document, and then from the document to the original insertion point.

◆ **Up.** Searches from the insertion point to the top of the document.

◆ **Down.** Searches from the insertion point to the end of the document.

■ **Search Options.** Choose from:

◆ **Match Case.** If selected, indicates that matching terms must have exactly the same capitalization. If this option is cleared, capitalization doesn't matter.

◆ **Find Whole Word Only.** If selected, specifies that FrontPage will match only complete words. The search term *basket*, for example, would not find the word *basketball*. Clearing the box searches for words of any length that contain the search term.

◆ **Find in HTML.** If selected, specifies that FrontPage should search each Web page's hidden HTML code as well as its visible text.

Chapter 14: Keeping Your Web Up-to-Date

5 After completing the entries in Figure 14-1, click the Find In Web button. The Find And Replace dialog box then assumes the form shown in Figure 14-2. The two buttons in the bottom right corner are captioned Stop and Cancel. Progress messages appear across the bottom of the window. Click Stop to pause or abandon the search.

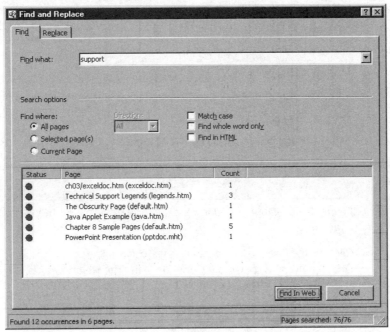

Figure 14-2. This window displays Find In Web progress and results.

6 When the search finishes, the caption on the Stop button changes to Find In Web. The large list box displays these column entries for each page containing the Find What text:

■ **Status.** Initially displays a red circle, indicating that no action has yet been taken.

■ **Page.** Displays the title and name of each page that contains the Find What text you specified in step 4.

■ **Count.** Reports the number of matches on each page.

7 To view or edit a found page, double-click its entry in the list box. As shown in Figure 14-3 on the next page, FrontPage opens the page and highlights the first instance of the Find What text.

The options in Figure 14-3 default to the values you assigned in Figure 14-1. Any changes you make apply to your search of the current page only. Repeatedly clicking the Find Next button searches the document from top to bottom or bottom to top, depending on the Direction setting.

Part 5: Publishing and Maintaining Web Sites

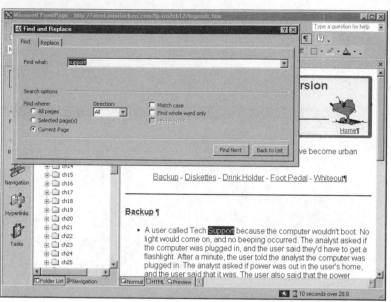

Figure 14-3.   Double-clicking a page located with Find In Web opens it in
Page view.

8 Clicking the Back To List button or searching past the last instance of the
Find What text displays the Continue With The Next Page? dialog box
shown in Figure 14-4.

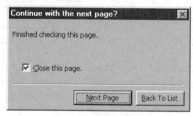

Figure 14-4.   This dialog box prompts for the disposition of Web pages
found and opened by Find In Web.

This dialog box has these options:

- ■ **Close This Page.** If selected, closes the editing window for the current
page. If you clear this box, FrontPage keeps the page open for further
editing.

- ■ **Next Page.** Opens the next document in the Find In Web list shown in
Figure 14-2.

- ■ **Back to List.** Terminates the process of opening successive documents
in the Find In Web list. It also leaves the current page open for further
editing.

Chapter 14: Keeping Your Web Up-to-Date

9 Opening a found page in FrontPage changes its Status icon (in Figure 14-2) from a red circle to a yellow circle followed by the word *Edited*.

As you might expect, the process of running a Replace In Web greatly resembles that for Find In Web. There are two major differences, however:

- When specifying the text to find, you must also specify the text to substitute.

- When you open a Web page from the Find Occurrences list, FrontPage displays both the search text and the substitution text in the resulting Find And Replace dialog box.

Replace In Web can be unattended or prompted. An unattended Replace In Web scans an entire Web, unconditionally replacing all instances of one string with another.

Here's the full procedure for performing an unattended Replace In Web:

1 Open your Web in FrontPage.

2 Close any editing sessions.

3 Choose Replace from the Edit menu.

4 When the dialog box shown in Figure 14-5 appears, configure the settings as described in step 4 of the Find In Web procedure.

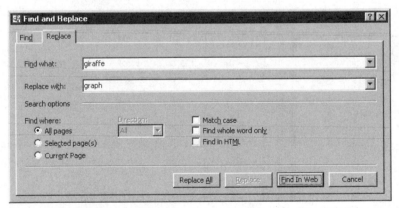

Figure 14-5. Begin a Replace In Web operation with this dialog box.

There is one additional box, namely:

■ **Replace With.** Specifies the word or phrase that should replace the found text.

Part 5: Publishing and Maintaining Web Sites

5 Click the Replace All button. FrontPage displays the following warning. If you click the Yes button, FrontPage summarily replaces all instances of the Find What string with the Replace With string.

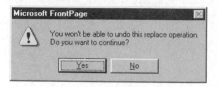

FrontPage can't undo an unattended Replace In Web, but it does display a list of files it modified. You should at least spot-check the results before discarding this list.

A prompted Replace In Web, like a Find In Web, involves two phases. The first phase searches your entire Web for all instances of the Find What string. (In fact, this phase of a Replace In Web *is* a Find In Web. You can run it with the Find tab selected and then click the Replace tab to run phase two.)

The second phase begins when a Find results list is on display and you click the Replace button. FrontPage sequentially opens each page in the list and displays a Find And Replace dialog box that applies only to that page. This dialog box is yours to operate. When the Find and Replace operations for the current page are finished, FrontPage asks whether to display the next matching page or suspend the entire operation.

Here's the detailed procedure for performing a prompted Replace In Web:

1 Perform steps 1 through 4 of the previous procedure.

2 Click the Find In Web button. FrontPage runs the Find In Web process and changes the Find And Replace dialog box to the form shown in Figure 14-2.

3 At this point in the process, no actual replacements have occurred. Click the Replace button to begin replacing text in the first listed page.

To begin replacing text on a different page, first select that page and then click the Replace button. Alternatively, double-click the desired page.

4 As shown in Figure 14-6, FrontPage opens each page for editing, finds the first instance of the Find What text, and offers to replace it. You can then do any of the following:

- **Replace All.** Click this to replace all instances in the current page without prompting.

- **Replace.** Click this to replace the current instance of the Find What text and advance to the next instance in the same page.

- **Find Next.** Click this to advance to the next instance of the Find What text in the same page.

- **Back To List.** Click this to redisplay the Replace In Web results list.

Chapter 14: Keeping Your Web Up-to-Date

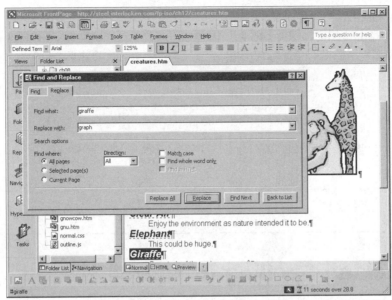

Figure 14-6. To replace text on a given page, double-click its entry
in the Replace In Web results list. FrontPage displays the Find And
Replace dialog box.

5 If you click Replace All or click either Find Next or Replace past the end
of the page, FrontPage offers to save the current page and open the next
page containing the found text, again using the dialog box in Figure 14-4.

Each page you examine will be marked Edited when you return to the list of matches,
even if you don't make any changes.

When the Replace In Web results list is on display, the Replace and Replace All buttons
work globally—that is, they affect the entire Web. When a Web page is open and the
results list is hidden, the buttons work only on the current page. Table 14-1 summarizes
these differences and provides a reference to other related commands as well.

Table 14-1. **Find and Replace Dialog Box Buttons**

Command	Replace In Web results list absent	Replace In Web results list present
Find In Web	Searches the entire current Web for pages that contain the Find What string and displays a Replace In Web results list. This command is available only when Find Where is set to All Pages or Selected Page(s).	
Replace All	Replaces all instances in the current page without prompting.	Replaces all instances in all listed pages without prompting.

(continued)

Table 14-1. *(continued)*

Command	Replace In Web results list absent	Replace In Web results list present
Replace	Replaces the current instance of the Find What text and advances to the next instance and in the same page.	Opens the current (or first) page in the results list, displays a normalFind and Replace dialog box, and finds the first instance.
Find Next	Advances to the next instance of the Find What text in the same page.	N/A
Back To List	Redisplays the Replace In Web results list.	N/A

Checking Spelling in Your Web

Like most word processors, Front Page features a spelling checker. You can use this tool to check spelling in a single page, or in all or part of your Web. In a process similar to Find and Replace, the spelling checker finds misspelled words and replaces them with correct ones. If you run the spelling checker on multiple files, it first builds a list of pages containing misspelled words, and then it provides choices for editing pages or adding them to Task view. If you choose to edit a listed page, FrontPage steps through the misspelled words.

To check spelling in all or part of a Web:

1 Close any pages that are open for editing.

2 If you plan to check less than the entire Web, select the pages you want to check.

Spelling

3 Choose Spelling from the Tools menu, or click the Spelling button on the Standard toolbar.

4 The Spelling dialog box shown in Figure 14-7 appears.

Figure 14-7. Use this dialog box to initiate Check Spelling In Web.

Configure the following settings:

Chapter 14: Keeping Your Web Up-to-Date

- **Check Spelling Of.** Specifies the range of pages to check for correct spelling:

    - **Selected Page(s).** Checks only the pages you selected in step 2.

    - **Entire Web.** Checks all pages in the current Web.

- **Add A Task For Each Page With Misspellings.** Indicates that you want to bypass the list of pages containing misspelled words and instead add each page to Task view.

5 Click Start. FrontPage checks the specified pages for spelling errors and then displays the dialog box shown in Figure 14-8, which lists all selected pages containing misspelled words.

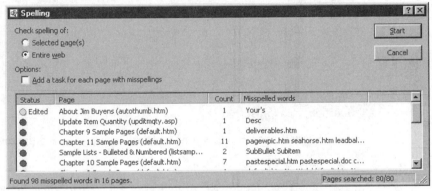

Figure 14-8. FrontPage displays this dialog box to identify pages with spelling errors.

The Status column displays the following:

- If you selected Add A Task For Each Page With Misspellings, FrontPage displays a yellow ball and a status of Added for each page that failed the spelling check.

- If you didn't select Add A Task For Each Page With Misspellings, FrontPage displays a red ball and no status for each page that failed.

6 As with the Find In Web and Replace In Web functions, scanning for errors doesn't correct them. To actually resolve spelling errors, double-click the entry for the first page you want to correct, and then click Start.

7 FrontPage opens the first page you selected in step 5, advances to the first spelling error, and displays the Spelling dialog box shown in Figure 14-9 on the next page. The following options are available:

- **Not In Dictionary.** Displays the misspelled word.

- **Change To.** Supplies a corrected word. You can accept the word FrontPage suggests, type a word on the keyboard, or pick a word from the drop-down list of suggestions.

419

Part 5: Publishing and Maintaining Web Sites

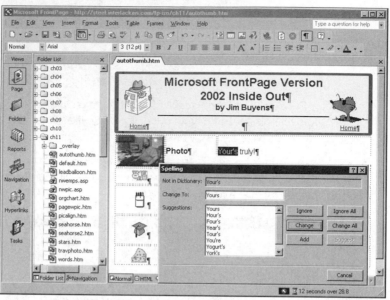

Figure 14-9. FrontPage uses this dialog box to correct spelling of
questionable words.

- **Suggestions.** Provides a list of possible corrections to the misspelling.

- **Ignore.** Bypasses the current word.

- **Ignore All.** Ignores the current word if it appears again in the same
  Web page.

- **Change.** Replaces the misspelled word with the contents of the
  Change To box.

- **Change All.** Replaces the current misspelled word with the contents
  of the Change To box everywhere on the page.

- **Add.** Adds the current word to the custom dictionary. Future spelling
  checks will no longer report this word as an error.

- **Suggest.** Checks the spelling of a word you typed by hand into the
  Change To box. This is useful when the correct word doesn't appear
  in the Suggestions list, you attempt a correction by hand, and you
  want to check your work before moving on.

For more information about checking spelling in individual Web pages, refer to "Searching,
Replacing, and Checking Spelling" on page 283.

8 Click the appropriate button in the Spelling dialog box. Clicking any button
except Cancel advances to the next spelling error in the same page. When
FrontPage reaches the end of the current page (or if you clicked the Cancel

button), it displays the Continue With The Next Page? dialog box shown in
Figure 14-4. As before:

- **Close This Page.** If selected, closes the editing window for the current
  page.

- **Next Page.** Opens the next document in the list of pages produced in step 4.

- **Back To List.** Terminates the process of opening successive documents
  that contain spelling errors. It also leaves the current page open for
  further editing.

> **note** FrontPage uses the Microsoft custom dictionary. Because this file is on the FrontPage
> designer's local machine, dictionary additions made by one designer won't be avail-
> able to other designers working on the same Web.

Re-Indexing Your Web

FrontPage maintains a number of databases and index files that cross-reference hyperlinks and other elements in your Web pages. If these files and your Web pages
get out of sync, FrontPage might produce incorrect search results, incorrectly size
pictures, or incompletely update hyperlinks.

FrontPage updates its indexes every time it makes changes to a Web, but other
programs and utilities don't. You should re-index your Web every time you make
changes with external tools, any time you suspect indexes of being corrupted,
or in general, any time your Web seems to be acting strangely.

> **caution** It's best to close any open files in your Web before recalculating hyperlinks.

To re-index a Web, open it in FrontPage and choose Recalculate Hyperlinks
from the Tools menu. This accomplishes three things:

- It updates the display for all current views of the current Web.

- It regenerates all dependencies. If, for example, you used an external editor
  to modify an included page, any pages that include it continue to display
  the old version. Recalculating hyperlinks refreshes the affected Include
  Page components.

- It rebuilds the text index used by the Web Search component. This can
  become outdated if you externally add, change, or delete files in your Web.

Stop

The Recalculate Hyperlinks dialog box in Figure 14-10 on the next page appears whenever you run the Recalculate Hyperlinks command. As noted, recalculating hyperlinks
can take several minutes for a large Web. When recalculation starts, the Stop button on

421

the Standard toolbar flashes until recalculation finishes. Only when it stops can you
do further work in FrontPage.

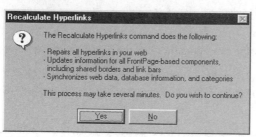

Figure 14-10. This dialog box presages a Recalculate Hyperlinks operation.

Checking Links in Your Web

A widely accepted principle of physics is that, left to itself, order inevitably reverts
to chaos. Hyperlinks provide a perfect example of such entropy at work. Although
FrontPage can greatly reduce instances of broken hyperlinks within your Web, typing
errors and changes at remote sites inevitably break even the most carefully created
hyperlinks. FrontPage provides the Broken Hyperlinks report to detect and correct
such errors.

All Web designers should check hyperlinks occasionally, because there's no reliable
means to catch changes as they occur throughout the entire World Wide Web. The
frequency of checking will vary, depending on the number of links, their volatility,
and the level of service you want to provide.

For more information about the Broken Hyperlinks report, refer to "Broken Hyperlinks" later
in this chapter.

Testing Your Web

Utilities such as the Broken Hyperlinks Report and Check Spelling In Web provide
excellent ways to check the content of your Web, and using FrontPage produces
error-free HTML. Nevertheless, there's no substitute for browsing your own Web
and testing its functions online.

Two fundamental things to check are the correct operation of all hyperlinks and
reasonable page transmission times under typical conditions. However, you should
also do a test drive to confirm proper appearance and operation under the following
conditions:

- **Different Browsers.** Test your pages with at least the current production
  versions of Internet Explorer, Netscape Navigator, and any other browser

used by your audience, plus the previous production version and perhaps the current pre-release version of each.

- **Different Browser Settings.** Remember that visitors can turn some browser features on and off, such as the ability to run scripts, run Java applets, and load ActiveX controls. If you use these facilities, make sure your pages degrade gracefully, rather than crash and burn, if visitors turn them off.

- **Different Color Depths.** View your pages in 256 color mode as well as 24-bit true color. Depending on your visitors' equipment, you might also want to test at 16 colors and in 64K high-color mode.

- **Different Screen Sizes.** Make sure your pages are usable, even if unattractive, on systems with 640 x 480 pixel displays.

- **Different Servers.** Don't assume that everything on multiple servers will work the same way (presuming your environment uses more than one, such as a Microsoft Web Server for authoring and an ISP's UNIX

Frequently Asked Question

How can programs other than FrontPage safely update a FrontPage-based Web?

The following methods all update FrontPage-based Webs or SharePoint team Web sites without invalidating the Web's internal indexes:

- In Microsoft Windows 95, Microsoft Windows 98, and Microsoft Windows NT 4.0, use the Web Folders feature that appears after you install Microsoft Office 2000, Office XP, or recent versions of Microsoft Internet Explorer.

  You can access Web Folders from My Computer and from most Open File and Save As dialog boxes in Microsoft Office applications.

- In Microsoft Windows 2000, use an HTTP location listed under My Network Places.

  You can access such HTTP locations from My Network Places, from most applications bundled with Windows 2000, and from most Open File and Save As dialog boxes in Office 2000 and Office XP applications.

- Have FrontPage launch the application you want to use. In this mode, FrontPage exports a temporary version of the file, runs the external program, watches for that program to end, and then imports the temporary file if its directory information has changed.

  If double-clicking a file in FrontPage doesn't launch the application you want, choose Options from the Tools menu, click the Configure Editors tab, and assign the desired program to the appropriate filename extension.

on the CD For more information about configuring FrontPage to launch other programs, refer to "Configuring External Editors" in the Bonus Content on the Companion CD.

server for production). The greater the difference between the servers, the more that can go wrong. Test and debug each server environment thoroughly.

Scripts are probably the most sensitive components in your Web. JavaScript, in particular, hasn't benefited from a formal language specification, nor does it have a comprehensive test suite. Bugs and features seem to come and go with each browser version, so testing is an absolute necessity. Remember that browser-side VBScript isn't supported by Netscape browsers.

Test after each change to your Web—each set of page changes, each Copy Web operation, each server upgrade, each new version of FrontPage, each new browser version that appears. Even if nothing else changes, hyperlinks will; verify them periodically.

Working with Reports View

FrontPage provides a sizable assortment of highly useful, interactive reports for managing your Web. There are three ways to display any desired report:

Reports ▾

Reports

- Choose Reports from the View menu, and then select the report you want from the resulting submenu.

- Choose Toolbars from the View menu, select Reporting, and then choose the report you want from the Report menu on the Reporting toolbar.

- Click the Reports icon on the Views bar. This displays either the last report you requested or, by default, the Site Summary report. (For more information, refer to "Viewing the Site Summary Report" later in this chapter.) Use either of the previous methods to select a different report.

 For more information about the Reporting toolbar, refer to "The Reporting Toolbar" in the Bonus Content on the Companion CD.

By their nature, reports pertain to collections of objects; one-line reports just aren't very interesting. For this reason, Reports view pertains only to FrontPage-based Webs. If you're just using FrontPage to edit a single page and haven't opened a Web, Reports view won't be available. If you *have* opened a Web, the reports pertain to that Web.

Here are the standard FrontPage reports, grouped by category:

- **Summary reports.** Provide overall Web statistics:
  - **Site Summary.** Accumulates and reports various high-level statistics about your Web, such as the number of files, their total size, and so forth.

- **File reports.** List Web pages and other files that meet various criteria:
  - **All Files.** Lists all files in a Web, regardless of folder.

Chapter 14: Keeping Your Web Up-to-Date

- ▣ **Recently Added Files.** Lists all files added to a Web within a given interval.

- ▣ **Recently Changed Files.** Lists all files changed within a given interval.

- ▣ **Older Files.** Lists files that haven't been updated within a given interval.

● **Problem reports.** Itemize errors that exist within your Web:

- ▣ **Unlinked Files.** Lists files your Web might not be using.

- ▣ **Slow Pages.** Lists Web pages whose total download time, including linked components, exceeds a given amount.

- ▣ **Broken Hyperlinks.** Reports links to files that don't exist and provides options for fixing them.

- ▣ **Component Errors.** Reports errors and inconsistencies involving FrontPage components. These can occur when, for example, you first configure the component correctly and then later delete a required file.

● **Workflow reports.** Display the status of a Web that several people are developing together:

- ▣ **Review Status.** Shows which pages are assigned for review, along with any further status the reviewer has assigned.

- ▣ **Assigned To.** Shows which pages are assigned to which designer.

- ▣ **Categories.** Lists all Web pages, including a column that shows assigned Category codes.

- ▣ **Publish Status.** Shows which pages are approved for publication and which are held back.

- ▣ **Checkout Status.** Shows which files are checked out for updates, and by whom.

newfeature!
● **Usage reports.** Display activity statistics collected by the Web server. These statistics are available only on Web servers running the FrontPage Server Extensions 2002 or SharePoint Team Services:

- ▣ **Usage Summary.** Displays overall statistics for your Web collected since inception. The inception date is one of the reported statistics.

- ▣ **Monthly, Weekly, and Daily Summaries.** Display total visits, total page hits, total hits of all kinds, and total download bytes by applicable period since inception.

- ▣ **Monthly, Weekly, and Daily Page Hits.** Displays, by period, the number of times Web visitors requested each page in your Web.

■ **Visiting Users.** Displays the identities of Web visitors to your site. However, unless you require Web visitors to identify themselves by user name and password, this report will be blank.

■ **Operating Systems.** Reports how many visits came from computers running Windows 95, Windows 98, Windows NT, Windows 2000, Macintosh, various forms of UNIX, and so forth.

■ **Browsers.** Reports how many visits came from various browsers, such as Internet Explorer 5.0, Internet Explorer 5.5, and various versions of Netscape.

■ **Referring Domains.** Reports the names of all Web sites—anywhere— that contain hyperlinks that Web visitors followed to your Web. (No, this isn't magic. Whenever a visitor clicks a hyperlink, the browser transmits the URL of the page that contained the link.)

■ **Referring URLs.** Reports the locations of all Web pages that contain hyperlinks Web visitors followed to your Web.

■ **Search Strings.** Reports a history of keywords Web visitors entered on Web Search forms. This provides an indication of your visitors' interests, and might also provide topics that warrant more intuitive links.

For more information about the Web Search component, refer to "Using the Web Search Component" on page 785.

Viewing the Site Summary Report

This report displays a series of statistics for the current Web: the number and total size of all files, the number and size of all picture files, the number of files unreachable from any hyperlink in the current Web, and so forth. Figure 14-11 shows a typical Site Summary report.

You can see at a glance that this Web currently has 220 files occupying 4,030 KB of disk space, that 119 of those files are pictures, and that 7 Web pages exceed the configured maximum download time. The Description column explains the meaning of each line.

Note the entries for recent, older, and slow files. The dialog box shown in Figure 14-12 determines which files fall into these categories. To display this dialog box, choose Options from the Tools menu and then click the Reports View tab.

The Site Summary report doesn't list individual files; it lists statistics tabulated from other reports. If the category name is underlined, clicking it displays the most relevant FrontPage report.

Chapter 14: Keeping Your Web Up-to-Date

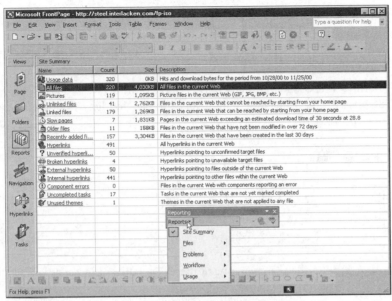

Figure 14-11. The Site Summary report displays statistics for the entire current Web.

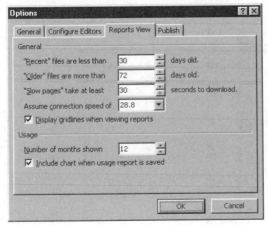

Figure 14-12. This dialog box determines what constitutes a recent, an older, and a slow Web page for Site Summary statistics and the corresponding detail reports.

Interacting with FrontPage Reports

FrontPage reports are, in fact, highly dynamic displays. You can move about, sort, filter, update, and launch other processes from FrontPage reports in a multitude of ways:

- To position any part of the report within the available window, use the scroll bars.

- To sort any report on any column, click the column heading. Clicking the same heading repeatedly alternates between ascending and descending sequence. To sort on multiple columns, click them in order from least significant to most.

- To filter a report so it displays only certain column values, click the drop-down arrow in its heading. This displays a selection list of values like the one shown here:

  - To filter the report on one of the listed values, select it as you would a value in any other drop-down list.

  - To remove a filter that's already in place, select (All).

  - To set up more complex filter criteria, select (Custom). This displays the Custom AutoFilter dialog box shown in Figure 14-13.

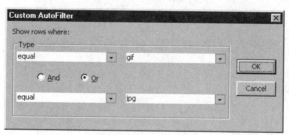

Figure 14-13. This dialog box applies either one or two filter conditions to any FrontPage report.

To enter one filter condition, choose a comparison operator under the Title heading and then select or type a value in the corresponding box to its right.

To enter a second filter condition, click either the And or Or option, select the second comparison operator, and then, as before, select or hand-type a value in the corresponding box to its right.

Click OK to apply the filter.

Chapter 14: Keeping Your Web Up-to-Date

In most reports, each line pertains to a file in your Web. Right-clicking any line in such a report displays the shortcut menu shown in Figure 14-14.

Figure 14-14. Right-clicking a line in any FrontPage report displays this shortcut menu. Depending on the context, some commands might be dimmed.

Here's an explanation of each choice on this menu:

- **Open.** Starts the default editor for the file on the clicked line. For Web pages, this is the Page view editing window. For everything else, it's whatever you see configured after choosing Options on the Tools menu and clicking the Configure Editors tab.

> For more information about configuring the editor associated with a given file type, refer to "Configuring External Editors" in the Bonus Content on the Companion CD.

> **note** Double-clicking any line is the same as right-clicking and choosing Open.

- **Open With.** Displays an Open With Editor dialog box so you can select the editor that will open the file.

- **Preview In Browser.** Launches your Web browser and tells it to request the given file.

- **Cut.** Loads the Clipboard with a pointer to one or more selected files in preparation for moving them.

- **Copy.** Loads the Clipboard with a pointer to one or more selected files in preparation for copying them.

Chapter 14

- **Copy Report.** Copies all the data in the current report into the Clipboard. From there, you can paste it into Microsoft Excel, Microsoft Access, or any other program for analysis.

- **Paste.** Completes a pending cut or copy operation at the current location.

- **Remove Filters.** Does away with any filters that were previously in effect. All possible lines will appear in the report.

- **Rename.** Opens the file name in the Name column to editing. Pressing the F2 key is equivalent.

- **Delete.** Deletes any selected files from the current Web.

- **Publish Selected Files.** Copies any currently selected files to the destination Web specified in the last full publishing operation.

> For more information about publishing a Web, refer to Chapter 13, "Publishing Your FrontPage-Based Web."

Don't Publish

- **Don't Publish.** Toggles the Publish or Don't Publish status of any currently selected files. (A white X in a red circle visually identifies files currently flagged for non-publication).

- **Properties.** Displays the Properties dialog box for the current file.

> For more information about the Properties dialog box, refer to "Working with Folders View" on page 174.

Report fields other than file names might also be editable. Here's how to update an editable field:

1 Select the line that contains the field you want to modify.

2 Click the field you want to modify.

3 If the field is editable, FrontPage displays it as an editable text box, a drop-down list, or another appropriate control. The following report segment shows how FrontPage displays a drop-down list for updating a file's Publish status.

This report segment shows a text field being updated. Note the dark border and the text insertion point.

footer.htm	Page Footer	Publish
adovbs.inc	ADO Constants for VBScript	Publish
autothumb.htm	About Jim Buyens	Publish

Viewing File Reports

This group of reports lists files in the current Web along with selected properties and attributes. The difference between these reports lies primarily in their selection criteria. In addition, the column headings change slightly depending on the report.

All Files

Figure 14-15 shows the All Files report, which is probably the most typical report in this group. It contains one line for every file in a Web, regardless of the folder.

Having a single list of all files in your Web can be convenient for locating files with a particular attribute. Clicking Modified Date, for example, makes it easy to identify all files—in any folder—changed within a certain time span. The All Files report provides all the capabilities of Folders view except for the ability to move files among folders.

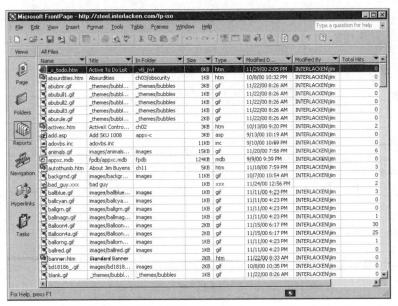

Figure 14-15. FrontPage's All Files report shows all files in the current Web.

Recently Added Files

This report lists files added to a Web within a certain number of days. This is very handy if you've forgotten where you put something or otherwise need to review recent changes. Figure 14-16 on the next page provides an example of this report.

To configure the default time period for this report:

1 Choose Options from the Tools menu.

2 Click the Reports View tab to display the dialog box shown in Figure 14-12.

3 Change the value of the "Recent" Files Are Less Than interval.

4 Click OK.

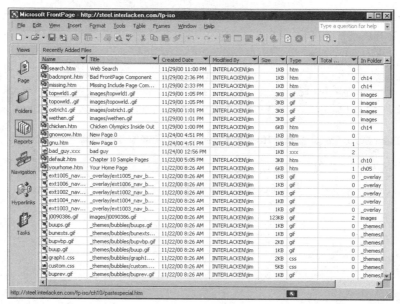

Figure 14-16. The Recently Added Files report shows the latest additions to your Web.

You can temporarily choose a different interval by using the Report Setting control on the Reporting toolbar.

 For more information about configuring default report settings, refer to "Customizing Reports View" in the Bonus Content on the Companion CD.

Recently Changed Files

Again using the format of the All Files report (Figure 14-15), this choice displays files changed within the specified Recent interval. This includes everything in the Recently Added Files report, plus any existing files that you or another designer updated during the Recent interval.

Use the Report Setting control on the Reporting toolbar to temporarily choose a different interval.

Older Files

This is yet another cousin of the All Files report. It includes any files in the current
Web whose most recent change was beyond the "Older" Files Are More Than interval
specified in the Options dialog box shown in Figure 14-12. It's a good idea to review
such files periodically, to see if they've become stale or outdated.

To temporarily choose a different interval, use the Report Setting control on the
Reporting toolbar.

Viewing Problem Reports

Each report in this group lists situations in your Web, which, at least on the surface,
appear to be errors. It's a very good idea to display these reports from time to time
and either account for or correct each error listed.

Unlinked Files

Any files that appear in this report have no apparent hyperlinks from other files within
the current Web. Again, this report closely resembles the format shown in Figure 14-15.

> **note** Some people call unlinked files *orphans*.

The fact that a file shows up as unlinked doesn't necessarily mean it's safe to delete it.
Nevertheless, it's usually worthwhile to review the Unlinked Files report from time
to time. Files can be unlinked for any of these reasons:

- The hyperlinks to the page are missing.

- All hyperlinks to the file are from outside the current Web.

- All hyperlinks to the file are built by script code too complicated for
  FrontPage to interpret.

- The file is obsolete and can safely be deleted.

 For more information about scripts, refer to Chapter 42, "Working with Script Code" in the
Bonus Content of the Companion CD.

Slow Pages

Files included in this report, shown in Figure 14-17 on the next page, simply take a long
time to download. The Download Time column displays the estimated time required.

FrontPage computes the download time by adding up the size of the base file and all its components (such as pictures), and then dividing by the Assume Connection Speed Of value that appears on the Reports View tab of the Options dialog box (Figure 14-12). If the download time is greater than or equal to the "Slow Pages" Take At Least limit, the base file appears in the Slow Pages report.

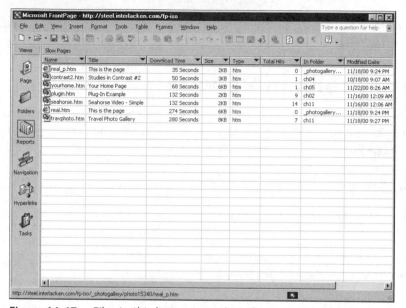

Figure 14-17. Files in this listing exceed configured guidelines for browser download time. Note the Download Time column.

To configure the default download speed and threshold:

1 Choose Options from the Tools menu.

2 Click the Reports View tab to display the dialog box shown in Figure 14-12.

3 To change the assumed download speed, choose a different value from the Assume Connection Speed Of drop-down box.

4 To choose the reporting threshold, change the value in the "Slow Pages" Take At Least box.

To temporarily override the default threshold, use the Report Setting control on the Reporting toolbar.

Report Setting

> **tip** To improve the download time for a Web page, decrease the number of pictures or the size of the picture files. Or split a single large page into multiple smaller ones.

You should generally consider changing any page that appears on this report, especially if you expect Web visitors to view it very often. No one enjoys slow-loading Web pages!

Broken Hyperlinks

Left to itself, the universe inevitably reverts to random bits. Broken hyperlinks are the living proof. Even if nothing within your Web changes during a certain period of time, hyperlinks outside your Web are sure to change and require correction. The Broken Hyperlinks report checks and corrects all the hyperlinks within your Web. Figure 14-18 shows a typical report.

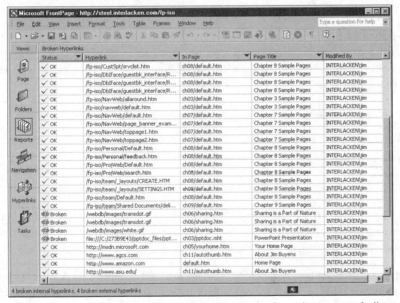

Figure 14-18. The Broken Hyperlinks report displays the status of all internal hyperlinks.

When you first display the Broken Hyperlinks report, FrontPage displays the Reports View dialog box shown in Figure 14-19 on the next page. To immediately check all the hyperlinks in your Web, click Yes. To defer this action until you issue a specific command later, click No.

Figure 14-19.   Answering Yes to this prompt verifies all the hyperlinks in your Web.

FrontPage uses internal indexes for verifying hyperlinks among pages in the same Web. As long as these indexes are correct, FrontPage will provide instant, always up-to-date information on these links. If you suspect that these indexes might be out of date, you can refresh them by choosing Recalculate Hyperlinks from the Tools menu. The number one cause of corrupt indexes is changing a Web through a means other than FrontPage.

To verify hyperlinks outside your Web, FrontPage tries connecting to them. This can be a time-consuming operation, especially when connections time out, and this might be a reason to answer No to the dialog box of Figure 14-19. Then to verify one or more external hyperlinks:

1 Make sure your connection to the Internet is working.

2 Select the external hyperlinks you want to verify.

3 Right-click any part of the selection.

4 Choose Verify Hyperlinks from the shortcut menu.

Verify
Hyperlinks

To verify all hyperlinks in a Web, either click the Verify Hyperlinks button on the Reporting toolbar, or right-click a blank line at the bottom of the report and then choose Verify Hyperlinks from the shortcut menu.

Verifying a long list of hyperlinks can take a long time, especially if your Internet connection is slow or you have many bad links. Bad links usually show up as timeouts, and a lot of timeouts can consume a lot of time. (You might want to make a sandwich here or visit your relatives in Madagascar.)

When Verify Hyperlinks ends:

● The good links will be flagged with green check marks and the word *OK*.

● Broken hyperlinks will have broken-link icons and the word *Broken*.

● Any links not yet checked will have question mark icons and the word *Unknown*.

436

Chapter 14: Keeping Your Web Up-to-Date

To display only broken hyperlinks, click the drop-down arrow on the Status heading and choose Broken. To display all hyperlinks, choose (All). To display only valid hyperlinks, choose OK.

The Edit Hyperlink dialog box shown in Figure 14-20 provides a handy way to modify the target location of any listed hyperlink. This is particularly appropriate for broken hyperlinks, of course, but it's also useful for correcting valid hyperlinks that point to the wrong place. To use this dialog box:

Edit Hyperlink

1 Use any of the following methods to display the Edit Hyperlink dialog box from the Broken Hyperlinks report:

- Double-click any page that contains the hyperlink you want to repair.

- Right-click any page that contains the hyperlink you want to repair, and then choose Edit Hyperlink from the shortcut menu.

- Select any page that contains the hyperlink you want to repair, and then click the Edit Hyperlink button on the Reporting toolbar.

2 To edit a page in Page view, click the Edit Page button. Because this button switches FrontPage out of Reports view, it renders the rest of this procedure inapplicable.

3 If you know the correct hyperlink address, type it directly into the Replace Hyperlink With box.

4 To locate the correct hyperlink by browsing, click the Browse button. This displays an Edit Hyperlink dialog box so you can locate the desired page. When you return to the Edit Hyperlink dialog box, FrontPage gets the current page location from the browser and inserts it for you.

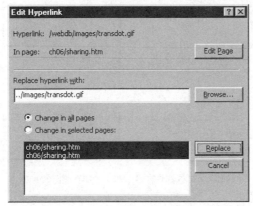

Figure 14-20. The Edit Hyperlink dialog box can correct a broken hyperlink.

437

5 To replace every instance of the original hyperlink location with a new location entered in the Replace Hyperlink With box:

    a Click the Change In All Pages option.

    b Click the Replace button.

6 To replace only some instances of the original hyperlink location:

    a Click the Change In Selected Pages option.

    b Selected the listed pages that should receive the corrected hyperlink.

    c Click the Replace button.

Component Errors

Figure 14-21 shows an example of the Component Errors report. This report lists
any errors or inconsistencies related to FrontPage components. Such errors tend
to be quite rare because FrontPage creates all the HTML code and won't let you
make a mistake. Nevertheless, anything that can go wrong sooner or later will, and
the Component Errors reports is here to tell you about it.

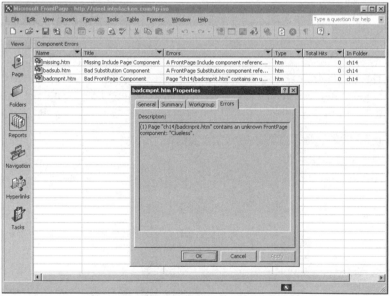

Figure 14-21. Web pages listed in this report have FrontPage components that are
improperly configured or that otherwise merit caution.

The report in Figure 14-21 lists the following three errors:

● The *missing.htm* page has an Include Page component that references
a page that doesn't exist.

Chapter 14: Keeping Your Web Up-to-Date

> For more information about the Include Page component, refer to "Using the Include Page Component" on page 750.

- The *badsub.htm* page contains a FrontPage Substitution component that references a site parameter that doesn't exist.

> For more information about the FrontPage Substitution component, refer to "Using Web Parameters and the Substitution Component" on page 762.

- The *badcmpnt.htm* page contains something that looks like a FrontPage component but that FrontPage can't recognize.

    If the Errors field is too long to fit on your screen, right-click the report line in question, choose Properties, and then click the Errors tab. As seen in Figure 14-21, this displays the full text of the error message.

The best way to repair a component error is to open the page in question and re-configure the component using the normal FrontPage dialog boxes. An alternative is to simply display the Web page and see if it looks OK. If it does, why worry? An unknown FrontPage component, for example, might be part of a third-party add-on package.

Viewing Workflow Status Reports

The Review Status, Assigned To, Categories, Publish Status, and Checkout Status reports are among FrontPage's workgroup features. Chapter 44, "Group Authoring with Workgroup Features," discusses these features in a unified way.

Review Status

FrontPage 2002 includes features for managing the work of several people creating a single Web. For example, FrontPage can remember who's assigned to work on a particular page, when each page was last reviewed, by whom, and the result. This information is then available for viewing in the Review Status report shown in Figure 14-22 on the next page.

The dialog box for entering Assigned To and Review Status information appears on the next page in Figure 14-23. To display this dialog box, right-click the corresponding file in any view or report, choose Properties from the shortcut menu, and then click the Workgroup tab.

You can enter both Assigned To and Review Status information either by typing it directly or by selecting from the drop-down lists. Initially the drop-down lists will be empty, but you can populate them by clicking the Names and Statuses buttons. To save your entries, click either the OK button or the Apply button.

Part 5: Publishing and Maintaining Web Sites

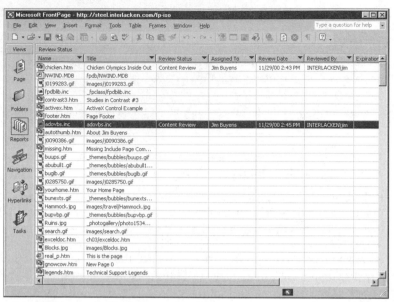

Figure 14-22. The Review Status report shows the person assigned to each page and the current status of all reviews.

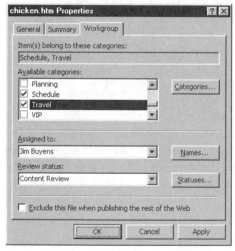

Figure 14-23. Use this dialog box to assign Web files to individuals and to indicate the status of reviews.

FrontPage automatically records the following information:

- **Review Date.** The date someone last changed the review status.

- **Reviewed By.** The logon ID of the last person who changed the review status.

Assigned To

This report, shown in Figure 14-24, primarily lists the Assigned To data entered in the
dialog box shown in Figure 14-23. FrontPage records the accompanying Assigned Date
and Assigned By fields whenever someone updates the Assigned To field.

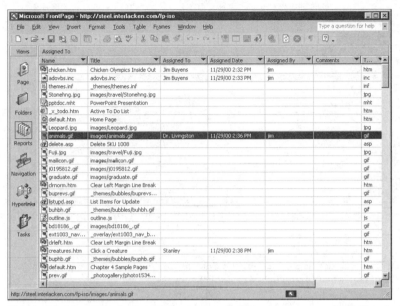

Figure 14-24. The Assigned To column in this report comes from the Assigned To field
in the dialog box in Figure 14-23. FrontPage records the Assigned Date and Assigned By
fields automatically.

Categories

Like the All Files report, the Categories report lists every file in the current Web. The
Categories report, however, also shows a list of category codes assigned to each file.
Figure 14-25 on the next page illustrates this report.

Near the top of Figure 14-23 you might have noticed a selection list called Available
Categories. (If you didn't, it's OK to look back.) In that dialog box, you can assign
any Web file to one or more categories by clicking the box in front of the category
name. To create new categories, click the Categories button in the same dialog box.

When you've assigned categories to one or more Web pages, you can use the Table Of
Contents Based On Page Category component to build a hyperlinked list of all files
in a category. Changing the categories for any file in your Web updates any applicable
Table Of Contents Based On Page Category components in the same Web. This is a very
nice feature, but as described so far, it doesn't provide a way to review all the category
codes in your Web. This is the purpose of the Categories report.

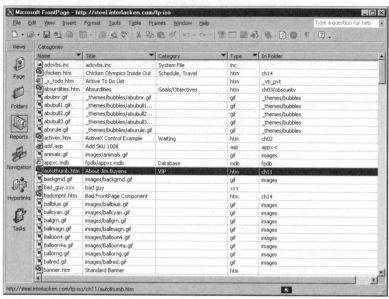

Figure 14-25. The Categories report shows the categories assigned to each page in a Web.

> For more information about the Table Of Contents Based On Page Category component, refer to "Using the Table of Contents Based on Page Category Component" on page 776.

The Report Setting control on the Reporting toolbar can filter this report by category name.

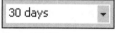

Report Setting

Publish Status

When publishing files from one Web to another (as when uploading files from your development environment to your public Web server), FrontPage normally assumes it should copy every file in your Web. (There are a few exceptions, such as files that haven't changed and files related to system configuration, but these aren't relevant to this discussion). For various reasons, however, you might occasionally want to hold back certain pages. Perhaps the file is a database you don't want overwritten every time you upload your Web, or perhaps the development copy of a page simply isn't ready for prime time.

FrontPage 2002 provides two ways to control whether or not a given file gets published with the rest of its Web. Both control the same internal setting:

Chapter 14: Keeping Your Web Up-to-Date

● Right-click the file in the Folder List, Folders view, or Reports view, and then choose Don't Publish from the shortcut menu. Each time you perform this action, it toggles the setting on or off.

● Display the Workgroup tab shown in Figure 14-23, and then either select or clear the check box titled Exclude This File When Publishing The Rest Of The Web.

The only nagging detail is figuring out, from time to time, which files are cleared for upload and which are not. This is the function of the Publish Status report shown in Figure 14-26.

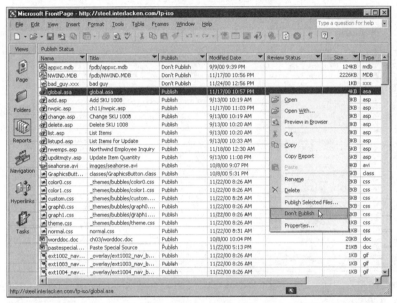

Figure 14-26. In the Publish Status report, files marked Don't Publish are blocked from transfer whenever you publish from the current Web to another.

If a file is marked for exclusion through either of the methods just described, its value in the Publish column will be Don't Publish. Otherwise, its Publish value will be Publish. As always, you can click the column heading to sort on this field.

Checkout Status

Using FrontPage's Document Check-In And Check-Out feature, Web designers can now take ownership of files in a Web. This guarantees that no other designers can edit or overwrite the file until the owner relinquishes it. Checking out a file also provides a measure of version control because the owner can undo the check-out and revert to the prior version of the file.

Document Check-In and Check-Out is a feature you or your Web's administrator must explicitly activate. The Checkout Status report won't be available until someone does this.

For more information about using document check-in and check-out, refer to "Using Page Level Check-In/Check-Out" on page 972.

The Checkout Status report shows which files are checked out to which designers, plus the current status of each file. A sample of this report appears in Figure 14-27.

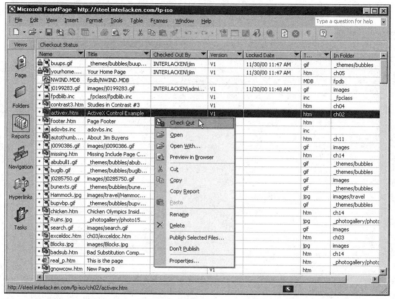

Figure 14-27. The Checkout Status report shows which designers have control of each file in a Web.

When Document Check-In And Check-Out is activated for a Web, most file-oriented shortcut menus display Check Out or Check In commands like the one pictured in Figure 14-27. This is how workgroup members gain and relinquish control of individual files.

newfeature!
Viewing Usage Reports

If your Web server runs SharePoint Team Services or the FrontPage Server Extensions 2002, you can view your Web's usage statistics without leaving FrontPage. Simply open the desired Web, choose Reports from the View menu, choose Usage, and then choose any of the reports listed.

Chapter 14: Keeping Your Web Up-to-Date

The same reports are available from the Reports list box on the Reporting toolbar.

Report Setting

Several factors might result in a usage report being blank or outdated. You should keep these in mind as you view the various reports:

- If your Web server isn't running SharePoint Team Services or the FrontPage Server Extensions 2002, no usage data will be available. If you can't upgrade the server to run this software, you'll need some other program to collect and display activity statistics.

For more information about SharePoint Team Services, refer to Chapter 35, "Using SharePoint Team Web Sites" and Chapter 38, "Understanding the FrontPage Server Extensions."

- The server extensions don't collect usage data continuously; they collect it from Web server activity logs on a daily, weekly, or monthly basis. This might account for the fact that a new Web has no statistics, or that daily statistics appear in bursts.

For more information about configuring the frequency of SharePoint Team Services usage analysis, refer to "Administering Installation Defaults" on page 1094.

- Some Usage reports rely on data that the Web server doesn't normally collect. If you need the data on these reports, the Web server administrator will need to activate the necessary logging. The following sections, which describe each report, indicate any special requirements of this type.

- Usage reports don't include usage by FrontPage itself, even if FrontPage desktop software communicates with the server extensions by HTTP.

For more information about configuring Web server log options, refer to "Configuring Site and Folder Level Options" on page 1059.

In all cases, remember that FrontPage displays statistics for the current Web only. This means that to display statistics for your production Web server, you need to open your production Web. Opening an off-line development Web displays statistics only for the development Web.

The Top 10 List component can create Web pages that display usage statistics for a given Web. However, other than using the same database of statistical information, that component has nothing in common with the Usage reports in Reports view.

For more information about the Top 10 List component, refer to "Creating Top 10 Lists" on page 843.

Usage Summary

Just as the Site Summary report provides overall statistics for your Web's content, the Usage Summary report provides overall statistics regarding its use. To display this report:

1 Choose Reports from the View menu, or open the Reports list box on the Reporting toolbar.

2 Choose Usage.

3 Choose Usage Summary.

A sample of the Usage Summary report appears in Figure 14-28. The first two lines report the time span of data that's available and the remaining lines present a variety of high-level statistics. If an entry in the Name column is underlined, this means that clicking it displays a relevant report with more detail.

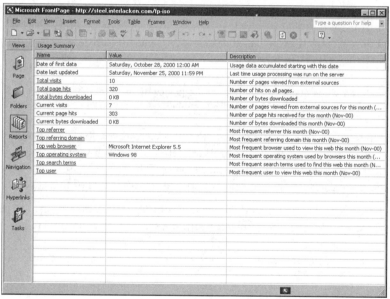

Figure 14-28. The Usage Summary report consolidates usage statistics for an entire Web.

Monthly, Weekly, and Daily Summary Usage

These three reports display the total number of visits, page hits, and total hits for the entire current Web. Each report contains one line of data for each month, week, or day within the time span available in the database. The interval, of course, depends on which report you select. Figure 14-29 shows a typical Daily Summary report.

Chapter 14: Keeping Your Web Up-to-Date

The following definitions apply to this report:

● **Visits.** Counts the number of requests from visitors at external locations (excluding any requests from FrontPage).

● **Hits.** Counts the number of requests from visitors at any location (excluding any requests from FrontPage).

● **Total Hits.** Counts the total number of requests from visitors at any location and using any program (including FrontPage).

● **Percentage Of Hits.** Reports the number shown in the Hits column on the current line divided by the sum of all numbers in the Hits column.

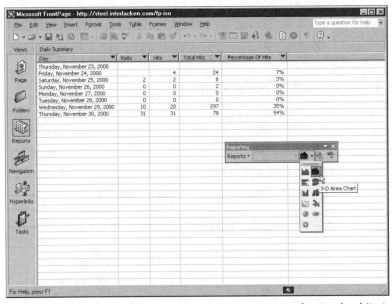

Figure 14-29. The Daily Summary report enumerates day-to-day hits to a Web.

If you find looking at numbers mundane and boring, FrontPage's ability to display graphs might be of interest. The procedure is quite simple:

1 Display the FrontPage report that contains the data you want to graph.

Chart Type

2 Open the Chart Type control on the Reporting toolbar and choose any available icon. Figure 14-29 shows this operation in progress.

Figure 14-30, on the next page, shows a graph of the data in Figure 14-29, using the 3-D Area Chart format.

447

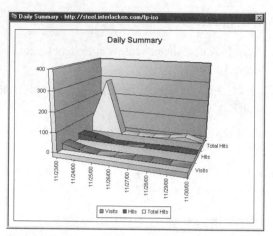

Figure 14-30. FrontPage can display usage data in graphs as well as reports. Just pick an icon from the Chart Type control on the Reporting toolbar.

Monthly, Weekly, and Daily Page Hits

For each file in your Web, this report lists the file's name, title, folder, total hits, and hits summarized by month, week, or day. The level of summarization depends on which of the three reports you choose. Figure 14-31 shows some typical results.

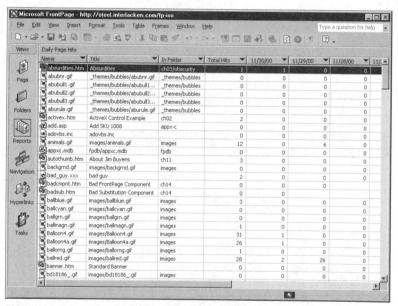

Figure 14-31. The Daily Page Hits report displays day-by-day hit counts for each file in a Web.

The statistics by month, week, or day appear in columns extending to the right. These columns can extend far outside the current window, so get your scrolling finger ready.

Chapter 14: Keeping Your Web Up-to-Date

Chart Type

Clicking the Chart Type control on the Reporting toolbar graphs only the lines you've selected. To select multiple report lines:

1 Select the first report line you want to chart.

2 Hold down the Ctrl or Shift key while selecting additional lines.

3 Choose the icon you want from the Chart Type control.

Visiting Users

This report displays the identities of people who visited your Web during a given month. Use the Report Setting control on the Reporting toolbar to choose the month. Figure 14-32 shows a typical example (if somewhat limited in volume). Charting this report depicts visiting users by percentage of hits.

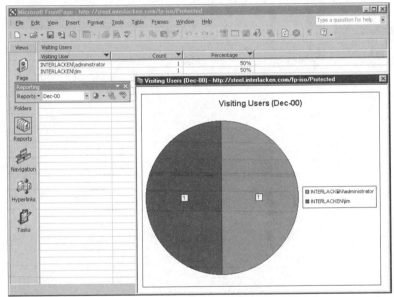

Figure 14-32. The Visiting Users report displays activity counts for each authenticated Web visitor.

This report will be blank unless both of the following conditions are satisfied:

● Anonymous Access must be unavailable. This requires Web visitors to identify themselves by user name and password.

For more information about configuring anonymous access to a Web, refer to "Configuring Directory Security" on page 1068 and "Administering Installation Defaults" on page 1094.

449

● The Web server must record Web visitor user names in its log files. For IIS, this means that the User Name (cs-username) property that appears in the Extended Logging Properties dialog box must be selected.

> For more information about configuring Web server log options, refer to "Configuring Site and Folder Level Options" on page 1059.

Operating Systems

If you want to know what operating systems visitors to your Web are using, this is the report for you. It summarizes hits by Web visitor operating system for a given month. Choose the month from the Report Setting control on the Reporting toolbar.

Figure 14-33 shows an example of this report. Charting it visually displays the data in the Operating System and Count columns.

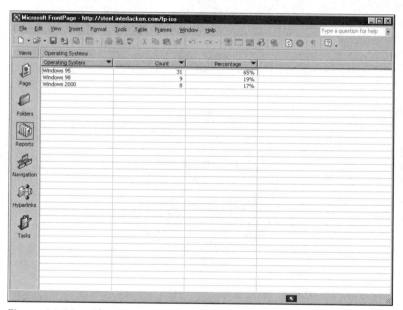

Figure 14-33. The Operating Systems report summarizes the computing environments that your Web visitors use.

The information in this report comes from the User-Agent field that browsers supply as header information with each HTTP request. If your Web server is IIS, this means the User Agent (cs-User-Agent) property in the Extended Logging Properties dialog box must be selected.

> For more information about configuring Web server log options, refer to "Configuring Site and Folder Level Options" on page 1059.

Browsers

This report arranges hits by type of Web browser for a given month. As usual, the
Report Setting control on the Reporting toolbar controls which month. Figure 14-34
provides a typical example.

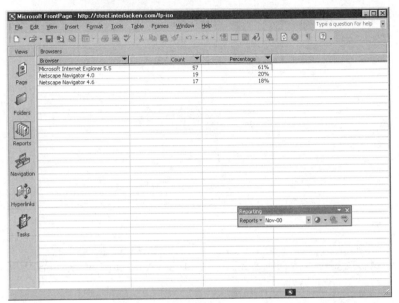

Figure 14-34. The Browsers report itemizes the browsers that your Web visitors use.

Like the Operating Systems report, the Browsers report uses information from the
User-Agent headers received with HTTP requests. Therefore, on your Web server,
the User Agent (cs-User-Agent) property in the Extended Logging Properties dialog
box must be selected.

For more information about configuring Web server log options, refer to "Configuring Site
and Folder Level Options" on page 1059.

Referring Domains

Although somewhat (all right, totally!) misnamed, this report tells you which other
Web servers are sending visitors into your Web. This information comes from a so-
called Referrer field that browsers supply as header information with each HTTP request. As seen in Figure 14-35 on the next page, this report actually lists host names
(that is, computer names) rather than domain names.

This is yet another month-at-a-time report. The Report Setting control on the Reporting toolbar controls which month.

If your Web server is IIS, the Referrer (cs(Referrer)) property in the Extended Logging Properties dialog box must be selected. Otherwise, the report will be blank.

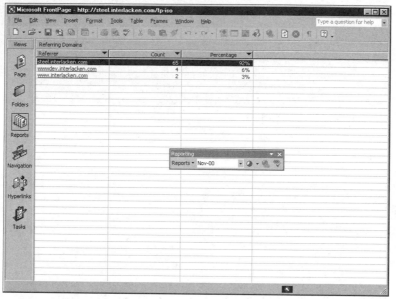

Figure 14-35. The Referring Domains report tabulates how often other Web servers send visitors to your Web.

> For more information about configuring Web server log options, refer to "Configuring Site and Folder Level Options" on page 1059.

Referring URLs

If the Referring Domains report contains too little detail for your tastes, the Referring URLs report might provide the cure. This report summarizes hits against your Web based on the URL of the page that contained the link. If you don't believe this, Figure 14-36 provides the proof.

The Report Setting control on the Reporting toolbar displays and optionally modifies the month reported.

Like the Referring Domains report, the Referring URLs report will be blank unless the Web server includes each request's Referrer field in its log. Therefore, the Referrer (cs(Referrer)) property in your Web server's Extended Logging Properties dialog box must be selected.

> For more information about configuring Web server log options, refer to "Configuring Site and Folder Level Options" on page 1059.

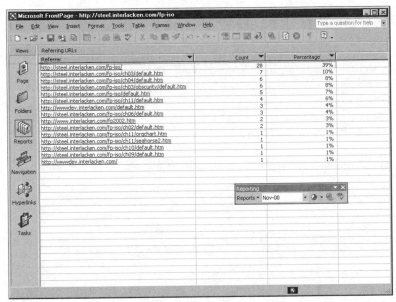

Figure 14-36. The Referring URLs reports show which pages are sending visitors to your Web, even if they're located on other servers.

Search Strings

This report summarizes the keywords that Web visitors used to find your site on one of the large search engines such as Yahoo! or AltaVista. This tells you how people are finding your site and what topics interest them. The more often Web visitors specify a given term, the more interested they likely are in that topic. You can use this information when deciding how to improve and expand your Web. Frequent searching for the same word might also indicate the need for a more prominent hyperlink on your home page. This report contains the following fields:

- **Keyword.** A word that one or more Web visitors entered on a Web Search form.

- **Count.** The number of times Web visitors submitted a Web Search form using the given word.

- **Percentage.** The value in the Count field divided by the sum of all counts.

The data for this report comes from strings that search engines append to the URL that transfers a visitor to your site. If a given search engine doesn't provide this information, it won't contribute to this report.

Using Hyperlinks View

This view provides the hyperlink-based structure analysis you might have expected when you first encountered Navigation view. It provides a display, centered on any page in the current Web, that illustrates graphically which other pages are related by hyperlink. This provides an excellent picture of the hyperlink relationships among pages that can be extremely useful when working with complex or unfamiliar Webs. Figure 14-37 illustrates this view.

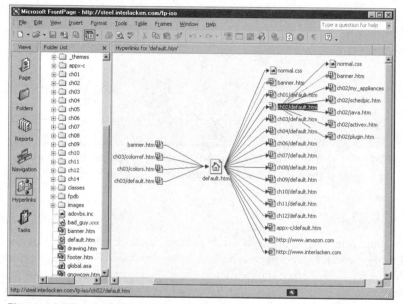

Figure 14-37. FrontPage's Hyperlinks view provides a graphical view of the hyperlink relationships within a Web.

In Hyperlinks view, the document pane displays a chart of hyperlinks to and from a so-called *center page*. Lines connecting one page to another indicate hyperlinked pages; the arrowhead points *from* the page containing the hyperlink *to* the page being linked.

You can specify the center page either of two ways: first, by selecting it in the Folder List, or second, by right-clicking a page in the document pane and choosing Move To Center from the shortcut menu.

Whenever FrontPage displays a new center page, it also displays:

- All pages in the current Web with hyperlinks to the center page. These appear to the left of the center page, connected with arrows showing the direction of the link.

Chapter 14: Keeping Your Web Up-to-Date

- All hyperlinks from the center page to any other page. These appear
to the right of the center page, again connected by arrows.

Any page flagged with a plus icon has additional hyperlinks not displayed. Clicking
the plus icon displays the additional links and changes the icon to a minus. Clicking a
minus icon collapses the link display and changes the icon to a plus.

Double-clicking the body of a Web page icon opens it in Page view for viewing or
editing.

Hyperlinks view identifies items by either title or file name. This is under control of
the following shortcut menu, which appears whenever you right-click the document
window's background:

Choosing Show Page Titles toggles display of page titles rather than the file names
shown in Figure 14-37.

> **tip** When Hyperlinks view is showing page titles, resting the mouse pointer over any
> page displays its file name and the type of link.

You can view the complete path and file name of an item in either pane by right-
clicking the item and choosing Properties from the shortcut menu. To see the file name
of any item in the right pane, rest the mouse pointer over it; FrontPage briefly describes
the type of item and displays its name:

Internal Hyperlink: indelinc.htm

By default, Hyperlinks view displays only hyperlinks from one Web page to another,
disregarding duplicates. To toggle display of additional items, use these commands
on the shortcut menu just shown:

- **Hyperlinks To Pictures.** Activating this option adds picture files to the
Hyperlinks view display. Designating a picture as the center of Hyperlinks
view displays all pages using that picture.

- **Repeated Hyperlinks.** Normally, if a page contains several links to the same
target, Hyperlinks view displays only one of them. Activating this option
shows all links, even duplicate ones.

Right-clicking a page in either pane produces a shortcut menu similar to the one shown
at the top of the next page.

Some of these options might be dimmed or omitted, depending on the context:

- **Move To Center.** Designates the selected file as the center page in the right pane. This option doesn't appear for pages in the left pane, or when the selected page already occupies the center position.

- **Verify Hyperlink.** Validates a file or hyperlink outside the current Web by attempting to retrieve it. This option is dimmed for locations inside the current Web because, in that case, FrontPage has other means of verification.

- **Open.** Starts the appropriate program to edit the selected page or file. Double-clicking the item accomplishes the same thing, as does choosing Open from the Edit menu. This option and the next are dimmed for links to pages located outside the current Web.

- **Open With.** Presents a choice of command editors you can use to edit the selected file. The Open With command on the Edit menu is equivalent.

- **Preview In Browser.** Launches your Web browser and tells it to request the given file.

- **Delete.** Removes a page or file from the current Web. The Delete command on the Edit menu is equivalent.

- **Properties.** Displays information about the selected file, such as its title and file name. You can also enter summary information about the page that might help you plan or maintain your Web.

New designers are frequently enamored of Hyperlinks view, especially if they have existing Webs. They can use this view to analyze the Web pages they've been tediously building and maintaining by hand, producing attractive diagrams as a result. This can be heady stuff, but most designers find Folders view and Navigation view more valuable for day-to-day work.

In Summary...

This chapter explained a number of ways that you can process groups of files in your Web with one operation. This included searching, replacing, checking spelling, content analysis, usage analysis, and hyperlink analysis.

The next chapter explains how to create Web pages from stored templates.

Structuring Individual Web Pages

Chapter 15

Using Page Templates

The easiest way to finish any job is to use work someone else has already done. This is the simple concept behind templates. Just as Chapter 8 explained how to create an entire Web from a template, this chapter outlines a similar process for creating a new Web page.

There are two times to think about page templates: once when you're just starting a page and again when you finish one. If a template can give you a head start on a page you're creating, you might as well take advantage of it. When you finish a page, that's an excellent time to consider making a template of it. If removing all the content that's unique to a page leaves a useful shell for creating new and similar pages, then the page you've created is an excellent candidate to become a template. As this chapter explains, creating templates is almost as easy as using them.

Creating Pages with Templates

Chapter 9 described several ways to create a new Web page ready for editing. Two of those procedures can create not just a blank page, but a page initialized with content, formatting, or both from a previously stored template. The first procedure uses the New Page or Web task pane. It begins like this:

1 Choose New from the File menu.

2 Choose Page Or Web.

3 When the New Page Or Web task pane shown in Figure 15-1 on the next page appears, click Page Templates.

459

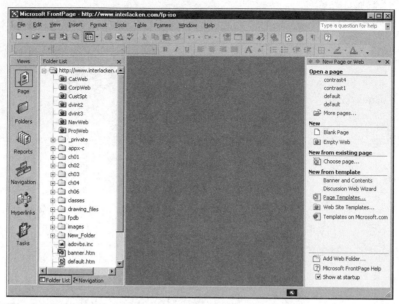

Figure 15-1. Click Page Templates to display the Page Templates dialog box shown in Figure 15-2.

The second procedure that creates a new Web page from a template uses the New Page menu on the Standard toolbar. It begins like this:

New Page

● Click the New Page button drop-down arrow, and choose Page.

Both of these procedures display the Page Templates dialog box shown in Figure 15-2. To continue creating a Web page that uses any of these templates, proceed as follows:

1 Click the General, Frames Pages, or Style Sheets tab to select the general category of page you want to create. Later sections in this chapter describe each of these categories.

2 Review the list of templates and click the one you want.

3 Check the Preview area. If a preview of the selected template is available, it will appear here.

4 Click OK. Microsoft FrontPage loads the template into the Page view editing window as a new Web page. Make any changes you want, and then choose either the Save or Save As command from the File menu to save it for the first time.

Chapter 15

Chapter 15: Using Page Templates

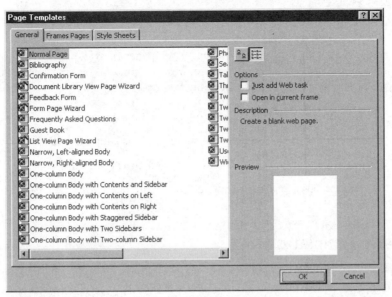

Figure 15-2. This dialog box offers a choice of types and formats for initializing new Web pages.

The following controls add additional flexibility to the Page Templates dialog box:

Large Icons

List

- **Large Icons.** This button, located above the Options frame, displays a full-sized icon for each available template. The name of each template appears beneath its icon.

- **List.** This button displays columns of available template names. A small icon precedes each name. This is the view shown in Figure 15-2.

- **Just Add Web Task.** This option adds a task to the Task list rather than creating a new page in Page view.

For more information about the Task list, refer to "Working with Task View" on page 964.

- **Open In Current Frame.** This option is available only if the active Page view document is a frames page. If this option is both available and selected, the new page will appear in the last frame you clicked before displaying the Page Templates dialog box. In any other case, the new page will be a freestanding Web page.

For more information about the using frames pages, refer to Chapter 17, "Using Frames for Page Layout."

Selecting General Templates

This category of templates creates ordinary Web pages (that is, pages that consist of a single HTML file containing text, pictures, components, scripts, and anything else you care to add). Within this grouping are four subtypes:

- Static templates that contain nothing but ordinary content
- Component templates that use Web components supplied with FrontPage
- Form templates that create pages containing an HTML form
- SharePoint Team Services templates that create pages for SharePoint team Web sites

Using Static Templates

Each template in this group creates a perfectly ordinary, self-contained Web page. One template, Normal Page, creates a blank page ready to receive whatever content you desire. The others contain sample content laid out in various formats.

Table 15-1 lists the Normal Page template plus two others that provide typical formatting for two common scenarios. The Bibliography template provides a suggested format for citing references to the works of others. The Frequently Asked Questions template provides a layout suitable for listing questions and answers.

Table 15-1. Page Templates with Simple Formatting

Template	Result
Normal Page	Blank Web page.
Bibliography	Bibliography page that makes references to printed or electronic works.
Frequently Asked Questions	Page that answers common questions about some topic.

Figure 15-3 shows a page created with the Bibliography template, which incorporates no high-tech wizardry but does remember the standard format of a bibliography entry.

The templates listed in Table 15-2 on page 470 lay out columnar text in various formats, many of which occur frequently in magazines or brochures. If one of these templates produces something close to the appearance you want, by all means use it. You should be aware, however, that there's nothing magic or automatic about the results. Text doesn't automatically flow from one body column to the next, for example, and the tables of contents are simply placeholders containing ordinary text. After replacing the mock-up text and pictures with your own, you'll need to do some manual layout work and set up your own hyperlinks.

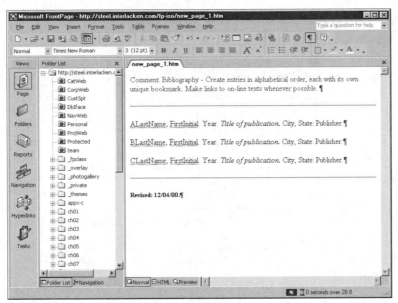

Figure 15-3. If you have trouble remembering the format of a bibliography entry, the bibliography page template is for you.

The best way to choose a template is to click each one in the Page Templates dialog box and find a Preview picture that fits your content. Figure 15-4 shows an unmodified page created with the One-Column Body With Contents And Sidebar template.

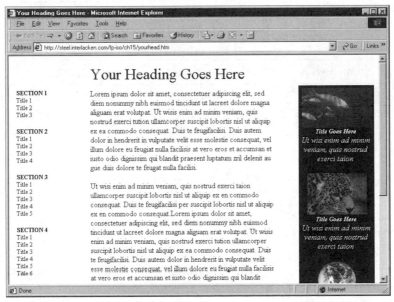

Figure 15-4. Static page templates have no unique content or interactive features, but they provide a head start in producing attractive page layouts.

Chapter 15

Table 15-2. **Templates for Columnar Text Layout**

Template	Body	Table of contents	Sidebar
Narrow, Left-Aligned Body	Narrow, left-aligned		
Narrow, Right-Aligned Body	Narrow, right-aligned		
One-Column Body	Centered		
One-Column Body With Contents And Sidebar	One-column	On left	On right
One-Column Body With Contents On Left	One-column	On left	
One-Column Body With Contents On Right	One-column	On right	
One-Column Body With Staggered Sidebar	One-column		Two-column, staggered, on left
One-Column Body With Two Sidebars	One-column		Staggered on left, normal on right
One-Column Body With Two-Column Sidebar	One-column		Two-column, on right
Three-Column Body	Three-column		
Two-Column Body	Two-column		
Two-Column Body With Contents And Sidebar	Two-column	On left	On right
Two-Column Body With Contents On Left	Two-column	On left	
Two-Column Staggered Body	Two staggered columns		
Two-Column Staggered Body With Contents And Sidebar	Two staggered columns	On left	On right
Wide Body With Headings	Wide with subheadings		

Using Component Templates

All three of the following page templates create Web pages that contain a specific FrontPage component. You can achieve essentially the same result by adding the component to any page. The three page templates are:

- **Photo Gallery.** Creates a page containing a Photo Gallery component. This component displays collections of photographs in any of four layout styles.

> For more information about the Photo Gallery component, refer to Chapter 22, "Using FrontPage Photo Galleries."

- **Search Page.** Creates a page that contains a Web Search component. This provides a way for visitors to search your Web for given words or phrases. To view or change the Web Search component's configuration, double-click anywhere within the dotted lines. Figure 15-5 shows a page created using this template.

> For more information about the Web Search component, refer to Chapter 28, "Providing a Text Search Capability."

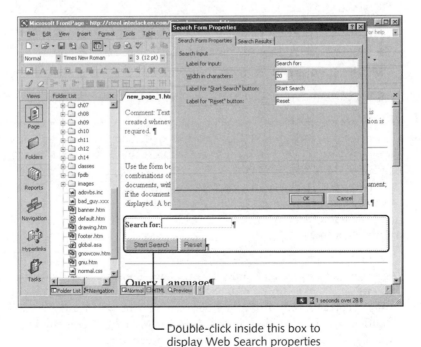

Double-click inside this box to display Web Search properties

Figure 15-5. To configure the properties of a Web Search component, double-click its area on the Web page.

● **Table Of Contents.** Creates a page that contains a Table Of Contents Relative To A Web Page component. This component displays an outline with links to every page in your Web.

> For more information about the Table of Contents For This Web Site component, refer to "Using the Table of Contents For This Web Site Component" on page 771.

Using Form Templates

The templates in the next group create HTML forms (that is, groups of text boxes, list boxes, check boxes, options, and buttons that submit data to a Web server). If these forms suit (or even approximate) your needs, then choosing a template might be easier than designing your own form from scratch.

> For more information about creating and modifying HTML forms, refer to Chapter 31, "Creating and Using Forms."

Of course, creating an HTML form is only half the battle. You must also arrange for a program on the Web server to receive and process any form data that the form submits. You have four options, with the first three available only if your Web server runs SharePoint Team Services or the FrontPage Server Extensions:

● The FrontPage Save Results form handler

● The FrontPage Discussion form handler

● The FrontPage Registration form handler

● A custom ISAPI, NSAPI, CGI, or ASP script

> **note** The acronyms ISAPI, NSAPI, CGI, and ASP all describe various ways of writing programs that run on Web servers when visitors submit suitably formatted requests. Here's what the acronyms mean:
> ISAPI: Internet Server Application Program Interface
> NSAPI: Netscape Server Application Program Interface
> CGI: Common Gateway Interface
> ASP: Active Server Pages

As you might suspect, all FrontPage form templates use FrontPage form handlers. This means that any form produced by a template—and not subsequently modified— will run correctly only if your Web server has SharePoint Team Services or the FrontPage Server Extensions installed. To see which handler is configured and how it's configured, or to make changes, follow this procedure:

1 Locate the form area in Page view. Dotted lines like those shown in Figure 15-5 surround this area.

2 Right-click it, and choose Form Properties from the shortcut menu.

This will display the Form Properties dialog box shown in Figure 15-6. Consult Chapter 32 regarding the use of this dialog box.

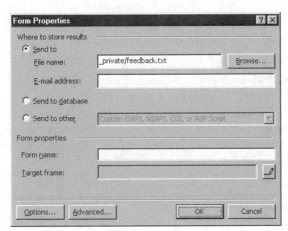

Figure 15-6. An HTML form with these properties would add data to a file named _private/feedback.txt_ every time a Web visitor clicks the form's Submit button.

For more information about processing submitted HTML forms, refer to Chapter 32, "Processing Data Submitted from Forms."

Here are the specific FrontPage templates that create HTML forms:

● **Form Page Wizard.** Prompts you for the type of information you want a form to collect, creates a form with typical form elements for that information, and incorporates that form into a new Web page.

For more information about the Form Page Wizard, refer to "Using the Form Page Wizard" on page 882.

● **Feedback Form.** Creates a form that collects comments about your Web, products, or organization. By default, it records this information in a file in your Web named _private/feedback.txt_.

● **Guest Book.** Creates a form Web visitors can use for appending comments to a public list. By default, this list appears in a Web page named _guestlog.htm_ and located in the same folder as the guest book page.

- **User Registration.** Creates a form where visitors can create their own security accounts for accessing protected Webs (that is, Webs that require entry of a user name and password for access). Use of such forms is subject to these restrictions:

  - They must be located in the root Web of the server that contains the protected Web. Locating them within the protected Web is useless because—by definition—unregistered visitors have no access there. Protecting Webs and setting up self-registration forms are usually jobs for an administrator of the server's root Web.

  - Some Web servers don't permit self-registration, and among these are the Microsoft Web servers for Microsoft Windows 2000 and Microsoft Windows NT. These Web servers control Web access by means of the same user account database that controls system logons. It would be a major security loophole if unknown Web visitors could use self-registration to create accounts that provided other kinds of logon access to the server.

 For more information about self-registration, refer to "Enabling User Self-Registration" in the Bonus Content on the Companion CD.

- **Confirmation Form.** This template, despite its name, doesn't create a form. Instead, it creates a Web page that's formatted as a thank-you letter and contains six confirmation components: Username, MessageType, Subject, UserEmail, UserTel, and UserFAX. This might be useful if all of the following are true:

  - You've developed another page that contains an HTML form.

  - The form uses the FrontPage Save Results component to save data on the Web server.

  - The form contains six form fields named Username, MessageType, Subject, UserEmail, UserTel, and UserFAX. The more your form fields differ from these, the more editing you'll have to do.

  - You want to acknowledge receipt of the data with a Web page that looks like a thank-you letter. Again, the more the desired format differs, the more editing you'll have to do.

If there's a lot of editing to do, you'll probably have more success creating a blank page, formatting it as you want, and inserting a confirmation component for each field on the HTML form.

Refer to the sidebar titled "Using Confirmation Components" on the next page for more information about confirmation components.

Chapter 15

Using SharePoint Team Services Templates

Two templates have no use unless your Web server has SharePoint Team Services installed. If your development and production Web servers are two different computers, both will need SharePoint Team Services. The two templates are:

● **Document Library View Page Wizard.** Creates a page for viewing a SharePoint Team Services document library. The key element on this page is a Document Library View component.

Unlike the other component templates mentioned earlier, this wizard produces results that are different than adding a Document Library View component to a new blank page. The Wizard creates a page that resembles the standard SharePoint-based team Web site pages in appearance and includes matching Link bars and other embellishments. Adding a Document Library View component to an ordinary page adds only the component with no special formatting.

> For more information about SharePoint Team Services and SharePoint team Web sites, refer to Chapter 35, "Using SharePoint Team Web Sites."

Using Confirmation Components

Whenever the FrontPage Save Results, Discussion, or Registration components process data from an HTML form, they send a so-called *confirmation page* to the Web visitor. If any errors occurred, the confirmation page reports them. If no errors occurred, the confirmation page shows the Web visitor what data was saved.

 For more information about the Discussion component, refer to "Creating and Managing Discussion Webs" in the Bonus Content on the Companion CD.

Normally, the form handlers of the Save Results, Discussion, and Registration components create their own confirmation pages on the fly. This approach is easy on the Web designer but not on the eyes; the pages are rather plain in appearance and usually bear no resemblance to other pages in the same Web.

To avoid these problems, Web designers can create confirmation pages. These are ordinary Web pages—formatted as the designer wants—that contain one or more *confirmation components*. Each confirmation component is coded with the name of one field on an HTML form. When a Save Results, Discussion, or Registration form handler processes the form, it also processes the confirmation page, replacing each confirmation component with the form field value having the same name.

> For more information about confirmation pages, refer to "Configuring Confirmation Page Options" on page 902.

● **List View Page Wizard.** Creates a page for viewing a SharePoint Team Services list. The key element on this page is a List View component. Again, the wizard produces a more complete page than merely adding a List View component to a new blank page.

If you want to use either template, the Web server you use for development and the Web server you use for production both need to contain the document library or list you want to configure.

Selecting Frames Page Templates

These templates create frames pages. A frames page—or, by its official name, a *frameset*—is a special kind of Web page that divides the browser window into two or more rectangular areas called, naturally enough, *frames*. Each frame typically displays a different Web page.

Because they consist of multiple files, frames pages are somewhat more difficult to create and manage than ordinary Web pages. They do, however, make it easy to update one part of the browser window (one frame) in response to clicks in another part of the window (another frame).

FrontPage contains a wealth of features that make working with frames pages easy, beginning with a useful assortment of starting points. That's the purpose of the templates on this tab.

To select the best template for your needs, select each offering by clicking it or by using the arrow keys, and watch the Preview area. When the correct layout appears, click OK.

> For information about frames pages, refer to Chapter 17, "Using Frames for Page Layout."

Selecting Style Sheet Templates

Templates in this category create cascading style sheet (CSS) files. These files have no visual appearance of their own; instead, they contain lines of code that change the typographical properties (that is, the style) of standard HTML objects or of objects that depend on a custom style.

If you're fairly new to creating Web pages, you might want to ignore cascading style sheets for a little while. As you gain experience, however, you'll probably recognize the futility of trying to maintain uniform appearance throughout your Web when you apply typographical formatting a word, a sentence, or a paragraph at a time. You'll wish there were some way to specify formats centrally and have any number of pages refer to them. When this happens, it'll be time to take another look at cascading style sheets.

For now, take it on faith that FrontPage provides an assortment of sample CSS files—templates—already coded and ready for use.

> For more information about style sheet files, refer to Chapter 20, "Managing Appearance with Cascading Style Sheets."

Creating Custom Templates

Creating and using FrontPage templates is both easy and productive. Templates relieve designers of repetitive tasks when creating new pages. To create a template:

1 Use any convenient method to create a Web page with the desired components and features. When in doubt, it's usually better to include optional page features than to omit them. Deleting features you don't need is easier than adding those you do.

2 With the page open in Page view, choose Properties from the File menu, make sure the General tab is visible, and enter the template title in the Title box. This is the name you (or other Web authors) will later use to select the template. Click OK after you've entered the title.

3 Choose Save As from the File menu to display the dialog box shown in Figure 15-7.

Figure 15-7. To save any Web page as a template, set Save As Type to FrontPage Template.

4 In the Save As dialog box:

    a Set Save As Type to FrontPage Template.

    b Verify that the file name is acceptable.

    c Click the Save button.

5 When the Save As Template dialog box shown in Figure 15-8 appears, enter or verify the following information:

    ▪ **Title.** The name by which you or other FrontPage designers will select the template.

    ▪ **Name.** The filename base used for saving the template's files and folders.

    ▪ **Description.** Any verbal explanation or notes.

    ▪ **Save Template In Current Web.** If selected, saves the template in the current Web. This instantly makes it available to all users of that Web, but *only* when creating pages *in that Web.*

    If the box isn't selected, FrontPage stores the template on your hard disk. This makes it available only to you, but it's available no matter what Web you open.

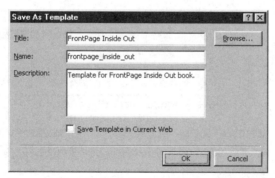

Figure 15-8. Specify the template's name, description, and location when this dialog box appears.

6 Click OK to save the template.

7 If the Save Embedded Files dialog box shown in the background of Figure 15-9 appears, the new template makes reference to other files in the current Web. For each such file, click the Set Action button and then, in the Set Action dialog box shown in the foreground of Figure 15-9, choose one of the following:

    ▪ **Save.** Retains a copy of the file along with the template. When you or someone else uses the template and saves the resulting page for the first time, FrontPage optionally adds a copy of the embedded file to the new page's Web.

- **Don't Save.** Doesn't retain a copy of the file. Anyone who uses this template will be responsible for providing the given file.

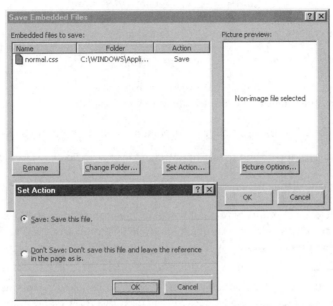

Figure 15-9. This dialog box controls which component files FrontPage saves as part of a template. Click the Set Action button to display the Set Action dialog box in the foreground.

The procedure for modifying a template is somewhat less intuitive. Here it is:

1 Use the template to create a new page.

2 Make whatever changes you believe are necessary.

3 Repeat the procedure described for creating a new template. When FrontPage prompts for permission to replace the existing template, click Yes.

When you save a template to your hard disk, FrontPage saves it in a folder that's usually located at

> C:\Windows\Application Data\Microsoft\FrontPage\<type>\<template>.tem

or, on Windows 2000 at

> C:\Documents and Settings\<username>\Application Data\Microsoft\FrontPage\<type>\<template>.tem

where:

- *<type>* is *CSS, Frames,* or *Pages* depending on the type of template.

- *<username>* is your Windows logon account.

Chapter 15

- *<template>* is the name you specified when saving the template.
  The *<template>.tem* folder normally contains a file named *<template>.inf*,
  and possibly a second named *<template>.dib*.

When you save a template to your Web, FrontPage saves it in a folder located at

/_sharedtemplates/<type>/<template>.tem

where *<type>* and *<template>* have the same meanings as on disk. This folder
is normally hidden, but you can use the following procedure to make it visible:

1 Choose Web Settings from the Tools menu, and click the Advanced tab.

2 Make sure the option titled Show Hidden Files And Folders is selected.

There are two reasons for knowing where FrontPage keeps templates:

- To delete a template, you must delete its *.tem* folder from the location just
  described. If you're working in Windows 2000, make sure you've displayed
  hidden files and folders in Windows Explorer before attempting a deletion.

---

tip Show Hidden Folders is an option on the View tab of the Folder Options dialog box
in Windows Explorer. Choose Folder Options from the Tools menu to display this
dialog box.

- To distribute a template stored on disk:

  1 Copy the *<type>\<template>.tem* folder to an intermediate location.

  2 Have the other users copy it to their *C:\Windows\Application Data
  \Microsoft\FrontPage\<type>\<template>.tem* folder (or, on
  Windows 2000, to their *C:\Documents and Settings\<username>
  \Application Data\Microsoft\FrontPage\<type>\<template>.tem*
  folder). In an organizational setting, this is something you could
  automate through a logon script or SMS package.

Changing a template doesn't change pages previously created from it. However,
any variables, Include Page components, or color masters specified by the template
remain as such on created pages, so you can maintain them globally.

In Summary...

This chapter explained how to create new Web pages based on templates, which
are images of Web pages saved for future use. It also explained how to avoid
repetitive work by creating templates of your own.

The next chapter explains how to create HTML tables and use them as grids for
page layout.

Using HTML Tables for Page Layout

Tables are a very useful addition to HTML. Before tables were available, HTML offered no practical means to organize content horizontally or in grids. The entire World Wide Web was left-justified.

Tables consist of horizontal *rows*, vertical *columns*, and *cells*—where rows and columns intersect. Each of these elements can have specific attributes—such as cell spacing, which determines the distance between each cell in a table. You can also apply certain attributes to the table as a whole. For instance, you can change the table's alignment on the page or add a border.

Tables serve two functions in HTML: Not only can they present tabular information the way a chart or spreadsheet does, they can also control page layout with precision. A table creates a grid on your page, and you can use the grid to position the various page elements. It's often a good idea to sketch your tables on paper before you create them in FrontPage. You'll save time and frustration by making most of your decisions about layout, spacing, and alignment before you create your grid.

Creating and Editing Tables

For ease of learning, the following discussion uses very simple grids as examples. A later section titled "Using Tables for Page Layout" describes how to use tables for laying out more complex content.

 For more information about the Tables toolbar, refer to "The Tables Toolbar" in the Bonus Content on the Companion CD.

Creating a New Table

FrontPage provides five distinct ways to create HTML tables. The method you choose depends on your preferences and the type of content you want to display. The five methods are as follows:

- Drawing with the mouse
- Using the Insert Table button
- Inserting a table using menus
- Converting text to a table
- Pasting tabular data

The remainder of this section will provide step-by-step instructions for each of these methods.

Drawing a Table with the Mouse

This method creates a one-celled table with a size and location you specify by dragging the mouse pointer across the desired area. To create more rows or columns, you subdivide an existing table, row, column, or cell by dragging the mouse pointer across it. Here's the procedure:

Draw Table

1 In Page view, choose Draw Table from the Table menu, or click the Draw Table button on the Tables toolbar. The mouse pointer will take on the shape of a pencil.

2 Point to where you want one corner of the table to appear, hold down the mouse button, and then drag diagonally to the table's opposite corner.

3 Release the mouse button to create the table. Note the following:

- All such tables are sized in pixels.

- All such tables initially consist of one cell. You can create rows and columns within the table by drawing lines with the Draw Table button.

- By default, FrontPage will position your table immediately beneath any content that precedes it. Your table will be left aligned, centered, or right aligned, depending on where you began to draw it.

- Drawing a line that connects two opposing sides of a table always creates a new row, column, or cell. If the line is too short or at too steep an angle, FrontPage will ignore it.

■ Lines that intersect the top, bottom, left side, or right side of a table are ignored.

■ Drawing a line that starts below an existing table and finishes inside the existing table creates a new table below the existing one.

■ Drawing a new table to the left or right of another table creates a new table inside the existing one. (Two tables can't exist side by side unless another, larger table contains them.) This method requires that the existing table be centered and the pencil be in table-drawing (as opposed to cell-splitting) mode.

When drawing tables, it's important to realize that the drawing pencil has two modes. And, just to make life confusing, there's no clear way to switch the pencil from one mode to another:

● In the first mode, a dotted rectangle forms as you drag the pencil diagonally across the screen. When you release the mouse button, FrontPage creates a table having approximately the same size, shape, and position as the rectangle.

The pencil is generally in this mode when it's not near an existing table, or immediately after drawing a table.

● In the second mode, a dotted line forms as you drag the pencil across the screen. When you release the mouse button, FrontPage either:

■ Slices an existing table row, column, or cell in half.

■ Discards the mouse movement if it wasn't clearly vertical or clearly horizontal, or didn't clearly indicate an existing table element.

The pencil is generally in this mode when it's near an existing table.

InsideOut

The table drawing feature is a carry-over from a similar feature in Microsoft Word. However, what works well for creating paper documents can be awkward for creating Web pages, and this feature is a case in point. Don't lock onto the table drawing tool as your only means for creating tables.

For information about changing a table after you've drawn it, refer to "Modifying an Existing Table" later in this chapter.

Using the Insert Table Button

This method inserts a table at the current insertion point. You specify the number of rows and columns by clicking or dragging the mouse.

To use the Insert Table button in clicking mode:

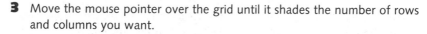

Insert Table

1 Place the insertion point where the table should appear.

2 Click the Insert Table button on the Standard toolbar. A small grid of table cells will appear.

3 Move the mouse pointer over the grid until it shades the number of rows and columns you want.

4 Click the mouse button again to insert the table, or click Cancel to cancel table creation.

To use the Insert Table button in dragging mode:

1 Place the insertion point where the table should appear.

2 Click the Insert Table button on the Standard toolbar and hold down the mouse button. A small grid of table cells will appear.

3 Drag the mouse pointer across the grid, selecting the number of rows and columns you want. The grid will grow larger if you try to drag beyond its right or bottom edge.

4 Release the mouse button to insert the table.

5 To cancel table creation, drag the mouse pointer beyond the grid's top or left edge, then release the mouse button.

In general, the dragging method is superior because it can enlarge the supplied grid. Of course, you can always enlarge the table later with more rows and columns, should you need them.

When you use either method, single line breaks will occur before and after the new table.

Inserting a Table Using Menus

Choosing a menu option and filling out a dialog box provides more control over a new table's attributes than either method above. To take this approach:

1 Place the insertion point where the table should appear.

2 Choose Insert from the Table menu, and then Table from the resulting submenu. The Insert Table dialog box shown in Figure 16-1 will appear.

Chapter 16

3 Specify the properties you want the talbe to have, and click OK.

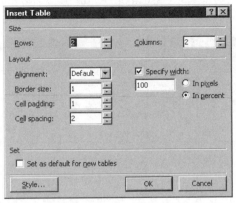

Figure 16-1. Set your table options in the Insert Table dialog box.

The available properties are described below. You can modify any of these properties later without re-creating the table:

- **Size.** These options control the dimensions of the table, that is, the number of rows and columns:

  - **Rows.** Enter the number of horizontal rows the table should have.

  - **Columns.** Enter the desired number of vertical columns.

- **Layout.** These options control page positioning and appearance:

  - **Alignment.** Specify the table's horizontal position on the page. The choices are Default, Left, Right, and Center. Default leaves the choice up to the Web visitor's browser—which usually results in a left-aligned table. Left and Right align a table to the corresponding margins, whereas Center positions it in the center of the page.

  - **Border Size.** If you want a border around your table and each of its cells, enter its thickness in pixels. A border size of zero specifies no borders.

  - **Cell Padding.** Enter the number of pixels to insert between a cell's margin and its contents.

  - **Cell Spacing.** Enter the number of pixels that should appear between the margins of adjacent cells.

> **note** If margins are visible and cell spacing is zero, the margins of adjacent cells will touch and blend together.

Figure 16-2 illustrates the difference between cell padding and cell spacing. They're easier to tell apart when cell borders are turned on. Figure 16-2 also illustrates tables within tables.

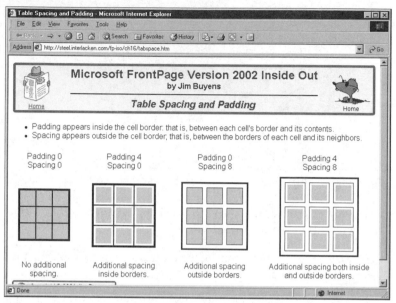

Figure 16-2. This Web page illustrates the difference between cell spacing and cell padding. Spacing occurs outside the border lines, and padding occurs within. Note also that the four 3x3 tables, their headings, and their captions are located within the cells of an invisible 7x3 table. Columns 2, 4, and 6 contain only white space.

- **Specify Width.** Enter the amount of horizontal space you want the table to occupy. To apply this setting, you must select the check box, specify a value, and indicate a unit of measure:

  - **In Pixels.** Select this option to specify the width of the table in pixels.

  - **In Percent.** Select this option to size the table as a percentage of available space in a Web visitor's browser window. A table width of 100 percent stretches the table across all available space.

> **caution** Most Web browsers treat table measurements as approximations, not as concrete specifications.

- **Set As Default For New Tables.** Selecting this check box applies the current table formatting to all new tables by default.

Chapter 16

tip Although the Set As Default For New Tables option is available only in the Insert Table dialog box, it affects all new tables you create by any method. It's worth creating a sample table and immediately deleting it just to set your defaults.

● **Style.** Click this button to apply cascading style sheet properties to the table.

Figure 16-3 shows the result of inserting a table with the properties given in Figure 16-1.

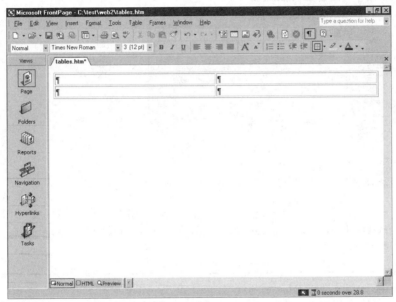

Figure 16-3. This table uses the default settings shown in Figure 16-1.

Converting Text to a Table

To create a table from existing text:

1 Select the text you want to convert by dragging the mouse pointer across it.

2 Choose Convert from the Table menu, then choose Text To Table.

3 In the Convert Text To Table dialog box shown in Figure 16-4 on the next page, choose one of the following:

■ To convert each paragraph in the text to a full row in the table, click Paragraphs.

■ To divide each row's text into columns based on the presence of tab characters or commas, click Tabs or Commas.

Chapter 16

■ To draw a one-celled table around the selected text, click None.

■ To divide each row's text into columns based on some other character, click Other and type the character you want in the text box.

4 Click OK.

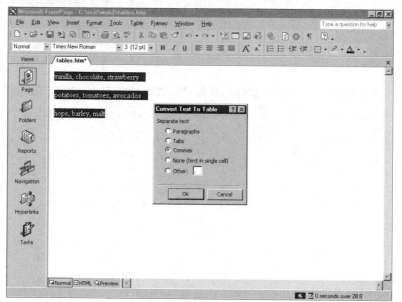

Figure 16-4. The Convert Text To Table command builds a table from existing text.

---

tip To convert an existing table to text, first select the table, then choose Convert from the Table menu, and then choose Table To Text. Each cell in the table will become an ordinary paragraph.

Pasting Tabular Data

Another way to create a table in FrontPage is to paste tabular content from other programs, such as a table from a word processor or database, or cells from a spreadsheet. If FrontPage doesn't automatically create a table, use the Paste Special command from the Edit menu to format the text as you paste it. Then, if necessary, use the Convert Text To Table command to complete the table.

Using the Table AutoFormat Feature

Within a table, you can specify different background colors, fonts, or typefaces for certain cells to create a more eye-catching presentation. FrontPage has a number of predetermined table designs, and you can use the Table AutoFormat feature to add one of them to your table in much the same way you'd add a theme to a Web. There are two ways to apply a design to your table: the Table AutoFormat dialog box and the Table AutoFormat drop-down list.

To use the Table AutoFormat dialog box:

Table
AutoFormat

1 Select the table you want to format by placing the insertion point inside it.

2 Click the Table AutoFormat button on the Tables toolbar. This will display the Table AutoFormat dialog box shown in Figure 16-5 on the next page.

3 Use the following options to control your table's appearance:

- **Formats.** Choose a design for your table from this list.

- **Preview.** When you choose a format, an example appears in this window.

- **Formats To Apply.** After choosing a table format, you can customize it by turning the following check boxes on or off. The Preview window will reflect your choices:

  - ◆ **Borders.** Toggles the use of borders in the table.

  - ◆ **Shading.** Determines whether the table will contain shaded areas.

  - ◆ **Font.** Toggles the use of style-specific type for certain text in the table.

  - ◆ **Color.** Switches between gray and a background color for the shaded areas of the table. The default is color.

  - ◆ **AutoFit.** Reduces the table size to fit the content of the table.

- **Apply Special Formats.** These options control the use of special formatting applied to rows and columns:

  - ◆ **Heading Rows.** Specifies whether or not the top table row is shaded.

  - ◆ **First Column.** Turns shading on or off in the first table column.

  - ◆ **Last Row.** Highlights the last row with shading, borders, or a combination, depending on the format you choose.

  - ◆ **Last Column.** Highlights the last column with shading, borders, or a combination, depending on the format you choose.

4 Click OK.

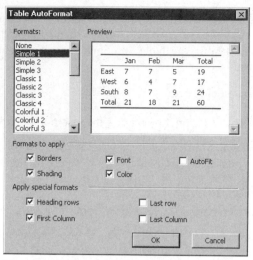

Figure 16-5. The Table AutoFormat dialog box adds predesigned formatting to an existing table.

To use the Table AutoFormat drop-down list:

Table AutoFormat

1 Select the table you want to format by placing the insertion point inside it.

2 Choose a table formatting option from the Table AutoFormat drop-down list on the Tables toolbar.

To remove previously applied formatting from a table, select the table and choose None from the Table AutoFormat drop-down list.

Modifying an Existing Table

Regardless of how you create a table, you probably won't get it exactly right on the first try. Most people spend considerably more time modifying and refining existing tables than creating new ones.

The Table Properties dialog box contains settings that affect an entire table. There are two ways to open this dialog box:

● Set the insertion point anywhere in the table, choose Table Properties from the Table menu, and then choose Table.

● Right-click anywhere in the table, and choose Table Properties from the shortcut menu.

Chapter 16

Either action displays the Table Properties dialog box shown in Figure 16-6.

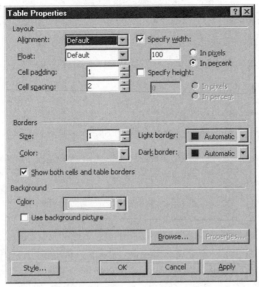

Figure 16-6. This dialog box provides access to settings that affect an entire table.

Several of the following settings also appear in the Insert Table dialog box shown in Figure 16-1. They work the same in both instances, but the Table properties dialog box provides a different layout and several new settings:

- **Layout.** These options control a table's page positioning and appearance:

    - **Alignment, Cell Padding, Cell Spacing, and Specify Width.** These options all work exactly as they do in the Insert Table dialog box (Figure 16-1).

    - **Float.** This option determines whether text will wrap around the table. The Left and Right options align the table to the left or right margin, respectively; both allow text to flow around the table. Default leaves the question of text wrapping up to the browser, which usually means it won't wrap.

    - **Specify Height.** Controls the amount of vertical space the table occupies. To apply this setting, select the check box, specify a value, and indicate a unit of measure. Choose In Pixels to declare a height value in pixels; choose In Percent to define the height value as a percentage of available space in the Web visitor's browser.

---

tip When you specify the dimensions of any Web-page object as a percentage, that percentage is relative to the object's immediate container. Thus, depending on where it appears, an object sized at 50 percent might occupy 50 percent of the browser window, 50 percent of a frame, or 50 percent of a table cell, whichever is most specific.

- **Borders.** These options control the size and colors of the table's border.

  - **Size.** Specifies, in pixels, the thickness of the border that surrounds the table. This option is also available in the Insert Table dialog box (Figure 16-1).

  - **Color.** Specifies a solid color for drawing the border that surrounds the table.

  - **Light Border.** Contributes to a three-dimensional, "raised" effect for the table by changing the color of the top and left table borders. (See the following note.)

  - **Dark Border.** Also contributes to the 3-D effect. It changes the color of the right and bottom table borders.

  - **Show Both Cells And Table Borders.** Displays single rule lines around the table's cells.

---

note According to common guidelines for computer graphics, the light source for three-dimensional pictures is above and to the left. Thus, to make a a table, or any other object, look three-dimensional:

- Make the top and left edges light, as if catching light directly.
- Make the bottom and right edges dark, as if in shadow.

Pages take on a very confusing perspective if different objects appear lighted from different directions.

- **Background.** These options control the table's background picture or color:

  - **Color.** Controls the table's background color.

  - **Use Background Picture.** Gives the table a background image. To use this option, select the check box and specify the background image's file name and location in the current Web.

  - **Browse.** Displays the Select Background Picture dialog box, through which you can search the current Web, the local file system, or the FrontPage clip-art library for a background graphic.

  - **Properties.** Displays the Picture Properties dialog box shown in Figure 11-20, which alters the properties of the specified background picture.

  - **Style.** Controls cascading style sheet properties for the current table.

Adding Rows and Columns to a Table

Three methods are available for adding rows or columns to a table: menus and the toolbar. To add rows or columns using menus:

1 Click any cell that will adjoin the new row or column.

2 Choose Insert from the Table menu, and then choose Rows Or Columns.

3 In the resulting dialog box, click either Rows or Columns.

4 Indicate the number of rows or columns to insert. The Number and Location labels change depending on whether you are inserting rows or columns.

5 For rows, indicate whether to insert the new row(s) above or below the current selection. For columns, specify right or left. Click OK.

To add rows to a table using the toolbar:

1 Select one or more existing rows that will appear under the new row. See the sidebar titled "Selecting Table Cells."

Insert
Rows

2 Click the Insert Rows button on the Tables toolbar.

With each click, FrontPage will insert, above your selection, the same number of rows that you have indicated.

> **tip** When you insert rows using the toolbar or right mouse button, FrontPage inserts them above the selected rows. When you insert columns, they appear to the left of whatever columns you selected.

To add columns to a table using the toolbar:

1 Select one or more existing columns that will appear to the right of the new column.

Insert
Columns

2 Click the Insert Columns button on the Tables toolbar.

3 To the left of your selection, FrontPage will insert the same number of columns you have indicated.

To insert rows or columns using the right mouse button:

● Right-click any part of an existing row and then choose Insert Rows from the shortcut menu.

● Right-click any part of an existing column and then choose Insert Columns from the shortcut menu.

Selecting Table Cells

There are three approaches to selecting cells, rows, columns, or an entire table:

- Using menus. Click any cell in the desired range, choose Select from the Table menu, and then choose one of the following commands:
    - Table
    - Column
    - Row
    - Cell
- Using mouse movements at the table margins. Move the mouse pointer over the top margin to select columns, or over the left margin to select rows:
    - To select a single column or row, click when the mouse pointer changes to an arrow.
    - To select multiple columns or rows, hold down the mouse button when the arrow appears, and drag along the appropriate margin.
- Clicking cells:
    - To select a single cell, press Alt and click the cell.
    - To select a range of cells one cell at a time, hold down Ctrl+Alt and drag the mouse pointer across each one. As an alternative to dragging, click each cell you want to select while pressing Ctrl+Alt.
    - To select a contiguous range of cells, drag from one corner of the selection to the opposite corner. You can also click one corner cell and then click the opposite corner while pressing the Shift key.
    - To add cells to a selection, hold down Shift while clicking the additional cells.
    - To deselect cells from a group of selected cells, click the cells while pressing Ctrl+Alt.
    - To select the entire table, click the top or left table margin while pressing the Alt key.

Adding and Removing Table Cells

HTML tables are quite flexible and don't require all rows to have the same number of cells. To add cells to a single row:

1 Click inside the cell just left of where you want the new cell inserted.

2 Choose Insert from the Table menu, and then choose Cell.

In Figure 16-7 the insertion point was in the cell numbered 3 when the Web designer inserted a cell. The new cell appeared between existing cells 3 and 4.

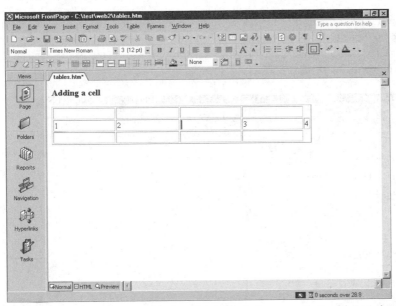

Figure 16-7. A cell was added to this table between cells 3 and 4 in the second row.

To delete cells:

1 Select the cell(s) you want to remove.

2 Choose Delete Cells from the Table menu.

FrontPage can also merge adjacent cells to span several rows or columns. Figure 16-8 on the next page illustrates this concept; note the large cells in the bottom left and top right corners that occupy the space normally occupied by two. Here's the procedure for merging cells:

1 Select the cells you want to merge. They must be contiguous and form a rectangular block—no L-shapes or other irregular shapes.

2 Choose Merge Cells from the Table menu or click the Merge Cells button on the Tables toolbar.

Merge Cells

The only tricky part of this procedure is selecting the cells. Refer to the sidebar "Selecting Table Cells" for details.

> **caution** Merging two cells into one produces quite a different result than deleting one of them. Merged cells span multiple rows or columns—whatever space the individual cells occupied before the merge. Deleting a cell forces adjacent cells to move in from below or from the right.

Split Cells

To split a cell or cells into further columns or rows, select the cell(s), and then either click the Split Cells toolbar button or choose the Split Cells command from the Table menu. In the Split Cells dialog box, you will be prompted to split the selected cell(s) into columns or rows.

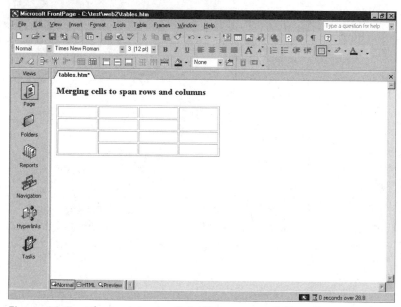

Figure 16-8. The oversized cells in the corners of this table resulted from merging cells in a 4x4 table.

Adding a Table Caption

To give a table a caption, click anywhere in the table, choose Insert from the Table menu, and then choose Caption. FrontPage will create a blank caption above the table and set the insertion point there. Type the caption text you want. To move the caption below the table:

1 Click the caption, choose Table Properties from the Table menu, and then choose Caption. (Alternatively, right-click the caption and choose Caption Properties from the shortcut menu.)

2 Choose the caption position you prefer: Top Of Table or Bottom Of Table, and click OK.

Figure 16-9 shows a simple 4x4 table containing some data. Inserting the text was a simple matter of placing the insertion point inside each cell and then typing. The same approach works for inserting pictures and other objects—even additional tables—into a cell. You can set the same properties for items within a cell that you can set for them elsewhere on the page.

490

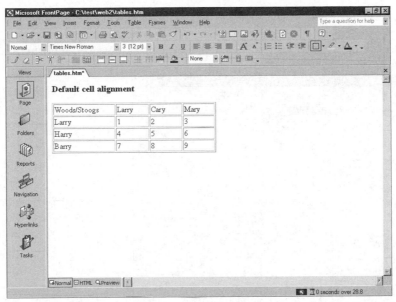

Figure 16-9. Like a browser, FrontPage adjusts default column height and row width, based on cell contents and window size.

By default, the rows and columns in a table grow in height and width to accommodate cell content. Browsers—and FrontPage as well—normally try to minimize white space by widening columns whose cells contain a lot of text. At the same time, they try to keep columns wide enough not to truncate any pictures or other fixed-width objects. If possible, the browser sizes the table horizontally to fit within the available display area.

Adjusting Cell Properties

Although the table layout in Figure 16-9 looks generally pleasing, several aspects beg improvement. The numeric entries should allow for two-digit numbers and, therefore, should be right-justified, for example, and the column headings might look better bottom-aligned. You can make these kinds of adjustments in the Cell Properties dialog box. To specify cell properties:

1 Select one or more cells using one of these methods:

■ Set the insertion point in a cell.

■ Select content in one or more cells.

■ Use any of the methods cited in the sidebar "Selecting Table Cells."

2 Choose Table Properties from the Table menu, and then choose Cell. Alternatively, right-click the selection and choose Cell Properties from the shortcut menu.

Chapter 16

491

Step 2 will display the Cell Properties dialog box shown in Figure 16-10. This dialog box controls many of the same properties as the Table Properties dialog box (Figure 16-6), but only for the selected cells. Other properties, however, apply to cells only.

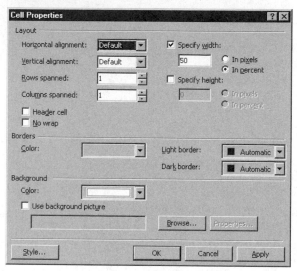

Figure 16-10. The Cell Properties dialog box exposes settings for any number of selected table cells.

Here's the complete list of properties that the Cell Properties dialog box controls:

- **Layout.** These options determine how objects in the selected table cell appear. You can apply all the following properties to a single cell or a block of cells:

  - **Horizontal Alignment.** Controls lateral positioning of the cell's contents. The Left and Right options align the contents to the left or right border, respectively. Center positions the contents an equal distance from the left and right borders, and Justify aligns the contents flush against both borders.

  - **Vertical Alignment.** Controls vertical positioning of the cell's contents. Again, there are four possibilities:

    - **Top.** Aligns the cell's contents to the top of the cell. Any white space appears at the bottom.

    - **Middle.** Distributes any vertical white space half above and half below the cell's contents.

    - **Baseline.** Aligns the baseline of the first line of text with the baselines in adjacent cells, as in the following example.

Chapter 16

◆ **Bottom.** Aligns the cell's contents to the bottom of the cell.
Any white space appears at the top.

note The baseline is the imaginary line on which characters such as m and x rest. Characters such as p and q extend below the baseline.

■ **Rows Spanned.** Indicates the height of the cell in terms of normal
table rows.

■ **Columns Spanned.** Indicates the width of a cell in terms of normal
table columns.

note Merging cells and setting a span accomplish similar end results, but they aren't the same. Merging combines two or more cells into one wider cell that spans multiple rows or columns; cells not involved in the merge retain their former positions. Setting a span widens one cell to cover multiple rows or columns, pushing any following cells down or to the right.

● **Header Cell.** When selected, this option indicates that the selected cell contains headings. This normally causes any text to appear in bold.

● **No Wrap.** When selected, this option indicates that the browser mustn't
wrap text in the selected cell.

● **Specify Width.** This option signifies that a minimum cell width is in effect.
To use this setting, you must select the check box, specify a value, and indicate a unit of measure. Click In Pixels to specify the width of the cell
in pixels; click In Percent to size the cell as a percentage of the table width.

caution If you specify column widths that exceed the width of a table, the results are unpredictable.

● **Specify Height.** This option signifies that a minimum height is in effect.
To use this setting, you must select the check box, specify a value, and indicate a unit of measure. Click In Pixels to specify the height of the cell
in pixels; or In Percent to size the cell as a percentage of the table height.

- **Borders.** These options control the border colors of the selected cell:

  - **Color.** Specifies a solid color for drawing the cell border.

  - **Light Border.** Specifies a color for drawing the top and left cell borders.

  - **Dark Border.** Specifies a color for drawing the right and bottom cell borders.

- **Background.** These options control the background picture or color for the selected cell:

  - **Color.** Controls the color of the cell's background.

  - **Use Background Picture.** If turned on, indicates that the cell will have a background picture. To use this option, select the check box and specify the background picture's file name and location in the current Web.

  - **Browse.** Displays the Select Background Picture dialog box, through which you can search the current Web, the local file system, or the FrontPage clip-art library for a background graphic.

  - **Properties.** Displays the Picture Properties dialog box, shown in Figure 11-20, which alters the properties of the specified background picture.

  - **Style.** Controls cascading style sheet properties for the selected cell(s).

Compare Figure 16-9 and Figure 16-11. The latter figure reflects the following edits:

- The cells in the top row have a background color of #999999.

- The text in the top row of cells is bold.

- The cells in the top row are bottom-aligned.

- The cells containing numbers are right-aligned.

FrontPage provides three commands that attempt to produce uniform row and column sizes. Each appears on the Table menu as well as on the Tables toolbar:

- **Distribute Rows Evenly.** This command sets the height of the currently selected table to its present value in pixels, divides this value by the current number of rows, and sets the height of each cell to the resulting value.

- **Distribute Columns Evenly.** This command sets the width of the currently selected table to its present value in pixels, divides this value by the current number of columns, and sets the width of each cell to the resulting value.

- **AutoFit to Contents.** This command removes all sizing attributes from the current table. The browser then sizes the rows and columns to minimize the height of the table while not exceeding the width of the available display area.

Unfortunately, the power of these commands is greatly diminished by HTML's weak control over the dimensions of table cells. Browsers consider cell dimensions specified in the HTML code as initial suggestions only. You can specify all the cell dimensions you want, but the browser, reacting to the Web visitor's current display window, will still apply its own cell-sizing logic.

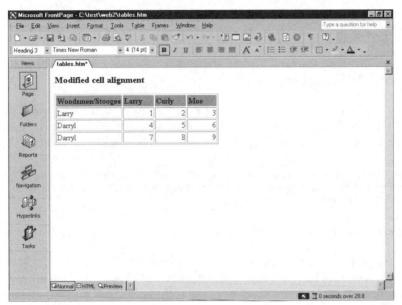

Figure 16-11. Although still simple, this table's appearance is enhanced from that in Figure 16-9.

Using Tables for Page Layout

It bears repeating that, despite its popularity, HTML is one of the clumsiest page description languages in use. Its inventors, in the interest of device independence, stripped HTML of virtually all capabilities to control page appearance. Designers, in the interest of visual communication, have tried to regain page control ever since.

HTML provides only a basic assortment of paragraph styles. Normal text, headings, code listings, and so forth are all flush left—that is, aligned to the left margin, with no provision for indentation. Only a few styles, such as bulleted lists, numbered lists, and definition lists, provide built-in horizontal alignment.

More advanced objects, such as pictures, tables, Java applets, and ActiveX controls, are flush left by default but can also be centered or flush right (aligned to the right margin). When nontext objects are aligned to the left margin, text can optionally flow around them. Text always flows around right-aligned objects.

For more complicated layouts, designers frequently resort to one of the most time-honored techniques in page layout: a grid. Newspapers have the most obvious layout grids, usually followed by magazines and brochures, in that order. From billboards to business cards, the elements of graphic design tend to be rectangular, and they tend to be aligned in rows and columns.

Tables and frames are the most common tools used for HTML page layout, and both of them arrange content in rectangular grids. Of the two, tables offer the most flexibility, but frames offer less repetition of content.

Grid Layout Principles

Robin Williams, in *The Non-Designer's Design Book*, identifies four key elements of effective page design: contrast, repetition, alignment, and proximity. The first two concepts are introduced in Chapter 4, "Planning Your Site."

> For more information about contrast and repetition, refer to "Defining Your Site's Style" on page 110. For more information about color contrast, refer to "Design Tips For Choosing Colors" on page 558.

Alignment and proximity are two topics best described here, in the context of tables:

- **Contrast.** This is the idea that different kinds of page objects should each be identified by a different look. Titles, headings, body text, hyperlinks, and legal disclaimers, for example, should each be differentiated by a unique appearance.

- **Repetition.** This concept postulates that similar page objects should look alike. All body text should look the same, as should all primary headings, all secondary headings, and so forth. Giving similar objects different appearances can be extremely confusing to the visitor.

- **Alignment.** This concept addresses the positioning of each element in a composition. Elements should appear to be organized according to a plan, not haphazardly.

  Proper alignment generally involves drawing imaginary horizontal and vertical lines through the composition, and then aligning related objects along those lines. Similar objects should generally be aligned in similar fashion. Unlike objects can likewise have unlike alignment, but they can also be differentiated in some other way.

  When you observe this principle with the elements aligned in a grid, the page automatically becomes more clean and usable. However, your Web can appear stale and dull if you repeat the same grid on every page. Of course global elements such as the logo and navigational graphics should remain in the same location throughout the site, but you should build some variety into your pages to create visual interest. Using different grids in different parts of your Web can help you accomplish this.

● **Proximity.** This principle holds that related objects should be closer together than unrelated objects. This leads to techniques such as ordering similar items together, decreasing blank space between related items, and increasing blank space between unrelated items.

HTML Tables as Layout Grids

Tables constitute a major weapon in the battle to control page layout. They provide a way to split the page into horizontal and vertical sections, and thus to lay out page elements spatially. Whoever invented HTML tables might have imagined only simple grids like that shown in Figure 16-9. But table-based layouts have evolved into some of the most attractive and complex pages seen today on the World Wide Web.

The cells in an HTML table can have visible or invisible borders. Tables are required for most page layouts, and invisible borders are usually preferable. Creating a page layout with tables involves first deciding how many horizontal and vertical cells the composition requires, and then merging cells for objects that need to span more than one row or column.

> **note** In graphic design, even text is rectangular. Designers often think of headlines, titles, body text, and other elements as though they were colored rectangles rather than words, letters, and punctuation. It's quite common to call body text gray space, for example.

HTML Frames as Layout Grids

Using HTML frames begins with defining a frames page that divides the browser window into zones called frames. Each frame displays a different Web page, and clicking hypertext in one frame can change the page displayed in another. A typical use of frames involves a menu list in one frame and an information display in another. As the Web visitor clicks different menu items, the information frame displays corresponding Web pages.

> For more information about using frames, refer to Chapter 17, "Using Frames for Page Layout."

Tables and frames both divide the browser window into horizontal and vertical areas, but they solve two quite different problems. Tables are relatively static x-y grids, but you can define as many rows and columns as you need. Frames provide a means to replace parts of the browser display while preserving others, but their size and positioning is much less precise. A 5x5 table is relatively easy to work with, but a 25-frame frames page would be a nightmare.

For more information about HTML page layout, refer to Chapter 10, "Adding and Formatting Text" and Chapter 20, "Managing Appearance with Cascading Style Sheets."

Table Layout Mechanics

Figure 16-12 illustrates a simple Web page laid out with HTML tables.

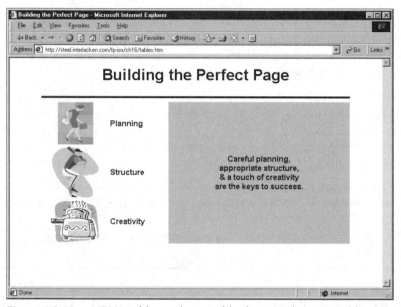

Figure 16-12. HTML tables make possible the two-dimensional layout of this Web page.

The heading and the horizontal line in Figure 16-12 are just ordinary, centered HTML elements. The icons, the category titles, and the slogan occupy a table three columns wide and three rows high, the table FrontPage makes visible in Figure 16-13. The cells in column 3 are merged and have a gray background color applied.

Notice how using a table aligns the category titles along a vertical gridline, even though the three icons are different widths. The titles are similar items, and therefore should have a similar appearance and similar alignment. Because each icon and its category title are related, they too should have similar alignment. The two-dimensional table uses one type of alignment—vertical—to indicate similar elements and another type of alignment—horizontal—to indicate associated content.

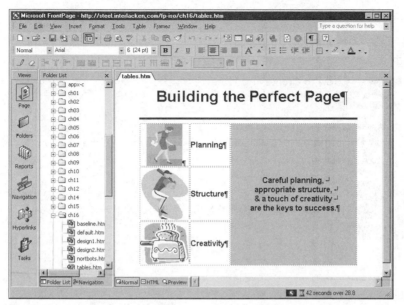

Figure 16-13.   Here is the Web page from Figure 16-12, displayed in FrontPage.

The slogan isn't associated with any one category, and therefore shouldn't be lined up with any of them. Centering it vertically ensures that it won't line up with any of the categories, and using a background color further signals the reader that this is something other than a category title. Centering it horizontally further differentiates it from the other, left-justified text, and fills in the large empty space a bit.

The layout table and the horizontal bar are set to 85 percent of the page width. This compresses the main content a bit, which is important because there isn't much of it. Too much white space (a Web designer's term for any kind of empty space) in the middle of the page makes the intended message seem unimportant. White space around the edges focuses attention inward.

Figure 16-14 on the next page, shows another, somewhat similar, layout done with an HTML table. There are three columns and four rows, which FrontPage makes visible in Figure 16-15 on the next page. Cells 2 and 3 in row 1 are merged to provide a large, somewhat encompassing space for the heading. Cells 3 and 4 in column 1 are not only merged but also given a gray background; this creates an area that's visually distinct from the rest of the page.

The gray area on the left will probably become a menu of hyperlinks, although no links currently exist. (After all, this is only an exercise done for the sake of example.) Each bulleted item is clearly associated with the icon to its left.

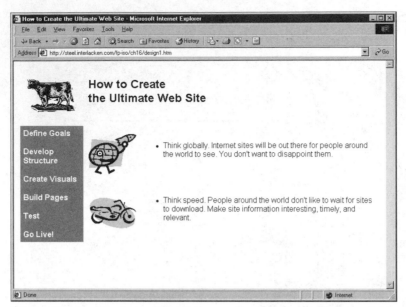

Figure 16-14. Here's another Web page that uses tables for page layout.

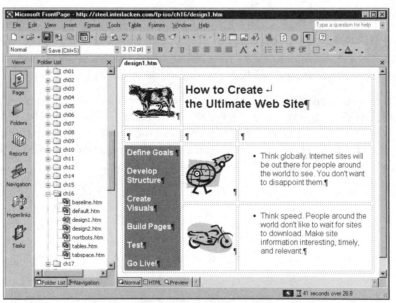

Figure 16-15. FrontPage shows the page layout table. Note the two large cells, which are merged, and the background color that visually bounds the menu area.

Figure 16-16 shows a considerably more complicated use of tables for page layout. This page uses a 4-column, 3-row table for its main grid, but two of the resulting cells themselves contain tables. The main grid itself is inside another table.

To create this page, the designer first inserted a one-cell table with a width of 85 percent. Next, the designer placed another table inside the first one. The second table holds all of the content. The first table defines the width, holds the content table, and is shaded gray, allowing what appears to be a border to display around the content area.

To understand which cells contain tables, you must first understand the merged cells in the content table. The following cells are merged:

- In row 1, cells 2 and 3. Cell 4 is divided into four equal parts by another nested table.

- In row 2, cells 2 and 3.

- In row 3, cells 3 and 4.

- In column 1, rows 2 and 3.

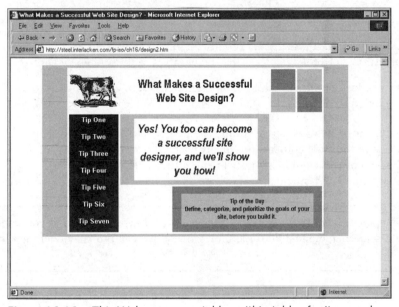

Figure 16-16. This Web page uses tables within tables for its page layout.

The nested tables are more visible in Figure 16-17 on the next page:

- A three-celled table occupies columns 2 and 3 (merged) of row 2. Its width is 100 percent, so it completely fills the cell that contains it, and it supplies the border and background color for the text.

- Another three-celled table occupies columns 3 and 4 (merged) of row 3. Its width is set the same as the above table.

- The widths of the inside tables are set so that they appear to overlap, creating visual interest.

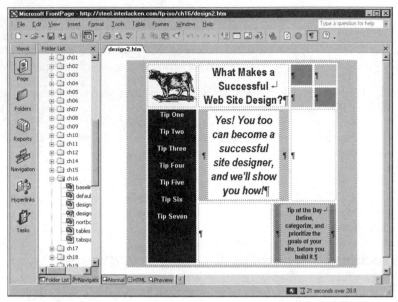

Figure 16-17. FrontPage makes the layout tables in this Web page visible.

- The inside tables are sized to different heights, to give emphasis to the upper, larger table.

This page uses the white space around the elements to create a flow from the main headline to the main content, and finally to the subcontent tip. The numbered tips in the left column would obviously link to other pages within the site. The content, although there isn't much of it, is well positioned to catch and guide a visitor's eye.

> **tip** A high percentage of Web visitors will never scroll down your page. If you don't get their attention in the first 800x600 browser window, you probably won't get their attention at all.

If you think the use of tables as described here seems convoluted compared to other page-layout techniques, you're right! HTML itself was never designed for this kind of work—nor, most likely, were tables. Nevertheless, advanced use of tables permits a degree of layout control that would be impossible using any other technique. Fortunately, FrontPage can make creating and formatting complex tables easier by reducing the need for arcane syntax and HTML tags.

> **tip** Most professional Web site designers draw out their tables on paper before they begin building the site's pages. You should follow their example. Attempting to add, remove, or rearrange tables after the fact can be difficult, and it might drive you to start over from scratch.

Using Transparent Pictures for Page Layout

In an effort to keep Web pages device-independent, HTML provides very little support for absolute positioning. HTML "thinks" in terms of flowing text, not in terms of objects placed on an x-y grid. This is greatly frustrating when presenting commercial art rather than, say, a research paper.

Tables and frames provide page designers with a rough method of x-y positioning, but for fine control, many designers have adopted the use of transparent GIF pictures. Anywhere they want some blank space on the page, they simply insert a completely transparent GIF.

Every pixel in a transparent GIF is the same color—transparent. Clever designers keep a one-pixel by one-pixel transparent GIF, commonly called a "spacer GIF," in their bag of tricks. This is the smallest possible file to download, and specifying an appropriate height and width for it (in the Appearance tab of the Picture Properties dialog box shown in Figure 11-20) will stretch the file to any required size. Remember to clear the Keep Aspect Ratio check box so that you can independently set the width and height. You can use the same file over and over again in different locations simply by specifying an appropriate size for it each time.

Working with one-pixel transparent GIFs presents a unique problem with WYSIWYG editors such as FrontPage: Such pictures are quite difficult to locate, select, and modify after you add them to a page. For this reason you might find it easier to work with slightly larger files. The CD accompanying this book contains these transparent GIF files for your use:

File Name	Pixels	File Size (Bytes)
trans1x1.gif	1x1	807
trans5x5.gif	5x5	814
trans9x9.gif	9x9	821

In Summary...

This chapter explained the various FrontPage commands for creating and modifying HTML tables. It also provided guidance on using tables for page layout in much the same way that traditional designers use grids.

The next chapter provides similar information regarding the use of framesets. Like tables, framesets divide the browser window into rectangles. That, however, is where the similarity ends. Frames present you with less flexibility and control than table cells. But you can use frames containing hyperlinks to update parts of the browser window while other parts remain static.

Chapter 16

Using Frames for Page Layout

When you start thinking about how best to lay out your Web site, you should consider using frames to divide the browser window into functional areas. Frames can show the Web visitor more than one Web page at a time, and the contents of one frame affect the contents of another. For example, many e-commerce sites use frames to display the contents of a shopping cart in one frame while visitors browse for additional items in another frame. Frames aren't the best option for every site, but they are for many.

When you create a site using frames, you must first create a special kind of Web page—a sort of master page—called a *frames page*. (Some people call this a *frameset*.) Regardless of name, this tells the browser how to display the frames and the pages they contain to the Web visitor.

In the past, frames were always tiled in a window. That meant frames never overlapped each other and the complete frames page always filled the entire browser window. With the advent of inline frames, all that changed. Using inline frames, Web developers can create frames that "float" within ordinary Web pages and display the contents of a separate Web page. The section "Using Inline Frames" later in this chapter explains how this works.

This chapter explains how FrontPage creates and manages frames pages. It also explains how to create hyperlinks that update the frame you want, or that replace the entire frames display with another page. Finally, the chapter explains some very simple scripting techniques that enhance the use of frames for both for the designer and the visitor.

Creating and Editing Frames

Two common methods of arranging content in a window are tables and frames. Whether they arrange simple columns of data or complex page layouts, tables are among the most powerful page composition tools for Web page design. A major shortcoming, however, is that tables aren't dynamic. Browsers can't replace the contents of a table or cell without redisplaying the entire Web page.

> For information on using tables, refer to Chapter 16, "Using HTML Tables for Page Layout."

A frames page gets around this shortcoming by dividing the browser window into zones called *frames*. The frames page defines the overall frame layout but provides no actual content. Instead, each frame displays a self-sufficient Web page. The frames page tells the browser what pages to load initially; later, hyperlinks reload individual frames in response to visitor selections.

Understanding Frame Fundamentals

Figure 17-1 displays a Web page that uses frames.

This "banner" frame displays *top.htm*

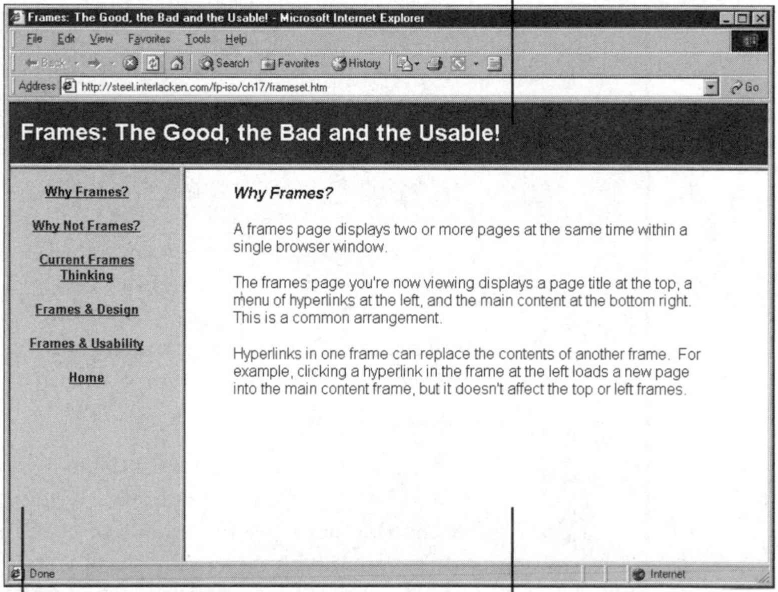

This "contents" frame displays *why.htm*   This "main" frame displays *why.htm*

Figure 17-1. This page uses four HTML files: one to define the three frame areas, and one per frame to provide content.

Creating this display requires four HTML files:

- One HTML file defines the frame areas, giving each frame a position, name, and frame source. This file is called the frames page, and it contains no visible content of its own.

- One HTML file occupies each defined frame. In Figure 17-1, three HTML files occupy three frames. Each frame has a property, called its *frame source,* that specifies the URL of the Web page that provides the frame's content. The frames page specifies an initial frame source for each frame.

The labels in Figure 17-1 show the frame names and sources for each of the three frames that make up the frames page. The fact that Figure 17-1 displays four HTML files *at once* is a key concept. The browser's Address box shows only one URL, but three more are hidden. To see the other URLs, right-click the content area of a frame and choose Properties from the shortcut menu. If you have the file open in FrontPage, right-click a frame and choose Page Properties from the shortcut menu. The Page Properties dialog box appears as shown in Figure 17-2 on the next page.

A frames page can also be the source of another frame (that is, you can have frames pages within frames). This can become extremely confusing, but it works.

When a frames page and its frame sources are on display, hyperlinks in any frame can display new content in the same frame, a different frame, the entire window, or a different window. A link attribute called the *target frame* specifies—by name—which frame should receive the content of a given hyperlink. The browser looks for the target frame specification in three locations. In order, these are:

- **The hyperlink itself.** Dialog boxes such as the Insert Hyperlink dialog box (shown in Figure 12-1) specify the target frame for an individual hyperlink. Click Target Frame and specify the frame where the new page should appear.

- **A default target frame.** The Web page that contains the hyperlink can specify a default target frame. This applies to all hyperlinks on that page that don't specify an explicit target frame. You specify the default target frame in the Page Properties dialog box.

- **The current frame.** If the hyperlink target frame and the default target frame are both absent, hyperlinks display their content in the frame in which they occur, just as you'd expect on a page with no frames.

If you specify a target frame that doesn't exist, the browser will usually display the named HTML file in a new window. Always double-check frame name spellings, especially if a frames page isn't working properly.

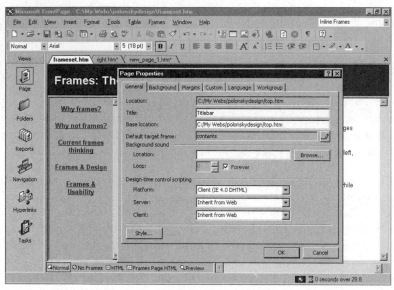

Figure 17-2. The Page Properties dialog box for the main title frame shows a URL different from that of the frames page.

Figure 17-1 illustrates the most frequent use of the target frame in current Web pages. Note the menu of hyperlinks in the left frame. When the Web visitor clicks one of these hyperlinks, the corresponding page appears in the main frame to the right. If the content appeared in the menu frame, it might obscure the other menu choices, making them unavailable. By setting each hyperlink's target frame (or the menu page's default target frame) to *main,* you ensure that the menu remains visible in the left frame and the content displayed in the right frame changes.

In addition to the frame names you create as part of a frames page, the four built-in target frame names listed in Table 17-1 might be useful. Microsoft FrontPage sometimes identifies these by the common target names listed in the table's second column.

An arrangement such as that shown in Figure 17-1 constantly displays your site's banner in the top frame and a menu of common hyperlinks in the left frame, no matter which page visitors browse in the main window. However, this structure has disadvantages as well:

● Managing frame names is a manual process, which is by nature tedious and error-prone.

● Adding hyperlinks to specific frames page combinations can be difficult. When another hyperlink loads the entire frames page, the default frame sources will always load.

To load the frames page with a different combination of sources, you have to create (and perpetually maintain) a second version of the frames page or do some fancy scripting.

For more information on the use of scripting in framesets, refer to "Scripting Frames and Frames Pages" later in this chapter.

Table 17-1. **Built-In Frame Names (No User Definition Required)**

HTML code	Common target name	Browser action
_new	New Window	Loads the hyperlink target into a new window.
_self	Same Frame	Loads the hyperlink target into the frame that contains the hyperlink. This is useful for overriding a page's default target frame on selected hyperlinks.
_parent	Parent	Loads the hyperlink target into the parent of the frame that contains the hyperlink. That is, the hyperlink target will replace the entire frames page that defines the frame containing the hyperlink.
_top	Whole Page	Loads the hyperlink target into the full window of the Web browser, replacing all prior frames pages. This is commonly used as the exit door from a framed page back to a single HTML, full-page display.

Creating and Modifying Frames Pages

Creating a new frames page in FrontPage is fairly simple. As with tables, you'll spend far more time modifying the frames than creating them:

1 Display the Page Templates dialog box:

  a Choose New from the File menu.

  b Choose Page Or Web from the submenu.

  c When the New Page Or Web task pane appears, click Page Templates in the New From Template section.

Here's another way to display the Page Templates dialog box:

  a Click the New Page button's drop-down arrow on the Standard toolbar.

New Page

  b Choose Page.

2 When the Page Templates dialog box appears, select the Frames Pages tab shown in Figure 17-3 on the next page.

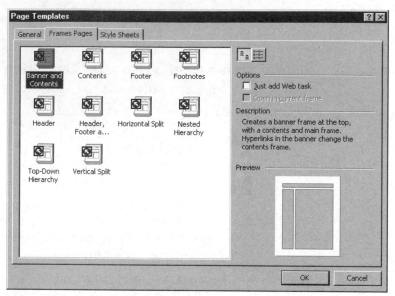

Figure 17-3. FrontPage offers a variety of pre-built frames pages that are useful as starting points for your own work.

3 Click the available frames page options until you find the one closest to your needs. The description and preview boxes display information about each selection and a depiction of the frames page layout.

4 When you find a frames page that meets your needs, click OK. FrontPage displays the new frames page as shown in Figure 17-4.

note The Database Interface Wizard is the only Web template that creates frames pages. There are no Web templates that create general purpose Webs organized with frames.

A new frames page contains no content. It is much like a picture frame with no picture. In place of content, FrontPage displays two buttons in each new frame:

● **Set Initial Page.** Click this button to display the Insert Hyperlink dialog box (a variation of the Insert Hyperlink dialog box shown in Figure 12-1). To initialize the frame with an existing Web page, use this dialog box to find the page, and then click OK.

● **New Page.** Click this button to create a new Web page whose content will fill the frame when the frames page opens. FrontPage doesn't offer templates for new pages used as frame targets; instead, it fills the frame with a blank page and prompts you for a name and title when you first save the frames page.

When FrontPage displays a frames page, it displays not only the frame positions but also their default targets in fully editable, WYSIWYG mode. Clicking each of the New Page buttons in the frames page of Figure 17-4 and supplying preliminary content produces the results shown in Figure 17-5.

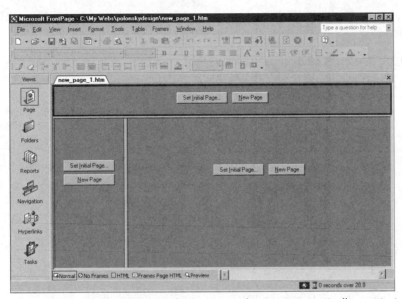

Figure 17-4. Creating a new frames page doesn't automatically create target pages for each frame.

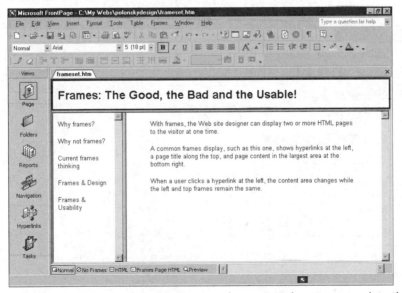

Figure 17-5. Now new target pages and some initial content populate the frames pages of Figure 17-4. Saving this view saves four files: the frames page itself, and each of three target Web pages. The dark line around the top frame indicates the active frame.

When you first save the frames page, FrontPage prompts you not only for the frames page file name, but also, in turn, for the file name of each new target. When you subsequently save the frames pages, FrontPage also saves any open target pages you've modified.

Here are some additional procedures you might find useful when working with frames pages:

- Save a specific target page without saving the frames page or any other target pages:

    1 Select the frame of the target page.

    2 Choose Save Page from the Frames menu.

- Save a target page under another name:

    1 Select the frame of the target page.

    2 Choose Save Page As from the Frames menu.

    3 Specify the file name and click Save.

- Change the default target for a frame:

    1 Select the frame of the target page.

    2 Choose Frame Properties from the Frames menu.

    3 In the Frame Properties dialog box, choose a new Initial Page, and then click OK.

When a frames page exists, it might be necessary to add a frame to the current layout. The only way to add a frame is to split an existing one. To do so:

1 Select the frame you want to split by clicking inside it once.

2 Choose Split Frame from the Frames menu. The Split Frame dialog box appears with the following options:

- Select Split Into Columns to divide the frame vertically.

- Select Split Into Rows to divide the frame horizontally.

3 Click OK.

> **note** You can also create a new, empty frame by positioning the mouse pointer on the border of an existing frame, holding down the Ctrl key, and using the mouse to drag the border to a new location.

4 FrontPage displays a new frame containing the same two buttons it displays in new frames pages. Click one of these two buttons:

■ **Set Initial Page.** Specifies an existing page.

■ **New Page.** Creates a new blank page.

To delete a frame, first select it, and then choose Delete Frame from the Frames menu. This deletes only the page from the frames page and *not* the Web page itself.

Troubleshooting

Loading and saving a target page doesn't update a frame's initial page setting

The Save Page As command on the Frames menu saves the contents of the current frame using a new file name. However, it *doesn't* automatically update the frame's Initial Page setting. This means FrontPage temporarily displays the *wrong* Web page in the saved frame. FrontPage recovers by reloading the last-saved version of the frame's Initial Page when you switch to another frame or, if you immediately close the frames page, the next time you open it.

Suppose, for example, that a frame's Initial Page is *apples.htm.* You modify the frame's content and then save the results as *oranges.htm.* FrontPage temporarily displays the contents of *oranges.htm* even though the frame's Initial Page remains *apples.htm.* FrontPage loads the last-saved version of *apples.htm* when you switch to another frame.

This behavior is perfect if you want to open the frames page, save a modified version of one source page, and leave the original frames page and source page unchanged. Obviously, your assessment of perfection will differ if you intend something else.

To save a frame's content as a new Web page *and* point the frame's Initial Page setting to it, first use the Frames menu's Save Page As command. Then, with the same frame displayed, use the Frame Properties dialog box to update the Initial Page property.

To change a frame's content and save it under *both* the existing name *and* a new one, you have to save the target twice—first using the Frames menu's Save Page command, and then using its Save Page As command.

You can specify the dimensions of a frame in three ways: by percentage, by relative sizing, or by pixels:

- Percentage states what fraction of the frames page's available height or width a given frame will occupy. This has the advantage of changing the frame size proportionately, depending on the size of the visitor's browser window.

- Relative sizing assigns a sizing factor to each frame, and then divides the available space proportionately. For example, if the frames page consists of three horizontal frames with relative heights of 10, 20, and 30, the three frames receive 10/60, 20/60, and 30/60 of the browser window, respectively. (To calculate the denominator, just add the values.)

- Specifying frame sizes in pixels seems at first to offer more absolute control, but only if you know in advance the size of all objects in the frame. Remember, for example, that in most cases you won't know the actual font sizes the visitor has chosen for various kinds of text.

There are two ways to resize a frame. The first of these methods resizes a frame visually:

1 Move the mouse pointer over the frame border until it becomes a double-headed arrow.

2 Hold down the mouse button and drag the border to the desired position.

The second method uses menus, and therefore controls frame sizes numerically. You can specify frame sizes relative to each other, as a percentage of available space, or as a specific number of pixels:

1 Select the frame you want to modify.

2 Display the Frame Properties dialog box in either of two ways:

- Choose Frame Properties from the Frames menu; or

- Right-click the frame, and then choose Frame Properties from the shortcut menu.

When the Frame Properties dialog box shown in Figure 17-6 appears, use the following settings to control the current frame:

- **Name.** Enter the name that hyperlinks will specify to load their contents into the selected frame.

- **Initial Page.** Specify the URL of the Web page that will initially appear in the frame (that is, when the browser first loads the frames page). Use the Browse button to locate the page.

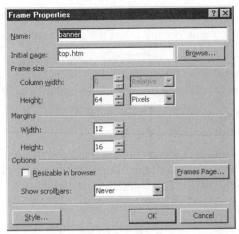

Figure 17-6. The Frame Properties dialog box controls the name, size, and other settings pertinent to a frame.

- **Frame Size.** Use this group of options to control the frame's display size. As you might expect, frames have two dimensions:

  - **Width/Column Width.** Use this setting to control the width of a frame or column.

    If the frame resides in a column with other frames of uniform width, the name of the setting box is Column Width (as it is in Figure 17-6) and the setting controls all frames in the column. Otherwise, the box's name is Width, and the setting controls one frame. In either case, specify both a width and the corresponding unit of measure.

  - **Height/Row Height.** Use this setting to control the height of a frame or row.

    If the frame resides in a row with other frames of uniform height, the name of the setting box is Row Height and the setting controls all frames in the row. Otherwise, the box's name is Height, and the setting controls one frame. In either case, specify both a height and the corresponding unit of measure.

The preceding measurements have three possible units of measure: Relative, Percent, and Pixels:

  - **Relative.** These units specify frame sizes relative to each other. If the frames page is divided horizontally into two frames with relative sizes of 1 and 4, the frame will occupy 1/5 and 4/5 of the available window space, respectively. Relative sizes of 2 and 8 would produce identical results, as would 5 and 20.

- ◼ **Percent.** These units allocate portions of the frames page. A frame sized at 33 percent would occupy 1/3 of the horizontal or vertical space available to the frames page.

- ◼ **Pixels.** These dimensions are straightforward. The frame will occupy the specified number of pixels or dots on the visitor's monitor.

- ● **Margins.** Use this group of options to control the size of margins within the selected frame:

  - ◼ **Width.** Use this setting to specify the number of pixels you want between the frame contents and the left and right borders. The number applies to both the left border and the right border.

  - ◼ **Height.** Use this setting to specify the number of pixels you want between the frame contents and the top and bottom borders. This number applies to both the top and bottom borders.

- ● **Options.** Use these two settings to control resizing and scroll bars:

  - ◼ **Resizable In Browser.** Select this box to let visitors resize the frame based on the size of their window. Otherwise, clear it.

  - ◼ **Show Scrollbars.** Use the choices in this list box to control when the browser will display scroll bars for the frame:

    - ◆ **If Needed.** Choose this option if the browser should display scroll bars whenever the frame's contents are larger than the window.

    - ◆ **Never.** Choose this option if the browser should never displays scroll bars for the frame.

    - ◆ **Always.** Choose this option if the browser should always display scroll bars for the frame, even if the entire contents of the page fit within the frame.

- ● **Frames Page.** Click this button to display the Page Properties dialog box for the frames page that contains the current frame.

The Page Properties dialog box for a frames page is quite similar to that of a normal page. It consists of five of the tabs described in Chapter 18, plus the Frames tab shown in Figure 17-7.

For descriptions of the other five tabs in the Page Properties dialog box, refer to "Specifying Page-Level Attributes" on page 537.

The Frames tab contains two settings. Both pertain to the frames page and not to individual frames or their targets:

- ● **Frame Spacing.** Specifies the number of pixels the browser should insert between frames. If Show Borders is also selected, the space will appear as a border; otherwise, the frame contents will be separated by this amount of neutral space.

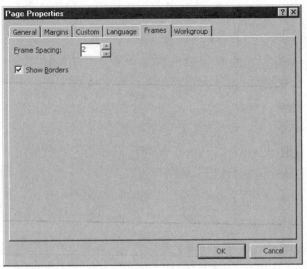

Figure 17-7. The Frames Page button on the Frame Properties dialog box opens this version of the Page Properties dialog box, which contains a tab pertinent to Frames.

- **Show Borders.** If this box is selected, the browser will display visible borders between frames of the thickness specified in Frame Spacing.

note FrontPage displays borders even if Show Borders is cleared. To view the page without frame borders, click the Preview button at the bottom of the FrontPage window, or preview the page in your browser.

To open a normal editing window for a page already open in a frame, click anywhere in that frame, and then choose Open Page In New Window from the Frames menu. You can edit in the larger window and switch back to the frames page to check its appearance.

tip To switch among several pages open in Page view, you have three options: click the tabs at the top of the editing window, select the page you want from the Window menu, or press Ctrl+Tab.

Today most browsers support frames, but this wasn't true when frames were first introduced. The frames specification, therefore, provides a way to embed an ordinary Web page in a frames page. A frames-capable browser will ignore the ordinary Web page, whereas a frames-deficient browser will ignore the frames page information.

> **note** A major tenet of HTML is that browsers should silently ignore anything they don't understand. This smooths adoption of new HTML features by allowing older browsers to run as they always have. Unfortunately, for designers, the lack of error messages can make debugging maddeningly difficult.

To display the page that a frames-deficient browser will display, open the frames page and then click the No Frames button at the bottom of the window (visible in Figure 17-5). FrontPage initializes the No Frames page with the following message:

This page uses frames, but your browser doesn't support them.

You can replace this message with a complete Web page if you want.

When designing a frame-based site, keep in mind that not all visitors have frames-capable browsers, and that some visitors simply don't like frames. This means you should either provide a parallel set of non-frames pages or include adequate hyperlinks on a single set of pages so that non-frame visitors can also navigate your site.

Frames pages appear in Navigation view as ordinary Web pages. A frames page's default target pages aren't automatically made children in Navigation view, nor are Navigation view children automatically designated default target pages.

> **For more information about Navigation view, refer to Chapter 7, "Managing Web Structure with Navigation View."**

Take great care when using themes and frames in the same Web. Backgrounds, color schemes, and graphic elements that look good on single Web pages are often distracting when displayed multiple times, once in each frame.

> **For more information about themes, refer to Chapter 19, "Using FrontPage Themes."**

Combining shared borders and frames is almost never a good idea because the shared border content will appear redundantly in every frame of a frames page.

> **For more information about shared borders, refer to "Using Shared Borders" on page 765.**

Scripting Frames and Frames Pages

This section explains how to work around four common stumbling blocks that many designers encounter when using frames. All of these explanations involve writing simple script code, and none of them has direct FrontPage support. If you're unfamiliar with the use of scripting for the World Wide Web, you should either skip this section or read Chapter 38 before proceeding.

Here are the requirements explained in the following sections:

- Reloading two frames with one mouse click
- Loading a frames page with non-default targets
- Reloading a stand-alone page with a frames page
- Helping visitors set up shortcuts

Reloading Two Frames with One Mouse Click

Web sites that use frames often run into trouble as the number of main menu options grows. A main menu with four, eight, or twelve options might be workable, but when the number runs into the dozens, visitors run for the hills.

A common solution to the problem of too many options—and not just with frames—is to adopt a multi-level menu structure. This, however, presents another problem, because when a visitor clicks a main menu option that loads a submenu, the visitor expects *both* the menu frame *and* the main content frame to change. Think about it: after the menu frame displays the new menu, why should the main content frame display a page that pertains to the previous menu? Figure 17-8 shows a frames page experiencing this dilemma. If a visitor clicks Mineral, they expect to see a new content page that introduces mineral pets *and* a new menu of mineral pet choices. Normally, however, clicking a hyperlink can replace the content of only one frame.

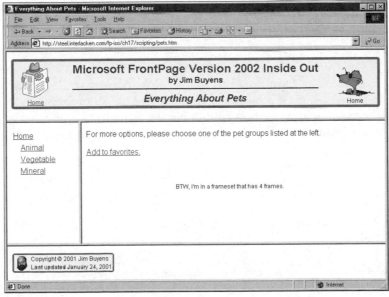

Figure 17-8. Clicking the Animal, Vegetable, or Mineral link in this layout should not only display a new menu in the menu frame, but also a new content page in the main frame.

Avoiding both prolonged meditation and self-denial, the solution to this problem is based on three facts:

● A single JavaScript statement can reload a page as easily as a hyperlink can.

● Scripts can contain as many JavaScript statements as you want.

● Clicking a hyperlink can run a script instead of requesting a new page.

The following JavaScript statements reload a given frame in a frames page:

```
parent.frames.main.location="introanimal.htm"
parent.frames.menu.location="menuanimal.htm"
```

The first statement loads the *introanimal.htm* page into the frame named *main*. The second statement loads the *menuanimal.htm* page into the frame named *menu*. The expression at the left of each equal sign says:

● Start at the parent of the current frame (that is, with the frames page).

● Go to the collection of all frames that belong to that parent.

● Go to the specified frame (*main* or *menu,* in this case).

● Go to the specified location (that is, the URL).

Loading a new URL by executing either of these statements reloads the given frame, which covers the first fact. As for the second fact, you can put as many JavaScript statements in a row as you like, as long as you put a semicolon between them. As for the third, here is the syntax for coding a hyperlink that runs JavaScript code:

```
javascript:<any javascript statements>
```

You can use the following expression as a hyperlink address, just as if it were an HTTP URL. In fact, entering as the target location of the Animals hyperlink in Figure 17-8 solves the problem of content frames not displaying updated content when a visitor clicks a new menu option. Don't enter a return; the entire expression is supposed to be one line:

```
javascript:parent.frames.main.location='introanimal.htm';
parent.frames.menu.location='menuanimal.htm'
```

Figure 17-9 shows the expression entered in the Address box of the Edit Hyperlink dialog box.

For more information about the Edit Hyperlink dialog box, refer to "Creating Hyperlinks with Menus" on page 358.

There's just one trick to this code: FrontPage always uses quotation marks ("…") to enclose URLs that appear in hyperlinks. This means you can't put quotation marks in JavaScript statements that appear in hyperlinks. Therefore, you have to use apostrophes ('…'). Diabolical.

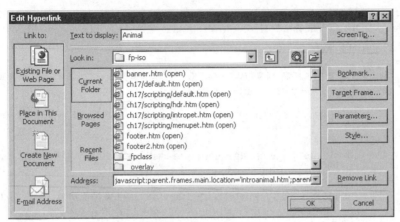

Figure 17-9. By entering JavaScript in place of a link address, you can make hyperlinks run script code.

You can test this technique yourself by loading */ch17/scripting/pets.htm* from the sample Web into your browser. Clicking the Animal, Vegetable, or Mineral link displays a new menu and a new main content page.

While you're at it, check out the *Home* hyperlink on the main menu and the *Main* hyperlink on the submenus. These are just ordinary hyperlinks, but they provide a much better way to move back through a Web site than by using the browser's Back button. If a visitor browses 20 or 30 frame combinations and then clicks the browser's Back button, the display backs up only *one* frame combination. To get out of the frames page, the visitor has to click the browser's Back button 20 or 30 times. A Home option that returns the visitor to the page that originally loaded the frames page is a welcome feature. Coding this hyperlink with a target frame of *_top* replaces the entire frames page.

Loading a Frames Page with Non-Default Targets

A common problem with frame-based sites has been the lack of ability to jump into the site at any point. Even within the same site, there's been no way of jumping to both a frames page *and* the exact combination of target pages you want. Until now.

In its simplest form, the HTML that creates a frame specifies nothing but the frame name and a default target page. It looks like this:

```
<frame name="main" src="intropet.htm">
```

This is the code that tells the browser to name the frame *main* and initially load it with the *intropet.htm* page. If there was some way to modify the *src* location on the fly, before the browser received this code, you could make the browser load whatever page you want.

Because ASP code modifies HTML code before the browser receives it, an ASP page is perfect for the task at hand. Here's how to make an ASP frames page load any combination of target pages you want:

1 Get an ordinary frames page working, as you want (except, of course, that it always loads the default target pages).

2 Rename or copy the existing frames page so it has an *.asp* filename extension.

3 Open the frames page in Page view, and click the Frames Page HTML button at the bottom of the Window.

4 Find the line of code that defines the frame you want to control. This will be a *<frame>* tag with a *name=* attribute that identifies the desired frame.

5 Replace the URL of the target frame with an expression like this:

```
<%=pgMain%>
```

Leave any other attributes in the *<frame>* tag unchanged. This will result in code that looks like the following (where the ellipses ("...") indicate any other attributes):

```
<frame name="main" src="<%=pgMain%>" ...>
```

The <%...%> tags mark a block of server-side scripting code. The equal sign is a shortcut notation that means, "Write the following expression into the HTML sent to the browser." The expression *pgMain* is automatically an ASP variable because it isn't anything else (such as a reserved word, function name, or built-in constant).

6 Add the following code to the *<head>* section of the frames page. To avoid disturbing any other tags in the *<head>* section, put the code either just after the *<head>* tag or just before the *</head>* tag:

```
<%
If request("main") = "" Then
  pgMain = "intropet.htm"
Else
  pgMain = request("main")
End If
%>
```

The expression *request("main")* retrieves the value of any form fields or query string values named *main* that arrived with the Web visitor's request:

■ The form field, for example, could be a drop-down list named *main* that contained a list of permissible locations.

■ The query string value is a *name=value* pair appended to the URL as shown in the following code. The example specifies two query string values, *main* and *menu*. Note that a question mark marks the beginning of the first name=value pair but that an ampersand marks the beginning of all others:

```
pet.asp?main=introanimal.htm&menu=menuanimal.htm
```

In order for the menu specification to work, you must make the same sort of changes to the menu frame that the preceding text described for the main page.

The original five lines of code in this step should now be easy to understand. If the visitor's request contains a *main* value, that value becomes the default target of the *main* frame. If it doesn't, the code sets the default target to *intropet.htm*.

7 Save the page and then test it. To test the code in step 6, for example, you should verify that the URL

http://<yourserver>/<yourpathj>/pet.asp

displays the *intropet.htm* page in the *main* frame and that the URL

http://<yourserver>/<yourpathj>/pet.asp?main=introveggie.htm

displays the *intropet.htm* page in the *main* frame.

The *ch17/scripting/pet.asp* page in the sample Web modifies two target frames this way: the *menu* frame and the *main* frame. In each case, a *<%=variable%>* expression replaces the normal target frame URL, and five lines of script code like those in step 5 copy a visitor-specified or default URL into that value.

One disadvantage of using an ASP page is that the Page view editing window no longer displays target pages for the modified frames, as shown in Figure 17-10 on the next page. This situation occurs because Page view doesn't execute ASP code, and therefore lacks a proper target URL. This is an inconvenience, although not a serious one if you develop the frames page and default page first, and subsequently incorporate the ASP modifications.

Because the technique that this section describes uses Active Server Pages, it requires that you use a Microsoft Web server, that the folder or folder tree that contains the ASP page be marked as executable, and that you load the page into the browser using an HTTP URL and *not* a disk location. Loading an ASP page directly from disk into a

Chapter 17

browser doesn't execute any server-side code because a Web server isn't performing the delivery.

> For more information about Active Server Pages, refer to "Processing Form Data with ASP Pages" on page 910 and "Server-Side Scripting" on page 55.

 For more information about Active Server Pages, refer to, "Introducing Active Server Page Objects" in the Bonus Content on the Companion CD.

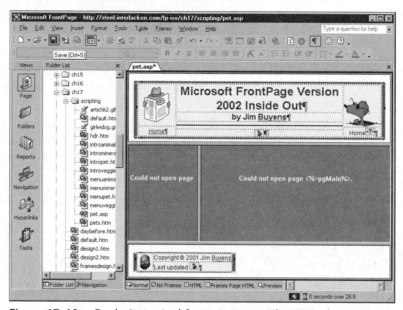

Figure 17-10. Replacing actual frame targets with ASP code prevents FrontPage from displaying a default target in WYSIWYG mode.

Reloading a Stand-Alone Page with a Frames Page

Some Web visitors, desperate to create shortcuts that point somewhere inside a frame-based site, right-click an interesting frame, display the Properties dialog box, copy the URL, and paste it into a shortcut on their Favorites menu or desktop. Of course, when they later use the shortcut, they see only the content page and not the entire frame lay-out. This often leaves visitors with no access to the rest of the Web. A similar situation occurs when an Internet search engine sends visitors to one of your content frames.

To resolve this problem, a page would have to somehow determine that it had been caught in public without its frames page and immediately tell the browser to load the proper frames page. (Of course, the frames page should appear with the current page, rather than the default page, displayed in the appropriate frame.)

> For more information about viewing a frames page with the desired target page, refer to "Loading a Frames Page with Non-Default Targets" earlier in this chapter.

As it turns out, there are at least two ways that a script running in a Web page can determine whether that page appears solely in the browser window or as part of a frame layout:

- The script can compare *document.location* (which contains the URL of the current Web page) to *window.top.location* (which contains the URL of the top-level page displayed in the browser window).

  If these values are equal, the current page is the top-level page and therefore occupies the entire browser window. No frames page is active. (This assumes, of course, that the script is running in a content page and not in the frames page itself.)

  If the values are different, the current page is on display but some other page controls the browser window as a whole. In other words, the current page is appearing as part of a frames layout.

- The script can evaluate the expression *window.parent.frames.length,* which returns the number of frames currently on display in the main browser window. If this value is zero, the window isn't displaying a frames page. If the value is nonzero, the value indicates the number of frames in the current layout.

The message in the center of the main frame in Figure 17-8 reflects both of these techniques. A script in the *intropet.htm* page, which in the figure occupies the *main* frame, compares *document.location* to *window.top.location*:

- If these values are equal, the script writes: "I'm the top dog. There are."
- If not, the script writes: "BTW, I'm in a frameset that has."

The script then displays the value of *window.parent.frames.length* and the word *frames.* Displaying the *intropet.htm* page in and out of a frameset thus produces two different results, proving that the page can determine its environment.

To summarize, each content page needs to contain a small script that determines whether or not the page currently appears within a frame. If it does appear within a frame, great, end of story. If it doesn't, it needs to reload the main window with the proper frameset using the technique described in the previous section (titled "Loading a Frames Page with Non-Default Targets") to make the current page appear in the proper window. Here's the script: five lines of code, including three that don't count:

```
<script>
if (document.location == window.top.location) {
  window.location = "pet.asp?menu=menupet.htm&main=intropet.htm";
}
</script>
```

525

If *document.location* equals *window.top.location,* the current page isn't in a frames layout. The script therefore changes the main window location to the URL of the *pet.asp* page, specifying the proper targets for the *menu* and *main* frames.

As explained thus far, the approach described in this section requires that you modify the script to specify proper target locations for each page that uses it. If you're good at scripting and willing to adopt some naming conventions, however, you could write code that inspects the *document.location* value (that is, the URL of the current page), and thereby determines the proper targets for the *menu* and *main* frames. This means you could insert exactly the same script in every page that appears within a given frames page. And, to ease both deployment and maintenance, you could replicate that script to every required page by means of an Include Page or Shared Borders component.

> For more information about the Include Page and Shared Borders features of FrontPage, refer to Chapter 26, "Organizing Reusable Web Content."

Helping Visitors Set Up Shortcuts

Another problem that occurs when using frames is that when Web visitors set up Internet shortcuts on their Favorites menu (that is, when they *bookmark* a page), the bookmark always points to the frames page and not to the combination of target pages on display. Although the most capable and determined visitors can dig out the URL of an interesting frame and bookmark it manually, this is no technique for the masses.

Microsoft Internet Explorer, in version 5 and later, has a script function that can help. Here's the syntax:

```
window.external.addFavorite(<URL>,<description>)
```

Executing this statement displays the Add Favorite dialog box shown in the foreground of Figure 17-11. Clicking the Add To Favorites hyperlink displayed in the foreground of the figure brought up the dialog box, which, although it doesn't appear visually, targets the page location specified in the script code.

> **note** You can't add shortcuts to your site without obtaining interactive approval from the Web visitor.

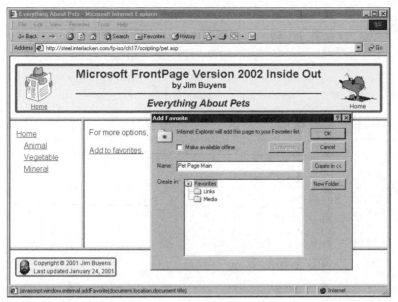

Figure 17-11. Clicking the Add To Favorites hyperlink displays the Add Favorite dialog box shown here.

When the visitor later selects the shortcut, the target page will notice that it's not surrounded by the proper frames page. It'll therefore use the technique described in the previous section (titled "Reloading a Stand-Alone Page with a Frames Page") to load the frames page, taking care to display the original target page in the proper frame.

The only drawback is that Netscape Navigator, at least through version 4, doesn't support the *window.external.addFavorite* statement. Depending on the exact version, Netscape either displays an error message or does nothing when a script tries to use this feature. Therefore, the hyperlink that invokes it should appear only for visitors using Internet Explorer.

Fortunately, both Internet Explorer and Netscape Navigator identify themselves by a string contained in the property *navigator.appName*. Internet Explorer provides the following value:

```
Microsoft Internet Explorer
```

and Netscape provides the following value:

```
Netscape
```

The following code therefore writes a paragraph containing the phrase "Add to favorites" only if the browser is Internet Explorer (The method *substring(0,9)* returns the first nine characters of a string):

```
if (navigator.appName.substring(0,9) == "Microsoft"){
    document.write("<p>Add to favorites.</p>")
}
```

Surrounding the "Add to favorites" text with a hyperlink that runs the *window.external.addFavorite* method results in the following code:

```
if (navigator.appName.substring(0,9) == "Microsoft"){
    document.write("<p><a href='" +
        "javascript:window.external.addFavorite" +
        "(document.location,document.title)'>" +
        "Add to favorites.</a></p>")
}
```

Notice that this code passes the *window.external.addFavorite* method a URL of *document.location* and a shortcut description of *document.title*. The *document.location* property always contains the URL of the current Web page and the *document.title* property always contains the text you assign that page in the Title box of the Page Properties dialog box. Using these properties rather than hard-coded values means you can insert the script in any page you like without modifying it. Just make sure you assign each page a meaningful title; otherwise your visitors will end up with shortcuts to pages like New Page 2.

You can use HTML view to insert this code, surrounded by *<script>* and *</script>* tags, anywhere on a Web page you want an Add To Favorites hyperlink to appear. After returning to Normal view, you can drag its JavaScript icon to different locations on the page, and you can even copy it and then paste it into other pages. To view the code and make corrections, either double-click the JavaScript icon or return to HTML view.

Assessing Frames

The scripting techniques described in this section provide elegant and relatively simple solutions to real-world problems. At the same time, they clearly illustrate some of the disadvantages of using frames. If frames themselves were a simple and elegant solution, none of this scripting would be necessary.

Before you launch into designing a frames-based site, consider whether a Navigation view site that used shared borders instead of frames might not provide results that are just as easy to use and clearly easier to maintain.

For more information about shared borders, refer to "Using Shared Borders" on page 765.

newfeature!
Using Inline Frames

Creating an inline frame in FrontPage is a simple process. Inline frames are inserted into a page much like any other element, such as an image. To create an inline frame:

1 Place the insertion point where you would like to insert the inline frame.

2 Select Inline Frame from the Insert menu. This creates a new inline frame as shown in figure 17-12.

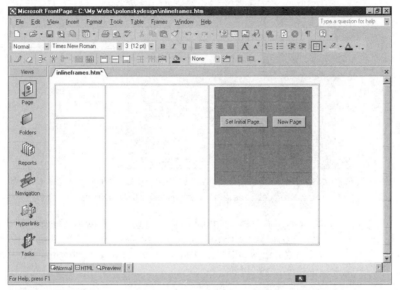

Figure 17-12. FrontPage inserts an inline frame just as it would any other frame. The page shown shows a new inline frame inserted into an existing table.

An inline frame behaves exactly like a frame in an ordinary frames page. Either set an initial page or create a new page by selecting the appropriate button.

Modifying the Properties of an Inline Frame

As with many of the elements you add to a page, inserting an inline frame consumes much less time than modifying it, both initially and over time. Here's how to perform some common operations:

To modify an inline frame's settings, use the Inline Frame Properties dialog box:

1 Select the inline frame by moving the mouse pointer to the top of the frame border and then clicking when the pointer changes to an arrow.

2 With the frame selected, either select Properties from the Format menu, double-click the frame or frame border, or right-click the frame border

Chapter 17

529

and select Inline Frame Properties. The Inline Frame Properties dialog box appears, as shown in Figure 17-13:

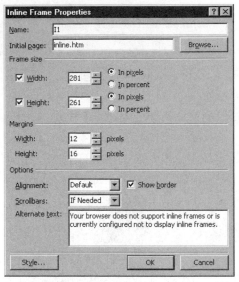

Figure 17-13. The Inline Frame Properties dialog box controls the name, size, and other settings pertinent to an inline frame.

- Specify the Name, Initial Page, Frame Size, and Margins the same as you would for a regular frame. The section, "Creating and Modifying Frames Pages with FrontPage," earlier in this chapter provides information about these features

- In the Options section, you can set the alignment of the frame relative to its position on the page. Because a visitor's browser might not support inline frames, consider using the default, Alternate Text option.

The procedure for resizing an inline frame is quite simple:

1 Click one of its handles.

2 Drag the frame to the appropriate size.

Figure 17-14 shows a Web page containing an inline frame as it appears in a browser.

> **note** Not all browsers support the use of inline frames. Netscape Navigator, at least through version 4, is a notable case in point. If the browser can't display an inline frame, it ignores it and the information in the frame simply doesn't appear. Certain browsers might also display an error message. If a visitor clicks a hyperlink intended to reload an inline frame, a non-compliant browser will open the target page in a full browser window.

The inline frame in Figure 17-14 appears within a table cell. This provides more control over its position on the page and over its background coloring.

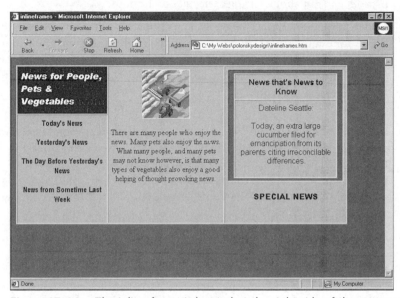

Figure 17-14. The inline frame is located at the right side of the screen with the heading *News that's News to Know*.

Design Tips: Using Frames

Although initially very popular among Web developers, the use of frames has dropped off recently. Designers were intrigued with the idea of being able to display the contents of more than one page at a time to their visitors. Having the ability to show all the navigational links, for example, was at one time thought to be great Web site architecture. Lately, that thinking has changed.

A designer should decide in the beginning stages of any new Web development endeavor whether or not to use frames. To make the best choice possible, it's important to understand the limitations of frames as well as their usability issues. A choice to use frames warrants careful consideration of their impact on the visitor's experience of the Web site.

Problems Using Frames

Below is a list of some problems associated with the use of frames. Keep these issues in mind when deciding how and when to use frames:

- **Reduced viewable screen area.** Keeping the contents of certain pages displayed at all times, such as menu pages in a navigation frame, reduces the main content area. This gives the visitor less screen space to see the page information. For most visitors, going to a Web site is about getting information, and not about staring at navigation buttons.

● **Misleading expectations.** When visitors click a navigation button within a frame, for example, new content is generally displayed within a new frame, and the navigation frame remains. When a visitor clicks a hyperlink located within a content frame, typically the content area changes. These two different results are potentially confusing to visitors as their expectations of "What happens when I click a link?" varies from frame to frame.

● **Inability to bookmark a page.** When a visitor displays a frames page, two or more Web pages are shown in the browser at the same time, but only one URL is listed in the address bar of the visitor's browser. If visitors travel through a frames site and comes across a page that they would like to bookmark, they can mark only the frames page URL, and not the specific page of content they're interested in.

● **Difficulty printing a frames page.** If a frames site is created with a navigation frame, the chances are that visitors are clicking only in that frame. When a visitor clicks in a frame, that frame becomes the active frame. If the visitor attempts to print the site, only the active page is printed, and as such, most visitors end up printing just the navigation buttons.

Many of the latest browsers have a way for visitors to distinguish which frame they would like to print from within the Print dialog box, but they must make an additional selection for that process to work. Unfortunately, that printing option is not available if visitors select the Print button on the browser's menu bar.

● **Slower download speed.** When creating a frames site, a designer must obviously create frames pages that tell browsers how to display the target pages. This means the browser must display one more than the total number of visible pages. This, in turn, means that displaying the pages correctly requires one more trip back to the Web server. Of course, each additional trip to the Web server takes time, potentially slowing down the display of the pages.

● **Limited search engine indexing.** Most designers would like the sites they create to be found and indexed by Web search engines. Unfortunately, many search engines have trouble finding the pages of frames-based sites.

Most search engines go to the *index.htm,* or home page, of a Web site and read its contents. When the search engine comes across a hyperlink, it follows that link and begins to read that Web page looking for its hyperlinks.

If a site uses frames, the search engine will go to the frames page looking for the links to the rest of the site, but those links are on a different page, not within the frames page. This type of setup can cause some search engines to look no further than the frames page, thus missing the full extent of the site.

● **Web visitor preference.** Another reason many designers avoid the use of frames is that many usability studies show that visitors simply don't like having to interact with them. When it comes to successful Web site design, meeting the visitor's needs and expectations, should always be a designer's highest priority.

In Summary...

This chapter explained how to create Web pages divided into frames. Frames divide the browser window into rectangular sections, each displaying a different Web page that hyperlinks can individually replace.

The next part of the book, "Formatting Your Web Pages," explains how to change the appearance of Web pages to convey the message you want.

Part 7

Formatting Your Web Pages

Chapter 18

Controlling Overall Page Appearance

Whenever you start working on a Web page—whether it's an existing page, a new blank page, or a page generated by a template or wizard—you no doubt have changes in mind that affect not only the page's content, but also its title, color scheme, and other general characteristics. Even for existing content, you might decide this is the time to standardize pages and apply uniform page attributes. This chapter explains how to make these kinds of page-level style changes.

Of the many attributes a Web page can have, color is probably the most striking and the most obvious. This chapter therefore concludes with some tips and things to keep in mind when designing color schemes.

Specifying Page-Level Attributes

Microsoft FrontPage provides the Page Properties dialog box to control the overall appearance of a page. To open the Page Properties dialog box, make sure you have a page open, and then take either of these actions:

- Choose Properties from the File menu.
- Right-click anywhere in the page's window and choose Page Properties from the shortcut menu.

The Page Properties dialog box has six tabs: General, Background, Margins, Custom, Language, and Workgroup. The next series of topics explains how to use the controls on each of these tabs.

General Page Properties

The General tab of the Page Properties dialog box appears in Figure 18-1. You should always specify a meaningful title, but use of the remaining elements is optional.

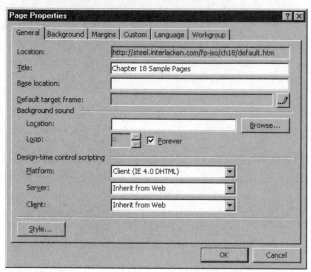

Figure 18-1. The General tab of the Page Properties dialog box controls a page's title and hyperlinking defaults.

The data options on the Page Properties General tab control the following characteristics:

- **Location.** This read-only box displays the Uniform Resource Locator of the current page—the URL a browser would use to retrieve it. If FrontPage opened the page from a file, a URL beginning with *file:///* appears. For new pages not yet saved, the location is *unsaved:///new_page_<#>.htm*.

- **Title.** Enter the name of the page in words. This is an often-overlooked but important attribute; it appears in many FrontPage windows and dialog boxes, as a page description in search results, and in the title bars of your visitors' browsers. Be certain that every page you maintain has a meaningful title suitable for public display.

- **Base Location.** Use of this box is rare, and you should normally leave it blank. For an explanation of its use, see the sidebar "Relative Addressing and Base URLs" later in this chapter.

Chapter 18: Controlling Overall Page Appearance

- **Default Target Frame.** Specify the name of the frame that clicking most hyperlinks on the current page should update. (This box applies only to pages that appear within frames pages).

Change
Target
Frame

Suppose, for example, that you want most hyperlinks on the current page to update a frame named *main*. To avoid coding a target frame on each hyperlink, you could code the frame name *main* in this box.

To update this box, click the accompanying Change Target Frame button.

> For information on using frames, refer to "Creating and Editing Frames" on page 506.

- **Background Sound.** These three options select and control a sound file that the visitor's browser will play when it displays your page:

    - **Location.** Enter the name of the sound file. This can be a local file or a URL. To browse the local file system or current Web, click the Browse button.

    - **Loop.** Enter the number of times the specified file should play.

    - **Forever.** Select this check box to have the sound file play indefinitely. This overrides the Loop setting.

> **tip** Avoid specifying large sound files or files in platform-specific formats. In general, MIDI files are the smallest and most widely supported.

- **Design-Time Control Scripting.** These drop-down lists control the actions of design-time controls, a type of ActiveX control that can supply FrontPage with additional editing and HTML-generation features. Use of these lists is very rare:

    - **Platform.** Specify where scripting should occur—Client or Server.

    - **Server.** Specify the language design-time controls should use for server-side scripting: JavaScript, VBScript, or the Inherit From Web default setting.

    - **Client.** Specify the language design-time controls should use for browser-side scripting: JavaScript, VBScript, or the Inherit From Web default setting.

- **Style.** Click this button to open the Modify Style dialog box, which specifies CSS information for the body of the current page.

> For information about cascading style sheets, refer to Chapter 20, "Managing Appearance with Cascading Style Sheets."

Chapter 18

539

Relative Addressing and Base URLs

Hyperlinks on Web pages needn't reference complete URLs. If a hyperlink doesn't include a host name, a browser uses the host that delivered the current page. If a hyperlink also contains no folder location, the browser uses the same folder as the current page. This is called relative addressing because hyperlink locations are relative to the current page unless a full and explicit path is included. Below are two examples:

Current Page:	*http://www.interlacken.com/info/default.htm*
Hyperlink:	*/products/toasters.htm*
Jump Location:	*http://www.interlacken.com/products/toasters.htm*

Current Page:	*http://www.interlacken.com/info/default.htm*
Hyperlink:	*contact.htm*
Jump Location:	*http://www.interlacken.com/info/contact.htm*

In general, it's best to use relative addressing wherever possible. This makes it very easy to move groups of pages from one Web server or folder to another. By contrast, specifying complete URLs means updating them whenever you move pages from one computer or Web to another.

Occasionally, you may find it convenient to base relative URLs not on the current page but on some other location. Specifying a base URL accomplishes this as follows:

Current Page:	*http://www.interlacken.com/info/default.htm*
Base URL:	*http://www.microsoft.com/info/*
Hyperlink:	*contact.htm*
Jump Location:	*http://www.microsoft.com/info/contact.htm*

Background Page Properties

Figure 18-2 illustrates the Background tab of the Page Properties dialog box. It controls most aspects of the page's overall color scheme:

- **Background Picture.** Select this check box if you want the page to have a background picture. The associated text box specifies the location of the picture file. Rather than typing the file location, you can click the Browse button to locate it.

note The Background tab doesn't appear on the Page Properties dialog box for any page controlled by a theme. The theme takes over these attributes.

Chapter 18: Controlling Overall Page Appearance

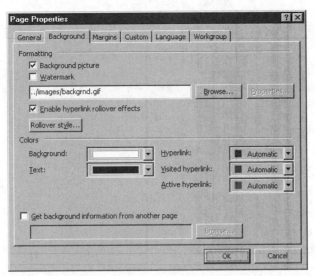

Figure 18-2. The Background tab of the Page Properties dialog box controls a page's overall color scheme.

---

tip You can also access the Background tab by choosing Background from the Format menu.

- **Watermark.** Select this box if, when the Web visitor operates the browser's scroll bars, you want the background picture to remain fixed and not scroll with other content on the page.

  Microsoft Internet Explorer supports this feature, but other browsers might not. FrontPage itself doesn't exhibit the watermark behavior; it scrolls the background picture even though watermarking is in effect. To see watermarking in action, browse the page with Internet Explorer.

- **Properties.** Click this button, when it's available, to display a Picture Properties dialog box that displays or alters the properties of the specified background picture.

For an explanation of the Picture Properties dialog box, refer to "Modifying Picture Properties" on page 337.

- **Enable Hyperlink Rollover Effects.** Select this check box if you want text hyperlinks in this page to change appearance when the mouse passes over them.

Using Background Pictures in Your Pages

A background picture appears behind any other pictures or text on the page. If the picture is smaller than the page, the browser repeats it left to right and top to bottom. With this "tiling" behavior, a small picture, which is fast to download, can fill the entire screen.

To keep the background picture from repeating left to right, make it wider than any typical computer screen display. A width of 1200 pixels is usually sufficient. Most picture editors have features called Add Margin or Extend Canvas that can widen pictures this way. Fill the added pixels with your background color, or make them transparent. Repeating pixels of the same color compress very well and add little to file size and download time.

Wide pictures of this kind are often used to create border designs along the left margin. The design occupies the leftmost 20 or 30 pixels, and the rest of the picture is either a solid color or transparent.

Avoid strong colors or patterns in background pictures. These can easily obscure your text.

- **Rollover Style.** Click this button to specify how text hyperlinks in this page should appear when the mouse passes over them. Clicking the button displays a Font dialog box like the one shown in Figure 10-20. This button is disabled unless the Enable Hyperlink Rollover Effects box is checked.

- **Background.** Use this setting to control the page's background color. This color appears if there's no background picture, if any part of the background picture is transparent, or if the browser is ready to start displaying the page before the background picture arrives.

> For instructions on using this and other FrontPage color controls, skip ahead to the section titled "Using FrontPage Color Dialog Boxes" later in this chapter.

- **Text.** Use this setting to control the color of ordinary text.

- **Hyperlink.** Use this setting to control the color of hyperlinked text.

- **Visited Hyperlink.** Use this setting to control the color of hyperlinked text whose target has recently been visited. The text reverts to hyperlink color when its target is cleared from the browser's cache on the visitor's computer.

- **Active Hyperlink.** Use this setting to control the color of hyperlinked text at the time the visitor clicks the link.

Chapter 18: Controlling Overall Page Appearance

● **Get Background Information From Another Page.** Select this check box
if you want the current page to inherit its color scheme from a different
page. Enter that page's location in the accompanying text box or use the
Browse button to locate it.

Selecting this check box dims all the other controls on the Background
tab except Enable Hyperlink Rollover Effects.

Margin Page Properties

The Margins tab of the Page Properties dialog box controls the *x-y* coordinates
of the first object displayed on the page, measured from the upper left corner.
This tab appears in Figure 18-3.

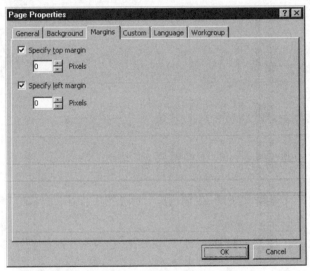

Figure 18-3. The Margins tab controls the top and left margins of a Web page.

Here are the actions you can take from the Margins tab:

● To specify the top margin for a Web page, select the Specify Top Margin
check box and enter the number of pixels.

● To specify the left margin for a Web page, select the Specify Left Margin
check box and enter the number of pixels.

Figure 18-4 on the next page shows how a Web page set to 0 top and left margins appears in the following three applications.

Note the amount of space between the window border and the corner pictures:

- Netscape Navigator, at least through version 4, honors different margin commands than Internet Explorer. Netscape therefore ignores any margin settings you specify in FrontPage and displays its default margins instead.

- Internet Explorer 4 or later correctly displays margins you specify in FrontPage.

- FrontPage displays the top and left margins correctly, but displays a default right margin. This is a bug-like feature carried over from FrontPage 2000.

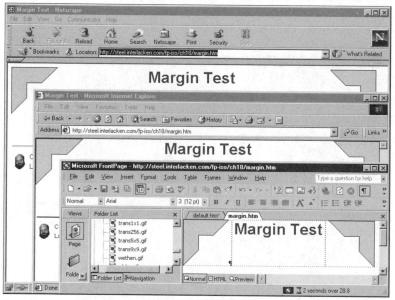

Figure 18-4. FrontPage and Internet Explorer 4 or later display a page with 0 top and left margins. Netscape Navigator 4 and earlier ignores this method of setting margins.

Custom Page Properties

Figure 18-5 displays the Custom tab of the Page Properties dialog box, which maintains two categories of variables. System variables are those defined as official HTTP headers, while user variables are any others you wish to specify. In Figure 18-5:

- The REFRESH system variable tells the Web visitor's browser to wait 10 seconds after displaying the current page and then jump to another page.

- The PICS-Label system variable characterizes the content of a Web page, folder, or entire site regarding violence, nudity, sex, and language.

- The GENERATOR user variable identifies the software that created this Web page. FrontPage supplies this information automatically.

Chapter 18: Controlling Overall Page Appearance

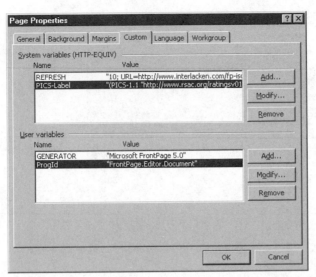

Figure 18-5. The Custom tab specifies HTTP header field equivalents and user variables. These appear in the <head> section of a page's HTML code.

● The ProgId user variable identifies the specific program that created the current page. This is another item that FrontPage supplies automatically.

To add a variable, click the appropriate Add button and then type the variable name and its initial value into the dialog box shown in Figure 18-6.

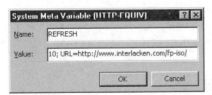

Figure 18-6. This dialog box adds a variable to the System Variables list shown in Figure 18-5.

To change the value of a variable, select the variable, click the Modify button, and replace the value. To delete a variable, select it and then click Delete.

> For information on system variables, refer to "Configuring HTML Header Properties" later in this chapter.

Language Page Properties

Figure 18-7 on the next page displays the Language tab, which controls the HTML character encoding for the current page (that is, the international character set).

 For more information on HTML encoding, refer to "Reviewing Web Settings" in the Bonus Content on the Companion CD.

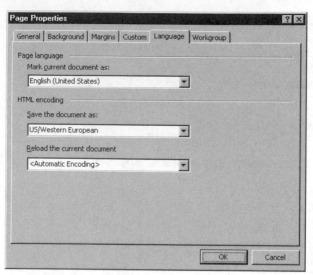

Figure 18-7. The Language tab of the Page Properties dialog box controls national language usage.

The choices available depend on the languages installed with your copy of FrontPage:

● **Mark Current Document As.** Specify the default language FrontPage should use when checking spelling. The default is the default language for your computer.

To mark part of a page as being in a different language, first select it in Page view, and then choose Set Language from the Tools menu. Select the language you want from the Set Language dialog box shown in Figure 18-8, and then click OK.

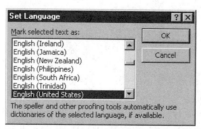

Figure 18-8. This dialog box marks the national language of a selected portion of text.

● **Save The Document As.** Select the character set FrontPage should use for saving the current page. The default comes from the Language tab of the Web Settings dialog box. To display the Web Settings dialog box, choose Web Settings from the Tools menu.

 For more information about the Web Settings dialog box, refer to "Reviewing Web Settings" in the Bonus Content on the Companion CD.

● **Reload The Current Document.** Select the character set a browser should use to display the current page. The default is <Automatic Encoding>, which lets the browser make this decision.

Workgroup Page Properties

The Workgroup tab of the Page Properties dialog box appears in Figure 18-9.

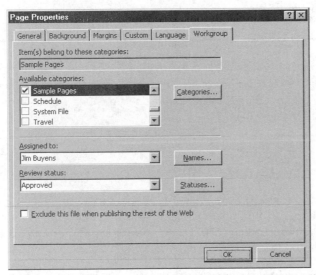

Figure 18-9. The Workgroup tab provides access to options that track a page's progress within a shared development environment.

This group of settings records and controls workgroup progress for developing the current page:

● **Item(s) Belong To These Categories.** This read-only box displays a list of categories assigned to the current Web page. Use the Available Categories list to modify this information.

● **Available Categories.** Check each listed category to which the current page belongs. Click the Categories button to modify the list of categories.

This setting works in concert with any Table Of Contents Based On Page Category components on other pages in the same FrontPage-based Web.

For more information about the Table Of Contents Based On Page Category component, refer to "Using the Table of Contents Based On Page Category Component" on page 776.

● **Assigned To.** Type or select the name of the person assigned to this page. To update the selection list, click the Names button.

● **Review Status.** Type or select the current review status for this page. To update the selection list, click the Statuses button.

- **Exclude This File When Publishing The Rest Of The Web.** When you publish the current Web to another location, any pages with this check box selected won't be transferred. This might be desirable for work in progress.

Configuring HTML Header Properties

This section describes a number of additional properties and features you can configure for pages in your Web.

InsideOut

Unfortunately, FrontPage provides no convenient check boxes or drop-down lists to control the highly useful settings described in this section. One way or another, you have to configure them by hand.

Using the REFRESH System Variable

The REFRESH system variable shown in Figure 18-6 is a very useful one. It instructs the browser to wait a specified number of seconds—10 in the example—and then automatically jump to the specified URL. This is how some sites introduce themselves with a timed series of pages.

Another use for the REFRESH system variable occurs when you move a popular page to another location. Then, in its old location, you might leave a blank or informative page containing a REFRESH system variable that automatically jumps visitors to the new location. Here are two tips for using this feature:

- An informative page should display long enough for the visitor to read at least the most important parts.

- If you decide to use a blank page, set the delay for one or two seconds. Setting the delay to 0 interferes with the Back button on your Web visitor's browser; the instant the visitor clicks the Back button, your REFRESH page kicks the view forward again.

Rating Your Web's Content

The Internet Content Rating Association (ICRA) has established a scheme whereby you can rate your Web's content in four categories: violence, nudity, sex, and language. Web visitors can configure their browsers to display warnings or block access to sites that exceed a given level of content in the four supported categories. Here are some reasons to categorize your Web this way:

- To be a good Internet citizen.

Chapter 18: Controlling Overall Page Appearance

- To permit access by visitors who block unrated sites.

- To protect yourself from complaints by visitors offended by your content.

To use the ICRA system you must complete a simple registration process. Here's the complete procedure for rating your site:

1 Browse the Internet Content Rating Association's Web site at *http://www.icra.org.*

2 Follow the Label Your Web Site Here link on the home page, and complete the rating process.

3 When this process is complete, the final Web page will contain a long string of characters you should add to your Web page. (You will also receive an e-mail message containing this string.) Copy this string to the Clipboard by selecting it and then pressing Ctrl+C.

4 Use FrontPage to open the Web page you want to rate.

5 Click the HTML tab at the bottom of the editing window.

6 Locate the *<head>* tag. This tag occupies one of the first few lines in the Web page.

7 Set the insertion point immediately after the closing ">" character in *<head>*.

8 Press Ctrl+V or Shift+Insert to paste the text you copied in step 3.

9 Click the Normal tab to resume editing.

Providing Information for Search Engines

Some additional system variables appear below. The large Internet search engines (such as Yahoo!, Lycos, and AltaVista) use these variables to improve the accuracy of their search results. To code any of these keywords for your Web page:

1 In the Page Properties box, display the Custom tab.

2 Click the Add button in the System Variables (HTTP-EQUIV) portion shown in Figure 18-5. This displays the System Meta Variable (HTTP-EQUIV) dialog box shown in Figure 18-6.

3 Choose an identifier from the first bulleted list below, and then enter it in the Name box.

4 Choose a value from the second bulleted list below, and then enter it in the Value box. Click OK.

You may wish to enter some of these identifiers (such as Copyright) for legal reasons:

- **Copyright.** Any copyright statement.

- **Description.** A sentence that describes the page's content.

- **Distribution.** One of two words: *global* or *local*. Local indicates pages of little or no interest to visitors outside a Web site's own organization.

- **Expires.** A date after which the page will no longer be relevant. Use this format:

    Tue, 02 Dec 2005 21:29:02 GMT

- **Keywords.** Likely search terms a prospective visitor might enter. Separate multiple keywords with commas.

- **Robots.** Instructions to control the actions of Web search "robots," such as the large search engines. Compliance is voluntary; some searching robots honor these commands, and some don't. To code this setting, enter *Robots* in the Name box. In the Value box, enter one or more of the following keywords, separated by commas:

    - **None.** Tells robots to ignore this page. This is equivalent to Noindex, Nofollow.

    - **All.** Indicates that there are no restrictions on indexing this page or pages referenced in its hyperlinks. This is equivalent to Index, Follow.

    - **Index.** Welcomes all robots to include this page in search results.

    - **Noindex.** Asks robots not to add this page to indexes.

    - **Follow.** Allows robots to follow hyperlinks from this page to other pages.

    - **Nofollow.** Asks robots not to follow hyperlinks from this page.

---

on the web   For more information about the Robot Exclusion Standard, browse *http://www.kollar.com/robots.html.*

Making an Icon Appear in the Favorites List

As you may have noticed, a custom icon identifies certain Web sites that you add to the Favorites list in Internet Explorer. These icons give a site additional visibility and encourage past visitors to browse your Web again. There are two ways to make such icons appear:

- Place an icon file named *favicon.ico* in your Web server's root folder. For example, put the file at *http://www.interlacken.com/favicon.ico.*

When the visitor adds any page from your server to his or her Favorites, your icon will appear next to the link in both the Favorites menu and the Favorites pane (which appears at the left side of the browser).

● If you don't have access to your Web server's root folder or want certain pages to display a different icon, add a tag such as the following to the *<head>* section of the Web page:

```
<link rel="shortcut icon" href="/fp-iso/iconjjb.ico">
```

This is a line of code you'll need to insert by hand. Switch to HTML view, and enter it just after the *<head>* tag or just before the *</head>* tag.

This technique adds an icon that behaves just as in the first method, but only for the Web page that contains the tag.

There are two restrictions to the use of such icons. First, they work only with Internet Explorer 5.0 and above. All other browsers ignore them. Second, the icon must be exactly 16 x 16 pixels in size and be in Windows icon file format. Files in this format usually have a filename extension of *.ico*.

If you don't have a graphics editor that creates *.ico* files 16 x 16 pixels in size, try Axialis AX-Icons. You can download and purchase this software from *http://www.axialis.com /order/index.html.*

Understanding RGB Color Values

The proper combination of red, green, and blue light can perfectly simulate any color humans can perceive. Computer video equipment leverages this effect to display color pictures. For each pixel (picture element) on the monitor screen, the application specifies the desired amount of red, green, and blue light. Most video equipment provides 256 intensities of red light, 256 of green, and 256 of blue. This produces 16,777,216 combinations, which is more colors than the eye can discern.

The Red, Green, Blue (RGB) system of color values describes colors just as video cards and monitors do: as three color intensities, each ranging from 0 to 255. Here are some examples:

● The RGB color 255-0-0 means pure, maximum-intensity red.

● 0-0-255 means pure, maximum-intensity blue.

● 0-0-0 means black.

● 255-255-255 means white.

Some HTML statements require RGB values coded as hexadecimal numbers. In this notation, the value 00 means none of a color and FF means maximum intensity. The color #00FF00 means no red, maximum green, and no blue. The leading pound sign indicates that what follows is hexadecimal.

> **tip** If you're not good at doing hexadecimal conversions in your head, use the Scientific mode of the Windows Calculator accessory. This mode has Hex and Dec options that toggle the calculator between these two number systems.

Using FrontPage Color Dialog Boxes

FrontPage provides three levels of control over most color settings. To fully exploit the use of color in your Web pages, you need to understand all three levels. They are as follows:

- A drop-down list with these choices: Automatic, the 16 original VGA colors, any other colors that already appear in the current page, and Custom.

- A second dialog box with 127 color swatches, 6 grayscale swatches, a black swatch, a white swatch, and a button for "picking up" any color currently displayed on screen.

- The standard Windows color picker with 48 basic color swatches, 16 configurable color swatches, and controls for specifying exact colors two different ways: via the Hue, Saturation, Luminance (HSL) color model and via the Red, Green, Blue color model.

Figure 18-10 shows the first level of detail, the drop-down list that appears when you click the arrow next to any color control in a FrontPage dialog box. The Automatic choice normally means a color configured in the visitor's browser. Clicking any of the 16 color swatches arranged in two rows selects that color. To see the name of any color, let the mouse pointer rest over it.

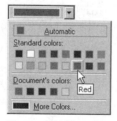

Figure 18-10. Most color choices in FrontPage begin by offering this drop-down menu.

It's usually best to choose Web colors with RGB components of 0, 51, 102, 153, 204, and 255. These are the so-called "safe" colors that even 256-color display systems can display accurately. Unfortunately, as illustrated in Table 18-1, only 8 of the 16 drop-down swatches comply with this advice.

> For information on "safe" colors, refer to "Achieving Accurate Rendition—Safe Colors" later in this chapter.

Chapter 18: Controlling Overall Page Appearance

Table 18-1. **Colors in the 16-Color VGA Palette**

Safe colors					Unsafe colors				
Standard name	FrontPage name	Color values			Standard name	FrontPage name	Color values		
		R	G	B			R	G	B
Black	Black	0	0	0	Gray	Gray	128	128	128
White	White	255	255	255	Light Gray	Silver	192	192	192
Red	Red	255	0	0	Dark Red	Maroon	128	0	0
Green	Lime	0	255	0	Dark Green	Green	0	128	0
Blue	Blue	0	0	255	Dark Blue	Navy	0	0	128
Cyan	Aqua	0	255	255	Dark Cyan	Teal	0	128	128
Magenta	Fuchsia	255	0	255	Dark Magenta	Purple	128	0	128
Yellow	Yellow	255	255	0	Dark Yellow	Olive	128	128	0

Even the eight compliant colors are rather boring: black, white, the three primaries, and their complements. These are wonderful colors and, used properly, they provide plenty of contrast. However, they're hardly intriguing. You'll produce more subtle and interesting Web pages by choosing custom colors with safe RGB components. To do so, click the More Colors choice and examine the More Colors dialog box shown in Figure 18-11.

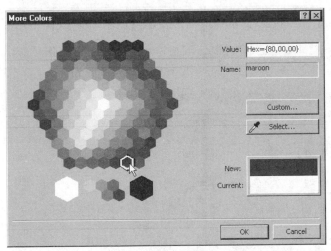

Figure 18-11. You can select any color shown in this dialog box simply by clicking the corresponding swatch. In addition, after clicking the Select button, you can use the mouse to pick up any color currently displayed on your screen.

InsideOut

To their detriment, the FrontPage and Windows dialog boxes for picking colors both carry a lot of historical baggage. Both make it difficult, for example, to lighten, darken, or wash out colors without changing their hue. And neither has any facility for choosing combinations of colors. Oh well, maybe next release.

The large hexagon in Figure 18-11 is actually a color wheel with red at five o'clock, green at nine o'clock, and blue at one o'clock. Dark shades occupy the edges, light tints occupy the center, and saturated colors lie in between. Below the color wheel are a white swatch, a black swatch and, between them, six grayscale swatches.

A safe-color version of the More Colors dialog box would have black, white, 4 shades of gray, and 210 colors. Instead, the box has 6 shades of gray and 127 colors, and some of each are unsafe. Rather than optimizing this feature with browser-safe colors, the FrontPage designers made it resemble the comparable one in Microsoft PowerPoint.

Fortunately, most of the 127 color swatches *are* browser-safe. To verify the browser safety of any color, hold the mouse pointer over it and check the value displayed in the Value box. If any of the two-digit Hex values *aren't* 00, 33, 66, 99, CC, or FF, the color *isn't* browser-safe. The color selected in Figure 18-11, for example, fails the test.

To pick up a color already displayed on your screen, first click the Select button, causing the mouse pointer to become an eyedropper. Move the eyedropper over the color you want, anywhere on the screen, and then click the mouse button.

Clicking the More Colors dialog box's Custom button displays the third FrontPage color picker: the Color dialog box, which appears in Figure 18-12.

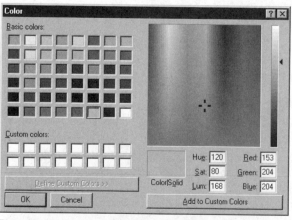

Figure 18-12. FrontPage's third color picker is the standard Windows Color dialog box.

Hue, Saturation, Luminance, and the Color Dialog Box

A large part of the standard Windows dialog box for color selection displays a continuous banded rectangle of colors you can choose by clicking. Figure 18-12 shows this dialog box. This banded rectangle, plus the slider bar just to its right, utilizes a color model called Hue, Saturation, Luminance (HSL).

Like RGB, HSL uses three numbers to denote each color. (Because the eye perceives color in three dimensions—red, green, and blue—most numerical color models use three dimensions as well.) Here's how the Color dialog box supports the HSL color scheme:

- The top edge of the banded rectangle represents a hue dimension that varies from 0 to 239. 0, at the right, means red; 80 means green; and 160 means blue. At 239, the scale wraps around to 0 (red) again.

  To select a hue, drag the crosshairs left and right within the banded rectangle, or type a number between 0 and 239 into the Hue text box.

- The vertical edge of the banded rectangle represents saturation. A saturation of 240, which is the top of the scale, means the color contains no gray. A saturation of 0, the bottom of the scale, means the color *is* gray. (Notice that the bottom of the banded rectangle is gray all across.)

  To select a saturation value, drag the crosshairs up or down within the banded rectangle, or type a number between 0 and 240 into the Sat text box.

- The slider at the right of the dialog box controls luminance. This dimension controls the brightness of gray referred to by saturation. The highest setting, 240, means white; 0 means black; and 120 produces the most vivid hue (no white or black added to the basic hue). Regardless of hue and saturation, the top of the slider is always pure white, and the bottom is pure black.

  To vary luminance, drag the slider up and down, or type a number between 0 and 240 into the Lum text box.

HSL's fascination with gray stems from its origins in the television industry. Luminance is the black-and-white portion of a television signal. The inventors of color television modified the black-and-white television signal, adding hue and saturation data in such a way that monochrome sets would ignore them.

Most Web designers find the HSL system more difficult to understand than RGB. However, it does provide a way to select colors visually, and its frequent appearance in Windows color dialog boxes makes learning it worthwhile.

The Color dialog box presents 48 standard color swatches (mostly unsafe), 16 configurable color swatches, and text boxes for specifying exact colors two different ways:

- Entering values of 0, 51, 102, 153, 204, and 255—and no others—into the Red, Green, and Blue text boxes at last provides access to all 216 browser-safe colors.

- Dragging the crosshairs around the large banded rectangle and moving the slider to its right chooses colors by means of a system called Hue, Saturation, Luminance (HSL). The sidebar titled "Hue, Saturation, Luminance, and the Color Dialog Box" provides more information about this system.

  After choosing a color by this means, you can correct it to the nearest safe color by rounding each of the red, green, and blue values to 0, 51, 102, 153, 204, or 255.

Achieving Accurate Rendition—Safe Colors

In the early days of the Web, display adapters capable of displaying all 16,777,216 combinations of red, green, and blue were both specialized and expensive. Most video cards of the time supported 16 fixed colors or 256 selectable colors at once. The 16-color display adapters had essentially no chance of displaying Web pages correctly and quickly passed out of use. The 256-color systems became the order of the day, and many of these systems are still in use.

> **note** A video card that contains 8 bits of memory for each pixel can display 2^8, or 256, colors at once. A video card that contains 24 bits of memory for each pixel can display 2^{24}, or 16,777,216, colors at once.

Nowadays, of course, video systems that display all 16,777,216 colors are common. They typically go by the name of 24-bit color, 32-bit color, or True Color. If you know that all your visitors—or at least the overwhelming majority of them—have such video cards, then you can use any colors you want and ignore the issue of safe colors. Otherwise, the safe choice is to optimize your color selections for visitors with 8-bit displays.

An 8-bit video card can display 16,777,216 different colors, but only 256 at once. This isn't a problem when displaying a single Graphics Interchange Format (GIF) picture, because most programs tell the video system to display the same 256 colors that appear in the picture. However, three problems arise when displaying pictures on a Web page:

- On most computers with 256-color displays, not all 256 colors are programmable. On Windows-based computers, for example, 20 colors are reserved for use by Windows so that window borders, menu bars,

Chapter 18: Controlling Overall Page Appearance

button faces, and other elements of the user interface maintain a consistent appearance. This leaves only 236 colors that can be adjusted to match those in a picture.

- Web pages can contain any number of GIF pictures. Each GIF picture can contain only 256 colors, but two pictures on the same page—if they have no colors in common—can require a total of 512. Three pictures can require 768 colors, and so forth. This presents a problem if the display hardware can accommodate only 256 colors in total.

- A single Joint Photographic Experts Group (JPEG) picture can contain far more than 256 colors: up to 16,777,216 (assuming the picture has that many pixels). A 256-color system has no hope of rendering such a picture accurately.

Most browsers solve this dilemma by programming 256-color displays with a fixed 216-color palette. The 216 colors are all combinations of six evenly spaced levels of red, the same six levels of green, and the same six levels of blue. Table 18-2 shows the six levels. These are the only colors you can be sure browsers will display as you intended, and for this reason those 216 are commonly called *the browser-safe colors.*

Table 18-2. **Safe Palette Color Intensities for 256-Color Video Systems**

Intensity	Decimal	Hex
Minimum	0	00
	51	33
	102	66
	153	99
	204	CC
Maximum	255	FF

To display colors with RGB intensities other than 0, 51, 102, 153, 204, or 255, the browser either *dithers* or *substitutes*. When dithering, the browser displays nonstandard colors as a mixed pattern of standard-color pixels. In theory, the viewer's eye perceives the mixed pattern as a smooth area, but in practice the perception is often grainy. Dithering usually works better on continuous-scale pictures, such as photographs. It's most objectionable on pictures with large solid areas, such as text, flood fills, and line art.

When substituting, the browser simply replaces nonstandard colors with its idea of the closest standard color. Browsers normally apply substitution rather than dithering for background colors, because dithering a background can seriously affect the readability of text.

Why should you care about all this? Well, both dithering and substitution result in Web visitors seeing something other than you intended. To avoid this, take one of these steps:

- Specify only the following RGB values for text, backgrounds, and solid pictures: 0, 51, 102, 153, 204, or 255; or

- If you must supply RGB color values in hexadecimal, specify only values 00, 33, 66, 99, CC, or FF.

Design Tips for Choosing Colors

Choosing color schemes is one of the most important aspects of creating new Web pages. It's no less important for maintaining existing pages and keeping your site looking fresh. For these reasons, the rest of this chapter makes some suggestions for picking colors for page backgrounds, text, and other elements on your pages.

Choosing Page Colors

Here are some quick guidelines for choosing colors on Web pages. They're just as relevant in this context are they are in brochures, magazines, posters, or any other artistic design. Even if you don't read the rest of this chapter, these tips should give you a good start:

- Choose complementary colors: earth tones, sky tones, ocean colors, and so forth. Colors that appear together in beautiful natural settings are likely to look good in other settings as well.

- Coordinate the color of your background and other page elements with those in any pictures you plan to use.

- Ensure that there's sufficient contrast between the various text colors and the background.

- Use dark text on a light background. This is easier to read than light text on a dark background.

- Strive for colors that contrast but don't clash.

- Avoid using background pictures that overpower normal text. The best background pictures are very light with low contrast.

- You'll seldom go wrong with red, white, and blue, especially in countries like the United States, Great Britain, and France, where these are the national colors.

- When in doubt, try black on white with red highlights.

Chapter 18: Controlling Overall Page Appearance

Attractive color schemes consist of three (or at most four) predominant colors. On Web pages, these are usually the background color, the normal text color, and a highlight color.

- For easy reading, the most contrast is between normal text and the background. The background is usually light and the text dark.

- The highlight color is used for elements such as edge trim, icons, and headings. Consider using a complement of the background hue, but with similar saturation and brightness. Contrast between the highlight and background should generally be less than the contrast between normal text and the background. However, if you apply the highlight color to heading text, make sure there's sufficient contrast against the background to make your headings readable.

- Use icons and pictures related to the background color. Against a light blue background, for example, use icons featuring either dark, cool colors or complementary earth tones. Avoid icons with poor edge contrast against the selected background color; these confuse the eye.

- Choose similar colors for hyperlink text and visited hyperlink text. These should probably be similar hues with equal saturation and brightness rather than equal hues of different saturation. Make sure that both hyperlink colors have enough contrast against the background to be legible but are near enough to each other to suggest a similar function. Hyperlink text and visited hyperlink text are usually brighter than normal text.

- Avoid not only more than three major colors per page, but also more than two or three types of contrast. Using too many kinds of contrast on the same page is visually disorienting.

Fine-Tuning Color Values

Here's how to perform some common color tuning using the RGB color scheme:

- To lighten a color, increase all three of its RGB values (except, of course, any RGB values already set to 255).

- To darken a color, decrease all three of its RGB values (except, of course, any RGB values already set to 0).

- To get the complement (that is, the opposite) of a color, subtract all three of its RGB values from 255.

Chapter 18

Emotional Dimensions of Color

Most people develop rich associations between colors, other sensory perceptions, and the moods they invoke. Some of these associations are physical, such as red—the color of fire—denoting warmth. Some are societal, such as purple being associated with royalty. Others seem quite arbitrary. Whatever the origins, these associations identify color as a communications channel—a channel by which your Web pages will, by design or by default, communicate with your visitors. Interpretation of color varies somewhat by culture, but the following associations are typical:

- **Hot.** A combination of highly saturated red hues produces red at its strongest and conveys a picture of heat. Hot colors are strong and bold, and they attract attention strongly. They stimulate the nervous system, sometimes to the point of raising blood pressure.

- **Cold.** Consisting of highly saturated blues, cold colors are directly opposite hot ones. They invoke sensations of snow and ice; they slow bodily functions and induce a sense of calm. Saturated greens and blue-greens are cold colors.

- **Warm.** Any hue containing red is warm, but mixtures of red and yellow are particularly so. Warm colors are spontaneous, soothing, and enticing.

- **Cool.** To obtain a cool color, start with a cold one and add yellow. This produces yellow-green, green, and blue-green hues such as turquoise. Cool colors are lush, deep, springlike, and soothing.

- **Light.** Light colors are mostly white, with just a tint of hue; hues appear in such small proportion that contrast among them is minimal. They convey airiness, free flow, rest, and relaxation. Light colors have all three RGB components at or near maximum.

- **Dark.** Vivid hues mixed with black produce dark colors. Electronically, none of the RGB components is likely to exceed 127. Dark colors are dense, somber, and masculine in effect, and they suggest autumn or winter. Compositions consisting entirely of dark colors are seldom effective, but dark colors provide excellent contrast against light.

- **Pale.** These are soft pastel colors formed with diminished hues and at least two-thirds white (that is, with all three RGB components at 170 or more). Pink, light blue, and ivory are typical results. Soft and calming, pale colors are frequently used for interiors of homes and offices.

- **Bright.** Colors lacking black or white dilution are vivid and saturated, and therefore bright. Bright colors attract attention from a distance, but if overused at close quarters they can be overpowering and harsh.

Examining Classic Color Schemes

Because human judgment and interpretation are involved, choosing effective color combinations can never be a completely scientific process. Nevertheless, some approaches are more consistently successful than others. The schemes listed in this section have been used repeatedly and have stood the test of time.

Several of these schemes refer to a color wheel. This is nothing more than a circle with the primary colors arranged equally around it. The easiest color wheel for Web designers to use has red, green, and blue spaced equally around the wheel, with inter-mediate colors occupying—you guessed it—intermediate positions. Figure 18-13 shows such a wheel.

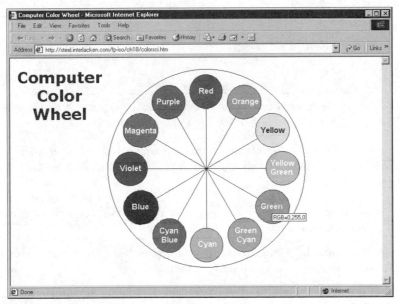

Figure 18-13. Arranging the colors red, green, and blue around the edge of a circle produces a useful tool for analyzing color relationships.

Despite the fact that the eye sees colors of red, green, and blue, artists and traditional designers consider the primary colors to be red, *yellow,* and blue. This is because most people think that the differences among red, yellow, and blue are more extreme than the differences among red green, and blue. (The difference between blue and green seems less than the difference between green and yellow, for example). As a result, many color wheels are laid out as shown in Figure 18-14 on the next page.

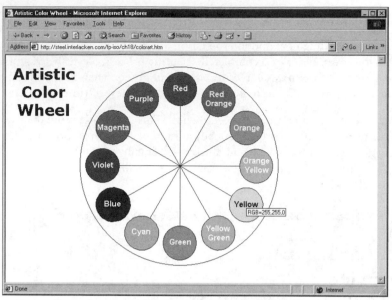

Figure 18-14. Design professionals and artists usually favor this arrangement of the color wheel, which features red, yellow, and blue as its primaries.

In the end, there's really no right or wrong color wheel. Use whatever works best for you. However, knowing even this much color theory prepares you for the following list of classic color schemes:

- **Achromatic.** Use no color at all; the Web page consists entirely of grays. A black-and-white photograph is achromatic.

- **Monochromatic.** Use various tints and shades, but only one hue. This lends a soft appearance and sense of unity.

- **Neutral.** Use a single hue, but neutralize it by adding its complement or black. The result is more muted than a monochromatic scheme might be.

- **Analogous.** Use tints or shades of three consecutive color-wheel colors.

- **Complementary.** Use two colors 180° apart on the wheel. Beware of excessive contrast, especially when choosing vivid colors. The upper left color wheel in Figure 18-15 illustrates this scheme.

- **Clash.** Choose a starting color for this extremely harsh yet eye-catching scheme, and then choose the hue to the left or right of its complement (that is, choose two colors 150° or 210° apart).

- **Split Complementary.** Use a starting color and the two colors adjacent to its complement (that is, 150° and 210° around the wheel). Two similar colors clashing with another often produces a certain balance, especially if you avoid vivid colors.

Chapter 18: Controlling Overall Page Appearance

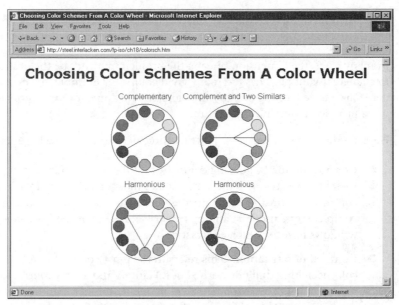

Figure 18-15. Choosing colors that are opposite, adjacent, or equally spaced around the wheel often yields pleasing results.

- **Compliment and Two Similars.** Use a starting color, its complement, and two colors adjacent to the complement. The upper right color wheel in Figure 18-15 illustrates this scheme.

- **Harmonious.** Use three or four colors that appear equally spaced around the wheel. Both color wheels in the lower half of Figure 18-15 illustrate harmonious color schemes.

- **Primary.** Use red, yellow, and blue.

- **Secondary.** Use green, violet, and orange.

- **Tertiary.** Use any colors other than red, yellow, blue, green, violet, and orange, but that are equally spaced around a color wheel.

Perhaps by now you've realized there are many ways to choose contrasting colors that are pleasing and compatible. In fact, there are seven ways, described in the next section.

Controlling Color Contrast

Contrasts between colors falls into seven basic dimensions. The more two colors differ in any of these respects, the more contrast visitors perceive between them:

- If your Web page has colors that clash (that is, if it contains too much color contrast), decrease one or more of the dimensions listed on the next page.

563

- If your page has colors that run together or appear dull (that is, if it contains too little color contrast), increase one or more of these dimensions.

In many cases, the dimension causing the problem may not be the best dimension to change. If your page has too many vivid colors, for example, the best answer isn't necessarily to reduce the number of colors. Making one or more colors less vivid will often produce a more pleasing result.

Here are the seven dimensions. The first three pertain to physical properties of light:

- **Contrast of hue.** Choosing colors from different positions on the color wheel (or spectrum) is the simplest and most obvious way to achieve color contrast. Contrast of hue is greatest among primary colors, less among their complements, and least among tertiary and other mixed hues. Stained glass windows have very high contrast of hue.

- **Contrast of saturation.** This refers to the purity of a color. A saturated color is neither dull nor washed out. Painters and artists control saturation by starting with an extremely vivid pigment and then diluting it with white, black, or gray. This is the kind of contrast you see in bright red on pink, or royal blue on baby blue.

Controlling Color Saturation

In computer pictures, saturated colors have RGB components as extreme as possible; the three primaries, red, green, and blue, for example, are fully saturated at RGB values of 255-0-0, 0-255-0, and 0-0-255. Cyan, magenta, and yellow are fully saturated at 0-255-255, 255-0-255, and 255-255-0. Intermediate hues are fully saturated when one RGB component is 0 and another is 255.

Here's how you can control the saturation of a color:

- To add white to a color, increase its low RGB values uniformly. Adding some white to vivid blue (0-0-255), for example, could produce 102-102-255. Adding even more white would produce colors like 151-151-255 and 204-204-255.

- To add black to a color, uniformly decrease its high RGB values. Adding some black to vivid blue (0-0-255) might produce a color like 0-0-153. Adding more black would produce 0-0-102 or 0-0-51.

- To add gray, increase the color's low RGB values and decrease its high RGB values simultaneously. Adding gray to vivid blue (0-0-255) produces colors like 102-102-153.

- To create the complement of a color, invert its RGB values. The complement of vivid blue (0-0-255) would be 255-255-0 (yellow).

Chapter 18: Controlling Overall Page Appearance

- **Contrast of light-dark (brightness).** Two colors of the same hue can differ greatly; a dark, near-black shade and a light, near-white tint of the same color exhibit this kind of contrast. A black-and-white photo consists entirely of light-dark contrasts, though this kind of contrast can occur with any hue.

  The human eye responds more precisely and reliably to differences in brightness than to differences in hue. That is, contrast between light and dark is usually more legible than contrast between different hues. In the absence of light-dark contrast, fine text is usually illegible.

The remaining four color contrasts pertain to human perception and interpretation of light:

- **Contrast of cold-warm.** Colors on the green-blue side of the color wheel are classified as cool, whereas those on the red-yellow side are warm. Web pages involving all warm or all cool colors are usually more pleasing than those in which colors of both types appear. Cool colors are usually deemed sedate and warm colors stimulating (wall and fixture colors in psychiatric wards and fast-food restaurants are designed accordingly).

- **Contrast of complements.** This is the contrast that occurs between any two colors that are directly opposite on a continuous color wheel. Combined, they always produce black, white, or gray; adding their respective RGB components produces three equal numbers. Using complementary colors, especially in combination with intermediate colors, can produce a strong yet pleasing sort of contrast. Vivid complements, however, can clash violently.

- **Simultaneous contrast.** When the eye shifts away from a bright color, such as yellow, to a dull color, such as gray, it experiences a sort of boomerang or overshoot effect and mistakenly senses the opposite of the "missing" color. This explains why a gray spot in a yellow background appears blue, or a black thread in a red fabric looks green. Color experts can use this effect constructively, but for beginners it's more often an explanation of why their work doesn't look as expected.

- **Contrast of extent.** The degree to which a color predominates in a Web page depends not only on its intensity but also on the amount of space it occupies.

  If all the major colors in a Web page have equal impact on the viewer, based on their intensities and extents, the result is harmonious. If not, the result is expressive. Expressive results have greater visual contrast.

  Contrast of extent is a tool, not a rule. To reduce the impact of a color, use less of it in terms of area, brightness, or both. To increase a color's impact, increase its brightness or surface area.

Frequently Asked Question

Why do some colors just look darker than others?

The human eye reacts more strongly to some colors than to others. Comparing yellow and violet colors of equal intensity, for example, the eye perceives yellow as about three times as bright. The following relative intensities are generally accepted.

Yellow	Orange	Red	Violet	Blue	Green
9	8	6	3	4	6

This explains why, for example, blue text on a black background is so hard to read. It is more difficult for the eye to detect blue light than almost any other color. That's why, to make blue on black text readable, you must add some white to it. Instead of an RGB color of 0-0-255, try 102-102-255 or 153-153-255.

The same chart of intensities explains why colored areas might appear darker or lighter than you expect. Because orange appears twice as bright as blue, for example, blue must have twice the area of orange for the two colors to have equal impact. Intermediate combinations are also possible. Here are three possible brightness effects controlled by the extent of the two colors:

Extent of color	Perceived brightness
Blue area is twice orange area.	Blue appears as bright as orange.
Blue area equals orange area.	Orange appears twice as bright as blue.
Orange area is twice blue area.	Orange appears four times as bright as blue.

In Summary...

This chapter explained how to control the overall attributes of a Web page. It also provides advice and background material that many people find helpful when choosing color schemes.

The next chapter explains how FrontPage themes can give your Web pages a uniform, professionally designed appearance.

Chapter 19

Using FrontPage Themes

Despite the fact that many beginning Web designers ignore it, communicating visually is something all successful Web pages must do. Human perception of information on a Web page is, after all, an artistic study, and many Web beginners, believing that they lack artistic talent, find this issue intimidating. The task of balancing color, graphic elements such as buttons and pictures, and the text that makes up the Web's content is not only difficult, but time-consuming as well. As a result, artistic design is often an expensive task.

Microsoft FrontPage themes provide a solution for people who don't know design techniques but can recognize something they like. Themes are professionally designed style packages that include a color scheme, a font scheme, and graphic page elements you can apply to single pages or an entire Web with one command.

Time and talent permitting, you can modify FrontPage themes to your heart's desire, even creating new themes if you want. To multiply the value of your efforts, any themes you create in FrontPage are available to other Microsoft Office applications as well.

This chapter first walks you through the process of assigning themes to existing pages or Webs, and then covers the mechanics of modifying themes to create new ones.

Introducing Themes

FrontPage can apply themes to a single page or an entire Web. Figure 19-1 on the next page shows the Themes dialog box, the focal point for applying, modifying, and removing themes. To display it, choose Theme from the Format menu.

Part 7: Formatting Your Web Pages

Figure 19-1. Choosing the Apply Theme To All Pages option applies the selected theme to every page in the current Web not already controlled by a theme.

Note the All Pages option in the upper left corner, under the heading Apply Theme To. Choosing All Pages and clicking OK applies the selected theme to every page in the current FrontPage-based Web, with one exception: Any pages controlled by an individually applied theme remain unchanged.

Applying a theme to all pages makes it the default theme for that Web. All existing pages take on a uniform appearance, and any new pages will automatically use the specified theme as well. Applying a theme to selected pages affects only those pages.

If you want to override a Web's default theme for certain pages, that's easy to do. Here are the steps:

1 Open those pages that you want to change in Page view.

2 Choose Themes from the Format menu.

3 Choose either the theme you want or (No Theme). Doing this applies changes to the currently open page only.

note Themes exist to give a Web a professional and consistent look. Applying an assortment of themes to individual pages can make your Web appear abrupt and confusing to visitors. If, however, your Web consists of several discrete sections, and each section acts almost like a separate Web, applying themes to the individual pages of each section might be advisable. Even then, however, you might consider creating a separate Web for each section.

The Apply Theme To All Pages option makes the selected theme the default for the current Web. FrontPage then displays the selected (now default) theme twice in the Themes dialog box:

- Once at the top of the list, preceded by the string (Default).

  If you assign this instance of the selected theme to one or more selected pages, subsequently changing the default theme will affect those pages.

- Once in its normal position.

  If you assign this instance of the selected theme to one or more selected pages, subsequently changing the default won't affect those pages. This holds true even if the specific theme you assign is currently the default.

Applying a theme to an entire Web is a somewhat irrevocable action. As indicated by the warning shown in Figure 19-2, the theme replaces all the fonts, colors, bullets, and lines in every page in a Web, with no possibility of undoing. You can remove the theme by applying the choice (No Theme) to All Pages, but this won't restore all the colors, fonts, and other formatting those pages used to have. Instead, these properties will revert to their HTML defaults. Alternatively, you can apply a different theme.

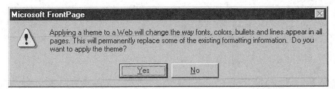

Figure 19-2. This dialog box warns you that applying a theme to an entire Web over-writes formatting information that can't be restored.

Applying any theme to a Web—whether to individual pages or the entire Web—copies the theme into a hidden folder named, not surprisingly, _themes. This makes the theme available to anyone who opens that Web, and overrides any like-named themes on that Web visitor's hard disk. Distributing a theme to all your Web visitors is as simple as adding a page that uses that theme to that FrontPage-based Web.

Using Existing Themes

To use an existing theme, open a Web in FrontPage and select Theme from the Format menu. This displays the Themes dialog box shown in Figure 19-1.

The large list box at the left of the dialog box shows the available themes. Selecting a theme previews its appearance in the large area titled Sample Of Theme. After finding a theme you like, click OK to apply it to one or more Web pages.

Part 7: Formatting Your Web Pages

The following controls manage the details:

- **Apply Theme To.** This option controls which pages clicking OK will affect:

  - **All Pages.** Select this option if the theme you specify should become the default theme for all pages in the current Web. This option is unavailable unless a FrontPage-based Web is open.

  - **Selected Page(s).** Select this option if the theme you specify should apply to the current page in Page view or, if another view is on display, to whatever pages are selected. Themes assigned with this option override themes assigned with All Pages.

- **Vivid Colors.** Select this option to preview and apply the vivid set of colors from a theme that provides both muted and vivid colors.

Troubleshooting

Netscape Navigator can't display some form fields when using cascading style sheet themes in a Web

If cascading style sheets specify a border width for the *<textarea>* or *<select>* tags, Netscape Navigator versions 4.5 and earlier are incapable of rendering scrolling text boxes or drop-down lists. This situation can arise when FrontPage themes that use cascading style sheets also specify a *border-width* attribute for these form field components.

There are three ways to work around this problem. Use the one that's most appropriate for your situation:

- Clear the Apply Using CSS check box in the Themes dialog box.
- Use the Modify Theme feature.

  After using this method, you can re-use the modified theme on other Webs in the future. To modify the theme, follow these steps:

  1 Choose Theme from the Format menu and select the theme you want to modify.

  2 Click the Modify button at the bottom of the Themes dialog box, and then click the Text button.

  3 When the Modify Theme dialog box appears, click More Text Styles.

  4 When the Style dialog box appears, select the style called *select* from the Styles list, and then click Modify.

  5 When the Modify Style dialog box appears, click Format, and then select Border from the drop-down list.

  6 When the Borders And Shading dialog box appears, make sure the Borders tab is selected, and then click the icon representing Default to remove the borders.

- **Active Graphics.** Select this option to activate animated pictures if a theme contains them. Tread carefully here: The novelty of flashing lights can wear off quickly.

- **Background Picture.** Select this option if you want pages to display a background picture. A background picture is a small graphic, usually with some sort of pattern, that's tiled across the entire background of the page. Most themes substitute a solid background color if you clear this option.

> **caution**   After you apply a theme, there's no Undo command that restores your Web to its prior appearance. Removing a theme returns pages to their default HTML state. Always back up your Web first or work from a copy.

7   Click OK in both the Borders And Shading and Modify Style dialog boxes.

8   In the Styles list, select *textarea*, and then click Modify.

9   Repeat steps 5 through 7 to remove the borders from the *textarea* style.

10   Click OK in both the Style and Modify Theme dialog boxes.

11   In the Themes dialog box, click Save or Save As and type a new name for the modified style if necessary. Click OK.

- Edit the Cascading Style Sheets file.

  This method resolves the problem by editing an individual file in the problem Web. If you reapply the theme after following this method, FrontPage will overwrite the changed file and the original problem will reappear:

  1   Choose Web Settings from the Tools menu and click the Advanced tab in the dialog box.

  2   Select the Show Hidden Files And Folders check box, and then click OK. Refresh the Web if prompted to do so.

  3   In the Folder List or Folders view, expand the *_themes* folder and select the folder of the theme that is causing the problem.

  4   Double-click the *theme.css* file to open it.

> **note**   Although the offending property values are usually in the *theme.css* file, you might also wish to check other CSS files in the same folder.

  5   Remove the border-width attribute for the *select* and *textarea* styles by deleting the attribute and its setting from each style.

  6   Save and close the file.

● **Apply Using CSS.** Select this option if you want FrontPage to apply theme attributes by using cascading style sheet (CSS) commands. If you clear the option, FrontPage uses standard HTML commands.

> For more information about cascading style sheets, refer to Chapter 20, "Managing Appearance with Cascading Style Sheets." For more information about the Delete and Modify buttons, refer to "Creating and Modifying Themes" later in this chapter.

After applying a theme and opening a Web page, you might be surprised to find it less elaborate than the preview. This happens because the preview includes page banners, Link bars, hover buttons, dividers, and other FrontPage components your pages don't necessarily contain. Alas, there's no solution but to edit each page and insert the desired elements.

> For more information about Link bars, refer to "Using Link Bars with Navigation View" on page 201. For more information about page banners, refer to "Using Page Banners" on page 212.

If an element on the page had a style set to it before a theme was applied—a Heading 1 style, for example—that element takes on the Heading 1 style of any theme you apply.

> For more information about applying HTML styles to text, refer to "Using HTML's Basic Paragraph Styles" on page 288.

You might also be surprised, after applying a theme, that FrontPage suppresses many of its normal formatting commands for the affected pages. You can't override colors, bullet types, and other element properties under theme control on an element-by-element, attribute-by-attribute basis. You can, of course, change the style of an element to one of the theme formats that's more to your liking.

For elements where the theme doesn't preempt color control, FrontPage extends the color drop-down menu as shown here to include the theme colors. This makes it easy to choose colors in line with the overall design.

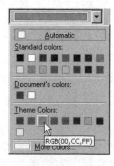

Creating and Modifying Themes

FrontPage themes are one area where you truly can't make something out of nothing. The only way to create a new theme is to modify an old one and save it under a new name. Here's the procedure for modifying a theme:

1 Display the Themes dialog box by choosing Theme from the Format menu.

2 Choose any theme as your starting point, and then click the Modify button beneath the theme preview. Clicking this button displays additional buttons between the theme preview area and the Modify button, as shown in Figure 19-3.

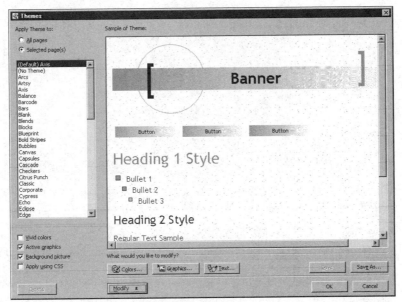

Figure 19-3. Clicking the Modify button on the Themes dialog box displays an additional row of buttons under the preview area.

3 Use the Colors, Graphics, and Text buttons to modify the existing theme, and click Save or Save As.

> For more information about using the Colors, Graphics, and Text buttons, refer to "Modifying Theme Colors," "Modifying Theme Graphics," "Modifying Theme Text," and the sidebar "Netscape Navigator can't display some form fields when using cascading style sheet themes in a Web" in this chapter.

> **note** If you make a change to a theme and click OK without choosing Save or Save As first, FrontPage displays a warning asking whether you want to save the changes to the current theme.

Modifying Theme Colors

Clicking the Colors button shown in Figure 19-3 displays the Modify Theme dialog box shown in Figure 19-4.

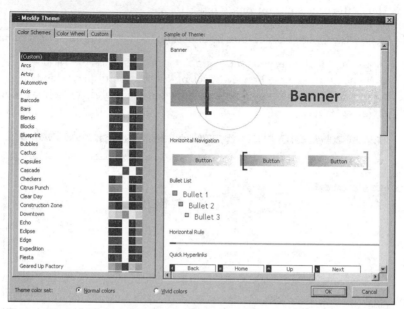

Figure 19-4.   Clicking a named color scheme at the left applies a set of colors to the current theme.

The Theme Color Set option buttons at the bottom of the dialog box control which set of colors you're configuring: normal or vivid. By default, a theme's normal and vivid colors are the same. The vivid color set, should you care to define it, is usually similar to the normal set but brighter or more vibrant. You can switch between color sets by clicking the Normal Colors or Vivid Colors option button.

> For an explanation of color terms such as *vivid, bright, and saturated,* refer to "Design Tips for Choosing Colors" on page 558.

The three tabs at the upper left offer three ways to choose a color scheme:

- **Color Schemes.** The Color Schemes tab (shown in Figure 19-4) presents preselected sets of colors grouped to look good together. To try out a given color scheme, just select its entry in the list and view the results in the Sample Of Theme area.

   Note that despite considerable overlap, the list of color schemes and the list of themes are different. Figure 19-4 shows Automotive and Downtown color schemes, for example, but no corresponding themes exist in

Chapter 19: Using FrontPage Themes

Figure 19-1. The color schemes that share a name with a theme show the colors in that theme.

● **Color Wheel.** The Color Wheel tab (shown in Figure 19-5) makes use of the Hue, Saturation, Brightness (HSB) color model described next.

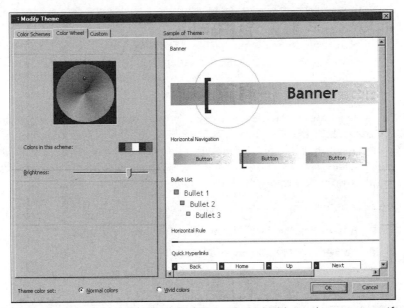

Figure 19-5. The Color Wheel tab provides an additional way to specify theme colors.

Note the tiny white dot superimposed on the color wheel inside the black rectangle. Dragging this dot around the circle changes the selected hue and saturation in the following ways:

■ **Hue.** Refers to a true, pure color value. The color wheel represents hue as degrees of rotation around the wheel inside the black rectangle. Red, blue, and green, for example, are at 9 o'clock, 1 o'clock, and 5 o'clock, respectively.

■ **Saturation.** Measures the purity of a color (that is, the lack of neutral colors diluting it). To increase saturation, drag the white dot closer to the center of the circle. To decrease saturation, drag it closer to the edge.

■ **Brightness.** Measures the intensity of a color. If brightness is zero, for example, the result is black. The Brightness slider on the Color Wheel tab controls brightness. To increase brightness, drag the slider to the right, and drag it to the left to decrease brightness.

Frequently Asked Question

Why can't a color wheel show all the colors?

Because the eye perceives color in three dimensions—red, green, and blue—all color measurement schemes involve at least three dimensions. Here are some examples:

Color Scheme	Dimensions
RGB	Red, Green, and Blue
HSB	Hue, Saturation, and Brightness
HSL	Hue, Saturation, and Luminance
CMY	Cyan, Magenta, Yellow

Because all these schemes are necessarily three dimensional, no two-dimensional arrangement can ever display a complete and continuous set of colors. A color wheel—which, being flat, is two-dimensional—can't display all combinations of three color values in any sort of continuous way. That's why the Color Wheel tab needs to display not only a color wheel, but a brightness slider as well.

Here's another way to look at this situation:

● A two-dimensional chart can graph only two variables.

● Measuring color requires three variables.

● No two-dimensional chart can ever display a continuous pattern of all possible colors.

The bar titled Colors In This Scheme shows the colors FrontPage uses to build the theme. These change as you drag the white dot around the wheel. The Sample Of Theme preview changes only when you *stop* dragging (that is, when you release the mouse button).

note Be careful when you change the colors in a theme. Modifying colors changes only the colors of HTML elements such as text and backgrounds, but doesn't change graphic colors for elements such as buttons and banners.

You might ask how, after you choose one color with the wheel and slider, FrontPage loads five colors into the Colors In This Scheme bar. Here's how it's done:

■ The color you select is the normal text color; it appears fourth in the color bar.

Chapter 19: Using FrontPage Themes

■ The color that appears third is the background color, which can't be changed from the Color Wheel tab. To change the background color, use the Color Schemes tab or the Custom tab.

■ FrontPage calculates the remaining three colors. The formulas for these calculations are buried somewhere inside the code for FrontPage, but they seem to apply the strategy of Complement And Two Similars illustrated in Figure 18-15.

The first color applies to the Heading 2, Heading 4, and Heading 6 styles. This color is diametrically opposed (180° distant) from the color you select.

The second color applies to the Heading 1, Heading 3, Heading 5, and Active Hyperlink styles. This color is about 150° counterclockwise from the color you select.

The fifth color applies to the Regular Hyperlink style. It's about 150° clockwise from the color you select.

Choosing colors using the Colors In This Scheme bar might seem confusing at first, but it's actually quite a convenient way to create an elegant color scheme.

● **Custom.** The Custom tab (shown in Figure 19-6 on the next page) provides direct control over 14 Web elements controlled by a theme. The elements are categorized as items in the Item drop-down list. To change the color of any item:

1 Select it from the Item drop-down list.

2 Click the Color drop-down arrow, and choose the exact color you want.

> For more background on choosing colors from a color wheel, refer to "Design Tips for Choosing Colors" on page 558. For specific instructions on choosing colors, refer to "Using FrontPage Color Dialogs Boxes" on page 552.

As you change the colors assigned to any item, the Sample Of Theme preview area changes accordingly.

Part 7: Formatting Your Web Pages

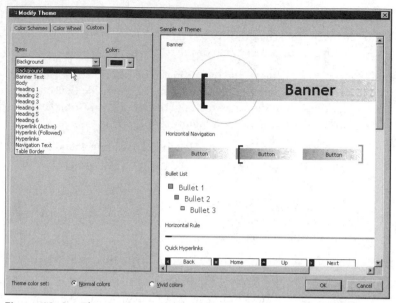

Figure 19-6. The Custom tab allows designers to modify the color of a specific element within a theme.

Modifying Theme Graphics

Clicking the Graphics button in the Themes dialog box produces the Modify Theme dialog box shown in Figure 19-7.

Figure 19-7. The Picture tab of this dialog box specifies the picture files FrontPage uses on pages controlled by a specific theme.

Chapter 19: Using FrontPage Themes

● The Picture tab specifies the pictures FrontPage uses for each of 11 groups of elements. To modify a specific group, select it from the Item drop-down list:

■ **Background Picture.** Controls the picture that fills the background of the page.

■ **Banner.** Controls the picture that appears behind the page title.

■ **Bullet List.** Controls the picture that marks each item in a bullet list.

■ **Horizontal Rule.** Specifies the picture used in place of HTML's normal horizontal rule element.

The remaining seven picture types (Global Navigation Buttons, Horizontal Navigation, Quick Back Button, Quick Home Button, Quick Next Button, Quick Up Button, and Vertical Navigation) all apply to the Link Bar component described in Chapter 7.

For a brief introduction to Link bars and to Navigation view, which provides the data for Link bars to work, refer to Chapter 7, "Managing Web Structure with Navigation View."

To specify a picture the current theme should use:

1 Select an element group from the Item drop-down list.

2 In the corresponding text box(es), enter or browse to the picture you want FrontPage to use. The Sample Of Theme area previews your choices.

Frequently Asked Questions

Themes do a great job of formatting page banner components. Is there any way to specify page-banner text without entering it in Navigation view?

Sorry, there isn't.

For more information about the Page Banner component, refer to "Using Page Banners" on page 212.

Themes do a great job of formatting navigation bars, too. Is there any way to create a navigation bar without arranging pages in Navigation view?

newfeature! Yes. FrontPage 2002 includes a feature called Link Bar With Custom Links that does exactly that.

For more information about the Link Bar With Custom Links component, refer to "Creating a Link Bar Based On Navigation Structure" on page 206.

Part 7: Formatting Your Web Pages

In Figure 19-7, for example, this procedure would apply to the Banner picture. To specify the picture for a different type of element, select a different group from the Item list box.

● The Font tab of the Modify Theme dialog box, shown in Figure 19-8, specifies the fonts FrontPage will use for textual elements that the theme controls. To specify the font for a given element:

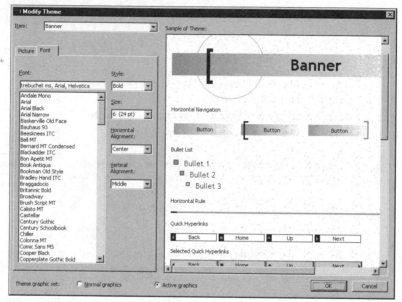

Figure 19-8. The Font tab controls the appearance of text that appears in page banners and Link bars.

> For more information about fonts for normal text and headings, refer to "Modifying Theme Text" later in this chapter.

1 Select an element from the Item drop-down list.

2 Specify one or more fonts by entering them in the Font text box. Clicking any font name in the provided list makes it the one and only suitable font. To specify additional fonts, enter their names by hand. You must separate individual font names with a comma.

> **tip** There's no guarantee that a given font will be available on the visitor's computer. That's why it's best to specify multiple fonts and to use common ones at that.

3 In the Style section, apply any desired formatting to the font, such as bold or italics.

4 Select a font size from the Size menu.

5 Adjust the alignment of the font, either horizontally or vertically, by selecting the appropriate menu item.

> For more information about how FrontPage superimposes text over pictures, refer to "Adding Text to Pictures" on page 649.

Modifying Theme Text

Clicking the Text button in the Themes dialog box displays the version of the Modify Theme Text dialog box shown in Figure 19-9. This specifies the font of body and heading text that appears on pages controlled by the theme.

> For more information about applying fonts to text elements other than normal text and headings, refer to "Modifying Theme Graphics," earlier in this chapter.

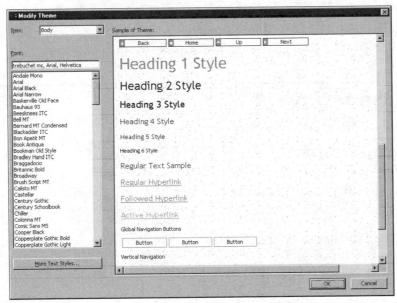

Figure 19-9. This dialog box controls the appearance of body and heading text.

Here's the procedure for modifying these properties:

1 Select the element you want to control from the Item drop-down list.

2 Click the desired font in the Font list. The font name appears in the Font text box.

3 To specify multiple fonts in order of preference, type the second and each subsequent font into the Font text box by hand, using the list as your guide. Be sure to separate the font names with commas.

As you select new fonts from the Font list, the Sample Of Theme preview area changes to reflect your selection.

The More Text Styles button provides access to CSS properties, using the dialog box first seen in Figure 5-23. This provides control not only over font family, but also over font size, weight, style, color, and all the usual CSS selectors and properties.

> For more information about controlling text properties with cascading style sheets, refer to "Assigning Style Sheet Properties" on page 613.

Saving Modified Themes

When you've modified a theme to your satisfaction, click the Save button to save your theme under the same name, or click Save As to save it under a new name. If you click Save As, FrontPage displays the Save Theme dialog box shown in Figure 19-10, which prompts you for a theme name.

Some themes, such as those supplied with FrontPage, are flagged read-only. In these cases, the Save button will be dimmed and you'll have to use Save As.

Troubleshooting

Themes dialog box flashes and then disappears

When you attempt to change the themes used in a Web, the Themes dialog box might flash into view and then disappear. This can occur for two reasons:

- The preference file, *cmdui.prf,* is corrupted.
- The FrontPage registry entry is corrupted.

To resolve the issue of a corrupted *cmdui.prf* file, first try deleting the file. Here's the necessary procedure:

1 Close all open instances of FrontPage.

2 In Windows, choose Search (on Windows 2000) or Find (on earlier operating systems) from the Start menu, and then click For Files Or Folders.

3 In the Search For Files Or Folders Named box, type *cmdui.prf.*

4 In the Look In drop-down list, select the drive where FrontPage is installed, and click Search Now.

5 When the file is found, right-click the file name in the Name column and choose Delete from the shortcut menu.

Chapter 19: Using FrontPage Themes

Figure 19-10. Enter a name for a newly created theme in the Save Theme dialog box.

After you've saved a theme, you can use it in any Web pages you create.

Distributing Themes

Themes you save in FrontPage reside in a folder accessible to other Office applications as well. Not all Office applications use such themes, but those that do—including Microsoft Word—have access to them immediately.

There are two ways to distribute themes from one computer to another: by copying the files directly, or by transferring over the Web.

If you find more than one *.prf* file, you can either delete them one at a time until the problem goes away or just delete them all. Any *cmdui.prf* file with a FrontPage folder in its path is a prime suspect.

The next time FrontPage starts, it will create a new, uncorrupted version of this file.

If the problem persists, try deleting the entire FrontPage registry entry. This is a rather drastic action, but FrontPage will create new, uncorrupted, default registry entries the next time it starts. Here are the steps for deleting the registry entry:

1 Close all open instances of FrontPage.

2 In Windows, choose Run from the Start menu.

3 Type *regedit* in the Open box, and then click OK.

4 If necessary, click the My Computer plus icon to expand the registry.

5 With My Computer still selected, choose Export from the Registry menu.

6 When the Export Registry File dialog appears, specify a safe location on your hard disk or removeable drive, and then click Save.

7 When your backup is complete, expand the following folder:
HKEY_CURRENT_USER\Software\Microsoft

8 Right-click the *FrontPage* folder and click Delete on the shortcut menu.

9 Close the registry editor and restart your computer.

Part 7: Formatting Your Web Pages

Distributing by Copying Files

To distribute a theme to computers other than your own requires copying one folder that contains three files. By default, this folder resides at the following path:

C:\Program Files\Common Files\Microsoft Shared\Themes\<theme name>

The folder, the three files, and the theme generally have similar names; for example, the Blends theme resides in the *blends* folder, and the three files are named *blends.elm, blends.inf,* and *preview.gif.*

To copy a theme from one computer to another, copy its folder to an intermediate location—such as a disk, file server, or FTP location—and then copy it from there into the *Themes* folder on the other computer.

Figure 19-11 shows the *Themes* folder, the *blends* folder, and the three *blends* files on a typical Microsoft Windows 2000 Professional installation.

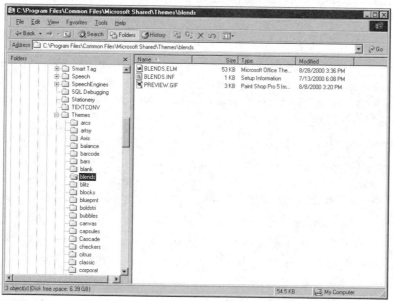

Figure 19-11. Themes reside in a common files area accessible to other Office applications. To install a theme on another computer, copy it to that computer's *Themes* folder.

Distributing over the Web

When you apply a theme to a page in a FrontPage-based Web, FrontPage copies the theme files into that Web. Then, when another FrontPage designer opens the same Web, their Themes list contains two kinds of entries:

● Themes residing on their local system.

● Themes residing in the current FrontPage-based Web.

If the second FrontPage designer applies a theme that resides only on the FrontPage-based Web, FrontPage offers to download the theme and install it locally. This provides an efficient means to propagate themes required by those who need them.

Using Themes in Real Life

These days just about anyone can create a Web site, and if you haven't been asked yet, it's probably not far from happening. There are as many types of people creating Web sites as there are sites on the Internet. Not all of these site developers have the creative knowledge or desire to actually "design" their sites. For a Web developer with limited knowledge of graphic design, but a desire to create a professional and consistent Web, using a theme is a simple choice.

Starting with a solid plan of attack makes sense. These three steps are just the beginning:

1 Create a list of goals that the Web needs to accomplish.

2 Define the target audience: Who is the Web for?

3 Choose a FrontPage theme that supports the goals of the Web and meets the needs of the audience.

Using Chapter 16 as a reference, add tables to lay out the content on the pages of the Web. Figure 19-12 on the next page shows a home page at this point in the plan—the "before" page.

The Web is not quite where it should be. The basic structure is there, the navigation is created, and all of the pages have content and headings letting the visitors know whose Web this is. There's just one more step: applying a theme.

Figure 19-13 on the next page shows the results of applying a FrontPage theme.

For elements where the theme doesn't preempt color control, FrontPage extends the color drop-down menu to include the theme colors. In the Widgets Web site shown in Figure 19-14 later in this chapter, the designer used one of these colors in place of the normal background in the lower left table cell. This emphasized the content of that cell, broke up the monotony of the page background, and generally made the page more balanced. The designer also added a clip art picture to anchor the corner of every page. This creates consistency and a measure of branding of the Web.

For more information about using tables for page layout, refer to Chapter 16, "Using HTML Tables for Page Layout." For more information about changing the background color of a table cell, refer to "Adjusting Cell Properties" on page 491.

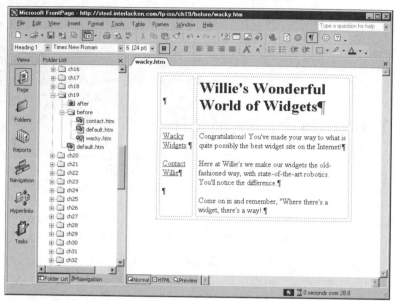

Figure 19-12. This Web page uses basic styles and tables. It's both simple and uninteresting.

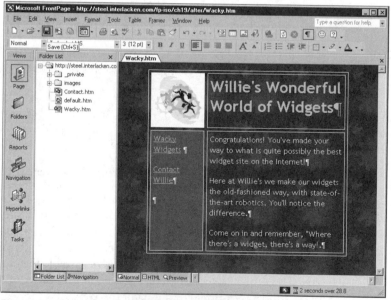

Figure 19-13. Applying a theme adds spice.

With a little planning, some trial and error, and a good helping of patience, a bland, boring Web can become something clean and professional.

Chapter 19: Using FrontPage Themes

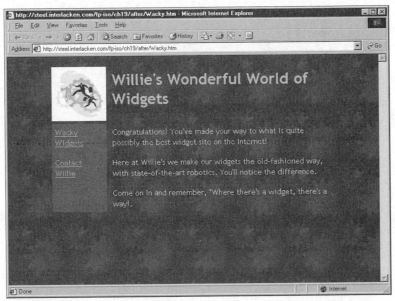

Figure 19-14. Here's the "after" page as it appears in a Web browser.

In Summary...

This chapter explained how to apply themes to an entire Web, how to modify themes, and how to create new themes from existing ones. Themes impart a uniform appearance to one, many, or all pages in a Web.

The next chapter explains cascading style sheets, which also control the appearance of multiple Web pages from a single source.

Chapter 20

Managing Appearance with Cascading Style Sheets

Early versions of HTML had almost no provisions for controlling fonts, colors, indentations, line spacing, or other aspects of typography. Later versions added simple control over fonts and colors, but only for specifically marked blocks of text. Centralized control of typography for an entire page or site remained lacking.

To provide full typographical control over Web pages, the World Wide Web Consortium (W3C) adopted a technology called *cascading style sheets* (CSS, or sometimes CSS1). This technology offers two primary advantages over other methods of formatting Web pages:

- CSS can control all the same typographical properties that ordinary HTML tags control, but with greater precision. CSS can also control many typographical properties that HTML tags can't. As such, CSS offers tremendous flexibility.

- CSS can define groups of typographical properties (styles) in one place and then apply them by name to many different blocks of text located in the same Web page or in many different Web pages. In this sense, it offers tremendous control.

CSS naturally has drawbacks as well. For one thing, not all browsers support it in the same way, or at all. For another, the people who designed CSS optimized it for designers who work with lines of code. This makes CSS extremely platform-neutral

589

but also a difficult fit for programs like Microsoft FrontPage. FrontPage does its best to shield designers from the intricacies of CSS code but nevertheless, using some CSS features means working with code. (Fortunately, you can work with code without leaving FrontPage.)

CSS Positioning (often called CSS2) is a later development that brings pixel-precise positioning to the Web. Using CSS2, you can specify an exact position for any and all elements on a page, not only in terms of height and width but also in terms of depth. (Depth involves a *z-order* property that controls which elements appear in front of or behind others.) CSS2 is almost a dream come true for designers with experience in media other than the Web, but it suffers from three major drawbacks:

- It's seldom possible to gain complete control over every dimension that appears on a Web page. A Web visitor can change the size of fonts by using a menu command, for example, and there's nothing the Web designer can do about it. And when some dimensions are fixed and others are variable, it's almost certain that something won't fit as intended.

- Browsers support CSS2 even less uniformly than they support CSS1.

- Lack of browser support for CSS2 is a more critical issue than lack of support for CSS1, as the following points illustrate:

  - When a browser that doesn't support CSS1 displays a Web page that contains CSS1 formatting, it displays the page legibly but with plain fonts.

  - When a browser that doesn't support CSS2 displays a Web page that contains CSS2 formatting, it usually displays a wild assortment of misplaced objects.

Despite the drawbacks inherent in CSS2, FrontPage does a reasonable job of supporting it. The second half of this chapter explains how this support works.

Lest you discard CSS as too complicated or too poorly supported, consider your only options for controlling typography:

- Forget typography, and make believe Netscape Navigator 3 is the state-of-the-art.

- Forget centralized control and the need for uniformity. Apply HTML formatting to each individual block of text.

- Make everything a picture and force Web visitors to suffer the download time.

- Use CSS and deal with browser differences.

It's hard to believe CSS isn't the best of these solutions.

Dealing with Browser Compatibility (or Lack Thereof)

Some designers are obsessed with the idea that their pages should look exactly the same no matter what browser the visitor uses. As a result, they use only the features that even the oldest browsers support.

Another group of designers have an opposite obsession; they exercise every feature of the very latest browsers and don't mind a bit if visitors running older versions get errors or incorrect displays. This gives the visitors an incentive to upgrade, or so goes the thinking.

The middle ground, of course, is to use features that degrade gracefully with older browser versions. That way, visitors with new browsers get the richest possible experience and those with older browsers experience whatever they're accustomed to. The use of CSS1 fits very well into this middle-ground strategy.

Introducing Cascading Style Sheet Concepts

Any browser that supports CSS starts out with a default set of styles based on built-in logic and whatever preferences the visitor has in effect. Any CSS rules found in Web pages then override, on a property-by-property basis, the default styles. If several styles apply to the same element, the overrides occur in the order the styles appear. This is part of the *cascading* idea in cascading style sheets.

Another aspect of cascading is that some styles *inherit* properties from others. This is usually based on the type of HTML tag involved. When you assign a CSS property to an entire numbered or unnumbered list, for example, any subordinate list items inherit the same properties. The rules of inheritance vary somewhat among browsers, but inheritance is still a very useful aspect of cascading.

The Web page in Figure 20-1 on the next page uses HTML default formatting throughout. Few Web pages are actually this dull, but many come close.

On the next page, Figure 20-2 shows the same content with several kinds of CSS formatting in place. Note the borders and backgrounds in place for the three heading styles, as well as the fact that they overlap. There are no pictures at work here: just ordinary text formatted with CSS1 and locked into position with CSS2. A style sheet also specifies the paragraph indentations, picture bullets, indents, and fonts.

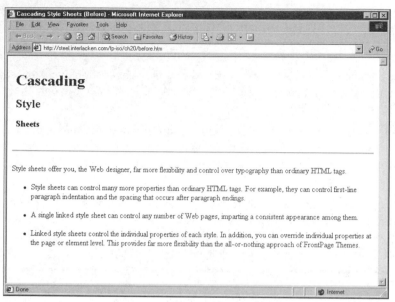

Figure 20-1. This Web page uses default HTML formatting throughout.

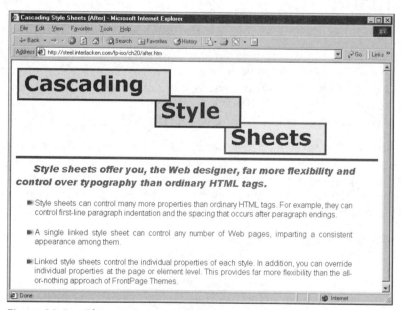

Figure 20-2. This page presents the same content as Figure 20-1, but the use of CSS styles and positioning have improved its appearance significantly.

Support for cascading style sheets in Netscape Navigator 4 lags somewhat behind that in Microsoft Internet Explorer 4 and above, as a glance at Figure 20-3 quickly confirms. Nevertheless, the page shown in Figure 20-3 is legible and generally follows the intended design. As all browsers increasingly conform to W3C standards, differences in page appearance should decrease.

Chapter 20: Managing Appearance with Cascading Style Sheets

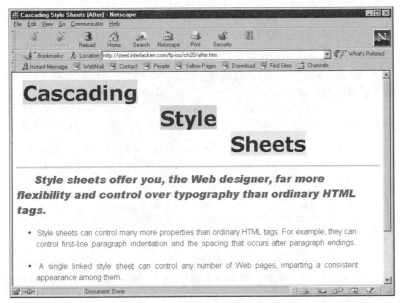

Figure 20-3. Netscape Navigator 4 supports fewer CSS features than Internet Explorer, but even so, pages formatted with CSS generally appear as designed.

Understanding Style Sheet Terminology

The language CSS consists of lines of code—code from which all the WYSIWYG editors and dialog boxes in the world can't shield you completely. Wherever possible, this book avoids showing code and displays the relevant FrontPage dialog boxes instead. But here, when considering fundamentals, code it is. Have faith, though; it'll be simple. First, some definitions:

- **CSS Style.** This is a collection of property names and values such as font name, font size, font weight, color, background color, border type, border width, and so forth. Here's how a CSS style looks in code:

  ```
  font-family: Arial, sans-serif; color: red;
  ```

  - **A colon.** Separates each property name from its value(s).

  - **Commas.** Separates multiple values assigned to the same property.

  - **Semicolons.** Indicates the end of a property setting and permit the beginning of the next.

- **Selector.** This is the name of a CSS rule. This book focuses on three types of selectors:

  - **Type Selector.** This selector has the same name as an HTML tag. Assigning properties to a type selector modifies all text controlled by the corresponding HTML tag. The *h1* selector, for example, controls the appearance of Heading 1 text. The *b* selector controls the appearance of bold text, and so forth.

Type selectors are among the best features of CSS. With one statement, you can change the appearance of your whole Web page or of all elements that use a given HTML style. And with one command you can make one set of type selectors control an entire Web. Later topics in this chapter explain how to define and use type selectors.

- ■ **Class Selector.** This selector has any name you choose to give it, except that the name must begin with a period and can't be the name of an HTML tag.

  Unlike type selectors, class selectors don't apply automatically to all similar elements of a Web page. Instead, you refer to the class by name anywhere you want to apply it.

  Whenever you want text in multiple places to have a consistent format, class selectors are an excellent solution. Suppose, for example, that you want error message paragraphs to look different from normal text paragraphs. Type selectors can't do this because both kinds of paragraphs use the same tag: <p>. If, however, you defined an *errmsg* class selector, then you could apply it to whatever paragraphs were appropriate. Defining the *errmsg* class selector centrally guarantees that all error message paragraphs will look the same. Later topics in this chapter explain how to define and use class selectors.

- ■ **ID Selector.** This selector works somewhat like a class selector, except that the ID is the name of something in your Web page. Instead of naming a style and then invoking it from page elements, you name the page elements and then define styles for them. ID selectors can have any name you like except the name of an HTML tag. In addition, they must begin with a pound sign ("#").

  You should never give two elements in the same page the same ID. This makes class selectors preferable for most uses. Later topics in this chapter explain how to define and use ID selectors.

- ● **CSS rule.** This is a statement that assigns properties to one or more selectors.

Coding Style Sheet Rules

Both CSS styles and the rules that define them are rather abstract entities, not particularly amenable to WYSIWYG display. To wrest every drop of function out of cascading style sheets, therefore, you'll sometimes need to click the HTML tab at the bottom of the Page view window and enter the rules by hand. As seems to be the way of art, the results might be beautiful but the techniques are messy.

Chapter 20: Managing Appearance with Cascading Style Sheets

 For more information about using HTML view, refer to Chapter 41, "Working with HTML Code," in the Bonus Content on the Companion CD.

The syntax (that is, the required format) of CSS statements is different from that of HTML. The following is a CSS rule that assigns two properties (font family and color) to the selector *h1:*

```
h1 { font-family: Arial, sans-serif; color: red; }
```

Note that in this example:

- The selector is the first item on the line.

- Curly braces enclose the entire list of properties.

- Each property consists of a property name, a colon, and then one or more values.

- Commas separate multiple values for the same property.

- A semicolon indicates the end of a property definition.

Rules and styles are many-to-many. A single rule can apply to any number of styles, and any number of rules can affect a single style. The following rule makes all Heading 1 and Heading 2 text appear in bold:

```
h1, h2 { font-weight: bold; }
```

The comma between the two selectors implies an *or* condition, meaning that the rule applies whenever the HTML tag is *h1* or *h2.* Lack of a comma implies an *and* condition. The following rule applies only to italic text located within table cells:

```
td i { color: rgb(153,0,0); }
```

Later topics in this chapter explain how to define and use CSS rules.

on the web   For more information about the features and use of cascading style sheets, browse these locations on the World Wide Web:
Microsoft: *http://msdn.microsoft.com/workshop/author/*
World Wide Web Consortium: *http://www.w3.org/Style/*

Locating Style Sheet Styles

You can specify CSS style information in the three general locations (or, if you prefer, the three levels) listed here:

- **Attached to a specific page element.** You can assign CSS style properties to individual HTML elements. Styles applied this way are called *inline styles.*

If you display the Properties dialog box for any element on a Web page, and if that dialog box contains a Style button, clicking that button displays another dialog box that applies CSS properties (font, paragraph, border, numbering, and position) to that element. In Figure 20-4, for example, the Style button in the lower left corner controls CSS properties for whatever table cells the designer selected before displaying the Cell Properties dialog box.

> For more information about using styles attached to specific page elements, refer to "Formatting Individual Page Elements" later in this chapter.

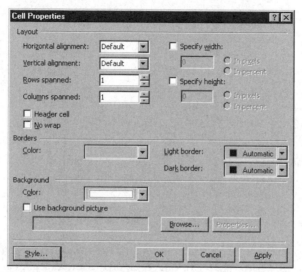

Figure 20-4. The Style button in this dialog box controls CSS properties for the selected page element.

- **In a style sheet located within a Web page.** Whenever you have a Web page open in FrontPage, choosing Style from the Format menu displays the Style dialog box shown in Figure 20-5. This dialog box can create, modify, and delete CSS rules applicable to the current page. (Clicking the Style button on the Style toolbar produces the same result.)

Style

> For more information about using style sheets located within a Web page, refer to "Formatting Single Web Pages" later in this chapter.

Chapter 20: Managing Appearance with Cascading Style Sheets

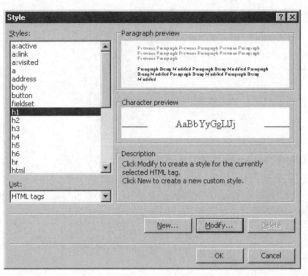

Figure 20-5. This is the launch point for creating or modifying CSS rules.

- **In a style sheet located in another file.** Centrally controlling the appearance of similar elements in the same Web page is all well and good, but what if you want similar elements in an entire collection of Web pages to look alike? You could set up identical style sheets within each page, but that would be boring, mundane, error-prone, and difficult to maintain. Linked style sheet files provide a welcome alternative. Using linked style sheet files involves four overall steps:

  1 Create a cascading style sheet file, mostly likely based on one of the CSS templates mentioned briefly in Chapter 15.

For more information about creating CSS files from templates, refer to "Selecting Style Sheet Templates" on page 470.

  2 Open the CSS file in Page view, choose Style from the Format menu, configure whatever styles you want, and save the page.

  Skip Step 3 if you want to apply your style sheet to an entire Web.

  3 Select one or more Web pages in which you want to use styles from the file you just saved. You can select an open Web page by leaving the insertion point in it, or you can select groups of files or folders in the Folder List or in Folders view.

  4 In Page view, select an open Web page, and then choose Style Sheet Links from the Format menu. This displays the Link Style Sheet dialog box shown in Figure 20-6 on the next page. If the file you saved in step 2 doesn't appear in the URL list, click Add to add it. To apply the style sheet to every file in the current Web, choose All Pages. To apply it to pages you selected in step 3, choose Selected Page(s).

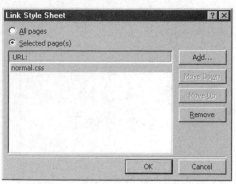

Figure 20-6. This dialog box links files containing CSS rules to selected Web pages or an entire Web.

> For more information about using one style sheet file in multiple Web pages, refer to "Linking Style Sheet Files" later in this chapter.

Assessing Browser Compatibility

Because CSS is a relatively new technology, not all browsers support it. CSS support first appeared in version 3 of Internet Explorer and version 4 of Netscape Navigator. Older browsers treat CSS instructions like they treat HTML tags they don't understand—they ignore them.

Even among browsers that do support CSS, levels of support and details of interpretation tend to differ. The more important the page, the more important it is that you test it using a variety of browsers. (This advice, of course, is universal. It applies whether you use CSS or not.)

Formatting Individual Page Elements

The most direct way to apply CSS styles is by individual page element. CSS refers to styles used this way as *inline styles*. Here's the procedure for applying inline styles to any element in an open Web page:

1 Right-click the element you want to modify.

2 When the shortcut menu appears, choose the Properties command that applies to the element you want: Picture Properties, Cell Properties, and so forth.

3 Look for a Style button on the resulting Properties dialog box. If the dialog box has multiple tabs, check each tab.

If there's no Style button, FrontPage doesn't support inline styles for the type of element you selected in step 1. Refer to the section titled "Coding Inline Styles" later in this chapter.

Chapter 20: Managing Appearance with Cascading Style Sheets

4 Click the Style button to display the Modify Style dialog box shown in Figure 20-7. The Name (Selector) and Style Type boxes are dimmed because they don't apply to inline styles.

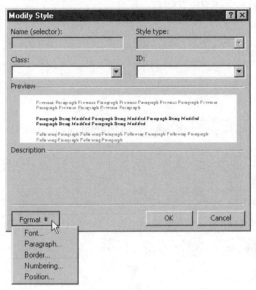

Figure 20-7. This dialog box applies a class selector, an ID selector, or inline styles to a Web page.

5 If you want the element you selected in step 1 to inherit the properties of an existing CSS class, enter the class selector in the box titled Class or select it from the Class drop-down list.

note The Class list in all CSS dialog boxes lists classes defined within the current Web page only. To apply a class defined in a linked style sheet, you must enter its name by hand.

For more information about CSS class selectors, refer to "Formatting Single Web Pages" later in this chapter.

6 If you want to assign an ID value to the element you selected in step 1, enter the ID value in the ID box. Entering such a value doesn't create an ID selector; it only assigns a name that an ID selector can reference.

No two elements in the same Web page should ever have the same ID value. A single element can have only one ID value. The ID values in the drop-down list already exist on the page, so you shouldn't choose anything from this list. You may refer to the drop-down list to identify previously de-fined ID values. Just type a new ID value in the text box.

For more information about creating ID selectors, refer to "Formatting Single Web Pages" later in this chapter.

7 The Preview box shows a rough approximation of how text formatted with the current styles will appear. The Description box shows the CSS properties currently in effect. However, neither of these displays includes properties specified on linked style sheets. This is a bug that some future version of FrontPage (hopefully yours) may fix.

8 To assign inline style properties to the element you selected in step 1, click the Format button in the lower left corner of the dialog box, and choose the category that contains the property you want to specify: Font, Paragraph, Border, Numbering, or Position.

> For instructions on setting these properties, refer to "Assigning Style Sheet Properties" later in this chapter.

Some of the HTML element types that FrontPage has Style buttons for include:

Page	Horizontal line	Hyperlink	Bulleted list
Table	Frame	Form	Numbered list
Table cell	Inline frame	Form Field	List item
Picture			

Three element types are notable exceptions to this list:

● **Paragraph.** The Paragraph dialog box has no Style button. FrontPage offers the following capabilities instead:

 ■ Setting any control in the Paragraph dialog box to a non-default setting causes FrontPage to create inline styles.

 ■ Similarly, FrontPage honors many of the settings in the Font dialog box by adding inline styles to the HTML. This obviates the need to set font properties at the paragraph level.

 ■ Scrolling to the bottom of the Style list on the Formatting toolbar displays a list of available class selectors. To format a given paragraph in accordance with any of these selectors, just select the paragraph and choose the selector you want from the list.

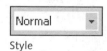

Style

● **Span.** This is a special HTML element that groups arbitrary portions of a Web page. A span has no default physical appearance. It begins wherever you put a ** tag in the HTML code and ends wherever you put a ** tag. Assigning CSS properties to a span assigns those properties to all the elements contained within it.

If you select part of a paragraph or other text element and then use the Font dialog box to change its properties, and if one of the properties you set can be controlled only by CSS, FrontPage creates a span and assigns the necessary CSS property to it. However, there's no command in FrontPage that directly creates a span, and there's no Span Properties dialog box where you can assign CSS properties.

● **Division.** This element works just like a span except that it forces line breaks before and after itself. Certain FrontPage features related to CSS positioning and dynamic HTML create divisions. But again, there's no command that directly creates a division, and there's no Division Properties dialog box where you can assign CSS properties.

InsideOut

Lack of direct support for the *<span>* and *<div>* tags is an unfortunate FrontPage omission. Perhaps some future build or version will include this.

Coding Inline Styles

If the Properties dialog box for a given element doesn't have a Style button (or if you're the type of person who does hexadecimal long division for fun) you can manipulate inline CSS styles directly in code. Here are the steps:

1 In the Page view editing window, select some or all of the text you want to affect.

2 Click the HTML tab at the bottom of the editing window.

3 Locate the HTML tag that controls the selected text. (In most cases, whatever you select before switching to HTML view will also be selected in HTML view.)

4 To apply CSS properties, add a *style=* attribute to the desired HTML tag. Here's an example:

```
<p style="text-align: right">
```

For a list of available property names and acceptable values, consult the various tables in the section titled "Assigning Style Sheet Properties" later in this chapter.

When you return to Normal view, any inline styles you applied in HTML view should be in effect. If not, you've probably misspelled something or used a property in an invalid context. (For example, specifying a font size for a horizontal line element has no effect.)

Formatting Single Web Pages

Using CSS at the page level is generally a two-step process:

1 **Define rules.** A rule assigns typographical properties to one or more selectors (that is, to one or more style names).

2 **Apply the rules to one or more blocks of text.** For type selectors, this is automatic. For class and ID selectors, you must designate the content that you want each rule to affect.

Here's the procedure for creating, modifying, and deleting CSS rules at the page level:

1 Choose Style from the Format menu or click the Style button on the Style toolbar. This displays the Style dialog box shown in Figure 20-8.

Style

If the current page has no page-level styles defined, the Styles list contains the names of all valid HTML tags. Note that by definition, this is also a list of valid type selectors.

The Styles list can also display a list of existing rules for the current page. This is the default if any style rules exist. To make this happen, select User-Defined Styles from the List box in the lower left corner.

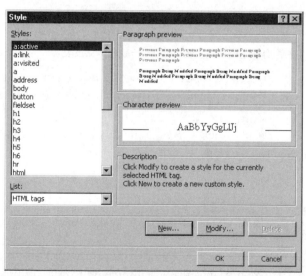

Figure 20-8. From this dialog box, you create, modify, and delete CSS style rules for the current Web page.

Chapter 20: Managing Appearance with Cascading Style Sheets

To alternate between these two displays, choose either HTML Tags or User-Defined Styles in the List box.

2 As you select each rule, the Paragraph Preview box shows the effect of that rule's paragraph properties, the Character Preview box shows the result of its font properties, and the Description box describes its properties in words.

The following steps explain how to create, modify, and delete rules, regardless of whether you've selected HTML Tags or User-Defined Styles in the List box:

a To create a new CSS rule of any type, click the New button. This displays the New Style dialog box shown in Figure 20-9.

> For instructions on using the New Style dialog box, refer to "Assigning Style Sheet Properties" section later in this chapter.

b To modify an existing rule, highlight its selector name in the Styles list and then click Modify. This displays the Modify Style dialog box shown in Figure 20-7, which is nearly identical to the New Style dialog box shown in Figure 20-9. This dialog box displays any properties already in effect for the given style.

> For instructions on using the New Style and Modify Style dialog boxes, refer to "Assigning Style Sheet Properties" later in this chapter.

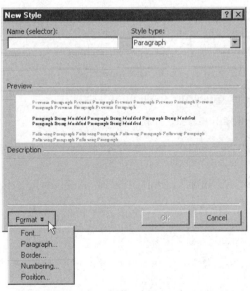

Figure 20-9. This dialog box is the entry point for setting the selector name and properties for a new CSS rule.

603

c To delete an existing rule, select it in the Styles list, and then click Delete. You can delete any style rules you've created, including those for type and ID selectors, but you can't delete valid HTML tag names.

> **tip** FrontPage also displays the dialog box shown in Figure 20-9 when you click the Style button in various Properties dialog boxes. However, in such cases, any properties you specify apply only to the current element.

Choosing Style Sheet Selectors

Type selectors, because they apply to Web page elements automatically, are by far the easiest to use. Here are some commonly used type selectors:

- *h1* through *h6.* Modifies the appearance of text formatted with the standard HTML styles Heading 1 through Heading 6.

- *body.* Modifies the appearance of everything that appears in the body of the Web page. You can use this selector to control the page background color, a background picture, or a default font for the page.

- *p.* Modifies the appearance of normal paragraphs.

- *td.* Modifies the appearance of normal table cells.

- *th.* Modifies the appearance of table heading cells. (To designate an ordinary table cell as a heading cell, select the cell, display its Cell Properties dialog box, and then select the Header Cell check box.)

- *ol.* Modifies the properties of an ordered list.

- *ul.* Modifies the properties of an unordered list.

- *li.* Modifies the appearance of list items.

- *a.* Modifies the appearance of hyperlinks. The *a* type selector has the following related sub type selectors:

  - *a:active.* Modifies the appearances of a hyperlink the visitor has just clicked.

  - *a:visited.* Modifies the appearance of a hyperlink the visitor has recently visited.

  - *a:link.* Modifies the appearance of a hyperlink the visitor hasn't yet visited.

> **tip** To remove underlining from all hyperlinks on a page, modify the *a* selector in the Style dialog box. Click Format, and then click Font. In the Effects section, select the No Text Decoration check box.

Chapter 20: Managing Appearance with Cascading Style Sheets

If your page requires special formatting for certain kinds of data (such as names, titles, part numbers, warnings, or error messages), class selectors are usually the best choice. Just remember to include a leading period when you define them:

```
.warning { color: red; }
```

but not when you call them:

```
<p class="warning">
```

Most designers seldom, if ever, use ID selectors. However, if you ever need one, remember to include a leading pound sign when you define the rule and not when you define the ID.

Troubleshooting

Tables and lists don't inherit body properties in Netscape Navigator

If you specify font properties on a *body* type selector, both FrontPage and Internet Explorer apply those properties, unless overridden, to all text on the page. This is because all page elements in FrontPage and Internet Explorer inherit font properties from the *body* element.

In Netscape Navigator, page elements such as *li* (list item), *td* (table data), and *th* (table heading) *don't* inherit text properties from the body element. As a result, you must control the properties of these selectors explicitly. Here are two ways of doing this:

- Use the Style dialog box to set up additional rules for *li, td, th*, and any additional selectors you require.
- Switch to HTML view and append the required selectors to the rule that already governs the body element. The following is an example of this:

```
body, li, td, th { font-family: sans-serif; }
```

Modifying Web Pages to Use Shared Classes and IDs

If you create a rule named with a type selector (that is, named with the name of an HTML tag), both the FrontPage editor and the browser will apply it automatically.

If you create a rule named with a class or ID selector, you must specially designate any content you want the rule to affect. There are three ways to do this:

- Using the Properties dialog box:
    1 Right-click the element you want to affect.

Chapter 20

Part 7: Formatting Your Web Pages

2   Select its Properties command from the shortcut menu.

3   Click the Style button when the Properties dialog box appears.

4   When the Modify Style dialog box previously shown in Figure 20-7 appears, enter the class selector name in the Class box or the ID selector name in the ID box.

You may find that the Class drop-down list doesn't display class selectors defined in linked style sheets. This is an apparent bug that may or may not be fixed in the version of FrontPage you receive. However, if you type the name by hand, FrontPage gladly adds it to your HTML and honors it in Page view. Just remember *not* to type the leading period that's required when you define a class selector, or the pound sign that's required when you define an ID selector.

● Using the Formatting toolbar:

1   Select the element you want to affect.

2   Open the Style list on the Formatting toolbar, scroll to the bottom, and choose the selector name you want. Unlike the Class list in the Modify Style dialog box, this list displays classes defined in linked style sheets as well as classes defined within the current Web page.

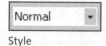

Style

● Using HTML view:

1   In the Page view editing window, select some or all of the text you want to affect.

2   Click the HTML tab at the bottom of the editing window.

3   Locate the HTML tag that controls the selected text. (In most cases, whatever you select *before* switching to HTML view is also selected *in* HTML view.)

4   To make the tag inherit the properties of a class selector, add the following attribute inside it:

```
class="class-selector"
```

The following paragraph tag inherits the CSS properties assigned to the class selector *onsale:*

```
<p class="onsale">
```

5   To give the tag an ID value, add the following attribute inside it:

```
id="identifier"
```

Chapter 20: Managing Appearance with Cascading Style Sheets

The ID attribute in the following table tag assigns the identifier *scores:*

```
<table id="scores">
```

Remember that no two elements in the same page should ever have the same ID. To assign the same style in two or more places, use a class selector.

Troubleshooting

Random names appear as IDs of *<table>* tags

When you assign CSS properties to an HTML table, you might discover that the ID field is already filled in with an automatically generated name.

This behavior is by design and supports a new feature of Microsoft Excel 2002 called Web Query. This feature extracts data from HTML tables anywhere on the World Wide Web and remembers which page and which table the data came from. Because Excel remembers these locations, it is easy to refresh the data at any time.

Remembering a URL is easy, but remembering a specific table is harder. Web queries can remember an ordinal position—meaning first table on the page, third table on the page, or whatever. But a better solution, if the table has an ID code, is to remember the ID code. Microsoft therefore changed FrontPage so that, by default, it assigns ID codes to every table.

There's nothing magical about the ID codes FrontPage assigns; you can change them or delete them at will. The only impact occurs if the page has been in use for some time and Web visitors have performed Web queries against it. In that case, changing the ID code might break those queries.

If you'd rather FrontPage didn't assign ID attributes to tables, choose Page Options from the Tools menu and clear the check box titled Assign Unique IDs To New Tables.

Formatting Multiple Pages

CSS rules that control an entire Web page provide more consistent control over appearance than inline styles or HTML attributes applied to individual elements. Page-level CSS rules, however, provide no control over groups of Web pages, and thus no guarantee of consistency among them.

To provide such consistency, a single collection of CSS rules would have to control multiple Web pages. This is exactly what linked style sheets provide. Using linked style sheets is a four-step process:

1 Add a style sheet file to your Web. These files contain nothing but CSS code and usually have a *.css* filename extension.

607

Part 7: Formatting Your Web Pages

2   Add as many CSS rules to the style sheet file as you like. Be sure to save the file after making any changes.

3   Modify any pages that should use the rules from step 2 so they refer to the file you created in step 1.

4   If any of the rules from step 2 have class or ID selectors, modify any necessary Web page elements so they refer to those classes or IDs.

The next four sections explain how to perform each of these steps.

Adding a Style Sheet File to Your Web

Using a template is the simplest and easiest way to add a style sheet file to a Web. As usual, there are two ways to begin. Here's the first:

1   Choose New from the File menu.

2   Choose Page Or Web.

3   When the New Page Or Web task pane appears, click Page Templates.

The second procedure uses the New Page menu on the Standard toolbar. Proceed as follows:

New Page

1   Click the drop-down arrow associated with the New Page button on the Standard toolbar.

2   Choose Page.

Following either of these procedures and then clicking the Style Sheets tab displays the Page Templates dialog box shown in Figure 20-10. To continue creating the style sheet file:

1   Review the available templates by clicking them and reviewing the Description and Preview areas in the dialog box. Here are some guidelines for choosing a template:

   ▪ If you're not seeking a specific predefined appearance, choose a template that controls the *kinds* of properties you want rather than one that provides correct property *values*. Values are easier to change later than the list of properties.

   ▪ To begin with a clean slate, choose the Normal Style Sheet template. This is probably the best choice 99 percent of the time.

Chapter 20: Managing Appearance with Cascading Style Sheets

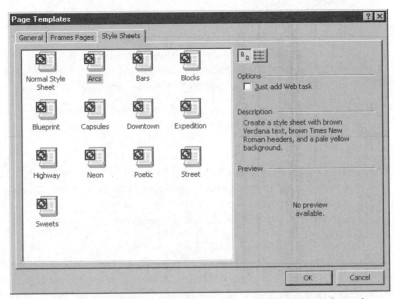

Figure 20-10. FrontPage provides a selection of page templates for creating new style sheet files.

2 When you've chosen the best available template, click OK. FrontPage loads the template into the Page view editing window and displays it as shown in Figure 20-11. The Arcs template created the results shown in the figure.

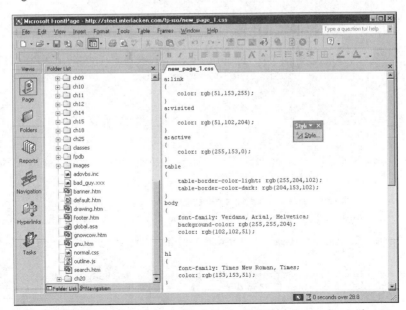

Figure 20-11. Selecting the Arcs style sheet template produces these results. Style sheets have no appearance of their own, so FrontPage displays them as code.

609

3 A quick glance at the figure reveals that CSS files don't appear in any sort of WYSIWYG view. The Normal, HTML, and Preview tabs that normally appear at the bottom of the window are completely absent. Although style sheets definitely control the appearance of Web pages, they have no appearance of their own. FrontPage must therefore display them as code.

4 Save a style sheet file as you would any other: for example, by choosing Save or Save As from the File menu. A common file name for a Web's main CSS file is *normal.css*.

The number of CSS files you add to a Web is totally at your discretion, but having only one such file is a good option to consider. Having only one CSS file implies that all the pages in your Web inherit the same general appearance from the same central location. If some pages contain unique elements, set up unique class rules to accommodate them.

If you don't want to use templates for creating CSS files—not even the Normal Style Sheet template, which is blank—you can create them in Microsoft Notepad or any other text editor, save them, and then import them to your Web.

For more information about importing files, refer to "Importing Web Pages" on page 166.

Adding Rules to a Style Sheet File

The procedure for adding and modifying rules in a CSS style sheet file is the same as that for adding and modifying rules in an ordinary Web page:

1 To display the Style dialog box shown previously in Figure 20-8, click the Style button on the Style toolbar, or choose Style from the Format menu.

Style

2 To create a new rule, click the New button. This displays the New Style dialog box shown in Figure 20-9.

3 To modify an existing rule, select it in the Styles box and then click the Modify button. This displays the Modify Style dialog box shown in Figure 20-7.

4 To delete an existing user-defined rule, select it and click the Delete button.

For instructions on using the New Style and Modify Style dialog boxes, refer to "Assigning Style Sheet Properties" later in this chapter.

If you understand CSS code, another option is to directly modify the CSS rules displayed in the Page view window.

Chapter 20: Managing Appearance with Cascading Style Sheets

Linking Style Sheet Files

In a universe consisting only of CSS files and Web pages, there are two ways of relating the two:

- First pick the style sheet file, and then select the Web pages it should control; or

- First pick the Web pages, and then select the style sheet file that controls them.

FrontPage uses the second of these approaches. Here are the procedural details:

1 Create a file containing the CSS rules you want, and then save it in your FrontPage Web with a *.css* extension.

2 If you want to control only certain files in your Web, select them. This will probably be easiest in Folders view. To select a page that's open in Page view, click anything within it.

3 Choose Style Sheet Links from the Format menu. The Link Style Sheet dialog box shown in the foreground of Figure 20-12 appears.

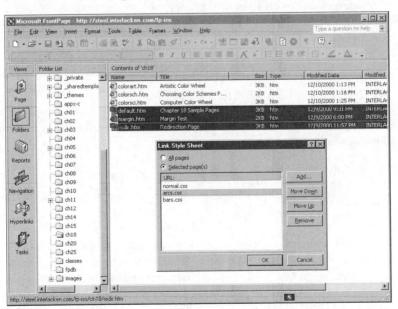

Figure 20-12. Use the options in the foreground dialog box to apply a cascading style sheet file to one or more pages in a FrontPage-based Web.

4 To apply a style sheet to every page in your Web, select All Pages. To apply it only to the pages you selected in step 2, select Selected Page(s).

5 If the style sheet file you want to apply isn't already listed, click the Add button to locate the file, and add it to the list. This button displays a typical file selection dialog box titled Select Style Sheet.

6 If you don't want a listed style sheet file to apply to the specified pages, select it in the URL list, and then click Remove. This action doesn't physically delete the file.

7 If the URL list includes more than one style sheet file, the browser will apply them in order. To change this order, select the CSS file you want to move and then click the Move Down or Move Up button. Continue this process until all the files are in the order you want.

8 Click OK.

---

caution   If the current Web is server-based (that is, if the top of your Folder List shows an HTTP location), the Link Style Sheet dialog box will fail unless the Web server is running FrontPage 2000 (or later) Server Extensions. Earlier versions of the extensions can't insert style sheet links based on commands from the FrontPage desktop software.

CSS merges style sheet rules on a property-by-property basis. Consider, for example, the following series of rules (the syntax is fairly self-explanatory and not critical to this discussion):

```
h1 { font-family: Arial; color: red; }
h1 { font-weight: bold; }
h1 { color: blue; margin-left: 10px; }
```

The presence of these three rules produces the same result as the presence of the following single rule:

```
h1 { font-family: Arial;
     font-weight: bold;
     color: blue;
     margin-left: 10px; }
```

The same results occur whether the rules appear sequentially in one file, separated by other rules in the same file, or interspersed with others rules in various files. The last value you assign to any selector property is the value the browser applies.

Similar considerations apply when one selector inherits properties from another. Consider, for example, the following series of rules:

```
body { color: red; }
h1   { font-family: serif; color: blue; }
body { font-family: sans-serif; }
```

The first rule says that all text in the body of the Web page should be red. The second rule says that all Heading 1 text should appear in the browser's default serif font and be blue. This second rule overrides the red color specified by the first rule, but only for Heading 1 text. The third rule presents a problem by specifying that all body text should appear in the browser's default sans-serif font. Does this override the more specific *font-family* setting in the second rule or not?

As it turns out, the third rule doesn't override properties established in the second rule because the second rule is more specific. But who needs these kinds of puzzles in life? And this is exactly what happens when you start assigning multiple CSS files to the same Web page. Save yourself a headache or three and confine yourself, if not to one CSS file per Web, at least to one CSS file per page.

Assigning Style Sheet Properties

All three procedures discussed so far (that is, the procedures for inline styles, for page level styles, and for linked style sheets) culminated in displaying the Modify Style dialog box shown previously in Figure 20-7 or the New Style dialog box shown in previously Figure 20-9. These dialog boxes create rules and display styles currently in effect, but actually setting CSS properties requires more pointing and clicking. Specifically:

1 Click the Format button that appears in the lower left corner of either dialog box.

2 Choose Font, Paragraph, Border, Numbering, or Position from the drop-down list.

The next four topics describe the first four options. Positioning deserves it own major heading, which follows shortly thereafter.

Assigning Style Sheet Fonts

The dialog box for assigning CSS fonts is shown in Figure 20-13 on the next page. If this looks hauntingly familiar, you're right; it contains most of the options that the box in Figure 10-20 contains—minus a few. The difference is that here, you're configuring an abstract style and not a specific Web-page element.

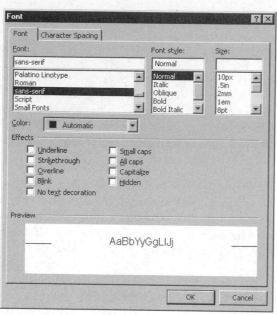

Figure 20-13. This dialog box specifies CSS fonts. Notice that you can type font names or choose from the Font list. The Size box accepts a plethora of measurement types.

Table 20-1 associates the options in this dialog box with the CSS properties they control, describes what they do, and itemizes the acceptable values. The same table also lists related CSS properties not accessible through FrontPage dialog boxes, just in case you're bold enough (sorry) to engage HTML view and modify your style rules directly.

No matter what font name you assign to a cascading style sheet property, there's no assurance the visitor has that font available. If the specified font *isn't* available, the visitor's browser does its best to pick another font that's similar, but this is far from an exact science. After all, if the visitor's system doesn't have a font like Gloucester MT Extra Condensed installed, how's it supposed to know enough about it to pick something similar?

Table 20-1. CSS Font Properties

Dialog box option	CSS property name	Description and values
Font	*font-family*	A list of font names available on the local system. Select any listed font, or type the name of another font. Although you must type them, the generic fonts listed in Table 20-2 are excellent choices.

Chapter 20: Managing Appearance with Cascading Style Sheets

Table 20-1. *(continued)*

Dialog box option	CSS property name	Description and values
Font Style	*font-style*	Can be *normal*, *italic*, or *oblique*. Normal text is upright. Italic text is slanted, thinned, and more curved. Oblique text is slanted but otherwise resembles normal.
	font-weight	The thickness of the strokes making up a font. Values include: A numeric weight from 100 to 900. The keywords *normal* (=400) or *bold* (=700). The keywords *bolder* or *lighter,* which thicken or weaken strokes compared to the object's parent.
Size	*font-size*	The height of a font, measured from the top of the tallest character to the bottom of the lowest. Any CSS unit of measure is okay.
Color	*color*	The color in which text should appear. FrontPage controls this using its standard sequence of color dialog boxes.
Underline Strikethrough Overline Blink No Text Decoration	*text-decoration*	Controls the following modifications to normal text: *underline*, *overline*, *strikethrough*, and *blink*. The default is *none.*
Small Caps	*font-variant*	Can be *normal* or *small-caps*. The value *small-caps* replaces lowercase letters with reduced-size capital letters.
All Caps Capitalize	*text-transform*	Presents text in a certain case, regardless of how it was entered. The options are: *capitalize* (first letter only, all others lowercase) *uppercase* (all uppercase) *lowercase* (all lowercase) *none* (as is, the default).
Hidden	*visibility*	Values of *hidden* (Internet Explorer) or *hide* (Netscape) make an element invisible. Values of *visible* (Internet Explorer) or *show* (Netscape) make it visible.
(none)	*font*	This is a shortcut property that accepts any of the values described above. CSS assigns each value to the correct property based on the value's syntax.

Chapter 20

There are three solutions to this problem:

- **Specify only commonly available fonts.** Fonts that come with Windows, fonts that come with Microsoft Office, and fonts installed with the visitor's browser are probably available to the vast majority of your visitors. Stick to these fonts.

- **Specify generic fonts.** The generic font names listed in Table 20-2 have reasonable equivalents on every user's system.

  It's true that the cursive and fantasy generic fonts still leave you wondering what you're going to get, but the serif, sans-serif, and monospace choices are reasonably specific and highly useful.

- **Specify multiple fonts.** The *font-family* property can accept a list of fonts the browser should use, in order of preference. In code, it looks like this:

```
h1 { font-family: Verdana, Arial, Helvetica, sans-serif; }
```

  This code makes the browser look first to see if the Verdana font is available, then Arial, then Helvetica, and then any sans-serif font. This virtually guarantees that what the visitor sees will conform to your original design.

  Unfortunately, FrontPage doesn't have a good facility for specifying a list of fonts. You can choose the first one from the Font list in Figure 20-13, but you must enter any additional fonts by hand, separating the font names with commas.

Table 20-2. **Generic CSS Fonts**

Generic font	Description
serif	The system-default serif font, such as Times New Roman or Times Roman.
sans-serif	The system-default sans-serif font, such as Arial or Helvetica.
cursive	A font that looks like handwriting.
fantasy	A highly decorative font.
monospace	The system-default monospaced font, such as Courier New or Courier.

The Character Spacing tab of the CSS Font dialog box is shown in Figure 20-14. Table 20-3 details the corresponding CSS properties.

Chapter 20: Managing Appearance with Cascading Style Sheets

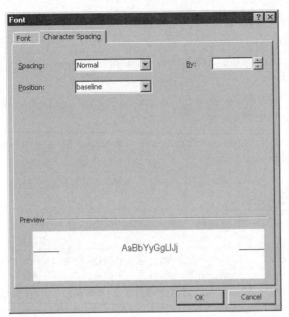

Figure 20-14. This CSS dialog box affects character spacing (kerning) and vertical alignment.

Table 20-3. **CSS Letter Spacing and Positioning Properties**

Dialog box option	CSS property name	Description and values
Spacing	*letter-spacing*	Expands or condenses the spacing between letters. The default measurement is in pixels. The accompanying By spinner controls the amount.
Position	*vertical-align*	A positive measurement raises the object above its normal position by the amount you choose. A negative measurement lowers it below. See the accompanying text for more options.

The Position (*vertical-align*) property specifies the alignment of an inline object relative to the surrounding text. Table 20-4 on the next page summarizes the permissible values. Despite its name, this property has nothing to do with CSS Positioning (CSS2).

> **note** The baseline is the imaginary straight line on which letters in a line of text rest. (The lowercase descenders of letters such as *j* and *g* extend below the baseline.)

Table 20-4. **CSS Font Position Properties**

Setting	Description
baseline	The baseline of the child (surrounded) object aligns with the baseline of the parent (surrounding) text.
sub	The baseline of the child object aligns with the parent's preferred baseline for subscripts.
super	The baseline of the child object aligns with the parent's preferred baseline for superscripts.
top	The top of the child object aligns with the top border of the surrounding text.
text-top	The top of the child object aligns with the top of the surrounding text.
middle	The object's vertical midpoint aligns with the parent's baseline raised by one-half the x-height (the height of a lowercase letter with no ascenders or descenders, such as *a, e, o,* and, well, *x*). In other words, the midpoint of the object would align with the midpoint of such letters as *a, e, o,* or *x* in the surrounding text.
bottom	The bottom of the child object aligns with the bottom border of the surrounding text.
text-bottom	The bottom of the child object aligns with the bottom of the parent.
percentage	If vertical alignment is a percentage, this value raises or lowers the child's position by that fraction of the parent's line height. The 50% setting raises the child object half a line. (Although no percentages appear in the drop-down list, you can enter a percentage by hand.)

Assigning Style Sheet Paragraph Properties

Cascading style sheets provide amazing control over the layout of paragraphs. The CSS Paragraph dialog box, which is shown in Figure 20-15, provides access to some of the available layout properties. The Border and Numbering dialog boxes, discussed later in this chapter, control even more such properties.

Table 20-5 correlates the options in the CSS Paragraph dialog box with the CSS properties they control, and then describes those properties.

Chapter 20: Managing Appearance with Cascading Style Sheets

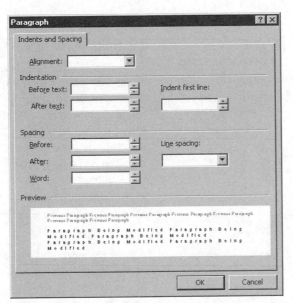

Figure 20-15. The Paragraph dialog box controls paragraph alignment, indentation, and spacing.

Table 20-5. **CSS Paragraph Properties**

Dialog box option	CSS property name	Description and values
Alignment	*text-align*	Controls the horizontal position of text. *left* aligns text to the left margin (left-aligned, flush-left).
		right aligns text to the right margin (right-aligned, flush-right).
		center aligns the center of each line with the center of the available area.
		justify aligns text to both the left and right margins, spreading the required space as evenly as possible between words in the line.
Indent First Line	*text-indent*	Specifies first-line paragraph indentation. Negative numbers produce "outdents" (where the first line extends to the left of second and subsequent lines).

(continued)

Table 20-5. *(continued)*

Dialog box option	CSS property name	Description and values
Indentation Before Text Indentation After Text Spacing Before Spacing After	*margin-left* *margin-right* *margin-top* *margin-bottom*	These four properties control the amount of blank space that surrounds a page element's border (or where the border would be, if its thickness weren't zero.) If you're working in code and want all four margins to be the same, code a *margin* property like this: margin: 10px
Spacing Word	*word-spacing*	Adjusts the normal spacing between words. Positive measurements increase spacing and negative values decrease it.
Line Spacing	*line-height*	Specifies the amount of vertical space reserved for a line. A common value is the point size times 1.2.

The Indentation Before Text, Indentation After Text, Spacing Before, and Spacing After options control the amount of white space reserved around the borders of an element, plus a small buffer zone called *padding*. Figure 20-16 illustrates the concepts of margins and of padding:

- The *content area* is the space that a picture, text, a table, or another type of content occupies.

- *Padding* surrounds the content area, matching its background color and certain other properties.

- If there's a visible *border*, it surrounds the padding area and not just the content area.

- *Margins* surround the padding area and borders, if there are any. Unlike padding—which matches the background of its contents—margins match the background of whatever surrounds them.

> **tip** Starting from the outside and proceeding inward, the areas that surround a content area are border, margin, and padding: M-B-P. Remembering this acronym might be easier than remembering the CSS property names.

Chapter 20: Managing Appearance with Cascading Style Sheets

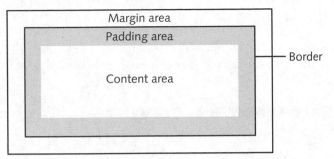

Figure 20-16. Padding surrounds a Web page object and matches its background. Margins surround the padding and match the exterior background. Borders, if specified, appear where the two meet.

You can specify margin width, border width, and padding width in terms of any CSS measurement. The most common, however, is pixels.

The line-height property controls the height of lines in a paragraph. FrontPage suggests measurements in pixels, but the CSS standard also provides for specifying a percentage or ratio of the font size (for example, either 120 percent or 1.2).

When you specify the *line-height* property (or most other text measurements) as a percentage, other objects will inherit not the percentage itself, but the result of multiplying the percentage and the font size. Consider the following example:

```
{ font-size: 12pt; line-height: 120%; }
fineprint { font-size: 10pt; }
```

The default style's line-height property will be 120 percent x 12 points = 14.4 points. Because the default style's line height is a percentage, the *fineprint* class inherits the multiplied result—14.4 points—as its line height. (Typographers would call this 10/14.4 spacing, meaning 10-point text and a 14.4-point line height. They might also speak of it as 10-point text with 4.4 points of leading. Leading refers to the strips of lead that early printers used to separate rows of movable type.)

```
{ font-size: 12pt; line-height: 1.2; }
fineprint { font-size: 10pt; }
```

In the second example, the default style's line height would again be 14.4 points—1.2 x 12 points. Because the default style's line height is a ratio, the *fineprint* class inherits the ratio and recalculates the effective line height as 1.2 x 10 points = 12 points. This results in a 10/12 spacing and a more attractive display of 10-point text.

Assigning Style Sheet Borders

Figure 20-17 illustrates the Borders tab of the CSS Borders And Shading dialog box. This appears after you click Format and choose Border in the New Style or Modify Style dialog box.

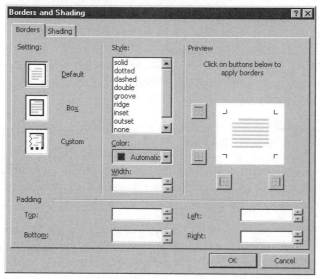

Figure 20-17. The Borders tab controls the visible border around Web page elements, as well as the amount of padding between the border and the page element's contents.

To operate this dialog box:

1 Double-click one of the Setting choices:

- **Default.** Means the current rule will have no effect on border settings.

- **Box.** Means you want borders on all four sides.

- **Custom.** Means you want borders on one, two, or three sides.

2 Choose the border style you want from the Style list. The Preview area will reflect your choice.

3 Use the Color drop-down list to specify what color the border should be.

4 Use the Width to specify how thick the border should be.

5 If you chose Custom (or just changed your mind), click any of the four icons at the left of and below the preview diagram. Each icon adds or removes borders on a different side—top, bottom, left, or right.

The Padding section is only marginally related to the parts of the dialog box described so far. Do you recall from the previous section that margin measurements control the amount of space between an element's surroundings and its border? Well, padding

Chapter 20: Managing Appearance with Cascading Style Sheets

controls the amount of space between the border and the element's regular content. Refer again to Figure 20-16 if a picture would clarify this.

Table 20-6 correlates each Borders tab setting with the CSS properties it controls.

Table 20-6. **CSS Border Properties**

Dialog box option	CSS property name	Description and values
Style	*border-style*	Specifies the type of line used to draw the border—none, solid, dotted, double, and so on.
Color	*border-color*	Indicates the color you want the border to be.
Width	*border-width*	Specifies the thickness of the border. You can specify width using generic values of *thick*, *medium*, or *thin*, or as a specific number of pixels. As before, the CSS specification supports additional units of measure.
Preview buttons	*border-top* *border-right* *border-bottom* *border-left*	These four properties control the type of border drawn on each side of a Web of a Web page element. Accepted values are those listed in the Style box in Figure 20-17, plus *none*.
Padding Top Padding Bottom Padding Left Padding Right	*padding-top* *padding-bottom* *padding-left* *padding-right*	These four settings control the amount of white space reserved between a page element's border and its content.
(none)	*border-top-width* *border-right-width* *border-bottom-width* *border-left-width*	These four properties specify the width of each border side independently. If all four sides should be the same width, it's much easier to use the *border-width* property.

If you're working with CSS rules by hand, it's often useful to use the *margin* and *padding* property names rather than the more detailed properties shown in Table 20-5 and Table 20-6. For example, it's perfectly OK to code:

```
.special { border: 2px solid #900; }
```

rather than:

```
.special { border-width: 2px; border-style: solid; border-color: #900; }
```

623

The order of any values you specify as border properties isn't important. CSS can figure out that measurements must be border widths, style names must be style values, and color values must be border colors.

If you manually code a CSS rule that uses the *border* and *padding* property names and then you modify the rule using FrontPage dialog boxes, FrontPage might rewrite the rule with detailed property names like *border-width* and *border-style*. The result on formatting, however, will be the same.

In the case of border width and padding width, you can specify anywhere from one to four values. Table 20-7 shows which values control which measurements, depending on the number of values you supply.

Table 20-7. CSS Border Width and Padding Width Property Values

Number of values specified	Source of value for:			
	Top	Right	Bottom	Left
1	1st	1st	1st	1st
2	1st	2nd	1st	2nd
3	1st	2nd	3rd	2nd
4	1st	2nd	3rd	4th

The second tab on the Borders And Shading dialog box is—you guessed it and won the bet—the Shading tab, shown in Figure 20-18. Table 20-8 relates the options on the Shading tab with their corresponding CSS properties and values.

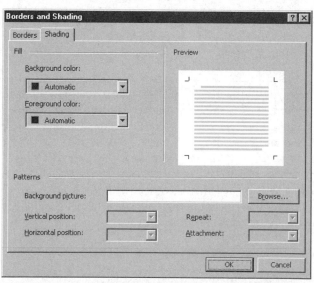

Figure 20-18. The Shading tab controls the foreground color and background appearance of styled elements on your Web page.

Chapter 20: Managing Appearance with Cascading Style Sheets

Table 20-8. **CSS Shading Properties**

Dialog box option	CSS property name	Description and values
Background Color	*background-color*	Specifies the default color used for filling the background of an element.
Foreground Color	*color*	Specifies the color used for presenting an object's contents. For many elements, this is the color in which text will appear.
Background Picture	*background-picture*	Specifies a picture that will fill the background of an element.
Vertical Position Horizontal Position	*background-position*	Controls positioning of the first (or only) background picture. These can be: The keywords *top, bottom, center, left,* and/or *right,* interpreted within the space the page element occupies. Percentages, again interpreted within the page element space. *0% 0%* means *top left*; *100% 100%* means *bottom right*. Any valid CSS measurement, interpreted from the element's top left corner.
Repeat	*background-repeat*	Controls the repetitive tiling of a background picture. *repeat* repeats the background picture both vertically and horizontally to fill the entire available area. *repeat-x* repeats the picture horizontally only. *repeat-y* repeats the picture vertically only. *no-repeat* displays the picture only once and doesn't repeat it.
Attachment	*background-attachment*	Scrolls the background picture or keeps it fixed. *scroll* moves the background picture along with other content. This is the default. *fixed* keeps the background picture stationary, even when other content scrolls.

Troubleshooting

FrontPage doesn't preserve CSS coding syntax.

In many cases, the CSS code that goes into FrontPage doesn't come out looking the same. Or, as insiders would say, FrontPage doesn't accurately *round-trip* CSS code.

In most cases, any changes FrontPage makes to CSS code are relatively harmless. If you code the following, for example:

```
.special { border-width: 2px; border-style: solid; border-color: 900#; }
```

FrontPage substitutes the more compact expression:

```
.special { border: 2px solid #900; }
```

Just to be inconsistent, FrontPage might also expand compact expressions to longer forms. For example, it converts this expression:

```
.test1 { padding: 3px 5px }
```

to the longer form:

```
.text1 { padding-left: 5px; padding-right: 5px,
         padding-top: 3px; padding-bottom: 5px }
```

This sometimes leads to curious results when CSS code contains errors. The following code, for example, tries to assign border properties to a margin:

```
.woeisme { margin: 2px solid #900; }
```

FrontPage converts this rule to the following which is definitely not equivalent:

```
.special { margin-left:solid; margin-right:solid;
           margin-top:2px; margin-bottom:#900 }
```

The original code wouldn't have produced correct results anyway, but the modified code is valid CSS that does something other than what the designer wanted. If your CSS code doesn't seem to be working as intended, either look at the CSS code directly in HTML view or review and correct all the values in CSS dialog boxes.

Assigning Style Sheet Numbering

The fourth Format option in the New Style and Modify Style dialog boxes is really a misnomer; the menu says Numbering but the dialog box controls unnumbered bullets

Chapter 20: Managing Appearance with Cascading Style Sheets

as well. Oh well, at least the resulting dialog box is titled Bullets And Numbering, as you can see in Figure 20-19.

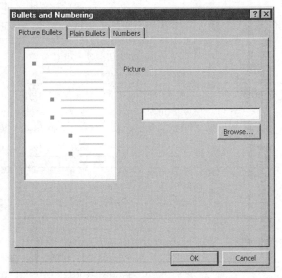

Figure 20-19.   Use this dialog box to specify what kind of bullets or numbers should appear for a bulleted or numbered list.

The three tabs are very simple and very much alike:

- **Picture Bullets.** This tab provides a text box and accompanying Browse button. Together, these specify a picture the browser will use for a bulleted list. This can be any picture the browser can display, though caution suggests a small one. Browse to the picture you want to display, and then click OK.

- **Plain Bullets.** This tab displays four ordinary bullet styles: none, solid round, hollow round, and solid square. Click the style you want, and then click OK.

- **Numbers.** This tab displays six numbering styles: none, Arabic numerals, uppercase roman numerals, uppercase letters, lowercase letters, and lowercase roman numerals. Click the style you want, and then click OK.

The Bullets And Numbering dialog box has the least direct correlation to CSS styles. Nevertheless, Table 20-9 on the next page lists the applicable CSS properties.

Table 20-9. **CSS Bullets and Numbering Properties**

Dialog box option	CSS property name	Description and values
Bullet Samples	*list-style-type*	Specifies the type of list bullet. Permissible values are *disc, circle, square, decimal, lower-roman, upper-roman, lower-alpha, upper-alpha,* and *none*.
Picture	*list-style-image*	Specifies the URL of a picture the browser will display as a list bullet. A relative URL like *../images/ballred.gif* or *mydot.gif* is best.
(none)	*list-style-position*	Specifies whether the list bullet should appear *inside* or *outside* the text area. The default is *outside* which produces hanging bullets like the ones in this book.
(all)	*list-style*	A shortcut property that accepts any combination of values described above. CSS assigns the values to the correct properties based on syntax.

Assigning Additional Style Sheet Properties

Table 20-10 lists some additional CSS properties that don't pertain to any of the FrontPage dialog boxes presented so far. These may be useful if you end up being a CSS fanatic and coding rules by hand in HTML view.

Table 20-10. **CSS Properties Not Supported in CSS Dialog Boxes**

CSS property	Description and values
width	The desired width of an element, using any valid CSS measurement.
height	The desired height of an element, using any valid CSS measurement.
float	Specifies an object's alignment: *left, center,* or *right*. Text will flow around left-aligned or right-aligned objects, but not around centered ones. If the property is blank, the object either flows in line with text or is left-aligned with text not flowing around it, depending on the type of object.

Chapter 20: Managing Appearance with Cascading Style Sheets

Table 20-10. *(continued)*

CSS property	Description and values
clear	Specifies that an element should be positioned far enough down the page that it clears any left-aligned elements, right-aligned elements, or both. Permissible values are *none* (the default), *left*, *right*, and *both*.
display	Controls how an element is displayed. *block* means the element starts on a new line, like a paragraph or heading. *inline* means the element flows within a line, as occurs with bold or italic text. *list-item* means the element appears as an indented box with a preceding label, like a bulleted or numbered list. *none* means the element does not appear.
white-space	Controls the treatment of spaces, tabs, line feeds, and carriage returns. *normal* treats all strings of such characters as if they were a single-space character. *pre* leaves all such characters in place. *nowrap* compresses white space characters like *normal*, but doesn't break lines wider than the browser window.

Positioning Content with Style Sheets

Pixel-precise positioning and layering of page elements has long been a dream of Web designers. They yearn for the relative simplicity of print design, where they can put things at specific page locations and not worry about readers changing the page dimensions after the fact. Well, CSS Positioning provides just that capability. Of course, nothing can stop Web visitors from having different-sized monitors or from resizing the browser window.

Introducing Style Sheet Positioning

Level 2 of the W3C's Cascading Style Sheets specification provides three kinds of positioning:

- **Static.** Browsers have supported this kind of positioning since the beginning. This remains the default.

- **Relative.** This kind of positioning lays out the Web page normally, but then, just before displaying any positioned elements, shifts them up, down, right, or left of their normal locations. The browser flows other content around the space where the relative position element *would have been* had it not been positioned.

● **Absolute.** This kind of positioning makes an element appear at specific *x-y* coordinates, measured from the top left corner of some *container* to the top left corner of the element. The browser reserves *no space* for the absolutely positioned element; the element just appears at the specified location. Other content doesn't flow around it.

The default container is the current Web page. You specify measurements in relation to top left corner, so the CSS statement to display something 20 pixels below the top of the browser window is:

```
top: 20px;
```

The command to place something 30 pixels from the left edge of the browser window is:

```
left: 30px;
```

Combining this with the command that invokes absolute positioning produces this HTML:

```
style="position: absolute; top: 20px; left: 30px;"
```

CSS Positioning supports more properties than just *position, top,* and *left,* but those three will do for now. If you're curious about the rest, browse through Table 20-11. If you're curious about whether FrontPage makes you type code like the above, you can be sure it doesn't. Subsequent topics will get to that shortly.

Table 20-11. **CSS Positioning Properties**

Property	Values	Interpretation
position	*static*	Tells the browser to position content normally. No special positioning is in effect.
	relative	Positions content relative to its normal page location.
	absolute	Positions content relative to the top left corner of its container.
top, left	*auto*, *<length>*, *<percent>*	Controls the placement of elements assigned relative or absolute positioning.

Chapter 20: Managing Appearance with Cascading Style Sheets

Table 20-11. *(continued)*

Property	Values	Interpretation
width, *height*	*auto,* *<length>,* *<percent>*	Controls the size of positioned elements.
z-index	*auto,* *number*	Controls the visual precedence of positioned elements that overlap. Static elements have a z-index of zero.
visibility	*inherit* *visible* *hidden*	Controls whether an element is visible. The *inherit* value adopts the visibility of the parent container.
clip	*auto,* *rect* *(upper-right,* *lower-left)*	Defines what portion of an absolutely positioned element is visible.
overflow	*visible*	If an element's content exceeds its height or width, enlarges the container to display all the content.
	hidden	If an element's content exceeds its height or width, hides the additional content.
	auto	If an element's content exceeds its height or width, displays scroll bars as necessary.
	scroll	If an element's content exceeds its height or width, displays scroll bars at all times.

So, what can you position? Well, all browsers can do static positioning because that's what they've been doing all along. In addition:

- Netscape Navigator 4 can apply:

  - *relative* or *absolute* positioning to spans, divisions, and block elements.

- Internet Explorer 4 and later can apply:

  - *relative* positioning to any page element.

  - *absolute* positioning to all the element types listed in Table 20-12 on the next page.

Table 20-12. **Valid Absolute Positioning Elements**

Navigator-positionable	Internet Explorer-positionable	Internet Explorer unique elements	Form elements
Divisions	Pictures	Fieldsets	Buttons
Spans	Applets	Frames	Input Elements
Block Elements	Objects		Select Lists
Tables			Text Areas

A *block element* is anything that causes line breaks before and after itself. Normal paragraphs are the most common block elements, followed by the various heading types.

Divisions and *spans* are two HTML tags that mark sections of a Web page. A division starts where you put a *<div>* tag, ends where you put a *</div>* tag, and creates line breaks before and after itself. A span starts with **, ends with **, and flows continuously with surrounding elements.

Both divisions and spans are normally invisible. This presents a problem for WYSIWYG editors like FrontPage, because what you see is nothing. FrontPage has a way of handling this, but once again, this is something that will come shortly.

A *container* is any page element that establishes a coordinate system for positioned elements within it. The default container, and the only one Netscape Navigator 4 recognizes, is the body of the Web page. Internet Explorer 4 and later also support divisions inside one another, positioning the inner division relative to the top left corner of the outer division. In the same situation, Netscape 4 positions both divisions relative to the top left corner of the page.

Why bother with all this? Well, the Page view editor supports only a portion of the total CSS Positioning specification. For example, FrontPage sometimes has trouble dealing with relative positioning, and it won't put one division inside another. Furthermore, it can't apply background colors, background pictures, borders, margins, and padding to any divisions or spans you create. If you want to use these sorts of features, you need to either take a reality pill or go into HTML view and deal with the code.

Controlling Position in FrontPage

There are two ways to control positioning in FrontPage:

● Through the Positioning dialog box that adds or modifies positioning properties for existing content.

● Through the Positioning toolbar that applies absolute positioning to existing content and modifies positioning properties.

Chapter 20: Managing Appearance with Cascading Style Sheets

Show All

When working with positioned content, it's best to have the Standard toolbar's Show All option enabled. With Show All in effect, FrontPage displays a hairline box around any positioned element.

In addition, whether or not Show All is in effect, FrontPage displays sizing handles around any positioned content you select. You can resize the positioned area by dragging its handles. To reposition it, move the mouse pointer over the area's outer edge and watch for it to take on this shape:

Whenever the pointer has this shape, you can hold down the mouse button and drag the positioned content around the page.

Using the Positioning Dialog Box

To position elements by menu, first select the content you want to position and then choose Position from the Format menu. The dialog box in Figure 20-20 appears.

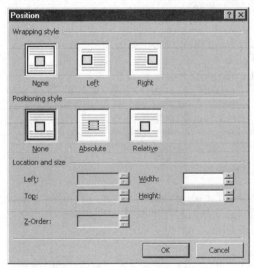

Figure 20-20. The Position dialog box controls the same properties as the Positioning toolbar, plus Wrapping Style and Relative Positioning.

The position dialog box provides these options:

- **Wrapping Style.** Controls how content outside the division or span flows around it. The choices are None (default alignment), Left (division or span aligned at the left margin with other content flowing around it at the right), and Right (aligned at the right margin with other content flowing around it at the left).

- **Positioning Style.** Controls the type of positioning: None (the default, which CSS2 calls static), Absolute, or Relative.

- **Left** and **Top.** Controls the positioned element's actual position, measured from the top left corner of the element's container to the top left corner of the element itself.

- **Width** and **Height.** Controls the positioned element's size.

- **Z-Order.** Controls the element's display precedence compared to that of overlapping elements (that is, it controls the element's *z-index*).

Using the Position dialog box to modify existing properties is trickier than it might first appear. A problem occurs when:

- The positioned element is a division.

- You select an element inside that division.

- You then display the Position dialog box.

When the Position dialog box appears, it won't show the existing positioning properties. Furthermore, after you enter some properties and click OK, FrontPage creates a *new* division or span inside the existing one. This is almost certainly not what you want. If you're trying to modify existing positioning and the existing properties don't appear, try clicking Cancel and selecting the division rather than its contents. If that doesn't work, try making your change through the Positioning toolbar.

> **tip**   To select a division, click the margin space to its right or left.

Using the Positioning Toolbar

FrontPage provides a special toolbar for controlling position properties, namely the Positioning toolbar described in Table A-9. All the controls on this toolbar have equivalents in the Position dialog box described in the previous section.

 For more information about the Positioning toolbar, refer to "The Positioning Toolbar" in the Bonus Content on the Companion CD.

The Positioning toolbar doesn't support relative positioning, but it can switch areas between static and absolute. To absolutely position one or more existing Web page elements:

1 Display the Positioning toolbar by choosing Toolbars from the View menu and then choosing Positioning.

2 Select the Web page element(s) you want to position. You can choose a single element or a contiguous set.

Chapter 20: Managing Appearance with Cascading Style Sheets

Position
Absolutely

3 Click the Position Absolutely button on the Positioning toolbar. At this point:

■ If you selected a single element (other than a block element) that appears in Table 20-12, FrontPage adds absolute positioning to that element's properties.

■ If you selected a block element, multiple elements, or an element not included in Table 20-12, FrontPage draws a division around the selected content and adds absolute positioning to that division's properties.

If the selection includes only part of a block element, FrontPage extends the selection to include the entire block element.

■ As usual, handles and possibly hairline borders appear around the positioned area.

■ Absolutely positioning an element or area generally won't cause it to move. The absolutely positioned area, however, no longer reserves any space on the ordinary page area. This means any elements that previously followed the now-positioned content may now flow under it, resulting in a sort of double exposure.

When positioning is in effect for an element, clicking it always displays handles. There are two ways to resize an absolutely positioned element:

● By dragging the handles with the mouse.

● By typing a measurement into the Width and/or Height boxes on the Positioning toolbar.

Width   Height

To relocate an absolutely positioned element or division, first click it to make handles appear, and then:

● Click the numeric values in the Positioning toolbar's Left or Top fields, and type the coordinate you want; or

Left   Top

● Drag the element by its edges. The "move" mouse pointer appears when the mouse is in the required position.

Figure 20-21 shows a Web page with absolute positioning in effect for five elements: the four mime pictures and the heading paragraph, "Great Leaping Mimes." Making such an arrangement work in Netscape Navigator 4 is a nuisance because FrontPage positions single pictures by adding inline style properties—attached directly to the pictures—and not by putting them inside positioned divisions.

Figure 20-21. The four pictures and the title string are each absolutely positioned elements. Z-indexing governs the display of overlapping elements.

To avoid this problem and force FrontPage to surround the picture with a new division:

1 Type a character or word next to the picture.

2 Select that character or word *and* the picture.

Position
Absolutely

3 Click the Position Absolutely button on either the Positioning toolbar or the Pictures toolbar.

4 Delete the character or word you typed in step 1.

Here's the reason this works. Recall from the previous section that Internet Explorer can position individual pictures but Netscape Navigator cannot. When you select a picture and then apply absolute positioning, FrontPage acts in accordance with Internet Explorer's behavior and just positions the picture.

Chapter 20: Managing Appearance with Cascading Style Sheets

The HTML looks like this:

```
<img border="0" src="images/mimerest.gif"
    style="position: absolute;
    width: 131; height: 107; top: 44; left: 286; ">
```

Unfortunately, Netscape Navigator, at least through version 4, ignores this positioning information. Netscape needs the picture positioned within a division, like this:

```
<div style="position: absolute;
    width: 131; height: 107; top: 44; left: 286;">
<img border="0" src="images/mimerest.gif"
    width="131" height="107">
</div>
```

Including some text along with the picture makes FrontPage create a division instead of just positioning the picture directly, and the division remains in place even after the text is deleted. The results appear in Figure 20-22.

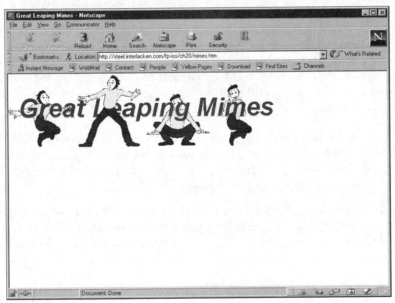

Figure 20-22. With care taken during page creation, Netscape Navigator 4 can also display positioned content.

Note in Figure 20-21 how three mimes appear behind the title and one in front. This is an example of z-indexing. Positioned content with higher z-index values appears in front of content with lower z-index values. Both positive and negative numbers are acceptable as z-index values; ordinary page content has an implied z-index of 0. If two overlapping elements have the same z-index, the one defined first in the HTML appears behind the one defined later.

To assign a z-index value via the Positioning toolbar, first select it, and then either:

- Click the Bring Forward or Send Backward button on either the Positioning Toolbar or the Pictures toolbar; or

Bring Forward   Send Backward

- Enter a new value in the Z-Index box and press Enter.

Z-Index

Using Positioning Wisely

When working with overlapping positioned content, selecting a particular division can be maddening. Selecting some other division that overlaps the same space is way too easy. For this reason, it's very good practice to keep divisions as short and narrow as possible, minimizing the overlap and hence the problems.

Mixing positioned and unpositioned content is tricky as well. With part of a Web page changing with the visitor's browser environment and part being "nailed in place," it's very easy to produce a page that looks right only under the most perfect conditions. Here are a few suggestions to minimize this problem:

- Reserve white space on your page with a 1-pixel-wide transparent GIF file. Make this file as tall as your positioned content (assuming, of course, the white space won't move and the positioned content is fixed in height), and then locate the positioned content over the white space.

- Use a relatively positioned division as a container for your absolutely positioned content, because normal page content flows *around* a relatively positioned division. Unfortunately, Netscape Navigator 4 doesn't deal well with positioned content inside other positioned content.

- Absolutely position everything on your page. This avoids mixing free-flowing and absolutely positioned content, but it may require your visitors to adjust their browser windows.

Specifying Style Sheet Measurements and Colors

The CSS specification provides great flexibility in the way you specify heights, widths, distances, and colors. This section explains all the available options.

Specifying Style Sheet Measurements

The values of many CSS properties involve measurements: the height of the characters, the width of a paragraph, the thickness of a border, or whatever. The format for specifying these measurements consists of a number followed by a unit of measure, with no intervening spaces. Table 20-13 lists the valid units of measure, and here are some examples:

CSS code	Meaning
12pt	12 points
1.5in	1½ inches
7mm	7 millimeters
125%	25 percent larger than would otherwise be the case

Table 20-13. Cascading Style Sheet Units of Measure

Type	Unit	Name	Description
Absolute	mm	Millimeter	25.4 millimeters equal 1 inch.
	cm	Centimeter	1 centimeter equals 10 millimeters.
	in	Inch	1 inch equals 25.4 millimeters.
	pt	Point	72 points equals 1 inch.
	pc	Pica	1 pica equals 12 points. 6 picas equals 1 inch.
Relative	%	Percent	Indicates a degree of magnification compared to the item's normal size. For example, 200% means twice normal size, and 50% means half normal size.
	em	Em	1 em equals the point size of the current font.
	ex	Ex	1 ex equals the x-height of the current font. The x-height is the height of the lowercase x character.
Device-Dependent	px	Pixel	1 pixel equals the smallest unit of resolution on the user's display screen.

When possible, it's best to use relative measurements. That way, if the visitor's browser magnifies or shrinks the entire page, your elements retain the correct relative proportions. The same is true when you resize an element's parent and expect subordinate items to scale proportionately.

If you can't use relative measurements, the device-dependent *pixel* measurement should be your second choice. This at least maintains proportion to any pictures on your page, which the browser always sizes in terms of pixels. In addition, it avoids difficult-to-resolve situations involving odd pixel sizes (for example, trying to display a font 7.5 pixels high).

The main problem with absolute measurements, such as *1 in,* lies in not knowing what the visitor's computer thinks an inch is. Most video drivers interpret 1 inch as 72 pixels, so that 1 point equals 1 pixel. This convention is far from universal, though, and still subject to the visitor's monitor size and video setting.

The meaning of percentage measurements varies with the type of object. For most types, it's a percentage of the measurement the object would otherwise inherit. For example, a paragraph width of *80%* would make the paragraph 80 percent as wide as it otherwise would be. The following are typical exceptions to this rule:

- For colors, the range 0% to 100% corresponds to the normal RGB values 0 through 255.

- For line height, the percentage value is applied to the surrounding text's point size.

In the context of CSS, an em is a unit of distance equal to the point size of text. Thus, within 12-point text, 1 em equals 12 points—1/6 inch. The advantage of using ems as a unit of measure is that they change proportionately when the point size changes.

Specifying Style Sheet Colors

There are five ways to specify colors:

- **By name.** You can specify colors using the names from Table 18-1, "Colors in the 16-Color VGA Palette." For example:

  ```
  { color: red; }
  ```

- **By hexadecimal 12-bit color value.** To specify red, green, and blue colors on a hexadecimal scale from 0 to F, specify three hex digits followed by a pound sign. For example:

  ```
  { color: #F00; }
  ```

- **By hexadecimal 24-bit color value.** Specify six hex digits followed by a pound sign. That's two digits each for red, green, and blue intensities, on a scale from 00 to FF. For example:

  ```
  { color: #FF0000; }
  ```

Chapter 20: Managing Appearance with Cascading Style Sheets

- **By decimal 24-bit color value.** To specify red, green, and blue color values on a scale from 0 to 255, use this notation:

    ```
    { color: rgb(255,0,0); }
    ```

- **By percentage color value.** To specify red, green, and blue color values as percentages of maximum intensity, use this notation:

    ```
    { color: rgb(100%,0%,0%); }
    ```

> **tip** Remember to specify browser-safe colors wherever possible. The required RGB components for the various notations are:
> 12-bit: 0, 3, 6, 9, C, and F.
> 24-bit: 00, 33, 66, 99, CC, and FF.
> Decimal: 0, 51, 102, 153, 204, and 255.

Design Tips—Typography

Typography is the umbrella term for the use of typefaces, a fundamental tool of graphic design, whether on paper or on screen. The shape, color, and style of the letters and symbols that make up text convey meaning as surely as the words and sentences themselves. Effective use of type enhances and amplifies your message, just as ineffective use weakens it and even confuses viewers or readers.

Originally, fonts used on the Web were totally outside the page creator's control. The page creator specified text styles such as "Heading1" or "Normal," and visitors configured their browsers with desired fonts for each style. In practice, most fonts ended up being a form of Times Roman or Courier.

Choosing fonts for normal text presents a problem because computer monitors typically display only 72 pixels per inch. At such resolutions, there simply aren't enough pixels to differentiate similar typefaces. Often, there aren't even enough pixels to make fonts legible. For these reasons, overriding the default font for normal text requires great care.

Headings and titles generally use larger type sizes and thus provide more opportunity for artistic type selection. The problem is that there's no good way to ensure that visitors have the specified fonts on their systems; nor is there any widely accepted technology for providing temporary, downloadable fonts as Web-page components. As a result, and as a workaround, many Web designers approach typography by rendering text as pictures. This works, but it increases both development and download time. These costs are worth considering before you adopt this approach.

For more information about how FrontPage can render text as pictures, refer to "Inserting Text On GIF Components" on page 330.

As always, similar page elements should look alike, and dissimilar elements should look different. This means, for example:

- All first-level headings should look alike.

- All normal text should look alike.

- First-level headings and normal text should look different.

Similarly, all hypertext links should look alike, but something other than a link should never look like one. Many other examples are possible.

The extent of contrast between different page elements is a matter of judgment, but the result should be a mixture of contrast and unity. If something deserves typographical treatment to make it look different, then make it look *really* different. Insufficient contrast makes the reader stop reading and start analyzing the tiny differences you've created. Insufficient contrast confuses and distracts the reader.

Excessive contrast is similarly distracting. Each Web page should have a unity among all its elements, and all Web pages on the same topic or site warrant a certain unity as well. Choosing different styles and conventions for every page forces your readers to constantly reorient themselves, diverting their attention away from your message.

There are two main uses for bolding and italics on Web pages. In normal text, **bold** indicates words bearing special emphasis, and *italic* denotes special terms—especially the first instance of a special term.

Bolding and italics can also be useful in designing heading fonts. In this context, the entire heading phrase is bolded or italicized to distinguish it from normal text, other headings, or other page elements.

Underlining, by the way, is a crude substitute for italics carried over from the days of typewriters. Now that italics are readily available, there's no longer any need to emphasize text by underlining. Such text can also be confused with a link because browsers are often configured to display hyperlinks with an underline.

The primary dimensions that provide contrast between different kinds of text are:

- **Size.** Font size is normally measured in points, where 1 point equals 1/72 of an inch. It refers to the vertical range of the entire typeface as measured from the top of the tallest character to the bottom of the lowest "descender," such as the tail of the letter *j*. Figure 20-23 illustrates the basic dimensions of any font.

- **Color.** Text, like any other page element, can appear in any selected color. Text color should naturally be integrated with the overall color scheme for the page.

Chapter 20: Managing Appearance with Cascading Style Sheets

Figure 20-23. The size of a font is the distance from its highest ascender to its lowest descender. The x-height is the height of a lowercase *x*.

- **Typeface.** There are thousands of typefaces, and more are being created every day. It's remarkable that there can be so many variations on an alphabet of only 26 letters, and even more remarkable that so many variations of the same letters can be recognizable. Characteristics that differentiate one typeface from another include the following:

  - **Presence or absence of serifs.** Serifs are small, angular extensions added to the ends of character strokes. Fonts such as Times Roman and Garamond have them; Arial and Helvetica don't.

  - **Slant of serifs.** Serifs may be angled relative to the baseline or parallel to it; this is particularly relevant for lowercase letters.

  - **Thickness of serifs.** Serifs may be hairline thin or as thick as main character strokes.

  - **Stroke transition.** Strokes are the lines and curves that form the body of a character. Stroke transition refers to the difference between the thickest portions of a character and the thinnest.

  - **Stress.** This term refers to the angle of an imaginary line drawn through the thinnest portions of a rounded, symmetrical character such as *O*.

  - **Weight.** The difference between bold and normal text is one of weight, but other degrees of thickness are possible as well. Some typefaces are always thicker than others by design; very thick fonts often have the words *black* or *ultra* in their names. In general, the heavier the font, the more attention it attracts. However, a predominance of heavy fonts greatly reduces their effectiveness.

  - **Direction.** This property sometimes refers to curvature or rotation of the baseline (effects that, by the way, are more often abused than used properly). Beyond baseline alignment, though, direction can refer to the dimensions of text flow. Sentences or paragraphs fitted into tall, narrow columns have a more vertical direction than text fitted into the full width of a page. The rows and columns of cells in a table have horizontal and vertical dimensions. Items in a list can appear horizontally, in sentence format, or vertically, as bullets in a list (like this one).

643

Chapter 20

■ **Proportional versus monospaced.** Most typefaces are proportional, meaning some characters are wider than others. This is and should be the normal situation; there's no reason for lowercase *i* and capital *W* to occupy the same amount of space on a line.

Monospaced typefaces allocate the same amount of space for every character, much like a typewriter. They're significantly less attractive and less readable than proportional fonts, but may be preferable for program code listings and other applications that need equally spaced characters to align text without using tabs.

■ **Form.** This property refers to the overall shape of the letters, numbers, and symbols in the typeface. Uppercase and lowercase letters in the same font obviously have different forms, as do the characters in distinctly different typefaces. In a sense, form is the sum of all the technical properties above.

■ **Style.** This is a catchall property that covers everything not covered above. Typefaces are collections of artistic pictures, after all, and combining a set of technical and artistic properties into a useful and legible font is an artistic endeavor.

Every typeface has a name, but the names may reveal little about their properties. Some, such as Garamond and Baskerville, have a rich history and are named for their designers of a century or more ago, but many are recent creations, driven by market forces, or derivations of the classics. To analyze the contrast or similarity of typefaces, general categories such as the following are more useful. Figure 20-24 provides visual examples:

● **Oldstyle.** These are some of the oldest, most readable typefaces in common use. They feature slanted lowercase serifs, moderate transition in strokes, and left-leaning diagonal stress. Typical oldstyle typefaces include Times Roman, Times New Roman, and Garamond.

> **note** Many oldstyle fonts are difficult to display on the limited resolution of computer monitors. The limit of 72 pixels per inch simply doesn't provide enough detail to display moderate stroke variations and slanted pixels, especially at small point sizes. In online environments, therefore, oldstyle fonts are less common than they are in print. One aid to viewing fonts is software that smooths (anti-aliases) the typefaces, such as Microsoft Plus! or Adobe Type Manager. Another is higher-resolution video cards, used on larger monitors, that can display type at resolutions up to about 120 pixels per inch, making each character more fully formed.

● **Modern.** These fonts were invented to have a more mechanical, colder look than oldstyle fonts. Stroke transitions are extreme, stress is vertical, and serifs are horizontal. Bodoni and Elephant are typical modern fonts.

Chapter 20: Managing Appearance with Cascading Style Sheets

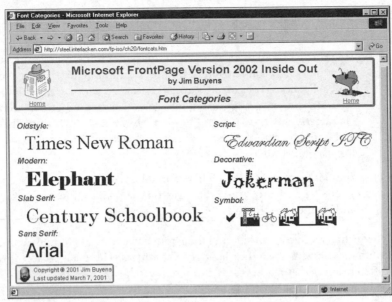

Figure 20-24. This Web page illustrates some of the most common font categories.

● **Slab serif.** Fonts in this category are designed for extra visibility by eliminating fine strokes. They have less stroke transition and thicker serifs than modern fonts, but retain the vertical stress. Century Schoolbook, New Century Schoolbook, and Clarendon are slab serif fonts.

● **Sans serif.** These fonts have no serifs and display uniform stroke thickness throughout. With no stroke transition, there is, of course, no stress. Sans serif fonts have a clean, technical appearance but in general aren't quite as legible as serif fonts. The contrast between serif and sans serif is quite extreme yet attractive, accounting for the common practice of using serifs for body text and sans serifs for headings. Common sans serif fonts include Arial and Helvetica.

● **Script.** Fonts that resemble handwriting or calligraphy fall into the script category. These are highly stylistic fonts typically used for wedding invitations and advertising. Most are inherently hard to read and even worse at computer monitor resolutions. Exercise great caution when considering a script font for use on a Web page. Edwardian Script ITC and Zapf Chancery are typical examples.

● **Decorative.** This category includes a wide variety of highly stylized fonts—you could almost call them fonts with a gimmick. They're eye-catching but hard to read, and overusing them can drive people screaming from the room. Small point sizes look terrible on computer monitors. Used properly, decorative fonts can produce eye-catching logos, headlines, and banners, but overuse is much more common than proper use. Tread carefully. Reading very much text in a font like Jokerman quickly grows tiresome.

- **Symbol.** These fonts range from useful symbols to visual clutter and don't even pretend to contain letters, numbers, and punctuation; they're actually icon collections. Formatting normal characters with a symbol font produces seemingly random sequences of mathematical symbols, foreign language characters, bullets, road signs, or pictures of almost anything. The Webdings and Zapf Dingbats fonts are examples. (A *dingbat* is a typographer's term for a symbol or decorative "thingie.")

  Symbol fonts are more useful in printed documents than in Web pages. There are far better (and more colorful) icon collections in clip-art libraries and on the Web than any symbol font can provide.

The primary value in considering these font categories lies in understanding the most common conventions and variations among fonts. The eye is so accustomed to reading different fonts that it takes quite a difference to be obvious.

> **note** Dozens of look-alike typefaces are modeled on (or ripped off from) the classic designs of Optima, Garamond, Times Roman, Helvetica, and the like.

Contrast in color and size are far more obvious than contrast in the shape of letters. If you decide to use multiple fonts on a page, topic, or site, make sure they're markedly different yet legible and that they work together. When in doubt, use the default font (typically an oldstyle) for body text and a larger sans serif font for headings.

In Summary...

This chapter explained the basics of cascading style sheets, a technology that provides far more flexibility and far more control over Web page typography than HTML tags alone can supply.

The next chapter explains how to modify, and in some cases create, pictures in FrontPage.

Part 8

Creating and Editing Web Pictures

Editing Pictures in FrontPage

Microsoft FrontPage provides a useful assortment of built-in picture editing functions. These functions certainly don't replace a full-tilt picture editor, such as Microsoft PhotoDraw, but they conveniently provide the right tool in the right place, most of the time you need it. If a quick fix is in order, these tools might be the solution. This chapter covers the tools available within FrontPage, as well as techniques to make the best use of them.

Adding Text to Pictures

Web designers frequently receive pictures that someone else created—a graphic designer, perhaps. Oftentimes, these pictures need to be changed with little notice, and many Web designers aren't equipped to do that. Suppose, for example, that a client gives the Web designer a button face to use for navigation around a site, but the text for that button isn't finalized. In such a case, the designer can build pages using the blank button face, and then use FrontPage to add the text later. FrontPage supports this operation with a feature called Text On GIFs. Figure 21-1 on the next page provides some examples.

Applying text to GIF files is quite simple:

1 Add the picture to the Web page if it isn't there already.

2 Make sure the Pictures toolbar is displayed.

 For more information about the Pictures toolbar, refer to "The Pictures Toolbar" in the Bonus Content on the Companion CD.

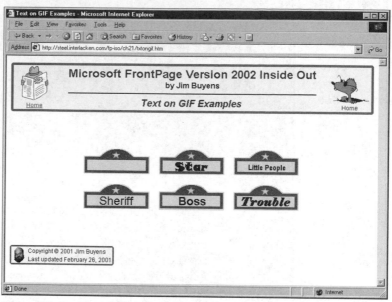

Figure 21-1. The picture at the upper left is the original picture; the others make use of the Text On GIFs feature.

3 Select the picture by clicking it.

Text

4 Click the Text button on the Pictures toolbar. If the picture is anything but a GIF file, FrontPage displays a prompt warning you that it's about to convert the picture to GIF.

There's very little risk in clicking OK and proceeding with this conversion If it turns out you don't like the results, you can either undo the change or delete the modified picture from the page and reinsert the original. If you keep the results and save the page, FrontPage displays the Save Embedded Files dialog box asking where to save the new GIF files. FrontPage doesn't delete the original picture file, nor does it update any other pages to use the GIF version.

5 A second set of handles appears within those surrounding the picture. Click inside the inner handles to place the insertion point, and then type your text. If the text doesn't fit, enlarge the text area by dragging its handles.

6 Set font, point size, alignment, color, and other attributes either by selecting the text and then choosing Font from the Format menu or by using the buttons on the Format toolbar.

7 When you're done, click outside the picture to stop text entry and editing.

To create headings, titles, and other small amounts of text using special fonts and colors, first use your picture editor to create a completely transparent GIF file. Add this file to your Web page, and then use the Text button to add and format the text.

The main advantage of this method, compared to just entering the text in your picture editor, is having the Text On GIFs feature readily available as you develop other parts of your page.

> For an explanation of transparency in picture files, refer to "Setting Transparency" later in this chapter.

It's tempting to stretch a small transparent GIF out to the size of a heading and then use the Text On GIFs feature to display the heading with full control over font and color. There are two precautions regarding this technique:

- The text must be a different color than the GIF file's transparent color; otherwise, you'll end up with transparent text. Note that a GIF file's transparent color usually isn't readily apparent because, by definition, it's invisible.

- FrontPage can't save text on a small picture you've merely resized on screen. Such resizing changes only the display size, and not the number of pixels stored on disk. And those pixels probably don't provide enough resolution to make your text legible. Resampling (described in "Cropping and Resizing Pictures" in this chapter) creates a picture permanently sized to the dimensions that appear on your screen.

Follow these steps to ensure that Text On GIFs works correctly:

Resample

1 Resize the GIF file by dragging its handles or entering dimensions in the Picture Properties dialog box.

2 With the picture still selected, click Resample on the Pictures toolbar.

3 Save the Web page, and give the transparent file a descriptive name when prompted.

4 Add the text, using the procedure described earlier in this section.

> The more often designers use cascading style sheets (CSS) to format text, the less they convert headings and other special text to pictures. For more information about CSS, refer to Chapter 20, "Managing Appearance with Cascading Style Sheets."

Saving Changes to Picture Files

Whenever you change a picture using any of the methods described in this chapter, you must eventually make a choice: Do you want to permanently alter the original picture file, or would you prefer to save the changes to a new file?

You don't have to decide immediately: As long as you have a Web page open, you can make as many changes to as many pictures as you want, without worrying about whether to make them permanent. But when you save the Web page, FrontPage displays a Save Embedded Files dialog box that asks you to confirm the file name and other details for each picture you changed. (This dialog box appeared previously as Figure 2-9, as Figure 9-9, and as Figure 11-2.) To change the proposed Save properties for any file listed, first select the file and then:

- To change the name of the saved file, click the Rename button, edit the proposed name, and then press Enter.

- To save the file in a different folder, click the Change Folder button, select a folder from the resulting dialog box, and then click OK.

> **tip** If a file's Folder column is blank, FrontPage saves the file in the same folder as the Web page itself.

- To change a file's action, click the Set Action button. The choices available vary with the circumstances but are usually Save, Don't Save, Overwrite, or Use Existing.

- To change a picture's format from GIF to JPEG or to change other format properties, click the Picture Options button.

Click OK when all these options are set the way you want them.

In most cases, you'll probably want to create a new file. This gives you the option to open the original file later and redo or undo your changes if you find them unsatisfactory.

> **caution** The Save Embedded Files dialog box offers you a default file name option for each picture you changed. With some picture changes, such as AutoThumbnail, the default is the original file name followed by _small_ (before the file extension). With others, such as brightness and contrast, the default is the original file name. Always double-check the default file name before choosing it.

> For more information about using the Save Embedded Files dialog box, refer to "Using the Save Embedded Files Dialog Box" on page 310.

Creating Thumbnail Pictures

To minimize download time for large pictures, it's common practice to display a small preview picture (a thumbnail) on the Web page a visitor would first encounter, and display the full-size picture only if the visitor clicks the thumbnail. Doing this gives the Web visitor the choice of whether or not to see a larger file, without having to wait to download it first. To do this in FrontPage:

1 Insert the full-size picture where you want its thumbnail to appear.

AutoThumbnail

2 Select the large picture, and press Ctrl+T or select Auto Thumbnail from one of the following places:

- The Tools menu.

- The Pictures toolbar.

- The shortcut menu that appears when you right-click the picture.

In one operation FrontPage removes the large picture, creates the thumbnail in its place, and sets up a hyperlink from the thumbnail to the large picture.

---

tip   To create a linked thumbnail in one operation, use the right mouse button to drag any picture file from the Folder List to an open Web page. Then when you release the mouse button, choose Auto Thumbnail from the shortcut menu.

---

3 Use the thumbnail's handles to resize it if desired.

4 When you save the Web page, FrontPage displays a Save Embedded Files dialog box to prompt for the thumbnail's file name (note that _small_ appears between the original file name and the file extension).

For more information about using the Save Embedded Files dialog box, refer to "Saving Changes to Picture Files" earlier in this chapter.

Setting AutoThumbnail Properties

As you might have noticed, the preceding discussion made no mention of the thumbnail picture's size and appearance. That's because FrontPage assumes you want all the thumbnails you create to look the same. (Surely you wouldn't want them all to look different, would you?)

To specify the default size and appearance of all thumbnails you create, choose Page Options from the Tools menu and click the AutoThumbnail tab. This tab appears in Figure 21-2 on the next page, and provides the following settings:

- **Set.** Controls the size of the thumbnail pictures. You should specify both a sizing strategy and a measurement. The sizing options are as follows:

    - **Width.** Choose this option if you want FrontPage to make all thumbnail pictures the same width.

    - **Height.** Choose this option if you want FrontPage to make all thumbnail pictures the same height.

    - **Shortest Side.** Choose this option if you want FrontPage to make the shortest side of each thumbnail a uniform size.

    - **Longest Side.** Choose this option if you want FrontPage to make the longest side of each thumbnail a uniform size.

653

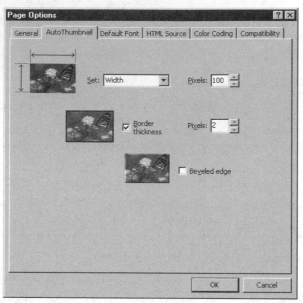

Figure 21-2. This tab on the Page Options dialog box controls how FrontPage creates thumbnail pictures.

No matter which strategy you choose, FrontPage sizes the remaining edge of the thumbnail in proportion to that of the full-size picture.

● **Pixels.** Specify the fixed size applied to the edge you chose.

● **Border Thickness.** Select this check box if you want FrontPage to create borders around each thumbnail picture. The Pixels spin box controls the border width.

● **Beveled Edge.** Select this check box if you want FrontPage to create beveled edges for each thumbnail picture.

Positioning Pictures

The Pictures toolbar has three buttons that support absolute positioning of pictures. Absolute positioning means you can specify the exact *x-y* coordinates, where the picture will appear. The coordinates are measured from the top left corner of the browser window to the top left corner of the picture, but FrontPage shields you from all that.

Absolute positioning requires the following short process:

1 Select the picture, and click Position Absolutely on the Pictures toolbar.

2 Drag the picture into position.

Position
Absolutely

After you flag a picture as absolutely positioned, you can drag it whenever it's selected, even during a subsequent editing session.

Absolute positioning works in three dimensions. Not only can it position objects up and down or right and left, it can also position them forward and backward compared to each other. This involves a property called *z-order*. A *z*-order can be positive or negative, but in either case, objects with higher *z*-order vales appear in front of objects with lower ones. If two objects have the same *z*-order, the one defined later in the HTML comes out on top. The default *z*-order value is zero.

To arrange pictures in layers:

1 Apply absolute positioning to each picture you want to arrange.

2 Select one picture, and on the Pictures toolbar, click Bring Forward or Send Backward.

Bring Forward   Send Backward

Repeat this for other pictures as necessary. You can set positioned pictures in front of or behind both regular page content and each other. Figure 21-3 shows a Web page with seven overlapping pictures. If you open this page in Page view, you can drag the pictures around at will.

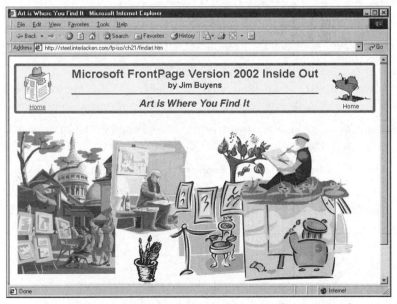

Figure 21-3. The montage in this Web page actually consists of seven pictures, each positioned absolutely in three dimensions.

> **tip** Using the Bring Forward and Send Backward buttons to arrange pictures can become confusing when working with many different pictures on the same page. Try to plan ahead: First insert and position the pictures you want in the background, and then insert your foreground pictures.

Microsoft Internet Explorer 4 was the first browser to support CSS2 positioning, which is the technology FrontPage uses for positioning pictures. Browsers that don't support absolute positioning will still display your page elements, but not in the expected layout. As always, test your pages in every browser environment you care about.

Rotating and Flipping Pictures

The Pictures toolbar provides four toolbar buttons for rotating pictures: two to rotate right or left in 90-degree increments, and two more for flipping top to bottom and right to left. To see their effects, look at Figure 21-5 on page 659. Rotating a picture merely reorients it, whereas flipping creates a mirror image of the original picture. You can flip or rotate the same picture any number of times.

Rotate Left   Rotate Right   Flip Horizontal   Flip Vertical

Controlling Contrast and Brightness

The Pictures toolbar contains four buttons for modifying brightness and contrast: one each for increasing and decreasing. Clicking these buttons repeatedly intensifies their effect:

- **More Contrast.** Makes high intensities higher and low intensities lower. That is, it darkens a picture's dark colors and brightens its light colors.

- **Less Contrast.** Makes high intensities lower and low intensities higher. In short, it pushes your picture in the direction of Seattle weather—all gray.

- **More Brightness.** Adds white to every color in the picture; the darker the color, the more white added. Eventually, the picture becomes pure white.

- **Less Brightness.** Adds black to every color in the picture; the lighter the color, the more black added. Eventually, the picture becomes pure black.

More Contrast   Less Contrast   More Brightness   Less Brightness

Figure 21-5, shown later in this chapter, shows some sample results from using these buttons.

656

Cropping and Resizing Pictures

Cropping is the process of making a picture smaller by choosing part of it and discarding the rest. To crop a picture in FrontPage:

Crop

1 Select the picture, and click Crop on the Pictures toolbar.

2 Within the selected picture, FrontPage draws a bounding box with handles. Move the handles so that the bounding box encloses the part of the picture you want to retain.

3 Click Crop again or press Enter. FrontPage discards any pixels outside the bounding box.

> **tip** It's best to keep all your pictures in an */images* folder rather than the root. FrontPage helpfully provides such a folder when you create your Web.

To resize a picture, simply select it and drag its handles. Dragging the corner handles resizes the picture proportionately; the height and width are forced to change by the same percentages. Dragging the top or bottom handle changes only the height, whereas dragging the left or right handle changes only the width.

Resizing a file with its handles doesn't alter the size of the picture file itself; it changes only the amount of screen space the picture occupies. Reducing the size of a picture in this way saves the Web visitor nothing in download time. To physically resize the picture, use the Resample command described later in this chapter.

Setting Transparency

All GIF and JPEG pictures are rectangular. Most real-life objects aren't. One solution to this dilemma, though a poor one, is to enclose all pictures in borders. This often produces unattractive results. A second and better approach is coloring the unused portions of the picture to match its surroundings—the Web page background. However, this solution also has drawbacks:

- It requires a different picture version for each background color.
- Smoothly matching a textured background picture generally isn't possible.
- Web visitors can instruct their browsers to ignore background pictures, background colors, or both.

The best solution is to make portions of the picture transparent, as if they were printed on a sheet of clear plastic. Figure 21-4 on the next page provides an example of this technique. The picture on the left, with a white background, doesn't blend with the colored background. The picture on the right has a transparent background that lets the page's background show through.

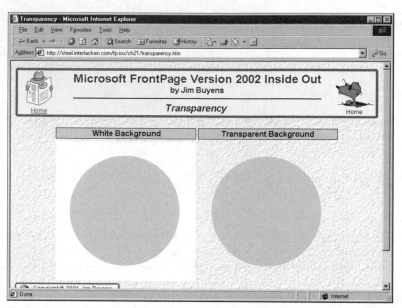

Figure 21-4. The picture on the left has a white background; the one on the right has a transparent background.

Most GIF file editors have features for handling transparency, though you can also control transparency from within FrontPage. The FrontPage procedure is as follows:

1 Add the picture to your Web page, if you haven't already.

2 Make sure the Pictures toolbar is displayed.

> **tip** To toggle the display of any toolbar, choose its entry from the Toolbars submenu of FrontPage's View menu.

Set Transparent Color

3 Click the picture to select it, and then click the Set Transparent Color button on the Pictures toolbar.

4 Move the mouse pointer over the selected picture and click any pixel of the color that should become transparent. All pixels matching that color in the picture will immediately become transparent.

5 To make a different color transparent, repeat steps 4 and 5. Only one color of a GIF can be transparent at a time.

6 To turn off transparency for a picture, repeat steps 3 and 4. However, in step 4, click the area that's already transparent.

> **caution** If you're setting transparency for an image with text, make sure that the texture or color of your Web page's background won't interfere with the text's readability.

Applying Monochrome and Washouts

Color

The Color button on the Pictures toolbar displays a drop-down list that contains four commands. Despite the button name Color, each of these commands modfiies the amount of black and white in the current picture. Here's the name and description of each command:

newfeature!

- **Automatic.** Displays a picture in its natural state. This command applies only to pictures contained within VML codes, such as pictures copied out of Microsoft Word and pasted into FrontPage. It doesn't apply to pictures (including VML drawings) added to Web pages using FrontPage alone.

- **Grayscale.** Removes all color from a picture (that is, it converts it to continuous shades of gray). You can undo this operation by clicking the button again, but not after the picture is saved.

- **Black & White.** Converts every pixel to either black or white, producing a silhouette effect. Like the Automatic command, this command applies only to pictures contained within VML codes.

- **Wash Out.** Lightens every pixel in a picture. You can wash out a picture only once before saving your changes.

To doubly wash out a picture, wash it, save it, and then wash it again.

Figure 21-5 illustrates these and other picture effects.

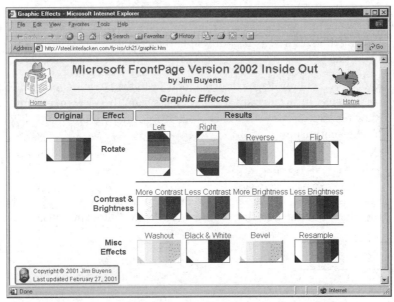

Figure 21-5. This page displays various picture transformations you can apply directly within FrontPage.

Beveling Edges

Bevel

This effect lightens the top and left edges of a picture while also darkening the bottom and right edges. This creates the effect of a three-dimensional button.

Resampling Pictures

Resample

To physically resize a picture, you must both resize *and* resample it in FrontPage. First resize the file, and then click Resample on the Pictures toolbar. Resampling creates a larger or smaller file than the original, rescaled by mathematically averaging pixels. This technique can make only minor adjustments to the quality of a picture. There's nothing better than using an original picture of a higher quality. Unlike resizing, resampling *does* change the file stored in your Web.

Restoring Pictures

Restore

Until you save a picture file, FrontPage can always revert to the version it originally loaded from your Web or other location. To return to this version, click Restore on the Pictures toolbar. Don't use Restore to reverse only the most recent of several changes; if you wish to do that, instead choose Undo from the Edit menu.

newfeature!
Creating Line Art Within FrontPage

During the layout and construction of Web pages, it might become necessary to draw a line. Or a box. Or maybe an arrow would do the trick. FrontPage has a collection of drawing tools, as well as a set of standard predesigned shapes that you can easily add to any page.

You can access FrontPage's drawing tools from the Drawing toolbar. To make this toolbar visible, if it isn't already, select Toolbars from the View menu, and then choose Drawing. You can also right-click a blank area of any toolbar and choose Drawing from the shortcut menu.

newfeature!
Creating AutoShapes

FrontPage comes with dozens of predesigned shapes from which to choose. Clicking AutoShapes on the Drawing toolbar presents the following categories:

AutoShapes

- **Lines.** Contain six basic line choices.

- **Basic Shapes.** Lists choices such as Octagon, Right Triangle, Cube, and even a Smiley Face. There are 32 basic shapes.

new feature!

Troubleshooting

Drawings, AutoShapes, and Word Art options on the Insert menu and various toolbars are dimmed

If, for reasons of browser compatibility, you've configured FrontPage not to create VML graphics, features that use VML are unavailable and appear dimmed on menus and toolbars. This includes drawings, AutoShapes, and Word Art.

To check your compatibility settings, choose Page Options from the Tools menu and select the Compatibility tab. This will display the Page Options dialog box shown in Figure 21-6.

Figure 21-6. If the VML Graphics check box isn't selected, the drawings, AutoShapes, and Word Art features won't be available when you edit a Web page.

Here are some guidelines for using this dialog box:

- To make the drawings, AutoShapes, and Word Art options available, make sure the VML box is selected.

- To create ordinary picture files for the benefit of browsers that don't support VML, make sure the Downlevel Image File box is selected.

on the CD For more information about the Page Options dialog box, refer to Chapter 45, "Configuring Page Creation Options" in the Bonus Content on the Companion CD.

- **Block Arrows.** Presents 28 block-outlined arrow shapes.

- **Flowchart.** Contains shapes similar to those found in Microsoft Visio. Use these shapes to create a flowchart site map, for example. There are 28 flow-chart shapes to work with.

- **Stars And Banners.** Call attention to a certain area of content on a page. For example, a star could highlight a new sale item. There are 16 stars and banners available.

- **Callouts.** Are what some people call speaking bubbles. To create that sophisticated Sunday morning comics look, select one of the 20 callout shapes.

- **More AutoShapes.** Brings up the Insert Clip Art dialog box.

To add an AutoShape to a page:

1 Select the desired shape from any AutoShape category.

2 Position the cross-hair mouse pointer on the page.

3 Click the left mouse button to insert the shape. Hold down the left mouse button and drag the shape to the dimensions you want.

> For more information about using clip art, refer to "Inserting Clip Art" on page 314. For more information about AutoShapes, refer to "Inserting AutoShapes" on page 334.

newfeature!
Creating Drawings

To use any FrontPage drawing tool, select the appropriate button from the Drawing toolbar. The mouse pointer then becomes the drawing tool; you click and drag on the page in the location where you want the drawn object to appear. Choose from the following drawing tools:

- **Draw.** Displays an extensive menu of commands and subcommands for grouping, ungrouping, ordering, aligning, and performing other operations on elements in a drawing. These commands generally follow the conventions of standard drawing programs.

- **Select Objects.** Prepares the mouse pointer for selecting objects by clicking them or by dragging the mouse across an area.

- **AutoShapes.** Displays a shortcut menu with submenus for various categories of predesigned shapes. The submenus include Lines, Block Arrows, Flowchart, Stars And Banners, and so forth.

Draw   Select Objects   AutoShapes

- **Line.** Draws a straight line of any length at any angle.

- **Arrow.** Works the same as drawing a line, except that the line ends with an arrow point.

- **Rectangle.** Creates rectangles of any dimension on the page. Hold down the Shift key while dragging out the rectangle to constrain the shape to a perfect square.

- **Oval.** Works the same as drawing a rectangle. Hold down the Shift key while dragging out the oval to constrain the shape to a perfect circle.

- **Text Box.** Creates a rectangle with a blinking insertion point. You can type text into a Text Box and then format it just as you would any other text on a page.

| Line | Arrow | Rectangle | Oval | Text Box |

For more information about working with text, refer to Chapter 10, "Adding and Formatting Text."

- **Insert WordArt.** Displays the WordArt Gallery dialog box shown in Figure 21-7.

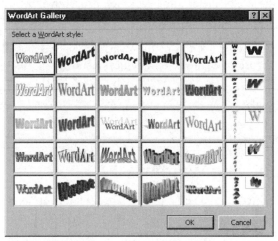

Figure 21-7. The WordArt Gallery dialog box shows the various text formatting options available.

- **Insert Clip Art.** Displays the Insert Clip Art task pane so you can add a clip art picture to the composition.

For more information about using Clip Art, refer to "Inserting Clip Art" on page 314.

● **Insert Picture From File.** Displays the Picture dialog box so you can add an existing picture in your Web or on your disk to the composition.

Insert WordArt   Insert Clip Art   Insert Picture From File

> For more information about adding pictures to a Web page, refer to Chapter 11, "Adding and Formatting Pictures." For more information about drawings, refer to "Inserting Drawings" on page 331.

newfeature!

Creating WordArt Objects

Insert
WordArt

To add special effects to a line of text, such as a 3-D effect, a curve, a drop shadow, or a color gradient, click Insert WordArt on the Drawing toolbar.

Selecting the WordArt option of your choice and clicking OK brings up the Edit WordArt Text dialog box, which presents the following options:

● **Text.** Type the text that you want formatted.

● **Font.** Choose a font to style the text. Since WordArt is designed for headlines, a heavy font such as Impact produces the best results.

● **Size.** Choose the size of the headline from the drop-down list. Click the Bold or Italic button, or both, to apply those attributes as you want.

Click OK when you're finished formatting the WordArt. The new headline will be displayed in Page view. Figure 21-8 shows some typical results.

> **caution**   WordArt is best suited for single lines of text, such as a headline. It's not intended to format paragraphs of text.

Formatting and Modifying WordArt

After you place a WordArt headline on a page, there are many options for customizing its appearance. Selecting the headline brings up the WordArt floating toolbar, which contains the following options:

● **Insert WordArt.** Displays the WordArt Gallery dialog box for creating a new WordArt headline.

● **Edit Text.** Displays the Edit WordArt Text dialog box already described.

Chapter 21

Figure 21-8. The FrontPage WordArt feature created and then modified this headline.

● **WordArt Gallery.** Displays the WordArt Gallery dialog box described previously. To choose a different style, select the new style and then click OK.

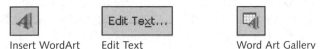

Insert WordArt   Edit Text   Word Art Gallery

● **Format WordArt.** Displays the Format WordArt dialog box, which changes the appearance of the current WordArt headline. Options in this dialog box control the color of the text, its transparency, its size, and other aspects of its appearance, as well as the alternative text for the picture.

● **WordArt Shape.** Displays a drop-down list when clicked; options on this list change the curve that the headline follows. For example, select Inflate Bottom to make the headline appear to bend out from the bottom. There are 40 shapes to choose from.

● **WordArt Same Letter Heights.** Adjusts the letters so that they all have the same height. Click this button again to restore the original formatting.

Format WordArt   WordArt Shape   WordArt Same Letter Heights

● **WordArt Vertical Text.** Draws the headline vertically from top to bottom. Click this button again to restore the original formatting.

- **WordArt Alignment.** Controls the alignment of the headline on the page, or in relation to adjacent elements. Select Left Align, Center, Right Align, Word Justify, or Stretch Justify.

- **WordArt Character Spacing.** Adjusts the kerning, or space between the letters of the word. Select from standard options of Very Tight, Tight, Normal, Loose, or Very Loose. Or type a percentage into the Custom box to create a nonstandard spacing option. If you've previously adjusted the kerning, select Normal to return the headline to its original spacing.

WordArt   WordArt   WordArt
Vertical Text Alignment   Character Spacing

For more information about WordArt, refer to "Inserting WordArt" on page 335.

Formatting and Modifying Line Art

After you place a drawing on a page, whether it's a rectangle, text box, WordArt object, or any other creation, you have many options for adjusting its appearance. Certain options might not be available with some types of art.

- **Fill Color.** Displays a relatively standard FrontPage color selection menu. However, the menu also includes a Fill Effects option where you can specify gradients, textures, patterns, and picture backgrounds.

For more information about using the standard FrontPage Color dialog boxes, refer to "Using FrontPage Color Dialog Boxes" on page 552.

- **Line Color.** Displays a relatively standard FrontPage color selection menu. However, there's also a Patterned Lines option where you can select line patterns.

- **Font Color.** Displays a standard FrontPage color selection menu that controls the color of text.

  This control has no effect on WordArt text. To modify the color of WordArt text, right-click the WordArt and choose Format WordArt from the shortcut menu, or click the Format WordArt button on the WordArt toolbar.

Fill Color   Line Color   Font Color

- **Line Style.** Displays a list of styles, including various thicknesses, double scores, triple scores, and so forth.

- **Dash Style.** Displays a list of dash patterns, including solid, fine dots, coarse dots, fine dashes, coarse dashes, and so forth.

- **Arrow Style.** Displays a list of arrowheads.

- **Shadow Style.** Applies one of 20 various shadow effects to the selected picture. Select No Shadow to return the selected picture to its original state. Shadow Settings displays the Shadow Settings floating toolbar, where you can make adjustments to the shadow's color and distance from the picture.

- **3-D Style.** Displays a list of 20 three-dimensional effect options. These options can, for example, transform a plain circle into a shaded cylinder or cone. Select No 3-D to return the selected picture to its original state. 3-D Settings displays the 3-D Settings floating toolbar, where you can make incremental adjustments to the degree of tilt applied to the picture. On this floating toolbar, you can also adjust the depth, lighting, surface, and color of the 3-D effect.

| Line Style | Dash Style | Arrow Style | Shadow Style | 3-D Style |

Figure 21-9 illustrates a number of Line Art and WordArt effects. Note the curved text, 3-D objects, and overlapping elements.

Selecting any picture displays selection handles that can rotate, skew, and stretch the picture to just about any shape or size you want. When working with art created within FrontPage, the key is experimentation. Try various shapes, sizes and colors to get the perfect effect that meets your Web's needs.

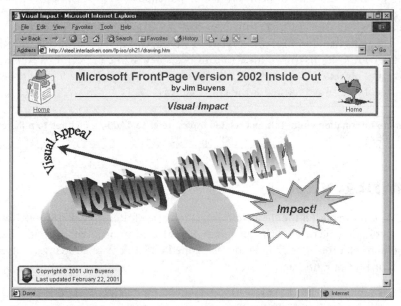

Figure 21-9. This page features various WordArt and Line Art creations.

Chapter 21

Displaying Line Art in the Browser

When you create artwork that uses the Drawings, AutoShapes, and WordArt components, FrontPage stores them as a collection of lines, curves, and other shapes rather than as pictures. The specific format FrontPage uses is Vector Markup Language (VML), which in turn stores the information in Extensible Markup Language (XML) format.

Transmitting VML data to the browser is much faster than transmitting an ordinary picture file that produces the same display. Of course, the VML data is useless to browsers that don't support it. Currently, only Internet Explorer 5 and later can display VML.

For the benefit of browsers that don't support VML, FrontPage can also save GIF versions of every Drawing, AutoShape, and WordArt object you create. Then, in the midst of the VML code, FrontPage inserts the HTML to display the GIF picture. Browsers that display VML will do so and, because of some special coding, never request or use the GIF file. Browsers that don't support VML will ignore it and display the GIF picture instead.

> For more information about options that control the use of VML and substitute GIF files, refer to the Troubleshooting sidebar, "Drawings, AutoShapes, and Word Art options on the Insert menu and various toolbars are dimmed," earlier in this chapter.

If your drawing is at all complex, it's often wise to first create a drawing area (or *canvas*) and then add objects to it. To create a drawing area:

1 Set the insertion point where you want the drawing composition to appear.

2 Choose Picture from the Insert menu, and choose New Drawing.

The canvas sets aside an area of the page for your drawing. To resize the canvas, select it and drag its handles. Browsers that don't support VML have a much easier time displaying compositions drawn inside a canvas display than compositions consisting of individual objects. This is because the GIF file FrontPage creates for such browsers consists of one large picture for the entire canvas.

> For more information about this and related topics, refer to "Adding Pictures to a Page" on page 305.

In Summary...

This chapter reviewed the tools built into FrontPage for editing pictures. Although it isn't a complete picture-editing program, FrontPage can make many kinds of common changes to pictures. The chapter also explained how to create Drawings, AutoShapes, and WordArt in FrontPage.

The next chapter explains how to use the new Photo Gallery component, which organizes snapshot collections for presentation on the Web.

newfeature!
Using FrontPage Photo Galleries

Working with photographs on a Web page can be challenging, even for the seasoned professional. How should you arrange the pictures on the page? Should you build your layout with tables? Should you create thumbnails? What about adding captions or descriptions of the photos?

Microsoft FrontPage's Photo Gallery component makes it easy to lay out multiple pictures on a Web page. This component arranges and displays pictures and provides a convenient way to add descriptive text and captions. As with other components, FrontPage does all the programming work for you, behind the scenes.

FrontPage creates a thumbnail version of each full-size picture you add to a photo gallery. The photo gallery Web page displays the thumbnail pictures; when a Web visitor clicks one of them, the browser requests and displays the full-size picture.

newfeature!
Creating a New Gallery

There are two procedures for creating a new photo gallery. The first procedure involves inserting a new photo gallery into an existing page:

1 Set the insertion point in the page where you want the gallery to appear.

2 Display the Photo Gallery Properties dialog box shown in Figure 22-1. There are two ways to perform this step. The first method initializes the new photo gallery with the default thumbnail layout:

a Select Picture from the Insert menu.

b Select New Photo Gallery from the shortcut menu.

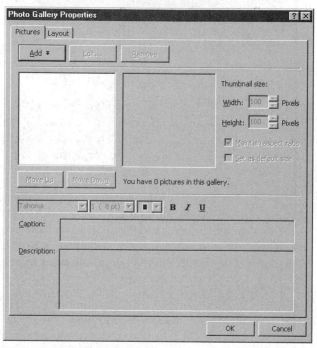

Figure 22-1. This is the Pictures tab of the Photo Gallery Properties dialog box.

The second method initializes the new photo gallery with a thumbnail layout you select:

a Select Web Component from the Insert menu.

b When the Insert Web Component dialog box appears, select Photo Gallery from the list box at the left, and choose the layout you want from the list at the right.

c Click Finish.

No matter which procedure for creating a new photo gallery you select, you can change the photos' thumbnail layout later.

The second procedure for creating a new photo gallery works best when you want to create a new Web page that contains a photo gallery:

1 Display the Page Templates dialog box using either of the following methods:

- Choose New and then Page Or Web from the File menu to display the New Page Or Web pane. Then click Page Templates.

- Click the arrow associated with the New Page button on the Standard toolbar, and then choose Page.

2 On the General tab, double-click Photo Gallery, or select Photo Gallery and click OK.

3 Save the new page in your Web as you normally would, clicking Cancel if the Save Embedded Files dialog box prompts you to overwrite the default photos.

Notice that creating a new gallery doesn't populate it with pictures. For that, you must click Add and choose one of two options for adding pictures to the gallery: Pictures From Files or Pictures From Scanners Or Cameras.

Adding Pictures from Files

Here's the procedure for adding a file from a local disk, from a file server, or from the Web to a photo gallery:

1 In the Photo Gallery Properties dialog box, click Add.

2 Choose Pictures From Files from the resulting drop-down list. This displays the standard FrontPage File Open dialog box. All of the picture file formats that FrontPage supports will be available.

For information about the File Open dialog box, refer to "Working with Page View" on page 171.

note If you add a picture in a format other than GIF or JPEG, FrontPage converts it to one of those formats when you save the page.

3 Locate and select one or more picture files that you want in the gallery, and then click Open. Each picture file you selected appears in the Photo Gallery Properties dialog box, as shown in Figure 22-2 on the next page.

To select multiple files in the File Open dialog box, hold down the Shift or Ctrl key while clicking them.

Chapter 22

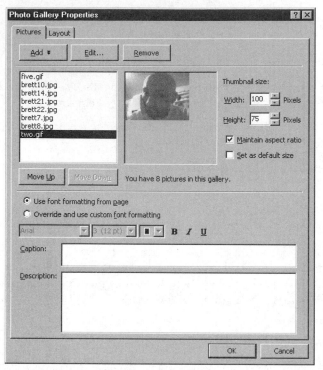

Figure 22-2. The Photo Gallery dialog box shows a list of picture files at the left, and a thumbnail of the selected picture at the right.

Adding Pictures from Scanners or Cameras

The Photo Gallery component can also accept pictures from a scanner or digital camera connected to your computer. Here's the procedure:

1 In the Photo Gallery Properties dialog box, click Add.

2 Choose Pictures From Scanner Or Cameras from the resulting drop-down list. This displays the Insert Picture From Scanner Or Camera dialog box shown in Figure 22-3.

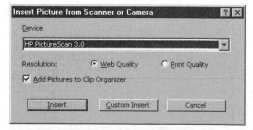

Figure 22-3. The Insert Picture From Scanner Or Camera dialog box lists available connected devices.

The following options are available:

- **Device.** This drop-down list shows the available devices (connected to your computer or network) from which FrontPage can import pictures. To launch a device, choose it from the list.

- **Resolution.** These options control the resolution (and hence the file size) of the pictures you import:

  - ◆ **Web Quality.** Select this option button to keep the file size down when FrontPage imports the picture. The resulting lower-resolution image will be perfectly adequate for Web viewing, but won't take a long time for visitors to download.

  - ◆ **Print Quality.** Select this option button if you expect visitors to print the picture. Selecting this results in a higher-resolution image that will take longer to download.

- **Add Pictures To Clip Organizer.** Select this check box to add the pictures you're importing from the scanner or camera not only to the Photo Gallery, but also to the FrontPage Clip Organizer on your hard disk.

3 Click Insert to launch the software associated with the device you chose from the Device drop-down list. Click Custom Insert if you want to insert a picture using the scanner or camera's custom picture insertion method rather than the standard FrontPage method.

4 Acquire the picture you want by following the instructions that came with the scanner or camera software.

5 The scanner or camera software should provide a command called Place Image, Insert Picture, or something similar. Choose this command to close the program and add the picture to your Web page.

6 The picture appears in the Photo Gallery Properties dialog box, as shown in Figure 22-2.

When you've added all the pictures you want, click OK in the Photo Gallery Properties dialog box. FrontPage generates the thumbnails for the pictures and displays the new gallery in your Web page.

For information on controlling the appearance of a photo gallery, refer to "Controlling Gallery Layout" later in this chapter.

To add more pictures to a photo gallery, open the Photo Gallery Properties dialog box, click Add, and make the appropriate selections. To remove a picture from the gallery, select the picture in the gallery list and click Remove.

newfeature!
Editing Picture Properties

If you're not satisfied with the look of pictures in a Photo Gallery, you might be able to correct them right from the Photo Gallery Properties dialog box. Here's the procedure:

1 Open the Photo Gallery Properties dialog box and select the picture you want to change from the list.

2 Click Edit to display the Edit Picture dialog box shown in Figure 22-4. The currently selected picture appears in the preview window. Use any of the following commands to change the appearance of the picture:

- **Picture Size.** Shows the current pixel width and height of the full-size picture. This is the same size that appears in the preview window. Choose from the following options:

  - To change the size of the picture, enter a new size in the Width and Height spin boxes.

  - To keep the picture's proportions the same while you resize it, select Maintain Aspect Ratio.

  - If all pictures in the gallery need to be the same approximate size, select Set As Default Size.

  - To adjust the size of the thumbnail pictures, see the next section of this chapter, "Editing Photo Information."

- **Rotate Picture.** Changes the orientation of the selected picture. Click the appropriate button to rotate the picture left or right, or to flip it horizontally or vertically.

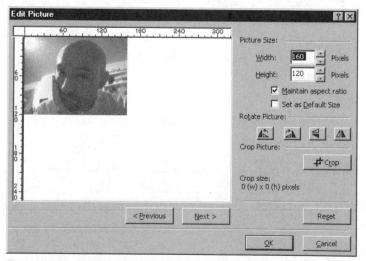

Figure 22-4. The Edit Picture dialog box presents options for changing the appearance of a picture.

■ **Crop Picture.** Discards unneeded areas of the picture. To crop the selected picture, click Crop. Within the picture, FrontPage draws a bounding box with handles. Move the handles so that the bounding box encloses the part of the picture you want to retain, and then click Crop a second time. FrontPage discards any pixels outside the bounding box.

■ **Reset.** Removes any changes you've made since opening the Edit Picture dialog box.

■ **Previous** and **Next.** Move backwards and forwards through all of the pictures in the current photo gallery.

When you're finished, click OK to save your changes and return to the Photo Gallery Properties dialog box.

newfeature!
Editing Photo Information

The following options are also available in the Photo Gallery Properties dialog box:

● **Thumbnail Size.** These options work just like the Picture Size portion of the Edit Picture dialog box described in the previous section. The difference is that these changes affect the thumbnail version of the picture. Make the appropriate selections in the Width and Height spin boxes.

● **Maintain Aspect Ratio.** Select this check box to keep the proportions of the thumbnail when resizing it.

● **Set As Default Size.** Select this check box to make all thumbnails the same approximate size.

● **Move Up** and **Move Down.** Use these buttons to change the order of pictures in the gallery. Select the picture you want to move, and then click either Move Up or Move Down.

This area also displays the total number of pictures currently in the gallery.

Editing Picture Captions and Descriptive Text

A photo gallery can display photo captions and descriptive text for each picture in the gallery. You can enter and format this information in the lower portion of the Photo Gallery Properties dialog box, shown in Figure 22-5 on the next page. These are your options:

● **Caption.** Use this option to give the picture a short, meaningful title.

● **Description.** Use this option to provide a sentence or two describing the picture.

Chapter 22

Figure 22-5. Use the Photo Gallery Properties dialog box to add formatted captions and descriptions to your pictures.

Some gallery layouts display both the caption and description, whereas others show only one text item. For information on which photo galleries display text, and how, see the next section, "Controlling Gallery Layout."

If you want the PhotoGallery to display text in the same font as the surrounding Web content, select the Font Formatting From Page Option.

If you want the PhotoGallery to display text in a custom font, select the Override And Use Custom Font Formatting option, select the Caption or Description text you want to modify, and then use font, font size, color, boldface, italics and underlining controls in the usual way.

As usual, select only fonts you believe your visitors are likely to have on their systems. In the absence of the font you specify, the visitor's browser chooses a substitute font, over which you have no control.

Controlling Gallery Layout

The main advantage of using a photo gallery is that it automatically displays multiple pictures in a professionally designed layout. You do, however, have some control over how those pictures appear on the page. The Layout tab of the Photo Gallery Properties dialog box is shown in Figure 22-6.

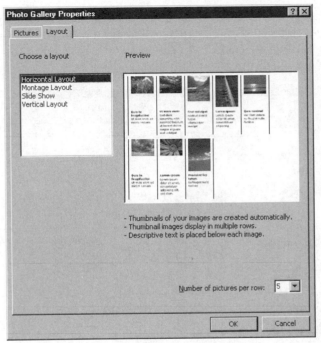

Figure 22-6. This is the Layout tab of the Photo Gallery Properties dialog box.

> **note** If you used the Insert Web Component dialog box to create your photo gallery, the Layout tab displays the selection you made at that time.

The Layout tab contains the following gallery layout options:

● **Choose A Layout.** Each of the four layout options in this list displays your pictures in a different way. When you select one of the following layouts, a preview appears in the Preview box, followed by a description of the layout:

■ **Horizontal Layout.** Choose this layout to display pictures in rows across the screen, with descriptive text below each picture. Use Number Of Pictures Per Row to control how many pictures appear in each row of the layout.

■ **Montage Layout.** Choose this layout to arrange pictures in a circular pattern much like a collage. The caption text appears when a visitor runs the mouse pointer over the picture. This layout doesn't display Description text.

■ **Slide Show.** In this layout, a full-size picture appears in the center of the page, while the thumbnail pictures scroll across the top of the page, where visitors can select them. Caption and Description text appears below the full-size picture.

677

■ **Vertical Layout.** Choose this layout to display pictures in columns with Description text arranged to the right of the pictures. An example of this is shown in Figure 22-7. Use Number Of Pictures Per Row to control the number of pictures that appear in each row of the layout.

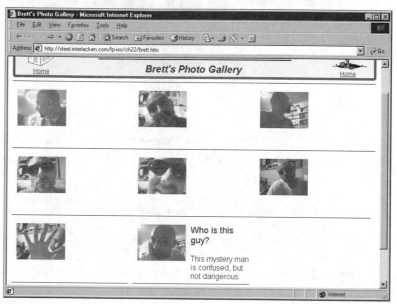

Figure 22-7. This figure shows a Photo Gallery as seen in a browser.

To access the Photo Gallery Properties dialog box at any time, right-click the photo gallery in Page view and select Photo Gallery Properties from the shortcut menu.

As a general rule, you should lay out your gallery in such a way that your visitors don't have to scroll left or right. Determine the screen resolution you're designing for, such as 800x600. Then make sure the width of your layout doesn't exceed the width of your target resolution. (In the case of 800x600, the width is 800 pixels.)

In Summary...

This chapter explained how to use the FrontPage Photo Gallery component to arrange multiple pictures on a Web page. The Photo Gallery component makes it easy to incorporate thumbnails, captions, and descriptions into a professionally designed layout.

The next chapter presents general information, tricks, and techniques for using pictures of all kinds on the Web.

Using Web Pictures Intelligently

This chapter discusses two important but often overlooked aspects of site design: the color palettes in your pictures and the total download time for your pages. This advice is far from all-encompassing, however. When choosing and positioning pictures for your Web pages, you should also consider color scheme, page layout, and the tendency for pictures to detract attention from text. In short, you should consider all the design tips sprinkled throughout this book.

Managing Picture Palettes

Pictures that contain large, flat, solid-color areas often appear properly in an editor or stand-alone viewer but appear grainy in browsers using 256-color display adapters. To correct this problem you need to convert the picture's *palette*. A palette is simply a collection of colors, and most picture editors can store, edit, and save palettes—both with individual pictures and as stand-alone palette files. If you open a picture having one palette and then open a palette file that defines another palette, most editors provide several options to reconcile the differences. For instance, you can usually convert each pixel in the picture to the nearest color in the new palette. If the palette consists solely of the 216 browser-safe colors, each pixel in the original picture takes on a safe color value. Your visitors' browsers won't perform dithering or color substitution on pictures you convert in this manner.

For more information about the 216 safe colors, refer to "Achieving Accurate Rendition—Safe Colors" on page 556.

> **note** Because many people have high-resolution display adapters capable of displaying millions of colors, it's nice to reward them with images that display well at a higher resolution. When creating a Web image from a photograph, for example, using the JPEG format provides enough colors to display pictures almost at print quality, but enough compression so that pictures download quickly to the browser. For visitors with a lower resolution, the same images display with acceptable quality in most situations.

The fixed 216-color palette explains two other problems Web designers often encounter:

● Black-and-white photograph rendition is usually terrible. This is because the browser has only six levels of gray, and four if you exclude black and white. Table 23-1 lists the six gray levels available to visitors who, because of their video equipment, must use the safe palette.

Table 23-1. Shades of Gray in the 216-Color "Safe Palette"

Color name	Decimal	Hexadecimal
Black	0-0-0	00-00-00
	51-51-51	33-33-33
	102-102-102	66-66-66
	153-153-153	99-99-99
	204-204-204	CC-CC-CC
White	255-255-255	FF-FF-FF

These six shades of gray aren't enough to display continuous-tone grayscale pictures, such as black-and-white photographs.

● Screen shots look terrible, because many of the 20 colors reserved by Microsoft Windows aren't in the safe palette. Table 23-2 shows the 16 colors available to early 16-color VGA adapters. These colors were indelibly fixed in VGA hardware, and by default, they're now fixed in the Windows mindset as well.

All the colors in the Bright column appear in the browser-safe palette, but none of those in the Dark column are in the browser-safe palette. This explains why screen shots converted directly into GIF files don't appear as clearly on Web pages as they did when originally displayed. To obtain a clear display, you'll need to use a picture editor to convert the dark VGA colors to their nearest safe palette equivalents.

Table 23-2. **RGB Values in the PC's Original 16-Color Palette**

Color name	Bright	Dark
Black	0-0-0	192-192-192 (light gray)
Red	255-0-0	128-0-0
Green	0-255-0	0-128-0
Blue	0-0-255	0-0-128
Cyan	0-255-255	0-128-128
Magenta	255-0-255	128-0-128
Yellow	255-255-0	128-128-0
White	255-255-255	128-128-128 (dark gray)

For more information about choosing colors, refer to "Design Tips for Choosing Colors" on page 558.

Making RGB and Hex Colors Match

Many picture editors use RGB as their color model, just as video adapters do. HTML, however, uses hexadecimal values to display colors in a Web browser. When creating or modifying an image, you might need to create Web-safe colors in decimal and then translate them to hex for use in HTML.

To make sure that the decimal and hex colors you create are part of the standard browser-safe color palette, choose color components from those listed in Table 23-3. For example, if the hex value in HTML is 99CC66, the matching RGB value is 153, 204, 102. Simply match the corresponding values from Table 23-3.

The table applies equally whether it's the hex or the decimal value that you already know. If, for example, you need to duplicate a safe background color that appears in a certain Web page, inspecting the HTML would give you a hexadecimal value. If you needed to enter decimal values into a photo editing software program, you could use Table 23-3 to convert the hex color values.

Table 23-3. **Equivalent Browser-Safe Palette Color Values**

Type	Equivalent Values					
Decimal	0	51	102	153	204	255
Hex	00	33	66	99	CC	FF

The Windows Calculator accessory provides a more general way of converting numbers between decimal and hexadecimal. Here's the procedure:

1 From the Windows Start menu, click Start, and then choose Programs, Accessories, and Calculator.

2 Choose Scientific from the View menu.

3 If the number you want to convert is hexadecimal, select the Hex option. If it's decimal, select the Dec option.

4 Enter the number you want to convert.

5 To convert the number you entered to hexadecimal, select the Hex option. Select the Dec option to convert it to decimal.

Managing Picture Download Time

Download time is a constant concern for all Web visitors. Even visitors with high-speed connections—who, by the way, are still a minority on the World Wide Web—don't want to be stuck waiting for huge picture files to download. As a Web designer, you should also be concerned with outbound bandwidth. The larger your pages, the fewer pages your server and your Internet connection can deliver per second (or minute).

In general, the time required to download a page is the combined size of all constituent files divided by the bytes per second of available bandwidth. Managing download time thus becomes an issue of managing download bytes. And, because most download bytes occur in picture files rather than the HTML, managing download bytes becomes an issue of managing picture file size.

Microsoft FrontPage estimates each page's download time for a typical modem visitor and displays it in the status bar; for example, the "49 seconds over 28.8" showing in the bottom right corner of Figure 23-1. You can use this feature to monitor the effect of pictures you add to a page.

> **tip** To configure the connection speed used for calculating download times, choose Options from the Tools menu, click the Reports View tab, and adjust the control titled "Assume Connection Speed Of." Although most designers now assume a minimum connection speed of 56K, it's still a good idea to know what the download time is at a 28.8K connection.

There are, however, three mitigating factors:

1 Most current browsers cache pictures and other files. That is, they keep local copies of recently used files. Before downloading any file, the browser checks for a local copy. If one exists, the browser does *either* of the following, depending on its configuration:

- Uses it without question, subject to certain timing constraints.

- Transmits the local copy's date stamp to the server. If the cached copy is outdated, the Web server transmits a new version. If the cached copy is current, the Web server responds with a status code instructing the browser to use the cached version.

You can maximize the benefits of caching by using stock pictures and not storing them redundantly on your server. This increases caching by reducing the number of different pictures. Storing all pictures in, say, an */images* folder ensures that the same picture has the same URL, no matter which page on your site displays it. Storing the same picture in two different server locations forces the browser to download and cache each copy separately.

2 To reduce total picture bytes on a Web page, you might be tempted to use many small picture files rather than one large or medium file. This process can go too far, however, because of a factor called *connection overhead.*

Unless both the browser and the Web server support a feature called *persistent connections,* the HTTP protocol forces the browser to open a new connection for every file it downloads. Thus, a Web page containing 10 pictures forces the browser to open and close 11 server connections: one for the HTML page and one for each picture. Each of these connections requires processing time on both the browser and server—time that might exceed what's required to download a smaller number of slightly larger files.

Stringent balancing of download bytes vs. required connections is seldom warranted, given the number of other variables in effect. Nevertheless, it's good practice to avoid large numbers of very small files.

> For information about displaying multiple images on a single page, refer to Chapter 22, "Using FrontPage Photo Galleries."

3 GIF picture compression works mainly by consolidating horizontal pixels. That is, rather than sequentially storing 100 white pixels on the same line, the file stores a single instruction to display 100 consecutive pixels, all white.

You can use this information to create pictures that compress well. Just remember that flat, horizontal areas compress well but complex horizontal areas don't.

JPEG compression is more two-dimensional and thus is less affected by the nature of the picture. Flat areas still compress better than highly variegated ones, however. With JPEG files you can also balance quality against picture size. To do this, vary the Quality setting in the Picture Properties dialog box. See Figure 11-3.

Chapter 23

683

Choosing Picture File Formats

Most current Web browsers can display only two picture file formats: Graphic Interchange Format (GIF) and Joint Photographic Expert Group (JPEG). A few browsers also support Portable Network Graphics (PNG), a new high-function alternative. Table 23-4 compares these formats.

Table 23-4. **Characteristics of GIF, JPEG, and PNG Formats**

	GIF	JPEG	PNG
Colors available	16,777,216	16,777,216	16,777,216
Colors per picture	256	16,777,216	16,777,216
Compression	Lossless	Lossy	Lossless
Transparency	One Color	No	Alpha Channel
Translucence	No	No	Alpha Channel
Animation	Yes	No	No
Remembers Gamma	No	No	Yes

> **note** FrontPage can import pictures in any of several other formats—BMP, TIFF, MAC, MSP, PCD, RAS, WPG, EPS, PCX, and WMF—and convert them to GIF or JPEG pictures.

Table 23-4 identifies some important differences between GIF, JPEG, and PNG pictures:

- **Lossy vs. lossless compression.** Storing a bitmapped picture might require several bytes of information for each pixel and, if the picture is large, might result in very large files. Most bitmapped file formats therefore include provisions for *compression*. Compression uses complex mathematical formulas to identify and abbreviate repeating patterns in the data.

  GIF compression uses a formula that results in zero loss of data from the compression/decompression process—that is, it provides *lossless* compression. The JPEG format supports varying degrees of compression, but most of them fail to guarantee an exact reproduction of the original. Depending on the creator's choice of settings, the resulting picture typically loses a measure of color fidelity, sharpness, or contrast. This is called *lossy* compression. The more data lost, the smaller the picture file.

- **Transparency.** All formats mentioned in this chapter save rectangular pictures. The number of horizontal and vertical pixels can be whatever you want, but there's no way to save a picture in these formats with circular, oval, or irregular borders.

Working with JPEG files

Every time you open and save a JPEG file, the quality of the picture goes down. This is what lossy compression means: if you save a picture and then reopen it, you don't get everything back. If you save it and reopen it again, you lose more quality. This process continues essentially forever.

For this reason, experienced graphic designers usually store original pictures in lossless formats such as TIFF, BMP, or their picture editor's native format. They convert to lossy formats such as JPEG only as a final step in preparing pictures for the Web.

One way to avoid rectangular picture shapes is to fill the edge with the same color as the background of your Web page. However, this won't work if the page uses a complex picture as a background, or if the visitor has configured the browser to override incoming background colors and pictures.

A better solution involves specifying a *transparent* color in the picture. Instead of displaying pixels having the transparent color, the browser displays whatever pixels lay behind them—usually the background color or picture.

For information about setting transparency in FrontPage, refer to "Setting Transparency" on page 657.

Even better is an *alpha channel*, which, for each pixel, specifies 256 levels of transparency as well as a base color.

The GIF format is well suited for setting a color to transparent. Typically, GIF images have large areas of a single color, such as in a clip-art image. Setting one color in the image as the transparent color would then let the page background show through. The JPEG format doesn't support the idea of transparency—but even if it did, JPEG files, which are typically photographs, have so many colors that setting a single color transparent would be like poking pinholes in the picture. Only a few pixels would be converted to transparent.

● **Animation.** The GIF format includes a provision to accommodate multiple pictures in the same file and to specify timing sequences among them. This provides a way to present simple animations within the browser without requiring the visitor to install additional animation software.

This type of animation typically loops continuously—in other words, it keeps playing over and over as long as the page is open in the browser. Take care when creating this type of animation so that it doesn't become distracting to the visitor. Every item placed on a page is one more thing that could distract visitors from the content on the page.

Chapter 23

685

> **tip** Microsoft PhotoDraw is one of many programs that can animate GIF pictures by making the picture shake, rattle, roll, rotate, fade, and so forth. However, using animated GIF files to display video is usually impractical.

- **Gamma.** Different computers make different assumptions about the relationship between software color brightness and the resulting monitor brightness. (This relationship, by the way, is nonlinear.) If you save a picture in PNG format, you can specify its *gamma factor*. Visitors' computers can then achieve better rendition.

Most Web designers prefer the GIF format for text, line art, and icons because of its lossless compression and transparency. JPEG finds use in backgrounds, photographs, and other areas where maximum compression and color fidelity are more important than sharpness.

A new picture format called Portable Network Graphics (PNG) supports full 32-bit color with an alpha channel, multiple compression methods, gamma information, and additional features that ease cross-platform difficulties. Unfortunately, PNG support in browsers remains far from universal, and PNG pictures tend to be larger than GIF or JPEG pictures.

> **on the web** For detailed information about Portable Network Graphics (PNG), browse *http://www.w3.org/TR/REC-png-multi.html.*

Pictures on Web pages remain in separate files and don't become part of the HTML. Instead, the HTML merely includes a reference to the picture file's name. As the browser receives the HTML for a page, it identifies any picture files needed and downloads them for display.

> **tip** When creating a top-level page—the beginning page of a section or area in your Web—it's a good idea to use no more than 30 to 40 KB of total file size. That includes all of the picture files and the HTML. Pages much larger than that can take a long time to download for visitors who connect to the Internet by modem. It's OK to make secondary pages more than 40 KB because visitors generally won't try to browse those pages unless they're interested in the content. Remember, though, that visitors are fickle and won't wait long, even for information they know they want.

Visualizing Transparency

At times it's quite desirable for parts of a computer picture to be transparent:

- When the edges of an object are irregular—that is, anything but rectangular.
- When parts of a picture must appear translucent.
- When parts of a picture should blend gradually into the background.

Accommodating Irregular Edges

Figure 23-1 shows a Web page containing two versions of the same picture. The version at the left has a solid white background that clashes with the textured background of the Web page. The picture at the right has a transparent background that allows the Web page background to show through clearly.

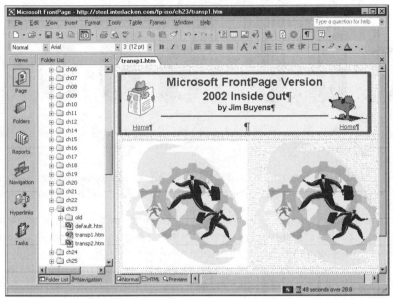

Figure 23-1. Compare the white background in the picture at the left with the transparent background of the picture at the right.

No amount of editing on the left picture will make it look as good as the picture on the right. No solid color can possibly blend evenly with the surrounding texture, and even adding a textured background to the picture will produce slight mismatches as the visitor resizes the browser window.

If your Web page background is solid rather than textured, you can achieve the effect of transparency simply by using pictures whose background color exactly matches the Web page background. The drawback is that if you change the Web page background color, you'll have to change all the pictures as well. Pictures with transparent backgrounds have no such drawback—you can use them on any Web page.

Smoothing Edges with Anti-Aliasing

Another application that greatly benefits from transparency is anti-aliasing. This is a technique that reduces the jagged appearance of curved lines when they're displayed on a computer monitor. Pixels along a curved edge, rather than being either the object's color or the background color, take on a mixture of the two. Figure 23-2 shows the string "abc" aliased at the left and anti-aliased at the right.

The right side of Figure 23-2 provides an enlarged view of anti-aliasing. Pixels entirely in the white area are entirely white, and those entirely in the black area are correspondingly black. Pixels along the border, however, are colored gray in proportion to the amount of black or white space that would be occupied at a much higher resolution.

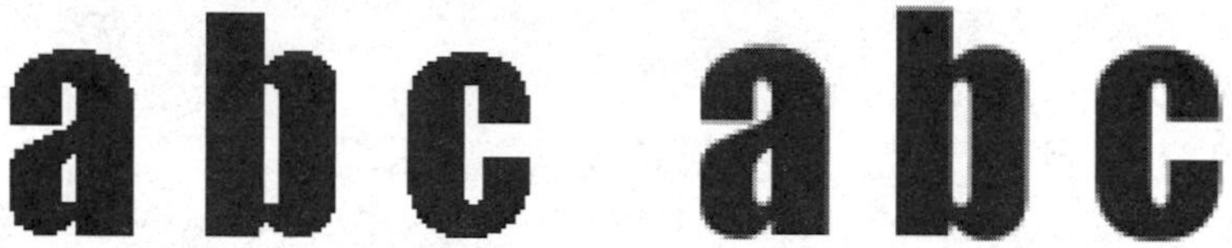

abc abc

Figure 23-2. Anti-aliasing, shown here at the far right, softens edges to make them look less jagged.

The use of anti-aliasing isn't confined to black-and-white drawings; the concept of proportionately shading edge pixels can apply to any intersection of two colors.

Many picture editors anti-alias everything by default, but this isn't always desirable. Anti-aliased edges sometimes appear blurry, like a slightly out-of-focus photograph, and sometimes the sharpness of aliased pictures is more important than the elimination of jagged edges. For this reason, it's important to have both aliasing and anti-aliasing tools at hand. Figure 23-3 provides an even larger view of anti-aliasing at work.

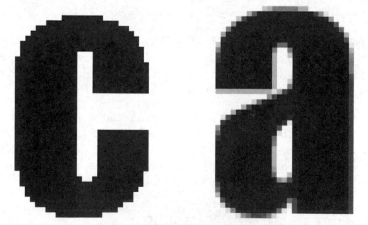

Figure 23-3. Pixels along the aliased curve are either light or dark. Pixels along the anti-aliased curve use various shades of gray for a smoother effect.

Using Transparency Effectively

Figure 23-4 shows a transparent AutoShape drawing positioned over a WordArt component. To make the WordArt show through, the designer positioned the AutoShape over the WordArt and adjusted the transparency of the AutoShape circle.

For more information about AutoShape drawings and WordArt components, refer to "Creating Line Art within FrontPage" on page 660.

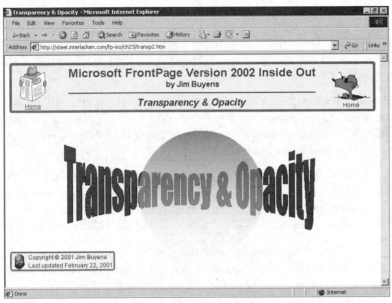

Figure 23-4. Experimenting with the transparency settings of FrontPage drawing features can result in interesting effects that add depth to your page.

A problem arises when preparing anti-aliased pictures (or, for that matter, nonrectangular pictures of any kind) for use on various colored or textured backgrounds. You know one color—that of the picture—but the second color varies depending on where the picture is used. The edge pixels need to be shaded not from one color to another, but from a solid color to various degrees of transparency—degrees that allow background colors to partially show through. To further complicate the problem, each pixel in the picture might require a different amount of transparency.

An *alpha channel* stores a fourth value along with the normal red, green, and blue intensities for each pixel. Each pixel's alpha value indicates the degree of transparency for that pixel, normally with the same precision used for red, green, and blue values. The addition of an alpha channel expands 24-bit color (8 bits each for red, green, and blue) to 32-bit color.

Unfortunately, neither GIF nor JPEG supports a true alpha channel. Advanced picture editors such as Adobe Photoshop *do* support alpha channels, but saving a picture in Web format converts the transparency information to fixed colors based on the editor's current background color. Having alpha channel support in the picture editor and its native file format is less useful than if Web pictures fully supported the feature, but it at least provides an easy way to create multiple versions of a picture with different background colors.

A common problem involves pictures anti-aliased for one background but used on another. This results in a sort of halo around the opaque portions of the picture. Unfortunately, even editing the picture with a program that supports alpha channels won't restore the original transparency information; the alpha channel was lost when the picture was saved with a fixed color background. Pixel-by-pixel editing along the edges is often the only remedy to this halo effect.

The JPEG file format doesn't support transparency at all, but the GIF format does support an all-or-nothing sort of transparency. The creator of a GIF file can designate one color in the picture as transparent. This is better than nothing—but nowhere near as powerful as a full alpha channel.

Of 16,777,216 possible colors, only 256 can exist within any given GIF file. These 256 are the GIF file's palette. Transparency works by designating one palette entry—out of the 256—as transparent. When the browser encounters this palette-entry color, it displays whatever lies behind the GIF picture instead of the palette-entry color.

If two palette entries represent the same color, only one of them can indicate transparency. This might explain why you occasionally get incomplete results when setting transparency on the basis of color.

In Summary...

Working with pictures inherently involves working with color. The results can be confusing, often resulting in pictures with undesired effects. Remember simply that JPEG images work best for photographs and images that contain varied tonal ranges. GIF images work best with images that contain large solid areas of color, and any single color in a GIF can be made transparent.

The next chapter discusses a number of ways Front Page can add animation to your Web pages.

Part 9

Incorporating Advanced Content

Enhancing Web Pages with Animation

You can use animation on your Web to call attention to something important. If your site sells designer mousepads, for example, you could create an animated image of a designer mousepad with a 3-D rotating effect, and use it to promote a sale.

But a spinning logo or image isn't the only form of animation. Animation also controls button images that change when a visitor moves the mouse pointer over them, or pages that fade out as a new page comes in. Video is another form of animation. This chapter explains how to use Microsoft FrontPage to apply these techniques, plus a couple of others.

Animating Page Transitions

Figure 24-1 on the next page shows, in frozen form, an animation effect in progress as one Web page replaces another. Instead of just erasing the screen and painting the new page normally—from top to bottom—the browser replaces it in an ever-decreasing circle. In this way the White On Black page gradually replaces the Black On White page.

To set page transitions, choose Page Transition from the Format menu. This opens the Page Transitions dialog box shown in Figure 24-2 on the next page. The following options are available:

- **Event.** Specifies when the page transition occurs:

  - **Page Enter.** Displays a transition effect as the currently edited page appears on the Web visitor's browser.

Figure 24-1. The page with the black background is gradually replacing the page with the white background. You control such effects using the Page Transition command on the Format menu.

- **Page Exit.** Displays a transition effect as the currently edited page disappears from the visitor's browser.

- **Site Enter.** Displays a transition effect as the currently edited page appears on the visitor's browser, provided that the previous page was from a different Web site.

- **Site Exit.** Displays a transition effect as the currently edited page disappears from the visitor's browser, provided that the next page is from a different Web site.

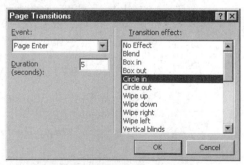

Figure 24-2. The Page Transitions dialog box defines animated transitions for Web pages.

- **Duration (Seconds).** Specifies how long the transition effect lasts.

- **Transition Effect.** Controls the animation pattern with more than 20 effects. You can guess from each transition's name the type of effect it produces. But the best way to become familiar with these effects is to simply try them on your own system.

One drawback to page transitions is that the browser must first wait for the *entire* new Web page to arrive, and then apply the effect. The visitor has no opportunity to start viewing early content while later content continues to arrive. The time to play the effect further increases the visitor's wait time. Also, the effects work only in Internet Explorer. Netscape Navigator ignores them.

Using Hover Buttons

Hyperlinked text, pictures, and push buttons are well-established fixtures on the Web. Some links, however, undoubtedly deserve something that gains more attention, and this is what the Hover Button component can provide.

A hover button is a small Java applet supplied with FrontPage. The applet displays a button—actually just a mouse-sensitive rectangle—with a solid-color background and a text caption. The button changes appearance when the visitor moves the mouse pointer over it, and jumps to a hyperlink location when the visitor clicks it.

Figure 24-3 shows a Web page with seven hover buttons, one for each background effect. Because the mouse pointer is positioned on the button with the Glow effect,

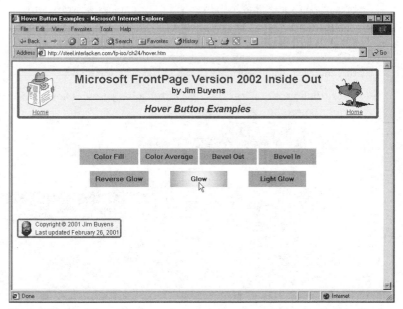

Figure 24-3. These buttons demonstrate all seven background effects available to hover buttons. Only the Glow effect is visible here, because that's where the mouse pointer is positioned.

it displays a gradient background while all the others are solid. The gradient remains in effect only while the mouse pointer is over the button. In its normal state, the button's background is solid like all the others.

Here's the procedure to create a hover button:

1 Open the Web page and set the insertion point where you want the hover button to appear.

2 Choose Web Component from the Insert menu.

3 Make sure Dynamic Effects is selected in the Component Type box at the left, and that Hover Button appears in the Choose An Effect list at the right. Click Finish.

4 The Hover Button Properties dialog box shown in the background of Figure 24-4 appears, prompting for the following settings:

- **Button Text.** Specifies the text the button displays. Remember that these are navigational buttons visitors will follow to move around your site. Give them names that are intuitive and easy to remember.

- **Link To.** Specifies the URL to which the button is linked. Type in a URL or click Browse to display a Select Hover Button Hyperlink dialog box that works like all other hyperlink dialog boxes.

- **Button Color.** Specifies the button's normal background color—that is, its color when the mouse pointer isn't over it. This displays the usual 16 boring and somewhat inappropriate color choices from the original VGA card. As usual, it's best to choose More Colors, and then choose Custom and specify RGB values having some combination of 0, 51, 102, 153, 204, and 255. If a Theme controls the page's appearance, the color list includes theme colors.

- **Background Color.** Specifies the button's background color when the mouse pointer is over the button.

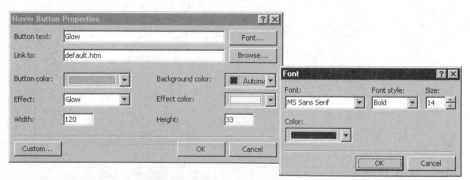

Figure 24-4. This is the dialog box for configuring hover buttons. Clicking the Font button displays the Font dialog box, which controls the font, style, color, and size of the button's label.

Chapter 24

Chapter 24: Enhancing Web Pages with Animation

▓ **Effect Color.** Specifies an accent color to display when the mouse pointer is over the button.

▓ **Effect.** Determines how the button appears when the mouse pointer passes over it:

◆ **Color Fill.** Means the effect color replaces the background color.

◆ **Color Average.** Means the background color changes to the average of its red, green, and blue components combined with those of the effect color.

◆ **Glow.** Means the button's center takes on the effect color, its left and right edges retain the background color, and areas in between display a gradient. This is the effect shown in Figure 24-3.

◆ **Reverse Glow.** Means the button's center retains the background color, the edges take on the effect color, and areas in between display a gradient.

◆ **Light Glow.** Means the button's left and right edges retains the background color, its center displays a lighter tint of the same hue, and areas in between display a gradient. This setting ignores the effect color.

◆ **Bevel Out.** Gives the effect of popping up the button by lightening the top and left edges, darkening the bottom and right, and lifting the text slightly up and to the left.

◆ **Bevel In.** Gives the effect of pressing the button by darkening the top and left edges, lightening the bottom and right, and moving the text slightly down and to the right.

▓ **Width** and **Height.** Determine the button's size in pixels. After selecting a hover button, you can also resize it by dragging its handles. (These are the eight small squares that appear around the edges.)

▓ **Font** and **Custom.** Open additional dialog boxes for setting more hover-button options.

The Font button displays the Font dialog box shown in the foreground of Figure 24-4. This dialog box controls the appearance of the button's label:

◆ **Font.** Sets the label's typeface. For maximum portability across systems, the list of typeface choices is limited.

◆ **Font Style.** Selects regular, bold, italic, or bold italic type.

◆ **Size.** Controls the font size in points.

◆ **Color.** Determines the color of the text. Choices, as usual, include the 16 VGA colors, plus default and custom.

Chapter 24

697

Part 9: Incorporating Advanced Content

The Custom button opens the Custom dialog box shown in Figure 24-5.

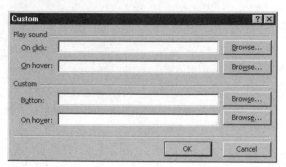

Figure 24-5. This Custom dialog box controls additional hover button effects.

The following settings are available for creating additional button effects:

Troubleshooting

Hover button or Banner Ad Manager doesn't work as expected

The Hover Button and Banner Ad Manager components each depend on two Java applets being available when visitors browse the Web page. If either applet is missing, the component won't work. The names of these applets are as follows:

- **Hover Button.** *fphover.class* and *fphoverx.class*.
- **Banner Ad Manager.** *fprotate.class* and *fprotatx.class*.

Whenever you save a page containing either component to a FrontPage-based Web, FrontPage checks the Web's root folder to see whether the required Java applets are present. If not, it adds them. Thereafter, whenever you use the FrontPage Publish feature for uploading to another Web server, FrontPage uploads the Java applets automatically. If you upload your files manually, you must upload the required Java applets as well.

If you add a Hover Button or Banner Ad Manager to a Web page and save it somewhere other than a FrontPage-based Web, FrontPage won't position the Java applets automatically. Instead, you'll need to copy, rename, position, and upload the Java applets yourself. By default, they're in the folder:

C:\Program Files\Microsoft Office\Office10\fpclass

and they have the filename extension *.cls*.

If you think the necessary Java applets are in place, but the Hover Button or Banner Ad Manager still isn't working, the button's HTML might be specifying the wrong location for the applets. This most often occurs when you copy a page containing these components from one Web to another.

■ **Play Sound.** Specifies sound files the browser plays under certain conditions. It's best to use small, brief sound files. Both of the following settings are optional:

◆ **On Click.** Specifies a sound that plays when the Web visitor clicks the button.

◆ **On Hover.** Specifies a sound that plays when the Web visitor moves the mouse pointer over the button.

■ **Custom.** Identifies picture files that display within the hover button. Both settings are optional. If you specify both a picture in this dialog box and a text caption in the main Hover Button dialog box, the caption appears superimposed over the picture:

◆ **Button.** Names a picture that appears inside the hover button when the mouse pointer isn't over it.

To recover from this situation:

1 Open the malfunctioning Web page.

2 Select the malfunctioning Hover Button or Banner Ad Manager.

3 Click the HTML tab at the bottom of the Page view window.

4 The first selected line should contain an *<applet>* tag, and that tag should contain a *codebase=* attribute. Modify the value of the *codebase* attribute so it points to the folder where the Java applets reside. Be sure to specify a relative folder path and not a file name.

Up to and including FrontPage 2000, these Java applets resided in a folder named *_fpclass.* You might still find this folder in your Web, and you might still have Hover Buttons or Banner Ad Managers that refer to it. This isn't a problem so long as the Web pages point to a location where the Java applets exist. (The *_fpclass* folder, if it exists, is hidden by default. To make it visible, select Web Settings from the Tools menu, click the Advanced tab, select the check box titled Show Hidden Files And Folders, and then click OK.)

If you include any transparent GIF pictures in a Banner Ad Manager, they appear with the applet's background (a plain gray) and not that of your Web pages. This is because the Banner Ad Manager component uses a Java applet to display your rotating pictures, and Java applets can't be transparent. To avoid this, don't use transparent pictures with the Banner Ad Manager component.

Any sound files you specify for a Hover Button (using the Custom dialog box shown in Figure 24-5) must be in a file format called AU (presumably short for *audio.)* This is a sound file format most commonly used on UNIX systems, and the only such format Java applets can play. If the file you want to use is currently in some other format, you'll have to find a program (usually a sound file editor) that can convert it.

Chapter 24

◆ **On Hover.** Names a picture that appears when the mouse pointer passes over the hover button.

> **tip** To avoid alignment problems, it's best if the hover button and any custom pictures are the same size.

You can use the Browse buttons next to each option to locate files in the current Web, on the World Wide Web, or on your local hard drive or network file server.

Using the Banner Ad Manager

This Web component displays a series of pictures, one at a time, at a particular location on your Web page. Clicking any picture in the series can jump the visitor to another Web location. The list of pictures, the time interval and transitions among them, and the hyperlink location are all under your control.

Many ad rotators on the World Wide Web rotate pictures only once, when a visitor requests a certain Web page. The Banner Ad Manager, by contrast, continuously rotates pictures even if the visitor doesn't reload the Web page. Many ad rotators also jump to a different Web page depending on the picture currently displayed, but the Banner Ad Manager always jumps to the same location.

> For information about an ad rotator that displays a different ad (with a different target location) each time a visitor displays a page, refer to "Using the MSWC.AdRotator Object" later in this chapter.

Figure 24-6 shows a page that contains a Banner Ad Manager. To insert a Banner Ad Manager you must first, of course, obtain or prepare the pictures. It's best but not required that all the pictures be the same size. When you specify a list of pictures that vary in size, the browser pads or crops them. This might not give the effect you want.

> **tip** The most common size for advertising banner pictures on the World Wide Web is 468 pixels wide by 60 pixels high.

Here are the steps to insert a Banner Ad Manager:

1 Open a new or existing Web page and set the insertion point where you want the Banner Ad Manager to appear.

2 Choose Web Component from the Insert menu.

3 Make sure Dynamic Effects is selected in the Component Type box at the left, and then select Banner Ad Manager from the Choose An Effect list at the right, and click Finish.

These steps display the Banner Ad Manager Properties dialog box shown in Figure 24-7.

Chapter 24: Enhancing Web Pages with Animation

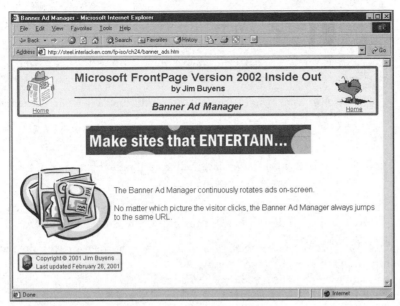

Figure 24-6. The Banner Ad Manager component replaces a picture at timed intervals. The picture on this page changes every five seconds.

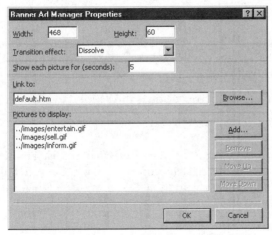

Figure 24-7. This dialog box is set to cycle through each of three pictures at five-second intervals.

When this dialog box appears, configure it as follows:

- **Width** and **Height.** Specify the amount of space to reserve for displaying the pictures. If a picture is smaller than the space you specify, FrontPage surrounds it with neutral space (gray). If a picture is larger, FrontPage crops the excess height or width.

- **Transition Effect.** Choose the effect for transitioning between pictures:

    - **None.** Switches directly from one picture to another with no special effect.

■ **Blinds Horizontal.** Replaces each existing picture with successively wider horizontal strips of its replacement.

■ **Blinds Vertical.** Replaces each existing picture with successively wider vertical strips of its replacement.

■ **Dissolve.** Fades out existing pictures until only a new picture remains.

■ **Box In.** Displays new pictures in a rectangle that grows inward from the edges of the existing picture.

■ **Box Out.** Displays new pictures in a rectangle that grows outward from the center of the existing picture.

● **Show Each Picture For (Seconds).** Specify the number of seconds each picture remains on display before transitioning to the next picture.

● **Link To.** Specify where the browser will jump if the visitor clicks any picture in the rotation. A single Banner Ad Manager jumps to a single location, no matter which banner picture the visitor clicks.

> **tip** You might expect that the Banner Ad Manager would jump to a different location for each picture it displays. Well, it doesn't. You can configure only one hyperlink location, and all the pictures jump there.

● **Browse.** Click this button to display the Select Banner Ad Hyperlink dialog box. You can browse the current Web, your local file system, or the World Wide Web to select the Link To location.

● **Pictures To Display.** This box lists the pictures the Banner Ad Manager will rotate. FrontPage displays the listed pictures in order, from top to bottom, and then restarts at the top.

● **Add.** Click this button to insert a picture at the bottom of the list. FrontPage displays its normal picture-browsing dialog box so that you can search the current Web, the World Wide Web, your local disk, or the Clip Organizer.

● **Remove.** Click this button to delete the currently selected item from the Pictures To Display list.

● **Move Up.** Click this button to move the currently selected picture one position higher in the Pictures To Display list.

● **Move Down.** Click this button to move the currently selected picture one position lower in the Pictures To Display list.

Whenever you save a Web page that contains a Banner Ad Manager, FrontPage first determines whether you're saving it to a FrontPage-based Web. If not, FrontPage offers to make the Web page's folder into a disk-based, FrontPage-based Web. You'll avoid trouble later by always saving pages that contain Banner Ad Manager components in a FrontPage-based Web.

Using the MSWC.AdRotator Object

Microsoft's premier Web server, IIS, has a very slick built-in feature for managing ad rotators: the *MSWC.AdRotator* object. If your Web server runs (or could run) IIS, this is an option worth considering. The *MSWC.AdRotator* randomly selects one of several ad pictures from a list and displays it (with a corresponding hyperlink) in any Web page you like. An *MSWC.AdRotator* object controls the ads in the Web page shown in Figure 24-8.

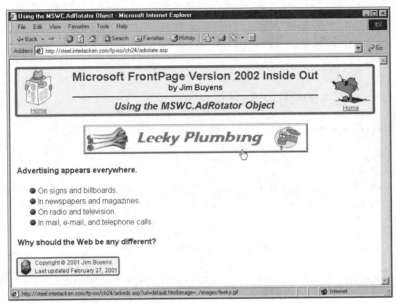

Figure 24-8. An *MSWC.AdRotator* object randomly selects one ad picture from a list and displays it on a Web page. Each picture in the list has a corresponding hyperlink.

Using an *MSWC.AdRotator* object really isn't difficult: it requires only three lines of code (two of which never change) and a text file that lists the ad pictures and corresponding hyperlinks. Understanding it does involve some new concepts, though, and running it requires a computer with Windows NT Server 4.0 or Windows 2000 running IIS.

One major restriction applies to the *MSWC.AdRotator* object: any page that uses it must be an ASP page. This means that the page must reside in an executable folder and that you can't see the rotator object work unless a properly configured Web server delivers the page.

For more information about marking folders as executable, refer to "Configuring Home Directory Settings" on page 1064.

For more information about marking folders as executable, refer to "Reviewing Web Settings" in the Bonus Content on the Companion CD.

Chapter 24

There are three steps in supporting ad rotation using ASP. Later sections explain each step in detail, but here's the overall approach:

- **ASP Redirection Script.** Place a special, one-line ASP page in an executable location somewhere on the Web server. There can be a single copy of this file, provided by the Webmaster, or each designer can have as many as required.

- **ASP Redirection File.** Create a simple text file on the server that lists the rotating ad pictures, associated URLs, and other related information.

- **AdRotator Object.** Add two or three lines of code to your Web page, wherever you want the ad to appear. Change the page's filename extension to *.asp* and make sure it resides in an executable directory on the Web server.

Creating the ASP Redirection Script

The *MSWC.AdRotator* object doesn't generate simple hyperlinks like:

```
http://ads.interlacken.com/heads.htm
```

That would be boring and mundane. Instead, it generates links such as the following, which are sure to become more interesting and useful as the section proceeds:

```
http://www.interlacken.com/fp-iso/ch24/
adredir.asp?url=http://ads.interlacken.com/heads.htm
```

The true URL that corresponds to the current ad appears as the value of the query string variable *url*. That isn't the location this URL requests, however. The actual location is a page named *adredir.asp* that contains, in total, one line of code. That code appears below:

```
<% response.redirect(request.QueryString("url")) %>
```

The *response.redirect* method sends an instruction to the browser, telling it to jump to another page. This uses essentially the same mechanism as the *refresh* system variable mentioned in Chapter 18. In this case, the *response.redirect* method tells the browser to jump to the page that the query string variable *url* specified: that is, to the location that *adredir.asp* finds in *request.QueryString("url")*.

For more information about the *refresh* system variable, refer to "Using the REFRESH System Variable" on page 548. To learn how browsers submit information by adding a query string to a URL, refer to "Coding URL Fields for Executable Programs" on page 384. To learn how ASP pages receive information submitted via query strings, refer to "Processing Form Data with ASP Pages" on page 910.

Chapter 24: Enhancing Web Pages with Animation

> **caution** The *adredir.asp* file in your server, if it exists, will probably have a different path. The path */exec/* is only an example. Contact your Webmaster, system administrator, or Internet service provider to find out (1) whether your Web server supports ASP, (2) whether there's a central copy of the *adredir.asp* file you can use, and (3) if not, where you can put one. Both *adredir.asp* and any Web pages that use it need to be in folders that have permission to execute ASP pages.

Instead of just telling the visitor's browser where to jump, the *MSWC.AdRotator* object tells the browser to request the *adredir.asp* page so that *adredir.asp* can tell the browser where to jump. So what, you ask? Well, this is the more interesting and more useful part. By counting hits to *adredir.asp*, you can tell how many people are clicking ad pictures. And if your Web server keeps query string data in its log files, you can also count which ads they clicked. Is that cool or what?

> **note** If you want to collect more information about people who click ads, you can just add more statements to *adredir.asp*. Each time *adredir.asp* runs, for example, you could write a data record with the date, time, requesting IP address, and requested URL.

Remember that the *adredir.asp* file, or whatever you decide to call it, *must* be present and that any number of *MSWC.AdRotator* Web pages can use the same *adredir.asp* page.

Creating the ASP Redirection File

One such file appears here, and also as */ch24/adrotate.txt* in the sample Web:

```
REDIRECT adredir.asp
WIDTH 468
HEIGHT 60
BORDER 1
*
../images/wurst.gif
default.htm
The Wurst Deli
5
../images/pierbuoy.gif
default.htm
Pier Buoy Sandwiches
5
../images/leeky.gif
default.htm
Leeky Plumbing
5
```

> **note** In this example, the *adrotate.txt* file, the *adredir.asp* file, and the Web page
> *adrotate.asp* that displays the ads all reside in the same folder. This accounts for the
> lack of server names and path names in the URLs. If your situation differs, so might
> the need for server and path names in your URLs.

Keywords identify the first four lines, all of which are optional. They specify:

- **REDIRECT.** The relative URL of the one-line redirection file.
- **WIDTH.** The width of the ad pictures.
- **HEIGHT.** The height of the ad pictures.
- **BORDER.** The border width for the ad pictures.

A line containing an asterisk comes next, then groups of five statements as follows:

- The relative URL of an ad picture (relative to the current ASP page).
- The URL that clicking the ad will follow.
- The text equivalent for the ad. (This appears as the hyperlink's *alt* attribute.)
- A relative frequency.
- A blank line.

The relative frequencies work like this: if all the ads described in the same file have the
same frequency values—such as 5—they appear equally often. If, however, one of the
ads has a frequency value of 10, it appears twice as often as those with 5. An ad with a
frequency of 50 would appear ten times as often as one with a value of 5. The actual
values are immaterial; you could use 1, 2, and 10 as easily as 5, 10, and 50, and achieve
identical results.

Defining the list of ads in a text file is actually a very good policy. It means that someone who doesn't know HTML—your client, for example—can keep the list up to date.

Displaying the MSWC.AdRotator Ads

Now that you know everything about the one-line, redirection ASP file *(adredir.asp)*
and about the rotation list file *(adrot.txt)*, you're finally prepared to look at the two
lines that actually display the ad. They are:

```
<% Set objAdRot = Server.CreateObject("MSWC.AdRotator")
   Response.Write(objAdRot.GetAdvertisement("adrotate.txt"))%>
```

This code does a lot. Specifically:

- The first line creates an *MSWC.AdRotator* object called *objAdRot*.

- The second statement tells the *objAdRot* object to generate ad rotation HTML based on the settings and the ad list in the *adrotate.txt* file.

- Acting on the generated HTML, the browser sends clicks on any ad to *adredir.asp* (or whatever page *adrotate.txt* specified).

- The *adredir.asp* page tells the browser where to jump.

- You can tell how many people are clicking ads by counting hits to *adredir.asp.*

If you're a perfectionist you might wish to add two more lines between the two listed above:

```
objAdRot.TargetFrame = "_blank"
objAdRot.Border = 0
```

The first line configures the *MSWC.AdRotator* object so that clicking the ad displays the advertiser's Web page in a new window. This provides some assurance that visitors will return to your Web page before quitting their Web surfing session.

The second line controls the width of the blue hyperlink border that surrounds the ad picture. This overrides the BORDER setting in the ASP redirection file.

To view a working example of this technique, open the files *adrotate.asp, adrotate.txt,* and *adredir.asp* in the */ch24/* folder of the sample Web. What could be more fun?

Using DHTML Effects

In addition to animating the appearance and disappearance of entire Web pages, FrontPage can animate the way individual elements arrive on screen, react to mouse activity, or both. Headings, pictures, and other objects can fly in from various borders, drop in one word at a time, spiral in, zoom in, and so forth. In addition, an object's appearance can change as the mouse pointer passes over it.

Figure 24-9 on the next page shows such a page-load animation in progress. The heading line, including the picture, has already slid in from the right edge of the window. The bookmark hyperlinks *Backup, Diskettes, Drink Holder,* and *Foot Pedal* have already dropped in from the top of the window, and the bookmark hyperlink *Whiteout* is en route.

FrontPage creates these effects by adding browser scripts to your Web page. These scripts are written in JavaScript and use the positioning and overlap features provided by dynamic HTML (DHTML). Internet Explorer 4 was the first browser to support these features; others have followed. Applying DHTML effects in FrontPage is quite simple:

1 Set the insertion point anywhere within the element you wish to animate. This will usually be a paragraph.

Part 9: Incorporating Advanced Content

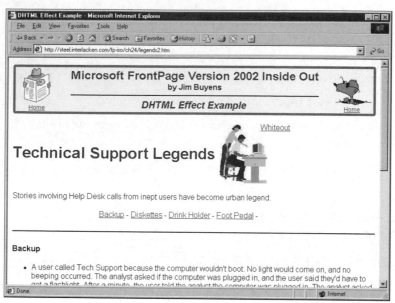

Figure 24-9. The hyperlinks on this Web page are dropping in word by word from the top.

2 Locate the DHTML Effects toolbar described in Table A-10 in Appendix A. If it isn't visible, choose Toolbars from the View menu, and then choose DHTML Effects.

3 Use the Choose An Event drop-down list (labeled On) to specify the event that triggers the effect. There are four options:

- **Click.** Means the effect occurs whenever the Web visitor clicks the element.

- **Double-Click.** Means the effect occurs whenever the Web visitor double-clicks the element.

- **Mouse Over.** Means the effect occurs whenever the Web visitor moves the mouse pointer over the element.

- **Page Load.** Means the effect occurs whenever the Web visitor loads or reloads the page.

4 Use the Choose An Effect drop-down list (labeled Apply) to choose the effect you want. As illustrated in Table 24-1, the choice of effects varies depending on the trigger event.

5 If the Effect Settings list is enabled, click the drop-down button and choose one of the listed options.

To remove an effect, first select the element, making sure the DHTML Effects toolbar displays the effect you want to remove. Then, click the toolbar's Remove Effect button.

Chapter 24: Enhancing Web Pages with Animation

Table 24-1. **Effects Available for DHTML Events**

Event (On)	Effect (Apply)	Description	Settings
Click, Double-Click	Fly Out	Moves the animated element off-screen	Direction of movement
Click, Double-click, Mouse Over	Formatting	Changes the appearance of text	Fonts (including font colors) and borders
Page Load	Drop In By Word	Moves text on screen from the top, a word at a time	(none)
	Elastic	Moves the entire element on screen from the right or bottom overshoots, and then corrects	From right or from bottom
	Fly In	Moves the element on screen from any side or corner	Side or corner, entire element or a word at a time
	Hop	Moves the element slightly up, right, down, and then left	(none)
	Spiral	Moves the element from the upper-right corner to its proper place, using a spiral motion	(none)
	Wave	Moves the element slightly down, right, up, and then left	(none)
	Wipe	Gradually reveals the element	Left to right, top to bottom, or from middle
	Zoom	Text starts out either very large or very small, and then zooms to normal size	In (reduced text becomes normal) or out (enlarged text becomes normal)

Highlight
Dynamic
HTML
Effects

FrontPage can visually indicate elements with DHTML effects by showing them with a light blue background. This occurs only in Page view, and not in the Web visitor's browser. However, if you find the blue background in Page view distracting, you can toggle it on and off by clicking the Highlight Dynamic HTML Effects button on the DHTML Effects toolbar.

Chapter 24

709

The various DHTML Effects animations run only once. There's no way to make them run continuously, and that's probably a good thing. After loading your page, you want Web visitors to read your content and not to sit there watching cartoons.

Highlighting hyperlinks is a common use for Mouse Over effects. When the mouse pointer passes over hyperlinked text, the text can change color, get larger, change font, and so forth. FrontPage calls this a *rollover* effect.

> For information about configuring rollover effects for all hyperlinks on a Web page, refer to "Background Page Properties" on page 540.

Swapping Pictures with DHTML Effects

When you select a picture and then use the DHTML Effects toolbar, the toolbar offers the effects shown in Table 24-2.

Table 24-2. Picture Effects Available for DHTML Events

Event (On)	Effect (Apply)	Description	Settings
Click	Fly Out	Moves the picture off the screen	Direction of movement
	Swap Picture	Replaces the picture with another picture	Location of the replacement picture
Double-Click	Fly Out	Moves the picture off the screen	Direction of movement
Mouse Over	Swap Picture	Replaces the picture with another picture	Location of the replacement picture
Page Load	Refer to Table 24-1.		

The Swap Picture effect offers a flexible alternative to Hover Buttons if you proceed as follows:

1 Create two versions of a picture you want to use as a button:

- One is the picture as it normally appears.

- The other is an alternate version that appears when the Web visitor passes the mouse pointer over the picture area.

Note: Both pictures should be the same size.

2 Add the "normal" picture to your Web page and build the desired hyperlink.

3 Select the "normal" picture, and then display the DHTML Effects toolbar.

Chapter 24: Enhancing Web Pages with Animation

4 In the DHTML Effects toolbar:

- ▦ Set On to Mouse Over.

- ▦ Set Apply to Swap Picture.

- ▦ Set the third drop-down list to Choose Picture.

5 Use the resulting Picture dialog box to specify the "alternate" picture.

Because of an apparent bug, you must perform these steps in the order given. If you specify the DHTML effects first and then the hyperlink, FrontPage might discard the DHTML effects.

Presenting Video

FrontPage can insert video clips into your Web pages as easily as it inserts still pictures. Delivering video requires no special software in FrontPage or on your Web server, but displaying it requires a player on the visitor's browser. The most common video formats on the Web are Audio Visual Interleaved (AVI) from Microsoft and QuickTime (formerly called Active Movie [MOV]) from Apple. Visitors can obtain player software from these companies' Web sites, or through their browser suppliers.

It's good practice and common courtesy to provide hyperlinks that download players for video clips or other multimedia elements used on your Web pages:

- For information about downloadable Microsoft browser features, browse:

  http://www.microsoft.com/windows/ie/download/default.asp

- For information about downloadable Netscape browser plug-in features, browse:

  http://www.netscape.com/plugins/index.html

- For more information about QuickTime, including download locations, browse:

  http://www.apple.com/quicktime/

For more information about presenting video, refer to "Inserting Video Files" on page 324.

Displaying a Marquee

The Marquee component displays a line of text that scrolls automatically across the browser window. Browsers lacking built-in marquee support display the marquee text statically.

Part 9: Incorporating Advanced Content

To add a marquee to your Web page:

1 Open the page in FrontPage.

2 To convert existing text to a marquee, select it. To create a marquee that uses new text, just set the insertion point where you want the marquee to appear.

3 Choose Web Component from the Insert menu.

4 Make sure Dynamic Effects is selected in the Component Type box at the left, and then select Marquee from the Choose An Effect list at the right. Click Finish to display the Marquee Properties dialog box shown in Figure 24-10.

InsideOut

Use of the marquee has fallen out of favor because no single rate of scrolling is right for all Web visitors, and because the constant motion distracts the visitor from other content. Use of marquees on Web pages has therefore dropped to near zero. If you want your Web to have a professional appearance and deliver a satisfying experience, avoid using this component.

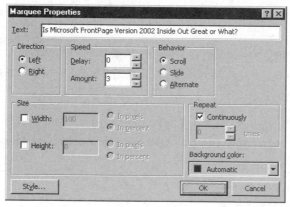

Figure 24-10. This dialog box configures a FrontPage marquee.

5 Configure the marquee by setting the dialog box options as described below, and then click OK.

The Marquee Properties dialog box provides the following options:

● **Text.** Specifies the message the marquee animates. Any text you selected before starting the marquee command appears here.

Chapter 24: Enhancing Web Pages with Animation

- **Direction.** Controls how the marquee text moves—toward the left (the usual choice) or toward the right:

  - **Speed.** Controls how quickly the marquee moves.

  - **Delay.** Specifies the number of milliseconds between each motion of the marquee.

- **Amount.** Specifies how many pixels the marquee shifts in each step.

- **Behavior.** Determines the type of motion:

  - **Scroll.** Advances the marquee continuously across the screen in accordance with the Direction setting. Motion continues until the trailing edge of the text reaches the end of the marquee area.

  - **Slide.** Like scroll, advances the marquee continuously across the screen. Motion continues until the leading edge of the text reaches the end of the marquee area, where it stops.

  - **Alternate.** Moves the marquee text back and forth within the available area. In this method the marquee text is always completely visible, for maximum impact.

- **Size.** Determines the screen area occupied by the marquee:

  - **Width.** Controls the marquee's horizontal dimension. The default is to occupy all available width: the entire browser window, table cell, frame, or other container.

    To choose a specific width, select the check box, enter a value, and then indicate the unit of measure as either pixels or percent.

  - **Height.** Controls the marquee's vertical dimension. The default is to accommodate only the marquee text, including its formatting.

    To choose a specific height, select the check box, enter a value, and then indicate the unit of measure as either pixels or percent.

- **Repeat.** Controls how often the marquee redisplays the moving text:

  - **Continuously.** Means the marquee continues moving text as long as the visitor's browser displays the Web page.

  - **Times.** Specifies how many times the marquee effect repeats.

> **caution** If you specify the Behavior setting as Scroll, and then set Repeat to a specific number of times, little or nothing might visible in the marquee area when movement stops.

- **Background Color.** Gives the marquee its own background color. The default is the Web page's background color.

- **Style.** Assigns cascading style sheet attributes to the marquee.

To modify an existing marquee, either select it and choose Properties from the Format menu, or right-click it and choose Marquee Properties from the shortcut menu.

To change a marquee's font, font size, text color, or other text properties, either select the marquee and use the normal format menus, or open the Marquee Properties dialog box and click Style to apply cascading style sheet attributes.

Figure 24-11 shows a marquee in an Internet Explorer browser window. Assigning a behavior of Scroll makes the text scroll from behind the icon on the right, travel across the screen, and then disappear behind the icon on the left. This effect is achieved by placing the two icons and the marquee in the left, right, and center cells of a one-row, three-column table.

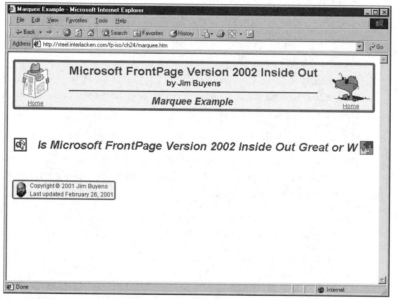

Figure 24-11. The marquee in this Web page scrolls from behind the icon on the right, and then disappears behind the icon on the left.

In Summary...

FrontPage features a number of exciting animated elements to spice up your Web pages. Using components such as hover buttons, page transitions, and DHTML effects, you can make your pages look like you spent a million dollars on technology.

The next chapter explains how to use programmed objects that operate within the browser or Page view window. This includes ActiveX objects, Plug-Ins, Java applets, and Design-time controls.

Chapter 25

Incorporating Advanced Objects

The astounding growth of the World Wide Web is a testament to the power and practicality of HTML. Even so, HTML remains basically a static medium. The designer lays out a page and hopes the visitors will look at it. Extending the functionality of HTML is difficult because designers can't count on visitors upgrading their browsers until years have passed.

Fortunately, current-day browsers can display various kinds of programmed objects in the browser window, and these objects can provide functions not present in the browser itself. This chapter describes how to use three types of such objects:

- **ActiveX objects.** These are Microsoft Windows software components that provide standardized interactive and background services. Many such objects are capable of operating in a Web page provided, of course, that the Web browser supports Active X controls. Currently, only Windows versions of Internet Explorer provide such support.

- **Plug-ins.** These are programs that take over parts of the browser window and display specially marked files. For a plug-in to work, the Web designer must configure the area the plug-in file will occupy, the Web server administrator must configure the server to properly identify the type of file, and the Web visitor must install a plug-in that can display the given file type. The fact that plug-ins work in both Microsoft Internet Explorer and Netscape Navigator is a significant strength.

- **Java applets.** These are another kind of program that takes over part of the browser window. These applets can run on any type of computer that has a Java virtual machine interpreter installed, and this encompasses a wide range of computers. Compared to ActiveX controls, Java applets are limited in capability. This reduces the security risk of running downloaded code on the visitor's computer, but also reduces the capability for useful work.

Design-Time Controls (DTCs) are a completely different type of ActiveX control not intended for use in a browser. Instead, DTCs extend the capabilities of an HTML editor. A DTC collects specifications from the Web page designer and emits the corresponding HTML whenever the designer saves the page. The browser never uses the DTC directly; it uses only the HTML that the DTC produces. General-purpose DTCs are relatively uncommon, but if you purchase software that provides them, Microsoft FrontPage can use them.

Incorporating ActiveX Controls

Microsoft's vision of uniting Windows and the World Wide Web naturally involves a merger of Windows programming objects and active Web pages. This section explains how to incorporate such objects, called ActiveX controls, into your Web page.

Introducing ActiveX

ActiveX controls are reusable software modules that provide functions other software can exploit. Because ActiveX controls are easy to distribute and use, they've become a very popular way to package and distribute software. Microsoft designed ActiveX controls with Windows in mind, but the concept extends to almost any other platform.

Physically, ActiveX controls are Windows dynamic link libraries (DLLs), but they usually have an *.ocx* filename extension. They come from a variety of sources: Some come with the operating system, some come as parts of other software installed on your computer, and others come from Web pages that use them and provide a download location.

Each ActiveX control provides one or more software objects. These objects might or might not display anything on the screen, but they all have *properties, methods,* and *events*:

- **Properties.** These are data values accessible by external processes as well as by the control. Depending on how a control is written, an external process might or might not be able to update a given property.

- **Methods.** These are software routines, programmed into the control, that external processes can trigger.

- **Events.** These are external incidents that trigger code to execute. Event routines run in response to external stimuli, such as mouse clicks, keystrokes, or incoming data.

Chapter 25: Incorporating Advanced Objects

Using ActiveX Controls on the Web

A typical Windows computer has hundreds—or even thousands—of ActiveX controls installed on it. Of these, only a fraction provide functions that are useful on a Web page. However, if a particular control is useful, a browser can run the control just as easily as any other piece of software can. Some ActiveX controls, of course, exist specifically for use in Web browsers. ActiveX controls have many capabilities, but the important ones that pertain to Web pages are these:

- ActiveX controls can display preset data. Chapter 11, for example, showed how the Microsoft ActiveMovieControl Object can display a video.

- ActiveX controls can interact with script code also contained within the Web page. Scripts, in this sense, are small blocks of program code delivered with the Web page, and they run on the Web visitor's browser. They're usually written in JavaScript and VBScript. Scripts can read and modify ActiveX properties, invoke their methods, and respond to their events.

- The HTML for an ActiveX control can specify a download location. Then, if a Web visitor doesn't have all the ActiveX controls that a given page uses, the browser can download and install those controls on the fly.

- ActiveX controls running in a Web browser can make any changes to the local system that the Web visitor could make.

The last capability is, of course, a potentially dangerous one. Browsing the Web could expose your system to any number of malicious, intrusive, or privacy-invading software components. A digital signature scheme ensures that whoever downloads an ActiveX control knows who created it and thus whom to prosecute if the control is mischievous or destructive! Figure 25-1 shows the Security Warning dialog box that appears before Internet Explorer downloads and installs any ActiveX control from the Web.

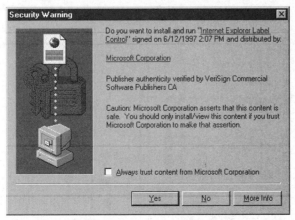

Figure 25-1. This dialog box asks for permission to install a new ActiveX control used in a Web page.

Lack of browser support is probably the greatest impediment to using ActiveX controls on the Web. Currently, Windows versions of Internet Explorer are the only browsers that support ActiveX controls. All other browsers simply ignore the controls and display a presupplied message or nothing in their place. Here, then, are some strategies for using ActiveX controls:

- Use ActiveX controls only in situations where you know all the Web visitors will be using a Windows version of Internet Explorer:

  - If you're delivering a specialized service over the Internet, for example, you can simply tell your clientele what browser to use.

  - On an intranet, a Windows version of Internet Explorer might be your corporate standard.

- Design your Web page to degrade gracefully if the browser can't run ActiveX controls. You might, for example, provide two different mechanisms for entering a quantity: an ActiveX slider or gauge as well as an ordinary text box, for example. This provides Web visitors with the best experience possible given their browsers' capabilities.

- Design two different Web pages, one for Internet Explorer users and another for everyone else. Before you recoil at the thought of doing twice the work, consider the following:

  - A number of forces are, in any event, driving a trend toward multiple representations of the same content. Wireless devices, personal digital assistants (PDAs), and Microsoft WebTV are cases in point.

  - Technologies that separate presentation from content—technologies such as database-driven and XML-driven Web sites—often make platform-dependent Web pages practical. For example, instead of hand-crafting 1000 Web pages to display 1000 catalog items, modern designers develop one Web database page that displays any item in a catalog database. That way, supporting five platforms requires creating five Web pages and not 5000. And for those five, you need to do the database development—which is usually the hard part—only once.

Inserting ActiveX Controls

Here's the procedure for adding an ActiveX control to a Web page that's already open in Page view:

1 Set the insertion point where you want the ActiveX control to appear.

Web
Component

2 Choose Web Component from the Insert menu or the Standard toolbar. This displays the Insert Web Component dialog box.

3 In the Component Type list, select Advanced Controls.

Chapter 25: Incorporating Advanced Objects

4 In the Choose A Control list, choose ActiveX Control, as shown in Figure 25-2.

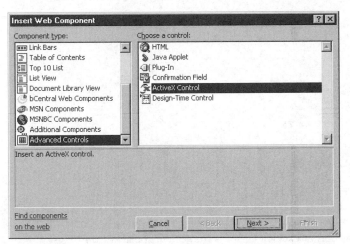

Figure 25-2. The Insert Web Component dialog box can insert ActiveX controls.

5 Click Next; the dialog box now resembles Figure 25-3. If the control you want appears in the Choose A Control list, select it and then click Finish.

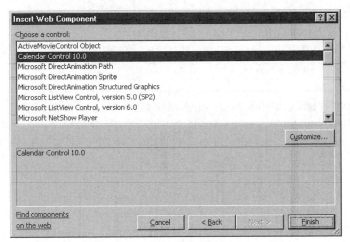

Figure 25-3. To add an ActiveX control to your Web page, select it from this list and then click Finish.

6 If the Choose A Control list doesn't include the control you want, click Customize to search for the control on your system. This displays the Customize ActiveX Control List dialog box shown in Figure 25-4 on next page.

Part 9: Incorporating Advanced Content

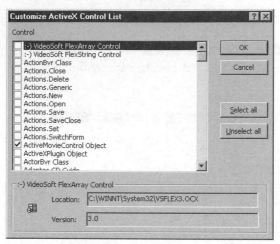

Figure 25-4. Click Customize in the Insert Web Component dialog box to include or exclude controls from the Choose A Control list.

This dialog box displays a complete list of the ActiveX controls installed on your system. You'll probably discover many more controls than you expect; the list includes all controls you've downloaded from Web pages, plus those installed by other software. The check box that precedes the name of each control specifies whether that control appears in the Choose A Control list shown in Figure 25-3.

If the control you want is present in this list, select its check box, click OK, and go back to step 5.

note The Location box in Figure 25-4 displays the file name and path of any control you select. This is important if you want to provide a copy of the control in your Web for visitors to download. You can't copy something into your Web if you don't know where it is!

7 If you still can't find the control you want, click the Find Components On The Web link in the lower left corner of the Insert Web Component dialog box (Figure 25-3). This closes the dialog box but starts Internet Explorer so you can find the control on the Web. After you've found the control, download and install it on your system. Finally, go back to step 1.

This step assumes, of course, that your default browser is Internet Explorer. Starting a browser such as Netscape Navigator that can't install Active X controls serves little purpose. It's almost as though your computer went on strike.

Chapter 25: Incorporating Advanced Objects

FrontPage adds any new ActiveX control to your Web page at the current insertion point. If the control generates a display, Page view displays it. If not, the control just occupies a blank space. Either way, FrontPage surrounds the area with sizing handles. You can drag, cut, copy, paste, and resize in all the usual ways.

ActiveX controls don't execute in Page view—objects in FrontPage need to "hold still" for editing. This means ActiveX controls don't respond interactively, as they would in a browser situation. Some controls don't even display in WYSIWYG mode. To see the control in action, switch to Preview mode, or choose Preview In Browser from the File menu.

As you might expect, there's an ActiveX Control Properties dialog box that sets the properties of any control on a Web page. Any of the following methods displays the ActiveX Control Properties dialog box:

- Double-click the ActiveX control.

- Right-click the control, and choose ActiveX Control Properties.

- Click the control, and choose Properties from the Format menu.

- Click the control, and press Alt+Enter.

Any of these techniques produces a dialog box resembling Figure 25-5. However, because no two ActiveX controls have the same properties and capabilities, no two of their Properties dialog boxes look the same.

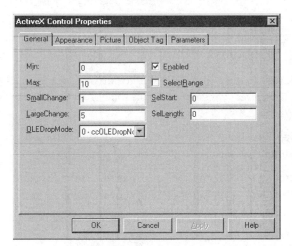

Figure 25-5. The Microsoft Slider control displays this ActiveX Control Properties dialog box. Other controls might display more or fewer tabs, but nearly all controls display the Object Tag and Parameters tabs.

The last two tabs in Figure 25-5, Object Tag and Parameters, are generic and appear for nearly all ActiveX controls. The rest are specific to the particular control. The Object Tag tab appears in Figure 25-6 on the next page.

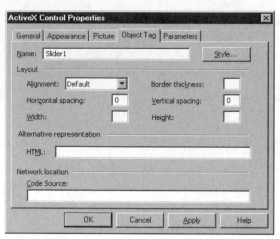

Figure 25-6. The Object Tag properties for an ActiveX control pertain to size and placement on the Web page, and to download location. The browser, and not the ActiveX control, uses this information.

The Object Tag tab contains these options:

- **Name.** Scripts on the same Web page can use this name to reference the control.

- **Layout.** Use these options to specify the control's page placement and appearance:

  - **Alignment.** Specify the control's position relative to surrounding text. Table 11-2, on page 338 describes the possible values.

  - **Border Thickness.** Enter a nonzero value to surround the control with a border. The specified value controls the border's thickness in pixels.

  - **Horizontal Spacing.** Enter the number of pixels that should separate the control from neighboring elements on the same line.

  - **Vertical Spacing.** Enter the number of pixels that should separate the control from any text or pictures above and below it.

  - **Width.** Specify, in pixels, the amount of horizontal space available to the control.

  - **Height.** Specify, in pixels, the amount of vertical space available to the control.

tip You can also resize the area available to an ActiveX control by selecting the control in Page view and then dragging its handles.

Chapter 25: Incorporating Advanced Objects

- **Alternative Representation.** Specify what a browser should display if it doesn't support ActiveX controls:

  - **HTML.** Supply any HTML that should appear if a browser doesn't support ActiveX controls. This can be plain text, HTML tags, or both.

- **Network Location.** Use this option to specify a network location for the control and its data. This feature allows capable browsers such as Internet Explorer to fetch and install the control on demand:

  - **Code Source.** Provide the URL of the file containing the ActiveX control. If a control isn't installed on a Web visitor's computer, browsers such as Internet Explorer can download and install it using this URL.

    If you want Web visitors to download an ActiveX control from your site, copy it into your Web from the location shown in Figure 25-4, and then specify its URL in the Code Source box. Alternatively, you might wish to specify a Code Source location at a supplier's Web site rather than your own to ensure that Web visitors will get the most current version.

> **note** Be sure to observe copyright restrictions when distributing ActiveX controls.

The Parameters tab, shown in Figure 25-7, provides a general-purpose way to establish settings for the control. Whether or not default entries appear depends on the control. Any entries that do appear might be redundant with settings on tabs other than Object Tag and Parameters. With luck, any parameters you need to work with will appear on control-specific tabs or with recognizable names on the Parameters tab. If good luck eludes you, you'll have to locate and consult documentation from the control's supplier. The next two sections in this chapter address these issues in greater detail.

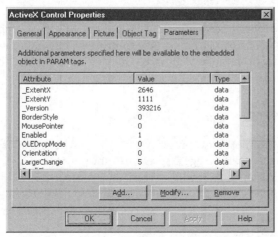

Figure 25-7. The Parameters tab lists values that the ActiveX control expects and uses.

Using Local-Property Editing

If an ActiveX control is installed on your computer and supports local-property editing, its property sheet displays three or more tabs. Figure 25-8 shows the General tab displayed for the Microsoft Calendar control. The Object Tag and Parameters tabs follow as usual.

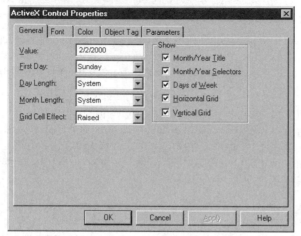

Figure 25-8. This is the local-property editing dialog box for the Microsoft ActiveX Calendar control.

The General, Font, and Color tabs list the Calendar control's available properties and current values. Use standard Windows dialog box procedures to modify these settings. When finished, click OK.

Each control that supports local-property editing displays its own set of tabs and properties. Recall, for example, the total of five tabs displayed for the Microsoft Slider control, shown in Figure 25-5.

As you can imagine, local-property editing is a much-appreciated feature among Web developers who use ActiveX controls, and most new controls include it. Local-property editing does increase the size of the control, however, making it bulkier and thus slower for the Web visitor to download.

Editing Object Parameters

Most ActiveX controls now support local-property editing. However, for those that don't (or aren't locally installed), FrontPage displays only the Object Tag and Parameters tabs. This is the case in Figure 25-9, which shows the properties for a Label control. Initially, the parameter table is blank, and you have to add all required parameters manually, one by one.

Chapter 25: Incorporating Advanced Objects

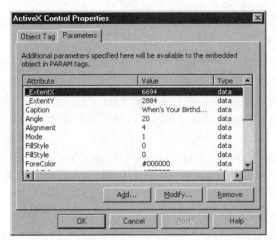

Figure 25-9. The Parameters tab manages parameters for ActiveX controls that don't support local-property editing.

Here's the procedure for adding a parameter:

1 Obtain a list of the control's required and optional parameters. This information usually comes as documentation from the control's supplier.

2 Open the ActiveX Control Properties dialog box for the given control, and click the Parameters tab.

3 Click Add. The dialog box shown in Figure 25-10 appears.

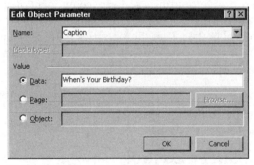

Figure 25-10. The Edit Object Parameter dialog box specifies parameters of ActiveX controls that don't support local-property editing.

4 Specify parameters using the following options:

■ **Name.** Enter the name of the parameter, spelled exactly as shown in the control's documentation.

■ **Media Type.** Specify the Multipurpose Internet Mail Extension (MIME) type of the specified value. You can specify a Media Type only if you choose the Page option under the Value heading in the lower part of the dialog box.

■ **Data.** Select this option if the parameter's value consists of data. Type the data into the associated text box.

■ **Page.** Select this option if the parameter's value is the URL of a file. Enter the URL in the associated text box, or click Browse to locate the URL.

■ **Object.** Select this option if the parameter's value is the name of another ActiveX control on the same page. Type the name of the control in the associated text box.

5 Click OK to close each dialog box.

To modify an existing parameter:

1 Select it from the list shown in Figure 25-9, and then click Modify. (Alternatively, double-click the parameter's line in the list.)

2 Change whatever settings require correction, and click OK to close each dialog box.

To remove a parameter setting, select it and click Remove.

Inserting and using ActiveX controls needn't be complex. Chapter 11, for example, explained how to use the Microsoft ActiveMovie control for displaying video files. In many cases, however, the reason for putting a software component on a Web page is so the Web visitor can interact with it. If this is your intent, you should know that connecting an ActiveX control to the rest of the Web page normally requires a small amount of program code you must write yourself. The next two sections explain Web pages that use ActiveX controls exactly this way.

> For more information about the ActiveMovie control, refer to "Inserting Video Files" on page 324.

Scripting the Microsoft Slider Control

The Microsoft Slider control displays a graduated scale that represents a range of numbers. A Web visitor can select any number within the given range by dragging a so-called *slider* or *thumb* along the scale. The Volume Control applet in the Windows operating system, for example, uses slider controls. The slider is an ActiveX control that's part of the Windows operating system; therefore, it's installed and ready for use on every Windows computer.

Chapter 25: Incorporating Advanced Objects

This section explains how a slider control can enhance a very simple HTML form. Under-standing this example requires some knowledge of material covered later in the book. For more information about HTML forms, refer to Chapter 31, "Creating and Using Forms."

 For more information about HTML code, refer to Chapter 41, "Working with HTML Code." For more information about scripting, refer to: Chapter 42, "Working with Script Code" in the Bonus Content on the Companion CD.

Figure 25-11 shows a Web page that uses the Microsoft Slider control. The Web visitor can choose a quantity either by dragging the slider left or right, or by typing it in the text box. No matter which control the visitor uses, a bit of script code keeps the other control in sync.

Figure 25-11. An ActiveX control displays the slider on this Web page. This particular slider selects a value between 0 and 10.

Clicking the Submit button submits the HTML form to the Web server for process-ing. Because the slider control isn't a standard HTML form element, the browser doesn't transmit its value. The browser does, however, transmit the text box's value, and that's just as good.

Scripts that run in the same Web page as an ActiveX control can access its properties using a very simple notation: *<element name>.<attribute name>*. The element name is whatever appears in the Name box of the Object Tag section of the ActiveX Control Properties dialog box. The object represented in Figure 25-6, for example, has a name of Slider1. The attribute names are those that appear in the Parameters tab of the same dialog box.

Scrolling down the list of attributes shown in Figure 25-7 reveals an attribute named Value. This attribute contains the value the Web visitor selects by dragging the slider. A script can use the expression *Slider1.value* to access or modify the current value of this attribute.

The Web page in Figure 25-11 contains two scripts:

● One updates the text box whenever the Web visitor moves the slider.

● Another moves the slider whenever the Web visitor changes the value in the text box.

The following script updates the text box whenever the Web visitor moves the slider. This script can appear almost anywhere in the Web page but somewhere in the *<head>* section is probably best:

```
<script LANGUAGE="JavaScript" FOR="Slider1" EVENT="Change">
if (navigator.appName.substring(0,9) == "Microsoft") {
  form1.qty.value = Slider1.value
}
</script>
```

Chapter 42, "Working with Script Code," in the Bonus Content on the Companion CD provides an overview of script code, but here are the details for this example:

● The first line denotes that this is the start of a script, that the programming language is JavaScript, that the script pertains to the *Slider1* element, and that the script should run whenever any property of the *Slider1* element changes.

● The second line verifies that the browser is Internet Explorer. This is the same technique as the one used in Chapter 17.

● If the browser *is* Internet Explorer, the third line copies the *value* property of the *Slider1* ActiveX control into the *value* property of the text box. The name of the text box is *qty*, a fact you could confirm by double-clicking the text box in Page view and inspecting the Name box in the Text Box Properties dialog box. The name of the form is *form1*, which you could verify by right-clicking anywhere in the form, choosing Form Properties from the shortcut menu, and again checking the Name box.

● The fourth line terminates the range of the *if* statement begun on line two.

● The fifth line marks the end of the script.

Chapter 25: Incorporating Advanced Objects

The script that updates the slider control whenever the Web visitor updates the text box is slightly more complicated. It starts with the following line, which is the HTML for the text box itself:

```
<input type="text" name="qty" size="10"
onChange="qtyChange(qty.value)">
```

The *onChange* attribute in this tag specifies a single JavaScript statement that executes whenever the value of the text box changes. As coded, that statement calls a function called *qtyChange* and passes the new value *qty.value* as an argument. The following is the code for this function:

```
<script>
function qtyChange(aqty){
  if (isNaN(aqty)) {
    alert("Quantity " + aqty + " is invalid,")
  }else{
    if (navigator.appName.substring(0,9) == "Microsoft") {
      form1.Slider1.value = aqty;
    }
  }
}
</script>
```

- Line one marks the beginning of a block of script code. The default language is JavaScript.

- Line two marks the beginning of the *qtyChange* function. The function takes one argument, named *aqty*.

- The *isNaN* function in line three returns true if *aqty* is not a number. (*isNaN* is not a number, get it?)

- If *aqty* is not a number, line four displays an error message.

- Otherwise, *aqty* must be a number, and:

    - Line six verifies that the browser is Internet Explorer.

    - Line seven copies the *aqty* value into the *Slider1* control.

    - Line eight terminates the range of the *if* statement begun on line six.

- The remaining lines close out the first *if* statement, the function definition, and the block of script code.

Submitting the form requests a Web page named *sliderqty.asp* from the Web server. This is a so-called Active Server Page (ASP) containing script code that runs on the Web server as well as ordinary HTML code. The inner workings of Active Server Pages are beyond the scope of this discussion, but at a high level, the *sliderqty.asp* page retrieves

729

the values submitted with the HTML form and adds them to the outgoing Web page for display. Figure 25-12 displays typical results.

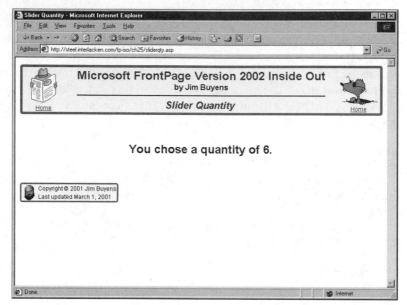

Figure 25-12. Submitting the HTML form shown in Figure 25-11 produces a Web page that incorporates the specified value.

> For more information about Active Server Pages, refer to "Processing Form Data with ASP Pages" on page 910 and "Server-Side Scripting" on page 55.

 For more information about Active Server Pages, refer to Appendix B, "Introducing Active Server Page Objects" in the Bonus Content on the Companion CD

To view this page in FrontPage, open the sample Web installed from the companion CD and then open *ch25/slider.htm*.

To actually submit the form and see the results shown in Figure 25-12, you must satisfy all of the following requirements:

- The sample Web must reside on a FrontPage-enabled Web server capable of running Active Server Pages.

> For more information about using server-based Webs, refer to "Using Server-Based Webs" on page 127.

- The sample Web (or at least the *ch25* folder) must be marked executable.

 For more information about marking Web server folders as executable, refer to "Reviewing Folder Settings" in the Bonus Content on the Companion CD.

Chapter 25: Incorporating Advanced Objects

For more information about marking Web server folders as executable, refer to "Configuring
Home Directory Settings" on page 1064.

- Even if the Web server is running on your own computer, you must use
  an HTTP URL to load the *slider.htm* page. Loading the *slider.htm* page
  directly from disk won't work, because then the browser will try to load
  sliderqty.asp from disk as well. And *that* won't work because:

  - Loading an ASP page from disk doesn't execute any script code that's
    marked to run on the Web server.

  - Even if you changed the server-side script code to browser-side script
    code, none of the software resources present on the Web server would
    be available.

Of course, a real Web page of this type would contain more than one field. The ASP
page or other process on the Web server would perform more complex processing than
simply echoing values back to the Web visitor. Nevertheless, this example illustrates the
use of ActiveX controls to enhance the Web visitor's experience.

This Web page, by the way, works perfectly well in Netscape Navigator. For proof, inspect
Figure 25-13. Netscape ignores the slider object and the script code bypasses any references to Slider1 when Netscape is the browser. The page therefore functions as a
perfectly normal HTML form.

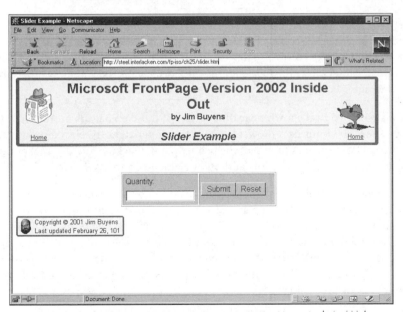

Figure 25-13. Netscape Navigator ignores ActiveX controls in Web pages. However,
with suitable precautions, the page can still be functional.

Part 9: Incorporating Advanced Content

Scripting the Microsoft Calendar Control

Figure 25-14 shows FrontPage displaying two ActiveX controls: a Label control and
a Calendar control. The Label control, which appears first, has no features for interact-
ing with the Web visitor. A WordArt component could display the same content, but
wouldn't have exemplified a control that lacked local-property editing. (See Figure 25-9.)

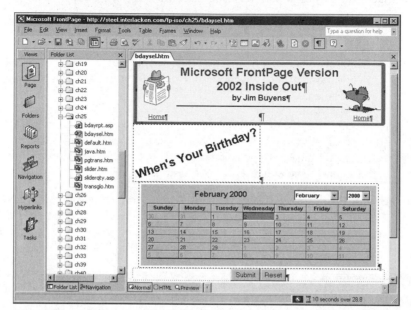

Figure 25-14. Here FrontPage displays two ActiveX controls on a page: a Label object
displaying slanted text and a Calendar control displaying a calendar. Neither object is run
in FrontPage.

The Calendar control shown near the bottom of the Web page is more interesting.
When the Web visitor uses the list boxes at the upper right to select a month and year,
the grid of days changes to reflect the proper dates. Clicking any day makes the month,
day, and year available to scripts and other elements in the Web page.

The Calendar control is an attractive way to collect dates from Web visitors, but, as
with the Slider control, clicking an HTML form's Submit button doesn't transmit the
Calendar control's values to the Web server. To overcome this limitation, this Web
page's Submit button is actually a Push button that runs a small script. The script copies
the Calendar control's currently selected year, month, and day values into three hidden
form fields and then submits the form. This transmits the three copied values to the
Web server for processing.

Chapter 25: Incorporating Advanced Objects

You can create most of the HTML code for the Push button code by choosing Form from the Insert menu and then choosing Push Button. The button's name isn't important, but if you want it to be *btnSub*, display the button's Properties dialog box and change the Name field. The code is as follows:

```
<input type="button" value="Submit" name="btnSub"
onClick="subForm();">
```

Notice that this button isn't a Submit button. Clicking it doesn't submit the form. Instead, the *onClick* attribute runs a function called *subForm* whenever the visitor clicks the button. You must add this attribute to the button's HTML code manually, in HTML view.

> **tip** If you select a button (or any other page element) in Page view, it will still be selected when you switch to HTML view.

The following information will help you understand the code for the *subForm* function:

- The Calendar control's name is *cal01*.

- Whenever the Web visitor selects a date, the Calendar control's *month, day,* and *year* attributes reflect that selected date. If no date is selected, all three attributes contain 0.

- The HTML form's name is *form1*.

- The HTML form contains three hidden form fields named *qmon, qday,* and *qyr*. These fields have no visual presence on the Web page, but the browser nevertheless submits their values when it submits the form.

  To view the definition of these hidden form fields:

  1 Right-click anywhere in the HTML form. (The Submit button is a good spot.)

  2 Choose Form Properties from the shortcut menu.

  3 Click Advanced when the Form Properties dialog box appears. Figure 25-15 on the next page shows the results.

When the Web visitor clicks Submit, the *subForm* function first checks to see whether *cal01.day*—the Calendar control's day of the month value—is greater than 0. If so, it copies the *cal01.month, cal01.day,* and *cal01.year* values to the hidden form fields *qmon, qday,* and *qyr* and then submits the form. Otherwise, it displays a message to the Web visitor and then exits.

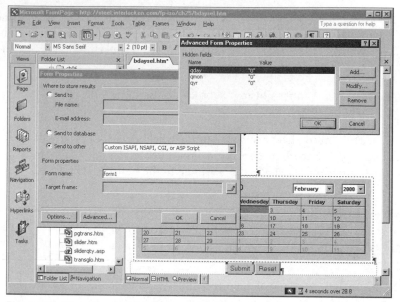

Figure 25-15. The HTML that creates the Submit button on this Web page has three hidden form fields.

The following is the actual code for this function:

```
function subForm() {
  if (cal01.day > 0) {
    form1.qmon.value = cal01.month;
    form1.qday.value = cal01.day;
    form1.qyr.value = cal01.year;
    document.form1.submit();
  }else{
    alert("You must select a date!");
    return;
  }
}
```

To view this page in a browser, open the sample Web and then open *ch25/bdaysel.htm*. Figure 25-16 shows the results.

As in the slider example, submitting the form shown in Figure 25-16 runs an ASP page that essentially displays the submitted data back to the Web visitor. All the requirements regarding a server-based Web, executable folders, and HTTP URLs apply. Figure 25-17 shows the results.

Chapter 25: Incorporating Advanced Objects

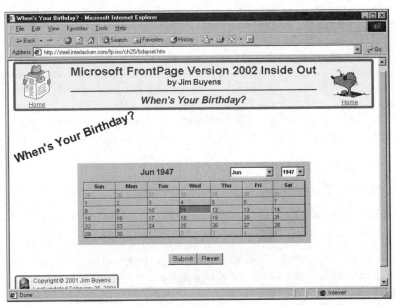

Figure 25-16. Internet Explorer correctly displays the page edited in Figure 25-14.

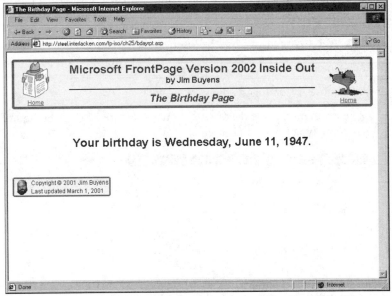

Figure 25-17. Submitting the HTML form shown in Figure 25-16 produces a Web page that incorporates the specified date.

Incorporating Plug-Ins

A plug-in is a piece of software that takes over a section of the browser window and displays something in it. Usually the display is from a file obtained from the Web server, and most often it's some kind of multimedia file. Netscape Communications originally devised plug-ins, and Internet Explorer now supports them. Plug-ins generally aren't as configurable (with HTML) as other approaches to multimedia, but support by both browsers is a strong point. Displaying a given file with a plug-in requires three things:

- The file has to be specially marked in the HTML.

- When the Web server delivers the file, it must properly identify the file type.

- The Web visitor's browser must have a plug-in available for the given file type.

Some plug-ins come with the browser itself. Web visitors can install more from various Internet sites. In general, a Web designer doesn't know which, if any, plug-in software will process a given file type. This can vary considerably depending on the type of computer, the type of browser, and the browser's configuration.

FrontPage can't install plug-ins on the Web visitor's browser or perform browser configurations. It can, however, flag files on a Web page for plug-in processing. To begin:

Web
Component

1 Choose Web Component from the Insert menu or the Standard toolbar.

2 In the Component Type list, select Advanced Controls.

3 In the Choose A Control list, choose Plug-In.

4 Click Finish to display the dialog box shown in Figure 25-18. The figure shows some typical values filled in.

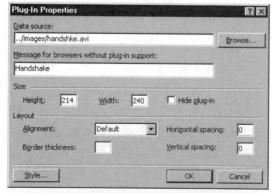

Figure 25-18. This dialog box creates instructions for the browser, telling it to display the named file using a plug-in.

Chapter 25: Incorporating Advanced Objects

5 When the Plug-In Properties dialog box appears, all its options are blank or default. Supply the following properties as required:

■ **Data Source.** Specify the relative or absolute URL of the file the plug-in should process, or click the Browse button to locate the file.

Although FrontPage accepts a blank value in this text box, telling the browser to process a missing file name as a plug-in is rather pointless. Therefore, you should consider this option mandatory.

■ **Message For Browsers Without Plug-In Support.** Supply any text you want to appear if the browser doesn't support plug-ins. For example, if the plug-in displays a clown saying "Hello," you might enter, "A clown says Hello."

■ **Size.** Specify how much window space the plug-in should consume:

◆ **Height.** Specify a height in pixels. You can also modify this property by selecting the plug-in in Page view and dragging its handles.

◆ **Width.** Specify a width in pixels. This is another property you can modify by dragging the plug-in's handles in Page view.

◆ **Hide Plug-In.** Select this box if you don't want the plug-in to occupy any window space. This can be appropriate for nonvisual files such as sound clips.

■ **Layout.** Specify how you want the plug-in to appear on the Web page:

◆ **Alignment.** Specify how the browser should position the plug-in relative to surrounding text. For a list of possible values, consult Table 11-2 on page 338.

◆ **Border Thickness.** Specify the thickness, in pixels, of a black border that will surround the plug-in. For no border, specify zero.

◆ **Horizontal Spacing.** Specify the number of pixels that should separate the plug-in from the nearest left and right elements on the same line.

◆ **Vertical Spacing.** Specify the number of pixels that should separate the plug-in from the nearest elements above and below it.

■ **Style.** Click this button to apply cascading style sheet properties to the plug-in display.

Figure 25-19, on the next page, shows Netscape Navigator using a plug-in to display the AVI file configured in Figure 25-18.

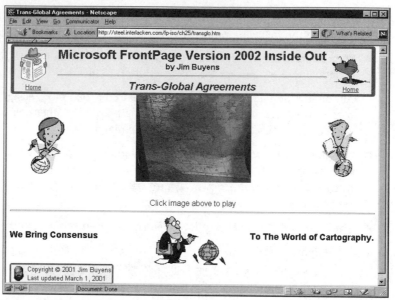

Figure 25-19.   Netscape Navigator uses a plug-in to display the AVI file configured in Figure 25-18.

Troubleshooting

Plug-In doesn't play correctly in browser

A common plug-in problem involves Multipurpose Internet Mail Extension (MIME) types. The file type a browser uses for selecting a plug-in usually isn't a filename extension; it's a MIME type that the Web server assigns. The MIME type for an AVI file, for example, is usually *video/x-msvideo*. Correctly displaying the file requires a two-step translation:

- First, the Web server translates the filename extension to a MIME type.
- Second, the browser uses the server-supplied MIME type to select a plug-in.

For more information about MIME types, refer to "MIME Types and Other Curiosities" on page 1039. For information about configuring MIME tables in Microsoft Web servers, refer to Chapter 37, "Installing and Configuring a Web Server."

Incorrect Web server configuration is a common cause of plug-in files that fail to appear properly. After eliminating browser configuration as the source of a problem, ask the Web server's system administrator to check the server's MIME type table. Be sure to provide the filename extensions you're using and the MIME type you'd like assigned.

Incorporating Java Applets

Java is a popular programming language closely resembling C++, but with restrictions that help the innocent avoid frustration. A team at Sun Microsystems invented Java, and Sun remains its guiding authority.

Java programs don't compile to a processor's native instruction set; instead, they compile to the instruction set of an imaginary computer called the *Java virtual machine*. Java programs are portable to any type of computer and any operating system that has a virtual machine emulator. The emulator is a piece of software that carries out Java virtual machine instructions using local native instructions so that the compiled Java program can run.

Java applets are small Java programs that run as part of a Web page. Applets are considerably less capable than ordinary programs—even ordinary Java programs. Applets can take up space on the screen, play sounds, modify the browser window, interact with scripts, and open various connections to the machine that delivered the applet to the visitor's browser. Applets can't, however, make changes to the local machine's files or hardware settings. The collective name for these restrictions is *the Java sandbox*. The idea is that an applet, playing within its sandbox, can't do anything at all to your computer; therefore it can't do anything bad.

Applets reside on a Web server. You can locate many freeware or shareware applets on the Web, download them to your own site, and use them in your pages. Browsers download applets just as they do pictures or other files used on a Web page, but of course the browser runs the applet rather than displaying it as a picture.

About GraphicsButton

The examples in this section use a freeware Java applet called GraphicsButton. It displays a button with a specified picture on its face and jumps to a specified Web location when a Web visitor clicks it. In addition, the edges of the button depress when the visitor clicks the button.

To obtain GraphicsButton, its documentation, and other information about Java, visit Pineapplesoft at *http://www.pineapplesoft.com/goodies/*

Applets, like ActiveX controls, have properties and methods. The ActiveX distinction between methods and events is discarded in Java; both are simply considered methods. To add a Java applet to one of your Web pages:

1 Obtain a copy of the applet and its documentation.

2   Use FrontPage to open the Web page that will contain the applet.

3   Import the applet file, which normally has a filename extension of *.class*, into your Web. You'll probably find it convenient, as many Web developers do, to place all Java applets in a folder called *classes*.

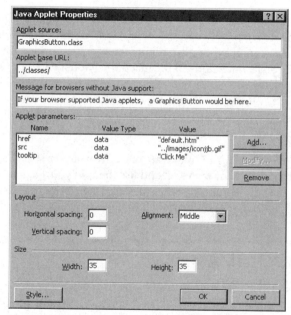

4   Choose Web Component from the Insert menu or the Standard toolbar.

Web
Component

5   In the Component Type list, select Advanced Controls.

6   In the Choose A Control list, choose Java Applet.

7   Click Finish to display the dialog box shown in Figure 25-20. The figure shows some typical values filled in.

Figure 25-20.   This dialog box adds a Java applet to a Web page.

8   When the Java Applet Properties dialog box appears, all its properties are blank or default. Supply the following options as required:

- **Applet Source.** Specify the name of the Java applet file. Don't specify a complete URL or a path of any kind.

- **Applet Base URL.** Specify the URL path to the applet file. Don't include *http://*, the computer name, the port number, or the name of the applet file itself.

- **Message For Browsers Without Java Support.** Specify any text the browser should display if it doesn't support Java applets.

Chapter 25: Incorporating Advanced Objects

■ **Applet Parameters.** Use this list to specify any settings the applet requires for proper operation. Click Add in this group box to specify a
name and value for each required applet parameter. Step 9 describes
this process in detail. Consult the applet's documentation for a list of
mandatory and optional parameter names and data values.

■ **Layout.** Specify how you want the applet to appear on the Web page:

◆ **Horizontal Spacing.** Specify the number of pixels that should
separate the applet from the nearest left and right elements on the
same line.

◆ **Vertical Spacing.** Specify the number of pixels that should separate the applet from the nearest elements above and below it.

◆ **Alignment.** Specify how the browser should position the applet
relative to surrounding text. For a list of possible values, consult
Table 11-2 on page 338.

■ **Size.** Specify how much window space the applet should consume:

◆ **Width.** Specify a width in pixels. You can also modify this property
by selecting the applet in Page view and dragging its handles.

◆ **Height.** Specify a height in pixels. This is another property that
you can modify by dragging the applet's handles in Page view.

9 Clicking Add in the Applet Parameters section of the dialog box (Figure
25-20) produces the Set Attribute Value dialog box shown in Figure 25-21
on the next page. Enter data using the following options:

■ **Name.** Specify the name of the parameter, spelled exactly as described in the applet's documentation.

■ **Specify Value.** Select this check box for parameters that take a value.
Clear it for keyword parameters.

■ **Data.** Select this option and fill in the accompanying text box if the
value you want to specify is a string.

■ **Ref.** Select this option and fill in the accompanying text box if the
value you want to specify is a URL.

■ **Object.** Select this option and fill in the accompanying text box if the
value you want to specify is the URL of an OBJECT element in the
same Web page.

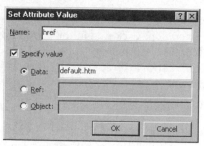

Figure 25-21. This dialog box sets parameter values for Java applets.

To modify a parameter setting:

1 Select its entry in the Applet Parameters list (Figure 25-20), and click Modify. (Alternatively, double-click the desired parameter.)

2 Change whatever settings require correction, and click OK.

To remove a parameter, select it and click the Remove button.

Figure 25-22 shows the GraphicsButton applet open in both FrontPage and Internet Explorer. Like ActiveX controls, Java applets don't execute within FrontPage; this accounts for the difference in their appearance.

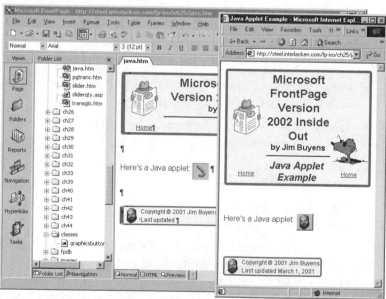

Figure 25-22. Because Java applets don't execute in FrontPage, you display their true appearance only by browsing them.

Chapter 25: Incorporating Advanced Objects

Incorporating Design-Time Controls

The use of ActiveX controls isn't limited to enhancing and extending Web pages. Most computers running Windows operating systems have hundreds, if not thousands, of ActiveX controls having little or nothing to do with Web browsing; they're used with Microsoft Office applications, by other programs from Microsoft and third-party vendors, and by Windows itself. Given all this, you might wonder whether adding ActiveX controls to FrontPage might add new editing features, just as adding controls to Web pages adds new browsing features. Design-Time Controls (DTCs) provide a glimpse of the answer.

The idea of a DTC is relatively simple. You add the control to an editing window—such as an open window in Page view—and the control displays whatever is useful to the Web designer. Opening the control displays a dialog box—with any luck, a self-explanatory and useful one—that configures a set of properties for the page. Whenever the Web designer saves the page, the application notifies the control and the control emits HTML that does whatever the designer specified.

Currently, most DTCs are designed for use with Microsoft Visual InterDev, a high-end Web development application geared more for programmers and hard-core HTML types than the general population. Nevertheless, FrontPage provides some support for DTCs.

The FrontPage procedure for adding a DTC to a Web page is relatively simple:

1 Set the insertion point where you want the control to appear.

Web
Component

2 Choose Web Component from the Insert menu or the Standard toolbar. This displays the Insert Web Component dialog box.

3 In the Component Type list, select Advanced Controls.

If no DTCs are installed on your computer, the Design-Time Control option is dimmed. Consider this procedure at end.

4 In the Choose A Control list, choose Design-Time Control. The dialog box shown in Figure 25-23 on the next page appears.

5 Choose the desired control. If the control you want isn't listed:

    a Click Customize to display the dialog box shown in Figure 25-24 on the next page.

    b Find the control you want in the Choose A Control list.

    c Select the control's check box, and click OK.

6 Click Finish.

743

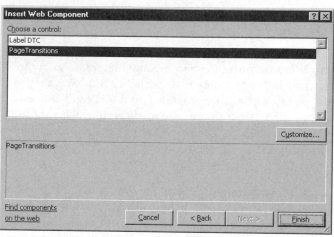

Figure 25-23. The Insert Web Component dialog box adds a DTC to your Web page.

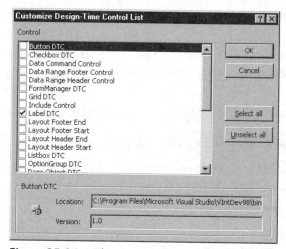

Figure 25-24. The Customize Design-Time Control dialog box controls which DTCs are available.

After you insert a DTC, it might or might not present a WYSIWYG appearance. There are two possible reasons for this:

● The control might not be written to provide WYSIWYG display. Remember, the two main functions of a DTC are collecting settings during Web-page editing and writing HTML as the Web page is saved. There's no specific requirement to collect settings in WYSIWYG fashion.

● The control's output might not consist of visible page elements. For example, the DTC might create a timer that controls other elements on the page, or that opens database connections.

Chapter 25: Incorporating Advanced Objects

Figure 25-25 shows FrontPage editing a page that uses the Page Transitions control supplied with Visual InterDev. This is a non-WYSIWYG DTC.

> To set up page transitions without using the Page Transitions DTC, refer to "Animating Page Transitions" on page 693.

This design-time control
consumes no space on the
finished Web page.

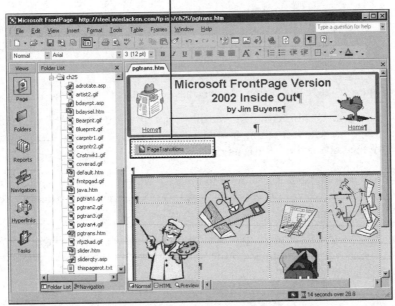

Figure 25-25. The Page Transitions DTC in this Web page controls effects such as fades and wipes between Web pages. However, it has no visual appearance of its own.

To configure a DTC, right-click it and then choose Design-Time Control Properties from the shortcut menu. Figure 25-26 on the next page shows a typical result, namely the Design-Time Control Properties dialog box for the Page Transitions DTC.

The Page Transition tab presents the following options:

- **Page Enter.** Use this group of controls to specify what effects the browser should use when switching to the current page from somewhere else:

  - **Transition.** Choose the desired effect. The drop-down list offers a variety of fades and wipes.

  - **Duration.** Specify how long the effect should last (in seconds).

  - **Preview.** Click this button to display the effect in the Preview box at the right. Figure 25-26 shows a preview in progress.

745

Part 9: Incorporating Advanced Content

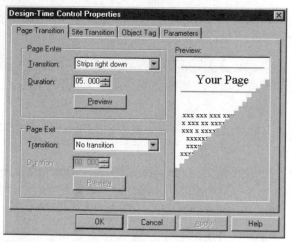

Figure 25-26. This dialog box specifies properties for the Page Transition DTC.

- **Page Exit.** Use this group of controls to specify what effects the browser should use when switching from the current page to another. The options are the same as those for Page Enter.

The Site Transition tab is very similar to the Page Transition tab, but specifies effects that occur when Web visitors enter and leave your site. The browser detects a change of site by comparing the computer names in successive URLs.

Figure 25-27 shows Internet Explorer starting to display the Web page from Figure 25-26. The new page appears from the top left corner of the window and extends downward and to the right.

caution The ability to display page transitions depends on the browser version. Netscape browsers up to and including version 4 lack this capability and ignore transition effects.

The major strength of Design-Time Controls is their potential to work in several different Web page editors. In theory, software developers can write modules once and sell them in a variety of environments. In practice, DTCs require very specific features from the Web page editor, and most of them work only with Visual InterDev. FrontPage, for example, has tended to stay with its original Microsoft WebBot approach (now called FrontPage Components). Nevertheless, if a Design-Time Control works with FrontPage, you might as well take advantage of it.

note Many of the DTCs that come with Visual InterDev integrate closely with that product's database features, and not with the database features in FrontPage.

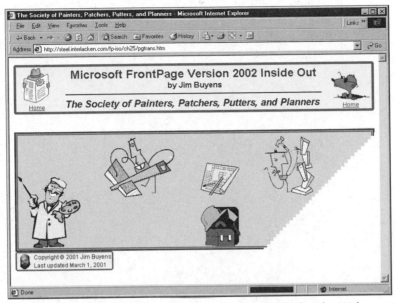

Figure 25-27. Here's Internet Explorer starting to display the Web page from Figure 25-26. The new page extends from the top left corner.

In Summary...

This chapter explained how to enhance Web pages with ActiveX objects, plug-ins, Java applets, and Design-Time Controls. All of these are programmed objects that operate within the browser or Page view editing window. Making full use of such objects—particularly ActiveX controls and Java applets—might require writing small amounts of script code.

The next chapter explains how to make content you create in one location appear in many others. This not only reduces initial development effort, but also makes it easy to keep the information updated over time.

Chapter 26

Organizing Reusable Web Content

Most Webs contain a great deal of repetitive content. This includes standard headers, footers, menu bars, names, dates, and places that occur on multiple pages or perhaps on every page in a Web. Coding this sort of content into every page is time-consuming and error-prone, and the pages become difficult to maintain over time. FrontPage, therefore, provides components that replicate a single copy of whatever content you want into as many pages as you want. This ensures that all copies look the same, and that they remain synchronized whenever you make changes to the original.

The most popular such component is called Include Page. This component copies the contents of one Web page (preferably a short one) into another. Subsequently changing the source page automatically updates all the other pages that include it.

Scheduled Include Page, a closely related component, displays the included content for a period of time specified by the designer. A Scheduled Picture component provides the same service for individual graphic elements.

The Substitution component provides the same service for words, names, and phrases that the Include Page component provides for pages. First you set up a so-called *Web parameter* that stores each word, name, or phrase as a named constant. Then the Substitution component can display those values wherever you want. Changing a Web parameter automatically updates each Substitution component that uses it.

Shared borders replicate identical content to the top, left, right, or bottom edges of all or selected pages in your Web. This would be boring and mundane if not for the fact that shared border content can be self-customizing. This means the content automatically changes depending on the properties of each page that uses the shared border. Webs organized through Navigation view are the most common place to put shared borders—but there are no restrictions on using them elsewhere if appropriate.

Using the Include Page Component

FrontPage's Include Page component merges the content of one Web page into another. This is a very useful feature for coding repetitive page segments once and using them on many pages. The concept is similar to that of boilerplate text in word processing.

Included pages usually contain page segments rather than full-blown page layouts—segments that appear on several or all pages in a site. Including the same segment on several pages guarantees that it will look the same everywhere. Later, if you must change the segment, you'll need to update only one location.

Figure 26-1 shows three typical candidates for the Include Page component.

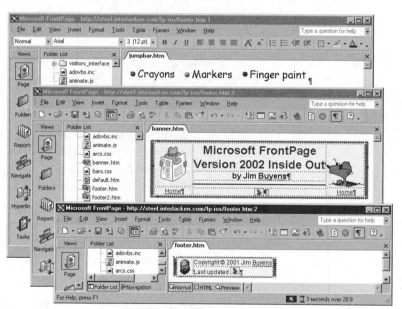

Figure 26-1. FrontPage displays two pages suitable for inclusion in other pages.

You've seen at least two of them before:

- The upper page contains a picture with hotspots. Its name is *jumpbar.htm*.

- The middle page contains the page banner that appears in most of the Web pages in this book. Its name is *banner.htm*.

- The lower page contains the copyright notice that appears at the bottom of most of the Web pages in this book. Its name is *footer.htm*.

Chapter 26: Organizing Reusable Web Content

> **tip** To simultaneously view the same Web page in two or more open windows, first open the Web normally. Then, to create additional windows, choose New Window from the Window menu.

Each segment is an ordinary, freestanding Web page, but its primary purpose is to be included as part of other pages. To include a segment in another Web page:

1 Construct the segment to be included as its own page, just as you would any other Web page.

> **note** The _private_ folder in a FrontPage-based Web is an excellent place to keep Web page segments used by the Include Page component. This folder (thanks to the leading underscore in its name) is accessible to you while editing but not to Web visitors when browsing.

2 In Page view, open the page that will include the segment.

3 Set the insertion point where the included content should appear.

4 Choose Web Component from the Insert menu or the Standard toolbar. This displays the Insert Web Component dialog box.

Web Component

5 In the Component Type list, select Included Content.

6 In the Choose A Type Of Content list, choose Page.

7 Click Finish.

8 The Include Page Properties dialog box shown in Figure 26-2 appears next.

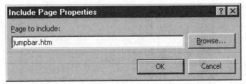

Figure 26-2. Specify the page segment to be displayed at the insertion point in your currently open page.

In this dialog box:

a Click the Browse button.

b Locate the page you wish to include.

c Click OK to confirm the page selection, and then click OK to insert the included content in your current page.

You can also type the path and file name directly into the text box.

Figure 26-3 shows a Web page that includes all three files shown in Figure 26-1. Included content takes on the properties of the page that includes it—background, color scheme, and so forth. The included portions look as though they've been created directly in the parent page.

There's an implied line break before and after every Include Page component. That is, the included content occupies the entire display width and doesn't flow continuously with surrounding content. If this presents a problem, locate the included content in a table cell or expand the amount of included content. Include entire paragraphs, for example, and not single words. Alternatively, use the Substitution component for words or phrases.

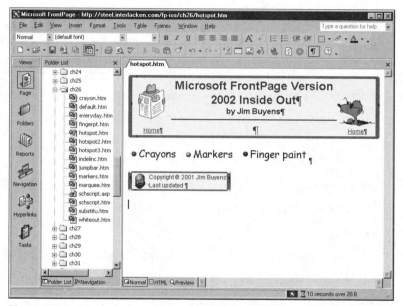

Figure 26-3. Included portions of a Web page take on the look of the parent page.

To change the included content, edit the source page. To change the properties of this or any FrontPage component, do any of the following:

- Double-click any area the component occupies.

- Select the component, and then choose Properties from the Format menu.

- Select the component, and then press Alt+Enter.

- Right-click the component, and choose Properties from the shortcut menu.

The Include Page component places a full copy of the included content in each Web page that uses it, for two reasons. First, merging content at browse time would consume more resources on the Web server. Second, merging content at authoring time produces pages that display correctly even on Web servers that don't have the FrontPage Server Extensions installed.

Of course, when you update a page that's included in other pages, you expect all the pages to reflect the new content. To accomplish this, FrontPage maintains, for each page, a list of other pages that include it. Then when you save the included page, FrontPage updates all of the host pages.

This indexing information is just the sort of thing you might expect to find in a FrontPage-based Web. The Include Page component can include only other pages in the same Web.

Updating an included page without going through FrontPage (or Web Folders, or an HTTP location in My Network Places) won't update FrontPage's various indexes, and won't propagate changed pages to others that include them. These are functions of the FrontPage software only. If you make changes to your Web using means beyond the control of FrontPage, open the Web in FrontPage and run the Recalculate Hyperlinks command afterwards.

Frequently Asked Question

What are Server-Side Includes?

Most Web servers have a feature called Server-Side Include (SSI) that searches outgoing Web pages for specially formatted comment lines. Each such comment line specifies the name of another file that resides on the Web server. The server transmits the contents of that file instead of the content line. The statement below, for example, replaces itself with the contents of a file named *promo.inc,* which resides in the parent folder of the current Web page:

```
<!-- #include file="../promo.inc" -->
```

FrontPage neither assists nor resists the use of SSIs. Lack of assistance means there's no Insert SSI menu anywhere; if you want to add an SSI statement to your Web page, you must do so in HTML view. Lack of resistance means that FrontPage will blissfully ignore the SSI and let it remain in place undisturbed.

By default, Microsoft Web servers perform SSI processing only on pages having an *.stm* or *.asp* filename extension. The *.stm* extension is the three-letter equivalent of *.shtml,* which is the extension that usually triggers SSI processing on UNIX-based Web servers.

If you plan on using FrontPage to create page segments for later inclusion via SSI, be aware that FrontPage adds *<html>, <head>,* and *<body>* tags to every page it saves. Inserting these tags along with other included content in the middle of a Web page might confuse the browser. Therefore, after you finalize the included content, you might need to give the file another filename extension such as *.inc,* then open it in a text editor and remove the offending tags.

> **note** FrontPage isn't the only program that can maintain the integrity of a FrontPage-based Web while making changes. The Web Folders feature in Windows 98, Windows Me, and Windows NT is actually a front-end to parts of FrontPage that correctly update Webs, as are any HTTP locations that appear under My Network Places in Windows 2000. For more information on this topic, refer to the Frequently Asked Question, "How can programs other than FrontPage safely update a FrontPage-based Web?" on page 423.

Troubleshooting

Include Page Component interferes with other FrontPage features

Because of the way they propagate content, the Include Page component and its close cousin, the Scheduled Include Page component, are occasionally troublesome when used together with certain other FrontPage features. Here are some situations to avoid:

- Don't mix shared borders and Include Page components. For example:
  - Don't add Include Page components to shared border areas.
  - Turn off shared borders on any page you're using as a segment to appear in other pages.

  Adding an Include Page component to a shared border sets up a sort of "double include" situation—ordinary pages include the shared border page, and then the shared border page includes the Include Page segment. FrontPage has a history of bugs in this situation—and even if it didn't, this practice can lead to very messy situations, such as pages including themselves.

- Don't use text animations on any page you're using as an included segment. FrontPage will include the page with the text animation, but it won't include the Dynamic HTML script that makes the animation work.

  You can work around this limitation by applying the same animation to something (for example, a space character) on each page that includes the page with the original animation. However, the need to specially configure each page that uses an Include Page component defeats the reason for using the Include Page component at all.

- Put all image maps (pictures with hotspots) in the same physical page.

  Hotspots assign different hyperlink targets to different parts of a single picture. The collection of all such links for a single picture is called an image map, and each image map on the same page must have a different name. FrontPage normally assigns unique image map names by numbering them FPMap0, FPMap1, FPMap2, and so forth. However, if an included page and the page that includes it each contain one image map, both image maps will have the name FPMap0, and one of them won't work properly.

Chapter 26: Organizing Reusable Web Content

Using the Scheduled Include Page Component

As often as content on the Web changes, it's not surprising that designers frequently need to make scheduled changes. Figure 26-4, for example, shows two Web page segments that might appear on the same page at different times—the upper during January and the lower during other months.

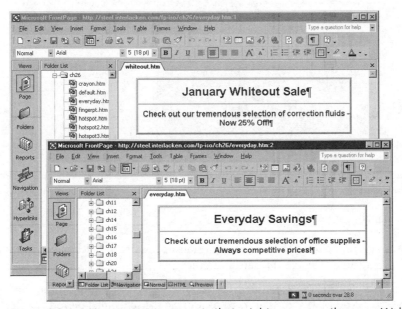

Figure 26-4. Here are two segments that might appear on the same Web page at different times.

FrontPage supports scheduled changes with the Scheduled Include Page component. This component resembles the Include Page component, but adds three features:

- A start date
- A stop date
- An optional URL

Inserting a Scheduled Include Page component is much like inserting an Include Page component:

1 Set the insertion point.

2 Choose Web Component from the Insert menu or the Standard toolbar. This displays the Insert Web Component dialog box.

Web
Component

3 In the Component Type list, select Included Content.

755

Part 9: Incorporating Advanced Content

4 In the Choose A Type Of Content list, choose Page Based On Schedule.

5 Click Finish.

The Scheduled Include Page dialog box appears in Figure 26-5.

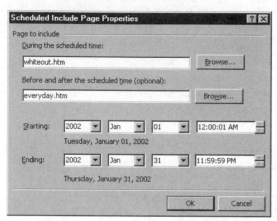

Figure 26-5. This dialog box controls the properties of a Scheduled Include Page component.

The available settings are as follows:

- **Page To Include.** Use these two options to specify the Web pages you want to include based on the date and time:

    - **During the Scheduled Time.** Enter the Web location of the content you want Web visitors to see during the scheduled period.

    - **Before And After The Scheduled Time (Optional).** Enter the Web location of the content you want Web visitors to see before and after the scheduled period. If you leave this box blank, nothing will appear.

- **Starting.** Specify the year, month, day, and time Web visitors should begin seeing the scheduled content. To start showing the content immediately, enter a past date.

- **Ending.** Specify the year, month, day, and time Web visitors should stop seeing the scheduled content. To keep showing the content indefinitely, enter a date far in the future.

Figure 26-6 shows Internet Explorer displaying the Scheduled Include Page component configured in Figure 26-5. The current month isn't January 2002.

Chapter 26: Organizing Reusable Web Content

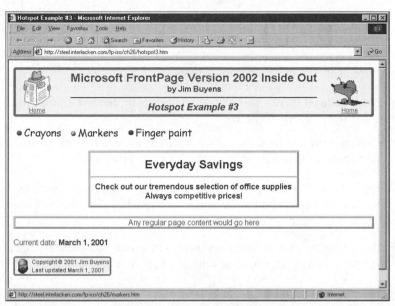

Figure 26-6. This is the Web page configured in Figure 26-5. The *everyday.htm* segment appears because the current date isn't January 2002.

Troubleshooting

Scheduled Include Page content doesn't change on schedule

The Scheduled Include Page component and the Scheduled Picture component both suffer one nagging flaw: The scheduled change isn't completely automatic. Even on a Web server running the FrontPage Server Extensions, there's no automatic process for the scheduled content to be inserted, replaced, or removed at the specified time. To ensure proper timing of Scheduled Include Page components, you must do *either* of the following:

● Make some change to your FrontPage-based Web every day. (For example, change the value of some configuration variable.)

● Arrange with your server administrator to recalculate hyperlinks in batch mode on a nightly basis.

The *fpsrvadm.exe* program can be run from a scheduled batch file to recalculate hyperlinks. For more information on this command, refer to "FrontPage Server Extensions Administration Tools" on page 1088.

Using the Scheduled Picture Component

The Scheduled Picture component works almost exactly like the Scheduled Include Page component. The differences are as follows:

- The Scheduled Picture component conditionally displays a single picture rather than a block of content.

- Conditionally displayed pictures flow in line with text. There are no automatic paragraph breaks before and after a scheduled picture.

Figure 26-7 shows the Scheduled Picture Properties dialog box. This dialog box and the procedure for invoking it parallel those for the Scheduled Include Page component exactly. Refer to the previous section for details.

Scheduled Pictures suffer the same timing nuisance as Scheduled Include Pages; for date changes to take effect, you must initiate a hyperlink recalculation.

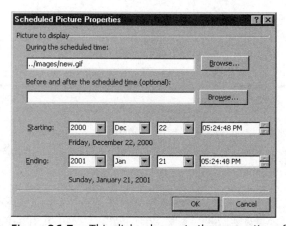

Figure 26-7.   This dialog box sets the properties of a Scheduled Picture component.

Scripting Time-Sensitive Content

The fact that the Scheduled Include Page and Scheduled Picture components take effect only when you save the pages that contain them—or recalculate hyperlinks for the Web that contains those pages—is a significant limitation. Many Web developers therefore prefer alternate approaches using server-side or browser-side scripting.

Server-side scripting requires more resources and features from the Web server than browser-side scripting does, but in this case it's easier to code. Here's the procedure for controlling time-sensitive content with server-side scripting:

Chapter 26: Organizing Reusable Web Content

1 Set the insertion point where you want the time-sensitive content to appear.

2 Click the HTML button at the bottom of the editing window.

3 The insertion point in HTML view will normally correspond to the insertion point in Normal view (that is, to the location you set in step 1). Verify that this is the case, and if necessary, move the insertion point so it doesn't lie within an HTML tag.

4 Enter the following code, changing the date if desired:

```
<%If (now() < #Jun 30, 2002#) Then%><%End If%>
```

Note that this expression will be true whenever the current date is prior to June 30, 2002. You can, of course, enter other dates or use different relational operators such as > (greater than) or >= (greater than or equal to). You can also code more complex expressions if you like. Here are some examples:

```
<%If (now() >= #Jan 1, 2001#) Then%><%End If%>
```

```
<%If (now() >= #Jan 1, 2001#) Then%><%Else%><%End If%>
```

```
<%If (now() > #Oct 1, 2002#) And
(now() < #Nov 1, 2002#)Then%><%End If%>
```

Keep in mind that the *now()* function actually returns a date *and* time. The following expression will be true only at the fleeting instant of midnight:

```
<%If (now() = #Jan 1, 2001#) Then%><%End If%>
```

You should use >= to specify an entire day.

5 Click the Normal button at the bottom of the Page view window. The two pairs of <%…%> tags you added in step 4 should appear as two VBScript icons.

If these graphics don't appear, click the Show All button on the Standard toolbar or press Ctrl+Shift+8 (Ctrl+Asterisk).

Show All

6 Select all the time-sensitive content and drag it between the two icons you identified in step 5. You can continue editing this content as much as you like, or drag the VBScript icons to include or exclude more content.

7 Be sure to give the modified page a filename extension of *.asp*:

   ■ If the page is new, select a Save As type of Active Server Pages (*.asp) the first time you save it.

   ■ If the page already has a filename extension of *.htm,* save and close the page in Page view and then rename it in the Folder List.

Because this technique uses Active Server Pages, it requires that you use a Microsoft Web server, that the folder or folder tree that contains the ASP page be marked executable, and that you load the page into the browser using an HTTP URL and *not* a disk location.

If you get an ASP error message when you load the page, you've probably entered some invalid ASP code. To correct the code, double-click the VBScript icon. FrontPage will display the Server Script dialog box shown in Figure 26-8, wherein you can modify the code. This technique is also handy for changing the cutoff date.

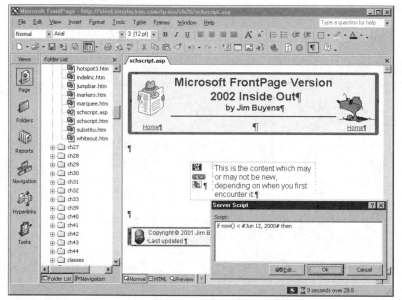

Figure 26-8. Double-clicking the VBScript icon for a server-side script displays the script in the Server Script dialog box. The Script box is editable.

For more information about Active Server Pages, refer to "Processing Form Data with ASP Pages" on page 910.

 For more information about Active Server Pages, you can also refer to "Server-Side Scripting," and Appendix B, "Introducing Active Server Page Objects," in the Bonus Content on the Companion CD.

Browser-side scripting requires nothing of the Web server. As a result, it works with Microsoft Web servers, non-Microsoft Web servers, and servers that won't give you executable folders, as well as with loading the page from disk. However, it requires writing all the time-sensitive HTML code into JavaScript statements. Here, for example, is a browser-side script that displays a New icon until June 12, 2002:

```
<script language="JavaScript">
<!--
  endDate = new Date("Jun 12, 2002");
  curDate = new Date();
  if (curDate < endDate){
    document.write("<img src=../images/new2.gif " +
                   "height=11 width=28 border=0>");
  }
// -->
</script>
```

Here are the salient points regarding this code. To conform with prevailing usage, the programming language is JavaScript:

- The first and last lines mark the beginning and end of a block of script code.

- The second and next-to-last lines are comment delimiters.

  If a browser doesn't support scripting, it will bypass the <script> tags and try to interpret the script code as HTML. Ugly. The comment indicators tell any such browser to ignore the script code as well. JavaScript, of course, will ignore the HTML comment indicators.

- Lines three and four create two date objects: one with a given date and one with the (default) current date.

- Line five compares the values of the two date objects created in lines three and four.

- If the comparison is true, lines six and seven write the HTML to display a picture. Notice that the entire *<img...>* tag is coded as a string constant and passed to the *document.write* method. This is how you must emit any time-sensitive content you control by this method.

To add a script such as this to your Web page, follow steps 1, 2, and 3 of the previous procedure and then type the script into HTML view.

Once you've entered the script, a JavaScript icon like the following will show where it resides. You can relocate this icon as usual by dragging.

As with Active Server Page scripts, you can edit a block of JavaScript code without leaving Normal view. Just double-click the JavaScript icon and work within the dialog box shown in Figure 26-9 on the next page.

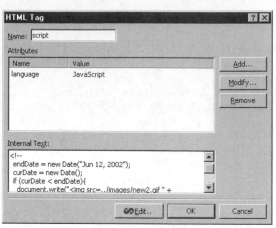

Figure 26-9. Double-clicking a JavaScript icon displays the script in this dialog box. The Internal Text box is editable.

For more information about browser-side scripting, refer to "Scripting Web Pages on the Browser" in the Bonus Content on the Companion CD.

Using Web Parameters and the Substitution Component

Web parameters are commonly occurring character strings you can establish centrally and then reference by name throughout a Web. Like included page segments, Web parameters provide uniformity and eliminate redundant maintenance. If the value of a Web parameter changes, you need to update it in only one place.

Suppose, for example, that the names of key people at your site change from time to time. You could:

1 Set up a site parameter for each key position in your organization chart (say, *veepmktg* for your Vice President of Marketing).

2 Assign each site parameter a value (Assign *veepmktg* the value "Janet Leverling," for example, if she's the Vice President of Marketing).

3 Have each page in the site reference the parameter *veepmktg* rather than the explicit name *Janet Leverling*.

When someone new takes over the Vice President of Marketing position, you can then change the value of the *veepmktg* parameter rather than finding and updating each affected page by hand, possibly missing some in the process.

Chapter 26: Organizing Reusable Web Content

Figure 26-10 shows the Web Settings dialog box for adding and maintaining site parameters. To display this dialog box, choose Web Settings from the Tools menu and then click the Parameters tab.

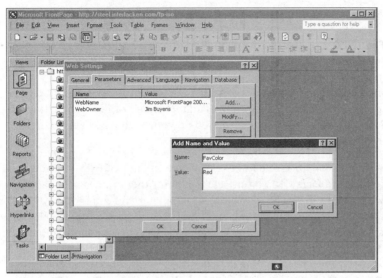

Figure 26-10. FrontPage can accommodate any number of global parameters for a site.

The Substitution component displays Web parameter values in a Web page. You configure the component with the Web parameter's name, and the component displays the parameter's value. Any text that will appear on multiple pages and be subject to occasional change is a candidate to become a Web parameter.

To display Web parameter values in a Web page:

1 Open the page in Page view.

2 Set the insertion marker where you'd like the Web parameter value to appear.

3 Choose Web Component from the Insert menu or the Standard toolbar. This displays the Insert Web Component dialog box.

Web Component

4 In the Component Type list, select Included Content.

5 In the Choose A Type Of Content list, choose Substitution. Click Finish.

6 When the Substitution Properties dialog box appears, shown in Figure 26-11 on the next page, choose the Web parameter you want to insert, and then click Finish.

Part 9: Incorporating Advanced Content

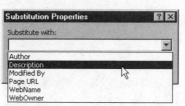

Figure 26-11. The Substitution Properties dialog box lists all the Web parameters you've defined in the Web Settings dialog box

After you click OK, FrontPage will insert a marker for the selected parameter. If you redefine the parameter later (from the Parameters tab of the Web Settings dialog box), FrontPage will update the value displayed on your Web pages everywhere the Web parameter appears.

There are four built-in Web parameters, shown in Figure 26-11: Author, Description, Modified By, and Page URL. FrontPage maintains these values on a page-by-page basis, as shown in Table 26-1. The only built-in parameter you can modify directly is Description; it displays any comments you enter on the Summary tab of the Properties dialog box displayed in the Folder List or Folders view. A Web designer manually created the Web parameters WebOwner and WebName.

Table 26-1. **Web Parameters Maintained by FrontPage**

Substitution name	FrontPage property	Description
Author	Created by	The user name of the person who created the page.
Description	Comment	Comments entered in a page's Properties dialog box in the Folder List or Folders view.
Modified By	Modified by	The user name of the person who most recently modified the page.
Page URL	Location	The location of the page, as seen from a browser.

Figure 26-12 shows a Web page with six Substitution components. There's one component for each of the four built-in parameters, plus two that display parameters configured under Tools, Web Settings: WebName and WebOwner.

The Substitution component for Description displays the placeholder [Description] in Figure 26-12 because the contents of the parameter are empty. In a browser, however, empty values appear blank.

Chapter 26: Organizing Reusable Web Content

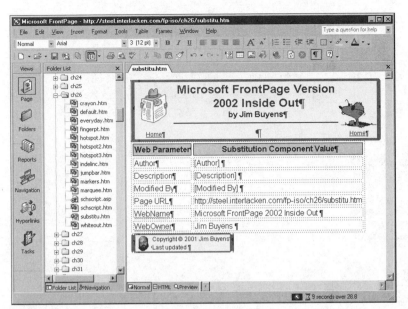

Figure 26-12. FrontPage shows system-maintained Web parameters as placeholders, but displays developer-defined Web parameters as values. Browsers display the final values in either case.

> The Description parameter displays a file's Comment property, as entered in the Folder List or Folders view. For more information about entering information in this parameter, refer to "Working with Folders View" on page 174. The Component Errors report lists all cases where Substitution components refer to missing or empty Web parameters. For more information about the Component Errors report, refer to "Component Errors" on page 438.

Using Shared Borders

This section discusses another FrontPage facility that standardizes content and appearance across an entire Web. *Shared borders* provide a way to insert standard content at the upper, lower, left, or right edges of any or all pages in the same Web.

Shared borders appear between your Web page's normal content and the upper, left, right, or lower edge of the browser window. You can put whatever you want inside the shared border area, but the *same* content appears in the *same* border for *every* page in your Web. The lower shared border for one page can't be different from the lower shared border of any other page, for example. When Microsoft decided to call these borders "shared," they weren't kidding!

A typical use of shared borders would include a Page Banner component in the upper shared border, a Link Bars component in the left shared border, and copyright, contact, or date and time information in the lower shared border. Figure 26-13 on the next page illustrates such a page.

765

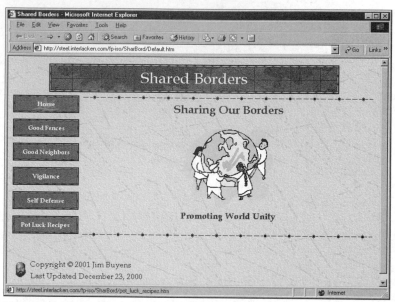

Figure 26-13. This page uses a Page Banner component in the upper shared border, a Link Bars component in the left shared border, and a Date and Time component in the lower shared border.

A Page Banner or Link Bars component included in a shared border produces different results in each page where the shared border appears. The same is true for other components, such as Date and Time or Substitution, that display values stored outside the Web page itself.

> For more information about the Date and Time component, refer to "Using the Date and Time Component" on page 769. For more information about the Substitution component, refer to the previous topic in this chapter.

To apply shared borders, choose Shared Borders from the Format menu. This will display the dialog box shown in Figure 26-14, which controls these settings:

- **Apply To.** Choose All Pages to apply shared borders to an entire Web. Choose Current Page to override the Web's default for this page.

- **Top, Left, Right,** and **Bottom.** For each side of the page where you want a shared border to appear, select the corresponding check box:

  - **Include Navigation Buttons.** Select this check box if you want FrontPage to include a Link Bars component within the shared border.

- **Reset Borders For Current Page To Web Default.** Select this check box if you want to remove all shared border overrides from the current page.

- **Border Properties.** Click this button to display the Border Properties dialog box shown in Figure 26-15.

Chapter 26: Organizing Reusable Web Content

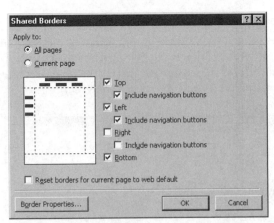

Figure 26-14. This dialog box controls the application of shared borders to any or all pages in a Web.

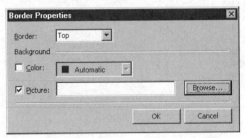

Figure 26-15. This dialog box modifies the background properties of any shared border.

The Border Properties dialog box modifies the background color and background picture of any shared border you select. Here's how to use the controls on this dialog box:

- **Border.** Choose the shared border you want to modify: Top, Left, Right, or Bottom.

- **Background.** Specify the background content of the shared border:

    - **Color.** Select this check box. Choose a color to specify a background color.

    - **Picture.** Select this check box. Choose a picture that will fill the background.

The first time you use shared borders in a Web, FrontPage will:

- Create a folder called _borders.

- Create Web pages called *top.htm, left.htm, right.htm,* and *bottom.htm* (or whichever of these you chose to use) within the _borders folder.

- Surround the content of each existing Web page with an HTML table.

- Include the *top.htm, left.htm, right.htm,* and *bottom.htm* files within the table cells along the corresponding borders.

767

Figure 26-16 shows FrontPage displaying the shared borders page from Figure 26-13. The visible boundaries around each shared border aren't visible when the page appears in a browser. You can edit information in the borders, but any changes will affect *every* page in the same Web that uses shared borders. That's the point of shared borders: to show zones of identical or self-customizing content on every page.

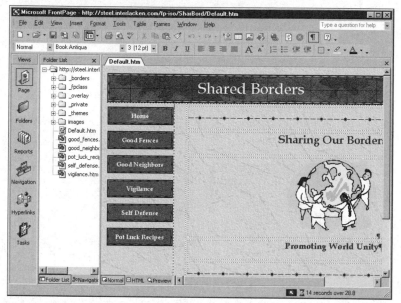

Figure 26-16. Shared borders can provide standard content along the edge of any or all pages in a Web. The choice of edges is configurable.

To override a Web's shared border settings for a specific page, first open it in Page view, and then choose Shared Borders from the Format menu. Make sure the Apply To choice is Current Page, then either:

- Indicate which shared borders the current page should use; or

- To return a page to its Web's default shared border settings, select the check box titled Reset Borders For Current Page To Web Default.

In Summary...

This chapter explained how to use several FrontPage components that replicate standard content to one or many pages. This decreases initial development time, but the real payoff comes during maintenance, when changing a single master copy updates all locations that use it.

The next chapter describes components that use information from a FrontPage-based Web to generate Web content.

Chapter 27

Displaying Derived Content

Wouldn't it be great if you didn't have to create your own Web content? What if Microsoft FrontPage could do it for you? Well, that's exactly what the components this chapter describes endeavor to do.

Of course, these components don't really create new content; they merely derive it from other content. The Date And Time component reports the date and time you, someone else, or an automated process updated a Web page. The Table Of Contents For This Web Site component creates a table of contents based on analysis of hyperlinks in your Web. The Table of Contents Based On Page Category component creates a table of contents based on category codes you assign to your Web pages.

Using the Date And Time Component

The Date And Time component displays the date a page was last saved manually or last updated by any means. FrontPage maintains these dates automatically and they don't necessarily correspond to the page's file system date.

To insert a Date And Time component, set the insertion point and then choose Date And Time from the Insert menu.

Figure 27-1 on the next page shows the Date And Time dialog box that appears.

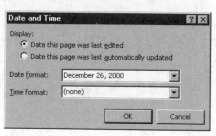

Figure 27-1. This dialog box configures the Date And Time component.

The following are the options available in the Date And Time dialog box:

- **Display.** Use this group of controls to choose which date to display:

  - **Date This Page Was Last Edited.** Select this option to display the date you or someone else last saved the page with FrontPage.

  - **Date This Page Was Last Automatically Updated.** Select this option to display the date a page last changed because of either manual editing or automatic updating caused by a change elsewhere in your Web.

Frequently Asked Question

How can a Web page display its file system date?

The following script displays the date and time of the last update to a file as indicated in the Web server's file system:

```
<script language="JavaScript">
<!--
document.write(document.lastModified)
// -->
</script>
```

To use this script in a Web page, follow these instructions:

1. Open the page in Page view.
2. Set the insertion point where you want the date to appear.
3. Click the HTML tab at the bottom of the Page view window, and make sure the insertion point isn't inside another HTML tag.
4. Enter the script as just shown.
5. Click the Normal tab at the bottom of the Page view window.

This script, like any other, won't execute in FrontPage. To see it display a date, switch to Preview mode or load the page into a browser.

- **Date Format.** Select a date format or (none) from the drop-down list.

- **Time Format.** Select a time format or (none) from the drop-down list.

> **tip** Avoid date formats that use numbers for months. The expression 2/10/2002 means February 10 in some parts of the world and October 2 in others.

A common use for the Date And Time component is to indicate a version date at the bottom of a Web page.

Using the Table Of Contents For This Web Site Component

The Table Of Contents For This Web Site component generates a hyperlinked table of contents based on any starting page in your Web. The first level of headings reflects all hyperlink targets referenced in the starting page. Below each of these page entries, indented, are its hyperlink targets. This process continues through any number of levels. Each entry is a hyperlink to the page it represents.

The Table Of Contents For This Web Site component lists pages in the current Web only. Hyperlinks to locations outside the current Web don't appear. Page titles, and not hyperlink text or file names, identify each listed page. To change a page's title, open it in Page view, choose Properties from the File menu, and update the Title box.

You can create a Table Of Contents For This Web Site in either of two ways. The first method adds the component to any new or existing page:

1 Set the insertion point where you want the Table Of Contents For This Web Site to appear.

2 Choose Web Component from the Insert menu.

3 In the Insert Web Component dialog box, choose Table Of Contents from the Component Type list at the left.

4 Choose For This Web Site from the Choose A Table Of Contents list at the right, and then click Finish.

The second method of creating a Table Of Contents For This Web Site component creates a new page using the Table Of Contents template:

1 Use either of two methods to display the Page Templates dialog box:

- Choose New from the File menu, and choose Page Or Web. Then when the New Page Or Web task pane appears, click the Page Templates link that appears under the New From Template heading; or

- Click the drop-down arrow associated with the New Page button on the Standard toolbar, and then choose Page.

New Page

2 When the Page Templates dialog box appears, select the Table Of Contents template, and then click OK.

3 When a new page appears in Page view, double-click the Table of Contents For This Web Site component. (Figure 27-3 shows an example of this component.)

This displays the Table Of Contents Properties dialog box shown in Figure 27-2.

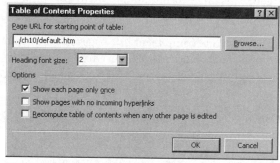

Figure 27-2. This dialog box configures the Table Of Contents component.

The settings in this dialog box work as follows:

- **Page URL For Starting Point Of Table.** Identify the page whose hyperlinks will become first-level headings in the table of contents. To display an entire FrontPage-based Web, specify its home page.

- **Heading Font Size.** Specify a heading style for the table of contents heading. Selecting 1 specifies the Heading 1 style, selecting 2 specifies the Heading 2 style, and so on. The title of the starting-point page provides the heading text.

  To omit the heading, specify None. This is generally desirable when the page that contains the table of contents is also the starting point. The heading, in that case, would represent a page linking to itself.

Chapter 27: Displaying Derived Content

● Options:

▨ **Show Each Page Only Once.** Select this check box to prevent pages from appearing more than once in the table of contents. Clear it if you want the table of contents to show a complete list of hyperlinks for each page.

▨ **Show Pages With No Incoming Hyperlinks.** Select this check box to display any orphan pages at the end of the table of contents. An orphan is a page that can't be reached by clicking any combination of your site's hyperlinks. If this check box is cleared, no orphan pages will appear.

▨ **Recompute Table Of Contents When Any Other Page Is Edited.** Select this check box to make FrontPage re-create the table of contents every time a page in the Web changes. This can be time-consuming. If you'd rather re-create the table manually—by opening and saving the Table of Contents page—leave this box cleared.

Unfortunately, the Page view window shows only a mock-up of the actual table. Figure 27-3 provides an example. To see the actual table, you must open the page with your browser as shown on the next page in Figure 27-4.

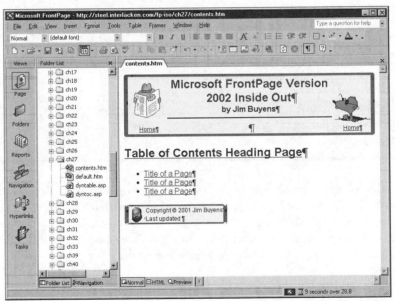

Figure 27-3. The Table Of Contents For This Web Site component that is based on the navigation structure appears in FrontPage as a mock-up.

InsideOut

Figure 27-4 illustrates one of the most frustrating aspects of the Table Of Contents For This Web Site component. The Web designer told the component to produce a table of contents for the *ch10* folder, and, in doing so, the component itemized all the pages in the Web. This was because the starting page *ch10/default.htm* had a hyperlink to the Web's home page. There's no real fix for this behavior other than removing the hyperlink to the Web's home page, an action the designer might rightfully be reluctant to take. Hyperlinks back to the home page are useful things.

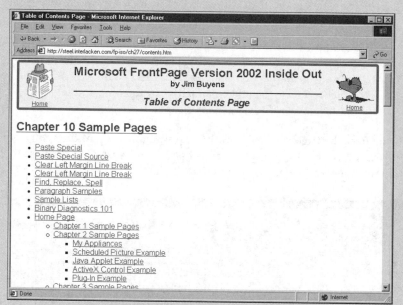

Figure 27-4. A browser displays a Table Of Contents For This Web Site component in full detail.

A *recursive hyperlink* is any pair of pages with links to each other, such as a home page with a hyperlink to a topic page that contains a hyperlink back to the home page. Not only are recursive hyperlinks possible on the Web, they're common. To avoid infinitely nested entries, the Table Of Contents For This Web Site component stops expanding hyperlinks for any page found subordinate to itself.

The Table Of Contents For This Web Site component has an almost punitive approach to errors, omissions, and tricky approaches. If you've forgotten to give any of your pages meaningful titles, for example, you might find yourself with a table full of pages with names like New Page 3 or with blank entries.

Troubleshooting

Applying fonts to a Table Of Contents component has no effect

Using the Font dialog box—which appears after you select Font from the Format menu—to modify a Table Of Contents component has no effect. Both FrontPage and the browser display the table of contents in a default font. (This occurs with the Relative To A Web Page and Based On Page Category components.)

> For more information about the Table Of Contents Based On Page Category component, refer to "Using the Table Of Contents Based On Page Category Component" later in this chapter.

This occurs because FrontPage uses a variety of HTML tags to format a table of contents and doesn't propagate conventional font attributes to each tag.

To work around this problem, set up a CSS style sheet that modifies the tags present within the Table Of Contents component:

- To modify the Table Of Contents heading, use a type selector in the range *H1* through *H6*, corresponding to the Heading Font Size you specified in the Table Of Contents Properties dialog box.

  For example, if you specified a Heading Font Size of 2, an *H2* type selector would modify its appearance.

- Use an *LI* type selector to modify the appearance of the individual page listings.

> For more information about cascading style sheets, refer to Chapter 20, "Managing Appearance with Cascading Style Sheets."

Also, the Table Of Contents For This Web Site component works by analyzing ordinary hyperlinks. Anything ingenious you've done with JavaScript, Active Server Pages (ASP), or frames is likely to disturb this analysis and produce a table that's, shall we say, surprising. Tossing a Table Of Contents For This Web Site component into your Web is no substitute for careful organization.

InsideOut

Approach the Table Of Contents For This Web Site component realistically. The concept of automatically creating a site table of contents is appealing, but few sites have pages so tightly organized that they automatically produce a well-organized table of contents. You might find that constructing a table of contents manually is easier than reorganizing your site so the Table Of Contents For This Web Site component produces satisfactory results.

Using the Table Of Contents Based On Page Category Component

Link bars and the Table Of Contents For This Web Site component are two very convenient ways to let FrontPage do the work of connecting pages in your Web. They both, however, take a rather structured, hierarchical view. Often, the pages you want to group cut across other boundaries, and then you're back to maintaining lists of hyperlinks by hand. Fortunately, the Table Of Contents Based On Page Category component provides an alternative.

> **caution** The Table Of Contents Based On Page Category component works only with disk-based Webs and with server-based Webs using the FrontPage 2000 or later Server Extensions.

Using the Table Of Contents Based On Page Category component is a two-step process:

1 Assign Category codes to all like pages in your Web. You can define as many of these categories as you want, and you can assign any number of categories (or none) to any page in the same Web.

2 Wherever you want a list of all Web pages in a certain category, insert a FrontPage Table Of Contents Based On Page Category component. Tell the component what categories to list and, when you save the Web page, FrontPage does the work of finding and listing all pages with matching categories.

To assign categories to a Web page:

1 Locate the page in Folders view or in any Folder List, right-click it, choose Properties from the shortcut menu, and then choose the Workgroup tab. A dialog box like the one shown in Figure 27-5 appears.

Alternatively, open the page in Page view, choose Properties from the File menu, and click the Workgroup tab. Except for its exterior shape, this tab is identical to the tab in the dialog box shown in Figure 27-5.

2 If the category you want to assign already exists, select its check box in the Available Categories list.

3 If you need to create a new category, click the Categories button to display the dialog box shown in Figure 27-6:

    a To add a new category, type it in the New Category box, and then click Add.

    b To remove a category, select it, and then click Remove.

Chapter 27: Displaying Derived Content

      c To undo all changes made since opening the dialog box, click Reset.

      d Click OK to save your changes and exit.

4 After you've selected all appropriate categories, click OK.

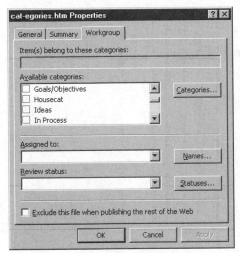

Figure 27-5. Define categories for a file on the Workgroup tab of the Properties dialog box.

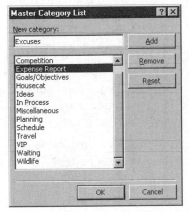

Figure 27-6. Clicking the Categories button in Figure 27-6 displays this dialog box, where you can alter the list of valid categories.

To insert a Table Of Contents Based On Page Category component:

1 Open the Web page where you want the component to appear.

2 Set the insertion point.

3 Choose Web Component from the Insert menu.

Part 9: Incorporating Advanced Content

4 Choose Table Of Contents from the Component Type list at the left of the Insert Web Component dialog box.

5 Choose Based On Page Category from the Choose A Table Of Contents list at the right of the dialog box, and then click Finish.

Figure 27-7 shows the resulting dialog box.

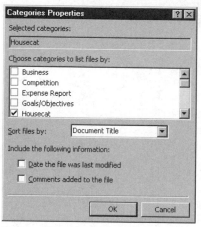

Figure 27-7. The Table Of Contents Based On Page Category component creates a hyperlinked list of all pages in a Web that are coded with given category codes.

Follow these instructions to configure each option:

- **Choose Categories To List Files By.** Select the check box for each category you want included in the list of Web pages. If you select multiple check boxes, a match to any one of them will include the page. For example, if you select both the Planning and the Waiting categories, the list will include any Web page coded Planning, Waiting, or both.

- **Sort Files By.** Indicate how you want the list sorted: by Document Title, or by Date Last Modified. Document Title arranges pages alphabetically from A through Z. Date Last Modified lists the most recent first.

- **Date The File Was Last Modified.** Select this check box if you want the list of matching pages to include the date someone last modified each page.

- **Comments Added To The File.** Select this check box if you want the list of matching pages to include comments made regarding each page.

> **note** The comments listed by the Table Of Contents Based On Page Category component are those entered in Folders view or any Folder List. For more information about entering such comments, refer to "Working with Folders View" on page 174.

As with the Table Of Contents For This Web Site component, FrontPage displays only a mock-up of the finished Table Of Contents Based On Page Category component. Figure 27-8 provides an example. Only saving the page and viewing it with your browser will display the actual list as it appears in Figure 27-9 on the next page.

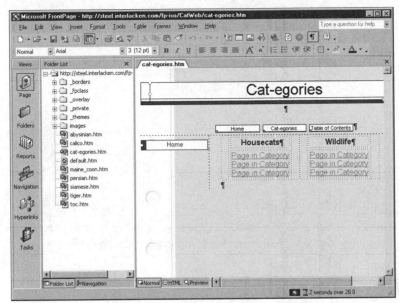

Figure 27-8. Table Of Contents Based On Page Category components appear as mock-ups when FrontPage displays them.

Table Of Contents Based On Page Category components are great for displaying lists of Web pages selected by product line, responsible person, type of status report, or almost any sort of criteria you can imagine. Any time you need to select and list Web pages, doing so with Category codes will almost certainly ease maintenance over time.

Troubleshooting

Table Of Contents Based On Page Category doesn't reflect new categories you assign to a page

Simply changing the Category of a Web page might not update all the Table Of Contents Based On Page Category components in the same Web.

If you encounter this problem, run the Recalculate Hyperlinks command from the Tools menu.

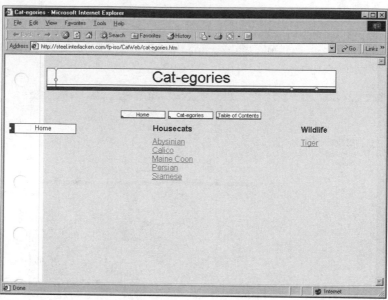

Figure 27-9.   Table Of Contents Based On Page Category components appear as expected when you save them into a Web and display them in your browser.

Scripting Dynamic Menus and Tables of Contents

If your Web changes very rapidly, tables of contents and other kinds of menus might become outdated faster than FrontPage components or your own most diligent efforts can update them. Often, these situations occur when external processes add files on no fixed schedule. Web visitors might upload files such as photographs or résumés, for example, or automated process might deposit files representing business activity in your Web.

The most expedient solution in such cases is often to make sure that both of the following are true:

● The folder where the incoming files reside doesn't contain a Web page with the Web server's default page name.

● The Web server is configured to permit directory browsing. The Web server's administrator must configure this setting.

If both of these conditions are true, browsing the given folder will display a listing like the one in Figure 27-10. The Web server sets up a hyperlink surrounding each listed file name so that clicking on any file requests that file.

Straight folder listings like the one in Figure 27-10 have their place, but for many applications you'll want something better—something that looks a bit more professional and a lot less like it came out of somebody's bit bucket. As a starting point, Microsoft provides the *dyntoc.asp* Active Server Page shown in Figure 27-11 on the next page. This ASP page runs a script on the Web server that lists the contents of a specified folder and lists all the files name that exist there.

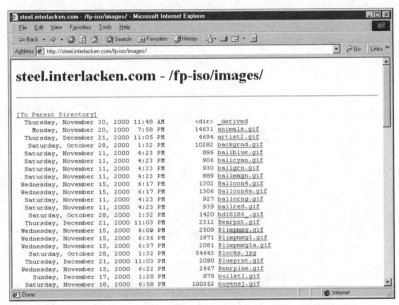

Figure 27-10. Web servers return a hyperlinked folder listing like this when Web visitors request a folder location that doesn't contain a file with the server's default file name and the Web server is configured to permit directory browsing.

---

on the web For more information about the *dyntoc.asp* page, refer to article Q218606 in the Microsoft Knowledge Base. The URL is
http://support.microsoft.com/support/kb/articles/q218/6/06.asp.

A copy of this page resides within the sample Web as *ch27/dyntoc.asp*. To view it, open the file in FrontPage. To view the ASP code, click the HTML tab at the bottom of the Page view window.

A line-by-line explanation of this ASP page is beyond the scope of this book, but the following statements are the ones that do all the work:

```
strDocsPath = "../images"
strDocsPhysicalPath = Server.MapPath(strDocsPath)
Set objFSO = Server.CreateObject("Scripting.FileSystemObject")
Set objFolder = objFSO.GetFolder(strDocsPhysicalPath)
Set objFiles = objFolder.Files
For Each objFile in objFiles
'  Code to display each file name goes here.
Next
```

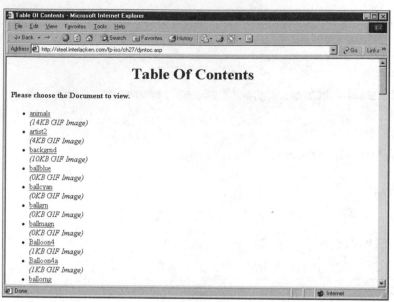

Figure 27-11. This ASP page reads a folder on the Web server and displays this table of contents in real time.

These statements do the following:

- The first statement stores a URL path in a variable named *strDocsPath*. The ASP page will list the contents of this path.

- The second statement converts the URL path in *strDocsPath* to a physical file path on the Web server.

- The third statement creates an element called *Scripting.FileSystemObject*. This is a software component that provides a number of useful methods for inspecting and modifying the server's local file system.

- The fourth statement uses the *FileSystemObject*'s *GetFolder* method to create a *Folder* object for the given physical file path. A *Folder* object provides access to the physical properties of the given folder.

- The fifth statement establishes *objFiles* as an alias for the *objFolder.Files* collection. The *Files* collection of any *Folder* object contains a *File* object corresponding to each file in the physical folder.

Chapter 27: Displaying Derived Content

After this statement executes, the *objFiles* variable points to a list of *File* objects: one for each file in the given folder.

● The sixth and eighth statements set up a loop that successively points the *objFile* variable to each File object in the *objFiles* collection. Within this loop:

   ▪ *objFile.Name* returns the file name (sans path) of the current file.

   ▪ *objFile.Type* returns the file type of the current file.

   ▪ *objFile.Size* returns the size of the current file.

Name, Type, and *Size* are properties that all *File* objects have.

The following is a listing of the code that displays each file name, somewhat reformatted from the Microsoft version for readability:

```
For Each objFile in objFiles
    strName = objFile.Name       ' get a file's name
    strFile = Lcase(strName)     ' make it lowercase for the URL
    strType = objFile.Type       ' get the file's type
    strName = MakeTitle(strName) ' make the name a title for display
    lngSize = objFile.Size\1024  ' get the file size in KB
    ' output the filename and URL
    Response.Write "<li>" & _
      "<a href=""" & strDocsPath & "/" & strFile & """>" & _
        strName & "</a><br>"
    ' output the file's size and type
    Response.Write "<em>(" & lngSize & "KB " & strType & ")</em>" & _
      "</li>" & vbCrLf
Next
```

Lines two through six copy various properties of the *objFile* object into ordinary variables and prepare them for display. The two *Response.Write* statements write into the output stream destined for the Web visitor's browser. When two quotation marks (as """") appear together within a literal, the literal's value contains one quotation mark.

Microsoft obviously designed this example to illustrate the ASP code and not to represent the state of the art in Web design. The Web page shown in Figure 27-12 on the next page provides a somewhat better appearance, the ability to move up and down a folder tree, and the ability for a query string to specify a folder location, but these are minor enhancements rather than significant new concepts. To view the ASP code or any other details relating to this page, open the *ch27/dyntable.asp* file in the sample Web.

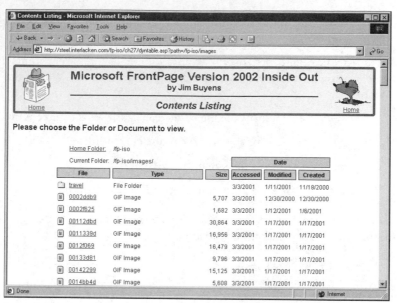

Figure 27-12. This Web page looks more like something you'd want visitors to see, but file names still don't provide much guidance as to what each hyperlink displays.

Unlike the browse listings that Web servers generate, directory listings that ASP pages create can filter the file listings, display only those informational fields you want, and let Web visitors switch to other folders or not. But the fact remains that file names, even with the best of naming conventions, usually make poor menu choices.

In Summary...

This chapter explained several components that generate Web content based on analysis of information tracked by or contained in a FrontPage-based Web.

The next chapter explains how to provide a text search capability Web visitors can use for locating content within your Web.

Chapter 28

Providing a Text Search Capability

Text searching is one of the most common and popular means for Web visitors to find content on the Web. No matter how well organized a site's Web pages and menus are, some visitors will always prefer entering a few keywords, reviewing a list of matching pages, and cutting to the chase.

This chapter explains several techniques that search all or part of a Web, an entire Web server, or the entire World Wide Web for given keywords. One of these techniques will almost surely be right for any requirement. However, for those rare cases when you need to create a custom text search capability, the chapter concludes with an introduction to writing text search pages yourself.

Using the Web Search Component

The Web Search component provides a text search capability for the local Web server, the current Web, or a folder tree within the current Web. This makes the Web Search component less powerful than the large Internet search engines, but limited searching has advantages as well:

- If you've done a good job of organizing your Webs and servers, each Web represents a specific body of knowledge. Searching that realm might very well be a reasonable thing to do.

- Searching only your Web limits the opportunities for visitors to wander off and visit other sites.

- If you want to search an entire group of servers, many other tools are available for that purpose. The Search The Web With MSN feature described later in this chapter is a case in point.

Scanning large numbers of files for every query would simply consume too much time. Fortunately, building an index ahead of time and using it later to satisfy queries are both practical operations. Virtually all full-text search engines therefore use a text index—a database of word locations—to satisfy queries. Microsoft FrontPage uses one of two markedly different text indexes, depending on your Web's operating environment. The first is a server-based catalog maintained by either Microsoft Index Server or Microsoft Indexing Service, depending on your server's operating system:

- If you have a server-based Web that resides in the following environment:

    - The operating system is Microsoft Windows NT 4,

    - Index Server is installed, and

    - Index Server actually indexes the file area where the server-based Web resides,

    FrontPage will use the Index Server catalog as its full-text index.

- Likewise, if you have a server-based Web that resides in this environment:

    - The operating system is Microsoft Windows 2000,

    - Indexing Service is installed, and

    - Indexing Service actually indexes the file area where the server-based Web resides,

    FrontPage will use the Indexing Service catalog as its full-text index.

> **note** For the most part, Index Server for Windows NT 4 and Indexing Service for Windows 2000 provide identical services and work alike. This chapter therefore mentions the two interchangeably. Unless otherwise noted, you should assume that any references to Indexing Service in this chapter apply to Index Server as well.

In any other case, FrontPage uses its own built-in full-text index. This index has fewer features and more restrictions, but is more universal. The text will indicate how and when differences between these two indexing techniques affect the Web Search component.

> **note** Regardless of other settings, searches configured in FrontPage don't search hidden folders—those whose names begin with an underscore. Such folders aren't available for normal Web browsing.

Chapter 28: Providing a Text Search Capability

Performing a Web search requires running a program on the Web server—a program that's part of the FrontPage Server Extensions. Therefore, in order for the Web Search component to work, the Web page that contains it must be part of a server-based Web, and you must load the page by giving your browser an HTTP URL.

Adding a Web Search Component

You can add a Web Search component to your Web using two different methods. The first method adds a Web Search component to any new or existing page. The process is much the same as for other Web components:

1 Set the insertion point where you want the Web Search component to appear.

2 Choose Web Component from the Insert menu. This displays the Insert Web Component dialog box.

3 Select Web Search from the Component Type list at the left and Current Web from the Choose A Type Of Search list at the right. Click Finish.

The second way to start using the Web Search component involves creating a new page with the Search Page template:

1 Use either of two methods to display the Page Templates dialog box.

Here's the procedure for the first method:

   a Choose New from the File menu, and then choose Page Or Web.

   b When the New Page Or Web task pane appears, click the Page Templates link that appears under the New From Template heading.

Here's the procedure for the second method of displaying the Page Templates dialog box:

   a Click the drop-down list associated with the New Page button on the Standard toolbar.

   b Choose Page.

New Page

2 When the Page Templates dialog box appears, select the Search Page template and then click OK.

3 When the new page appears in Page view, locate the Web Search component (an HTML form with a text box labeled Search For, like that shown in Figure 28-1 on the next page), and then double-click it.

Following either procedure opens a two-tabbed dialog box named Search Form Properties. The first tab appears in Figure 28-2 on the next page and controls the appearance of the input form.

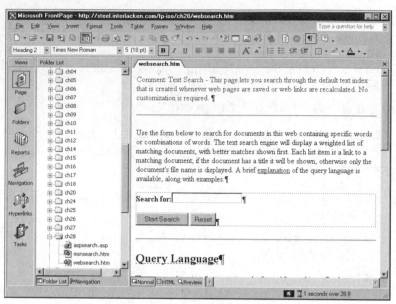

Figure 28-1. The Search Page template produces a Web page like this.
The Web Search component is the HTML form containing the Search For
text box.

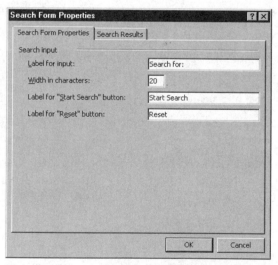

Figure 28-2. Use this dialog box to configure your search page.

Here are the available options for controlling the appearance of the input form:

- **Label For Input.** Supply the phrase that prompts visitors to enter keywords.

- **Width In Characters.** Specify the width, in typical characters, of the text
  box provided for entering search terms.

- **Label For "Start Search" Button.** Supply a caption for the button that initiates the search.

- **Label For "Reset" Button.** Supply a caption for the button that reinitializes the search form.

The second tab, Search Results, controls the presentation of items found in the search. There are two versions of this tab: one for Internet Information Server running with Indexing Service, and one for all other environments.

Searching with Indexing Service

Figure 28-3 shows the Search Results tab of the Search Form Properties dialog box as it appears when Indexing Service is available.

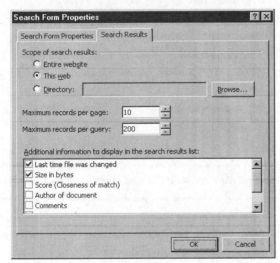

Figure 28-3. This dialog box controls the format of search results when Indexing Service is present.

This tab contains the following options:

- **Scope Of Search Results.** Use this group of options to limit the range of Web pages to search:

  - **Entire Website.** Select this box to search the entire Web server where the Web resides. This includes the root Web and all other Webs on the same server.

  - **This Web.** Select this box to search only the current Web and any subwebs it might have.

  - **Directory.** Select this box to search a single folder (plus its subfolders) in the current Web. Specify the folder in the text box provided.

Troubleshooting

Search returns results from wrong Web

Searches performed with the Web Search component sometimes return a list of pages from the wrong Web. This occurs on Webs that use Indexing Service, and most often on new or physically relocated virtual Web servers. This occurs because the search component is using a different Indexing Service catalog than the one that indexes the current Web. Here's how to resolve this problem:

1 Open the Web where the problem occurs, choose Recalculate Hyperlinks from the Tools menu, and then click Yes. Try the search again after the re-calculation finishes.

2 If the problem persists, ask the server administrator to verify that an Indexing Service catalog exists for your virtual Web server:

- If it doesn't, ask the administrator to create one. Microsoft Knowledge Base article Q203796 provides instructions.

- If it does, ask the administrator to reapply the catalog to the virtual Web server. Consult Microsoft Knowledge Base article Q214835 if necessary.

In either case, ask the administrator for the name of the catalog and its starting location.

3 Repeat step 1.

4 If the problem persists, gain file system access to the area where the problem Web resides. Locate the Web's root folder and then look for a subfolder

- **Maximum Records Per Page.** Specify the maximum number of matching pages reported on one page of search output. The visitor must click a Next button to see each additional page of results.

- **Maximum Records Per Query.** Specify the maximum number of matching pages reported by an entire search.

- **Additional Information To Display In The Search Results List.** Specify what information should be presented with search results. Scroll down for more selections. Here are the options:

  - **Last Time File Was Changed.** Select this box to display the date and time that matched pages were last modified.

  - **Size In Bytes.** Select this box to display the size in bytes of each matching page.

  - **Score (Closeness of Match).** Select this box to display a number indicating match quality.

Chapter 28: Providing a Text Search Capability

named *_vti_script.* Use Notepad to examine any files in this folder that have a filename extension of *.idq.* If you find any line that begins *cicatalog=* and doesn't point to the starting location identified in step 2, correct it and save the file.

> For more information about configuring Indexing Service, refer to "Locating an Indexing Service Catalog" on page 797 and "Adding a Catalog to Indexing Service" on page 1079.

Suppose, for example, that you open an IDQ file and discover that it contains the following line:

```
cicatalog=C:\InetPub
```

Any searches performed by this IDQ file will refer to files that reside within the *C:\InetPub* folder tree. If your Web doesn't physically reside in this folder tree, the IDQ file will return results from the wrong Web. If you decide to update the *cicatalog* location, be sure to specify the starting location of an existing catalog.

Normally, FrontPage identifies and inserts the correct catalog name automatically. However, FrontPage doesn't detect changes or make corrections in this area until you run the Recalculate Hyperlinks command. This is the reason for recommending step 1.

Of course, running the Recalculate Hyperlinks command won't help if no suitable catalog exists, or if the registry information for the correct catalog is incomplete. These are the reasons for recommending steps 2 and 3. Step 4 mainly provides information but also provides a manual fix.

- **Author Of Document.** Select this box to display the name of the person who created the document (if known).

- **Comments.** Select this box to report any notes recorded with each matching file.

- **Document Subject.** Select this box to report the names of matched documents. For Web pages, this is the title field. (This field and the next don't appear in the screen shot. To display them, scroll down the Additional Information To Display In The Search Results List.)

- **Matches.** Select this box to report the number of matching documents found.

Indexing Service detects *all* file changes—whether made by FrontPage or other means—and updates its indexes as soon as the Web server has processing time available. This means text searches will always be up to date, with little or no time lag.

Chapter 28

791

Searching with the FrontPage Text Index

If your Web doesn't use Index Server, the FrontPage Server Extensions use a text index that FrontPage updates incrementally whenever it saves Web pages, or *en masse* whenever it recalculates hyperlinks. Changing a Web with tools other than FrontPage might therefore result in incorrect search results until someone runs the Recalculate Hyperlinks command.

Within a Web that uses the FrontPage text index, the Search Results tab looks like Figure 28-4. The properties you can configure in this case are different from those available with Indexing Service.

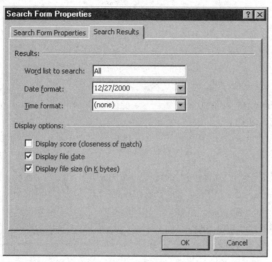

Figure 28-4. This dialog box controls the format of search results not produced by Index Server.

The following are the properties you can configure on the Search Results tab:

- **Word List To Search.** Specify either *All*, to search all pages in the current Web, or the name of a subfolder. For example, to search the contents of a Discussion Web, you would specify the folder where that Web resides.

- **Date Format.** Specify the format for displaying file dates. This field will be dimmed unless the Display File Date check box is selected.

- **Time Format.** Specify the format for displaying file times. This field will be dimmed unless the Display File Date check box is selected.

> **tip** It's always best to use 4-digit year, alphabetic month, and 24-hour time formats on the Web. These are less confusing to international visitors. Depending on the country, 01/02/03 can be January 2, 2003, February 1, 2003, or February 3, 2001.

Chapter 28: Providing a Text Search Capability

- **Display Score (Closeness Of Match).** Select this box to display a number
  indicating match quality.

- **Display File Date.** Select this box to display the date and time that
  matched pages were last modified.

- **Display File Size (In K Bytes).** Select this box to display the size in kilobytes of each matching page.

newfeature! Searching the Web with MSN

This Web component displays an HTML form that your visitors can use to search the
World Wide Web for a given string. A page that contains this component appears in
Figure 28-5.

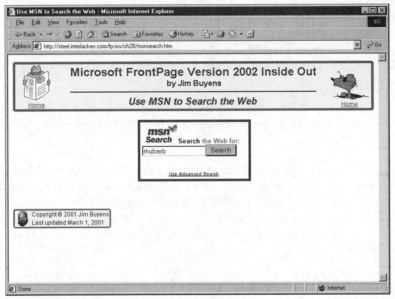

Figure 28-5. The Search The Web With MSN component in the center of this Web
page submits search terms to the public MSN search engine. The border around the
search form is actually a one-cell table added later.

Entering search terms and clicking the Search button submits a request to the Microsoft
Network search engine at *http://search.msn.com*. Figure 28-6 on the next page shows
some typical results.

Here's the procedure for adding this component to a page in your Web:

1 Set the insertion point.

2 Choose Web Component from the Insert menu. This displays the Insert Web
Component dialog box.

793

Figure 28-6. Submitting the search request shown in Figure 28-5 produced these results.

3 Choose MSN Components from the Component Type list at the left and Search The Web With MSN from the Choose A MSN Component list at the right. Click Finish.

Unlike most other Web components, Search The Web With MSN doesn't have a persistent identity or a custom dialog box for configuration. Instead, the result of inserting this component is some ordinary HTML that appears in your Web page. Right-clicking this area doesn't offer a Search The Web With MSN Properties choice, for example. Instead, it offers a Form Properties choice that directly configures the properties of the HTML form.

> **For more information about HTML forms, refer to Chapter 31, "Creating and Using Forms."**

Two details of the MSN Search form are critical. As long as you preserve these details, you can modify the MSN Search form as much as you like:

● Submitting the form must request the location *http://search.msn.com /results.asp* as shown in the Action box of the Options For Custom Form Handler dialog box in Figure 28-7. This is the location of the MSN search engine.

● The *Name* property of the text box for entering the search terms must be *q*. This is the form field name that identifies the list of search terms to the MSN search engine.

Chapter 28

Chapter 28: Providing a Text Search Capability

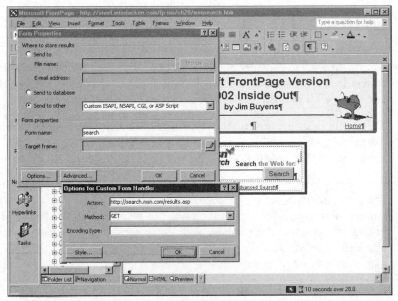

Figure 28-7. The Search The Web With MSN component doesn't have its own Properties dialog box. To configure it, just modify its HTML form properties. If you want, click Options to display the Options For Custom Form Handler dialog box.

One drawback of using this component is that it sends visitors away from your Web. One minute a visitor is happily browsing your Web, the next minute the visitor discovers the MSN Search form, and the minute after that your visitor is browsing some other site. One way of reducing this effect is to make the MSN search results appear in a new window instead of yours. Here's the procedure:

1 Right-click anywhere in the MSN Search form, and choose Form Properties from the shortcut menu to display the Form Properties dialog box.

2 Click the Target Frame button (the pencil button that appears at the far right of the Target Frame box) to display the Target Frame dialog box.

3 Select New Window from the Common Targets list, and then click OK. Click OK again to close the Form Properties dialog box.

You might wish to make a similar change to the Use Advanced Search hyperlink, which also jumps to a page outside your Web.

> **tip** Hyperlinks that point outside your Web are a sure way to lose visitors. Many Web designers therefore avoid such links or at least open them in a new window. That way, the window displaying the designer's Web remains on the visitor's desktop and eventually regains the visitor's attention.

Scripting Web Searches

If the Web Search component seems close to what you want but lacks in some detail, you might wish to consider developing your own search page. This is far from being the easiest, best-documented, and most intuitive aspect of Web development, but it works, and when all is said and done, it doesn't require many lines of code.

This method, by the way, isn't applicable to the FrontPage built-in full-text index. It works only with Indexing Service or Index Server, and this means it also requires a server-based Web residing on a Windows NT 4 or Windows 2000 computer.

> **note** The material in this section is cursory and not intended as a complete reference. For more information, refer to "Locating Additional Documentation" later in this chapter. In addition, you should be familiar with the material in the following chapters of this book: Chapter 31, "Creating and Using Forms"; Chapter 32, "Processing Data Submitted from Forms"; and Chapter 33, "Accessing Databases with FrontPage."

> **on the CD** You should also be familiar with Chapter 40, "Processing Databases with Active Server Pages"; Chapter 41, "Working with HTML Code"; Chapter 42, "Working with Script Code"; Appendix B, "Introducing Active Server Page Objects"; and Appendix C, "Introducing ActiveX Data Objects" in the Bonus Content on the Companion CD.

Figure 28-8 shows a Web page that performs a custom-coded Web search. Because it has some special debugging features, this probably isn't a Web page you'd choose to let your Web visitors see. It does, however, illustrate the important points. To examine this page in detail, use FrontPage to open the file *ch28/aspsearch.asp* in the sample Web installed from the CD-ROM that accompanies this book.

The gray rectangle near the top of the page is an HTML form with these input elements:

- **Text.** Specify the word or phrase you want to find.

- **Scope.** Specify the URL of a folder on the Web server. This limits the search to the folder tree that begins at that point.

- **Catalog.** Specify the name of the Indexing Service or Index Server catalog that indexes the server where the Web resides. In a default installation, this is the *Web* catalog. The presence of this field is a debugging feature; in a real application, this isn't something you'd expect Web visitors to know or experiment with.

- **SQL.** Select this box to display the SQL statement (shown in Figure 28-8) that locates the requested pages. This is also a debugging feature.

    A form designed for Web visitors wouldn't have Scope, Catalog, and SQL choices shown in Figure 28-8. The SQL statement appears only for debugging proposes.

Chapter 28: Providing a Text Search Capability

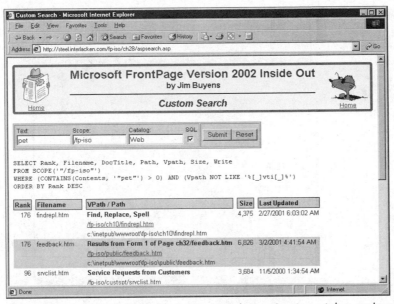

Figure 28-8. This Web page queries an Indexing Service catalog and produces custom output.

Locating an Indexing Service Catalog

In the hope that additional detail will provide more clarification than confusion, Figure 28-9 on the next page shows a list of Indexing Service catalogs on a Windows 2000 server named STEEL. To display this information on your own Windows 2000 system:

1 Choose Programs from the Start menu.

2 Choose Computer Management from the Administrative Tools menu.

> **note** If your system doesn't have an Administrative Tools menu, right-click the Windows task bar, choose Properties, and then click the Advanced tab. Finally, select Display Administrative Tools in the Start Menu Settings list, and then click OK.

3 When the Computer Management window appears, click the plus sign next to Services And Applications.

4 Select the Indexing Service item.

> **note** If your system doesn't have Indexing Service installed, choose Start, Settings, and Control Panel; double-click Add/Remove Programs; and then click Add/Remove Windows Components. Then, select the option titled Indexing Service and click Next until the wizard installs Indexing Service. Supply your Windows 2000 CD when prompted.

Part 9: Incorporating Advanced Content

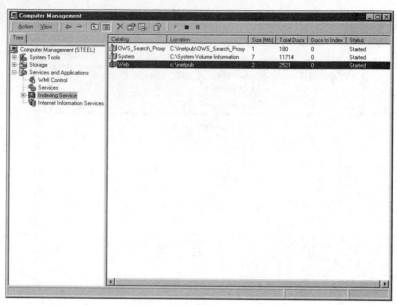

Figure 28-9. To configure Indexing Service, open its entry in the Computer Management administrative tool.

> **note** To inspect the Index Server configuration of a Windows NT 4 system, choose Start, Programs, Windows NT 4 Option Pack, Microsoft Index Server, and Index Server Manager.

Figure 28-9 shows that the computer STEEL has three catalogs: *OWS_Search_Proxy*, *System*, and *Web*. The Location column in the right pane shows where each of these catalogs physically resides. To view the folder trees that a particular catalog indexes:

1 Click the plus sign that appears in the left pane in front of Indexing Service.

Virtual Servers, Virtual Directories, and Indexing Service

In the simplest case, a computer providing Web services has one IP address and one DNS name. As a result, it appears to be one Web server. This is eminently simple, but installing a new computer for each Web site is an expensive proposition when the sites are small. Most providers therefore offer *virtual servers*.

A virtual server is a single computer that responds to multiple IP addresses and delivers content from a different HTTP root depending on the IP address. Each IP address has a different DNS name and thus appears to be a stand-alone site. Each virtual server that requires Indexing Service thus also requires its own catalog. Otherwise, content that normally appeared on two distinct Web sites would appear mixed together in search results.

Chapter 28: Providing a Text Search Capability

2 Click the plus sign that appears in front of the catalog you're investigating.

3 Select the Directories icon that appears beneath the catalog in question.

Figure 28-10 shows that the *Web* catalog indexes content in six folder trees. The first tree listed is the HTTP root for the default Web server on this computer. The remaining five trees are the physical locations of virtual directories on the default server. In general, each virtual server on the same computer will have its own Indexing Service catalog, and that catalog will index all physical or virtual directories that belong to that server.

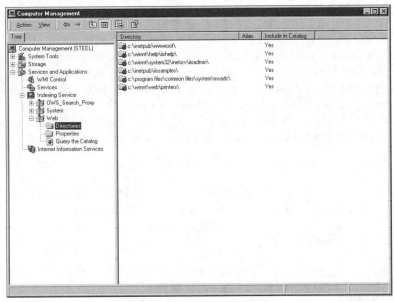

Figure 28-10. A single Indexing Service catalog can index multiple folder trees. In this case, each tree is a virtual directory belonging to the same Web server.

A virtual directory, on the other hand, is a folder tree that appears to be part of a Web server's folder tree, but physically resides elsewhere. In other words, the logical folder tree a Web visitor sees might be larger and more complex than the folder tree that physically resides on the Web server. The added branches come from virtual directories defined in the Web server's configuration.

For Indexing Service to produce complete results, each catalog must index not only the Web server's physical folder tree, but all of the virtual folder trees as well. That's why additional physical directories appear in the display shown in Figure 28-10. Each one of the extra *physical* directories hosts a *virtual* directory defined by the Web server.

(Indexing Service normally detects the need to list additional directories by means of interfaces to the Web server software.)

If your Web server's HTTP root resides somewhere not indexed by Indexing Service, the server's administrator will need to create a new catalog. (To start this process, right-click the Indexing Service entry in the Computer Management tree, choose New from the shortcut menu, and then choose Catalog). The name you give this catalog is the name you'd enter in the Catalog box of the form pictured in Figure 28-8.

Coding an Indexing Service Query

The code required to open a connection to Indexing Service, submit a query, and read through all the matching records (the hits) is very similar to that for accessing a database. Here are the salient points:

- The following statement creates a connection string named *cnStIx*. A connection string is the specification for opening a connection to a data provider, such as a database or Indexing Service. In the following connection string, *msidxs* means Microsoft Indexing Service. The *source=* setting specifies the name of the Indexing Service catalog. The *qcatalog* variable contains the value entered in the Catalog box of the form in Figure 28-8:

  ```
  cnStIx = "provider=msidxs;data source=" & qcatalog
  ```

- The next two statements create and open an *ADODB.Connection* object named *cnIx*. ADODB stands for ActiveX Data Objects Database. Notice that the Open method on the second line specifies the *cnStIx* connection string as an argument:

  ```
  Set cnIx = Server.CreateObject("ADODB.Connection")
  cnIx.Open cnStIx, "", ""
  ```

- The next three statements create and open an *ADODB.Recordset* object. For a normal database, this type of object contains all records that match a given database query. For an Indexing Service catalog, it contains one record for each matching file (that is, one record for each search hit):

  ```
  Set rsIx = Server.CreateObject("ADODB.Recordset")
  sql = "SELECT ... "
  rsIx.Open sql, cnIx, adOpenForwardOnly
  ```

To view the code that creates the SQL statement shown in Figure 28-8, open the *ch28/aspsearch.asp* page in the sample Web and switch to HTML view. For more information about its format, refer to the next topic in this section.

The value *adOpenForwardOnly* is a constant defined in a file named *adovbs.inc*. To include this file in any Web page that needs it, add the following line near the top of the *<head>* section:

```
<!-- #include file="../adovbs.inc" -->
```

As coded, this statement assumes that the *adovbs.inc* file is in the parent folder of the folder that contains the *ch28/aspsearch.asp* page. Be sure to adjust the *file=* URL if the two files reside in different relative locations.

- The first statement in the following code defines the start of a loop that continues until the current record position of the *rsIx* recordset is past the last record. The *rsIx.MoveNext* statement advances to the next record. Between these two statements you would place whatever code is necessary to create the HTML that displays the search hit:

```
Do While Not rsIx.EOF
   ' Code to display each record goes here.
   rsIx.MoveNext
Loop
rsIx.Close
cnIx.Close
```

The Loop statement marks the end of the loop, and the last two statements close the recordset and the connection, respectively.

Coding SQL Statements for Indexing Service

The SQL statement shown in Figure 28-8 appears again here:

```
SELECT Rank, Filename, DocTitle, Path, Vpath, Size, Write
FROM SCOPE('"/fp-iso"')
WHERE (CONTAINS(Contents, '"pet"') > 0) AND (Vpath NOT LIKE
'%[_]vti[_]%')
ORDER BY Rank DESC
```

In this statement:

- The field names listed on line 1 are field names in the Indexing Service catalog, not in a database table. To view a list of the available properties, locate the Indexing Service catalog using the Computer Management tool (see Figure 28-9). Then click the plus sign that precedes the catalog name, and select the Properties icon. The list of available fields appears in the Friendly Name column, shown at the right of Figure 28-11 on the next page. (The Rank field isn't part of the catalog; it's generated as part of running a query.)

- The FROM SCOPE clause specifies the folder tree to search.

- The WHERE clause in this example specifies two conditions. The first condition demands that the *Contents* field contain the word *pet*. This field contains the main contents of a file, such as the textual portion of a Web page. The second condition demands that the file's virtual path (that is, its

URL) not contain the string _vti_. This excludes FrontPage system files from the search results.

The percent signs are wild cards that mean "any string of text." Underscore characters are normally wild cards that mean "any single character," but the square brackets tell the data provider to treat them as ordinary characters.

● The ORDER BY clause specifies how to sort the results.

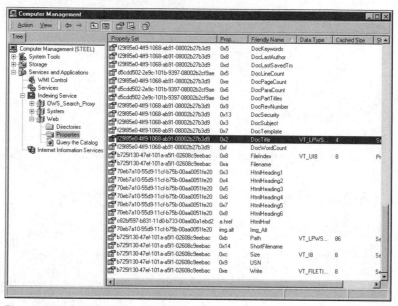

Figure 28-11. The Friendly Name column in the right pane lists the field name you can use in SQL statements.

Accessing a field in an Indexing Service result set follows the same pattern as accessing a field from a database query. The following expression, for example, retrieves the value of the file name field of the *rsIx* recordset and writes it into the outgoing HTML:

```
<%=rsIx("filename")%>
```

Locating Additional Documentation

If your Web server runs Windows 2000, you can get additional information about Indexing Service at *http://windows.microsoft.com/windows2000/en/server/help*. To locate the Indexing Service topic, first open the Files And Printers topic as shown in Figure 28-12.

Chapter 28: Providing a Text Search Capability

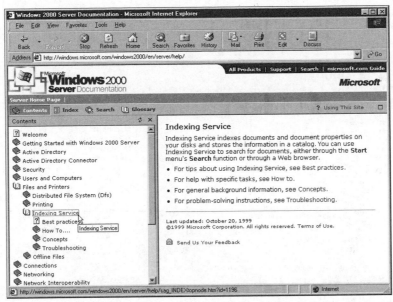

Figure 28-12. Information about the Windows 2000 Indexing Service is available from Microsoft's Web site.

To find out more about ADO access to the Indexing Service catalog, browse the Microsoft Developer Network Library at *http://msdn.microsoft.com/library.* Expand the following topics in the order listed. Figure 28-13 on the next page illustrates this path. Be forewarned, however, that it changes somewhat from time to time:

> *Platform SDK Documentation*
> > *Data Services*
> > > *Microsoft Data Access Components (MDAC) SDK*
> > > > *Microsoft ActiveX Data Objects (ADO)*
> > > > > *ADO Programmers Guide*
> > > > > > *Section V: Appendices*
> > > > > > > *Appendix A: Providers*
> > > > > > > > *Microsoft OLE DB Provider for Microsoft Indexing Service.*

Another method for finding information about this topic is to browse the search page at *http://search.microsoft.com/us/dev/default.asp* and search for the phrase "Microsoft OLE DB Provider for Microsoft Indexing Service," or for the provider name *msidxs.*

If your server runs Windows NT 4 with the Windows NT Server Option pack, you can find documentation under the heading "Microsoft Index Server" at the path *http://<yourserver>/iishelp/iis/misc/default.asp.* To learn more about accessing Index Server catalogs through ADO, open the Microsoft Index Server entry and then choose the topic titled "SQL Access to Index Server Data." Figure 28-14 on the next page illustrates this location.

Part 9: Incorporating Advanced Content

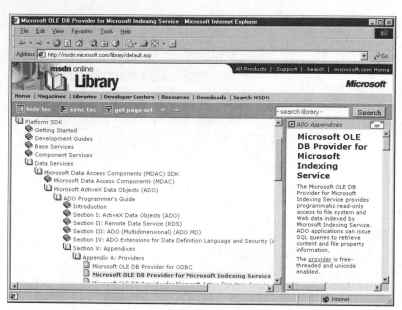

Figure 28-13. Documentation on using ADO to search Indexing Service catalogs is available from the Microsoft Developer Network Library location shown here.

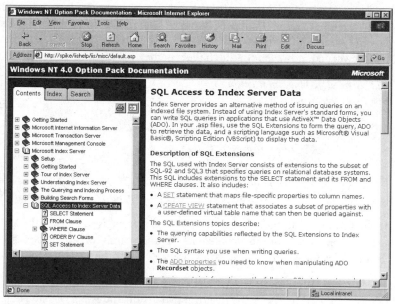

Figure 28-14. The topic highlighted in this screen shot provides more information about accessing Index Server catalogs through ADO.

Chapter 28

In Summary...

This chapter explained several techniques that provide a full-text search capability for visitors to your Web site. This helps visitors find the information they want without traversing a series of hyperlinks.

The next chapter describes some additional components that, like the Search The Web With MSN component, enhance your Web with real-time information from public sources.

Chapter 29

newfeature!
Using Automatic Web Content Components

Before the current release of Microsoft FrontPage, developing new Web components was a complex job best done by professional programmers. Even simple problems required a complex solution. Now, however, with Automatic Web Content components, FrontPage 2002 provides a simple solution for simple problems.

In its simplest form, an Automatic Web Content component is a selection that appears in the Insert Web Components dialog box. Choosing that component inserts a block of predefined HTML at the current insertion point. The effect is much like that of boilerplate text assigned to a special keystroke or command in a word-processing program—except that in FrontPage, the boilerplate can be a hyperlink or an HTML form that points to a useful function anywhere on the Web. The Search The Web With MSN component described in the previous chapter was a component of this type, and the Stock Quote feature described in this chapter is another.

Selecting an Automatic Web Content component can also connect you to a Web site that sends out wizard prompts that help you configure the component. After you've answered all the prompts, the Web site sends customized HTML to FrontPage for inclusion in your Web page. The Weather Forecast from MSNBC, bCentral Banner Ad, and FastCounter components discussed in this chapter are examples of such components.

Automatic Web Content components are so useful and so easy to develop that they'll probably start popping up all over. They'll arrive with FrontPage, with Office Updates, and as downloads from a variety of online services. In addition, you can develop custom Automatic Web Content components for yourself or your organization. Therefore, you should consider the Automatic Web Content components described in this chapters as examples rather than a comprehensive list.

newfeature!
Using the Stock Quote Component

This component creates an HTML form where your visitors can enter a stock exchange symbol and receive the current price and other statistics for that stock. The form submits the request to *http://moneycentral.msn.com* for processing, and MSN MoneyCentral sends back the stock quotation Web page shown in Figure 29-1.

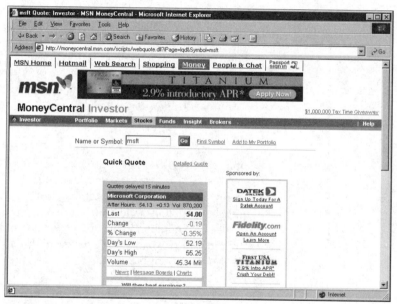

Figure 29-1. The Stock Quote component provides stock quotes like this for your Web visitors.

The procedure for inserting this component is much like that for inserting any other component. Here it is:

1 In Page view, open the Web page that will contain the stock quote request form.

2 Set the insertion point where you want the request form to appear.

3 Choose Web Component from the Insert menu.

Chapter 29: Using Automatic Web Content Components

4 When the Insert Web Component dialog box appears, choose MSN Components from the Component Type list at the left of the dialog box.

5 Make sure Stock Quote is selected in the Choose A MSN Component list at the right of the dialog box.

6 Click Finish.

These actions insert the HTML form titled Quick Quote that appears in the Web page in Figure 29-2. This is just an ordinary HTML form, not a full-fledged component with a Stock Quote Properties dialog box and other accoutrements. To change the properties of the form, right-click anywhere within the dotted rectangle and choose Form Properties from the shortcut menu. However, don't change either of the following options:

● After opening the Form Properties dialog box and clicking Options, don't disturb the URL in the Action box. Changing this URL prevents MSN MoneyCentral from receiving and processing the visitor's request.

● After right-clicking the Quick Quote text box and choosing Form Field Properties, don't change the Name field to anything other than *SYMBOL*. If you do, MSN MoneyCentral won't know what stock the Web visitor requested.

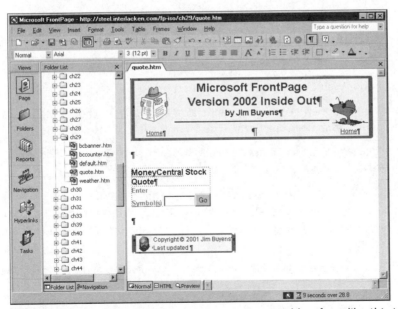

Figure 29-2. Inserting a Stock Quote component adds a form like this to your Web page.

By default, the Stock Quote component doesn't display the quote in a new window. To modify this behavior, right-click the HTML form, choose Form Properties, and click the Target Frame button.

new feature!

Using the Weather Forecast From MSNBC Component

This component displays the current and forecasted weather conditions for any city you select, courtesy of the MSNBC Web site. As well as delivering different content, the Weather Forecast From MSNBC component differs from the stock quote component in two ways:

- It displays its results in the current Web page. To view some typical results, refer to Figure 29-3.

- Your computer must be connected to the Internet any time you insert or modify the component.

Here's the procedure for adding a Weather Forecast From MSNBC component to your own Web page:

1 Make sure your connection to the Internet is working.

2 Use Page view to open the Web page that will contain the weather forecast.

3 Set the insertion point where you want the weather forecast to appear.

4 Choose Web Component from the Insert menu.

5 When the Insert Web Component dialog box appears, choose MSNBC Components from the Component Type list at the left of the dialog box.

6 Make sure Weather Forecast From MSNBC is selected in the Choose A MSNBC Component list at the right of the dialog box.

7 Click Finish. FrontPage connects to the MSNBC Web site and begins running a configuration wizard. The wizard's exact form and content might change over time, but at some point you should receive a prompt like the one shown in Figure 29-4.

8 Enter the name or U.S. ZIP code of the city you want, and then click Next.

Chapter 29: Using Automatic Web Content Components

9 The wizard queries the MSNBC Web site and responds with a list of matching cities, as shown in Figure 29-5 on the next page. Select the city you want, and then click Finish.

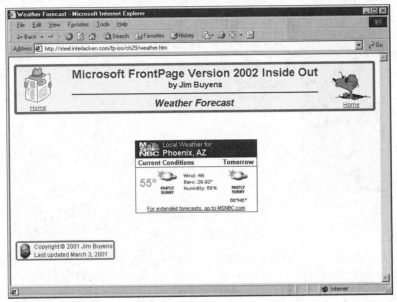

Figure 29-3. With the Weather Forecast From MSNBC component, a weather forecast like this can appear on any Web page you like.

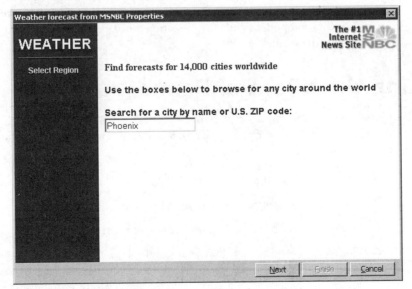

Figure 29-4. This dialog box prompts you for a city.

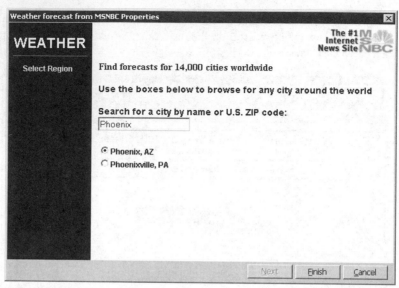

Figure 29-5. Choose the exact city you want from the list provided.

At this point, MSNBC sends FrontPage the HTML to retrieve and display the current weather for the city you requested. FrontPage adds this HTML to your Web page, but it won't actually run it. Instead, FrontPage displays an imitation weather forecast for Seattle, Washington. (55° Fahrenheit, damp, and dreary. What a surprise.)

Unlike the Stock Quote component, the Weather Forecast From MSNBC component actually inserts a component (albeit a generic one). Right-clicking Weather Forecast From MSNBC component and choosing the FrontPage Component Properties command reruns the wizard.

newfeature!
Using the bCentral Banner Ad Component

If you're looking for a way to place free advertising on Web sites other than your own, this is the component for you. Basically, it trades advertising for advertising according to the following scheme:

1 Create a Microsoft bCentral account.

2 Give bCentral your banner and your link address.

3 Start displaying bCentral banner ads on your own site.

4 Finally, for every two ads that your site displays, bCentral displays your ad once on some other site. (Example: Suppose you have a page that contains a bCentral banner ad and gets 1,000 hits a month. bCentral displays your ad on other member sites 500 times.)

Chapter 29: Using Automatic Web Content Components

Like the weather forecast component, the bCentral Banner Ad component connects to a Web site every time you create or modify it. Here's the procedure for joining the bCentral Banner Network and placing a bCentral banner ad on your Web:

1 Make sure your connection to the Internet is working.

2 Use Page view to open the Web page that will contain the bCentral banner.

3 Set the insertion point where you want the banner to appear, and choose Web Component from the Insert menu.

4 When the Insert Web Component dialog box appears, choose bCentral Web Components from the Component Type list at the left of the dialog box.

5 Make sure bCentral Banner Ad is selected in the Choose A bCentral Component list at the right of the dialog box.

6 Click Finish. FrontPage connects to the bCentral Web site and begins running a configuration wizard.

7 Read the introductory material, and then click Next to display the dialog box shown in Figure 29-6.

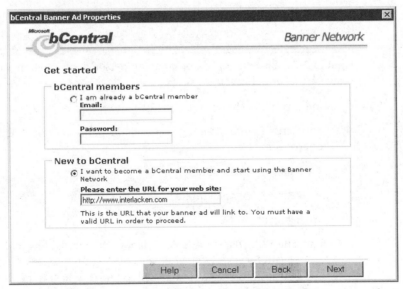

Figure 29-6. Using components from Microsoft bCentral requires a free membership account.

8 If you already have a bCentral account, select I Am Already A bCentral Member, fill in your e-mail address and password, click Next, and advance to step 12.

9 Select I Want To Become A bCentral Member And Start Using The Banner Network, fill in your Web site URL, and click Next.

Part 9: Incorporating Advanced Content

10 Read the terms and conditions, then select I Agree With These Terms And Conditions and click Next.

11 When the dialog box shown in Figure 29-7 appears, fill in your personal information, and then click Next.

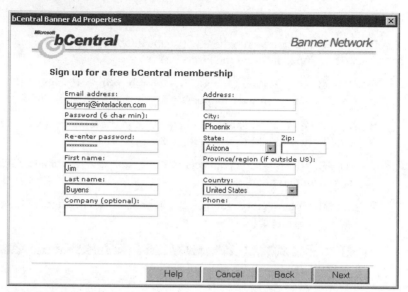

Figure 29-7. This dialog box prompts for personal information required to establish a bCentral account.

12 Fill in the dialog box shown in Figure 29-8 as follows:

■ **Your Site's Rating.** Identify the target audience for your site. The options are:

  ◆ **Rating 1** (children only).

  ◆ **Rating 2** (General Interest).

  ◆ **Ratings 1 and 2.**

■ **Your Site Will Display Ads For.** Identify the type of ads that would be appropriate for display on your site. This uses the same rating scale as the previous drop-down list, except Rating 2, which is identified here as Business Friendly/General Interest.

■ **Language Of Your Site.** Identify your site's primary spoken language.

■ **Your Web Site Is.** Select Business or Non-business.

■ **Your Web Site Title.** Enter the name of your site as it will appear on your banner ad.

■ **URL Your Ad Will Link To.** Enter the URL of the Web page that clicking your banner should display.

Chapter 29: Using Automatic Web Content Components

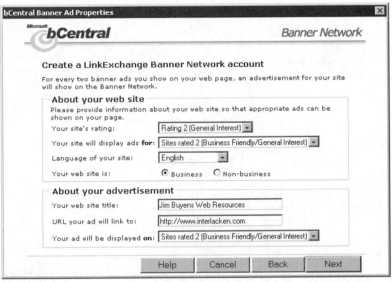

Figure 29-8. Use this dialog box to categorize your site and your advertising audience.

■ **Your Ad Will Be Displayed On.** Identify the type of site that should display your banner ad. This uses the same scale as in the Your Site Will Display Ads For list.

When all these entries are complete, click Next.

13 The dialog box shown in Figure 29-9 on the next page displays a preview of your banner ad. Use the following controls to modify its appearance:

■ **First Line.** Enter the text that should appear on the first line of your banner.

■ **Second Line.** Enter the text that should appear on the second line of your banner.

■ **Update Text.** Click this button to generate a new preview of the banner.

■ **Banner Background.** Select Color and specify a background color, or select Picture and choose a background picture.

■ **Line 1 Font Color, Font Size, and Font.** Specify the font properties for the first line of the banner.

■ **Line 2 Font Color, Font Size, and Font.** Specify the font properties for the second line of the banner.

14 Click Next and then Finish to add the HTML for the banner to your Web page.

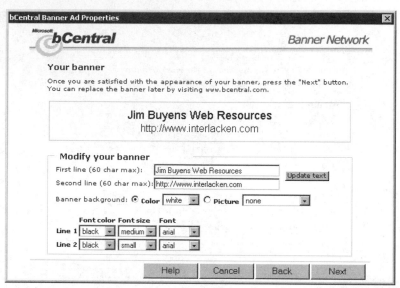

Figure 29-9. This dialog box controls the appearance of your banner ad.

Figure 29-10 shows how the banner appears when displayed in your Web page. Ads on your page, of course, will always point elsewhere. There's little purpose in advertising a site to visitors who are already there.

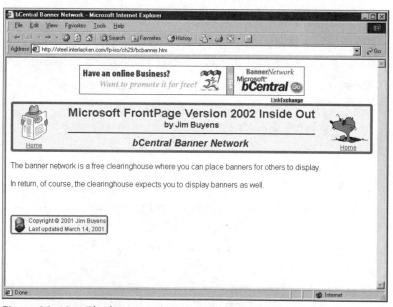

Figure 29-10. The banner ad at the top of this Web page came from the bCentral Banner Network site.

Chapter 29: Using Automatic Web Content Components

newfeature!
Using the FastCounter Component

Like most hit counters, the FastCounter displays a number that increases by one every time a Web page displays it. FrontPage has its own hit counter, and this means you have a choice as to which hit counter to use. Here are some factors that might help you decide:

> For more information about the FrontPage Hit Counter component, refer to "Using the Hit Counter Component" on page 827.

- The FrontPage hit counter displays digits that are larger and more prominent than those that the FastCounter displays.

- bCentral sends you monthly or weekly e-mail reports of hit counter activity. The FrontPage hit counter doesn't have this feature, but FrontPage does have a variety of built-in Usage reports.

> For more information about FrontPage Usage reports, refer to "Usage Summary" on page 446.

- The FrontPage hit counter offers your visitors more privacy. For more information on this topic, refer to the sidebar titled "Cookies, Counters, Banners, and Privacy" later in this chapter.

Here's the procedure for adding a FastCounter component to your Web page:

1 Make sure your connection to the Internet is working.

2 Use Page view to open the Web page that will contain the FastCounter.

3 Set the insertion point where you want the FastCounter to appear.

4 Choose Web Component from the Insert menu.

5 When the Insert Web Component dialog box appears, choose bCentral Web Components from the Component Type list at the left of the dialog box.

6 Choose FastCounter from the Choose A bCentral Component list at the right of the dialog box.

7 Click Finish. FrontPage connects to the bCentral Web site and begins running a configuration wizard. Click Next when the introductory dialog box appears.

8 If you don't have a bCentral account or aren't logged in, the dialog box shown in Figure 29-6 appears. Login or create an account as described in the previous section.

Chapter 29

9 If you're already logged in to bCentral and have a FastCounter account, the dialog box shown in Figure 29-12 appears. If this happens, skip ahead to step 12.

10 If you're already logged in to bCentral but don't have a FastCounter account, the dialog box shown in Figure 29-11 presents these options:

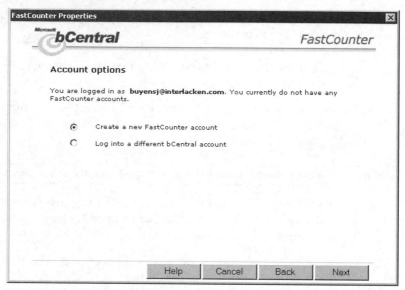

Figure 29-11. Using a FastCounter requires special enrollment in addition to a regular bCentral account.

- **Create A New FastCounter Account.** Select this option if the dialog box shows the bCentral account you want to start using for FastCounter service.

- **Log Into A Different bCentral Account.** Select this option if you want to use a different bCentral account for FastCounter service.

After selecting either of these options, click Next.

11 Read the terms and conditions, then select I Agree With These Terms And Conditions and click Next.

12 When the dialog box shown in Figure 29-12 appears, fill in the available options as follows:

- **Counter Starting Value.** Enter the first value the hit counter should display.

- **Email My Stats To Me.** Select the reporting frequency you desire: Monthly, Weekly, or Never.

- **Select A FastCounter Style.** Select the counter style you prefer.

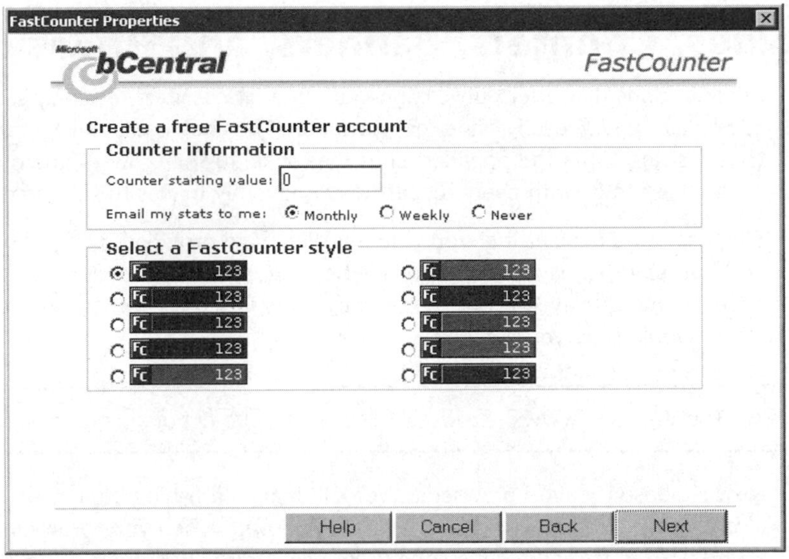

Chapter 29: Using Automatic Web Content Components

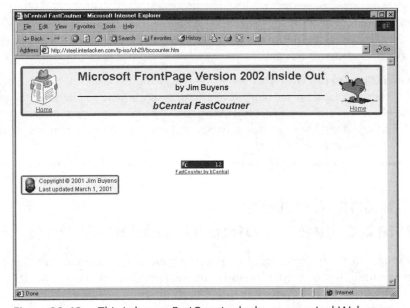

Figure 29-12. Use this dialog box to select the type of FastCounter your
site will display.

13 Click Next and Finish to complete the process.

Figure 29-13 shows how the FastCounter appears on your Web page. As usual, the
counter doesn't operate in FrontPage; instead, a placeholder appears.

Figure 29-13. This is how a FastCounter looks on an actual Web page.

Chapter 29

Cookies, Counters, Banners, and Privacy

Organizations that offer public banner ads and hit counters routinely send a so-called *cookie* along with each banner or hit counter. The cookie is usually a random number or text string. After the provider sends the cookie to the browser, the browser includes the cookie with every request it subsequently makes to the same provider.

Suppose, for example, that you visited a Web page provided by a fishing magazine, and that page displayed an ad provided by *http://www.falseads.com/*. If you had never before displayed an ad provided by *www.falseads.com*, the *www.falseads.com* server would send you a cookie.

> **note** The Web site *www.falseads.com* is meant to be fictional and not a real site.

Now suppose that you browsed a Web site that sold fishing equipment, and that site also displayed ads provided by *www.falseads.com*. When your browser requested the ad from *www.falseads.com* (as the fishing equipment web page told it to do), your browser would also send *www.falseads.com* the saved cookie. Can you see where this is going? After a while, *www.falseads.com* might not know who you are, but it knows you like fishing. The next time you request an ad from *www.falseads.com*, you're very likely to get something fishy.

As time passes, a provider like *www.falseads.com* builds a history of Web sites accessed by the same cookie value (that is, by the same browser). Even if the provider never learns the visitor's true identity, the provider learns what kind of Web sites the person visits and uses this information to customize the ads it displays. Whether or not this kind of electronic dossier and ad targeting constitutes invasion of privacy is, of course, a matter of opinion.

Occasionally, you can enter your name and e-mail address on a site that also displays banner ads. Perhaps the site requires registration, or perhaps you decide to buy something there. This creates at least the possibility that someone could merge your Web surfing habits, your purchasing habits, and your identity to target advertising directed at you even more precisely.

newfeature!
Developing Custom
Automatic Web Content Components

With only a little coding effort, you can create your own Automatic Web Content components and integrate them seamlessly into the FrontPage environment. Figure 29-14, for example, shows the Insert Web Component dialog box displaying four components developed just for this book.

Chapter 29: Using Automatic Web Content Components

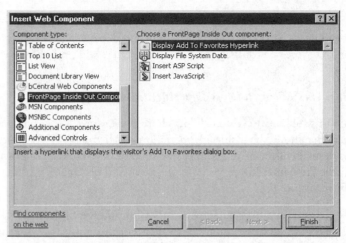

Figure 29-14. The four Web components listed in the components list on the right are unique to this book.

The components developed for this book are as follows:

- **Display Add To Favorites Hyperlink.** Adds a browser-side script that determines whether the current browser is Internet Explorer and, if so, displays a hyperlink to the Web visitor's Add To Favorites dialog box. This makes it easier for Web visitors to bookmark your page.

- **Display File System Date.** Adds a browser-side script that displays the last date the Web page was changed, as indicated in the Web server's file system.

- **Insert ASP Script.** Adds an empty block of Active Server Page script code to a Web page at the current insertion point. By running this component and then double-clicking the resulting icon to display the Server Script dialog box, you can add server-side script code to your Web page without ever switching to HTML view.

- **Insert JavaScript.** Adds an empty block of browser-side JavaScript code to a Web page. To add JavaScript code to your Web page without using HTML view, run this component, double-click the resulting icon to display the HTML Tag dialog box, and then enter the script code.

For more information about Add To Favorites hyperlinks, refer to "Helping Visitors Set Up Shortcuts" on page 526. For more information about displaying a Web page's file system date, refer to the Frequently Asked Question sidebar, "How can a Web page display its file system date?" on page 770. For more information about the Server Script dialog box and about the HTML Tag dialog box, refer to "Scripting Time-Sensitive Content" on page 758.

Chapter 29

To try these components on your own system, you must first locate the Microsoft Office *webcomp* folder. The exact path varies somewhat depending on your system and the version of Office or FrontPage that you have, but it will probably resemble the following:

C:\Program Files\Microsoft Office\Office10\1033\webcomp

One way to find this folder is to search all local hard drives for a folder named *webcomp*. This folder should be inside a *\Program Files\Microsoft Office* folder tree, and it contains a small collection of INI files and like-named folders. For example, you'll probably see file names like *bcentral.ini*, *msn.ini*, and *msnbc.ini*, plus matching folders *bcentral*, *msn*, and *msnbc*.

To install the four components listed above, simply copy all the files and folders from the \webcomp folder on the companion CD to the webcomp folder on your hard disk. That's it. The next time you display the Insert Web Components dialog box, the components should be there. (If not, renew your search for the real *webcomp* folder.)

> **tip** Whenever you use Windows Explorer to copy files from a CD, Explorer marks the copied files and folders as Read-Only—making them impossible to update. To remove the Read-Only designation, first right-click the file, folder, or selected files or folders, and then choose Properties from the shortcut menu. Clear the Read-Only box in the resulting dialog box, and then click OK.

To see how this works, open the *fpiso.ini* file with Notepad or your text editor of choice. The first few lines contain the following code:

```
[Component]
Name="FrontPage Inside Out Components"
Caption="Choose a FrontPage Inside Out component:"
Sorted=True
Type=IconAndText
ImageFile="icojjb.ico"
```

Here's what each statement in this block of code does:

- **[Component].** A required entry that indicates the start of the Automatic Web Content component definition.

- **Name.** Specifies the text that appears on the Component Type list of the Insert Web Component dialog box. For proof, compare the value shown above to the highlighted entry in Figure 29-14.

- **Caption.** Provides a title that appears over the selection list on the right side of the Insert Web Component dialog box. Again, you can verify this by comparing the code to the figure.

Chapter 29: Using Automatic Web Content Components

- **Sorted.** Tells FrontPage whether to sort the list of components alphabetically, or to present them in the order they appear in the INI file:

  - **True.** Specifies sorting.

  - **False.** Specifies no sorting.

- **Type.** Tells FrontPage how to display the Component Type list entry:

  - **IconAndText.** Tells FrontPage to format the list of components with an icon followed by a text description.

  - **Text.** Tells FrontPage to format the list of components with a text description only.

- **ImageFile.** Specifies the name of a Windows icon file. The picture in this file appears in the Component Type list—that is, at the left side of the Insert Web Component dialog box.

  The icon file you specify must reside in a folder that (1) is a subfolder of the *webcomp* folder and (2) has the same name as the INI file, less the *.ini* filename extension. For example, any icons that you specify in the file *webcomp\fpiso.ini* must reside in the folder *webcomp\fpiso*.

  You can specify any size icon you want, but FrontPage expands or shrinks it to 16 pixels square. Therefore, you might as well specify a 16x16 pixel icon.

> **note** If you don't have a graphics editor that works effectively with ICO files, try Axialis AX Icons. You can download and purchase this software from *http://www.axialis.com /order/index.html.*

The next group of statements provides an internal name for each Automatic Web Content component in the current group:

```
[Component.Options]
Option1=InsAddFavs
Option2=InsFsDate
Option3=InsASP
Option4=InsJscript
```

Here's what each of these lines do:

- **[Component.Options].** Tells FrontPage that the following statements enumerate the internal names of the Automatic Web Content components in this group.

- **Option1** through **Option***n*. Supplies the internal name of one component. Number these statements sequentially and use as many of them as you have components. Pick any names you want, but keep them short, free of punctuation, free of spaces, and meaningful.

823

The next block of statements describes the first option defined above; that is, it describes the *InsAddFavs* option:

```
[InsAddFavs]
Name="Display Add To Favorites Hyperlink"
Description="Insert a hyperlink that displays the visitor's Add To
Favorites dialog box."
ImageFile="favorite.ico"
```

Here's the function of each of these lines of code:

- **[InsAddFavs].** Tells FrontPage that this block of statements describes the InsAddFavs option just defined.

- **Name.** Specifies the text that appears in the component selection list that appears at the right side of the Insert Web Component dialog box. (Again, compare the value shown above to the highlighted entry in Figure 29-14.)

- **Description.** Specifies the text that appears in the large gray box near the bottom of the Insert Web Component dialog box. Enter this text on one long line.

- **ImageFile.** Specifies the name of a Windows icon file. The picture in this file precedes the component's name in the component selection list.

The last block of statements for the *InsAddFavs* component supplies the HTML that FrontPage adds to the Web page:

```
[InsAddFavs.HTML]
HTML1=<script language="JavaScript">
HTML2=if (navigator.appName.substring(0,9) == "Microsoft"){
HTML3=   document.write("<p><a href='" +
HTML4=      "javascript:window.external.addFavorite" +
HTML5=      "(document.location,document.title)'>" +
HTML6=      "Add to favorites</a></p>")
HTML7=}
HTML8=</script>
```

This code is fairly self-explanatory, but here, nevertheless, are the explanations:

- **[InsAddFavs.HTML].** Identifies this block of statements as the HTML that constitutes the component.

- **HTML1 through HTML*n*.** Provides the required HTML or script statements.

Chapter 29: Using Automatic Web Content Components

That's it! With no more work than this you can add an option to the Insert Web Component dialog box that inserts whatever HTML or script code you want. There are, however, two precautions regarding any HTML you insert:

- In almost every case, the easiest way to create and test the HTML is in a stand-alone Web page. Get the code working first, then make an Automatic Web Content Component out of it.

- FrontPage writes no line endings into the HTML that an Automatic Web Content component inserts. In the previous example, no line ending occurs between the HTML1 code and HTML2 code. This usually isn't a problem for HTML and JavaScript, which treat line endings the same as spaces anyway. Line endings are significant, however, in all forms of Visual Basic. Take this into account when you enter VBScript code. Separate statements with colons, and don't code line continuation characters.

The code for the three remaining sample Automatic Web Content components follows the same pattern: the *InsFsDate* option has [InsFsDate] and [InsFsDate.HTML] sections, the *InsASP* option has [InsASP] and [InsASP.HTML] sections, and so forth.

To create your own groups of components, just add an INI file and a matching folder to the *webcomp* folder and create INI file entries like the ones described here. For more examples, open and inspect any other INI files in the *webcomp* folder.

InsideOut

Unfortunately, Microsoft decided not to document how Automatic Web Content components work, at least not with the initial release of Office XP. This makes Automatic Web Content components that use more advanced features difficult or impossible to code. The best advice is to watch for further information on Microsoft's Web site.

In Summary...

This chapter explained the concept of Automatic Web Content components and explained how some typical ones work. It also explained how to create simple Automatic Web Content components yourself.

The next chapter explains how FrontPage can make usage statistics for your Web available to Web visitors.

Chapter 30

Monitoring and Reporting Site Activity

Popularity is a common measure of success on the Web. The more often people visit your Web page, the more successful you're deemed to be.

Hit counters are the most common form of usage analysis. Every time a visitor requests your page, a count displayed somewhere on that page (usually near the bottom) increases by one. This chapter explains how to use the Hit Counter component that comes with Microsoft FrontPage and then, as a bonus, explains how to create a Web page that displays the current value of all hit counters in your Web.

The second and more comprehensive form of usage analysis involves logs where Web servers keep detailed records of each visitor request. The FrontPage Server Extensions analyze such logs to produce the Usage reports described in Chapter 14. This chapter describes how the Top 10 List component can display the same data to Web visitors, and how you can write scripts that access and display much of the same data any way you want.

Using the Hit Counter Component

Simple hit counters are a favorite way to measure activity against a given Web page—and to publicly brag (or moan) about the results. Hit counters involve three components:

● A count kept in a small file on the Web server. For FrontPage, this is a file in the *_private* folder of your Web.

Part 9: Incorporating Advanced Content

- A program on the Web server that increments the count and creates a displayable version for output. For FrontPage, this is part of the FrontPage Server Extensions.

- HTML that triggers the server-side program and indicates where to insert the displayable output. This is what the Hit Counter component in FrontPage creates.

Figure 30-1 shows a page displaying a typical FrontPage hit counter. The displayed count is actually a picture whose source—rather than being a GIF or JPEG file—is a program that increments a count and generates data in GIF format. Each execution of the program increments the count by 1 until you reset the counter.

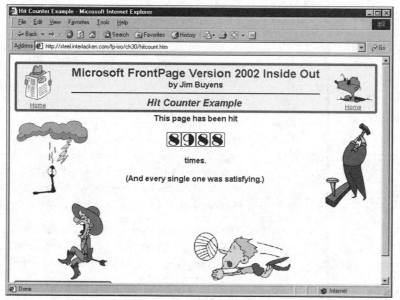

Figure 30-1. Show Web page activity using the FrontPage Hit Counter component.

Adding a hit counter to your page is simplicity itself. Here's the procedure:

1 Choose Web Component from the Insert menu.

2 In the Insert Web Component dialog box, select Hit Counter in the Component Type list that appears at the left and the Hit Counter appearance you want from the Choose A Counter Style list at the right.

3 Click Finish to display the Hit Counter Properties dialog box shown in the foreground of Figure 30-2.

The options in the Hit Counter Properties dialog box work as follows:

- **Counter Style.** Select an option for the style of digits that will display the hit count.

Chapter 30: Monitoring and Reporting Site Activity

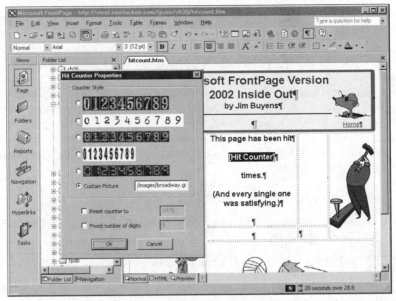

Figure 30-2. Use this dialog box to create or configure your hit counter.

- **Custom Picture.** Select this option to specify a digit style you designed
  or obtained yourself. Specify a file location relative to the root of your
  FrontPage-based Web, such as */images/decocnt.gif*. This should be a picture
  file containing the digits 0 through 9, in left-to-right order. The hit counter
  will use the leftmost 10 percent of this picture to represent 0, the next 10
  percent to represent 1, and so forth. Obviously, the width of the picture
  should be a multiple of 10 pixels.

> **tip** To create an invisible hit counter, specify a custom picture that's completely trans-
> parent or the same color as the background of your Web page. To view the counts
> accumulated by such a counter, refer to the section titled "Accessing Hit Counts with
> Scripts" later in this chapter.

- **Reset Counter To.** Select this option to set or reset the hit counter's starting value. To set a new start value, select this check box, specify the new
  starting count, and then save the Web page.

> **tip** After resetting the counter to a new value, save the page, clear the Reset Counter
> To check box, and save again. Otherwise, FrontPage will keep resetting the counter
> every time you save the page.
>
> When FrontPage publishes a Web, it doesn't copy hit counts from the source Web to
> the destination Web. Therefore, to reset hit counts on the destination Web, you must
> open it in FrontPage and do it yourself.

● **Fixed Number Of Digits.** Select this option to control how many digits
are displayed in the count. If the check box is cleared, FrontPage displays as
many digits as necessary to represent the count without leading zeros. If the
box is selected, FrontPage always displays the number of digits you specify.

FrontPage doesn't display hit counters interactively; instead, as you can see in Figure
30-2, it simply displays the text "Hit Counter." To see the hit counter in action, preview
the page with your browser.

As usual, there are four ways to display the Hit Counter Properties dialog box for an
existing hit counter:

● Double-click the Hit Counter component.

● Right-click the counter, and then choose FrontPage Component Properties
from the shortcut menu.

● Select the counter, and then choose Properties from the Format menu.

● Select the counter, and then press Alt+Enter.

If the counter doesn't work, the problem usually lies on the Web server. Verify that all of
the following are true:

● Either SharePoint Team Services or the FrontPage Server Extensions are installed. If they aren't, ask your server administrator to install them. If you
administer the Web server yourself—perhaps because it runs on your own
computer—try using the FrontPage Server Health features on the server or
reinstalling the FrontPage Server Extensions.

Troubleshooting

Cannot add multiple hit counters to a single page

When you add multiple hit counters to a single page, one of the following situations
could occur:

● If you use the same counter style, both hit counters display the same number.

● If you use different styles, each hit counter increases independently.

● Resetting the counter on one Hit Counter component resets the counter on
any other Hit Counter components on the same page to the same number.

The Hit Counter component in FrontPage isn't designed for multiple uses on a single
page. To resolve such problems, use only one hit counter per page.

Chapter 30: Monitoring and Reporting Site Activity

> For more information about installing and configuring the FrontPage Server Extensions, refer to Chapter 38, "Understanding the FrontPage Server Extensions."

- Anonymous visitors have security permission to execute the Server Extensions, as well as to update the *_private* directory in your Web.

 on the CD For more information about FrontPage Security, refer to "Controlling Web Security Through FrontPage" in the Bonus Content on the Companion CD.

- The hidden folder */_vti_bin*, in your Web, contains a program called *fpcount.exe*, and that the folder is executable by anonymous visitors.

> **note** In some versions of the FrontPage Server Extensions, the */_vti_bin* folder physically resides within each Web. For others, the */_vti_bin* folder in each Web is only a pointer to a single shared copy of all the programs.

Troubleshooting

Hit counter shows red X on all virtual servers on UNIX

Browsing a page that resides on a UNIX Web server and contains a FrontPage hit counter might display a red X instead of the hit counter. When this occurs, it occurs on all virtual servers on a UNIX host. Permissions are incorrect on the following path:

/usr/local/frontpage/version4.0/exes/_vti_bin

To resolve this problem, follow these steps:

1 Change the directory to */usr/local/frontpage/version4.0*.

2 Type *./set_default_perms.sh*

This resets the permissions on */usr/local/frontpage* and below to the correct default settings.

The correct permissions for */usr/local/frontpage/version4.0/exes/_vti_bin* are as follows:

```
dr-xr-xr-x    4 bin     bin            4096 May 23 08:56 .
dr-xr-xr-x    3 bin     bin            4096 Mar 26  1999 ..
dr-xr-xr-x    2 bin     bin            4096 May 23 08:56 _vti_adm
dr-xr-xr-x    2 bin     bin            4096 May 23 08:56 _vti_aut
-r-xr-xr-x    1 bin     bin         1536933 May  2 11:21 fpcount.exe
-r-xr-xr-x    1 bin     bin         3691284 May  2 11:21 shtml.exe
```

Troubleshooting

Hit counter doesn't work in subweb on Netscape servers

When you open a Web page that contains a hit counter, the counter doesn't increment past 1. This usually occurs for Web pages located in a subweb on a Microsoft Windows NT or Microsoft Windows 2000 computer running one of the following Netscape Web servers:

- Netscape Fasttrack (2.01 and prior)
- Netscape Enterprise (2.0 and prior)

This behavior occurs because of the way that Netscape Web servers determine the path to a subweb. Specifically, the PATH_TRANSLATED parameter doesn't consistently include a trailing slash.

To work around this problem, proceed as follows:

1 In FrontPage, open the root Web and create a new subweb. The URL should be similar to the following:

   http://<servername>/<webname>

   where *<servername>* is the name of the Web server, and *<webname>* is the name of the new subweb.

2 Switch to Page view and open the home page.

3 Insert a hit counter as described earlier in this chapter, and choose Save from the File menu.

4 View the page in your Web browser. (For example, choose Preview In Browser from the File menu.) If the page exhibits the problem, you see either of the following:

   ■ A broken image icon instead of the hit counter.

   ■ A hit counter that always displays one hit. That is, if you reload or revisit the page, the hit counter remains at 1.

5 Close your copy of FrontPage and perform this step entirely in Windows. Attempting to make this change through FrontPage will only reproduce the problem.

   Manually convert the subweb to a folder in the root Web. To do this:

   a Select Programs from the Web server's Start menu, then select Accessories, and then click Windows NT Explorer or Windows Explorer.

   b Expand the *_vti_pvt* folder in the Web server's content root. By default, the content root folder is located at *C:\Netscape\Suitespot\docs*.

   c Double-click the *Services.cnf* file. This opens the file in Microsoft Notepad.

Chapter 30: Monitoring and Reporting Site Activity

d Find your Web name and delete it from the list. The entry should look similar to the following:

/<Webname>

where *<Webname>* is the name you gave to your Web when you created it in step 1.

e Choose Save from the File menu, and close the file. Your FrontPage-based Web is now an ordinary subfolder in the root Web.

6 In FrontPage, open the root Web, and then open the subfolder *<Webname>* that you created in step 1.

7 In Page view, open the page that contains the hit counter and delete the hit counter. Then reinsert the hit counter as described earlier.

8 Open the page in your Web browser, using the URL from step 1. Verify that the hit counter is working correctly. If you reload or revisit the page, the hit counter should increment correctly.

9 In FrontPage, follow these steps to create a new Web:

a Choose New from the File menu, and then choose Page Or Web.

b When the New Page Or Web task pane appears, click Empty Web to display the Web Site Templates dialog box.

c In the box titled Specify The Location Of The New Web, enter the same location you specified in step 1, and click OK.

The content from the Web you created in step 1 is imported automatically from the subfolder in the root Web into the new subweb. The hit counter will continue to function correctly.

The Netscape servers listed earlier intermittently change the query string that the Hit Counter component constructs and passes to the hit counter executable file (*fpcount.exe*). The following examples explain how the hit counter constructs and passes query strings to *fpcount.exe,* and how the Netscape server determines the location of the file that contains the hit counter information:

● **For hit counters on pages in the root Web.** If the hit counter is on a page in the root Web, the hit counter constructs the following query string and passes it to *fpcount.exe:*

```
_vti_bin/fpcount.exe/?Page=hitcounttest.htm|Image=4
```

In this example, the Netscape server correctly determines the location of the file that contains the hit counter information and constructs the path:

C:\Netscape\Server\docs_private\hitcounttest.htm.cnt

(continued)

Troubleshooting *(continued)*

● **For hit counters on pages in a subweb.** If the hit counter is on a page in a subweb, the hit counter constructs the following query string and passes it to *fpcount.exe:*

```
_vti_bin/fpcount.exe/myweb/?Page=hitcounttest.htm|Image=4
```

In this example, the query string specifies a relative location that doesn't include the name of the subweb. As a result, the Netscape Enterprise server incorrectly determines the location of the file that contains the hit counter information and constructs the path as follows:

C:\Netscape\Server\docs\myweb_private\hitcounttest.htm.cnt

Because this path refers to a file that doesn't exist in the content root, the hit counter will not work in a subweb on either of the previously mentioned Netscape servers.

In this example, the correct location for the file that contains the hit counter information should be:

C:\Netscape\Server\docs\myweb_private\hitcounttest.htm.cnt

Accessing Hit Counts with Scripts

Hit counters provide a good snapshot of usage for a single page, but if you have many pages, checking all the current values can be tedious. The Web page shown in Figure 30-3 provides a solution by displaying, on one page, all the current hit values in a Web.

note Did you notice the quirk in the hit counts shown in Figure 30-3? The table in the center of the page shows a hit count of 17 for the *hitreport.asp* page, and the actual hit counter shows a count of 18. This is because the code that generates the report runs *before* the HTML for the Web page leaves the Web server. The code that increments the hit counter and displays the new value, by contrast, runs *after* the browser receives the HTML and requests the hit counter picture.

Unfortunately, there's no Web component or wizard that can produce a page like that in Figure 30-3. Producing such a page requires that you be at least slightly proficient in Microsoft Visual Basic Scripting Edition (VBScript). In addition, you must have a server-based Web that resides on a Windows NT or Windows 2000 computer. Finally, the folder where the Web page resides must be marked executable.

For more information about this example, refer to Chapter 41, "Working with HTML Code"; Chapter 42, "Working with Script Code"; and Appendix B, "Introducing Active Server Page Objects," in the Bonus Content on the Companion CD.

Chapter 30: Monitoring and Reporting Site Activity

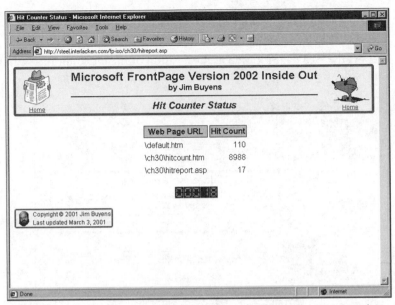

Figure 30-3. This Web page displays a list of all hit counts in a Web.

The first challenge in reporting hit count data is finding out where the data resides. As some poking and nosing about might reveal, the hit count for each file resides in a file named _private/<path>/<pagename>.cnt. The Folder List in Figure 30-4 on the next page, for example, shows the three hit count files listed in Table 30-1.

> **tip** If the _private folder isn't visible in your Web, choose Web Settings from the Tools menu, click the Advanced Tab, select Show Hidden Files And Folders, and click OK.

Table 30-1. **Location of Some Hit Count Files**

Web page URL (relative to root of current Web)	Hit count file location
ch30/hitcount.htm	_private/ch30/hitcount.htm.cnt
ch30/hitreport.asp	_private/ch30/hitreport.asp.cnt
default.htm	_private/default.htm.cnt

Figure 30-4 on the next page also shows the content of a hit count file: one record containing the identifier *FPCountFile* followed by a space and the current count value. Here, then, are the requirements for displaying the data shown in Figure 30-3:

- Walk the folder tree that starts at the _private folder of the current Web.

- Within each folder, locate all files that have a filename extension of *.cnt*.

- Open each such file, read the first record, and select the string of characters that follows the first space. Report this as the count.

- Report the Web page location as the location of the hit count file, minus the folder tree prefix *_private* and the filename extension *.cnt*.

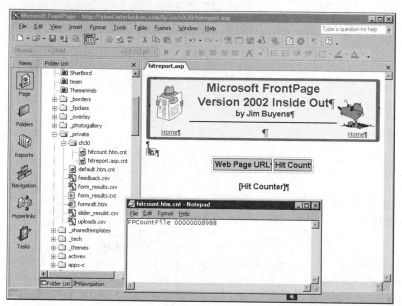

Figure 30-4. Each hit counter in a Web stores its count in a file that resides within Web's *_private* folder. The X icons indicate that publishing a Web doesn't copy hit counts to the destination Web.

Because virtually every one of these requirements involves accessing a folder or file, it should be no surprise that the script makes heavy use of the *Scripting.FileSystemObject* used in Chapter 27. To view the complete solution as you read the explanation, use FrontPage to open the file *ch30/hitreport.asp* in the sample Web installed from the CD, and then switch to HTML view.

For another example that uses the *Scripting.FileSystemObject,* refer to "Scripting Dynamic Menus and Tables of Contents" on page 780.

The script begins by declaring the variables it's going to use, and then initializing one object and one variable as follows:

```
Set FSO = Server.CreateObject("Scripting.FileSystemObject")
begDir = Server.MapPath("../_private/")
```

The first of these statements creates a *Scripting.FileSystemObject* that other parts of the script use for performing file operations. The second statement obtains and stores the physical folder path that's equivalent to the relative URL *../_private.* This is the correct

Chapter 30: Monitoring and Reporting Site Activity

starting point to use when scanning for hit counter files—assuming, of course, that the Web page doing the scanning resides in a first-level subdirectory of the Web's root folder. (Remember that double dot means "Go back one folder.") If your hit counter analysis page resides in a different location, you'll need to adjust this relative URL.

The following statement appears later in the Web page and kicks off the entire reporting process:

```
CheckDir (begdir)
```

CheckDir is a subroutine that searches for folders and *.cnt* files within a directory. Here's how this subroutine works:

- For each file it finds, it checks for a filename extension of *.cnt*. Then, for each file that satisfies this condition, it opens the file, gets the count, and writes one row of an HTML table.

- For each subfolder it finds within the given path, it calls the *CheckDir* sub-routine again, passing it the current path (including the subfolder).

Did you notice that the *CheckDir* subroutine calls itself? This is perfectly acceptable in all forms of Visual Basic. Each time you call a subroutine, Visual Basic loads a new copy into memory, and it has no problem having several copies of the same subroutine in memory at once.

> **note** Problems can result from having hundreds of copies of a Visual Basic subroutine in memory at once, but this is seldom a problem when processing subfolders. There's only one copy of the subroutine in memory for each folder level, and file system restrictions limit the number of subfolder levels.

Here are the statements that make up the *CheckDir* subroutine:

```
Sub CheckDir(aDir)
   Dim curDir
   Dim File
   Dim relPath
   Dim folder
   Dim url
   Dim cnt

   Set curDir = FSO.GetFolder(aDir)

   For Each File In curDir.Files
     If LCase(Right(File.Path, 4)) = ".cnt" Then
       url = Mid(File.Path, Len(BegDir) + 1)
       url = Left(url, Len(url) - 4)
       cnt = GetCount(File.Path)
```

```
        response.write "<tr>" & _
          "<td>" & url & "</td>" & _
          "<td align=right>" & cnt & "</td>" & _
          "</tr>" & vbCrLf
    End If
  Next

  For Each folder In curDir.Subfolders
    relPath = LCase(Mid(folder.Path, Len(BegDir) + 1))
    If InStr(relPath, "\_vti") < 1 Then
      CheckDir (folder.Path)
    End If
  Next

  Set curDir = Nothing
End Sub
```

- The following statement defines the start of the subroutine and accepts a single argument (which specifies the folder to process):

```
Sub CheckDir(aDir)
```

- The following six statements declare variables used within the subroutine. This guarantees that each copy of the subroutine has its own copy of these variables:

```
Dim curDir
Dim File
Dim relPath
Dim folder
Dim url
Dim cnt
```

- The following statement creates a folder object that represents the folder received as an argument:

```
Set curDir = FSO.GetFolder(aDir)
```

- The first statement in the following group sets up a loop that sequentially selects each file in the *Files* collection of the *curDir* folder object. The second statement checks to see whether the last four characters of the file name are *.cnt*. If so:

  - The third statement discards the leading portion of the file's physical path name: the part corresponding to *../_private/*.

  - The fourth statement discards the last four characters of the file name ("*.cnt*").

Chapter 30: Monitoring and Reporting Site Activity

■ The fifth statement calls a function named *GetCount* that extracts the hit counter value from a given file.

■ The next four statements write out one row of an HTML table.

■ The *End If* and *Next* statements terminate the *If* and *For* statements, respectively:

```
For Each File In curDir.Files
  If LCase(Right(File.Path, 4)) = ".cnt" Then
    url = Mid(File.Path, Len(BegDir) + 1)
    url = Left(relPath, Len(relPath) - 4)
    cnt = GetCount(File.Path)
    response.write "<tr>" & _
      "<td>" & url & "</td>" & _
      "<td align=right>" & cnt & "</td>" & _
      "</tr>" & vbCrLf
  End If
Next
```

The third statement warrants some additional explanation:

■ A typical value for File.Path is *C:\InetPub\wwwroot\fp10-iso _private\ch30\hitreport.asp.cnt*.

■ A typical value for *BegDir* is C:*InetPub\wwwroot\fp10-iso_private*. The length of this path is 36 characters.

■ The expression *Mid(File.Path, Len(BegDir) + 1)* selects a substring of the *File.Path* string starting at position 37 *(Len(BegDir) + 1)* and ending at the end of the string.

■ The result is *ch30\hitreport.asp.cnt*.

● The next block of statements in the *CheckDir* subroutine follows. The first statement in this group sets up a loop that sequentially selects each folder in the *Subfolders* collection of the *curDir* folder object.

The second statement discards the leading portion of the current subfolder's physical path name (the part corresponding to *../_private/*) and stores the result in a variable named *relPath*.

The third statement checks to see whether the subfolder name contains the string *_vti*. If it does, the subfolder is a FrontPage system folder and doesn't actually contain hit count files:

```
For Each folder In curDir.Subfolders
  relPath = LCase(Mid(folder.Path, Len(BegDir) + 1))
  If InStr(relPath, "\_vti") < 1 Then
    CheckDir (folder.Path)
  End If
Next
```

If the subfolder isn't a FrontPage system folder, the fourth statement calls the CheckDir subroutine with the subfolder as an argument. Notice that the loop runs the CheckDir subroutine once for each nonsystem subfolder in each folder.

The *End If* and *Next* statements terminate the *If* and *For* statements, respectively.

This nearly completes the explanation of this Web page. The only loose end is the *GetCount* function that extracts the hit counter value from a given file name. The following is the code for this function:

```
Function GetCount(aFile)
   Dim ctrFile
   Dim ctrRcd
   Dim ctrFld
   Dim hitCount
   Dim fld

   Set ctrFile = FSO.OpenTextFile(aFile)
   ctrRcd = ctrFile.readline
   ctrFld = Split(ctrRcd, " ")
   hitCount = 0

   For Each fld In ctrFld
     If IsNumeric(fld) Then
       hitCount = CLng(fld)
       Exit For
     End If
   Next

   ctrFile.Close
   Set ctrFile = Nothing
   GetCount = hitCount
End Function
```

- The following statement defines the start of the function and accepts a single argument (which specifies the file to process):

  ```
  Function GetCount(aFile)
  ```

- The following five statements declare variables used only within the function:

  ```
  Dim ctrFile
  Dim ctrRcd
  Dim ctrFld
  Dim hitCount
  Dim fld
  ```

Declaring Variables in VBScript

Unlike many other programming languages, Visual Basic doesn't require the programmer to explicitly declare variables before using them. If you want to keep a count of something, for example, you can just code this:

```
cnt = 0
```

If Visual Basic hasn't encountered the *cnt* variable previously, it creates a *cnt* variable on the fly. This is a wonderful convenience until you try to increment the count with a statement such as the following:

```
cnt = cmt + 1
```

Did you spot the spelling error in this statement? The expression *cmt + 1* always evaluates to 1 because when Visual Basic encounters the variable name *cmt* for the first time, it assigns it a null value that evaluates numerically to zero.

Most experienced programmers grow tired of the testing and debugging problems caused by misspelled variable names. As a result, they begin every Visual Basic program with the following statement:

```
Option Explicit
```

With this option in effect, you must use a *Dim* statement to declare every variable you use. Before using a *cnt* variable, for example, you must declare it with the following statement:

```
Dim cnt
```

This has the advantage that if you misspell a variable name, Visual Basic will refuse to run your program and display an error message instead. Of course, the same thing happens if you forget a *Dim* statement, but most experienced programmers find this a small price to pay.

To use the Option Explicit statement in an ASP page, add the following statement as the first line in the ASP file:

```
<% Option Explicit %>
```

Because of an oversight, early versions of FrontPage 2002 added three variables to every ASP page without bothering to declare them. Unless this oversight is fixed in later versions, you might need to declare these variables yourself. Their names are *FP_LCID, FP_CharSet,* and *FP_CodePage.*

- In the block of statements repeated next:

  - The first statement opens the file received as an argument and creates an object named *ctrFile* that manipulates the open file.

  - The second statement reads one line from the open file and stores the content in a variable named *ctrRcd*.

  - The third statements splits the *ctrRcd* into an array named *ctrFld*, using a space character as a delimiter.

  - The fourth statement sets the hit count value (in a variable named *hitCount*) to a default of zero.

```
Set ctrFile = FSO.OpenTextFile(aFile)
ctrRcd = ctrFile.readline
ctrFld = Split(ctrRcd, " ")
hitCount = 0
```

- The next block of statements sets up a loop that inspects each element in the *ctrFld* array. As soon as it finds one that's numeric, it sets the *hitCount* variable to that value and exits the loop:

```
For Each fld In ctrFld
  If IsNumeric(fld) Then
    hitCount = CLng(fld)
    Exit For
  End If
Next
```

Note that if the file is corrupted and the first record doesn't contain any numeric fields, the default value of zero will remain after the loop ends.

- The last group of statements closes the open file, destroys the open file object, and sets the function's return value to the hit count stored in *hitCount*:

```
  ctrFile.Close
  Set ctrFile = Nothing
  GetCount = hitCount
End Function
```

This example is somewhat more complicated than the one in Chapter 27—but after all, that was three chapters ago. If you don't understand everything about this page, you can add it to your own Web and display your own counts rather easily. Just copy it into an executable subfolder in your Web, delete the Include Page components at the top and bottom of the page, and browse it using an HTTP URL. After you get it working, format to suit.

The code as presented doesn't account for certain error conditions, such as the *OpenTextFile* method failing because a hit count file is in use. A hit count file containing no records is another error not handled. However, these conditions are rare.

newfeature!
Creating Top 10 Lists

Chapter 14 explains in detail how to display and view the comprehensive Usage reports built into FrontPage. Those techniques require opening the Web in question with the FrontPage desktop software. This means that to view Web statistics, you must have authority to open the Web in FrontPage (and consequently, authority to make changes).

Top 10 Lists provide a quick and easy way to display Web statistics to Web visitors with no special authority. Seven Top 10 Lists are available, and you can provide all, some, or none of them to visitors as you choose. The seven lists are as follows:

- **Top 10 Visited Pages.** Displays the 10 pages in your Web that visitors requested the most. Figure 30-5 provides a sample of this report.

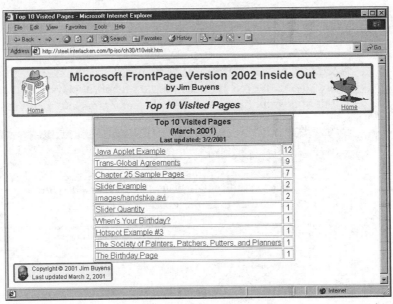

Figure 30-5. The Top 10 Visited Pages report lists the 10 most popular pages in your Web for the current month.

- **Top 10 Referring URLs.** Displays the 10 most common pages outside your Web that directed visitors into your Web. Figure 30-6 on the next page illustrates this report.

- **Top 10 Referring Domains.** Displays the 10 most common Web servers (other than yours) that directed visitors into your Web. Figure 30-7 on the next page illustrates this and the remaining four reports.

- **Top 10 Operating Systems.** Displays the 10 most common operating system that visitors to your Web were using.

- **Top 10 Browsers.** Displays the 10 most common browsers that visitors to your Web were using.

Part 9: Incorporating Advanced Content

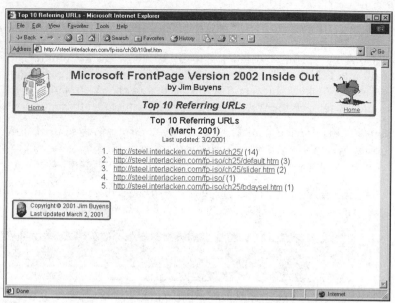

Figure 30-6. The Top 10 Referring URLs report displays the 10 pages outside your Web that most frequently sent visitors into your Web.

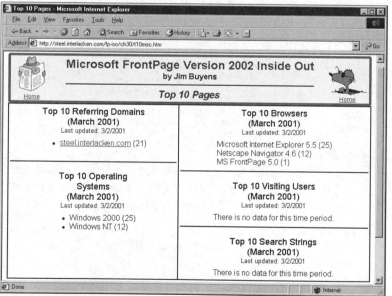

Figure 30-7. These Top 10 Lists report various centers of high activity.

● **Top 10 Visiting Users.** Displays the usernames of the 10 visitors who accessed your Web most frequently.

● **Top 10 Search Strings.** Displays the 10 most common keywords that visitors used to locate your site on one of the large Internet search engines.

Chapter 30: Monitoring and Reporting Site Activity

Figure 30-8 shows the Reports view Usage reports that correspond to the Top 10 Referring Domain and Top 10 Operating System reports shown in Figure 30-7.

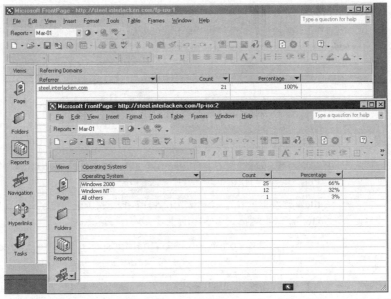

Figure 30-8. Top 10 Lists are essentially extracts of the Usage reports that FrontPage itself provides.

Here's the procedure for making any of these reports available to your Web's visitors:

1 Set the insertion point where you want the Top 10 List to appear.

2 Choose Web Component from the Insert menu. This displays the Insert Web Component dialog box.

3 Select Top 10 List in the Component Type list that appears at the left and the type of list you want from the Choose A Usage List box at the right.

4 Click Finish to display the Top 10 List Properties dialog box shown in Figure 30-9.

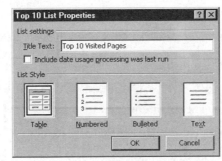

Figure 30-9. This dialog box configures the properties of a Top 10 List.

5 Specify the options on the Top 10 List Properties dialog box as follows:

■ **Title Text.** Enter the heading you want to appear at the top of the Top 10 List.

■ **Include Date Usage Processing Was Last Run.** If you select this box, the Top 10 List will display the most recent date that the FrontPage Server Extensions collected usage statistics from the Web server. In effect, this is the "Current as of" date for the statistics in the list.

■ **List Style.** Select the presentation format you want:

◆ **Table.** Select this icon if you want the statistics displayed in an HTML table. Figure 30-5 provides an example of this format.

◆ **Numbered.** Select this icon if you want the statistics displayed as a numbered list. Figure 30-6 provides an example.

◆ **Bulleted.** Select this icon if you want the statistics displayed as a bullet list. See the lists on the left side of Figure 30-7.

◆ **Text.** Select this icon if you want the statistics displayed as plain text. The lists on the right side of Figure 30-7 use this format.

6 Click OK to insert the Top 10 List.

After you've created the Top 10 List, FrontPage shows a mockup where the actual list will reside. After you save a page containing a Top 10 List component, the FrontPage Server Extensions will update it every time they perform usage analysis log processing.

Getting the Top 10 List component to display data can be a long, strange journey. As explained in the "Top 10 List doesn't display any data" troubleshooting sidebar, the Web server and the FrontPage Server Extensions both require proper configuration.

Frequently Asked Questions About the Top 10 List Component

Can the Top 10 List component show more than one month of data?

No.

Can the Top 10 List component show other than the current month's data?

No.

Can the Top 10 List component show more or less than 10 report details?

No, unless there are fewer than 10 lines of information to report.

Can an existing Top 10 List component display a different statistic?

No, you must delete the existing Top 10 List and create a new one in its place.

Chapter 30: Monitoring and Reporting Site Activity

Troubleshooting

Top 10 List doesn't display any data

The Top 10 List component displays a mockup of itself in both the Normal and Preview modes of Page view. In addition, browsing a page that contains a Top 10 List and resides in a disk-based Web displays the following message:

Publish this web to a server that supports the FrontPage Server Extensions to see usage data here.

To understand the reasons for this, you must understand where the numbers come from. Almost all Web servers keep a log of every request they receive—one log record per request. This log record contains the date and the time of the request, the requested Web page, the status code, the visitor's IP address, and so forth. On a scheduled basis, the FrontPage Server Extensions 2002 scan these logs and accumulate the data that appears in Top 10 Lists, the Usage reports in Reports view, and so forth.

Of course, if you don't have a Web server, you don't have a Web server log. Even if you did have a log, you wouldn't have the FrontPage Server Extensions to summarize it. Therefore, the Top 10 List component displays data only when:

● The Web page that contains the Top 10 List component resides in a server-based Web.

● The Web server is running the FrontPage Server Extensions 2002 or SharePoint Team Services. Earlier versions of the extensions don't collect usage statistics.

● The Web server must log the data you're interested in seeing. There are two aspects to this requirement:

  ▓ If the Web server isn't configured to keep a log, your statistics will obviously be zero.

  ▓ If the Web server isn't configured to log the data for a particular Top 10 List, that list will be empty. On Internet Information Server for Windows NT 4 or Internet Information Service for Windows 2000, the log should include at least the following information: Date, Time, Client IP Address, User Name, Method, URI Stem, HTTP Status, Bytes Sent, User Agent, Referrer.

  This list of fields is something you must configure in the Web server and not in FrontPage.

For more information about configuring Web server log options, refer to "Configuring Site and Folder Level Options" on page 1059.

(continued)

Troubleshooting *(continued)*

● The FrontPage Server Extensions must be configured to perform usage
analysis. The Web page shown in Figure 30-10 controls this. These settings apply to the entire Web server; you can't configure them on a Web-
by-Web basis:

■ If the option in the Usage Processing Is section is set to Off, no data
will appear.

■ If the option in the Usage Processing Is section is set to On and you
have a new Web, no data will appear until the next time the server
extensions run usage analysis log processing. This might require waiting a day, a week, or a month.

> For more information about configuring the frequency of Web server usage analysis, refer to
> "Administering Installation Defaults" on page 1094 and "Administering Server-Level Settings"
> on page 1090.

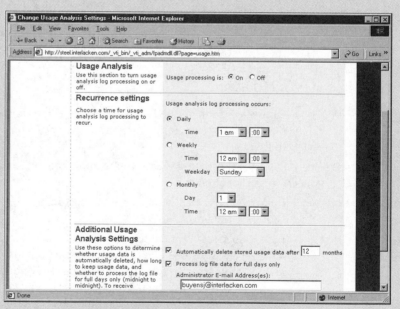

Figure 30-10. This Web page controls how often, if ever, the FrontPage
Server Extensions update usage statistics.

Creating Your Own Statistics Pages

Given that Top 10 Lists display much less data than the Usage reports available in Reports view, an inquiring mind might want to know where FrontPage stores the summarized usage data and whether an Active Server Page could make use of it. This section
answers those questions.

Chapter 30: Monitoring and Reporting Site Activity

Searching for data isn't hard if you know its approximate location and some data values it contains. All you need to do is:

1 Click the Windows Start button.

2 Click Search or Find (depending on your operating system).

3 Click For Files Or Folders, or Files Or Folders (depending on your operating system).

4 Enter one of the data values (preferably a reasonably unique string) in the Containing Text box.

5 Enter the approximate location in the Look In box.

6 Click Search Now and make a sandwich.

When both the search and the sandwich are finished, the Search Results window shows you the files that contain that data you want. In the case of FrontPage usage data, they turn out to be the ones listed in Table 30-2. All these files reside in a _vti_pvt_ subfolder of each Web's root folder.

Table 30-2. **Usage Report Data Files**

File name	Description
_x_browsers.xml_	Browsers
_x_domains.xml_	Visiting hosts
_x_pagehits.xml_	Visited pages
_x_referrers.xml_	Referring URLs
_x_refdomains.xml_	Referring domains
_x_systems.xml_	Operating systems
_x_users.xml_	Visiting users

The root folder of every FrontPage-based Web contains a _vti_pvt_ subfolder where FrontPage routinely keeps system files. This folder won't appear in FrontPage even if you select the Show Hidden Files And Folders setting, but if you have access to the Web server's file system you can see it in Windows Explorer. Figure 30-11 on the next page shows the proof. (Be sure to select the folder option Show Hidden Files And Folders before trying to display the _vti_pvt_ folder on your own system.)

If you haven't already noticed the _.xml_ filename extensions in Table 30-2, do so now. XML, the Extensible Markup Language, is an emerging standard for storing and exchanging information in a universal way. XML and HTML are related, but not very closely. Whereas HTML concerns itself mostly with format and presentation, XML concerns itself entirely with data. Opening the _x_browsers.xml_ file in Microsoft Internet Explorer, for example, produces the results shown in Figure 30-12 on the next page.

849

Part 9: Incorporating Advanced Content

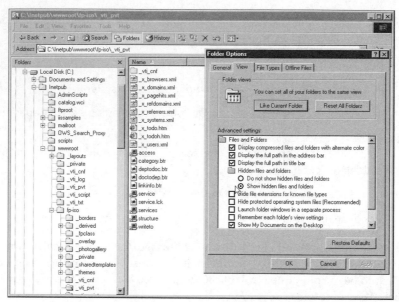

Figure 30-11.   The XML files in the _vti _pvt folder of this Web contain FrontPage
usage data. This folder is inaccessible to both browsers and FrontPage.

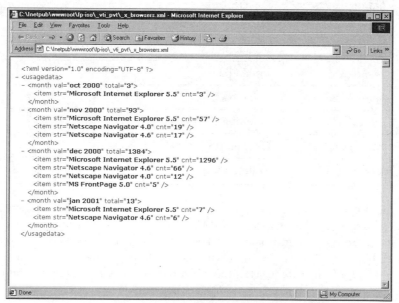

Figure 30-12.   Because XML files contain no formatting information, Internet Explorer
displays them as is.

Chapter 30: Monitoring and Reporting Site Activity

As shown in the figure, XML, like HTML, makes extensive use of tags enclosed by angle brackets. In the case of XML, however, the tags contain data identifiers (field names) rather than formatting codes:

- A pair of *<usagedata>...</usagedata>* tags, for example, mark the beginning and end of the data portion of the file.

- Pairs of *<month>...</month>* tags enclose the data for each month.

- *<item.../>* tags mark the bounds of each detail record.

- The actual data values are coded much as the attributes in an HTML tag.

Writing a script that reads this file as text and parses out its contents would be quite a headache. Fortunately, there are plenty of free software programs around that do this job very easily. They're called *parsers,* and the one Microsoft provides is called *Microsoft.xmldom.* You can use a *Microsoft.xmldom* object either at the browser or in an ASP script. This example uses an ASP script because FrontPage locks browsers out of the *_vti_pvt* folder where the necessary data resides.

Here's the VBScript code that creates a *Microsoft.xmldom* object and loads it with the contents of the *_x_browsers.xml* file:

```
Set xmlDoc = server.CreateObject("Microsoft.xmldom")
xmlDoc.async = False
xmlDoc.Load (Server.MapPath("../_vti_pvt/_x_browsers.xml"))
```

> **note** The ASP file for this exercise will reside in a subfolder of the current Web's root folder—*ch30* to be exact. In the relative URL *../_vti_pvt/_x_browsers.xml*, the double dots say, "Go to the parent of the folder where this Web page resides." The rest of the URL says, "Go to the *_vti_pvt* folder," and, "Go to the *_x_browsers.xml* file."

In this code:

- The first statement creates a *Microsoft.xmldom* object called *xmlDoc.*

- The second statement configures the *xmlDoc* object to suspend script execution while it loads an XML file.

- The third statement loads the *xmlDoc* object with the file at the relative location *../_vti_pvt/_x_browsers.xml.* The *Sever.MapPath* method converts the relative URL to a physical file path.

  Because the second statement set the *async* property to *False,* any statements after the *xmlDoc.load* statement won't execute until the *xmlDoc* object succeeds in loading the file or gives up.

So much for getting data into an *xmldom* object. Now, how do you get it out?
Well, all *xmldom* objects contain a *documentElement* object that represents the
highest level of the XML data structure. In the XML document shown in Figure
30-12, *documentElement* points to the *<usagedata>* node. So, with that document
loaded into the *xmldom* object named *xmlDoc,* the following expression provides
a path to whatever you want to know about the *<usagedata>* node:

```
xmlDoc.documentElement
```

All the *<month>* nodes are children of the *<usagedata>* node. This is because they
appear between the *<usagedata>* tag at the top of the file and the *</usagedata>* tag at
the end. The collection of all such nodes resides in an object named *ChildNodes.* The
paths to the four *<month>* nodes shown in Figure 30-12 are therefore:

```
xmlDoc.documentElement.childNodes.Item(0)
xmlDoc.documentElement.childNodes.Item(1)
xmlDoc.documentElement.childNodes.Item(2)
xmlDoc.documentElement.childNodes.Item(3)
```

Here are three more interesting and amusing facts about this data structure:

- The following expression returns the number of *Item* nodes in a *ChildNodes*
  collection:

  ```
  xmlDoc.documentElement.childNodes.length
  ```

- The *GetAttribute* method returns the value of any attribute coded within a
  node. The following expression, for example, would return "oct 2000":

  ```
  xmlDoc.documentElement.childNodes.Item(0).getAttribute("val")
  ```

- Because expressions such as this are long and tiresome to code, experienced
  programmers often set up aliases to parts of the structure they plan to access frequently. The first statement that follows, for example, sets up an alias
  named *xmlHdrData* that the programmer can use instead of the longer expression *xmlDoc.documentElement.childNodes.* The second statement that
  follows is therefore equivalent to the one just shown:

  ```
  Set xmlHdrData = xmlDoc.documentElement.childNodes
  xmlHdrData.Item(0).getAttribute("val")
  ```

Now you know everything necessary to code a loop that traverses the *xmlDoc* document and display all four pairs of *val* and *total* values. Go for it.

Done already? Got it all tested and debugged as well? No doubt you got something very
much like the following:

Chapter 30: Monitoring and Reporting Site Activity

```
Set xmlHdrData = xmlDoc.documentElement.childNodes
For hPos = 0 To xmlHdrData.length - 1
  cnt = xmlHdrData.Item(hPos).getAttribute("total")
  mon = xmlHdrData.Item(hPos).getAttribute("val")
  Response.Write "<tr>" & vbCrLf & _
    "<td>" & mon & "</td>" & vbCrLf & _
    "<td>Total</td>" & vbCrLf & _
    "<td>" & cnt & "</td>" & vbCrLf & _
    "</tr>" & vbCrLf
Next
```

In this code:

- The first statement sets up *xmlHdrData* as an alias to *xmlDoc.documentElement.childNodes*.

- The second statement initiates a loop that varies *hPos* from zero to one less than the number of *Item* nodes in *xmlHdrData*. (If there are four such nodes, the loop varies *hPos* from 0 to 3).

- The third and fourth statements retrieve the values of the *total* and *val* attributes from the current node, storing them in two variables named *cnt* and *mon*.

- The fifth statement (which continues to line nine) writes the *cnt* and *mon* values into one row of an HTML table.

- The last statement marks the end of the loop.

Compared to the easy job of displaying the *<month>* node data, displaying the *<item>* node data is downright trivial. It's strictly a case of "once more, with feeling." The following code goes just before the Next statement in the previous loop:

```
Set xmlDetData = xmlHdrData.Item(hPos).childNodes
For dPos = 0 To xmlDetData.length - 1
  cnt = xmlDetData.Item(dPos).getAttribute("cnt")
  bsr = xmlDetData.Item(dPos).getAttribute("str")
  Response.Write "<tr>" & vbCrLf & _
    "<td> </td>" & vbCrLf & _
    "<td>" & bsr & "</td>" & vbCrLf & _
    "<td align=right>" & cnt & "</td>" & vbCrLf & _
    "</tr>" & vbCrLf
Next
```

In this code:

- The first statement sets up *xmlDetData* as an alias to *xmlHdrData.Item(hPos).childNodes*.

Just as *xmlHdrData* pointed to all children of the *<usagedata>* node, *xmlDetData now* points to all children of the current *<month>* node. In case you're keeping score, *xmlDetData* is also equivalent to the following expression:

```
xmlDoc.documentElement.childNodes.Item(hPos).childNodes
```

● The second statement initiates a loop that varies *dPos* from zero to one less than the number of *Item* nodes in *xmlDetData*. (If there are two such nodes, the loop varies *hPos* from 0 to 1).

● The third and fourth statements retrieve the values of the *total* and *val* attributes from the current node, storing them in two variables named *cnt* and *bsr*.

● The fifth statement (which continues to line nine) writes the *cnt* and *mon* values into one row of an HTML table.

● The last statement marks the end of the loop.

To see how all this fits together in a Web page, carry out the following procedure:

1 Open the sample Web installed from the companion CD.

2 Open the Web page *ch30/custbrow.asp*.

3 Click the HTML tab at the bottom of the Page view window.

Figure 30-13 shows how the finished page looks in a browser. Because this is an ASP page, and because it makes use of FrontPage usage information:

● The page must reside on a server-based Web.

● The server-based Web must reside on a Windows NT 4 system with Internet Information Server installed, or on a Windows 2000 system with Internet Information Services installed.

● The folder where the ASP page resides must be marked executable.

● The Web server must conform to all the requirements listed in the troubleshooting sidebar, "Top 10 List doesn't display any data."

By the way, all seven files listed in Table 30-2 use the same format. Therefore, to display a different report, simply change the file name in the following statement to another file name from Table 30-2:

```
xmlDoc.Load (Server.MapPath("../_vti_pvt/_x_browsers.xml"))
```

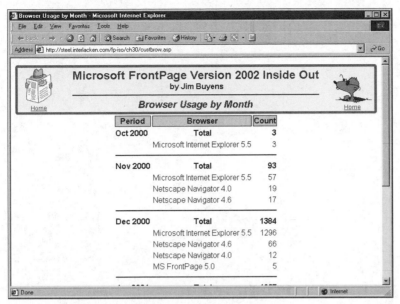

Figure 30-13. This Web page reports usage data the FrontPage Server Extensions extracted from Web server log files and stored in XML format.

In Summary...

This chapter explained two forms of Web-based Usage reporting available in FrontPage: the Hit Counter component and Top 10 Lists. It also explained how to extend these features with scripting.

The next chapter explains how to create HTML forms that display input fields in a Web visitor's browser, how to send any data the visitor enters to the Web server, and how to make the Web server process the data as you want.

Using Forms and Databases

Creating and Using Forms

Pages that collect input data are a familiar feature of the Web. Visitors use forms to identify themselves, submit search terms, make purchases, file comments or complaints, and perform virtually any kind of task that requires entering data and submitting it for processing. If you've ever used a Web page that included text boxes, check boxes, drop-down lists, submit buttons, and the like, you've used an HTML form.

Microsoft FrontPage can create HTML forms as easily as it creates any other sort of Web content. You just set the insertion point, choose the type of object you want from a menu, and move on to the next task. Each form field does require configuration, of course, as does the entire form. This chapter and the next two explain all these details.

This chapter deals primarily with individual form fields: what types are available, what types are best for a given job, and what configuration each type of field requires. Chapter 32 explains how to tell the Web server what to do with any data that Web visitors submit. Chapter 33 explains how to use the database capabilities built in to FrontPage.

Creating and Modifying HTML Forms

An HTML form is a bounded area of a Web page that contains objects for data input and buttons for data submission. Figure 31-1 provides an example.

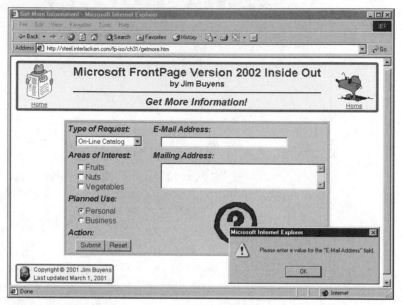

Figure 31-1. This page shows a typical HTML form. It collects data from the Web visitor and submits it to some process.

Here are some useful facts about HTML forms:

● Each form occupies a specific area on a Web page. A single Web page can contain one or more forms.

● Within each form are one or more form elements. Table 31-1 lists the available types.

● Each element on the form has a name and a value. The name internally identifies the input field, whereas the value reflects its current value.

● One element in the form—either a push button or picture-form field— must act as the submit button. When the Web visitor clicks this element, the browser:

  ■ Encodes all the element names and values in the form.

  ■ Transmits the data to a Web server for processing. The form's Action property contains a URL (referred to as the *Action URL*) that starts the necessary program on the Web server.

Table 31-1. **Form Element Types**

Description	Typical uses
Text Box	Short, one-line text strings.
Text Area	Multiple-line text, such as suggestions or comments.
File Upload	Uploading a file. The visitor types a file name by hand or uses a browse button to locate the file.
Check Box	Independent fields having only two values, such as yes/no or true/false.
Option Button	A list of choices where only one at a time can be selected.
Group Box	A titled border that surrounds a group of related fields.
Drop-Down Box	A list of choices. A Web visitor can select one listed item or several, depending on restrictions set by the page creator. If the menu is sized so that only one choice is visible, a button at the right drops it down to permit selection. If the menu is sized so that two or more choices are visible, a scroll bar replaces the drop-down button.
Push Button	A button that transmits the form contents to the *Action URL*, clears the form, or invokes a script.
Advanced Button	A button that works like an ordinary push button but can display HTML content on its face.
Picture Form Field	A picture that, when clicked, transmits the form contents to the *Action URL*.
Label	An invisible element that surrounds a form field and its title. Clicking the title is then equivalent to clicking the form field.
Hidden	An invisible element the browser transmits with the *Action URL*.

Figure 31-2 on the next page illustrates the appearance of the visible form fields with one exception: the picture form field. A picture form field looks like any other picture.

The original—and still the most common—way of processing HTML forms is submitting them to programs that run on a Web server. More recently, script languages like Microsoft VBScript and JavaScript have also gained access to form elements. Script code can respond to form-element events such as gaining focus, losing focus, mouse pointer movements, and clicking. (Scripts running on the browser can't directly access resources or update files on the server, but they *can* send requests to the server, just as clicking a push button can.)

 For more information about using browser scripts, refer to "Scripting Web Pages on the Browser" in the Bonus Content on the Companion CD.

> **note** *Browser scripts* are small blocks of program code that appear within HTML and ex-
> ecute on the Web visitor's computer. The capabilities of browser scripts are intention-
> ally limited for security reasons, but two capabilities they retain are setting
> form-element properties and responding to form-element events.

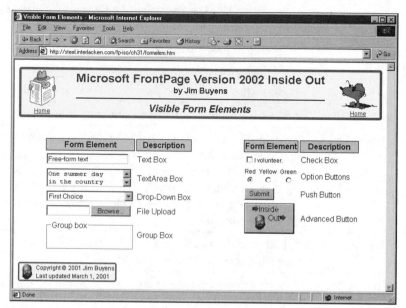

Figure 31-2. This Web page shows the appearance of each visible form field element.

Drawing Forms in FrontPage

FrontPage can easily add forms and form elements to your Web pages. To add an
HTML form to any Web page:

1 Set the insertion point where you want the first form element to appear,
choose Form from the Insert menu, and then choose Form from the resulting
menu. This creates a form, indicated in FrontPage by dashed lines, containing only a Submit and a Reset button.

2 For each element you want in the form, choose Form from the Insert menu,
and select the type of form element you want.

> **tip** If you add a form element outside any existing HTML form, Front Page will create a
> new form that surrounds the new form element.

Form elements appear in line with text. Thus, to put two form elements on different
lines, you must insert a paragraph ending or line break between them. To line up form
elements horizontally or vertically with others—or with surrounding HTML objects—

organize them into a table. One common approach is to place field captions and corresponding form elements in consecutive columns. Another is to place each caption and field element pair within a single cell.

To expand the form, simply add more content—whether it's text, pictures, tables, more form elements, or any other valid objects. You can add content by direct insertion, by dragging, or by cutting and pasting. To create a second, separate form, insert a form element *outside* the boundaries of the existing form.

Figure 31-3 shows the form of Figure 31-1 open in FrontPage. The gray background and raised edges come from an HTML table and not from the form itself.

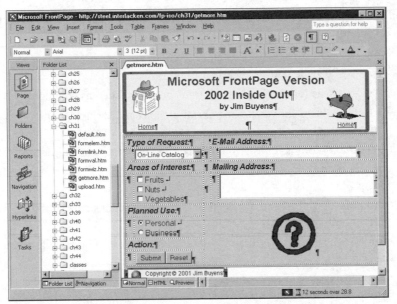

Figure 31-3. FrontPage created the form pictured in Figure 31-1.

Creating an HTML form visually is only part of the job. You must also:

- Configure the properties of both the form itself and each form element. The next section in this chapter describes how.

- Provide a way to process the data after it reaches the Web server. Chapters 32 and 33 will provide the details.

Nothing prevents you from adding two or more HTML forms to a single Web page. However, submitting a form transmits only the form field values inside that form. If you want a Submit button to transmit all the form field values on a Web page, make sure the page contains only one form and that all the form field elements appear within that form.

A single HTML form can contain any number of Submit buttons. A program on the Web server can tell which button the visitor clicked, based on the button's Name property.

Choosing and Arranging Form Elements

Some general guidelines will help you choose form element types and arrange them effectively:

- Place required fields, key fields, and other important fields near the upper left area of the form to give them top prominence.
- Group fields in naturally expected sequences such as Name, Address, City, State/Province, ZIP Code/Postal Code.
- Group related fields by placing them close together. Make the groups distinct by using white space, indentation, or picture elements.
- Put lengthy fields—such as comments or special instructions—at the bottom of the form.
- Use ordinary HTML text for field captions.
- Use text boxes for single fields consisting of plain text.
- Use text areas for multiple lines of free-form text, such as comments.
- Use check boxes for yes/no or true/false choices. Checked means Yes or True. For a list of yes/no items, use a series of check boxes.
- Use option buttons for lists where only one item at a time can be selected.
- Use drop-down boxes that allow multiple selections as a substitute for check boxes.
- Use drop-down boxes that permit only single selections as a substitute for option buttons.
- Use HTML tables to align captions and form elements horizontally and vertically.
- If groupings appear repeatedly—such as an order form requiring a similar group of fields for each item ordered—create an HTML table with a row for each grouping and a column for each field.
- Put the Submit and Reset buttons at the bottom of the form. This provides some assurance that the visitor has reviewed the entire form before submitting it.

Setting Form Element Properties

There are three ways to modify the basic properties of a form element:

- **Double-clicking.** Double-click the element you want to modify.
- **Right-clicking.** Right-click the element you want to modify, and then choose Form Field Properties from the shortcut menu.

864

● **Clicking.** Select the element you want to modify, and then choose Properties from the Format menu.

● **Using keystrokes.** Select the form element you want to modify, and then press Alt+Enter.

The dialog box you see depends on the type of form element. The "Form Element Properties" section later in this chapter discusses the dialog boxes for each type of form element.

Validating Form Input

Most applications involving HTML forms require constraints on form input. Quite often, for example, it's an error to leave certain fields blank. Other fields must conform to certain patterns—a U.S. Postal Service ZIP code, for example, should consist of five numeric digits.

FrontPage supports these requirements with a feature called *validation.* In FrontPage, the page designer specifies value constraints using convenient dialog boxes. FrontPage then enforces these constraints by adding JavaScript or VBScript code to the Web page. If the visitor violates the constraints, the browser transmits no data to the server but instead displays an error message. Figure 31-1 provides an example of this.

Validation is available for text boxes, drop-down boxes, and option buttons. Check boxes have only two values, both presumably valid, and therefore need no validation. Similarly, there's no validation for either push buttons or picture form fields because there's no wrong way to click them.

The Advanced tab of the Web Settings dialog box controls the language FrontPage uses when creating script code. The setting that governs validation script code is the Client drop-down list in the Default Scripting Language section. Choosing JavaScript or VBScript instructs FrontPage to create validation scripts in those languages.

on the CD For more information about the Advanced tab of the Web Settings dialog box, refer to "Controlling Advanced Web Settings" in the Bonus Content on the Companion CD.

caution VBScript validation scripts won't work in Netscape Navigator versions 4 and earlier. Check later versions for compatibility.

To specify validation rules for a form element that supports them, open the form field's Properties dialog box and click Validate. The following sections about each form element discuss the applicable validation rule settings.

Controlling Form Element Properties

You can change the position of an existing form element by dragging or by cutting and pasting. For other kinds of changes, however, you'll need to display the element's Properties dialog box by right-clicking the element and choosing Form Field Properties.

The following fields appear in nearly every dialog box that controls the properties of a form element:

- **Name.** For a given field to be processed, you must give it the name expected by the script or server-side form handler. If you—rather than the form-handling programmer—get to name the field, use short, lowercase names with no special characters or hyphens.

- **Tab Order.** Many form elements have a Tab Order field. This property controls the order in which fields receive the focus when the visitor presses the Tab key. The current field receives the focus after any fields with lower tab-order values, but before any fields with higher values. It's a mark of good design when form fields receive the focus in sensible order.

- **Style.** Click this button to specify CSS properties for the element.

> For information on CSS, refer to Chapter 20, "Managing Appearance with Cascading Style Sheets."

The following sections describe the available settings and validation rules for each type of HTML form element.

Setting Text Box Properties

Figure 31-4 displays the Properties dialog box for a text box. This dialog box provides the following entries:

- **Name.** Specify an internal name for the text box.

- **Initial Value.** Supply a data value, that should appear when the browser initially displays the form or when the Web visitor clicks the Reset button.

- **Width In Characters.** Specify the width of the field in typical display characters. You can also change the width of a text box by selecting it and then dragging the handles on its left or right side.

- **Password Field.** Select Yes if you want the browser to display asterisks in place of whatever characters the visitor actually types. Otherwise, select No.

Clicking the Validate button in the Text Box Properties dialog box displays the Text Box Validation dialog box shown in Figure 31-5. This figure is actually a composite shown with all fields active, for clarity; in practice, one or more fields will be dimmed, depending on the Data Type you select.

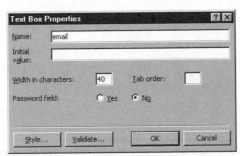

Figure 31-4. Use this dialog box to modify the properties of a text box.

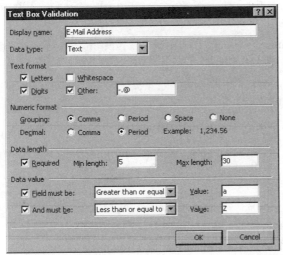

Figure 31-5. This dialog box sets constraints on values entered in a text box.

These are the available properties:

- **Display Name.** Enter a name that will appear in error messages. Normally, this should agree with the text box's caption on the Web page. If you don't specify a display name, error messages will use the internal name from the Text Box Properties dialog box shown in Figure 31-4.

- **Data Type.** Specify the type of data the text box can contain:

    - **No Constraints.** Select this option if the text box can contain any type of data.

    - **Text.** Select this option if the text box can contain alphanumeric or linguistic expressions.

    - **Integer.** Select this option if the text box can contain only whole numbers.

    - **Number.** Select this option if the text box can contain only whole or decimal numbers.

Chapter 31

- **Text Format.** Indicate what kinds of text characters are valid. FrontPage enables this section only if the Data Type is Text.

    - **Letters.** Select this check box if alphabetic characters are valid.

    - **Digits.** Select this check box if numeric characters are valid.

    - **Whitespace.** Select this check box if spaces, tabs, carriage returns, and line feeds are all acceptable.

    - **Other.** Select this check box if any additional characters are acceptable. Enter the acceptable characters in the text box provided.

- **Numeric Format.** Set the format of numbers. FrontPage enables this section only if the Data Type is Integer or Number.

    - **Grouping.** Indicate which characters, in addition to numeric digits, are valid in a numeric field.

        - **Comma.** Means the comma character is permissible, as in 12,345,678.

        - **Period.** Means the period character is permissible, as in 12.345.678.

        - **Space.** Means the space character is permissible, as in 12 345 678.

        - **None.** Means that no punctuation is permissible, as in 12345678.

    - **Decimal.** Indicates which character is acceptable as a decimal point. FrontPage dims this field if Data Type is Integer. Note that the grouping character and the decimal character can't be the same.

        - **Comma.** Means the comma is acceptable as a decimal point.

        - **Period.** Means the period is acceptable as a decimal point.

- **Data Length.** Set the length restrictions on data entered in the text box.

    - **Required.** Select this box if the visitor can't leave the text box blank.

    - **Min Length.** Specify the fewest characters the text box can contain.

    - **Max Length.** Specify the most characters the text box can contain.

- **Data Value.** Use these properties to set range constraints on the text box values. If the data type is Number or Integer, FrontPage uses numeric comparisons. If the data type is Text or No Constraints, FrontPage uses alphabetic comparisons.

    - **Field Must Be.** To set a range limit on the value Web visitors enter, select this check box and then specify a comparison and a boundary value. The available comparisons are Less Than, Greater Than, Less Than Or Equal To, Greater Than Or Equal To, Equal To, and Not Equal To.

▨ **Value.** Specify the boundary value. Comparison against this value must be true or an error occurs. If, for example, Field Must Be reads *Greater Than 10* and the visitor enters *9*, the visitor gets an error message.

▨ **And Must Be.** Select this check box and specify a comparison to enforce a second range limit on the value in the text box. The Value property on this line works as it does with the Field Must Be drop-down list.

Setting TextArea Box Properties

The dialog box for changing the properties of a TextArea box appears in Figure 31-6.

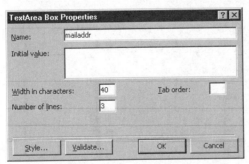

Figure 31-6. Use this dialog box to modify the properties of a TextArea box.

The available properties are the following:

● **Name.** Designates an internal name for the TextArea box.

● **Initial Value.** Supplies a data value that appears when the browser first displays the form or when the visitor clicks the Reset button.

● **Width In Characters.** Sets the width of the TextArea box in units of typical display characters.

● **Number Of Lines.** Sets the height of the TextArea box in lines.

> **tip** You can change the Width In Characters and Number Of Lines properties of a TextArea box by selecting the box and then dragging its handles.

● **Validate.** Displays the same Text Box Validation dialog box as for text boxes. Refer to the previous section for details.

Setting Check Box Properties

The dialog box shown in Figure 31-7 controls the properties of a check box. The following properties are available:

- **Name.** Give the check box an internal name.

- **Value.** Specify a string the browser will transmit to the server or script if the check box is selected. If the check box configured in Figure 31-7 is selected when the visitor clicks Submit, the browser transmits *fruits=on.* If not, the browser sends neither the name nor the value.

- **Initial State.** Specifies how the browser should initialize the check box—selected (Checked) or cleared (Not Checked)—when it first displays the form or later responds to the press of a Reset button.

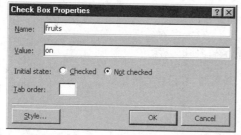

Figure 31-7. This dialog box controls the properties of a check box.

Setting Option Button Properties

Like lobbyists, heartaches, and rock-band aficionados, option buttons appear in groups. Of all option buttons in a group, only one at a time can be selected. No other HTML form elements interact this way.

> **note** The official HTML term for an option button is *radio button.*

The grouping mechanism for option buttons within a form is quite simple: all buttons with the same name are in the same group. Conversely, to group a set of option buttons, give them all the same name.

Assigning duplicate names to form elements is usually an error, but in the case of option buttons it's a necessity. Each like-named option button, however, must have a different value so the server can determine which button was selected when the Web visitor clicked Submit. The browser transmits the selected option button's value and no others.

Figure 31-8 shows the Properties dialog box for option buttons.

Figure 31-8. This is the Option Button Properties dialog box.

It provides access to the following settings:

● **Group Name.** Specify an internal name for the option buttons. Be sure to give each option button in the same group the same name.

● **Value.** Designate the string the browser will transmit if the visitor selects this option button before clicking Submit. Be sure to give each option button in the same group a different value.

● **Initial State.** Specify how to initialize the option button—Selected or Not Selected—when the browser first displays it or when the visitor clicks the Reset button.

note Setting the initial state of one option button to Selected sets the initial state of all other buttons in the same group to Not Selected.

● **Validate.** Displays the Option Button Validation dialog box that appears in Figure 31-9.

  ■ **Display Name.** Gives the button group a name that will appear in error messages. This option is dimmed unless the following check box is selected.

  ■ **Data Required.** Displays, if selected, an error if the visitor clicks Submit and no option buttons in the group are selected.

Figure 31-9. This is the Validation dialog box for option buttons.

Normally, a visitor can't clear all the option buttons in a group. The only way to clear a button is to select another button in the same group. It's possible, however, to have all option buttons in a group cleared when first displayed. This, together with the Data Required validation rule, ensures that the visitor made a conscious choice and didn't simply take the default.

Changing the validation rules for one option button automatically changes them for all buttons in the same group.

Setting Drop-Down Box Properties

The Properties dialog box for drop-down boxes appears in Figure 31-10.

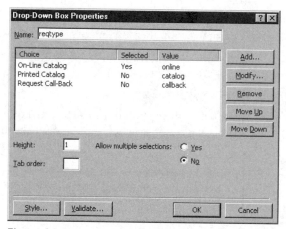

Figure 31-10. Use this dialog box to control property settings of drop-down boxes.

It offers access to the following settings:

- **Name.** Assign an internal name to the drop-down box.

- **Choice-Selected-Value.** This table contains a row for each entry in the drop-down box. Use the five buttons at the right to make changes:

  - **Add.** Click this button to display the Add Choice dialog box, which contains the same choices as the one in Figure 31-11. Configure the following options:

    - **Choice.** Specify the text the browser will display to the Web visitor.

    - **Specify Value.** This box controls the value the browser transmits if the current choice is selected when the visitor clicks the Submit button:

      If you select the box, the browser transmits the value in the associated text box.

If you clear the box, the browser transmits the value in the Choice box.

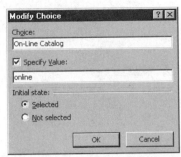

Figure 31-11. The Add Choice and Modify Choice dialog boxes contain identical fields for adding or modifying entries in a drop-down box.

◆ **Initial State.** Indicate whether the browser should select the current choice when it first displays the drop-down box or when the visitor clicks Reset. There are two settings: Selected and Not Selected.

   If the Allow Multiple Selections option described on the next page and shown in Figure 31-10 is No, setting the initial state of one choice to Selected also sets the initial state of all other choices to Not Selected.

▪ **Modify.** Click this button to alter the currently selected choice. When the dialog box shown in Figure 31-11 appears, make any desired changes and then click OK.

● **Remove.** Click this button to delete the currently selected choice.

● **Move Up.** Click this button to move the currently selected choice one position higher in the list.

● **Move Down.** Click this button to move the currently selected choice one position lower in the list.

● **Height.** Specify the height of the displayed list in lines. A one-line list has a drop-down button at the right. Lists two or more lines high have scroll bars at the right.

   You can also change the height of a drop-down box by selecting it and then dragging the handles on its top or bottom side.

note Microsoft Windows displays a drop-down box with a height of one as a drop-down box. Windows displays drop-down boxes with heights greater than one as scrollable list boxes.

- **Allow Multiple Selections.** Click No if the visitor should select only one choice at a time. Click Yes if the visitor can select two or more items simultaneously.

- **Validate.** Displays the Drop-Down Box Validation dialog box shown in Figure 31-12.

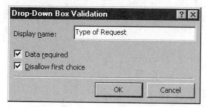

Figure 31-12. This is the Validation dialog box for drop-down boxes.

The following options are available:

- **Display Name.** Give the drop-down box a name that will appear in error messages.

- **Data Required.** Select this check box if the browser should display an error message when the visitor clicks Submit and no choices in the drop-down box are selected. A drop-down box can have zero selections in two circumstances:

    - When the browser initially displays the form and, in the Drop-Down Box Properties dialog box, you didn't set any Selected values to Yes.

    - When you set Allow Multiple Selections to Yes and the visitor Ctrl+clicks the last selected choice.

- **Disallow First Choice.** Select this check box if the browser should display an error message when the visitor clicks Submit and the first choice in the drop-down box is selected.

    This setting is appropriate when the first menu choice is actually a prompt to select a different choice. This ensures that the visitor makes a conscious choice and doesn't simply accept the default.

Setting Push Button Properties

Figure 31-13 shows the dialog box for push buttons. The following options are available:

- **Name.** Give the push button an internal name.

- **Value/Label.** Enter the text, if any, for the button's visible caption.

If the push button has both a Name and a Value/Label, the browser transmits the name=value pair when the Web visitor clicks the button. This tells the Web server which of several buttons the visitor clicked.

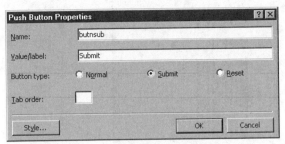

Figure 31-13. This dialog box controls push button properties.

- **Button Type.** Specify the type of push button.

  - **Normal.** Click this option if the button neither submits nor resets the form. This is normally the correct choice when a browser-side script will respond to the button. Choosing this button type sets the default label to Button.

  - **Submit.** Click this option if clicking the button should submit the form. Choosing this button type sets the default label to Submit.

  - **Reset.** Click this option if clicking the button should reset the form to its initial state. Choosing this button type sets the default label to Reset.

There are no validation features for push buttons—either you click a push button or you don't.

Setting Picture Form Field Properties

A picture form field works much like a Submit push button. Clicking a picture form field submits the form's data using the form's *Action URL*.

To insert a picture form field, choose Form from the Insert menu in FrontPage, and then select Picture. Using the Picture command inserts only an ordinary picture (that you designate in the resulting Picture dialog box), even when inserting into a form area.

Figure 31-14 on the next page shows the dialog box for setting the properties of a picture form field. The Name property on the Form Field tab identifies the picture form field and is transmitted to the server when the Web visitor clicks the picture. No validation is available. The remaining tabs are the same as those shown in the Picture Properties dialog box described in Chapter 11.

For more information about the Picture Properties dialog box, refer to "Modifying Picture Properties" on page 337.

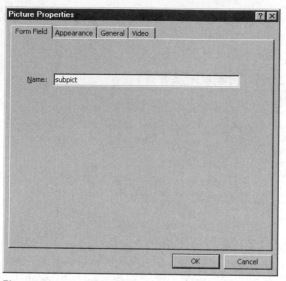

Figure 31-14. This dialog box controls the properties of picture form fields.

Setting Label Properties

Normally, the text that visually identifies form elements to the Web visitor is just that: ordinary text. Only visual proximity associates the label with its control.

HTML *labels* associate a form field's descriptive text with the form field itself. Clicking the descriptive text then has the same effect as clicking the form field. To "officially" designate text as the label of an HTML form element:

1 Enter the label text inside the HTML form and directly adjacent to the form element. If you want the label above or below the form element, separate them with a line break.

2 Select both the text and the form element.

3 Choose Form from the Insert menu, and then select Label.

This designates the selected text as the selected control's label. In Normal view, Page view displays a thin dotted line surrounding the text. In HTML view, you'll see a *<label>* tag preceding the text you selected and referencing the internal name of the form element.

To remove the label designation, select the label, choose Form from the Insert menu, and then select Label as you did before.

Setting Advanced Button Properties

If plain text labels on push buttons don't satisfy your needs (or your tastes), consider creating an advanced button. An advanced button can contain any HTML content you like on its face; otherwise, it works exactly like an ordinary push button.

When you first add an advanced button to a form, it looks like this:

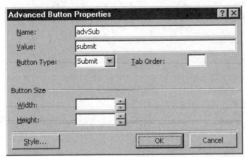

The black highlighting indicates that the Type Here text is selected. Typing into this area modifies the button's caption just as though you were typing into any other area. You can also modify text styles, insert tables and pictures, and so forth. Figures 31-2 and 31-16 both show highly stylized advanced buttons.

Right-clicking an advanced button and choosing Advanced Button Properties from the shortcut menu displays (what else?) the Advanced Button Properties dialog box shown in Figure 31-15.

Figure 31-15. The properties of an advanced button are very similar to those of an ordinary push button.

This dialog box controls the following properties:

- **Name.** Supply an internal name for the advanced button.

- **Value.** This option appears to serve no purpose. Whether you enter anything in this field or not, the browser transmits a value containing all the HTML inside the advanced button.

- **Button Type.** Specify what function the advanced button performs.

  - **Normal.** Click this option if the button neither submits nor resets the form.

  - **Submit.** Click this option if clicking the button should submit the form. This is the default.

  - **Reset.** Click this option if clicking the button should reset the form to its initial state.

877

● **Button Size.** These two properties are optional. If you leave them blank, the browser makes the advanced button just large enough to surround your content:

■ **Width.** Give the advanced button a specific width in pixels.

■ **Height.** Give the advanced button a specific height in pixels.

You can also change the width of an advanced button by selecting it and then dragging the handles on any side.

Figure 31-16 shows an HTML form that contains two advanced buttons. Unfortunately, Netscape Navigator, at least through version 4, doesn't display advanced buttons. It displays any HTML you put on the button face, but not the button. Ordinarily this would limit use of advanced buttons to environments that run Microsoft Internet Explorer exclusively. But in this case, there's a workaround: Simply code a conventional button *inside* the advanced button.

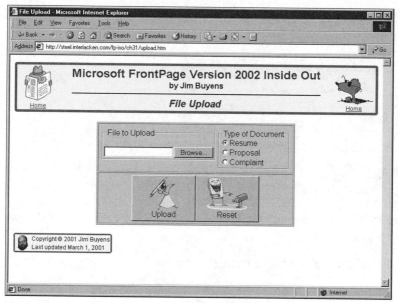

Figure 31-16. This Web page illustrates the file upload element, two group boxes, and two advanced buttons.

Here's the reason this works:

● Browsers capable of displaying advanced buttons ignore any regular buttons found within them.

● Browsers that can't display advanced buttons still detect and display all the HTML you supply for the button face. This includes any regular buttons.

Figure 31-17 shows the same Web page open in FrontPage. FrontPage displays both the advanced button and the regular button. Just be sure, if you decide to do this, that you configure the standard button and the advanced button with all the same properties. The standard button *doesn't* inherit the properties of the advanced button.

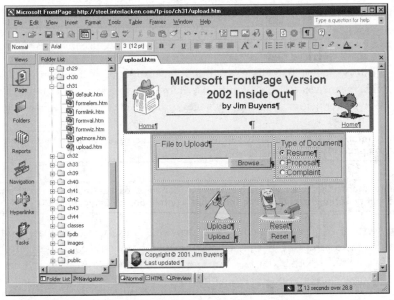

Figure 31-17. Note the ordinary push buttons within the two advanced buttons. No browser displays both buttons.

Setting Group Box Properties

This form element is entirely cosmetic. It provides a shaded and titled border that surrounds any content you place within it. The File To Upload and Type Of Document boxes in Figure 31-16 are group boxes.

When you first insert a group box, it contains no content. You can add content by dragging elements into it, by cutting and pasting, or by setting the insertion point within the group box and using any of the standard FrontPage insert commands.

To change the title of a group box, set the insertion point inside the text and edit as usual. To change the title, CSS style, or text alignment of a group box, right-click it and choose Group Box Properties from the shortcut menu.

InsideOut

The group box has one annoying habit: It fills the entire space—from left to right—that contains it. This means that if you insert it normally on a Web page, it fills the entire width of the page. To make the group box narrower, place it inside a table cell. That way, the group box fills the table cell instead of the entire width of the page.

newfeature!
Setting File Upload Properties

This component provides a way for Web visitors to upload files to your Web. This immediately raises issues of data security. You don't want Web visitors randomly or maliciously replacing your Web's content, and you don't want them uploading programs that run on your Web server. The file upload element therefore involves two restrictions:

- Visitors can't upload files to Webs that have anonymous browsing enabled. This means visitors must enter a username and password acceptable to the Web server before accessing any pages in that Web.

> For more information about security settings for FrontPage-based Webs, refer to "Managing Users" on page 1107.

 For more information about security settings for FrontPage-based Webs, refer to "Controlling Web Security Through FrontPage" in the Bonus Content on the Companion CD.

- A visitor can upload files only after providing a username and password that have authoring permissions to the Web that would contain the uploaded file. In other words, if you can open a Web in FrontPage and make changes, you can upload files. Otherwise, you can't.

These limitations are serious but necessary. They prevent unknown visitors from uploading documents such as resumes or proposals. On the other hand, the file upload element is perfectly adequate for SharePoint team Web sites. And in fact, this seems to be the environment that Microsoft provided the file upload element to serve.

When displayed in FrontPage or a Web page, the file upload element looks very much like two form elements together: a text box and a push button titled Browse. Figures 31-2 and 31-16 both show examples of file upload elements. Figure 31-18 shows the File Upload Properties dialog box, which you can display in all the usual ways.

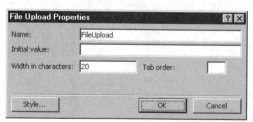

Figure 31-18. This dialog box controls file upload properties.

This dialog box controls the following options:

- **Name.** Specify an internal name for the file upload element.

- **Initial Value.** This field appears to serve no purpose. Whether you enter anything in this field or not, the file upload text box initially displays nothing.

Clicking the Browse button displays a default location, not a location you specify here. In short, the Web visitor, and not the designer, picks the file to upload.

● **Width In Characters.** Specify the width of the file upload element in typical display characters.

You can also change the width of a file upload element by selecting it and then dragging the handles on its left or right side.

Configuring the file upload element requires configuring HTML form properties as well as file upload element properties.

> For more information about configuring form properties for the file upload element, refer to "Configuring File Upload Options" on page 904.

newfeature! Using the List Form and List Field Elements

These two form elements work only in the context of SharePoint team Web sites.

> For more information about using the List Form and List Field elements, refer to "Creating Custom List Pages" on page 1011.

Using Hidden Form Fields

Hidden form fields have both their names and their values hard-coded into the HTML. The Web visitor can neither see nor alter these fields; they're totally under the page designer's control. Hidden fields usually contain application data that's constant or parameters that control the actions of a server-side program. This permits changing the behavior of the server-side program through changes to the HTML—a much easier process than changing the program itself.

Here's the procedure for adding, changing, and deleting hidden form fields:

1 Display the Form Properties dialog box by using either of these methods:

  ■ Right-click anywhere in the form and then choose Form Properties from the shortcut menu.

  ■ Select anything in the form, then choose Form from the Insert menu, and then choose Form Properties.

2 Click the Advanced button on the Form Properties dialog box. This displays the Advanced Form Properties dialog box shown in Figure 31-19 on the next page. In this dialog box:

  ■ To add a hidden field:

    a Click Add.

b When the Name/Value Pair dialog box appears, enter the hidden field's name and value in the respective text boxes, and click OK.

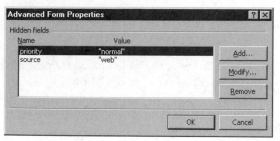

Figure 31-19. This dialog box maintains hidden fields on an HTML form.

■ To change a hidden field:

a Select the field to change, and click Modify.

b When the Name/Value Pair dialog box appears, correct the field value, and click OK.

■ To delete a hidden field, select it and click Remove.

Using the Form Page Wizard

FrontPage provides a wizard to help you get started creating HTML forms. This wizard has so many options that only a representative sample appears here.

The Form Page Wizard is unlikely to produce a finished page tailored to your complete satisfaction, but it can give you a good starting point or at least some quick ideas. If you don't like the initial results, keep rerunning the wizard with different options until results improve.

To run the wizard:

1 Display the Page Templates dialog box using either of these methods:

■ Choose New from the File menu, and then select Page Or Web. When the New Page Or Web task pane appears, click Page Templates.

■ Click the drop-down arrow next to the New Page button on the Standard toolbar, and then choose Page.

New Page

2 When the Page Templates dialog box appears, on the General tab, choose Form Page Wizard and click OK.

3 When the Form Page Wizard displays its banner page, click Next to display the dialog box shown in the left side of Figure 31-20. This dialog box contains a list of the major questions the form asks. To add questions, click Add to display the dialog box shown at the right of Figure 31-20.

4 From the list at the top of the right dialog box in Figure 31-20, select the type of input to collect for the current question. In the text box at the bottom, review the suggested prompt and make any necessary changes. Click Next.

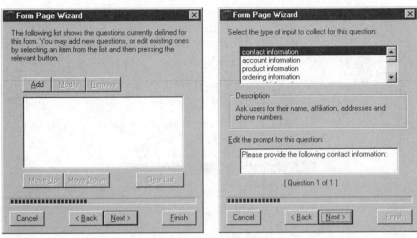

Figure 31-20. These dialog boxes build a list of major questions for the Web visitor and prompt the designer for the type of input to collect for each question.

5 The left side of Figure 31-21 displays a typical dialog box the wizard might display next. Each type of input in the previous step results in a different dialog box with different options in this step. Select the items you want to collect, revise the base name for those items if necessary, and then click Next.

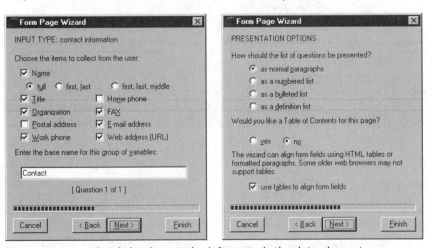

Figure 31-21. The dialog box at the left controls the data elements a form collects from the visitor. This dialog box at the right controls high-level aspects of form page layout.

6 Repeat steps 3, 4, and 5 as often as necessary to collect all the input you need. To start over, click Clear List in the dialog box shown at the left of Figure 31-20. When finished, click Next.

7 When the dialog box shown at the right of Figure 31-21 appears, indicate how you want the list of questions presented, whether you want a table of contents, and whether to use tables for form field alignment. Click Next when finished.

8 The next dialog box, pictured in Figure 31-22, controls how you want to capture the input fields you've specified. The following options are available:

■ **Save Results To A Web Page.** Appends the data to a Web page whenever a visitor submits the form.

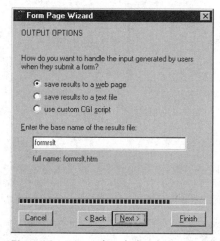

Figure 31-22. This dialog box controls how form data is saved.

■ **Save Results To A Text File.** Saves submitted data in a text file on the server. Various programs can import data from such files at a later time.

■ **Use Custom CGI Script.** Assumes a Web programmer will write a custom process to store the data.

■ **Enter The Base Name Of The Results File.** Designates the name of the Web page or text file (minus the *.htm* or *.txt* filename extension) where the Web server saves the data. Specify a relative location inside your Web or an absolute path in the Web server's file system. If you choose Use Custom CGI Script, this field is dimmed.

For details on saving form results, refer to "Setting HTML Form Properties" on page 893.

> **caution** The options Save Results To A Web Page and Save Results To A Text File use facilities in the FrontPage Server Extensions. Make sure the extensions are installed on any Web servers you plan to use, and check that your application is properly configured.

9 Clicking Next once more displays the final dialog box in the Form Page Wizard, which has no input fields. You can use the Back and Next buttons to review and correct your work. When done, click Finish to create the page as specified.

10 FrontPage will display the new page in Page view but won't save it. Make any further edits you think are necessary and then either discard the work and start over or save the page in the usual way.

Figure 31-23 and Figure 31-24, on the next page, show typical results from running the Form Page Wizard. Rerun the wizard as often as necessary to optimize results, and then finalize layout and appearance by editing the page directly. It's a good idea to test data collection features often. This makes it easy to localize and correct any errors.

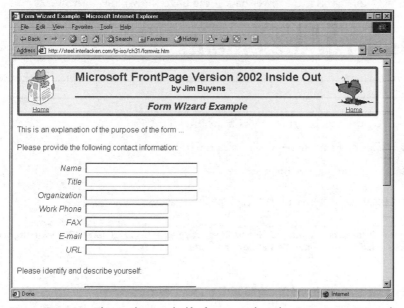

Figure 31-23. This is the top half of a page that the Form Page Wizard created.

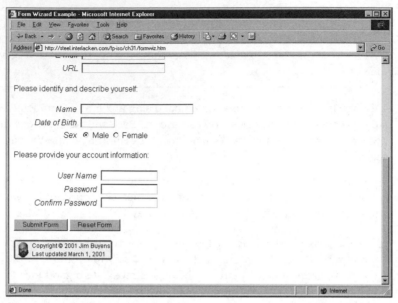

Figure 31-24. This is the lower half of the page shown in Figure 31-23.

Scripting Form Elements

There are many aspects to working with form elements with scripts, but three in particular deserve mention here:

- Responding to form events on the browser.

- Reading form element values on the browser.

- Recycling form element values.

The next three sections address each of these issues.

For more information about working with script code, refer to Chapter 42, "Working with Script Code," in the Bonus Content on the Companion CD.

Responding to Form Events on the Browser

In a perfect world, every element on a Web page would trigger a standardized and uniform list of events: *onClick, onChange, onMouseOver, onMouseOut,* and so forth. Sadly, in the real world, the available triggers vary depending on the type of browser, the browser version, and the element type. Fortunately, support for the following events is nearly universal as they pertain to visible form elements:

- *onClick.* This event occurs when the Web visitor clicks the form element with the mouse pointer.

● *onChange.* This event occurs when the Web visitor changes the value of a form element:

■ **Check boxes** and **option buttons.** For these items, an *onChange* event occurs as soon as the visitor clicks the form element.

■ **Text boxes.** The *onChange* event occurs when the element loses the focus and its value is different than it was upon gaining the focus.

■ **Drop-down boxes.** The *onChange* event occurs when the visitor releases the mouse button and the element's value is different than it was upon gaining the focus.

To write code that responds to these events, simply add the corresponding values to their HTML tags. For example, here's the HTML for a push button that jumps to a configured Web page:

```
<input type="button" value="Home" name="btnHome"
       onclick="window.location.href = '../'">
```

When the visitor clicks this button, the browser displays the default page in the current page's parent folder (because the relative URL is ../).

For another example that uses the *onClick* event, refer to "Scripting the Microsoft Calendar Control" on page 732.

Here are some additional tips for using the *onClick* and *onChange* events effectively:

● Code the *onChange* event the same way as the *onClick* event; that is, switch to HTML view and add an *onChange* attribute to the tag.

● The *onChange* event for push buttons is meaningless. Use the *onClick* event instead.

● You can put only one line of JavaScript code inside an *onClick* or *onChange* attribute value. To preserve your own sanity and that of whoever succeeds you, put lengthy code in a function located elsewhere and just put the function call in the *onClick* or *onChange* attribute.

Reading Form Element Values on the Browser

A script running on the browser can interactively read and modify the values of form elements. The expression you must use, however, varies with the type of element.

● **Text box** and **TextArea box.** Read or write the *value* property as shown:

```
document.<form-name>.<element-name>.value
```

● **Check box.** The *checked* property is *true* if the box is selected and *false* if it's cleared. Use the following expression to access this property:

```
document.<form-name>.<element-name>.checked
```

● **Option buttons.** The *checked* property is *true* if a particular option is selected and *false* if it's cleared. Use the following expression to access this property:

```
document.<form-name>.<element-name>[<subscript>].checked
```

The first option with a given group name has subscript zero. The next option having the same group name has subscript one, and so forth. The alert box in Figure 31-25 shows an example of this in action.

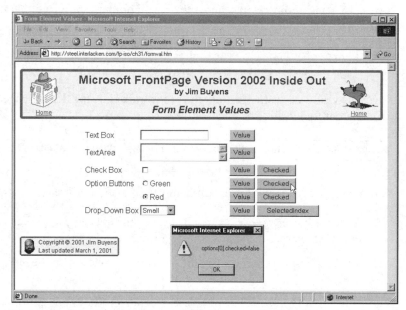

Figure 31-25. This Web page from the sample Web shows how browser-side scripts can query form field values.

The following expression displays whatever you entered in the Value box of the Option Button Properties dialog box for a particular option button. However, this value doesn't change depending on which button the visitor selects:

```
document.<form-name>.<element-name>[<subscript>].value
```

● **Drop-down box.** The *selectedIndex* property indicates which entry in the list is currently selected. If the first entry is selected, *selectedIndex* is zero and so forth:

```
document.<form-name>.<element-name>.selectedIndex
```

Figure 31-25 shows a Web page that displays the current values of various form elements. To try this out, load the *ch31/formval.htm* page into your browser from the sample Web. Clicking the Value, Checked, or SelectedIndex buttons to the right of each form element displays the corresponding property values for that element. The code that does this is very simple and should be apparent as soon as you find it in HTML view.

Figure 31-26 shows a Web page that uses HTML form elements as hyperlinks.

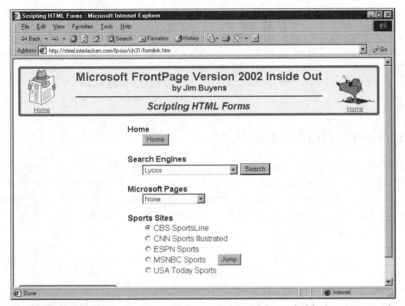

Figure 31-26. This page uses various kinds of form field elements to display a different Web page.

Here's how this page works:

- The Home button has an *onClick* attribute that sets *window.location.href* to the relative hyperlink location *../.*

> **tip** Setting a browser's *window.location.href* property to an absolute or relative URL makes the browser display that page.

- The Search button has an *onClick* attribute that runs a function called *jmpSearch,* passing it the value of *schform.schdest.selectedIndex* as an argument. The name *schdest* identifies the drop-down list titled Search Engines and *schform* identifies the form that contains it. The *jmpSearch* function sets *window.location.href* to a different location depending on the argument value.

889

- The drop-down list titled Microsoft Pages has an *onChange* attribute that runs a function called *jmpMS*, passing it the value *this.selectedIndex* as an argument. The *jmpMS* function sets *window.location.href* to a different location depending on the argument value.

---

tip   Within an event attribute such as *onClick* or *onChange,* the reserved word *this* refers to the element that contains the event attribute.

- The Jump button under Sports Sites has an *onClick* attribute that runs a function called *jmpSports*. This function inspects the *checked* property of each option button and sets *window.location.href* to a corresponding value.

To inspect this page in further detail, open the file *ch31/formlink.htm* from the sample Web.

Recycling Form Element Values

When the visitor submits an HTML form, the form's *action* property specifies the program or Web page the browser should request. This is something Chapter 32 discusses in detail, but for now it's important to realize that the *action* property can specify either a different page from the one that contains the form or the same page that contains the form.

If the *action* property specifies a different page and that page reports an error, the Web visitor can click Back, correct the field in error, and then try resubmitting the form. There are, however, two problems with this approach: First, it requires developing two Web pages instead of one. Second, after clicking Back, the visitor can no longer see the error message.

If the *action* property specifies the same page, there's only one page to develop and the Web visitor can see any and all error messages while making corrections. However, this approach has two problems of its own: First, the program or Web page must differentiate between the initial display of a form and an actual request for processing. Second, the browser doesn't restore the visitor's form field entries when the server transmits a new copy of the form. Instead, the server must modify the HTML so that all the form elements retain the visitor's previous selections.

Here's how to satisfy the second of these requirements if you're using an Active Server Page to both display and process the form. The exact approach depends on the type of element:

- **Text box** and **TextArea box.** Display the element's Properties dialog box and then enter an expression such as the following in the form field's Initial Value box:

```
<%=Request("<field-name>")%>
```

890

- **Check box.** Carry out the following procedure:

    1 Select the check box in Normal view.

    2 Switch to HTML view. The HTML for the same check box will be selected.

    3 Insert the expression shown in bold:

    ```
    <input type="check box" name="cbox1" value="ON"
      <%If (Request("cbox1") <> "") Then
          Response.Write " checked"
        End If
      %>>
    ```

    If the visitor clicked Submit with the check box selected, the expression *Request("cbox1")* equals *ON* and the code inserts the word *checked* into the outgoing HTML for the check box. Otherwise, *Request("cbox1")* will be empty and the code won't insert the word *checked*.

    The word *cbox1,* by the way, is the value you entered in the Name box of the Check Box Properties dialog box. This can be any valid name, but it *must* be the same in both the *name=* attribute and the *Request("")* expression.

    The order of the individual HTML attributes doesn't matter.

- **Option button.** The procedure that applies to option buttons is essentially the same.

    1 Select the option button in Normal view.

    2 Switch to HTML view. The HTML for the same option button will be selected.

    3 Insert the expression shown in bold:

    ```
    <input type="radio" name="optbox" value="V1"
      <%If (Request("optbox1") <> "") Then
          Response.Write " checked"
      %>>
    ```

- **Drop-down list.** The HTML for a drop-down list consists of:

    - An opening *<select>* tag.

    - A set of *<option>…</option >* tags for each option.

    - A closing *<select>* tag:

    ```
    <select size="1" name="ddbox1">
        <option value="1">First</option>
        <option value="2">Second</option>
        <option value="3">Third</option>
    </select>
    ```

891

To highlight a particular option, you must add the keyword *selected* to its *<option>* tag. Therefore, add the following expression inside each *<option>* tag:

```
<%If (Request("ddbox1") = "1") Then
    Response.Write " selected "
  End If
%>
```

Of course, there's nothing inviolate about these particular scraps of code. Any piece of code that incorporates the submitted values back into the outgoing HTML will do as well.

In Summary...

This chapter explained how to create HTML forms that display input fields in a Web visitor's browser and submit the visitor's entries to the Web server for processing.

The next chapter explains how to configure the form so the Web server provides the type of processing you want.

Processing Data Submitted from Forms

Designing an HTML form (and, presumably, imagining how it will work) is an interesting and satisfying exercise but it's only half the battle. The remaining half involves configuring the Web server so it does something useful after the visitor submits the form. That's the topic of this chapter.

Programming the Web server to save form data in files, in a database, or as mail isn't particularly difficult unless, of course, you're not a programmer. In that case, you'll be glad to know that the Microsoft FrontPage Server Extensions provide an assortment of prewritten server-side programs that satisfy most requirements with no programming required on your part. Instead, you describe your requirements by clicking through some dialog boxes, and FrontPage does the rest.

If you do have some programming skills, you'll probably find Active Server Pages a very easy way to get started with server-side programming. The last part of this chapter briefly describes how Active Server Pages receive data from forms.

Setting HTML Form Properties

An HTML form is only a data-entry template and does no processing on its own. To process or save data entered on HTML forms, you'll need to follow one of these approaches:

- Correctly invoke features of the FrontPage Server Extensions.

- Write Active Server Pages to process the data exactly as you want.

893

- Obtain server-side programs or scripts from another vendor and correctly invoke them.

- Arrange for custom script or custom server-side programming.

In the first case, your job consists of making sure the FrontPage Server Extensions are available on your Web server and then using dialog boxes in the FrontPage desktop software to specify the kind of processing you want. For the others, you'll need to configure your form so it asks the Web server to run the correct program. In all cases, the properties of the HTML form provide the necessary configuration. To view or modify the properties of an HTML form, use either of the following procedures:

- Right-click anywhere in the form and choose Form Properties from the shortcut menu.

- Set the insertion point anywhere within the form, choose Form from the Insert menu, and then choose Form Properties.

Both procedures display the Form Properties dialog box shown in Figure 32-1.

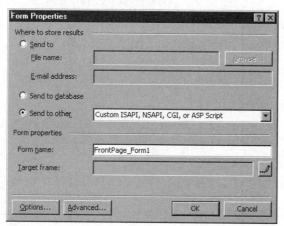

Figure 32-1. This is FrontPage's Form Properties dialog box.

The Form Properties dialog box controls the following properties:

- **Where To Store Results.** Use this group of controls to select a type of processing for the data in the form:

  - **Send To File Name.** Adds the form data to a file on the Web server. This file can be either a Web page that gets longer and longer with each submission, or a data file suitable for later processing in Microsoft Excel, Microsoft Access, or some other offline program. The associated text box specifies the name of the file—on the Web server—that will receive the data.

■ **Send To E-Mail Address.** Sends the form data as an electronic mail message. Each time a Web visitor clicks the form's Submit button, the Web server generates one message. Enter the receiving e-mail address in the associated text box.

■ **Send To Database.** Appends the form data to a database on (or accessible to) the Web server. This can be a Microsoft Access database that resides within your Web or any database accessible to the Web server via Open Database Connectivity (ODBC).

■ **Send To Other: Custom ISAPI, NSAPI, CGI, Or ASP Script.** Sends the form data to a server-based program that's not part of FrontPage. You must consult the program's documentation or designer to determine what input it requires for proper operation.

> For more information about sending form results to a file or as e-mail, refer to "Saving Form Results as Files or E-Mail" later in this chapter. For more information about saving form submissions in a database, refer to "Saving Form Results to a Database" on page 917. For more information about custom scripts, refer to "Using a Custom Form Handler" later in this chapter.

■ **Send To Other: Discussion Form Handler.** Places the information entered into the form onto a discussion site.

■ **Send To Other: Registration Form Handler.** Collects registration data from visitors to a site.

> For more information about discussion sites, refer to "Creating and Managing Discussion Webs." For more information about self-registration, refer to "Enabling User Self-Registration." Both these topics can be found in the Bonus Content on the Companion CD.

● **Form Properties.** Controls the form's name and, if it appears with a frames page, the frame where results of its processing should appear:

■ **Form Name.** Gives the form a name. This text box is optional unless a script or custom form handler needs a name in order to process the form.

■ **Target Frame.** Specifies the name of a frame in which output from the server-based program should appear. This property is optional.

● **Options.** Displays different dialog boxes, depending on your choice under Where To Store Results.

● **Advanced.** Displays the Advanced Form Properties dialog box, which configures hidden form fields.

> For more information about frames pages, refer to "Creating and Editing Frames" on page 506. For more information about hidden form fields, refer to "Using Hidden Form Fields" on page 881.

Saving Form Results as Files or E-Mail

The FrontPage Save Results component receives data from an HTML form and then saves it on a Web server, sends it by electronic mail, or both. Save Results can format data as Web pages or simple ASCII text, build data files ready for importing into database or spreadsheet applications, or add information directly to databases.

> For more information about HTML forms, refer to Chapter 31, "Creating and Using Forms."

The Save Results component absolutely requires presence of the FrontPage Server Extensions, both on the Web server you'll use for testing and on the server your visitors will use. If this is a problem, you'll have to get your system administrator to install the extensions, find another provider, or change your approach.

> **note** The Save Results component is an extremely powerful and flexible one; so powerful and so flexible that it never appears in FrontPage at all. For example, the Send To File Name, Send To E-Mail Address, and Send To Database options all use the Save Results component.

There are two ways to start using the Save Results component:

1 Use the Feedback Form template to create a new Web page. This creates a working Save Results page you can modify to suit your requirements.

2 Create or modify your own form, choosing and configuring the Send To option in the Where To Store Results section of the Form Properties dialog box.

Figure 32-2 shows a form that the Feedback Form template created, along with its form properties. The setting Send To File Name is the sole unique feature of pages created with this template; you can discard or modify anything else on the page. You can also choose this setting on existing forms or forms you create yourself.

> **tip** To display the Form Properties dialog box shown in Figure 32-2, right-click anywhere on the form and select Form Properties from the shortcut menu.

To configure the Save Results component, click the first Send To option (for either a file name or an e-mail address) in the Form Properties dialog box shown in Figure 32-2, and then click Options. This displays the Saving Results dialog box, which includes the following tabs:

● **File Results.** Specifies the format and location of files that collect the form data.

● **E-Mail Results.** Specifies the format and destination of e-mail messages that transmit the form data.

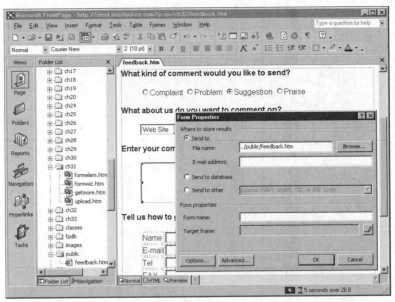

Figure 32-2. The Feedback Form template creates a Web page that, using the Save Results component, accumulates data in files on the server.

- **Confirmation Page.** Optionally specifies a custom page that assures the Web visitor that the Web server has accepted the data.

- **Saved Fields.** Specifies which form fields to save.

- **File Upload.** Tells the server extensions how to handle any files uploaded along with the form submission. (This tab appears only if your form contains a File Upload component.)

Refer to the following sections for screen shots and descriptions of each tab.

Configuring File Results Options

The first Save Results configuration tab controls the format and location of text files that accumulate the data. This tab appears in Figure 32-3 on the next page.

Set the options on the File Results tab as follows:

- **File Name.** Specify the name and location of the data collection file:

  - For locations within the current Web, specify a relative URL.

  - For locations outside the current Web, specify a file name and folder in the server's file space. Specify the folder as a Universal Naming Convention (UNC) or drive-letter path. If the file doesn't exist, the FrontPage Extensions create it when the first data arrives.

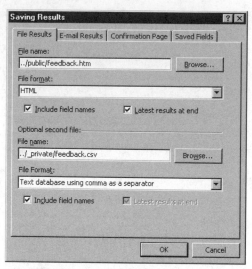

Figure 32-3. This dialog box configures settings for the Save Results component.

- If File Format (the next option) specifies HTML, use an *.htm* filename extension and a folder location that Web visitors can browse.

- If File Format specifies text, use a *.txt* or *.csv* filename extension. To locate the file within your Web but hide it from Web browsers, specify a location in the *_private* folder of your Web.

● **File Format.** Choose a format for the results file. Table 32-1 lists the choices.

● **Include Field Names.** Select this check box to save both the name and value of each form field. If the box isn't selected, FrontPage saves only the values.

● **Latest Results At End.** Select this check box to append data to the end of a Web page. Clearing the check box adds new data at the top of the page. FrontPage ignores this setting if the File Format isn't one of the HTML types; new data in such cases always appears at the end of the file.

---

caution Think carefully before saving form results to a location accessible by HTTP. This makes it very easy for you to view or download results, but equally easy for ordinary Web visitors to do so. If you consider form results confidential, save them in a file location on the server that's within a password-protected Web or FTP area.

In the section titled Optional Second File, specify the name, format, and other settings for a second file where the component can save results. This permits saving form results twice in different formats, such as HTML and comma-separated, or in two different file locations to reduce the risk of loss. Configure this section with the same four fields just described.

Table 32-1. **Format Options for the Save Results Component**

File format	Description
HTML	The component appends the data to a Web page, formatting the data as normal text with each field on a new line. This is the default.
HTML definition list	As above, but the component formats the *name=value* pairs as a definition list.
HTML bulleted list	As above, but the component formats the data as a bulleted list.
Formatted text within HTML	As above, but the component formats the data as Formatted (monospaced) text.
Formatted text	The component saves a plain text file formatted for easy reading.
Text database using comma as a separator	The component writes all data values on one line, separating them with commas. This is useful for databases, spreadsheets, and other programs that can import the comma-separated values (CSV) format.
Text database using tab as a separator	As above, but tab characters separate the data values.
Text database using space as a separator	As above, but spaces separate the data values.

Figure 32-4 on the next page shows the effects of saving results with the HTML file format setting. The Save Results component keeps appending form results to the same HTML page indefinitely in the manner shown. Following is the identical data (numbered for clarity) in the format Text Database Using Comma As A Separator. Note that the first data record contains field names rather than data; this is a common convention and very useful when performing spreadsheet and database imports:

```
1  "MessageType","Subject","SubjectOther","Comments",
   "Username","UserEmail","UserTel","UserFAX",
   "ContactRequested","Remote Name","Remote User",
   "HTTP User Agent","Date","Time"

2  "Suggestion","Web Site","","While viewing your Web
   site I was startled by a spider crawling across the
   computer screen. Please have your site sanitized so
   this doesn't happen again","Phil","phil@localhost",
   "1-555-555-5555","1-555-555-5556","ContactRequested",
   "192.168.180.102","",
   "Mozilla/4.0 (compatible; MSIE 5.5; Windows NT 5.0)",
   "07 Jan 2001","14:55:09"
```

899

3 "Problem","Web Site","","My pet rock abandoned me
  after five years of faithful service holding up the
  corner of my bookcase. Do you know of a detective agency
  that can track him down?","Herman from Huron",
  "herman@deadletter.msn.com","","","","192.168.180.102","",
  "Mozilla/4.0 (compatible; MSIE 5.5; Windows NT 5.0)",
  "07 Jan 2001","15:01:38"

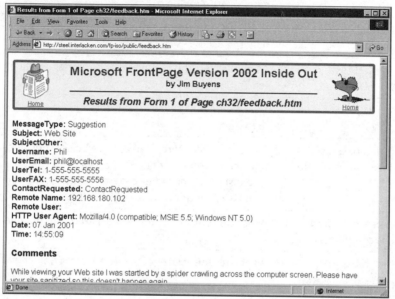

Figure 32-4. Saving form results as HTML produces an ever-growing Web page formatted like this.

---

tip If you decide to edit a Web page that the Save Results component updates, don't delete the component that displays *Form Results Inserted Here*. This is an internal component called *FormInsertHere* that marks the location where FrontPage inserts any additional data it collects from forms.

Configuring E-Mail Results Options

Figure 32-5 shows the E-Mail Results tab of the Saving Results dialog box. Set the options as follows:

● **E-Mail Address To Receive Results.** Enter the electronic mail address that receives the mailed data.

● **E-Mail Format.** Select a data format for the mailed data. Formatted text is the most universally readable and is the default.

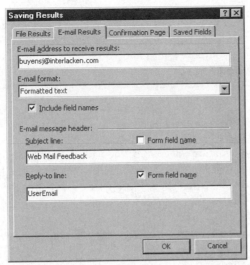

Figure 32-5. Use this tab to send HTML form data as electronic mail.

- **Include Field Names.** Select this box if you want to include field names in the message as well as field values.

Options in the E-Mail Message Header section control the subject line and Reply To address of the mailed data:

- **Subject Line.** This property is optional but recommended. Your options include:

  - If the associated Form Field Name box is cleared, enter some text to serve as the message's subject line.

  - If the box is selected, enter the name of a form field. Any data entered in that field then becomes the subject of the message.

- **Reply-To Line.** This property is optional; it adds a Reply To header to the message that transmits the form data. If the recipient of the form data replies to that message, the reply will be delivered to the address you specify here. Your options include:

  - If the associated Form Field Name box is cleared, enter the e-mail address of a person who will receive all such replies.

  - If the box is selected, enter the name of a form field. Any data entered in that field then becomes the Reply-To address.

tip Saving results to a file and sending e-mail aren't mutually exclusive. If the need arises, the Save Results component can send mail as well as saving zero, one, or two result files.

> **note** Saving form results as e-mail won't work unless your Web server's administrator has identified a Simple Network Management Protocol (SNMP) mail server to the FrontPage Server Extensions. For more information about this configuration, refer to "Changing Configuration Settings" on page 1115.

Configuring Confirmation Page Options

Figure 32-6 shows the Confirmation Page tab of the Saving Results dialog box. If the URL Of Confirmation Page (Optional) text box is blank, the Save Results component generates a confirmation page like that shown in Figure 32-7. If this format isn't acceptable, you can design your own page and specify its URL on the Confirmation Page tab.

> For more information about creating confirmation pages, refer to "Managing Confirmation Pages" later in this chapter.

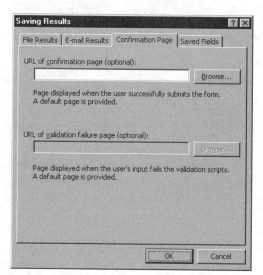

Figure 32-6. The Confirmation Page tab specifies the URL of a custom confirmation page.

In some cases, you can also specify the relative or absolute URL of a validation-failure page. The Save Results component displays this page if any submitted fields fail validation. If you don't specify a validation failure page, the Save Results component creates one.

> For more information about creating validation failure pages, refer to "Managing Confirmation Pages" later in this chapter.

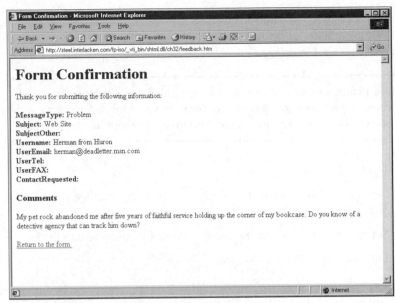

Figure 32-7. By default, the Save Results component generates form confirmation pages such as this.

Configuring Saved Fields Options

The fourth tab in the Saving Results dialog box is titled Saved Fields and appears in Figure 32-8.

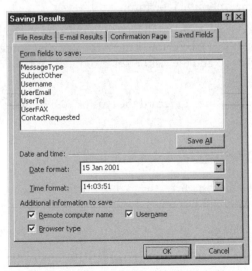

Figure 32-8. Use the Saved Fields tab to control which HTML form fields and system fields the Save Results component saves.

The upper half of the Saved Fields tab specifies which fields to save and in what order. Clicking Save All lists all fields defined in the current form. To remove a field, select it and then press the Delete key.

> **tip** The field names you must use on the Saved Fields tab are the names you assigned in the Name property of each field in your form. If your form fields still have default field names like T1 and R3, now is the time to regret it and fix them.

To reposition a field:

1 Select it (including the carriage return at the end), and then press Ctrl+X or Shift+Del to cut it.

2 Set the insertion point at the beginning of a line elsewhere in the list.

3 Press Ctrl+V or Shift+Ins to paste.

The remaining options record data not derived from the form itself. Activating any of these options appends the relevant information to the form data:

- **Date Format.** Choose *(None)* or a date format. If you specify a format, the form results will contain the date the visitor submitted the form.

- **Time Format.** Choose *(None)* or a time format. If you specify a format, the form results will contain the time the visitor submitted the form.

- **Remote Computer Name.** Select this check box to record the name or IP address of the computer that submitted the form.

- **Username.** Select this check box to record the name of the visitor who submitted the form. This data will be blank unless the Web page containing the form resides in a restricted Web and the visitor was prompted for both a name and a password.

- **Browser Type.** Select this check box to record the type of Web browser used to submit the form.

Configuring File Upload Options

If your form contains a File Upload component, the Saving Results dialog box displays a fifth tab titled File Upload. Figure 32-9 illustrates this tab.

Configure the properties of the File Upload tab in accordance with the following instructions. All these entries are optional:

- **Destination.** Specify the folder where uploaded files will reside. FrontPage retains the file name base and extension that the Web visitor specified, but discards the file's original path, instead using the location you specify here. If you leave this option blank, FrontPage stores the uploaded files in the folder where the Web page resides.

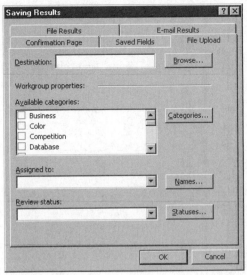

Figure 32-9. The File Upload tab configures the destination folder and other attributes of uploaded files.

● **Available Categories.** Specify any workgroup categories FrontPage should assign to uploaded files. A Table Of Contents Based On Page Category can then display a categorized list of uploaded files.

For more information about workgroup categories, refer to "Using the Table of Contents Based On Page Category Component," on page 776.

● **Assigned To.** Type or select the name of the person who's assigned to any files that the current form uploads. Click Names to update the selection list.

● **Review Status.** Type or select the current review status of any uploaded files. Click Statuses to update the selection list.

It's worth noting that FrontPage stores all these properties, plus the properties of the File Upload component itself, in the Web page that initiates the upload. This means that a malicious, mischievous, or misdirected individual could create a Web page and use it to attack your Web. That's why FrontPage requires that visitors who want to upload files identify themselves and have authority to update the current Web through the FrontPage desktop software and related means.

Managing Confirmation Pages

Certain FrontPage components prompt your Web visitors for data, and then submit the data to a Web server for processing by the FrontPage Server Extensions. Three of these components—Save Results, Registration, and Discussion—confirm successful server-side processing by echoing the data back to the person who entered it. A Web page that echoes submitted data this way is called a *confirmation page*. The same three components also support *validation failure pages*—pages that report failures caused by invalid input.

If you don't specify a confirmation page or a validation failure page, the component's form handler generates default pages as required.

Enabling Confirmation Prompts

The dialog boxes for the Save Results, Registration, and Discussion components each contain a Confirmation Page tab as shown in Figure 32-6. This tab has the following properties:

- **URL Of Confirmation Page (Optional).** Specify the location of a page for FrontPage to use as a template when it reports successful processing. If this option is left blank, the form handler generates a default format. You can click Browse to select a confirmation page from the current Web.

- **URL Of Validation Failure Page (Optional).** Specify the location of a page FrontPage should use when informing the visitor of rejected input. This option is dimmed if none of the form's elements have validation rules. If it's left blank, the form handler generates a default format. Again, you can click Browse to select a validation failure page from the current Web.

> For more information about form field validation, refer to "Validating Form Input," on page 865.

A Validation Failure Page appears only when the Web server, rather than the browser, detects a validation failure. This is rare because validation usually occurs on the browser, before the visitor submits the page. However, if the visitor's browser doesn't support scripting, bad data can still arrive at the Web server. The Save Results component therefore validates input on both the browser and the Web server. If the server detects an error, it displays a Validation Failure Page.

Using the Confirmation Field Component

You can design a confirmation page as you would any other Web page, but you need some means to tell the Server Extensions where to display the submitted data values. The Confirmation Field component provides this. Each Confirmation Field component contains the name of one data field. The Server Extensions replace each component with its named data value during transmission to the visitor.

Figure 32-10 shows a confirmation page created for a FrontPage Discussion Web. The discussion form handler sends this form to the visitor whenever an article is submitted successfully. The visible text *[Subject]* is actually a FrontPage component that will, on output, display whatever the visitor typed in the form field named Subject.

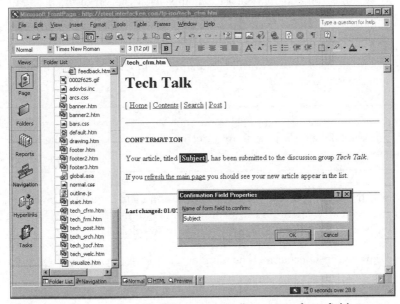

Figure 32-10. Confirmation pages generally contain form field components the form handler replaces with visitor input values, such as *[Subject]* in this figure.

To help you get started with confirmation pages, FrontPage provides a Confirmation Form template. There's nothing terribly unique about this template; it contains some sample text and a few sample Confirmation Field components. If you find creating something from something easier than creating something from nothing, take the following approach:

1 Use FrontPage to open the Web where the confirmation page will reside.

2 Use either of the following methods to display the Page Templates dialog box:

New Page

■ Choose New from the File menu, and then choose Page Or Web. When the New Page Or Web task pane appears, click Page Templates.

■ Click the drop-down arrow associated with the New Page button on the Standard toolbar, and then choose Page.

3 Choose Confirmation Form from the General tab and then click OK.

To add a Confirmation Field component—that is, an object the server replaces with a submitted data value—to any Web page, proceed as follows:

1 Set the insertion point where you want the component to appear.

2 Choose Web Component from the Insert menu.

3 When the Insert Web Component dialog box appears, select Advanced Controls in the Component Type list that appears at the left of the dialog box.

4 Choose Confirmation Field from the Choose A Control list that appears at the right of the dialog box, and then click Finish.

5 When the dialog box shown in Figure 32-10 appears, enter the name of the input field and click OK.

---

tip To find the name of a submitted field, open the Web page containing the HTML form, and then double-click the form element. The Name option in the element's Properties dialog box contains the name the Confirmation Field component expects.

Normally, the name you enter in the Confirmation Field Properties dialog box should be the name of an element on the form the visitor submits. However, for the registration component only, the following names are also valid:

● **Registration-Username.** The name of the visitor attempting to register.

● **Registration-Password.** The password the visitor requested.

● **Registration-Error.** A text explanation of a run-time error condition.

You can include any text, pictures, hyperlinks, or other Web page objects you want on a confirmation page. Confirmation pages are normal Web pages in every way, except that a form handler replaces any Confirmation Field components you insert with data that your visitors submit. You can format the page in any style and with any text or pictures you want.

Using a Custom Form Handler

Just because you used FrontPage to create an HTML form doesn't mean you must use the FrontPage Server Extensions to process it. In fact, you can use any type of server-side program you want. Here's how to configure an HTML form for processing by a custom program that runs on the Web server:

1 Open the Web page that contains the HTML form.

2 Use either of the following procedures to display the Form Properties dialog box:

- Right-click anywhere in the form, and choose Form Properties from the shortcut menu.

- Set the insertion point anywhere within the form, choose Form from the Insert menu, and then choose Form Properties.

3 Under Where To Store Results, select the Send To Other option, and make sure Custom ISAPI, NSAPI, CGI, Or ASP Script is selected in the accompanying drop-down list.

4 Click Options to display the Options For Custom Form Handler dialog box shown in Figure 32-11.

Figure 32-11. Use this dialog box to specify a custom program for processing form data.

Here's how to specify the settings in the Options For Custom Form Handler dialog box:

- **Action.** Must contain the URL of the server-side program. It's your responsibility to provide this program or ensure that it exists. Server-side programs usually have file names that end in *.exe, .dll, .cgi,* or *.asp.*

- **Method.** Specifies POST or GET, whichever the server-side program requires. These are two different ways of transmitting form data to a Web-server program. POST, which transmits data in the HTTP headers, is newer, less restrictive, and generally preferred. GET is subject to length limits and other restrictions because it transmits the form data as part of the URL.

- **Encoding Type.** Indicates the encoding method used for passing form data to a server-side program. This method permits transmission of reserved characters such as carriage returns and slashes. The only valid entries are as follows:

  - Blank, the default, which means the body of the request contains data from ordinary form elements.

  - application/x-www-form-urlencoded, which has the same effect as Blank.

  - multipart/form-data, which means the body of the request contains multiple sets of form data. Normally, the first set contains data from ordinary form elements and any additional sets contain files being uploaded.

Of course, the HTML form must collect the form elements that the server-side program expects, and identify them by the correct names. Otherwise, it's like mailing the government a magazine subscription form instead of your annual tax statement. Something's not going to work right.

Processing Form Data with ASP Pages

Submitting an HTML form to an ASP page is relatively simple. When you configure the Action property described in the previous section, just specify the relative path to the ASP page.

When the ASP page starts running on the Web server, it automatically has access to the following five objects:

- **Request.** Provides information about the Web visitor's current request.
- **Response.** Sends a Web page or other response back to the Web visitor.
- **Server.** Provides access to information and resources located on the Web server.
- **Session.** Stores information about multiple requests from the same Web visitor.
- **Application.** Provides shared information for all visitors using the same application (that is, using Active Server Pages in the same designated folder tree).

If someone asked you which of these objects contains form field values and you answered, "The *Request* object," you'd be right. The *Request* object contains the following five collections, two of which contain form field values:

- **Request.QueryString.** Contains any *name=value* pairs submitted from forms having a method type of GET.

> **note** The *Request.QueryString* collection also contains any *name=value* pairs you code in the query string portion of a URL (for example, *request.asp?name=Jim*).

- **Request.Form.** Contains any *name=value* pairs submitted from forms having a method type of POST.
- **Request.Cookies.** Contains any cookie values that arrived with the request.

> **note** If you add something to the *Response.Cookies* collection and the browser sends it back, it'll appear in the *Request.Cookies* collection.

- **Request.ClientCertificate.** Contains any information from digital certificates that accompany the request. This is primarily security information.

- **Request.ServerVariables.** Contains a variety of information about the incoming request and about the Web server.

The syntax for accessing data in any of these collections is as follows:

```
Request.<collection>("<name>")
```

Suppose, for example, the visitor submitted an HTML form, that the form contained an element named *color,* and that the visitor specified the value *green.* If the form specified the GET method, the following expression would equal *green:*

```
Request.QueryString("color")
```

If the form specified the POST method, the *Request.Form* collection would contain the form field value. Here's the necessary expression:

```
Request.Form("color")
```

If you specify the *Request* object but don't specify a collection, the Request object searches all five collections in the order just listed. Therefore, the expression:

```
Request("color")
```

would return the value *green* no matter which submission method the form used.

Figure 32-12 on the next page shows a simple ASP page that displays the complete contents of all five collections. This is a handy sort of page to have when testing HTML forms or looking for the *Request.ServerVariables* property that contains some particular scrap of data. The code for this page contains five calls to a subroutine named *ShowCollection.* Each call specifies one of the five *Response* collections in an argument named *acoll,* and the subroutine then runs a loop coded much like the following:

```
for each val in acoll
   response.write "<tr><td>" & val & "</td>" & _
                  "<td>" & acoll(val) & "</td>" & _
            "</tr>" & vbcrlf
next
```

As you can infer from Figure 32-12 on the next page, the actual code has a few embellishments having to do with cell alignment and the alternating white and gray background. To view the code for this page, load the file *ch32/request.asp* from the sample Web.

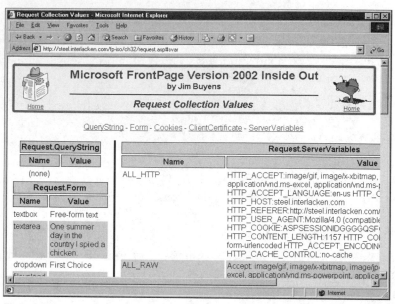

Figure 32-12. This is a generic Web page that displays all the Request information available to it. The actual display extends some distance below the portion shown here.

Sending Custom E-Mail

The Save Results component does an adequate job of sending the contents of a form as e-mail, but it's not flexible enough to handle all situations. You can't, for example, format the message exactly to your liking, and you can't send e-mail to different recipients depending on the circumstances. If you have these kinds of requirements, you'll need to locate other tools and do some custom coding.

One such tool is the set of Collaboration Data Objects (CDO) that came with Microsoft IIS 4 and now comes with every copy of Microsoft Windows 2000. This set of objects sends and receives mail in the background, under the control of other programs. The ASP code for making CDO send an e-mail message can be as simple as the code that follows:

```
Set objNewMail = Server.CreateObject("CDONTS.NewMail")
objNewMail.From = buyensj@interlacken.com
objNewMail.To = herman@deadletter.msn.com
objNewMail.Subject = "Happy Birthday"
objNewMail.Body = "If your birthday is today, have a good one."
objNewMail.Send
Set objNewMail = Nothing
```

The first line creates a CDO object for sending new mail. The next four lines assign from and to addresses, a subject line, and the body of the message. The *objNewMail.Send* command sends the mail, and the last line destroys the CDO object.

The documentation for CDO is part of the Microsoft Windows Platform System Development Kit (SDK) Documentation. To find this information on the Web, browse *http://msdn.microsoft.com/library/default.asp* and then open the following topics:

> *Platform SDK Documentation*
> > *Messaging And Collaboration Services*
> > > *CDO 1.2.1*
> > > > *CDO for NTS*
> > > *CDO for Windows 2000*

The topic CDO for NTS pertains to Microsoft Windows NT Server 4. Similarly, CDO for Windows 2000 pertains to the Windows 2000 version of CDO.

If your Web server doesn't run a Windows operating system or somehow has CDO disabled, ask the server's administrator whether another mail program is available and, if so, where to find the documentation. Sending mail is such a common requirement that nearly all Web servers provide a way to do it.

In Summary...

This chapter explained how to configure an HTML form to request the correct services from a Web server (that is, the services that fulfill the purpose of the form).

The next chapter explains how to use the database capabilities built into FrontPage. This includes the ability to save form results in a database, and to develop simple reporting and update capabilities without programming.

Accessing Databases with FrontPage

As the Web progresses from passive viewing to interaction between Web visitor and server, databases are critical and inevitable building blocks. If your applications involve Web visitors querying, entering, or updating persistent data, you need Web access to database services.

Microsoft FrontPage 2002 isn't a full-blown client-server database development system, but it does provide a number of useful database features:

- **Save Results To Database.** An enhancement to the Save Results component described in Chapter 32. This feature appends form data directly to a database table rather than, as previously described, to Web pages or a text file.

- **One-Button Database Publishing.** An option within the Save Results To Database feature. It creates a database file, creates a new table named *Results* within that database, and creates columns within that table for each field in an HTML form.

- **Database Results Wizard.** A tool for creating Web-based database queries. The wizard prompts you for the name of the database, the name of a table or query, the columns you want to list, and formatting options. Then it creates Web pages that look up and display the requested data on demand.

- **Database Interface Wizard.** Creates a series of Web pages that can display, add, change, and delete records in any database you decide to support.

Database systems are inherently complex, and the usual way of approaching complex topics is to start with fundamentals and proceed with rigorous, ever-increasing detail. That would produce an incredibly boring chapter with no payoff until the end, so this chapter does it backwards: practical information up front, supporting details to follow.

Database Requirements and Restrictions

Creating Web database pages requires that you work in a FrontPage-based Web. If it's a disk-based Web, the database must be accessible from your computer. If it's a server-based Web, the database must be accessible from the computer where the Web physically resides.

You need to use a FrontPage-based Web because FrontPage stores certain information about databases at the Web level, and not within each page. The database needs to be readable during design so that FrontPage can retrieve the table names and field names for various selection lists.

For database pages to actually run against the database—that is, to insert records, make queries, and display results—a disk-based Web won't suffice. Instead, you'll need a server-based Web running on a Web server that supports ASP pages and ActiveX Data Objects (ADO). This includes the combinations shown in Table 33-1.

Table 33-1. **Supported Web Servers for FrontPage Database Components**

Web server	Operating system	Server extensions	Status
Microsoft Internet Information Server 5	Microsoft Windows 2000	Microsoft FrontPage 2002	Preferred
Microsoft Internet Information Server 4	Microsoft Windows NT Server 4	Microsoft FrontPage 2000	Supported
Microsoft Personal Web Server 4	Microsoft Windows NT Workstation 4	Microsoft FrontPage 2000	Supported
Microsoft Personal Web Server 4	Microsoft Windows 95 or Microsoft Windows 98	Microsoft FrontPage 2000	Obsolete

As for database types, FrontPage database pages can access:

- File-oriented databases (such as Microsoft Access, Paradox, and dBase) located in the same Web.

- Any database defined as an ODBC System Data Source on the Web server.

- Other network databases such as Microsoft SQL Server and Oracle, provided that they have drivers installed on the Web server.

For more information about ODBC data sources, refer to "Configuring ODBC Data Sources" in the Bonus Content on the Companion CD.

If you don't already have a database, FrontPage can create an Access database for you. The next section explains how.

Saving Form Results to a Database

Chapter 32 discussed using the FrontPage Save Results component to save data from HTML forms as a file on the server or to transmit it as mail. This section explains how to save the same sort of data directly to a database.

Figure 33-1 shows a simple HTML form designed for reporting sightings of birds. Here are the steps required to save this data directly to a database:

1 Design the HTML form, making sure to give each form field an intuitive name.

For more information about creating HTML forms and naming form fields, refer to Chapter 31, "Creating and Using Forms."

2 Save the page containing the HTML form with an *.asp* filename extension. For this example, the file name is *sighting.asp.*

 ASP pages contain program statements (scripts) that execute on the Web server whenever a Web visitor requests that page. For more information about Active Server Pages, refer to "Scripting Web Pages on the Server" in the Bonus Content on the Companion CD.

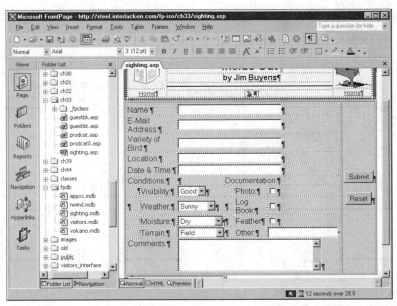

Figure 33-1. This data collection form is a candidate for saving results directly to a database.

3 Right-click anywhere in the form area and choose Form Properties from the shortcut menu.

4 When the Form Properties dialog box appears, select the option titled Send To Database and then click Options. FrontPage displays the Options For Saving Results To Database dialog box shown in the foreground of Figure 33-2. Note the four options under the Connection heading:

■ **Database Connection To Use.** Selects an existing database connection to use for storing the collected data.

> A database connection is a pointer to a database—a pointer defined at the Web level. For more information about database connections, refer to "Configuring a FrontPage Data Connection" later in this chapter.

■ **Add Connection.** Creates a new connection to an existing database. In essence, this is a shortcut to choosing Web Settings from the Tools menu, and then displaying the Database tab.

■ **Create Database.** Creates a new database to store the form results. In that database, FrontPage creates a new table with a column for each element in the form. Finally, FrontPage creates a connection to the new database.

■ **Update Database.** Revises the structure of an existing database to reflect the current collection of form fields.

To follow the example, click Create Database.

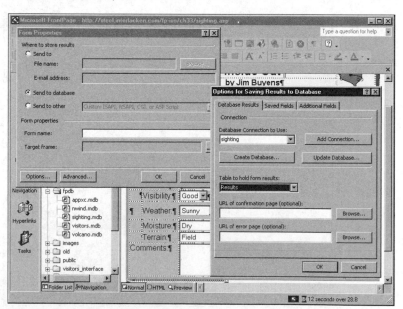

Figure 33-2. The Database Results tab of this dialog box controls basic options for saving form data to a database.

918

> **note** Clicking Create Database in step 4 constitutes the One Button Database Publishing feature promoted as part of FrontPage. Although FrontPage provides additional features related to saving HTML form data to a database, they're all optional.

5 When you click Create Database, FrontPage creates a database named *sighting.mdb* in the Web's */fpdb* folder, and creates a database connection named *sighting.* The string *sighting* comes from the name of the Web page: *sighting.asp.*

6 Clicking the Saved Fields tab displays the dialog box pictured on the left side of Figure 33-3. The Form Fields To Save list itemizes which form fields will be saved in the database, and in what database fields.

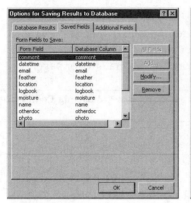 

Figure 33-3. The Saved Fields tab displays each field in the HTML form and the database field, if any, that will receive its values. The Additional Fields tab controls fields received not from the HTML form, but from the HTTP transaction that submits it.

The four buttons along the right edge provide these functions:

- **All Fields.** Adds every field in the HTML form to the list.

- **Add.** Adds one field from the HTML form to the list. A dialog box prompts for the specific field.

- **Modify.** Selects the database field that receives data from the currently selected form field. A Modify Field dialog box displays the form field name and a drop-down list of available database columns.

- **Remove.** Stops recording data from the currently selected field.

If you're entering data from a new form into an existing database table, you must display the Saved Fields tab and correlate your form fields to database field names. Otherwise, the Save Results component won't save any fields. Likewise, if you've changed either the database structure or the HTML form, once again you'll need to display the Saved Fields tab and hook up the correct form fields to the correct database fields.

7 The Additional Fields tab, shown on the right side of Figure 33-3, saves up to four additional fields in the database. The data for these fields isn't part of the HTML form; instead, the browser transmits it as HTTP headers along with the form data. Again, you can remove or reinsert these fields as you want.

8 Returning to Figure 33-2, note these additional options:

■ **Table To Hold Form Results.** Names the table that will receive the data from the HTML form you selected in the Database Connection To Use box. Clicking Create Database in step 4 creates a table called Results.

■ **URL Of Confirmation Page.** Provides the URL of a page the Web visitor will receive if the server can successfully update the database. If you leave this option blank, FrontPage will construct a default confirmation page.

■ **URL Of Error Page.** Provides the URL of a page the Web visitor will receive if the server fails to update the database. Leaving this option blank tells FrontPage to construct a default error page.

For more information about confirmation pages, refer to "Managing Confirmation Pages" on page 906.

9 When all three tabs are configured to your satisfaction, click OK twice.

To actually run the page and add data to the database, both the Web page and the database need to be on a server that meets the requirements given in Table 33-1. Furthermore, the Web page must be in a folder that can execute ASP scripts.

Executable Web Folders

Programs that run on Web servers present a significant security risk. Allowing Web designers (or Web visitors!) to store and execute programs on the server grants them the capability to do *anything* a program can do. This could be useful work, certainly, but it could also interfere with normal server operation or invade the privacy of others. For this reason, most server administrators allow programs to execute solely if they reside in certain folders that only a few trusted individuals can update.

ASP files contain source code rather than executable programs, but because they trigger executable processes, they too must reside in an executable folder. For FrontPage database development, the executable folder can reside on any enterprise, workgroup, or personal Web server that has access to a test or production copy of the database.

For information about configuring Web folders as executable, refer to Chapter 37, "Installing and Configuring a Web Server."

Chapter 33

Figure 33-4 shows some data entered in the Bird Sighting Report form, and Figure 33-5 shows the default confirmation page sent after FrontPage added this information to the database.

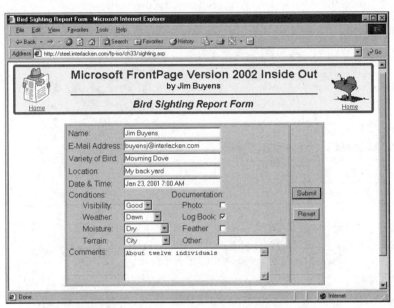

Figure 33-4. This is the HTML form shown in Figure 33-1, this time displayed by a browser and filled out by a fictitious visitor.

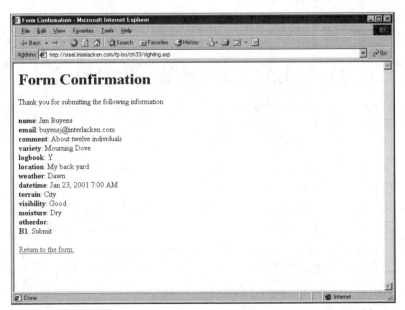

Figure 33-5. Clicking Submit on the Bird Sighting Report page adds a record to the database and displays this confirmation page.

Figure 33-6 shows Microsoft Access 2002 displaying some data collected from the Bird Sighting Report form described in this section. To process the database with Access, you would either download the database to your computer, open it through a file-sharing connection to the Web server, or run Access directly on the server.

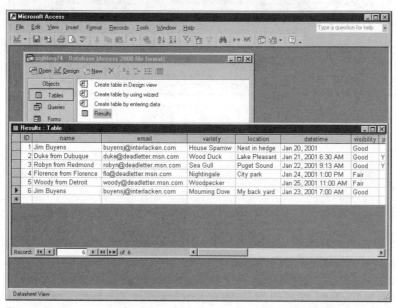

Figure 33-6. Access displays some data collected through the Bird Sighting Report form.

Of course, you're perfectly free to process the data with additional Web database pages as well.

Using the Database Results Wizard

The previous section showed how to use the database features of the Save Results component for adding records to a database. This section shows how to query and display database information, and this requires some new FrontPage components:

- **Database Column Value.** A placeholder that's replaced by the value of a database field when a Web visitor displays the page.

- **Database Results Region.** Contains one or more Database Column Value components, and repeats once for each record that a database query returns.

- **Database Results Wizard.** Displays a series of five screens that configure a Database Results region and any Database Column Values the region contains.

Don't confuse the Database Results Wizard with the database features of the Save Results component:

- The Database Results Wizard—described in this section—queries a database and formats the results.

- The Save Results component—described in the previous section—accepts and saves data from an HTML form, optionally in a database.

Displaying a Simple Query

To illustrate the Database Results Wizard, this section will create a Web page that displays data collected by the Bird Sighting Report page. The example displays selected fields from the table, using a custom sort order. Figure 33-7 shows the finished product.

> **note** The Web page in Figure 33-7 incorporates the same formatting enhancements as most of the other Web pages in this book. The designer added a standard header and footer, and applied a standard linked style sheet.

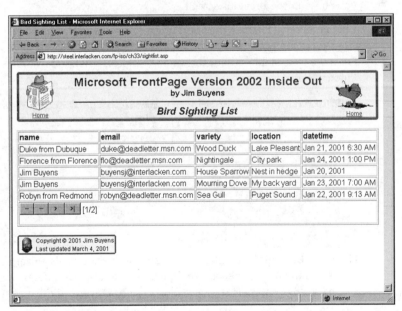

Figure 33-7. This Web page queries and displays the Bird Sighting database constructed in the previous section.

Here's the step-by-step procedure to create this Web page:

1 Create a new blank Web page in Page view.

923

2 Choose Database from the Insert menu, and then choose Results to launch the Database Results Wizard. The wizard's first dialog box (the left side of Figure 33-8) offers these choices:

■ **Use A Sample Database Connection (Northwind).** Adds a sample database to your Web, builds a connection to it, and selects that connection.

■ **Use An Existing Database Connection.** Selects a database connection already defined within the current Web.

■ **Use A New Database Connection.** Enables the Create button, which displays the Database tab of the Web Settings dialog box, shown on the left side of Figure 33-29.

For this example, use the existing database connection *sighting,* created in the previous section.

3 Click Next to display the second dialog box in the Database Results Wizard (the right side of Figure 33-8), which offers these choices:

■ **Record Source.** Selects a table or query from the database connection you chose in the previous screen.

■ **Custom Query.** Enables the Edit button, which displays a dialog box where you can enter a Structured Query Language (SQL) statement. For more information about this option, refer to "Refining Database Queries" later in this chapter.

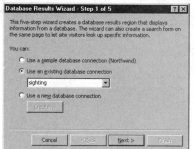

Figure 33-8. The first dialog box in the Database Results Wizard selects the database connection that provides the displayed data. The second dialog box specifies the table or query that provides the data.

> **note** Most people pronounce the acronym "SQL" as if it were the word "sequel." A sizable minority, however, say, "es-cue-el."

For the example, choose the *Results* table as the record source for this query and click Next. *Results* is the one and only table in the *sighting* database.

4 Figure 33-9 shows the wizard's third dialog box. There are two options:

■ **Edit List.** Controls which fields the Web page displays.

■ **More Options.** Controls selection criteria, sequence, default criteria values, and some additional display options.

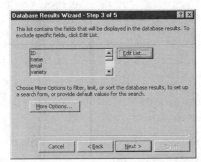

Figure 33-9. The Edit List button controls which table fields the Web page will display. The More Options button controls selection criteria, reporting order, default criteria, and other display options.

5 Click Edit List to display the Displayed Fields dialog box shown on the left side of Figure 33-10.

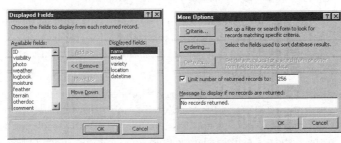

Figure 33-10. Click Edit List in the third dialog box of the Database Results Wizard (Figure 33-9) to display the Displayed Fields dialog box, which selects and orders fields for appearance on the Web page. To display the More Options dialog box, click More Options.

This dialog box configures the following options:

■ **Available Fields.** Lists fields from the database table that don't currently appear on the Web page.

■ **Displayed Fields.** Lists fields that do appear on the Web page, and specifies their order.

■ **Add.** Moves any selected fields out of Available Fields and into Displayed Fields.

■ **Remove.** Moves any selected fields out of Displayed Fields and into Available Fields.

925

- **Move Up.** Moves any selected field one position higher in the Displayed Fields list.

- **Move Down.** Moves any selected field one position lower in the Displayed Fields list.

For the example, select and arrange the fields as shown on the left side of Figure 33-10.

6 Clicking the More Options button displays the More Options dialog box shown on the right side of Figure 33-10. The More Options dialog box has the following options:

- **Criteria.** Controls which database records the Web page will display, based on their data values.

- **Ordering.** Controls the order in which records appear—from top to bottom—on the Web page.

- **Defaults.** Dimmed unless you specify criteria. In the presence of criteria, it provides substitutes for any criteria the Web visitor leaves blank.

- **Limit Number Of Returned Records To.** If selected, limits the number of records retrieved from the database. This option provides no way to view additional records beyond the given limit.

   This option exists to prevent runaway queries (that is, queries that retrieve thousands or tens of thousands of records). This is far more records than the Web visitor can assimilate, and is thus a considerable waste of resources.

   The Split Records Into Groups option described in step 9 shows a few records at a time to the Web visitor, and gives the Web visitor buttons for moving forwards and backwards through the result set. However, the result set can't be larger than any limit you specify here.

- **Message To Display If No Records Are Returned.** Specifies the text FrontPage will display if there are no database records to display.

The example uses only the Ordering option. Topics later in this chapter explain the remaining options.

> For more information about using advanced query settings, refer to "Using Advanced Query Settings to Select and Sort Records" later in this chapter.

7 Click Ordering in the More Options dialog box (the right side of Figure 33-10) to display the Ordering dialog box pictured in Figure 33-11.

Each field in the current database query initially appears in the Available Fields column, and initially has no effect on sorting the results of the query. The Sort Order column lists fields that do affect the order of query results.

926

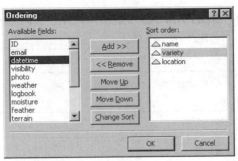

Figure 33-11. The Ordering dialog box specifies which data fields control the order of query results.

Fields higher in the column have precedence over fields below them, and an Up or Down arrow icon indicates ascending or descending sequence for each field.

The Ordering dialog box contains the following buttons:

- **Add.** Moves any selected fields out of the Available Fields column and into the Sort Order column.

- **Remove.** Moves any selected fields out of the Sort Order column and into the Available Fields column.

- **Move Up.** Moves one selected Sort Order field one position higher in the list. This and the next two buttons will be dimmed unless one and only one Sort Order field is selected.

- **Move Down.** Moves one selected Sort Order field one position lower in the list.

- **Change Sort.** Toggles one selected Sort Order field between ascending and descending sequence.

8 To follow the example, select and arrange the fields as shown in Figure 33-11. Click OK twice, and then click Next.

The left side of Figure 33-12 on the next page shows the fourth dialog box in the Database Results Wizard, which controls the layout of the displayed data:

- **Choose Formatting Options For The Records Returned By The Query.** Determines how FrontPage will display each record returned by the query. There are three overall formats, each with variations:

  - **Table - One Record Per Row.** Means FrontPage will create an HTML table where each column corresponds to a field in the database and each row contains these fields from a different record. The left side of Figure 33-12 shows this option selected. Table 33-2 on the next page lists additional options for this choice.

927

Table 33-2. **Formatting Options for Table—One Record per Row**

Option	Effect (if selected)
Use Table Border	Specifies that the table will have borders.
Expand Table To Width Of Page	Sets the table's width to 100 percent.
Include Header Row With Column Labels	Provides a row of column headings above the table The captions are the field names.

◆ **List - One Field Per Item.** Means FrontPage will display each field on a separate line, with formatting breaks between records. Table 33-3 lists the additional options.

◆ **Drop-Down List - One Record Per Item.** Means FrontPage will populate a drop-down list with choices from the selected database records. The list then works like any other drop-down list in an HTML form. Table 33-4 lists additional options for this choice.

Typically, the reason for displaying one field and submitting another is to show the visitor a choice in words (such as employee name) but send the Web server a code (such as employee number).

9 Click Next after you've selected the formatting options you need.

10 The Database Results Wizard's final dialog box provides another way of limiting the number of records displayed per page.

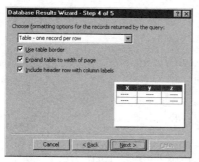 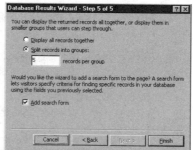

Figure 33-12. The fourth dialog box in the Database Results Wizard controls arrangement of the displayed data. The Wizard's last dialog box displays either an unlimited number of records per Web page or a set number with forward and back buttons.

Table 33-3. **Formatting Options for List—One Field per Item**

Option	Effect (if selected)
Add Labels For All Field Values	Precedes each field value with the corresponding field name.
Place Horizontal Separator Between Records	Separates the records with a horizontal rule.

List Options:
  Paragraphs
  Line Breaks
  Bullet List
  Numbered List
  Definition List
  Table
  Formatted
  Text Fields
  Scrolling Text Fields
	Determines the paragraph style used for fields within a record.

Table 33-4. **Formatting Options for Drop-Down List—One Record per Item**

Option	Effect
Display Values From This Field	Select the field that contains the values the visitor will see in the drop-down list box.
Submit Values From This Field	Select the field that contains the values the form will submit to the Web server.

The final dialog box provides the following options:

- **Display All Records Together.** Displays all selected records on one Web page.

- **Split Records Into Groups.** Displays a limited number of records per Web page. FrontPage creates first, last, forward, and back buttons so the Web visitor can move through the database. The Records Per Group text box specifies the number of records per page.

- **Add Search Form.** If selected, creates an HTML form that prompts for and submits any form field values you specified as record selection criteria. (The next section in this chapter describes how to do this.) If you didn't specify any criteria involving form fields, this option will be dimmed.

To follow the example, choose 5 records per group.

Clicking Finish on the final Database Results Wizard dialog box creates the Web page shown in Figure 33-13. The two shaded table rows are just for information and don't appear on the Web visitor's browser. The middle row is the Database Results region, which repeats once per record displayed.

FrontPage Preview mode won't display data in pages containing Database Results regions; Preview mode actually displays Web pages temporarily saved to disk and doesn't have access to all the facilities of a Web server. To view the page in action, save it with an *.asp* filename extension in an executable folder in a server-based Web, and then choose the Preview In Browser command or toolbar button. Figure 33-7 shows the Web page displayed after you've taken these actions.

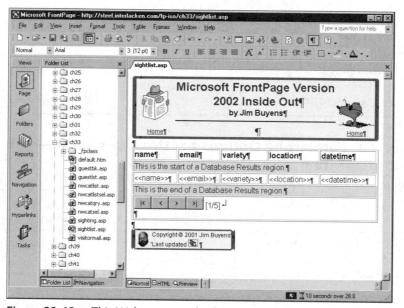

Figure 33-13. This Web page results from the selections shown in this section's preceding figures.

Refining Database Queries

Selecting Record Source in the second dialog box of the Database Results Wizard (the right side of Figure 33-8) generates the simplest possible database query—it selects all fields from all records in the given table, and presents them in the table's default sequence. FrontPage provides two alternatives that query the database with more specific options:

- Using the Custom Query option in the second dialog box of the Database Results Wizard (the right side of Figure 33-8), you can query the database any way you want by writing your own SQL statement.

For more information about SQL, refer to "Introducing SQL" later in this chapter.

- To specify more complex queries:

    1 Choose the Record Source option in the second dialog box of the Database Results Wizard (the right side of Figure 33-8).

    2 Click the More Options button in the third dialog box of the Database Results Wizard (Figure 33-9). This displays and enables the following buttons:

    ◆ The Criteria button in the More Options dialog box (the right side of Figure 33-10) can select records based on comparisons to either form fields or constants.

    ◆ The Ordering button in the same dialog box controls the sequence in which the records will appear.

Figure 33-14 shows the type of Web page these techniques can produce. Entering a Category ID in the text box and clicking Submit Query displays products in that category, in Product ID order. The next two sections will describe each alternative in detail.

note A designer manually formatted the Web page shown in Figure 33-14 using a combination of table attributes and CSS properties. For clarity in the example, the column headings remain equal to the database column names. This is the default, but something you'd want to change in a real application. Changing the column headings is a simple matter of editing them as text in FrontPage.

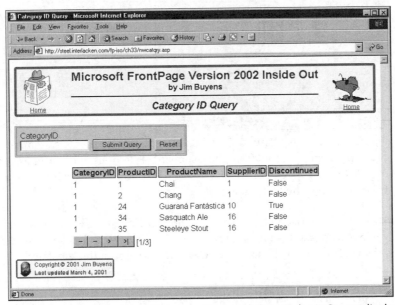

Figure 33-14. Entering a Category ID and clicking Submit Query displays matching records in Product ID order.

Using a Custom Query to Select and Sort Records

Selecting Custom Query and clicking the Edit button in the second dialog box of the Database Results Wizard (the right side of Figure 33-8) displays the dialog box pictured on the left side of Figure 33-15. This option provides great flexibility by accepting any SQL statement you want to enter, but it requires knowledge of SQL. This dialog box contains the following options:

- **SQL Statement.** Contains a SQL command. It tells the database software what data to retrieve.

- **Insert Parameter.** Displays the dialog box shown on the right side of Figure 33-15. Here you can enter the name of an HTML form field.

- **Paste From Clipboard.** Copies any text currently in the Clipboard to the SQL Statement text box.

- **Verify Query.** Submits the current SQL statement to the database software and reports any errors. Use this button to test the query before closing the dialog box.

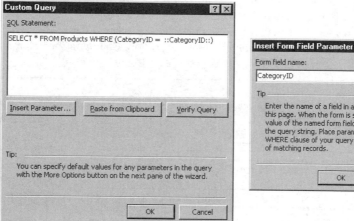
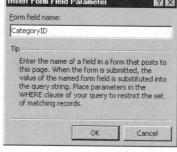

Figure 33-15. The Custom Query dialog box accepts a SQL statement typed by hand or pasted from the Clipboard. The Insert Form Field Parameter dialog box specifies the name of an HTML form field whose value will become part of the SQL statement.

Be sure to set the insertion point properly before clicking the Insert Parameter button—usually where a constant would appear in a HAVING or WHERE expression. FrontPage inserts the HTML form field name based on the insertion point's location.

> For more information about using form fields to supply query values, refer to "Using Form Fields to Supply Query Values" later in this chapter.

If you want, you can skip pressing the Insert Parameter button and just insert the form field code yourself. Just type two colons, the name of the form field, and two more colons wherever you want the form field's value to appear.

> **tip**
> Be sure to surround any form field parameters with the usual delimiters required by SQL. Values compared to character fields must be enclosed in apostrophes, whereas values compared to numeric fields must not.

You can create and debug queries in Access, and then transfer them to FrontPage using the Paste From Clipboard button. Here's the procedure:

1 Open the database (or a copy of it) in Access.

2 Open or create a query that displays the data you want. Use constants in place of any form field values you plan to use.

3 Choose SQL View from one of these locations:

- The View menu

- The View button drop-down list on the Query Datasheet toolbar

- The View button drop-down list on the Query Design toolbar

Figure 33-16 shows this operation in progress.

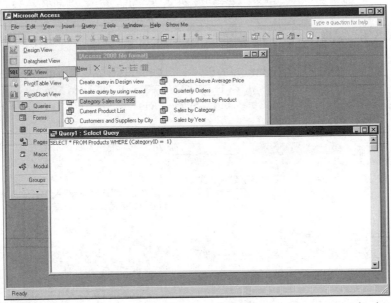

Figure 33-16. After you get a query working in Access, you can display the SQL code and copy it to the Clipboard for pasting into the Database Results Wizard.

933

4 Select all the text in the SQL statement, then copy it to the Clipboard by choosing Copy from the Edit menu, pressing Ctrl+C, or pressing Ctrl+Insert.

5 Switch to FrontPage and display the Custom Query dialog box shown on the left side of Figure 33-15.

6 Click Paste From Clipboard to insert the SQL statement.

7 If, in step 2, you used any constants in place of form field values, select each one and then use the Insert Parameter button to insert the form field name.

Using Advanced Query Settings to Select and Sort Records

Writing SQL statements gives you total control over selection of records from a database table and the order in which they appear. The catch, of course, is that you have to know SQL. This section describes another way to control record selection and ordering—a way that's slightly less flexible but requires no SQL proficiency.

To use this method, advance to the third dialog box of the Database Results Wizard (Figure 33-9), and then click More Options. This displays the More Options dialog box shown on the right side of Figure 33-10.

> **note** If you selected the Custom Query option in the second dialog box of the Database Results Wizard (Figure 33-8), clicking the More Options button in the third dialog box results in the Criteria, Ordering, and Defaults buttons being dimmed in the More Options dialog box. This is because a SQL statement entered as a custom query might contain options the Advanced dialog box can't preserve.

Clicking the Criteria button in the More Options dialog box displays the Criteria dialog box shown on the left side of Figure 33-17. The list headed Specify Criteria To Filter Which Records Are Displayed, Or Select Fields To Use In A Search Form lists criteria currently in effect.

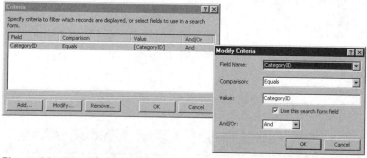

Figure 33-17. Clicking the Criteria button in the More Options dialog box displays the Criteria dialog box, which controls selection of database records for display. The Modify Criteria dialog box specifies selection criteria for database records.

These buttons modify the list:

- **Add.** Click this button to display an Add Criteria dialog box very similar to the Modify Criteria dialog box (the right side of Figure 33-17). The Add Criteria dialog box adds a new criterion to the list.

- **Modify.** Click this button to display the Modify Criteria dialog box shown on the right side of Figure 33-17. This dialog box changes the properties of an existing criterion.

- **Remove.** Click this button to delete the currently selected criterion.

Here's how to use the options in the Add Criteria and Modify Criteria dialog boxes:

- **Field Name.** Select the field whose value you want to test.

- **Comparison.** Specify the operator for the comparison: Equals, Not Equal, Less Than, and so forth.

- **Value.** There are three ways to use this option:

  - If you want to select records based on the value of an HTML form field, enter the name of the form field and then select the check box titled Use This Search Form Field.

  - If you want to select records based on a fixed value, enter the value and then clear the check box titled Use This Search Form Field.

  - If you chose a Comparison operator of Is Null or Not Null, the Value option will be dimmed.

> **note** A null value in a database field means the field currently has no value. This is different from a numeric field being zero, or a character field containing a zero-length string: in both those cases, the field *has* a value. A field whose value is null has no known value—not even zero or an empty string.

- **And/Or.** Choose *And* if other criteria, as well as this one, must be true for the record to be selected. Choose *Or* if this is one of several criteria, any one of which, if true, is sufficient to select the record.

Clicking the Defaults button in the More Options dialog box (the right side of Figure 33-10) displays the Defaults dialog box shown in Figure 33-18 on the next page. This dialog box specifies default values for criteria received from HTML forms. That is, if the HTML form value is blank or missing, the default supplied here takes effect.

Initially, the Input Parameters list contains each field having defined criteria based (as shown on the left side of Figure 33-18) on an HTML form value. To supply a default value for any field, either double-click it or select it and click Edit. The result will be the dialog box in the foreground of Figure 33-18. Enter the default value, and then click OK.

Chapter 33

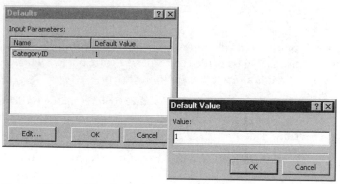

Figure 33-18. The Defaults dialog box lists each database field.

The Ordering button in the More Options dialog box (the right side of Figure 33-10) controls the sequence of records listed in the reports. For details on using this option, refer to step 7 in the section titled "Displaying a Simple Query."

Using Form Fields to Supply Query Values

If you specified database selection criteria based on HTML form fields—either by entering parameters in the Custom Query dialog box (the left side of Figure 33-15) or criteria in the Criteria dialog box (the left side of Figure 33-17)—the final dialog box in the Database Results Wizard (the right side of Figure 33-12) will contain a check box titled Add Search Form. Selecting this check box creates an HTML form like the one that appears near the top of Figure 33-19.

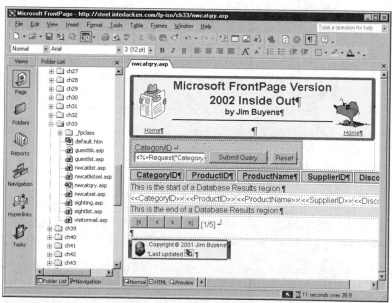

Figure 33-19. The HTML form at the top of this page collects and submits input that controls data displayed by the Database Results region below it.

This Web page handles both input and output of database queries. The Web visitor enters a *CategoryID* and clicks Submit Query. Then, as seen in Figure 33-20, the form's Action property submits the form value to the same ASP page that contains the form.

> **note** To display the dialog boxes shown in Figure 33-20, right-click the HTML form area and choose Properties from the shortcut menu. When the Form Properties dialog box appears, click the Options button.

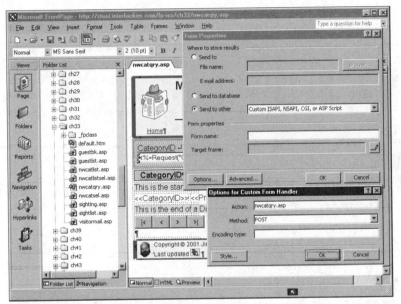

Figure 33-20. Pressing the Submit Query button on this ASP page re-executes the same page. The results will be different if either the form input or the database has changed.

Figure 33-21 shows the properties of the text box from Figure 33-19. Its name is *CategoryID*, the same as the name of the database field it selects. The use of similar names is a convention followed by the Database Results Wizard, and not a firm requirement.

Figure 33-21. The CategoryID text box in Figure 33-19 has these properties.

Chapter 33

The Initial Value field might look a bit peculiar until you realize it's a piece of ASP code. Whenever the Web server processes the ASP page, the inline expression *<%=Request("CategoryID")%>* obtains the form field value named *CategoryID* and writes it out as part of the Web page. Thus, the text box is always initialized to its previous value.

Nothing prevents having the HTML form and the Database Results region on different Web pages. To make them separate pages, just cut the HTML form out of the database results page and paste it wherever you want. Adjust the relative URL in the form's Action property if necessary.

Figure 33-22 shows a Web page with an HTML form that submits input to the *nwcatqry.asp* page. However, instead of using a text box for the *CategoryID* field, this page uses a Database Results component configured to display a drop-down list. The list contains one entry for each record in the Categories table, a table that defines the list of valid categories for the *nwind.mdb* database. The Database Results drop-down list displays the alphabetic *CategoryName* field, but submits the numeric *CategoryID* field.

Troubleshooting

Page containing HTML form and database results component displays error when first displayed

If you create a Database Results component that received criteria from an HTML form on the same Web page, displaying the page might display a message such as the following:

```
Database Results Error
Description: [Microsoft][ODBC Microsoft Access Driver] Extra ) in
query expression '(CategoryID =)'.
Number: -2147217900 (0x80040E14)
Source: Microsoft OLE DB Provider for ODBC Drivers
One or more form fields were empty. You should provide default
values for all form fields that are used in the query.
```

This occurs because the database query in an Database Results component runs every time a visitor requests the Web page—including the first time, before the Web visitor has entered any query fields. With missing criteria values, the database query fails. To avoid this problem, either:

- Put the HTML form and the Database Results region on different pages, or
- Use the Defaults dialog box shown in Figure 33-18 to assign defaults for all input fields used in the query.

Assigning default values to the forms field has no effect. The browser fills in form field defaults after receiving the Web page, which is after the reported error occurs.

938

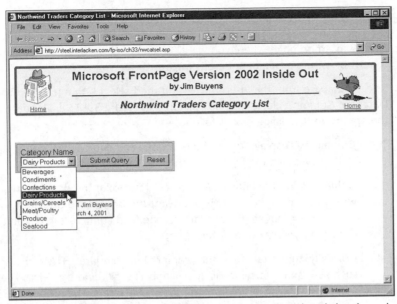

Figure 33-22. The Database Results component populated the drop-down list in this Web page with values from a database.

InsideOut

Whenever a visitor displays a page that contains a Database Results drop-down list, the list is always positioned to the first entry. This limits the usefulness of Database Results drop-down lists in pages that, as in Figure 33-14, use the same page for input and output. When a forms page displays itself, the visitor expects any drop-down list selections they made on input to remain in effect on output. To learn how to create a database-driven drop-down list box that retains its value, refer to "Recycling Form Element Values" on page 890.

For more information about creating a database-driven drop-down list that retains its value, refer to "Processing Databases with Active Server Pages" in the Bonus Content on the Companion CD.

Configuring Database Column Value Components

The objects displayed as *<<CategoryID>>*, *<<ProductID>>*, *<<ProductName>>*, *<<SupplierID>>*, and so forth in Figure 33-19 are Database Column Value components. These components are valid only inside a Database Results region, and each one contains the name of a database field to display. Whenever the Database Results region has a record to display, it replaces each Database Column Value component with the value of its corresponding field.

939

Here are the steps to insert a new Database Column Value component:

1 Set the insertion point where you want the component to appear. However, it must be within a Database Results region.

2 Select Database from the Insert menu, and then select Column Value. The Database Column Value dialog box pictured in Figure 33-23 will appear. Use the options in this dialog box as follows:

- **Column To Display.** To specify or modify the database field you want to display, select the field you want from the drop-down list.

- **Column Value Contains HTML.** Select this box if the database field you specified contains HTML you want the browser to display. This choice is appropriate if, for example, the field contains the HTML to display a hyperlink or a picture.

  Normally, the Database Results component translates HTML characters such as < and > to symbolic equivalents like < and >. This keeps the browser from misinterpreting these characters when they appear in normal text—in a description field, for example. However, it interferes with display of HTML you've purposely included in the query results. Selecting this option turns off the translation.

- **Display As Hyperlink.** Select this box if the database field contains URLs that the visitor should be able to click. FrontPage will display a hyperlink that uses the field contents as both the displayed text and the hyperlink location.

  Suppose, for example, that one row of a database table contained a field with the value *http://www.microsoft.com*. A Database Column Value component with the Display As Hyperlink option selected would use the following HTML to display the field:

  ```
  <a href="http://www.microsoft.com">http://www.microsoft.com</a>
  ```

  This HTML displays the text *http://www.microsoft.com* underlined like any other hyperlink, and clicking it would jump to Microsoft's Web site.

  Although the example shows a fully qualified URL, relative URLs work equally well.

3 Click OK.

To modify a Database Column Value component, double-click it, right-click it and choose Database Column Value Properties from the shortcut menu, or select it and choose Properties from the Format menu. This again displays the dialog box shown in Figure 33-23.

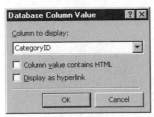

Figure 33-23. This dialog box configures the database field a Database Column Value component will display.

Creating Query Columns that Contain HTML

The previous section explained how, if some column in a database table or query contains HTML, you can select the Column Value Contains HTML box in the Database Column Value dialog box to display the HTML as Web content instead of odd-looking text. However, it didn't explain how the HTML got there. Not many database tables contain columns full of HTML.

In many cases, the tables that physically reside in the database don't contain HTML at all. Instead, the query that retrieves the records surrounds ordinary column values with HTML code. Figure 33-24 shows a Web page that uses just such a query.

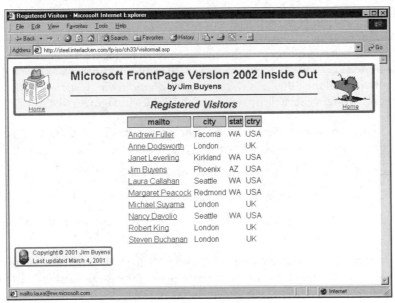

Figure 33-24. A database query generated the HTML for the clickable names in the *mailto* column of this database results page.

Chapter 33

The *city, stat,* and *ctry* fields are part of an ordinary table called *visitors.* The *mailto* column, however, isn't physically part of the database at all. Instead, it contains a string that Access assembles, based on a formula, for each row in the query. Here's the formula:

```
mailto: "<a href=" & Chr(34) & "mailto:" & [mail] & Chr(34) & ">" &
[name] & "</a>"
```

This formula contains five kinds of items:

- The initial expression *mailto:* assigns a column name to the calculated field.

- Expressions in quotes appear verbatim in the results.

- The *Chr()* function accepts a numeric argument and returns the corresponding ASCII character. *Chr(34)* returns a quotation mark character.

- Expressions in square brackets return the values of other fields in the same row. The expression *[mail]* returns the value of the *mail* field in the current table row.

- The ampersand character ("&") joins two strings together.

Note that the expression includes values from two different columns in the table: *[mail]* and *[name].* In fact, you can include values from as many fields as you want. This isn't a requirement, but it's certainly a powerful feature.

Figure 33-25 shows this formula entered as a column specification in Microsoft Access Design view. The designer saved the query as *vismailto.* Figure 33-26 shows the same query in Access Datasheet view. There's no distinction between the *mailto* field, which is calculated, and the other fields, which reside physically in the database. To run this query and produce clickable hyperlinks like the ones in Figure 33-24:

1 Set up a database connection to the database that contains the data (and the saved query)—unless, of course, you already have one.

2 Open a Web page, and set the insertion point.

3 Choose Database from the Insert menu, and then choose Results.

4 In the first dialog box of the Database Results wizard (the left side of Figure 33-8), specify the database connection you set up in step 1.

5 In the wizard's second dialog box (the right side of Figure 33-8), specify the query that contains the calculated expression. (The Record List will include a choice for the query name, plus the word VIEW.)

6 In the wizard's third dialog box (Figure 33-9), be sure to include the calculated field in the output.

7 In the fourth dialog box, *don't* specify Drop-Down List - One Record Per Item.

8 When the wizard finishes:

a Right-click the Database Column Value component titled *<<mailto>>*, and choose Database Column Value Properties from the shortcut menu.

b Select the box titled Column Value Contains HTML, and click OK.

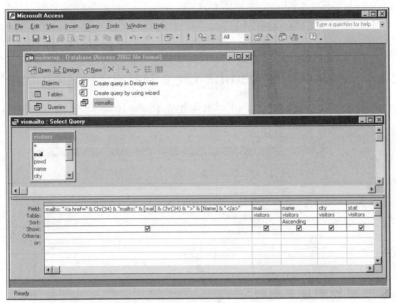

Figure 33-25. This query defines a field named *mailto* that comes from a formula rather than a physical field in a table.

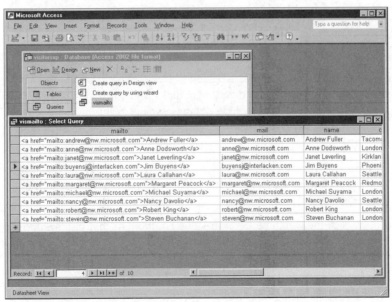

Figure 33-26. Running the query shown in Figure 33-25 produces these results. You can treat the calculated column like any other.

The same general technique works for all sorts of HTML: *<a href=…>* tags for hyperlinks, *<img src=…>* tags for pictures, and so forth. In the case of an *<img>* tag, the database would contain the name of the picture file and not the picture itself.

If for some reason you don't want to create a stored query, you can use calculated fields in a Custom Query. To do this, include the expression that defines the calculated field in the SQL statement you enter in the Custom Query dialog box shown at the left side of Figure 33-15.

Creating an Ordinary Hyperlink for a Database Column Value

Figure 33-27 shows another way of adding hyperlinks to a Database Results region.

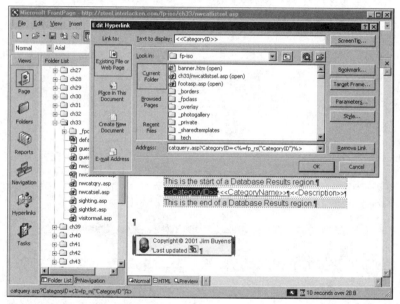

Figure 33-27. You can build ordinary hyperlinks that surround Database Column Value components and, if you want, include database values from the same record.

Here's the full procedure:

1 Create an ordinary Database Results region that displays the text you want to hyperlink as well as all the field values you want to include in the hyperlink URL.

2 Right-click the Database Column Value component that displays the desired text, and then choose Hyperlink or Hyperlink Properties (whichever appears) from the shortcut menu.

3 Enter any address you like in the Address option of the Insert Hyperlink or Edit Hyperlink dialog box.

4 Wherever you want a value from the database to appear in the URL, enter an expression such as the following:

```
<%=fp_rs("CategoryID")%>
```

Replace *CategoryID* with the name of the field you actually want.

Figure 33-28 shows the Web page from Figure 33-27 in use. Note that the mouse pointer is over the *CategoryName* for category 5, and that the status line at the bottom of the window displays a URL that includes the query string *CategoryID=5*. The digit *5* comes from the *CategoryID* field listed in the first Database Results column. Clicking this hyperlink displays the *nwcatqry.asp* page previously shown in Figure 33-14, instructing that page to display products with a *CategoryID* of 5.

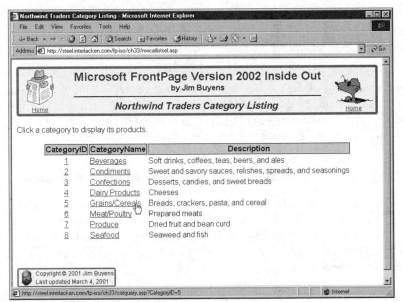

Figure 33-28. The hyperlinks in the CategoryName column of this Web page jump to the *nwcatqry.asp* page and tell it to display records with a specified CategoryID code.

Two additional points regarding this approach are worth noting. First, in the expression:

```
<%=fp_rs("CategoryID")%>
```

● The <% and %> tags mark the beginning and end of a block of ASP code. In other words, the code between these tags is going to execute on the Web server.

Note that the code that reads the database and formats the contents as HTML runs on the Web server and not on the browser. This is because the database resides on the server.

- The equal sign is a shortcut that tells the ASP processor to evaluate the subsequent expression and write it into the outgoing HTML.

- The string *fp_rs* is the name of the *recordset* object that contains the records the database region will display. FrontPage automatically generates code that positions the recordset to each available record and then reports that record.

  A *recordset,* as you might suspect, is an object that contains the results of a database query.

 For more information about recordset objects, refer to "Processing Databases with Active Server Pages" in the Bonus Content on the Companion CD.

- The string *CategoryID* is the name of the field that contains the value you want to retrieve. Be sure to include this field in the Database Results Wizard's third dialog box (Figure 33-9).

The second point regards the query string variable name *CategoryID.* This actually refers to the name of the text box in the upper left corner of Figure 33-14, and not directly to the name of the database field. When FrontPage creates a form like the one in Figure 33-14, it just happens to use the same name for the form field as the corresponding field in the database.

Re-Creating and Formatting Database Results Regions

You can rerun the Database Results Wizard at will simply by double-clicking any part of the Database Results region that isn't another FrontPage component or HTML element. You can also rerun the Wizard by right-clicking the Database Results region and choosing Database Results Properties, or by selecting the region and choosing Properties from the Format menu.

You can format Database Results regions and their accompanying forms as much as you like, but keep in mind that rerunning the Wizard might discard your formatting when it overwrites the Database Results region. You can never solve this problem completely, but here are some ways to minimize it:

- First get the Database Results region working as you want it, and then worry about formatting.

- As much as possible, format the Database Results region using CSS styles. Because CSS styles appear in the *<head>* section and not intermixed with the HTML, overwriting the HTML won't overwrite the CSS styles.

- FrontPage uses a fake HTML attribute called *BOTID* to associate the HTML form with its Database Results region. Whenever called upon to generate an input form, the Wizard inserts *BOTID="x"* into the *<form>* tag, where *x* is an arbitrary number. The *BOTID* attribute isn't an official attribute of the

Chapter 33

<form> tag, so browsers and other programs will ignore it. However, the Database Results Wizard uses this attribute to locate and replace the correct HTML form.

If you have trouble with the Database Results Wizard replacing the wrong form (or not replacing the correct one), view the page in HTML view and look for BOTID attributes.

Using the Database Interface Wizard

Chapter 8 described the basic procedure for creating a set of Web pages known collectively as a Database Interface. To briefly reiterate, this procedure uses a wizard you select from the Web Site Templates dialog box to create any combination of the following Web pages:

- **Results Page.** This is an ordinary Web page that contains a Database Results component. You could create exactly the same page using the procedures described in the "Using the Database Results Wizard" section earlier in this chapter. Furthermore, you can use any of the techniques described in that section to modify any results page that the Database Interface Wizard creates.

- **Submission Form.** This is another ordinary Web page, but it contains an HTML form that uses the Save Results component for adding records to the database. You could create the same page, or modify a page created by either method, by following the instructions in the "Saving Form Results to a Database" section earlier in this chapter.

Despite the similarity in results, there's a difference in mindset between creating a Save Results to Database page as described in this chapter and creating one using the Database Interface Wizard:

- ▪ The procedures in this chapter assume that you first want to create an HTML form, and then hook it up to a database.

- ▪ The Database Interface Wizard described in Chapter 8 assumes that you want to select or create the database first, and then have FrontPage create an HTML form for the database fields you select.

For more information about using the Database Interface Wizard, refer to "Using the Database Interface Wizard" on page 240.

- **Database Editor.** This is a frames page that displays, adds, changes, and deletes records in whatever database you selected when you ran the Database Interface Wizard. The target pages that display and add information are, of course, based on your old favorites—the Database Results component and the Save Results to Database component.

(continued)

Chapter 33

Using the Database Interface Wizard *(continued)*   Surprisingly, the pages that modify and delete records also use the Database Results component. Both of these pages—*update.asp* and *delete.asp*—contain Database Results components that run custom queries and select no fields for display:

- The custom query in the *update.asp* page uses the SQL verb UPDATE to locate the record with the key you selected, copy your form field values into the record, and save the record in the database. The wizard specifies no fields for display because the UPDATE verb doesn't produce any records to display.

- Similarly, the custom query in the *delete.asp* page uses the SQL verb DELETE to delete the record having the key you selected.

You can modify any Database Editor pages you like—the wizard puts them in a folder named *<connection>_interface/Results/editor*—but try to keep your changes cosmetic. Major change are likely to update the page itself or the way it interacts with other pages in the same frames page.

If, while running the wizard, you decided to protect the Database Editor with a password, the editor remembers that the visitor is logged in by sending the visitor a cookie. As long as the visitor's browser keeps sending the cookie back, the Database Editor won't ask that visitor to log in again.

Developing Custom Web Database Applications

The database facilities in FrontPage are relatively easy to use and require no programming skills, but they hardly represent the limit of what you can do with the combination of databases and Web pages. In fact, more and more Web sites store little or none of their content in Web pages at all; all the content resides in databases. The Web pages use technologies such as ASP pages to format the data on demand for Web visitors. This is a tremendously powerful approach because you can change the site's content without editing any Web pages, and you can redesign your Web pages without disturbing your content. This is the epitome of a so-called *data-driven Web site*.

The downside of this approach is that the more self-customizing your Web pages, the more awkward a WYSIWYG editor becomes. After all, if the page is going to rearrange or create its own HTML on the fly, what should the Page view editing window display? There's no good answer to this dilemma except that if you want to program your Web site, you need to be somewhat of a programmer.

 For more information about writing your own ASP pages that process databases, refer to "Processing Databases with Active Server Pages" in the Bonus Content on the Companion CD.

The difference in mindset between FrontPage components and ASP pages is a classic one: ASP pages are *procedural,* whereas the FrontPage WYSIWYG editor is *specification-oriented:*

- The procedural approach requires lines of program code that describe, step by step, how to produce the desired result. Its statements are imperative (that is, they're commands).

- The specification-oriented approach involves describing what you want rather than how to produce it. Its statements are declarative (that is, they're descriptions).

Specification-oriented approaches might be easier for nonprogrammers to learn and use, but only for relatively simple and well-known problems. Specification orientation deals poorly with both complex logic and conditions that require change to the specified output. When the output is too variable, specifying it declaratively becomes very awkward.

It's worth noting that WYSIWYG editing of any kind is inherently specification-oriented. When you format content in any of the Microsoft Office applications, you specify what you want and *not* how to program the printer. When you write a SUM formula in Excel, you say what cells you want added and not how to loop through an array or increment an accumulator. Drawing Access forms, reports, and queries is specification-oriented as well.

True to its membership in the Office family, FrontPage is also specification-oriented. You tell FrontPage what you want a Web page to look like, and FrontPage does the work of writing the HTML. This is probably, after all, why you bought FrontPage.

FrontPage is also a *static* environment. Animated GIF files don't play, nor do video clips. Scripts don't run. ActiveX controls and Java applets don't start. The reason is that FrontPage displays a point in time, not an active environment. Editing a document that constantly changes itself would be an exercise in reflexes—perhaps an exercise in futility. The experience of playing a video game comes to mind.

Although ASP and ADO undoubtedly provide a rich, full-function database environment, their procedural nature doesn't mesh as well with FrontPage. If your requirements go beyond simple queries, you'll have to create your own ASP code, enter it, and debug it. FrontPage can insert such scripts, but it can't write them for you.

 For more information about writing Active Server Page scripts in FrontPage, refer to "Scripting Web Pages on the Server" in the Bonus Content on the Companion CD.

Configuring a FrontPage Data Connection

FrontPage reads and writes database information through named *connections*. A database connection names a Microsoft Access database located in the current Web, an Open Database Connectivity (ODBC) data source on the Web server, or a direct connection to some other database. Connections might initially strike you as yet another abstract entity between you and your data, but they provide a number of advantages:

- You can define all the information about a database once, and then use that definition in multiple Web pages.

- You can create or upload databases to your Web, and then access them with Web pages, without assistance from the server administrator. For example, you don't need the administrator to set up an ODBC data source.

- You can access databases in your Web, ODBC Data Sources on the Web server, and any other databases available to the Web server, all in a uniform way.

 on the CD For more information about ODBC data sources, refer to "Configuring ODBC Data Sources" in the Bonus Content on the Companion CD.

tip Whenever you drag and drop an Access file into the Folder List or Folders view, FrontPage offers to create a database connection.

If you're planning to use an Access database stored within the same Web, first create it or upload it to the desired location—somewhere your Web visitors won't find it by accident. The */fpdb* folder is a good choice. Then:

1 Choose Web Settings from the Tools menu.

2 Click the Database tab. This displays the dialog box shown on the left side of Figure 33-29.

3 Click the Add button, displaying the New Database Connection dialog box shown in the top right corner of Figure 33-29. The following options are available:

- **Name.** The identifier you plan to use when accessing the connection from a Web page. Simple names of 6 to 8 characters are best. Using the name of the database as the name of the connection is usually a good choice because it gives you one less thing to remember.

- **File Or Folder In Current Web.** Connects to a database in the current Web.

- **System Data Source On Web Server.** Connects to an ODBC System Data Source Name defined on the Web server.

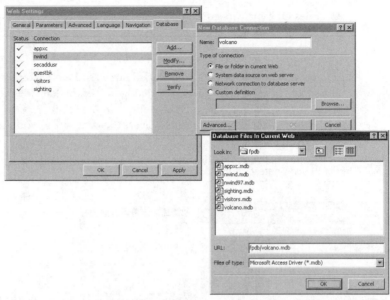

Figure 33-29. The Database Web Settings tab lists a Web's currently defined database connections. The New Database Connection dialog box adds a new database connection to a Web. The Database Files In Current Web dialog box locates a database in the current Web.

- **Network Connection To Database.** Connects to another database driver installed on the Web server.

- **Custom Definition.** Connects to either a Data Source Name (.*dsn*) or Universal Data Link (.*udl*) file that you designate by clicking Browse and choosing the file you want in the Connection Files In Current Web dialog box, similar to that in the bottom right corner of Figure 33-29.

 For more information about Data Source Name (.*dsn*) and Universal Data Link (.*udl*) files, refer to "Configuring ODBC Data Sources" in the Bonus Content on the Companion CD.

- **Browse.** Displays a dialog box for selecting the specific database.

4 Click OK.

The Browse button in the New Database Connection dialog box displays different dialog boxes depending on the Type Of Connection selection. Clicking the Browse button after choosing File Or Folder In Current Web displays the Database Files In Current Web dialog box shown in the bottom right corner of Figure 33-29. The following options are available:

- **Look In.** Selects folders in the current Web.

- **URL.** Specifies the database for this connection. Clicking a file listed in the center of the dialog box updates this option.

951

- **Files Of Type.** Specifies the type of database. This can be Access, dBase, FoxPro, Paradox, or any file-oriented database with a driver installed on the Web server.

If you click Browse after choosing Data Source On Web Server, FrontPage displays the System Data Sources On Web Server dialog box of the left side of Figure 33-30. The listed items are ODBC System DSNs defined in the ODBC32 Control Panel applet on the computer where the Web resides. Select the data source you want, and then click OK.

 For more information about ODBC data sources, refer to "Configuring ODBC Data Sources" in the Bonus Content on the Companion CD.

Figure 33-30. The System Data Sources On Web Server dialog box locates an ODBC System DSN defined on the Web server. The Network Database Connection dialog box locates a database through another database driver installed on the Web server.

Clicking Browse after choosing Network Connection To Database Server displays the Network Database Connection dialog box pictured on the right side of Figure 33-30. Select the type of database system, specify the server where it runs, and enter the name of the database on that server.

Clicking the Advanced button in the New Database Connection dialog box (the top right corner of Figure 33-29) is seldom necessary, especially with file oriented databases, but it displays the dialog box shown on the left side of Figure 33-31. You can obtain this information from the creator of the database or, in enterprise environments, from the database administrator:

- **Authorization.** Specifies logon credentials needed to access the database:
  - **Username.** A logon account permitted to use the database.
  - **Password.** The authentication code assigned to the given account.
- **Timeouts.** Specifies time limits which, if exceeded, will cancel a database operation:
  - **Connection.** Specifies the number of seconds allowable for opening a connection to the database.

■ **Command.** Specifies the number of seconds allowable for completing a database command—a query, for example.

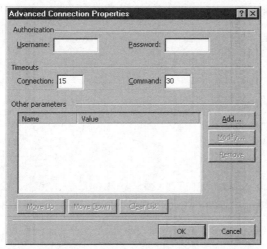

Figure 33-31. Clicking the Advanced button in the top right corner of the dialog box displayed in Figure 33-29 displays the additional options in this dialog box.

● **Other Parameters.** A list of named values required by the database driver. The Add, Modify, and Remove buttons control individual parameters. The Move Up and Move Down buttons reorder selected items in the list, and the Clear List button removes all entries.

The remaining buttons on the Database tab of the Web Settings dialog box (the left side of Figure 33-29) are Modify, Remove, and Verify:

● **Modify.** Displays a Database Connection Properties dialog box identical to the New Database Connection (the top right corner of Figure 33-29). This updates an existing database connection.

● **Remove.** Deletes the database connection.

● **Verify.** Attempts a connection to the database and reports the results. A check mark means the connection succeeded, whereas a broken link means the connection failed. Unverified connections have a question mark icon.

---

tip It's a good idea to set up FrontPage database connections for every Access database in your Web, even if you plan to use a certain database for custom development only. Existence of a database connection tells FrontPage to set up (and preserve) correct file system security for the database.

Introducing SQL

Virtually all modern relational databases use SQL as the means for accepting database commands. A typical SQL statement looks like this, with line numbers added to facilitate discussion. All fields named in the SQL statement must exist in the specified table:

```
1   SELECT <field>, <field>...
2     FROM <table>
3     WHERE (<field><op><value>)
4     GROUP BY <field>, <field>...
5     HAVING (<field><op><value>) AND/OR (<field><op> ¿
          <value>)...
6     ORDER BY <field>, <field>...
```

- The fields named after the SELECT keyword are the only fields returned. To return all fields in a table, specify an asterisk (*) rather than a field list.

- The FROM clause specifies the table being queried.

- The WHERE clause specifies one or more field comparisons that filter the records selected from the database.

- The GROUP BY clause consolidates rows with equal values in the named fields.

- The HAVING clause specifies one or more field comparisons that filter the output of the consolidation process.

- The ORDER BY clause controls the order in which returned records appear.

Of these six clauses, the last four are optional.

Unfortunately, FrontPage provides only a simple point-and-click means for generating SQL statements or for looking up the properties of a database. One alternative is to get a listing of table names and field definitions from the owner or administrator of the database, and then to type the required SQL statement manually. Another is to create the query graphically in Access, copy it to the Clipboard, and paste it into FrontPage using the Paste From Clipboard button. The "Refining Database Queries" section earlier in this chapter describes this procedure in detail.

> **For more information about SQL statements, refer to the documentation that came with your database application or one of the many books available on SQL.**

Databases on the Web—An Overview

Despite the widespread use of databases and the long efforts of many smart people, using databases remains somewhat complex. Multiple layers of software are required, each with its own eccentricities and configuration requirements. Web server interfaces add yet another layer of complexity.

This section explains, as simply as possible, what you need to know about database technology and configuration to create Web database pages with FrontPage.

Understanding the FrontPage Database Environment

Figure 33-32 is a simple block diagram illustrating how database access on the Web typically occurs. The step-by-step process flow consists of the following:

1 An ordinary HTML form, as described in Chapter 31, collects any required or optional input fields from the Web visitor.

If database function requires no visitor input, no HTML form is required. Instead, the ASP file or program that contains the database code is simply the target of a hyperlink.

2 The form's Action property specifies the Web page or program containing the database code. For database applications created in FrontPage, this will be an ASP file residing on the Web server.

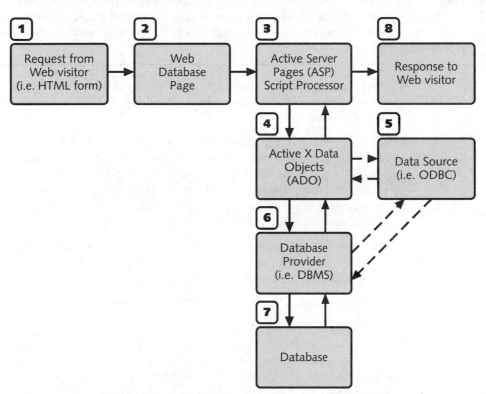

Figure 33-32. This diagram illustrates the operation of a typical Web database page.

Chapter 33

3 As it delivers the requested ASP file, the Web server calls the ASP script processor into play. The script processor executes Microsoft VBScript code FrontPage has placed in the HTML. This code performs three key functions:

a It merges any variable data into a SQL statement that specifies what data to retrieve.

b It opens a connection via ADO to the database and sends the SQL statement.

c When ADO returns the data, VBScript code in the HTML reads each record and replaces itself with HTML that displays the results.

ASP is an interpreter that executes specially marked lines of VBScript, JavaScript, or other languages embedded within HTML. Server-side script code isn't transmitted to the Web visitor, but the Web visitor *does* receive any HTML such scripts generate.

> **note** If you look at an ASP file on the server, you'll see any server-side script code it contains. If you browse the same file using an *http://* URL and choose your browser's View Source command, you'll see either generated HTML or nothing where the script code resided.

4 ADO provides database capability for server-side scripts. ADO objects are ActiveX objects with no user interface—they operate in background mode only.

5 ODBC is a software component that provides a relatively standard interface for applications despite differences in database systems. It consists of general-purpose modules that make up ODBC itself, plus specific drivers for each database system. An initial set of ODBC drivers comes with the Windows operating system. Upgrades and additions typically come with various kinds of database software.

An ODBC System Data Source Name is a definition, made through the ODBC Control Panel applet, that equates a DSN to a database driver, the name of a database, and other settings, depending on the database type.

FrontPage Database Connections are a type of ODBC data source created on the fly.

6 A database provider (usually a Database Management System, or DBMS) accepts high-level transaction commands—usually SQL statements—and manipulates the physical files that constitute databases. SQL Server and the Microsoft Jet database engine in Access are examples.

7 A relational database consists of data arranged in rows and columns—that is, in tables. Each row is in essence a record, each column a field. All records in the same table contain the same fields (but not, of course, the same values).

If two tables have identifying fields in common, the DBMS can match rows having like values and present the results as a joined table. The DBMS can present any desired combination of columns to the calling program, and can select records based on data values.

8 The response delivered to the Web visitor consists of ordinary HTML (plus, of course, any script or CSS code). Except for the *.asp* filename extension and the variability of output, the Web visitor won't be aware that a server-side script is involved.

Of the eight components shown in Figure 33-32, FrontPage can create and maintain items 1, 2, and 7: the submitted HTML form (if any), the Web page containing the Save Results coding or Database Results region, and in some cases the database itself. All these files must reside on the same Web server that accepts transactions from Web visitors, runs the database query, and returns the response. In addition, the page containing the Database Results region must reside in an executable folder on that Web server.

Design and configuration of the databases, the database management system, and the ODBC interface all occur completely outside FrontPage. If these resources don't already exist, use standard database development tools such as SQL Server or Access to develop and implement them. If they do exist, get the necessary file locations, record layouts, and permissions from their owner or administrator.

Locating a Web Database Facility

Running database applications on a Web server is more difficult than delivering simple Web pages for two reasons: complexity and resource consumption:

- Complexity issues arise because database management systems require much more effort to install, configure, and manage than ordinary Web servers. In addition, DBMSs are usually administered at the system rather than the user level. Not many system administrators are willing to turn over administration of a DBMS to end users; the potential problems and the difficulty in analyzing them are simply too extreme. However, these same administrators frequently lack the time to do database administration for a large base of diverse users.

- Issues of resource consumption arise because a database transaction can consume far more processor time, memory, and disk activity than delivering any simple Web page.

These issues usually aren't serious obstacles on intranets and public Web sites having dedicated communication lines and servers. Intranets usually have plentiful bandwidth and server capacity, together with a more homogeneous community of developers and visitors than, say, a public Internet service provider. Most public Web sites belonging to corporations, government agencies, and other organizations also enjoy adequate bandwidth and dedicated servers.

If you have a typical dial-up ISP account, you might lack the capability to run ASP pages, to use databases, and thus to offer database services on your personal Web pages. Obtaining these capabilities might require paying additional service charges or changing ISPs.

In general, however, any service that provides Windows 2000 or Windows NT servers running the FrontPage Server Extensions 2002 will probably support use of FrontPage database connectors pointing to Access databases within the same Web. After all, these capabilities are built into the Server Extensions and require no special configuration by the ISP.

Configuring a Web Database Environment

Table 33-5 lists the Web servers that support ASP, ADO, and ODBC. You can use any database system that has thread-safe ODBC drivers, though the most common are Access and SQL Server.

Table 33-5. Web Servers Supporting ASP, ADO, and ODBC

Web server	Operating system	Status
Internet Information Services	Windows 2000	Current
Internet Information Server	Windows NT Server 4	Supported
Personal Web Server	Windows NT Workstation 4	Supported
Personal Web Server	Windows 95 and Windows 98	Obsolete

The issue with thread-safe ODBC drivers is this: the ADO facility pushes database requests into ODBC as fast as they arrive, rather than waiting for one request to be completed before submitting another. Thread-safe ODBC drivers can cope with this, but others can't; the ones that can't malfunction or fail completely when two requests arrive too close together. The current drivers for Access and SQL Server are thread-safe.

Microsoft's top-of-the-line, industrial-strength server components are Windows 2000 Server, IIS, and SQL Server. All three components are designed for high-volume use. Extensive multithreading ensures optimal performance under heavy load. Their system management and administration are also enterprise-strength.

> **tip** Don't forget that the Windows 95 and Windows 98 won't run the FrontPage Server Extensions 2002, and that Windows Me won't run a Web server at all. In addition, Windows 95 won't run the FrontPage 2002 desktop software. The era of developing Web database applications on these platforms is definitely waning.

The combination of Windows 98, Personal Web Server, and Access consists entirely of tools designed for individual desktop use. This is both its greatest strength and greatest weakness. In terms of strength, the Windows 98/Personal Web Server/Access combination is undoubtedly the easiest for new Web designers to learn and deal with. Its performance and stability as a production environment, however, are moderate at best.

Likewise, few production environments have such casual requirements that Windows 98 and Access can satisfy them. Windows NT Server and Access might be adequate for light database use, but Windows NT Server and SQL Server are clearly optimal in most cases.

The best production and development environments for your project will lie somewhere between Access on Windows NT 4 Professional (at the low end) and SQL Server on Windows 2000 Server (at the high end).

Choosing a Web Database Development Environment

Running the combination of Windows 2000 Server, IIS, and a full-blown copy of SQL Server is probably overkill for any developer. Windows 2000 Professional, IIS, and a developer version of SQL Server provide essentially the same software at a much lower price (albeit with license restrictions that prevent use as a production server).

The degree of separation between your test and development environments depends on their natures. For informal intranet applications with no critical service requirements, the development and production environments can be one and the same. For mission-critical and highly secure applications, elaborate implementation and quality assurance procedures will generally be necessary, and these will involve development and production environments that are quite distinct.

The risk of problems moving from your development environment to production environment is least if you develop on Windows 2000 Professional and run on Windows 2000 Server. Transitioning from Windows 98 and Personal Web Server might involve additional problems because Windows 98 doesn't provide all of Windows NT Server's security features.

Moving from an Access development environment over to a SQL Server production environment can also be difficult. These two database systems use different dialects of SQL, and at least some SQL statements will likely need adjustment. Copying database and table definitions from Access to SQL Server is more problematic than copying them between like systems. In short, whatever problems you sought to avoid by developing with Access, you're likely to encounter anyway when you transfer the system to production.

If you decide on a development environment using SQL Server, remember that not every developer needs a private copy. In most cases, a single copy of SQL Server running on a local Windows 2000 system can easily support an entire workgroup of developers.

Don't overlook the possibility of running FrontPage on Windows 98, Windows Me, Windows NT Workstation, or Windows 2000 Professional while locating your Web and database servers on Windows NT Server or Windows 2000 Server. Remember, FrontPage manages the files in your Web using HTTP and doesn't require local-file access.

In Summary...

This chapter explained how to use the capabilities built into FrontPage for creating Web pages that access and update databases. Using databases on the Web has become a popular practice because it's much more accurate and much less time-consuming than creating Web pages for each item in a collection (for each product, department, or employee, for example).

The next chapter explains the features FrontPage offers for coordinating a team of designers all working on a single Web.

Part 11

Collaborating with Teams and Workgroups

Chapter 34

Managing Design Teams

Every day, it seems, FrontPage-based Webs and Web sites in general get larger and larger. Couple that with the natural law that says, "The more work you have to do, the sooner it needs to get done," and eventually you find yourself working in a group rather than alone. And of course, this leads to the minor chaos and pandemonium that groups everywhere seem to experience.

If you have a server-based Web or a disk-based Web residing on a file server, several people can access the same Web at the same time. This is far from being a problem; in fact, it's something Microsoft FrontPage has special features to support:

- **Tasks View.** Maintains a list of pending work items for the current Web. FrontPage can create such tasks as part of other functions, associate these tasks with specific Web pages, and prompt for task status when a designer saves the associated page.

- **Workflow Status And Reporting.** Records the following items for each page in a FrontPage-based Web: Assigned To, Assigned By, Assigned Date, Review Status, Reviewed By, and Review Date. By viewing reports that display these fields, you can instantly check on the status and progress of assigned changes.

- **Page Level Control Over Publishing.** Provides a Publish/Don't Publish indicator for each file in a FrontPage-based Web. This is useful when some parts of a Web, but not others, are ready for publication.

- **Page Level Check-In/Check-Out.** Reserves a file on behalf of one designer so others can't make conflicting updates.

Although less powerful than full-scale project management and source control systems, these features are highly integrated with FrontPage and provide all the functions many small projects need. At the very least, they can record the status of each Web page in process so that team members working on the same Web can avoid stepping on each other's work.

Working with Tasks View

Developing and maintaining any Web involves a multitude of small, interrelated tasks. Changes made to one page require updates on another. New pages require links from others. Errors in spelling, missing pictures, and hyperlinks to nowhere require follow-up and correction. To keep track of these pesky details, you need a task list.

As shown in Figure 34-1, FrontPage provides an automated, highly integrated Tasks view, which displays a list of pending tasks for the current FrontPage-based Web. You can create tasks either manually as you think of them or automatically as a result of other processes.

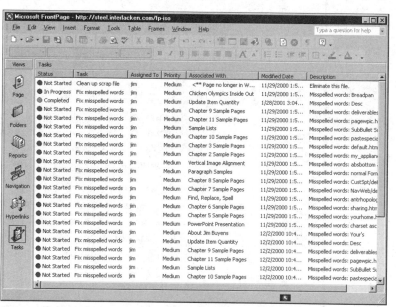

Figure 34-1. FrontPage's Tasks view helps you remember unfinished tasks in a highly integrated way. As you resolve each issue, you can mark the task complete.

Chapter 34: Managing Design Teams

The Tasks view column headings, as shown in Figure 34-1, are straightforward. Clicking any column heading sorts the list on that column. To display the task list, click the Tasks icon in the Views bar.

Creating Tasks Manually

FrontPage provides a variety of convenient ways to create tasks. Here's how to create a task manually:

1 Display the New Task dialog box shown in Figure 34-2 using any of these methods:

- In any FrontPage view, choose New from the File menu, and then choose Task.

- In any FrontPage view, choose Tasks from the Edit menu, and then choose Add Task.

- In Tasks view only, right-click any blank area in the main Tasks window and choose Add Task from the shortcut menu.

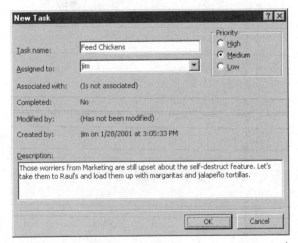

Figure 34-2. Use this dialog box to create new tasks.

2 When the New Task dialog box appears, enter a title in the Task Name box.

3 In the Priority section, select High, Medium, or Low.

4 Choose a name from the Assigned To drop-down list.

5 Optionally, enter a comment in the Description box. Click OK.

Chapter 34

Creating Tasks Associated with a Specific File

Note that in Figure 34-2, the Associated With field indicates no link. Creating a task directly from the file menu or the Tasks view background has this effect. To manually create a task associated with a specific page, do any of the following:

- Locate and select the page in the Page view Folder List or anywhere in Folders, Reports, or Navigation view. Next, choose Tasks from the Edit menu, and then choose Add Task.

- Open the page in Page view. Then, with the focus in the open page, choose New from the File menu, and then choose Task.

- In some New Page dialog boxes, you can create a New Page task rather than the new page itself.

To create a task linked to a hyperlink, create it from Hyperlinks view.

Creating Tasks Automatically

Certain global FrontPage operations also create tasks. For example, you can check the spelling on your entire Web and, rather than stopping at each error, simply create tasks pointing to any pages that contain errors. Here's a complete list of the ways FrontPage can create tasks automatically:

- **Pages that contain spelling errors.** Set the insertion point anywhere outside the Page view editing window, and then choose Spelling from the Tools menu. This displays the Spelling dialog box shown here. If you select Add A Task For Each Page With Misspellings, FrontPage creates a task for each page containing so much as a single misspelled word.

- **New pages that need detail filled in.** When FrontPage creates a new page, it can either open the page immediately or create a blank page and a task reminding you to edit the page later. Figure 34-3 shows how a designer might create a hyperlink to a new page. (Note that the designer selected the Just Add Web task box.)

> For more information about creating new pages, refer to "Creating a New Web Page" on page 255.

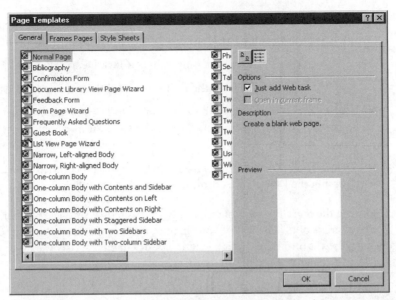

Figure 34-3. FrontPage uses the Page Templates dialog box to create new
Web pages. The option Just Add Web Task adds an entry to the Task list
rather than opening the new page.

Working with Tasks

Tasks view behaves in most respects like any report in Reports view. Clicking the
column headings sorts the report on that heading. Single-clicking the Assigned To,
Priority, and Description fields on any row opens those fields to editing.

By default, Tasks view displays only tasks that are Not Started or In Progress. To display completed tasks as well, choose Tasks and then Show History from the Edit menu,
or right-click a blank area in the main Task window and select Show History from the
shortcut menu. Right-clicking a task in Tasks view displays the shortcut menu shown.

The commands on this menu work as follows:

- **Edit Task.** Displays the Task Details dialog box, which is similar to the New
  Task dialog box shown in Figure 34-2. Here you can modify the properties
  of a task. You can display the same dialog box by:

  - Double-clicking the task you want to edit, or

  - Choosing Tasks from the Edit menu and then choosing Edit Task.

Part 11: Collaborating with Teams and Workgroups

- **Start Task.** Opens a task's associated file, if any, with the appropriate editor, such as Page view for an HTML page. You can also perform this action by:

  - ■ Clicking the Start Task button in the Task Details dialog box.

  - ■ Choosing Tasks from the Edit menu and then choosing Start Task.

- **Mark Complete.** Changes the task's status to Completed. You can also make this change by choosing Tasks from the Edit menu and then choosing Mark Complete.

- **Delete Task.** Removes a task from the list after you confirm your choice. Pressing the Delete key accomplishes the same result.

Choosing the Start Task command by any means tells FrontPage to open the associated file (if there is one). Then, after you change and save the file, FrontPage displays the message box shown here , asking whether your changes satisfy the task's requirements. Clicking Yes instructs FrontPage to mark the task completed.

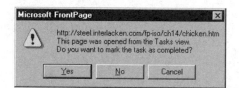

Controlling and Reporting Workflow Status

Tasks view records who's assigned to various tasks involving pages, but it doesn't show overall responsibility, overall status, review responsibility, or review status. FrontPage includes several features related specifically to these areas. All involve data you enter in the Properties dialog box for files in a FrontPage-based Web. Figure 34-4 shows this dialog box. To display it:

- Right-click any file in the Page view Folder List, or in Folders, Reports, or Hyperlinks view.

- Choose Properties from the shortcut menu.

- Choose the Workgroup tab.

For pages open in Page view, you can display an equivalent tab by choosing Properties from the File menu and then choosing the Workgroup tab.

Chapter 34: Managing Design Teams

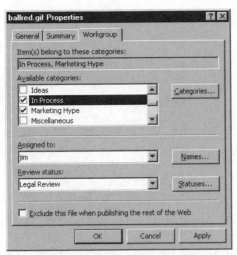

Figure 34-4. The Workgroup tab on a file's Properties dialog box specifies the file's assigned designer and review status.

Here are the properties available in the Workgroup tab:

- **Available Categories.** Lists the category names defined within the current Web:

  - If the current page already belongs to a given category, FrontPage automatically selects the corresponding box.

  - To assign additional categories to the page, select them yourself.

  - To create or delete categories, click Categories.

  A list of all categories assigned to the current file appears in the Item(s) Belong To These Categories box.

For more information about the use of categories, refer to "Categories" on page 441 and "Using the Table of Contents Based On Page Category Component" on page 776.

- **Assigned To.** Specifies who's assigned to work on this file. You can either type the name by hand or select it from the drop-down list. Clicking the Names button displays the dialog box shown in the left side of Figure 34-5 on the next page, which adds designers to or deletes them from the list.

  Whenever it changes the Assigned To field for a file, FrontPage records the name of the designer making the change, the date, and the time. This is where the Assigned Date and Assigned By columns in Figure 34-6 on the next page come from.

Part 11: Collaborating with Teams and Workgroups

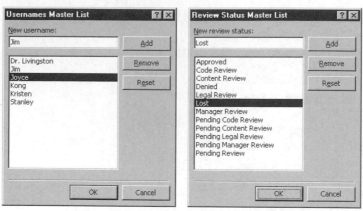

Figure 34-5. To add or remove names in the Assigned To list for a file's workgroup properties, click Names to display the dialog box at the left. To modify the Review Status choices, click Statuses to display the dialog box at the right.

Figure 34-6 shows the FrontPage Assigned To report. To locate all files assigned to a specific person, click the Assigned To column heading and then scroll down to that name. You can also change the Assigned To field directly in this report by first selecting the correct line, and then single-clicking the Assigned To field.

For more information about the Assigned To report, refer to "Assigned To" on page 441.

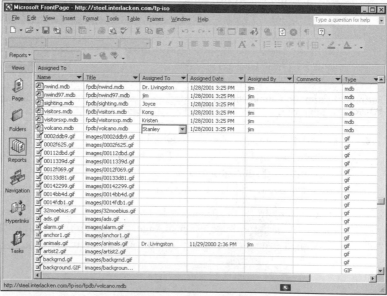

Figure 34-6. The Assigned To report lists each file in a FrontPage-based Web, showing who is currently assigned, by whom, and when.

Chapter 34

Chapter 34: Managing Design Teams

● **Review Status.** Records the results of the most recent review for the current file. As with Assigned To, either type the Review Status or select it after clicking the drop-down list button. FrontPage records the given status, plus the user name, date, and time.

Clicking the Statuses button in the dialog box shown in Figure 34-4 displays the dialog box shown in the right side of Figure 34-5. As with the Usernames Master List dialog box, you can add statuses, remove them, or reset the list.

Figure 34-7 shows the Review Status report, which summarizes the review status of each file in the current Web.

For more information about the Review Status report, refer to "Review Status" on page 439.

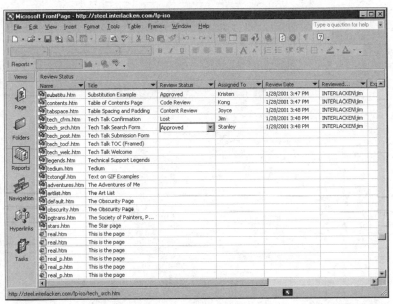

Figure 34-7. The Review Status report lists status, reviewer, and date for each file in a FrontPage-based Web.

● **Exclude This File When Publishing The Rest Of The Web.** Prevents (if selected) or permits (if cleared) publication of the current file when you run the Publish Web command. The next section explains this further.

Controlling Publishing at the Page Level

The check box titled Exclude This File When Publishing The Rest Of The Web, on the Workgroup tab of a file's Properties dialog box (Figure 34-4), prevents publishing the current file to another FrontPage-based Web. To prevent publishing of the current file, select this box. To allow publishing, clear it. You can also control this setting by right-clicking any file in the Page view Folder List, in Folder view, or in Reports view, and then clicking the Don't Publish option in the shortcut menu.

This feature doesn't affect your ability to import, move, or copy the given file, even among different FrontPage-based Webs or servers. It affects only the operation of the FrontPage Publish feature.

> **For more information about the Publish feature, refer to Chapter 13, "Publishing Your FrontPage-Based Web."**

The Publish Status report shown in Figure 34-8 shows which files are enabled and disabled for publishing. You can also update publishing status directly in this report. In the figure, an update is in progress where the drop-down list appears.

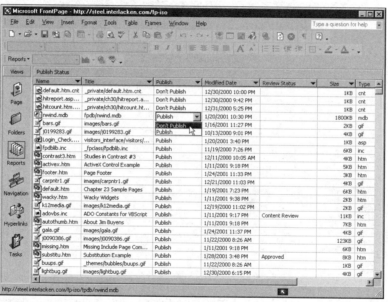

Figure 34-8. The Publish Status report shows which pages in a Web are enabled or disabled from publishing to another FrontPage-based Web or server.

> **For more information about The Publish Status report, refer to "Publish Status" on page 442.**

Using Page Level Check-In/Check-Out

When several people work on the same Web, there's always a chance that two people might start working on the same page at the same time. The result is a battle of dueling versions; whoever saves the file last overlays the first person's updates.

Chapter 34: Managing Design Teams

To compound the problem, changing a Web page can take days or weeks if the change is part of a general site upgrade or requires multiple approvals. Of course, that doesn't mean someone's going to keep the page open in FrontPage all that time, but it does mean that the designer wants the file safe from being updated by other people during that interval.

Page Level Check-In/Check-Out provides an answer to this problem. Here's how this feature works:

- The Web's administrator turns on the Page Level Check-In/Check-Out feature.

- Before a designer begins changing a file, he or she checks the file out—that is, takes ownership by using a right-click menu option. This does two things:

  - It prevents any other designer from making changes to the file.

  - It saves a copy of the file for possible restoration.

- After the file is checked out, it shows up as locked to other designers and administrators of the same Web. If they try to open the file, they'll get an error message with two options: either give up editing the file or open a read-only copy. They can save the read-only copy under another name, but they can't update the checked-out original.

- When the designer who checked out the file is finished with any updates, he or she can take either of two actions:

  - Check the file in, which relinquishes ownership and deletes the backup copy.

  - Undo the checkout, which restores the backup copy (undoing all changes) and then relinquishes ownership.

The option that makes Page-Level Check-In/Check-Out available or unavailable appears on the General tab of the Web Settings dialog box. To display it, choose Web Settings from the Tools menu, and then click the General tab. Figure 34-9 on the next page provides an example.

> **tip**   Page Level Check-In/Check-Out is available only for disk-based Webs and for server-based Webs using the FrontPage 2000 Server Extensions or later. Older versions of the Server Extensions don't support this feature.

Chapter 34

Part 11: Collaborating with Teams and Workgroups

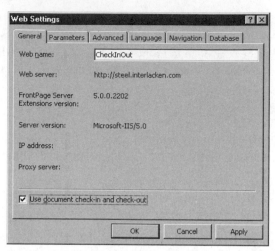

Figure 34-9. The Use Document Check-In And Check-Out option in this dialog box makes the use of source code control for a FrontPage-based Web available or unavailable.

To activate Page Level Check-In/Check-Out, select the check box titled Use Document Check-In And Check-Out. To disable it, clear the same box. When you click OK, FrontPage prompts you that it needs to recalculate the Web's hyperlinks. Click Yes to continue.

tip The user name FrontPage uses for Check-In/Check-Out is normally the one that provides access to the FrontPage-based Web. For Webs with no user-level security, FrontPage uses your Windows user name.

When Page Level Check-In/Check-Out is in effect, all FrontPage Folder Lists display an icon in front of each file name:

- **Green Dot.** Means the file is available for checkout.

- **Red Check Mark.** Means the file is checked out to you.

- **Gray Padlock.** Means the file is checked out to someone else.

Figure 34-10 shows a typical FrontPage Folder List with Page Level Check-In/Check-Out in effect. All three icon types are visible. The designer has right-clicked the file *checkers.htm,* and can use the Check Out option on the shortcut menu to take ownership.

If you try to open a file you haven't checked out, FrontPage presents the following dialog box. Clicking Yes checks the file out and then opens it. Clicking No opens the file

Chapter 34: Managing Design Teams

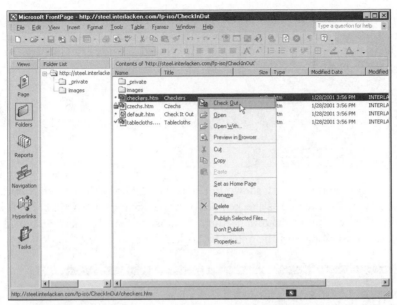

Figure 34-10. With Page Level Check-In And Check-Out in effect, each file in a Web is either available for checkout (green dot), checked out to the current user (red check mark) or checked out to someone else (padlock).

and permits saving it, but with no source code control in effect. (This might be acceptable for making quick, simple changes.) Clicking Cancel abandons the edit.

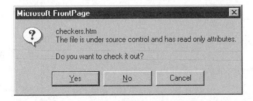

If you try to open a file someone else has checked out, you'll receive the following dialog box. Clicking Yes opens the file despite the fact that user *mary* has checked it out, but won't let you update Mary's version. To save it, you'll have to use another file name. Clicking No abandons the edit.

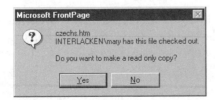

Part 11: Collaborating with Teams and Workgroups

Attempting to save a file that's checked out to someone else produces the following dialog box. There are no real options here other than clicking the OK button and saving the file under another name, or talking to Mary and asking her to incorporate your change with hers.

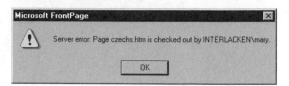

The Checkout Status Report, shown in Figure 34-11, shows the checkout status of every file in a Web. To find all files checked out by a specific person, sort the report by clicking the Checked Out By column heading. To look for files that have remained checked out suspiciously long, sort the report by Locked Date.

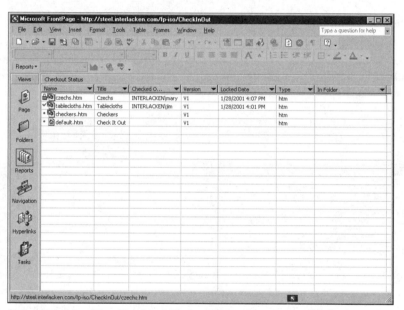

Figure 34-11. The Checkout Status report shows who checked out each file in a Web, and when.

Figure 34-10 also shows the shortcut menu for a file checked out to the current designer. Choosing Check In relinquishes control of the file and deletes the backup copy made at checkout. Choosing Undo Check Out restores the backup copy—in effect reversing all changes—and then relinquishes control.

There are two additional precautions related to creating and deleting files in a Web with Check-In/Check-Out in effect. First, creating a new file doesn't automatically check it out to you. If you want the file checked out, you have to do it yourself. Second, you can't delete a file checked out to someone else. To delete a file checked out to someone else, you must first ask that person to check it in.

on the Web   Even greater source-code control, including backout through multiple versions, is available by installing Microsoft Visual SourceSafe on a server-based Web. For details, browse *http://www.microsoft.com/frontpage/wpp/serk/admin.htm*

In Summary...

This chapter explained four FrontPage features that help coordinate the actions of a design team working on a single Web. These are Tasks view, Workflow Status, Page Level Publishing, and Page Level Check-In/Check-Out.

The next chapter explains how to create, administer, and use SharePoint team Web sites, a new and powerful type of Web for coordinating groups of all kinds (even groups allergic to Web development).

Chapter 35

newfeature!
Using SharePoint Team Web Sites

If you install SharePoint Team Services on your Web server, workgroups throughout your organization can use SharePoint team Web sites to coordinate their work. Team Web sites help people work together by providing an easy-to-use repository of project documents, discussions, and lists of virtually anything the project needs to record.

Lists are central to the operation of a SharePoint team Web site. Physically, a list is just a database table. But the power of lists comes from the fact that you can create them, update them, display them, and if necessary delete them using standard Web pages that team members can quickly learn to use.

SharePoint team Web sites provide the following services to anyone with a Web browser, connectivity to your server, and the necessary permissions:

- **Document Libraries.** A SharePoint team Web site document library has two components: a folder full of documents and a list that describes them. You can search for documents using either the document content itself or the data in the list:

    - **Web Discussions.** After an Office 2000 or Office XP user saves a document to a Web server as HTML (and recall: this is an integrated, one-step process), Web visitors browsing that document can make comments using a *discussion toolbar*. SharePoint Team Services stores these comments separately from the document itself. Then, when the document creator opens the document, all the comments appear seamlessly merged.

■ **Search page.** This feature uses Microsoft Indexing Service to search for documents within the current SharePoint team Web site.

The clients for these features are either a browser (for the Web-based tasks) or standard Office applications (for document creation and retrieval).

● **Discussion Boards.** This is the sort of feature most people call a threaded discussion group. Within a team Web site, you can create as many Discussion Boards as you like, and each board can accommodate an almost unlimited number of threads and messages. You can sort and present the messages any way you like, and purge old messages automatically.

● **Lists.** These are the basic unit of storage in a SharePoint team Web site. They can contain a list of announcements, a list of upcoming events, a list of scheduled tasks, a list of team members or contacts, a list of excuses, or anything else you like. The number of lists and the fields they contain are totally at your discretion.

● **Subscriptions.** With this feature, team members can ask to be notified whenever a specified document or folder changes. SharePoint Team Services detects such changes and sends the notifications by e-mail.

● **Administration.** This Web-based tool provides control over the preceding applications.

newfeature!
Creating a New SharePoint Team Web Site

SharePoint Team Services runs on Microsoft Windows 2000 computers with Microsoft Internet Information Services (IIS) 5.0 installed. SharePoint Team Services is a server-based application, so installing it requires Administrator privileges on the target machine. At a high level, here are the tasks required:

1 Install Windows 2000 Professional, Windows 2000 Server, or any later version.

> **note** Although Windows 2000 Professional will run SharePoint Team Services, Microsoft intends this as a development platform. Windows 2000 Professional isn't licensed for use as a widely accessible Web server.

2 Install IIS.

> For more information about installing IIS, refer to Chapter 37, "Installing and Configuring a Web Server."

3 Install SharePoint Team Services by running *sharept\setupse.exe* from your Office XP CD, or by downloading it from Microsoft's Web site at *http://www.microsoft.com/servers* and following the accompanying instructions.

Chapter 35: Using SharePoint Team Web Sites

As always, it's generally best to upgrade Windows 2000 and IIS to the latest release or service pack, and to install the most up-to-date release of SharePoint Team Services. For information about using SharePoint Team Services on other operating systems, monitor Microsoft's Web site.

Installing SharePoint Team Services installs the following items:

- **SharePoint team Web site application components.** These include Web pages, ASP pages, ActiveX controls, and so forth.

- **Microsoft FrontPage Server Extensions 2002.** If the Web server already contains an earlier version of the extensions, installing SharePoint Team Services will upgrade them.

- **Microsoft Data Engine (MSDE).** This is essentially a version of Microsoft SQL Server, but it lacks the tools you need to design and manage your own databases. If you already have a copy of SQL Server running on your network, SharePoint Team Services can use that installation rather than MSDE.

Installing SharePoint Team Services also installs a SharePoint team Web site in the Web server's root folder. If the server already contains a home page, the Setup program will prompt you before replacing it with the SharePoint team Web site's home page. If you choose not to replace the existing home page, Setup saves the SharePoint team Web site's home page using a different name.

If your computer has only one virtual Web server, installing SharePoint Team Services adds the FrontPage Server Extensions and other SharePoint Team Services features to that server automatically. Otherwise, SharePoint Team Services Setup asks you which servers to extend. After you install SharePoint Team Services, you can install it on or remove it at will from any virtual server on the same system.

> For more information about installing and removing the FrontPage Server extensions on individual virtual servers, refer to Chapter 38, "Understanding the FrontPage Server Extensions."

Microsoft designed SharePoint team Web sites for use by as many as 500 to 600 people who work together as a group (such as a department or project). The optimal number of users is smaller. If you have a lot of people, you probably have a lot of departments or projects, and you should generally create a separate SharePoint team Web site for each one. Fortunately, a single Web server can host any number of SharePoint team Web sites.

> For more information about creating SharePoint team Web sites, refer to "Creating a SharePoint Team Web Site" on page 248.

Figure 35-1 on the next page illustrates the home page for a typical SharePoint team Web site located in the Web server's root folder. Additional team Web sites on the same server would, of course, have folder paths in their URLs:

- The menu bar at the top of the page provides access to all features in the site.

- The Quick Launch area at the left provides hyperlinks to whatever high-usage features you select.

- The Search Documents text box and accompanying Go button search all documents libraries for a given string of text.

- The Announcements and Events areas provide links to the *Announcements* and *Events* lists and display recent additions to those lists.

- The Links area provides hyperlinks that team members might frequently use. This data resides in a list called, logically enough, *Links*.

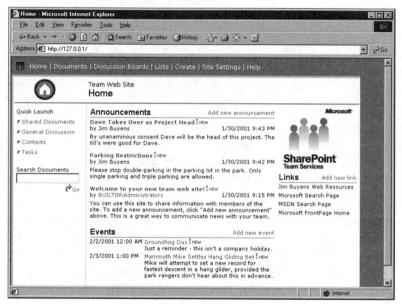

Figure 35-1. The home page for a SharePoint team Web site is highly configurable, but this version is fairly typical for a new site.

In general, it's best to block anonymous access to SharePoint team Web sites. Otherwise, the Web server won't prompt team members for usernames and passwords, and none of the data in the team Web site will be identified by team member.

> For more information about controlling access to SharePoint team Web sites, refer to "Administering SharePoint Team Web Site Settings" later in this chapter.

newfeature!
Using Document Libraries

Click Documents on the SharePoint team Web site menu bar to display the Document Libraries page shown in Figure 35-2. This page displays an icon representing each document library in the current team Web site. The one library shown in the figure—Shared Documents—appears automatically in every new team Web site, but you can create as many document libraries as you want. The New Document Library link jumps to a New page that creates new libraries, as do various other links located conveniently throughout the team Web site.

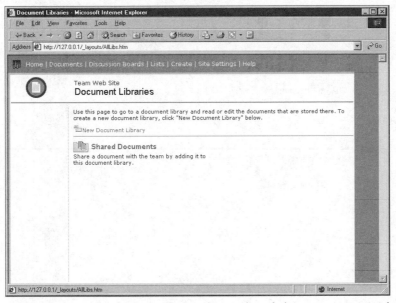

Figure 35-2. This page provides a selection list of SharePoint team Web site document libraries. The one library shown here appears by default in every new team Web site.

How Document Libraries Work

SharePoint team Web site document libraries have three major components:

- A folder named *Shared Documents,* where all the documents reside.
- A database table—stored in MSDE—that records additional information about each document in the library.
- A series of Web pages that update the document library, perform queries against it, and so forth.

Adding a document to the library requires updating two of these components in unison: the *Shared Documents* folder and the database table. That's why you should always update team Web site document libraries through the Web pages provided, or directly from Office XP using Web Folders (or, on Windows 2000, an HTTP location in My Network Places).

Part 11: Collaborating with Teams and Workgroups

Click the icon for any library, or click the Shared Documents link, to display a Document Library View page like the one in Figure 35-3. This page lists the documents in the library.

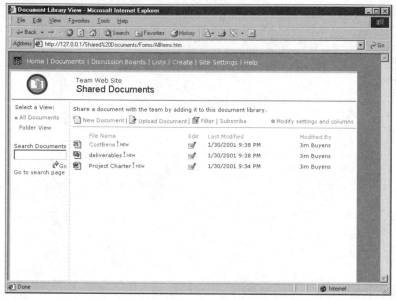

Figure 35-3. Click a library name or icon in a Document Libraries page (Figure 35-2), or click the Shared Documents link, to display a list of documents like this.

Here are its notable features:

- **Main Document Area.** This is the large area with a white background that appears in the center of the Web page. It lists all the documents in the current library. To sort this listing on any field, click the field's column heading. (That is, click File Name, Last Modified, or Modified By.)

- **Select A View.** This area in the top left corner selects among all available formats for listing documents in the library. By default, there are two such formats:

  - **All Documents.** Displays one line of text for each document in the library. Figure 35-3 illustrates this format.

  - **Folder View.** Displays one icon for each file or folder in the library. The icons appear from left to right across the available display area, then wrap to the next line.

  To create additional views, click the Modify Settings And Columns link to display a Customization page, and then click the Create A New View link at the bottom of the page.

● **Search Documents.** This area appears just below the Select A View area. To locate documents that contain a given word or phrase. Enter the text in the box provided, and click Go.

● **New Document.** Click this link to begin editing a new document you plan to store in the current library. If the library specifies a template, the Web page downloads it, starts the appropriate editor, and specifies the current library as the default save location. If the library has no defined template, the Web page starts Microsoft Word.

tip When saving documents into a SharePoint team Web site library (or saving them to disk in preparation for upload to a team Web site library), it's usually best to save them in HTML format. That way, other team members can view and annotate the document directly in their browsers. If you save or upload a non-HTML document in its native format, other team members will have to download the document, open it with another program, and then upload it again if they've made any changes.

● **Upload Document.** Click this link to display an Upload Document page that uploads a document from your computer and adds it to the library.

● **Filter.** Click this link to limit the list of documents based on criteria you specify. The team Web site redisplays the current Web pages, adding selection controls above each selectable column heading.

● **Subscribe.** Click this link to display a New Subscription page. This page tells SharePoint Team Services to send you an e-mail message whenever someone changes the contents of a document or folder within the library.

note Subscription is a pervasive feature. You can subscribe to receive change notifications regarding almost any aspect of a team Web site.

● **Modify Settings And Columns.** Click this link to display a Customization page that modifies the name of library, its assigned template, its presence or absence on the quick launch bar, and so forth.

Significantly, clicking this link also provides options that add or remove columns (that is, fields) from the document listing. You can use these extra columns to record anything you want about the documents in the library, and then to sort or filter documents on that basis. For example, you could add fields to record the:

▪ Name of the product that the document describes.

▪ Product version.

▪ Document version.

▪ Contract or customer for whom you created the document.

Troubleshooting

SharePoint team Web site document search displays the message, "Service is not running"

When using a Sharepoint team Web site, entering a search phrase in a Search Documents box and clicking Go might result in the following message:

Service is not running.

This message appears if Microsoft Indexing Service isn't running on the Web server where the Team Web Site resides. To start this service:

1 Choose Programs from the Windows Start menu.

2 Choose Computer Management from the Administrative Tools menu.

3 By default, the Computer Management application manages the local computer. To control Indexing Service on a different computer, right-click Computer Management (Local), choose Connect To Another Computer, select the name of the server where the SharePoint team Web site resides, and click OK.

4 Expand the Services And Applications entry.

5 Right-click the Indexing Service entry, and then choose Start from the shortcut menu. Click Yes when prompted to start Indexing Service. (If no Indexing Service entry appears, Microsoft Indexing Service isn't installed on the computer. The topic "Installing IIS on Windows 2000" in Chapter 37 explains how to install Indexing Service.)

6 Click the Indexing Service entry once, and observe the display in the right pane of the Computer Management window. This display contains one line for each Indexing Service catalog. Here are your options:

- If none of the catalogs include your Web server's root folder, right-click Indexing Service, choose New from the shortcut menu, and then choose Catalog. In the Name field, give the catalog a name that relates it to your Web server. In the Location field, specify the physical location of your Web server's root folder. Finally, click OK.

- If a suitable catalog already exists, observe the Total Docs and Docs To Index columns in the Computer Management window's right pane. When Total Docs is not zero and Docs to Index *is* zero, Indexing Service has finished analyzing your Web server.

7 Try rerunning the SharePoint team Web site search. If you still get the same error message, try stopping and restarting IIS. If the search still fails, try rebooting the server.

Chapter 35: Using SharePoint Team Web Sites

Each line in the main document area of a Document Library View page (Figure 35-3) contains the following clickable areas:

- **File Name.** Click any file name (or its icon) to open the file for viewing. If the file is a type that the browser can display, the browser displays it. Otherwise, the browser treats it as a download and starts the application on your computer that's associated with the file type.

- **Edit.** Click this icon to display an Edit Item page that updates the corresponding file or any information that describes it.

- **Modified By.** Click any name in this column to display a Personal Settings page that displays information about that team member.

Click any Edit icon in the Document Library View page to display the Edit Item Form page shown in Figure 35-4.

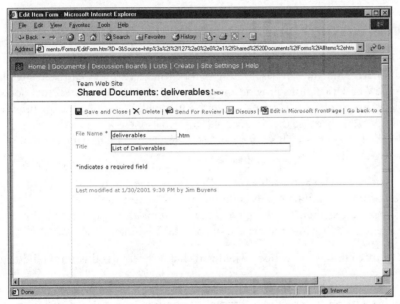

Figure 35-4. This SharePoint team Web site page displays a list of document properties you can edit.

This form provides the following capabilities:

- **Save And Close.** Click this link to save any changes you've made and return to the document library listing.

- **Delete.** Click this link to delete the current document from the library.

- **Send For Review.** Click this link to send e-mail to anyone you specify, asking that person to review the current library document.

- **Discuss.** Click this link to open the current document for review and annotation.

- **Edit In <application>.** Click this link to start the application associated with the current document and tell it to load the document from the Web server.

- **Go Back To Document Library.** Click this link to abandon any changes you've made and return to the document library listing.

- **Document Information Fields.** The central portion of the form contains form elements for all the editable fields that describe the document. To change any of this data, update the corresponding field and then click Save And Close.

With two exceptions, these options are relatively straightforward. The exceptions involve the options Discuss and Send For Review (which uses Discuss).

Using Web Discussions

The Discuss option is what most Office applications call *Web Discussions.* Despite the similarity in names, it has nothing to do with SharePoint team Web site Discussion Groups. Web Discussions provide a way to add yellow "sticky notes" to a document and to share those notes with others—all without actually updating the document itself. This is possible because the "sticky note" information resides in a database on a so-called *discussion server.* This can be any SQL Server or MSDE database that services a team Web site.

This is a very useful approach, because several people can review and annotate the same document simultaneously, and then the document owner can see all their suggestions merged together. There are no concerns about someone accidentally updating the document itself, because no one can update the document at all.

One of three things can happen when you click the Discuss link on the Edit Item Form page:

- If Microsoft Internet Explorer isn't configured to use a discussion server, it displays the dialog box shown in Figure 35-5 asking whether you'd like to specify one.

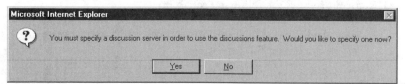

Figure 35-5. Discussing a document requires access to a discussion server that stores any comments you make. If Internet Explorer doesn't know the name of the discussion server, it displays this prompt.

Chapter 35: Using SharePoint Team Web Sites

● If the document is in HTML format, reviewers can view the document
and add their sticky notes using nothing but a Web browser. This mode of
operation integrates perfectly with other SharePoint team Web site features,
and it's a very good reason to save all documents in a team Web site in
HTML format.

● If the document isn't in HTML format, reviewers must download the document into the Office application that created it, choose Online Collaboration from the Tools menu, and possibly specify a discussion server by hand.

tip The Save As Web Page option in most Office applications saves all the properties and
features that saving in the native application format does. That is, saving and opening
a document in HTML format provides all the same features as saving and opening a
document in *.doc*, *.xls*, or *.ppt* format.

Figure 35-6 shows Internet Explorer accepting discussion comments for a document.
The Web visitor:

1 Displayed the Document Library View form shown in Figure 35-3.

2 Clicked the Edit icon for the *deliverables* file. This displayed the Edit Item
Form page shown in Figure 35-4.

3 Clicked the Discuss icon in the Edit Item Form page, and then displayed the
Enter Discussion Text dialog box.

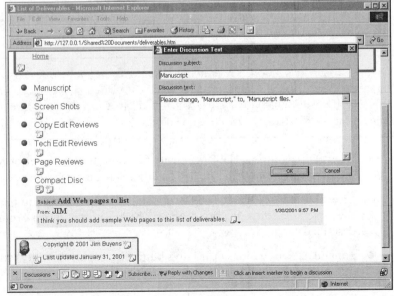

Figure 35-6. The sticky note icons show where you can append comments
to the document. Click one to display the Enter Discussion Text dialog box.

Click the Discuss icon to immediately display the Discussion bar shown at the bottom of Figure 35-6. (In Internet Explorer 5.5 or later, you might need to choose Explorer Bar from the View menu, and then choose Discuss.) The same command hides the Discussion bar if it's already on display. Here's how to use the buttons on this bar (note that these buttons will be available or unavailable depending on the type of document):

- **Discussions.** Click this button to display a menu containing the following options:

    - **Insert In The Document.** Choose this command to display or hide all possible locations for inline sticky notes (those that appear inline with the document text). There's basically one sticky note location per paragraph. To add text to a new or existing sticky note, click it.

    - **Insert About The Document.** Choose this command to display an Enter Discussion Text dialog box where you can enter discussion comments about the document in general.

    - **Refresh Discussions.** Choose this command to retrieve a current set of discussion comments from the discussion server. Your display will then reflect changes other visitors might have made after you first displayed the page.

    - **Filter Discussions.** Choose this command to display discussion comments from only a certain participant, or within a certain time span.

    - **Print Discussions.** Choose this command to print the discussion comments.

    - **Discussion Options.** Choose this command to select the discussion server and the discussion fields to display.

> **note** To host discussions on one server about documents on another, first open the document and then, on the Discussions toolbar, choose Discussion Options from the Discussions drop-down list. Finally, select the server that records discussion items from the Select A Discussion Server drop-down list.

- **Insert Discussion In The Document.** Click this button to perform the same function as the Insert In The Document menu command just described.

- **Insert Discussion About The Document.** Click this button to perform the same function as the Insert About The Document menu command just described.

- **Expand All Discussions.** Click this button to display the title, text, and all other fields for each discussion comment.

● **Collapse All Discussions.** Click this button to hide the contents of all discussion comments. A sticky note with a plus icon appears in place of each comment. To expand a particular comment, click the plus icon.

● **Show General Discussions.** Click this button to display all general (non-inline) discussion comments made about an HTML document.

● **Previous.** Click this button to display the previous discussion comment.

● **Next.** Click this button to display the next discussion comment.

● **Subscribe.** Click this button if you want to get an e-mail notification whenever someone updates either the current document or any document in the same folder.

● **Stop Communication With Discussion Server.** Click this button if you want to disconnect an HTML document from the discussion server.

● **Show/Hide Discussion Pane.** Click this toggle button to display or hide the discussion pane.

● **Close.** Click this button to close the Web discussion.

● **Reply With Changes.** Composes an e-mail message to the originator of a document, informing that person that you've added discussion comments to it.

Discussion text also appears—in almost identical format—when the original user opens the HTML file in Word. In fact, all discussion text from all users is merged seamlessly into place. (If no discussions appear, choose Online Collaboration from the Tools menu, and make sure the correct discussion server is specified.)

newfeature!
Using Subscriptions

Click any Subscribe link on a SharePoint team Web site page (such as the Document Library View page shown in Figure 35-3) to display the New Subscription page shown in Figure 35-7 on the next page. To display the Document Subscription dialog box shown in Figure 35-8 on the next page, click Subscribe on the Discussion bar. Both this dialog box and the New Subscription page serve the same function: you can subscribe to change notices on the current document or on any document in a specified folder (subject to filters); set notification criteria; specify your e-mail address; and indicate how long SharePoint Team Services should accumulate changes before sending them.

Figure 35-9 on page 993 shows a typical change notification message. Although the message in the figure provides only one notification, a single message can report multiple changes.

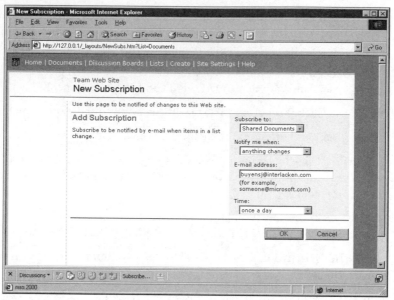

Figure 35-7. This Web page subscribes an e-mail user to change notifications for a given document or folder.

The notification process periodically scans a database and combines all notifications to the same recipient. The less often you choose to receive messages, the more notifications each message will contain.

The Subscription feature of a SharePoint team Web site isn't limited to Web Discussion comments that team members make using Internet Explorer. On the contrary, team members can subscribe for notification of almost any change to a team Web site.

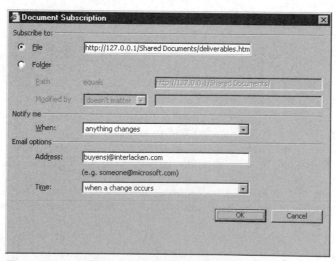

Figure 35-8. This is the dialog box version of the Web page that appears in Figure 35-7.

Chapter 35: Using SharePoint Team Web Sites

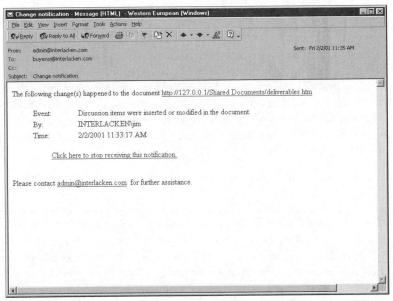

Figure 35-9. A SharePoint team Web site sent this change notification automatically.

Troubleshooting

Subscribers don't receive SharePoint team Web site change notifications

SharePoint team Web site members who subscribe to receive change notifications might not receive the expected mail for any of the following reasons:

- **Not enough time has passed.** SharePoint team Web sites send notifications at intervals even if a team member chose to receive them "When A Change Occurs." These intervals apply to the entire Web server, and are thus something an administrator must control. The following settings are the defaults, but your server's configuration might vary:

  - Immediate Notifications. Every five minutes.
  - Daily Notifications. Midnight.
  - Weekly Notifications. Sunday midnight.

- **Server settings might be incomplete.** The server administrator must configure SharePoint Team Services with the name of an SMTP mail server and an address that will appear in the From and Reply To fields of each outgoing message.

- **The Web Subscriptions feature might be disabled.** The server administrator can turn off the Web Subscriptions features at the server level. Obviously, this inhibits the transmission of notification messages.

Using Discussion Boards

A SharePoint team Web site discussion board works a lot like an Internet newsgroup or a FrontPage Discussion Web. Team members can post new messages, respond to existing messages, and view messages in their entirety or in condensed lists. Whoever administers the team Web site can purge and correct messages, alter discussion board settings and defaults, and so forth. If security settings permit, team members can initiate and control their own discussion boards, and whoever posts a message can subsequently revise or delete it.

Figure 35-11 shows a summary view of a typical discussion board. To display this Web page:

1 Choose Discussion Boards from the menu bar of any page in the SharePoint team Web site. This displays the Discussion Boards page shown in Figure 35-10, which displays the name and description of each available discussion board. The General Discussion board appears by default as part of every new team Web site. You can do the following:

- To create additional boards, click the New Discussion Board link. This displays a New page that initializes a new discussion board.

- To discuss a specific document on the Web, click Discuss A Document. This provides an entry point to the Web Discussions feature described in the section titled "Using Web Discussions" earlier in this chapter.

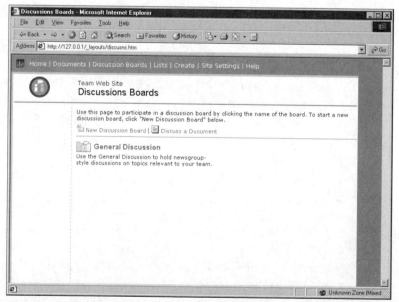

Figure 35-10. This page provides a selection list of SharePoint team Web site discussion boards. The single discussion shown appears by default in every new team Web site.

Chapter 35: Using SharePoint Team Web Sites

2 To view or modify the contents of an existing discussion board, click its icon or title. This displays a Discussion Board View page like the one shown in Figure 35-11. Figure 35-12 illustrates expanded view.

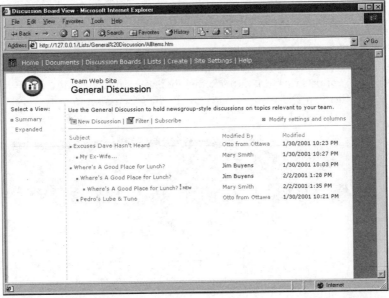

Figure 35-11. Click a discussion board name or icon in Figure 35-10 to display a list of messages like this.

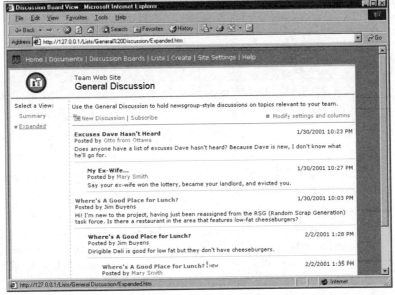

Figure 35-12. Click the Expanded link in a Discussion Board View page (Figure 35-11) to display this view of the messages in a discussion board.

Chapter 35

Here's how to use the various links on a Discussion Board View page:

- **Select A View.** Click any link in this area (at the left of the page) to display the discussion in the format you want. Summary view, the default, is the mode shown in Figure 35-11. To create additional views , click the Modify Settings And Columns link near the right border of the page.

- **New Discussion.** Click this link to initiate discussion on a new topic (that is, to create a new top-level message). Figure 35-13 shows the Web page that supports this function. (Remember, to create a new discussion *board,* click the New Discussion Board link in the Discussion Boards list, shown in Figure 35-10.)

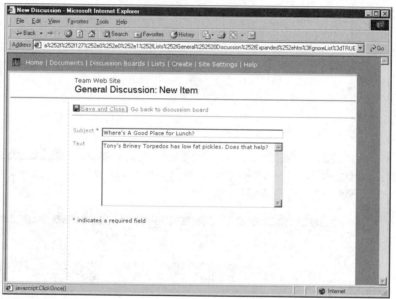

Figure 35-13. This Web page starts a new discussion thread. To display it, click any New Discussion link.

- **Filter.** Click this link to limit the displayed messages based on criteria you specify.

- **Subscribe.** Click this link if you want to receive e-mail notification whenever someone changes the contents of the discussion board.

- **Modify Settings And Columns.** Click this link to display a Customization page that modifies the name of the discussion board, its description, its columns, or its views. The SharePoint team Web site keeps all this information in its database, and then adds it—on the fly—to any relevant Web pages.

- **Subject, Modified By, and Modified.** Click any of these column headings to sort the display on that column.

- **Subject Titles.** Click any entry in the Subject column to select and display it.

- **Modified By Names.** Click any entry in the Modified By column to display information about that person.

Click the title of a message in the Discussion Board View page (Figure 35-11) to bring up the Display Discussion Article page shown in Figure 35-14. The title and body of the current message appear under the second menu bar.

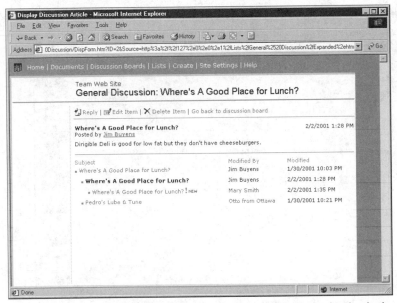

Figure 35-14. Click the Subject text of any message to display both the message and its position in the thread.

The menu bar itself contains the following links:

- **Reply.** Click this link to create a new message that responds to the current one. The new message appears beneath the existing one, indented one level to the right. Figure 35-13 shows the New Discussion page that appears when you click the Reply link.

- **Edit Item.** Click this link to modify the current message. Depending on settings in effect for the discussion board, this might be possible only for an administrator or the person who originated the message.

- **Delete Item.** Click this link to delete the current message. Again, this might be possible only for an administrator or the person who originated the message.

Part 11: Collaborating with Teams and Workgroups

● **Go Back To Discussion Board.** Click this link to back up one screen (usually to the Discussion Board View page shown in Figure 35-11).

newfeature!
Using Lists

Click the Lists link on the menu bar of any page in a SharePoint team Web site to display the Lists page shown in Figure 35-15. This is basically a list of all the lists in the current team Web site. All five lists itemized in the figure appear by default in any new team Web site.

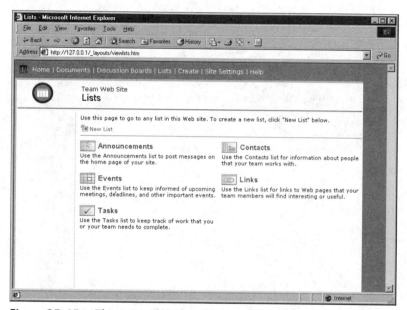

Figure 35-15. This page identifies the lists in a SharePoint team Web site. The lists shown here appear by default in every new team Web site.

Physically, a list is nothing more than a table in a database. Each list item is a table row and, as you've probably guessed, each list column is a table column. The SharePoint team Web site can create new tables (that is, lists), add columns, modify columns, and delete columns using Web pages that are part of (and integrated with) the team Web site.

Click the entry for any list in the List page to display a List View page like the one shown in Figure 35-16. The links on this page work much like those already described for document libraries and discussion boards (are you noticing a pattern?), but here's a brief summary:

● **Select A View.** Click any link in this area to display the list in the format you want.

● **New Item.** Click this link to display a page named New Item Form that adds a new item to the list.

Chapter 35: Using SharePoint Team Web Sites

● **Filter.** Click this link to limit the displayed messages based on criteria you specify.

● **Export.** Click this link to download a Microsoft Excel Web Query file that downloads the data in the list. Such files have a *.iqy* filename extension that's normally associated with Microsoft Excel. When you open such a file, Excel connects to the SharePoint team Web site database and downloads the data for the list you requested.

This is a highly useful approach because every time you open the Web Query file, Excel connects to the database server and downloads a fresh copy of the data in the list. This saves you from downloading fresh copies of the data manually. If you want to save a copy of the data as of some specific point in time, copy it from the query region and paste it into another spreadsheet.

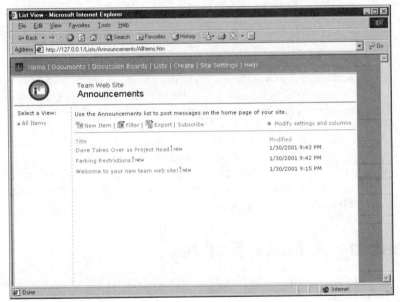

Figure 35-16. Click a list name or icon in a List page (Figure 35-15) to display the items in the list.

● **Subscribe.** Click this link if you want to receive e-mail notification whenever someone changes the contents of the list.

● **Modify Settings And Columns.** Click this link to change the properties of the list. This includes the name, description, columns, views, and other settings.

The five lists shown in Figure 35-15 all contain different combinations of fields and different views. Nevertheless, they're all simple database tables that operate using the same basic principles.

newfeature!

Creating New
Libraries, Discussions, and Lists

Click the Create link on any SharePoint team Web site menu bar to display the Create Page page shown in Figures 35-17 and 35-18. This page has the following options:

- **Custom List.** This option, the first on the page, creates a list with only one column: Title. After the list exists, of course, you can display it and then click Modify Settings And Columns to add more columns, delete the Title column, or make any other changes you want.

- **Import Spreadsheet.** This option, the last on the page, creates a list from data contained in a spreadsheet. Each row of spreadsheet data becomes one list record, and each column of spreadsheet data becomes a list column. The values in the first row will become the column names in the list.

When using this option, the SharePoint team Web site doesn't actually upload the spreadsheet as a file and then process it on the server. Instead, it opens Excel on your computer. Excel then opens the spreadsheet you specified, prompts for a range of cells to upload, and then transmits the values of those cells. This is much more flexible than uploading the entire file and converting its contents to a list.

All the other choices are basically variations of the Custom List choice, with the exception that each of them initializes the new list with a different collection of fields and formats. If one of these list types is nearly or exactly what you want, choose it. Otherwise, it'll probably be easier to use the Custom List choice than to delete all the extra columns another choice provides.

newfeature!

Creating a New Survey

Surveys are a particularly interesting type of list. As with all surveys, there are four basic steps:

1 Decide what questions you want to ask.

2 Design a form people can use to record their answers.

3 Let the survey population fill out the form.

4 Analyze the results.

Although a SharePoint team Web site can't choose questions for you, it does most of the work for the three remaining steps. This section explains how to create a survey and, along the way, how to perform a myriad of tasks useful for creating other lists as well. Here's the procedure:

Chapter 35: Using SharePoint Team Web Sites

1 Click the Create link on any SharePoint team Web site menu bar. This displays the Create Page page shown in Figures 35-17 and 35-18.

2 Click the Survey link shown in Figure 35-17. This displays the New Survey page partially shown in Figure 35-19 on the next page.

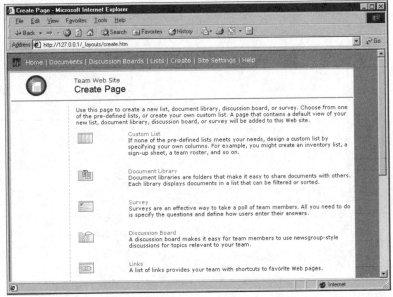

Figure 35-17. This Web page has links for creating lists, discussion boards, and document libraries of all kinds.

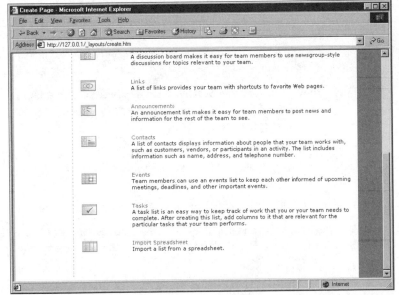

Figure 35-18. This is the bottom half of the Web page that starts in Figure 35-17.

Part 11: Collaborating with Teams and Workgroups

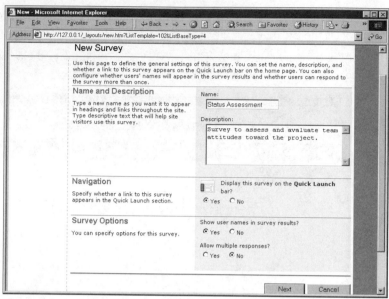

Figure 35-19. Click the Survey link in a Create Page page (Figure 35-17) to display this Web page for creating a new survey.

Fill out the input options as follows:

- **Name.** Give the survey a short, descriptive name.

- **Description.** If you want, enter a few sentences that explain the survey and its purpose.

- **Display This Survey On The Quick Launch Bar?** Click Yes if you want all Quick Launch areas in the current SharePoint team Web site to contain a link to this survey. Otherwise click No. Use this feature judiciously; a Quick Launch bar containing hundreds of links isn't much of a time saver.

- **Show User Name In Survey Results?** Click Yes if displays of survey results should include then name of each respondent. Click No to keep these names private.

- **Allow Multiple Responses?** Click Yes if the same person can fill out the survey multiple times. Click No if each person can submit responses only once.

Click the Next button when you're satisfied with your entries.

3 The next page to appear is the Create New Question page shown in Figures 35-20 and 35-21. This Web page constructs the first survey question.

Chapter 35: Using SharePoint Team Web Sites

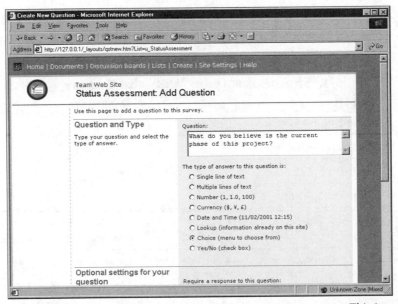

Figure 35-20. This page adds a question to an existing survey. This is quite useful because creating a new survey creates only one question.

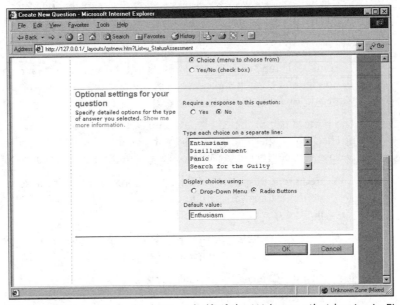

Figure 35-21. This is the bottom half of the Web page that begins in Figure 35-20.

Here's how to use the input options provided:

▧ **Question.** Enter the text for the first question in the survey.

■ **The Type Of Answer To This Question Is.** Indicate what type of data
constitutes the survey answer. Table 35-1 summarizes the result of
each choice.

Table 35-1. SharePoint team Web site Survey Answer Types

Type of answer	Input form
Single Line Of Text	Text box
Multiple Lines Of Text	Text area box
Number (1, 1.0, 100)	Text box
Currency ($, ¥, £)	Text box
Date And Time (11/02/2001 12:15)	Combination of text box (for date) and drop-down lists (for hour and minute)
Lookup (Information Already On This Site)	Drop-down list
Choice (Menu To Choose From)	Drop-down list or option buttons
Yes/No (Check Box)	Check box

The Lookup choice warrants a bit of additional explanation. This choice
populates a drop-down list with all values that occur in a given list and column within the SharePoint team Web site. For example, this could include
all Full Name values in the User Information list, all Titles in the Shared
Documents library, all E-Mail Addresses in the Contacts list, and so forth.
To configure a Lookup choice, you specify first the name of the list you
want and then the column.

4 The bottom half of the Edit Question page changes depending on the type
of answer you specify. Figure 35-21 shows the format that appears if you
choose Choice (Menu To Choose From). Enter each option as follows:

■ **Require A Response To This Question.** Click Yes if the survey respondent must answer the question before proceeding. Click No if answering the question is optional.

■ **Type Each Choice On A Separate Line.** Enter the list of choices. Separate choices by entering a carriage return.

■ **Display Choices Using.** Select either Drop-Down Menu or Radio Buttons depending on how you want respondents to view the choices.

■ **Default Value.** Enter the name of the choice that will be selected when
the respondent first displays the Web page that contains this question.

Click OK to finish creating the survey question.

5 The Customization page partially shown in Figure 35-22 is the next page to
appear.

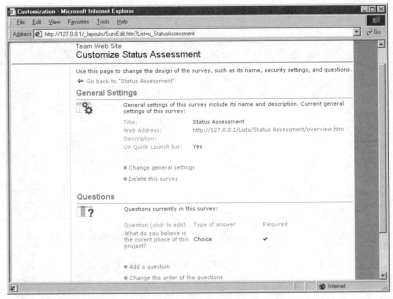

Figure 35-22. This page modifies the overall properties of a survey.

It provides the following links:

- **Change General Settings.** Displays a Change General Settings page very similar to the one shown in Figure 35-19. This provides a way to update these settings without recreating the survey.

- **Delete This Survey.** Removes the survey forms, links, and data from the SharePoint team Web site.

- **Question (Click To Edit).** Click the text of any question listed under this heading to change the text or format of that question, or to delete the question completely.

- **Add A Question.** Click this link to add the second, third, and all sub-sequent questions in the survey. Basically, you must click this link and then repeat steps 3 and 4 once for each question.

- **Change The Order Of The Questions.** Click this link to display a list of current questions and question numbers. The question numbers appear in drop-down lists that you can manipulate to put the questions in any order.

Figure 35-23 on the next page shows how the Status Assessment survey appears to a survey respondent. This is a custom survey created by using the procedure just de-scribed, and not a standard element of every new SharePoint team Web site.

Chapter 35

Part 11: Collaborating with Teams and Workgroups

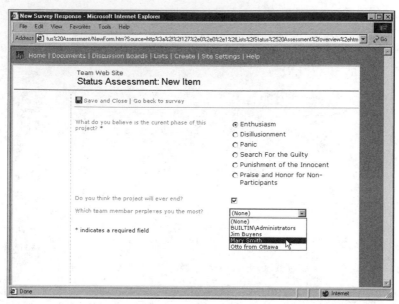

Figure 35-23. This is how the survey looks to a survey respondent. The survey itself is just a list with a column for recording each answer.

Here's how to display this page:

1 Click the Lists link on the menu bar of any page in a SharePoint team Web site.

2 Click the survey's list title or its preceding icon. This displays the Overview page shown in Figure 35-24.

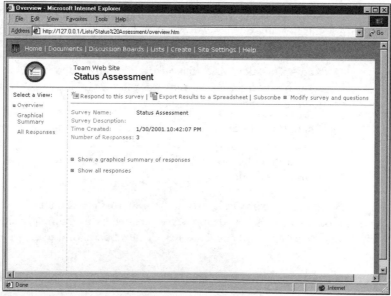

Figure 35-24. The entry point for analyzing survey results is this Web page.

Chapter 35: Using SharePoint Team Web Sites

The Overview page contains the following choices:

■ **Respond To This Survey.** Click this link to answer all the survey questions.

■ **Export Results To A Spreadsheet.** Click this link to download an Excel Web Query (*.iqy*) file that downloads the survey data into a spreadsheet.

> For more information about downloading list data, refer to "Using Lists" earlier in this chapter.

■ **Subscribe.** Click this link if you want to receive e-mail notification whenever someone completes or changes the survey.

■ **Modify Survey And Questions.** Click this link to change the properties of the survey. This includes the name, description, questions, and other settings. In short, it displays the Customization page partially shown in Figure 35-22.

■ **Show A Graphical Summary Of Questions.** Click this link to display a graphical summary of survey responses like the one shown in Figure 35-25.

■ **Show All Responses.** Click this link to display a textual listing of survey responses like the one shown in Figure 35-26 on the next page.

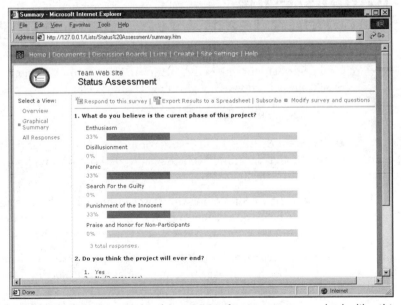

Figure 35-25. The graphical summary of survey responses looks like this.

Creating other kinds of lists follows basically the same pattern as creating a survey. This is because, in fact, a survey is nothing but a list where each row is a survey response and each column an answer.

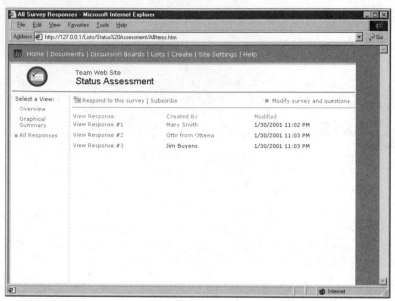

Figure 35-26. This Web page displays all responses to a survey.

newfeature!
Administering
SharePoint Team Web Site Settings

To modify and configure settings that apply to the entire SharePoint team Web site, click the Site Settings link in the menu bar of any team Web site page. This displays the Site Settings page shown in Figures 35-27 and 35-28.

On this page are the following:

- **Web Site Settings.** The first portion of the Site Settings page controls the SharePoint team Web site's name, description, and home page layout. These are the links in this portion:

  - **Change Site Name And Description.** Click this link to display a Change Site Name And Description page that modifies the name and description of the SharePoint team Web site.

  - **Customize Home Page Layout.** Click this link to display a Home Page Layout page that determines which lists should appear in the center column of the SharePoint team Web site's home page and which should appear in the right column. (Recall that the left column of the home page contains the Quick Launch area, and that the Customization page for each list controls whether that list appears in the Quick Launch area.)

Chapter 35: Using SharePoint Team Web Sites

In general, only the most popular lists should appear on the home page. Team members should click Documents, Discussion Boards, or Lists to access the rest.

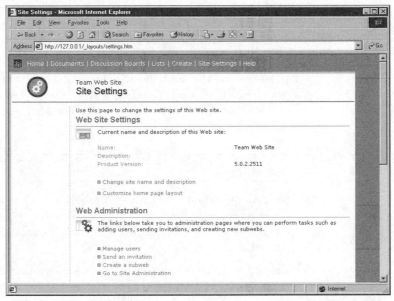

Figure 35-27.   The Site Settings page controls properties that affect an entire SharePoint team Web site.

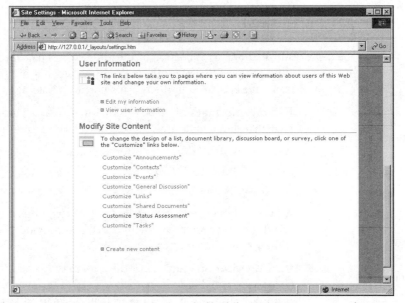

Figure 35-28.   This is the bottom half of the Site Settings page that appears in Figure 35-27.

- **Web Administration.** This portion of the Site Settings page contains links that add or remove users, create subwebs, and jump to overall site administration. Here are the links:

  - **Manage Users.** Click this link to display the Web page that adds, removes, or changes the roles of users who have access to one or more Webs on the current server.

    If a SharePoint team Web site has no designated users, the Manage Users link and the Send An Invitation link described next won't appear. Instead, a Change Permissions link appears. Use the Change Permissions link to add one or more users. The Manage Users and Send An Invitation links will then appear.

> For more information about managing user access to FrontPage-based Webs, refer to "Managing Users" on page 1107.

  - **Send An Invitation.** Click this link to run a wizard that gives team members access to the SharePoint team Web site and sends them e-mail. The e-mail describes the team Web site and invites them to participate.

  - **Create A Subweb.** Click this link to create a subweb within the SharePoint team Web site.

  - **Go To Site Administration.** Click this link to display the Administration page for the SharePoint team Web site.

> For more information about the Administration page for FrontPage-based Webs, refer to "Administering SharePoint Team Services Web Settings" on page 1101.

- **User Information.** This portion of the Site Settings page provides options to modify your own SharePoint team Web site account or, if you're an administrator, the accounts of others. This portion's links are as follows:

  - **Edit My Information.** Click this link to display a Personal Settings page that shows and modifies your own user account information.

    A hyperlink titled Edit User Information updates your full name, the address to use for sending e-mail, and any notes you care to provide.

    A hyperlink named Change Password changes your password.

    A hyperlink named Manage Personal Subscriptions displays all subscriptions you currently have in effect, and provides a way to delete those you no longer want.

  - **View User Information.** Click this link to display a list of users who have participated in or been invited to use the current SharePoint team Web site. This page contains hyperlinks to add or remove users, to invite new users, and to modify the full names, e-mail addresses, and notes pertaining to any known user.

● **Modify Site Content.** This portion of the Site Settings page contains links to customize each document library, discussion board, and list in the current SharePoint team Web site. These links display the same pages that displaying the list and clicking Modify Settings And Columns would display.

newfeature!
Creating Custom List Pages

SharePoint team Web sites provide a wealth of methods for modifying their features and appearance. Even so, there might be times when you need more flexibility and need it badly enough to dive in and work directly with the Web pages. This section explains the options and techniques for doing just that.

> **tip** The easiest way by far to create a new list is by clicking the New List link or the SharePoint team Web site Lists page. Similarly, the easiest way to modify a list is by clicking the Modify settings and columns link on its main Web page.

The first option, of course, is simply to open the SharePoint team Web site, find the team Web site page you want to change, and open it in Page view. This works subject to one large restriction: team Web site pages submit input to and receive output from a number of programs that run on the Web server, and you can't readily change these programs. (They're not ASP pages, for example). Therefore, anything you do that upsets the interface between team Web site pages and team Web site server programs breaks the site. Chapters 8 and 9 explained the structure of a SharePoint team Web site and gave some precautions for modifying constituent pages.

> For more information about creating a SharePoint team Web site, refer to "Creating a SharePoint Team Web Site" on page 248. For more information about creating, saving, and opening files in a SharePoint team Web site, refer to "Saving and Opening Files in SharePoint Team Web Sites" on page 266.

Creating and Modifying Library View Pages

Figure 35-29 on the next page shows a Web page that's a curious mix of SharePoint team Web site and custom features. The menu bar and data in the center of the page come from the Share Documents library of a SharePoint team Web site. Nevertheless, the page contains custom formatting and could contain custom content as well. What's more, this is a page you can create yourself from scratch. Here's the procedure:

1 Start FrontPage and create a new empty Web page.

2 Choose Web Component from the Insert menu.

3 When the Insert Web Component dialog box appears, choose Document Library View from the Component type list at the left, and a View Style from the Choose A View Style list at the right. Don't agonize over the View Style; you can easily change this later. Click Finish.

Part 11: Collaborating with Teams and Workgroups

4 When the Choose Document Library box shown at the left of Figure 35-30 appears, choose the SharePoint team Web site shared document library you'd like to display, and then click OK.

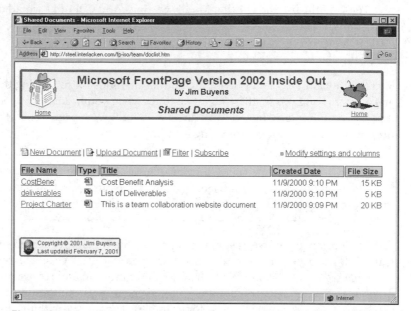

Figure 35-29. You can construct replacement Team Web pages that look any way (and display any additional content) you want.

When the Document Library View Properties dialog box shown at the right of Figure 35-30 appears, review the settings list at the right of each vertically arranged button.

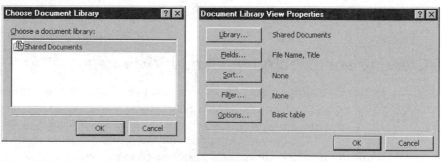

Figure 35-30. The dialog box at the left selects the document library that a Document Library View area will report. The dialog box at the right provides entry to all configurable aspects of a Document Library View area.

5 Click Library to choose a different document library. This redisplays the Choose Document Library box shown at the left of Figure 35-30 so you can choose a different library.

Chapter 35: Using SharePoint Team Web Sites

6 Click Fields to change the information displayed for each document. The Displayed Fields dialog box shown at the left of Figure 35-31 appears.

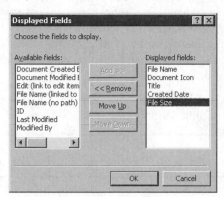
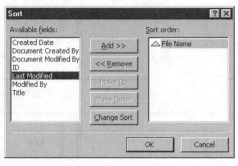

Figure 35-31. The Displayed Fields dialog box at the left controls which fields a Document Library View area will display. The Sort dialog box at the right controls which fields affect the item display order.

Make any necessary changes by using the following options:

- **Available Fields.** This list contains all the fields in the shared document library that the current Web page doesn't already display. To display any of these fields, either double-click it or select it and click Add.

- **Add.** Click this button to move any selected fields from the Available Fields list to the Displayed Fields list.

- **Remove.** Click this button to move any selected fields from the Displayed Fields list to the list Available Fields. (Compared to the Add button, this is a case of "Second verse, played in reverse.")

- **Move Up.** Click this button to move any fields selected in the Displayed Fields list one position higher in that list.

- **Move Down.** Click this button to move any fields selected in the Displayed Fields list one position lower in that list. (A clear case of "What goes up...")

- **Displayed Fields.** This box lists all the document library fields that the current Web page displays. To remove any of these fields, either double-click it or select it and click Remove.

After some field names, the Displayed Fields dialog box displays a suffix that refers to a link. One of these, for example, is Edit (Link To Edit Item). If you included such a field on your page (that is, if you add it to the Displayed Fields list), a visitor can click the displayed value to invoke the corresponding action (for example, Edit).

InsideOut

Unfortunately, linked fields in a Document Library View area suffer a major restriction: you have no control over the linked field's URL. If you plan to use such links, you must put the pages where the SharePoint team Web site software expects them to be, and that means replacing the standard pages created when you initialized the team Web site, document library, or list.

Currently there appears to be no workaround for this restriction. Try searching Microsoft's knowledge base for more information; the URL is *http://search.microsoft.com*.

7 Click Sort to change the initial order of the listed documents. This displays the Sort dialog box shown at the right of Figure 35-31, which provides the following controls:

- **Available Fields.** This list contains all the fields in the shared document library that don't currently control the order of listed records. To use a field for sorting, either double-click it or select it and click Add.

- **Add.** Click this button to move any selected fields from the Available Fields list to the Sort Order list.

- **Remove.** Click this button to move any selected fields from the Sort Order list to the Available Fields list.

- **Move Up.** Click this button to move any fields selected in the Sort Order list one position higher in that list.

- **Move Down.** Click this button to move any fields selected in the Sort Order list one position lower in that list.

- **Change Sort.** Click this button to reverse the order of any selected Sort Order fields (from ascending to descending or vice versa).

- **Sort Order.** This box lists all the document libraries that the current Web page displays. To remove any of these fields, either double-click it or select it and click Remove.

8 Click Filter to display only selected records from the current document library. This displays the Filter Criteria dialog box shown in Figure 35-32, which lists any criteria already in effect.

The following options appear in the Filter Criteria dialog box:

- **Add.** Click this button to define an additional filter. When the Add Filter dialog box shown in the center of Figure 35-32 appears, configure the following options:

  - **Field Name.** Select the field whose value you want to test.

Chapter 35: Using SharePoint Team Web Sites

◆ **Comparison.** Specify the operator for the comparison: Equals,
Not Equal, Less Than, and so forth.

◆ **Value.** Enter the value that forms the basis for the comparison.
For date fields, click Choose and then use the Date Value dialog
box that appears at the right of Figure 35-32 to specify the
value you want. Current Date means the date that the Web
server processes the visitor's request. Specific Date means a date
you type by hand.

For non-date fields, enter the desired value in the text box provided.

◆ **And/Or.** Choose *And* if other filters, as well as this one, must be
true for the record to be selected. Choose *Or* if this is one of several filters, any of which, if true, are sufficient to select the record.

■ **Modify.** Click this button to change an existing filter. This displays a
Modify Filter dialog box that looks and works very much like the Add
Filter dialog box just described. This button is dimmed unless you've
already selected a filter.

■ **Remove.** Click this button to remove an existing filter. The button is
dimmed unless you've already selected a filter.

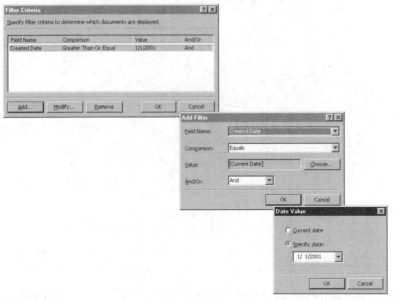

Figure 35-32. The Filter Criteria dialog box lists any current restrictions on
the items displayed. Click its Add button to display the Add Filter dialog box,
which adds a new filter to the list. If the filter involves a date field, click the
Choose button to display the Date Value dialog box.

Chapter 35

9 Click Options to display the View Options dialog box shown in Figure
35-33. This dialog box configures the following settings:

- **Choose A Style.** Choose a page layout design for the document
  library records.

- **Toolbar Type.** Choose the type of toolbar that will appear above the
  library listing:

  - **Full Toolbar.** Choose this option to display a toolbar with five
    links: New Document, Upload Document, Filter, Subscribe, and
    Modify Settings And Columns.

  - **Summary Toolbar.** Choose this option to display a toolbar with
    two links: Shared Documents and Add New Document.

  - **None.** Choose this option if you don't want to have a toolbar at
    all.

  The links on these toolbars follow the standard conventions that apply
  to SharePoint team Web sites. You can't, for example, change them so
  they jump to custom pages.

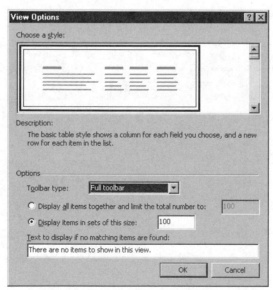

Figure 35-33. Use this dialog box to specify the style, toolbar type,
item limit, and zero-items message for a Document Library View area.

- **Display All Items Together And Limit The Total Number To.** Select
  this option if you want the query to display all results on a single Web
  page. To avoid runaway queries, you should also enter a workable
  maximum record count in the accompanying text box.

Chapter 35: Using SharePoint Team Web Sites

■ **Display Items In Sets Of This Size.** Select this option if you want the query to display a specific number of records on the first Web page, and then provide a Next link that displays the next group of like records.

■ **Text To Display If No Matching Items Are Found.** Enter the message you want visitors to see if the library is empty or fails all filtering criteria. (For example, you might display "Thanks, you've just deleted our last six months' work.")

10 When you're done adjusting options, click OK on the Document Library View Properties dialog box (the right side of Figure 35-30).

At this point your new Web page should display a recognizable SharePoint team Web site document list, albeit crudely formatted. Figure 35-34 provides an example. You can apply any formatting or add any additional content you want.

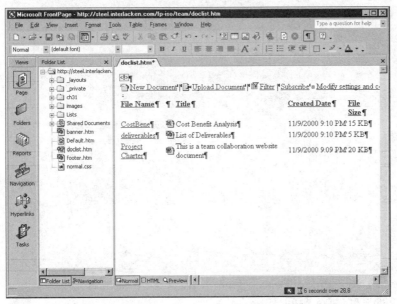

Figure 35-34. By default, creating a new Document Library View area provides very little formatting.

To change any structural aspect of the Document Library View area, double-click it or right-click it and choose View Properties from the shortcut menu. Both actions display the Document Library View Properties dialog box already described. It works the same for changing a view area as it does for creating one.

To perform more radical surgery, right-click the Document Library View area and choose Layout Customization View from the shortcut menu. This changes the Page view display to the format shown in the background of Figure 35-35 on the next page. The library view area in the figure now looks like a table with six rows, but four of them are comments and two are very special. (If you chose a different layout style, your row numbers might differ, but the concepts are the same.)

InsideOut

After you've switched a Document Library View area to Layout Customization View, you can change it back by right-clicking the area and choosing Live Data View from the shortcut menu. When you do so, however, FrontPage discards any changes you made while in Customization view. This is the price for making changes in a more flexible way than Live Data View can accommodate. Think carefully before changing back to Live Data View.

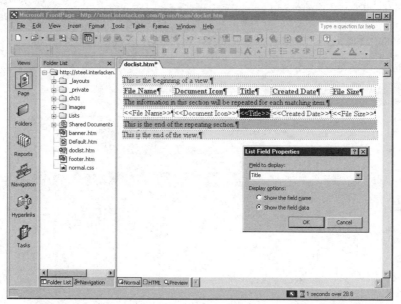

Figure 35-35. The List Field component displays the name or current value of any field in a document library or list.

In the library view area:

- The comment rows are 1, 3, 5, and 6.

- Row 2 contains the column headings. This row appears only once whenever a visitor displays a page that contains it.

- Row 4 contains a template for record values. The SharePoint team Web site software duplicates this row once for every record it displays from the given document library.

By default, each cell in rows 2 and 4 contains a special component called a List Field. These components work a lot like Confirmation Field components in a Confirmation form, or Column Value components in a Database Results region: that is, they're place-holders that the SharePoint team Web site software replaces with actual values when a Web visitor requests the page. You can use List Field components to display any document library field names or field values you want.

Double-clicking an existing List Field component displays the List Field Properties dialog box shown in the foreground of Figure 35-35. Right-clicking the component and choosing either List Field or List Field Properties accomplishes the same thing. Use the following fields to modify a List Field component:

- **Field To Display.** Select the document library field that the List Field component should display.

- **Display Options.** Select Show The Field Name to display the name of the field. This is the usual setting for List Field components used in the heading area of the List View area.

  Select Show The Field Data to display the contents of the field. This is the usual setting for List Field components used in the repeating area of the List View area.

  To add a List Field component to an existing List View area, set the insertion point where you want it to appear, choose Form from the Insert menu, and then choose List Field.

Creating and Modifying List View Pages

If you can create and modify Library View pages, you can create and modify List View pages. The procedures are nearly identical. To get started:

1 Start FrontPage and create a new empty Web page.

2 Choose Web Component from the Insert menu.

3 When the Insert Web Component dialog box appears, choose List View from the Component Type list at the left, and a View Style from the Choose A View Style list at the right. Don't agonize over the View Style; you can easily change this later. Click Finish.

Did you catch the difference? In step 3, you choose List View rather than Document Library View from the Component Type list. That's it. Virtually everything that pertains to document libraries pertains to lists as well. This is just what you should expect, because a Document Library View doesn't actually display the documents in a library; it displays information from the SharePoint team Web site list that describes the documents.

There are a few other differences, such as the fact that SharePoint team Web site toolbars for document libraries and ordinary lists are slightly different. Keep an eye out for
these and you shouldn't have any problems.

Creating and Modifying List Forms

SharePoint team Web sites use a specialized Web component to create three of their
most common forms. You can insert this component, and thus initialize such a form, by
following this procedure:

1 Start FrontPage and create a new empty Web page.

2 Choose Form from the Insert menu, and then choose List Form. This displays
the List Or Document Library Form dialog box shown in the foreground of
Figure 35-36.

3 Set the options in the List Or Document Library Form dialog box as follows:

- ■ **List Or Document Library To Use For Form.** Select the list or document library you want the form to update.

- ■ **New Item Form (Used To Add New Items To The List).** Select this
  option to create a form that adds new items to the list or document
  library.

- ■ **Edit Item Form (Used To Edit Existing List Items).** Select this option
  to create a form that modifies existing items in the list or document
  library.

- ■ **Display Item Form (Used To View List Items).** Select this option to
  create a form that displays items in the list or document library.

- ■ **Show Standard Toolbar.** Select this box to display the standard
  SharePoint team Web site toolbar for the form type.

4 Click OK to create the form.

As with Document Library View and List View components, Page view should now
display a crudely formatted but recognizable SharePoint team Web site form. You can
add whatever formatting and content you want, but there isn't much you can do to the
form itself except double-clicking it to redisplay the List Or Document Library Form
dialog box.

Chapter 35: Using SharePoint Team Web Sites

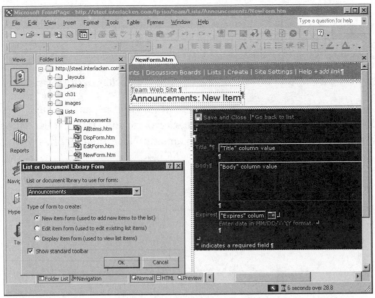

Figure 35-36. This dialog box controls the properties of a SharePoint team Web site form page.

Again, as with Document Library View and List View components, you have very little flexibility regarding the location of pages that contain SharePoint team Web site forms. Specifically, you must locate forms that pertain to lists as follows:

Form Type	Location relative to start of Web
New item form	/Lists/<list-name>/NewForm.htm
Edit item form	/Lists/<list-name>/EditForm.htm
Display item form	/Lists/<list-name>/DisplayItem.htm

Here are the locations for forms that pertain to shared document libraries:

Form Type	Location relative to start of Web
New item form	/<library-name>/Forms/NewForm.htm
Edit item form	/<library-name>/Forms /EditForm.htm
Display item form	/<library-name>/Forms /DisplayItem.htm

These, of course, are the locations of the forms that appear automatically when you create a new document library or list. You can create pages from scratch and overlay the default ones, but in most cases it'll be easier (and safer) to just open the default pages and modify them. That's why Figure 35-36 shows a default list form open in the background.

In Summary...

This chapter explained how team members can use the features of a SharePoint team Web site to share documents and coordinate their activities. It also explained how to administer such a site, and how to create custom pages that perform standard functions.

The next chapter explains some terms and concepts that pertain to the Internet in general and Web servers in particular. This is background material that, if you had need of it, you've probably skipped ahead and read already. Nevertheless it has to go somewhere, and it might as well be here.

Part 12

Managing a Personal Web Server

Looking at the Web—Inside Out

Surfing the Web is such a simple and enjoyable pastime that people tend to forget how much technology lies behind those nice page displays and simple button clicks. Only when things stop working does complexity once again rear its ugly head.

This chapter isn't a step-by-step guide to solving every problem that could go wrong on the Web, but it does explain the basic technologies involved. This knowledge should help you design applications that work the first time, fix some of those that don't, or at least make an informed guess about whom to contact.

Relationships Between Browsers and Servers

Like most Internet applications, the Web is a client/server system. The clients are machines where Web visitors submit commands and view responses using software called a *browser*. Microsoft Internet Explorer and Netscape Navigator are the most popular browsers. The servers typically are located some distance from the visitors, fulfill simultaneous requests from multiple visitors, and have no need for a keyboard, mouse, or monitor other than for system administration.

In one sense, a server is any computer that runs applications or provides services on behalf of other computers. One such computer can provide any number of applications or services (provided, of course, that it doesn't run out of memory, disk, processing power, or other resources.) The application that delivers pages on the World Wide Web is called an *HTTP server*. HTTP stands for "Hypertext Transfer Protocol."

> **note** The term *server* is a bit ambiguous. Sometimes it refers only to the hardware, sometimes to a specific piece of background software, and sometimes to the combination of all hardware and software on a machine. Because this is a book about the Web, the term *server* means all the hardware and software required to fulfill HTTP requests—that is, requests to deliver Web pages.

Another distinction between clients and servers is that clients generate requests and servers provide responses. Obviously, the client must formulate its requests and submit them in a way the server understands. Likewise, the server must formulate its responses in a way the client can deal with. The rules governing these interchanges are called *protocols*.

> **note** A protocol is nothing more than a way of acting. Life is full of little protocols, such as the conventions we use to avoid bumping into people on sidewalks, in hallways, and when entering and leaving elevators. If an individual (or computer) acts outside established protocols, interaction with others will generally fail.

There are millions of computers on the Internet, and they interact in quite a variety of ways. As a result, many different Internet protocols are used. People can hardly talk about anything on the Internet without talking about protocols. Protocols govern how telephone numbers must be dialed, how modems link to each other, how dial-up networking software negotiates settings and logs on to the network of an Internet service provider (ISP), and how machines on a local network (or intranet) communicate via Ethernet. There are hundreds more protocols, but fortunately, a discussion of browsers and HTTP servers can ignore most of them. The two most important protocols involved in Web browsing are HTTP and TCP/IP. Later sections in this chapter describe both protocols.

Understanding TCP/IP

All communication on the Internet uses a group of protocols collectively called Transmission Control Protocol/Internet Protocol (TCP/IP). For any sort of Internet client and server to communicate, both must be running TCP/IP and have an active network link between them.

> **note** If your working environment doesn't include a TCP/IP network, you might decide to use a disk-based Web for development rather than a Web server. See "Using Server-Based Webs" on page 127.

Browsers and HTTP servers always communicate by TCP/IP. This means each computer running these applications needs working TCP/IP software, configured with an *IP address*. IP addresses are four bytes long, with the value of each byte typically stated as a decimal number. For example, 192.168.180.2 is a typical four-byte IP address.

> **tip** TCP/IP software usually comes with operating systems, and not with browsers or HTTP servers. To install TCP/IP on most versions of Microsoft Windows, open Control Panel, Network, Add, and then Protocol. Select TCP/IP and then follow the prompts.

Period Speech

In the interest of brevity, technical people often refer to punctuation marks using the following shorthand terms:

period	.	dot
exclamation point	!	bang
slash	/	whack
backslash	\	hack
ampersand	&	amper
parentheses	()	paren
asterisk	*	star

If you connect to the Internet by dial-up link, your computer probably has no assigned IP address. Instead, software at your Internet service provider assigns a temporary address every time you dial in. HTTP servers, browsers, and applications such as Microsoft FrontPage can use this temporary address to connect to Web servers on the Internet or on your local machine, but after you disconnect, the IP address disappears and even a Web server on your own computer becomes inaccessible. Some Internet service providers will provide a permanent, or *static,* IP address for an additional fee.

If your computer is on a campus or enterprise local area network (LAN), your network administrator has probably assigned the computer an IP address. For this discussion it makes little difference whether the administrator assigned your address manually or via an automated network service, or whether the administrator configured your network software personally or simply provided instructions. If your computer has an IP address, FrontPage can communicate with Web servers also running on your computer or elsewhere on the network.

> **warning** It's absolutely critical that no two computers on the same network have the same IP address. Duplicate IP addresses prevent both computers from working and lead to other network problems as well. Never give your computer an IP address you guessed at, chose randomly, or copied from someone else's computer.

Chapter 36

Regardless of type, servers are usually situated on local area networks and generally have administrator-assigned IP addresses. Administrators also publicize the server's IP address by assigning an easy-to-guess, easy-to-remember name and providing lookup through a globe-spanning network service called the Domain Name System (DNS).

Talking to Yourself—The Loopback Address

Whenever you have trouble connecting from a client to a server, both running on the same computer, try using 127.0.0.1 or the name *localhost.* These are special values that mean *myself* on every computer running TCP/IP.

The number 127.0.0.1 is a special IP address—called the *loopback address*—that always refers to the local machine. If you're running a Web server and a client such as FrontPage or a browser on the same machine, the client can access the local Web server by connecting to 127.0.0.1. This can be extremely convenient if you don't know your IP address or if it changes frequently (for example, each time you dial into your Internet service provider). In most cases, the name *localhost* is synonymous with 127.0.0.1.

Port Numbers

When a single server provides several TCP/IP services, clients need a way to identify which of these services they want to use. Port numbers provide such a method.

When a TCP/IP service starts up, it registers with the local machine's network software and asks to receive all traffic directed to certain ports. The network software then forwards all incoming traffic on those ports to that service.

If a service requests a port that's already in use, it receives an error code. Allowing two services to register the same port would be ambiguous; the network software would again be unable to identify which service should receive traffic arriving on that port.

By default, HTTP servers listen on port 80. This is also the default port number in an *http://* URL. If a system administrator wants to run several kinds of Web-server software at the same time on the same machine, the administrator must configure each piece of software to listen on a different port number, and visitors must specify the same port numbers in their URLs. For instance,

> *http://www.interlacken.com*

will access an HTTP server on port 80, and

> *http://www.interlacken.com:8080*

will access an HTTP server on port 8080. Port 8080 is a common choice for Web servers running on computers where port 80 is already in use.

Building a Private TCP/IP Network

If you have more than one computer in your home or office, connect them together! This makes it easy to share printers and data among your computers, and you can even set up your own intranet.

The complete details of setting up a small LAN are beyond the scope of this book, but generally it involves these steps:

1 Install a network card in each machine, and then connect the cards to each other with suitable wiring. Ethernet network cards cost less than $100, and hubs to connect them are just as cheap.

2 Install the driver software for your network card. All versions of Windows since Windows 95 include all the software you need for a wide variety of network cards. If Windows won't recognize your card, the manufacturer should provide a driver.

> **tip** The Windows Plug and Play feature will usually detect the new network card, prompt you for the necessary disks and CDs, and walk you through the installation. If not and you're running Windows 2000, open Control Panel, double-click Add/Remove Hardware, and then proceed through the Add/Remove Hardware Wizard. On earlier operating systems, open Control Panel's Network applet, select the Adapters tab, and then click Add.

3 When the network setup program prompts you for protocols, be sure to choose TCP/IP.

4 Give each machine an IP address from Table 36-1 on the next page. Unless you need to connect more than 255 computers, this means choosing 192.168.*xxx*.*yyy* where:

- All the machines have the same *xxx* number between 1 and 254.

- Each machine has a different *yyy* value between 1 and 254.

> **tip** Unless you've installed network cards, cabling, and software before, get help from someone with experience or from another book. The material presented here is only an overview.

5 Assign a Subnet Mask of 255.255.255.0.

6 The Default Gateway specifies the IP address of a network device that can route network packets to locations other than your local network. You might need to enter this field if you're connected to a large internal network or to a small network that includes a gateway to the Internet. Contact your network administrator or the instructions that came with your Internet gateway for details. In the absence of another guidance, leave the Default Gateway, DNS, and WINS dialog boxes blank.

Table 36-1. Private Network IP Addresses

Class	From IP address	To IP address	Subnet mask	Maximum computers per network
A	10.0.0.1	10.255.255.255	255.0.0.0	16,581,375
B	172.16.0.1	172.31.255.255	255.255.0.0	65,025
C	192.168.0.1	192.168.255.255	255.255.255.0	255

note Private IP addresses are assigned by an Internet standard called RFC 1597.

Private network IP addresses aren't valid on the Internet; you can use them only to connect private networks for a home or small business. No conflict results if machines on the private network occasionally dial into an Internet service provider, or if you later connect the private network to the Internet using software called a proxy server.

For more information about proxy servers, refer to the sidebar "Proxy Servers and GET Requests" later in this chapter.

There's one more step in setting up a private TCP/IP network, namely setting up a *hosts* file so the computers can find each other by name. The section "Using a Hosts File," later in this chapter, explains.

Server Names and the Domain Name System

Computers on the Web actually connect by means of numeric IP addresses and not by name. Site names such as *www.microsoft.com, ftp.microsoft.com,* and *www.msn.com* are only for the convenience of visitors. Names such as *www.microsoft.com* are simply easier to remember than numeric addresses such as 207.68.137.36. With visitors preferring names and computers using numbers, a method is clearly needed to translate from one to the other. The Domain Name System (DNS) provides that service.

DNS names have built-in levels. Periods separate the levels, with the highest level at the right end of the name. DNS servers look up names a level at a time—first *com,* then *microsoft,* and then *www*—and possibly on different servers for each level. Table 36-2 lists a few of the most common high-level DNS names. DNS names aren't case sensitive, but they're usually shown in lowercase.

> **note** The rightmost portion of a DNS name—the suffix—indicates the country that registered the name. The suffixes *com, gov, mil, net,* and *org* all indicate the United States. Other suffixes are unique to each country, such as *ca* for Canada, *fr* for France, *jp* for Japan, and *uk* for United Kingdom.

Table 36-2. Common Domain Name Suffixes (Root Domains)

Suffix	Meaning	Example	Site
com	Commercial	www.microsoft.com	Microsoft Corporation
edu	Educational	www.nd.edu	University of Notre Dame
gov	Government	www.odci.gov	Central Intelligence Agency
mil	Military	www.army.mil	United States Army
org	Nonprofit Organization	www.pbs.org	Public Broadcasting Service
ca	Canada	www.canoe.ca	Canadian Online Explorer
uk	United Kingdom	www.ox.ac.uk	Oxford University, England
us	United States	www.state.az.us	State of Arizona

Your Internet service provider or network administrator will either give you the IP address of a local DNS server or arrange to have it configured into your computer automatically. This is an important setting because without it you can connect to other machines only by numeric IP address.

Because IP addresses are difficult to remember and subject to change, Internet authorities (such as they are) invented the Domain Name System—DNS. Essentially, DNS is an online, distributed database that translates easily remembered names such as *www.intel.com* and *ftp.microsoft.com* to IP addresses. When your browser, for example, tries to open the URL

   http://www.microsoft.com/frontpage

it actually begins by using DNS to translate *www.microsoft.com* to an IP address. The browser then connects to the IP (numerical) address and not to the DNS name.

Like most Internet applications, DNS is a client/server system. The client software is called a *resolver,* and in the case of Windows, it's part of the TCP/IP software that comes with the operating system. *Name resolution* is the process of translating computer names to IP addresses and vice versa.

A DNS server usually resides centrally on a network and contains the databases that allow DNS to work. When a Web visitor requests a connection to a named host, the visitor's computer sends the name to the local DNS server, and with any luck the DNS server responds with the corresponding IP address. If the local DNS server can't resolve the request, it might contact additional DNS servers until it can.

> **tip** Your Internet service provider or information services department will normally provide a DNS server for you to use. Your TCP/IP software might get the DNS server's IP address automatically when you dial in or otherwise connect to the network; otherwise, you might need to enter it manually. Contact your service provider or system administrator if you need assistance using DNS.

Each dot (period) in a DNS name normally indicates a different database and possibly a different machine. If your network software asks your local DNS server for the IP address of *www.microsoft.com*, the following steps occur:

1 The local server first contacts a root DNS server that knows all the *.com* entries in the world.

2 The root server provides the names and IP addresses of all DNS servers in the *microsoft.com* domain.

3 Your local server would contact one of the *microsoft.com* DNS servers to get the IP address for *www.microsoft.com*.

The inner workings of DNS really aren't important for Web authoring. However, if people ask you for your DNS name, you should know what they're talking about. You'll also need to understand a little about DNS so that you can ask your Internet service provider or network administrator to establish a name for your server, as well as understand the error messages you'll get if DNS isn't working.

Using a Hosts File

It's common in small environments—such as home and small office networks—to have small Web servers not included in any DNS server's database. To access such servers by name rather than IP address, you can provide name-to-IP-address translation using a hosts file. This is a simple text file named *hosts* (with no extension) and located in the following folders:

● **Windows 95** and **Windows 98.** The Windows folder (that is, *c:\windows*)

● **Windows 2000** and **Windows NT.** *<systemroot>\system32\drivers\etc* (where *<systemroot>* is typically *c:\winnt*)

You can create this file using any simple ASCII editor, such as Notepad. Each line in the file contains an IP address, one or more spaces, and a computer name. After saving the file in the correct location, you should find that your computer translates the entered names to corresponding computer names as if they were in DNS.

> **tip** If you use Save As to save the hosts file with Notepad, be sure to enclose the file name—*hosts*—in quotes (*"hosts"*). Otherwise, Notepad adds a *.txt* extension and the file won't work.

The primary disadvantage of hosts files is that each computer needs its own copy of the file. Keeping all these files up to date becomes unwieldy in large environments.

Hypertext Transfer Protocol—A Simple Concept

Using Web browsers such as Internet Explorer to retrieve and view Web pages is generally a pleasant and easy experience. The data you see, however, is obviously stored somewhere else on the network, and your browser retrieves it using a relatively hidden transfer mechanism. In the case of the World Wide Web, the data comes from a Web server, and the transfer mechanism is Hypertext Transfer Protocol (HTTP).

Like so many other technologies, HTTP started out simple and later grew to be complicated. As originally conceived, this is the procedure that occurred:

1. The browser opened a connection to the computer and port specified in the desired Web page address.

2. The browser transmitted the word GET followed by a space, a folder path, an optional file name, and a carriage return (equivalent to pressing Enter). A typical GET request, for example, was

   ```
   GET /sports/hockey/standings.html
   ```

3. The server sent back a status code, a file type indicator, a blank line, and the contents of the requested file.

4. The server then closed the connection.

Notice that the GET command in the previous paragraph contains less information than a normal URL. The corresponding URL might have been

http://fictitious.msn.com:80/sports/hockey/standings.html

where *http* specifies the protocol, *ficticious.msn.com* is the name of the Web server, and *80* is a port number on that server. The browser uses the information in *http://ficticious.msn.com:80* for connecting to the Web server, and it transmits the rest as a command to locate and deliver the file (as the GET request just shown).

> For an explanation of port numbers, refer to "Port Numbers" earlier in this chapter.

The file *standings.html* probably contains HTML and might call for additional files. If so, the browser retrieves each additional file by issuing another GET request. The server handles all ordinary GET requests identically, regardless of file type. The job of assembling multiple files and formatting the finished page falls entirely on the browser.

Proxy Servers and GET Requests

There's one instance where a browser sends out GET requests containing the remote hostname and port number: when it uses a proxy server.

For security reasons, many organizations provide access to external Web sites only through a proxy server. A proxy server is simply a relay agent that retrieves Internet Web pages for people at that site but prevents Internet visitors from accessing the site's internal resources. To use a proxy server, each browser must be configured to do both of the following:

● Send all GET requests to the proxy server and not to the host specified in the URL.

● Include the full URL, including the server name and port, in all GET requests.

Essentially, the browser sends the proxy server GET requests containing host names. The proxy server then connects to the named host and sends a GET request with the host name removed. With or without a proxy server, the remote Web server receives GET requests not containing its host name.

Nowadays, in addition to the basic GET request, browsers transmit *headers* that convey additional information about the connection. In the following request, for example, the browser indicates what kinds of files it can accept, what human language it prefers (English), the size and color depth of the Web visitor's screen, the visitor's operating system and CPU type, the name and version of the visitor's browser, the computer name the browser is trying to contact, and an indication that the browser is willing to use the same connection for several transfers rather than opening new connections for each file:

```
GET / HTTP/1.0
Accept: image/gif, image/x-xbitmap, image/jpeg, image/pjpeg, */*
Accept-Language: en
UA-pixels: 1024x768
UA-color: color8
UA-OS: Windows 2000
UA-CPU: x86
Visitor-Agent: Mozilla/4.0 (compatible; MSIE 5.5; Windows 2000
Host: www.interlacken.com
Connection: Keep-Alive
```

In response to this GET request, the server responded with the headers at the top of the facing page. They indicate the status code "200 OK," the name and version of the Web server software, the willingness to reuse connections, the date and time, the file type "text/html," the ability to supply a byte-numbered portion of a page, the date the returned page was last modified, and the length in bytes of the returned page:

```
HTTP/1.0 200 OK
Server: Microsoft-IIS/4.0
Connection: keep-alive
Date: Fri, 09 Feb 2001 22:41:10 GMT
Content-Type: text/html
Accept-Ranges: bytes
Last-Modified: Fri, 09 Feb 2001 03:50:15 GMT
Content-Length: 5574
```

Web pages that contain HTML forms often use a second type of request called POST. The POST method uses additional HTTP headers to transmit all the names and values from an HTML form. This provides more flexibility and data-handling capacity than using the GET method with a query string.

A complete explanation of HTTP headers is beyond the scope of this book, but Web designers should be aware that browsers and Web servers exchange a variety of information about themselves during each request. Information supplied by the browser, for example, can be used on the server to customize the server's response.

Secure Sockets Layer

Security is always a concern on the Web, especially for activities that involve transfer of money, exchange of credit card numbers or bank account numbers, or other financial transactions. Both parties in any such transaction want such data encrypted so no one else can tap into the communication, modify or duplicate the transaction, or capture the data for later (and presumably fraudulent) use.

Secure Sockets Layer (SSL) provides just such the type of encryption required on the Web. SSL works like this:

1 The Web visitor submits a URL—perhaps by clicking a hyperlink or form button—with a protocol identifier of *https.*

2 The browser contacts the Web server on port 443.

3 The browser and server negotiate an encryption key for the current session. This key includes factors specific to the Web visitor's computer, such as its IP address, that make it very unlikely that any other computer would get (or guess) the same key.

4 After the encryption key is agreed on, all communication (using *https* URLs) between that browser and server will be encrypted using that key. Then the following occurs:

    a The browser sends the encrypted data to the SSL service on port 443.

    b The SSL service decrypts the transmission and forwards it internally to the requested server and port.

HTTP and Stateless Connections

The greatest limitation of HTTP connections is that they are *stateless*. This means that the connection is closed immediately after a page is transmitted, and the server retains no useful memory of it. This becomes a real nuisance when a single transaction requires several Web pages to complete. Suppose that a Web visitor brings up the first Web page, submits some information, and gets a second screen prompting for more data. When the visitor submits the second page, the server has no memory of what transpired on the first.

Here are three common solutions to this dilemma:

- Have the server write out all the data about a transaction to each Web page, and have the browser transmit it back with every transaction. This usually involves a hidden form field for each item of data.

- Have the server and browser exchange transaction data as cookies. *Cookies* are data fields that the browser and server exchange by means of special HTTP headers. Cookies might apply to a specific Web page, folder, or site, but cookies from one site can never be sent to another.

- Have the server keep transaction data in a file or database record designed for that purpose. Transmit a transaction identifier to and from the server using hidden form fields, path data, query strings, or a cookie.

By default, cookies reside in the browser's memory and disappear when the visitor closes the browser. However, a Web page can specify that its cookies should be saved persistently in a special file on the visitor's hard disk. As long as cookies exist for a given Web page, folder, or site, the browser transmits them with every request to that location until the cookies expire. The server specifies an expiration date every time it sends the cookies.

---

   c The SSL server receives the Web server's response, encrypts it, and transmits the results to the browser.

   d The browser decrypts and displays the results.

Note that the client software—the browser or FrontPage, for example—always initiates SSL communication. In addition, the Web server must support SSL and be properly configured to use it.

Server Root Folders

It's hard to imagine a case where any server administrator would want to make a Web server's entire file system available to everyone on the World Wide Web. Web servers therefore assign a *root folder* as the starting point for all GET requests. The term *root folder* is used interchangeably with any of the following: *home directory, home folder, root directory, HTTP root, document root,* and *home root.* If the server's root folder was

    H:\inetpub\wwwroot

and the server received

    GET /sports/hockey/standings.html

it would actually look for and deliver the file

    H:\inetpub\wwwroot\sports\hockey\standings.html

> **caution**   Don't assign your computer's root directory as your Web server's root directory. This makes the entire content of your computer accessible to anyone on the same network. And if you're on the Internet, that's a lot of other computers.

Virtual Folders

It's frequently convenient to view data as though it resided within a Webserver's root folder, even though it doesn't. The data might reside on a different drive letter for space management or historical reasons or it might reside on another machine. *Virtual folders* solve this dilemma by making folder locations outside the server's root folder appear to be within it.

Suppose, for example, a site kept its local announcements in a folder at

    I:\sitenews

but its server root folder was

    H:\wwwroot

The server administrator could define a virtual folder called */news* that represented *I:\sitenews.* If the server then received

    GET /news/default.html

it would look for and deliver

    I:\sitenews\default.html

rather than

    H:\wwwroot\news\default.html

A frequent reason for setting up virtual folders is security. An administrator might feel more confident of a system's security if important files are physically located outside the server's root folder. In addition, many Web servers use virtual folders to implement folder-level security provisions. Any folder-level settings used by the Web server but not by the local file system usually reside in virtual folder definitions.

Virtual Servers

Contrary to popular belief, no law of nature dictates that all Web sites have DNS names beginning with *www* and ending in *com*. Nevertheless, this is what most Web visitors now expect, and it creates problems for large and small sites alike.

For large Web sites, problems arise when trying to build servers powerful enough to handle hundreds (or thousands) of incoming requests per second. The solution is normally to keep upgrading hardware and software, or to set up additional servers for menu choices one or two levels removed from the home page. Systems are also available to randomly distribute incoming requests to one of several identically configured servers, even if all the requests specify the same IP address.

For small Web sites, the problem is the cost of building a separate server, even if the number of hits per day is small or moderate. The obvious solution is locating several small Web sites on one server, but the site owners want direct, custom names such as *www.<my-site>.com* and *www.<your-site>.com,* not *www.<provider>.com/<my-site>* and *www.<provider>.com/<your-site>.*

Virtual servers provide an elegant solution to this common dilemma. An administrator sets up a different DNS name and IP address for each Web site, and then configures one computer's network software to respond to several such addresses. Finally, the administrator configures the Web server software to access different root folders, depending on which IP address the Web visitor specified. This allows different DNS names such as *www.<my-site>.com* and *www.<your-site>.com* to access different root folders on the same physical server.

> **tip** To display the dialog box that makes a Windows 2000 computer respond to more than one IP address, right-click My Network Places and choose Properties from the shortcut menu. Then, right-click Local Area Connection, choose Properties from the shortcut menu, double-click Internet Protocol (TCP/IP), and click Advanced.

Server-Side Programming

Delivering prewritten Web pages is quite a useful function, but generating pages on the fly offers considerably more flexibility. Generating pages on the fly does require custom programming, but it means the same URL can produce different results depending on the date, the time, the type of browser, or any other information available to the Web server. The same technologies can also process input from HTML forms and display database data.

> FrontPage provides a number of server-side programming features that don't require programming knowledge on your part. For examples, refer to Chapter 28, "Providing a Text Search Capability," and Chapter 32, "Processing Data Submitted from Forms."

Here are some popular ways to deliver Web pages customized by programming:

- **Common Gateway Interface (CGI).** When the Web visitor clicks a hyper-link or a form button, the associated URL identifies not a file the server should transmit, but a program the server should run. Such programs typically receive input from HTML forms or from data appended to the URL, and as output they generate HTML for delivery to the Web visitor. They can also update files or databases on the server, send mail, and perform other useful functions.

- **Internet Server Application Programming Interface (ISAPI).** This approach is similar to CGI in function but implemented differently. ISAPI programs are dynamic link libraries (DLLs) that the operating system needs to load only once for any number of executions. By contrast, CGI programs are EXE files that must be loaded, initialized, run, and unloaded for each incoming request. The visitor submits a URL containing the name of the DLL.

- **Active Server Pages (ASP).** Unlike CGI and ISAPI, ASP pages consist of ordinary HTML intermixed with program code. The Web server interprets and executes the program code as it delivers the Web page. Web pages containing server-side scripts have the filename extension *.asp*.

  Programmers usually create code for ASP pages using simple script languages such as JavaScript and Microsoft VBScript. These languages can then invoke services from built-in server functions, ActiveX controls, Java applets, and other objects.

Because of the damage an errant or mischievous program can inflict, server-side programming raises significant security concerns. No Webmaster or system administrator wants visitors interfering with normal operation or tampering with content. For this reason, most Web servers are configured to execute only programs in specially designated folders. Administrators then allow just a few trusted individuals to place programs there.

MIME Types and Other Curiosities

The GET response on page 1035 includes the following line in the HTTP headers:

```
Content-Type: text/html
```

The string *text/html* is a MIME Content Type code that indicates the type of data that follows. MIME stands for Multipurpose Internet Mail Extensions and, as you might expect, was first defined as a way to handle e-mail attachments. A *MIME type* simply provides a system-independent way to indicate the format of a file; mail programs use it to launch an appropriate viewing program when file attachments arrive with electronic mail. It makes sense to use the same MIME-type associations for viewing Web files as well.

The Web doesn't use filename extensions to identify file types sent between computers, because not all operating systems support them. The Macintosh is a case in point. Instead, Windows-based Web servers usually have a table that translates filename extensions to

MIME types, and browsers use local MIME tables to select appropriate viewer programs. If you run into problems with Web content appearing incorrectly or prompting the Web visitor for a download location, investigate the MIME tables on both the server and the client.

Figure 36-1 shows the Windows dialog box for configuring MIME types. To display it, choose Folder Options from the Tools menu in any Windows Explorer window, and then click the File Types tab. Each file type in the resulting table has associations with one or more file extensions, a MIME type, and a program capable of opening the file.

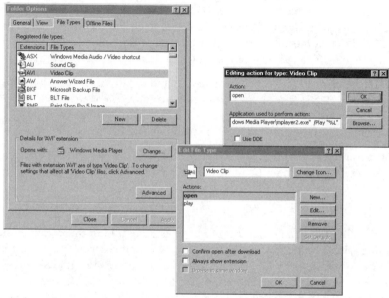

Figure 36-1. Web servers identify file types with MIME Content Type codes. The browser uses this information to invoke the proper viewing program.

You have the following options:

- To display the Edit File Type dialog box, select a file type from the Registered File Types list, and then click Advanced.

- To display the Editing Action For Type dialog box, select an entry from the Actions list in the Edit File Type dialog box, and then click Edit.

The flip side—some would say the server side—of MIME configuration appears in Figure 36-2. This dialog box controls the MIME types that Internet Information Services 5 transmits. The server translates each filename extension to a MIME type, and the browser uses these MIME types in deciding how to handle the file.

> For more information about the File Types dialog box, refer to, "Configuring Master Properties," on page 1058.

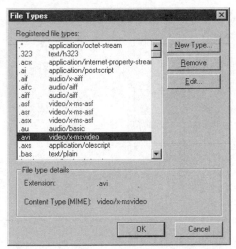

Figure 36-2.   This is the dialog box that configures MIME types transmitted by IIS.

Using a Proxy Server

To configure Internet Explorer 4, Internet Explorer 5, and FrontPage 2000 or FrontPage 2002 to use a proxy server, follow these steps. You can safely ignore them if your environment doesn't include a proxy server. If it *does* contain a proxy server, contact your network administrator or help desk for exact settings. Here's the procedure:

1 The first step varies depending on your current application:

- In Internet Explorer 4, choose Internet Options from the View menu.

- In Internet Explorer 5 and later, choose Internet Options from the Tools menu.

- In FrontPage 2000 or FrontPage 2002, choose Options from the Tools menu, and then click the Proxy Settings button.

2 When the Internet Options (or Internet Properties, if you used the FrontPage method in step 1) dialog box appears, take one of these actions depending on which browser is installed on your system:

- For Internet Explorer 4, click the Connection tab. The dialog box shown in Figure 36-3 on the next page results.

- For Internet Explorer 5 and later, first click the Connections tab, and then click the LAN Settings button. Figure 36-4 on the next page shows the resulting dialog box.

3 Select the check box titled Use A Proxy Server (or Access The Internet Using A Proxy Server in Internet Explorer 4).

4 In the Address box, specify the proxy server's name or IP address.

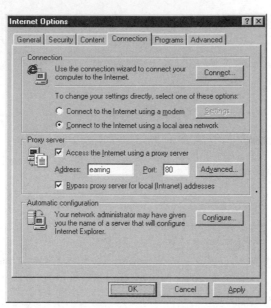

Figure 36-3. To configure a proxy server in Internet Explorer 4, use the Proxy Server section's settings on the Connection tab of its Internet Options or Internet Properties dialog box.

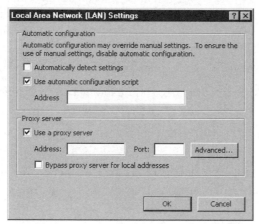

Figure 36-4. To configure a proxy server in Internet Explorer 5 and later, click LAN Settings on the Connections tab of its Internet Options or Internet Properties dialog box.

5 In the Port box, specify the proxy server's port number (usually 80).

6 To choose not to use the proxy server for computers on your local network, select the check box titled Bypass Proxy Server For Local Addresses. Your Internet service provider, system administrator, or Help desk can tell you if this setting is required in your environment.

7 If your environment requires additional settings, click Advanced. This displays the Proxy Settings dialog box shown in Figure 36-5.

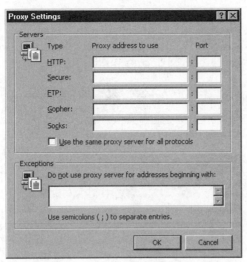

Figure 36-5. The Proxy Settings dialog box provides a detailed level of control over proxy server usage.

8 The Servers section of the Proxy Settings dialog box works as follows:

- If the check box titled Use The Same Proxy Server For All Protocols is cleared, the settings for HTTP apply to all protocols. This is the default.

- If the same check box is selected, you can specify a different proxy server, a different port, or both for each listed protocol.

9 The Exceptions section optionally contains a list of servers for which connecting through the proxy server isn't appropriate. As you enter the list, place a semicolon after each computer name. Again, contact your network support staff for settings.

---

tip The need for proxy server settings is much more common if your computer is connected to a large organizational network or a network with a security firewall or gateway to the Internet. Dial-up Internet accounts generally don't involve proxy servers.

Hypertext Markup Language

HTML, or Hypertext Markup Language, arose from an earlier format called Standard Generalized Markup Language (SGML). SGML had been a fixture in the technical publishing industry for years because of its ability to assemble uniform documents from the writings of many contributors. This was possible because the contributors submitted only plain text intermixed with style codes that indicated headings, captions, bulleted and numbered lists, and other structural elements. Publishing specialists then chose fonts, margins, and other aspects of page layout independently from the original authors.

The first use of HTML was to publish technical papers at the European Laboratory for Particle Physics in Geneva, Switzerland. The technical contributors there were familiar with SGML, so HTML was designed along the same principles—plain ASCII text marked up with ASCII style codes. This produced documents like the one in Figure 36-6.

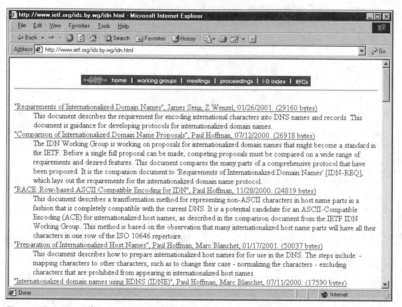

Figure 36-6. This is HTML doing what its inventors intended—displaying simple text documents.

As use of the Web grew beyond the scientific community and entered the mainstream community, Web page designers wanted to match the appearance of other high-visibility mass media. Browser manufacturers sought market share by adding markup tags that would appeal to these designers, resulting in pages such as that shown in Figure 36-7.

The designer of a page like the one in Figure 36-6 has very little control over paragraph formatting, font selection, page width, or line endings. The designer *can* specify paragraph styles such as Heading Level One and font styles such as Bold, but the Web visitor's browser and computer system control the typeface, point size, and color used for each style. There are no controls for paragraph indentation, line spacing, or margins. Everything is flush left (left-aligned).

By contrast, the page shown in Figure 36-7 is divided into *frames* and makes considerable use of pictures, even though the text within each frame follows the same rules as the text in Figure 36-6. The limitations of HTML tempt many Web designers to make each page a single large picture, but this usually results in unacceptably long download times for visitors who access the Web by modem.

For more information about frames, refer to "Creating and Editing Frames" on page 506.

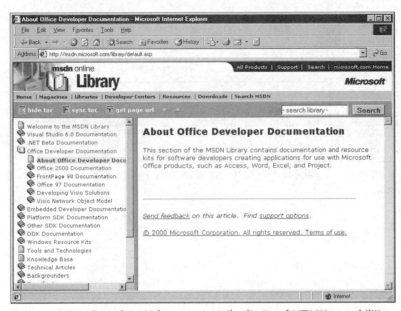

Figure 36-7. Complex Web pages test the limits of HTML's capabilities.

The original HTML specification provided no means for placing text, pictures, or other objects spatially on the page; contents flowed left to right and top to bottom, and were left-aligned only. Frames provide a way to divide a page into areas and control each area, but *tables* provide an additional technique for *x-y* positioning.

Figure 36-8 on the next page shows a Web page that uses a myriad of tables—including tables within tables—to organize topics into recognizable zones. Note how the contrasting colors, typography, and pictures set off each block of content. Nevertheless, similarities in style give the page a unified look.

For more information about tables, refer to "Creating and Editing Tables" on page 475.

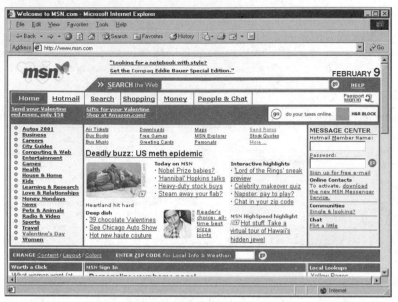

Figure 36-8. This page uses HTML tables to arrange information horizontally and vertically.

HTML Forms

Forms created in HTML provide a limited *graphical user interface (GUI)* that's useful for constructing data-entry screens. Figure 36-9 shows FrontPage creating such a form. Note the use of an HTML table to arrange the field titles and form.

> For more information about HTML forms, refer to Chapter 31, "Creating and Using Forms."

Each element within the form has a name assigned by the Web designer plus a value assigned by the Web visitor. When the visitor clicks the form's Submit button, the browser sends the name and value of each field to a program on the Web server. The server program uses the form data to send mail, update a database, or perform some other action.

Figure 36-9 shows the configuration of a radio button (or option button). The value in the Group Name box (*location,* for example) identifies all option buttons in the same group; selecting one button deselects all other buttons with the same Group Name identifier. The Value box specifies the string transmitted to the server if the form is submitted with this button selected. The Initial State buttons controls whether this button is selected when the form is first displayed. The value in the Tab Order box optionally indicates the sequence this button occupies as the visitor tabs from one form element to another.

> **caution** Radio (option) buttons are the only form elements where duplicate names are valid. Normally, each element in the form must have a unique name.

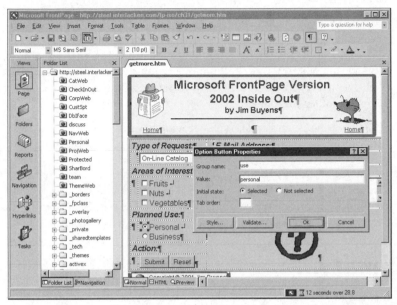

Figure 36-9. FrontPage provides a graphical way to easily construct HTML forms.

A single Web page can contain any number of HTML forms. If there are several forms on a single page, clicking any Submit button transmits only those elements in the same form.

What Activating the Internet Is All About

During the first few years of the Web's existence, most activity consisted of publishing information in fixed HTML pages and building hyperlinks. What was termed progress consisted of getting HTML to render more and more attractive pages—a challenging task both technically and artistically. This kind of progress hasn't reached its zenith and probably never will, but a second challenge has arisen: that of making pages respond more interactively than simple hyperlinks ever can. Microsoft calls providing this kind of interactivity "activating the Internet."

The software foundation for activating the Internet has four layers:

- HTML provides basic page layout and presentation.

- Scripts provide simple application logic and coordinate interaction among other components. Script languages typically require no compilation, no declaration of variables, and no installation. They are comparable to macro languages in applications. On the Web, scripts typically reside within the

HTML files of pages they affect. The script can execute either on the server, just before the HTML is transmitted, or on the browser. Browser scripts can execute as the page loads, later as timers go off, or as visitors operate controls on the Web page.

- Components usually provide more complex or intricate services than scripts. Programmers write them in rigorous, compiled languages such as C++, Java, and Visual Basic. Because of the development time required, it usually isn't practical to write component objects for a single Web page. Well-written components are versatile, fast, and designed to be used by scripts or other components.

- The operating system and services provide basic functions such as file input and output, database management, and network communication.

These layers are arbitrary and, in practice, the lines between them sometimes blur. Nevertheless, they provide a useful model. Components and services provide a way to implement functions of any complexity in a reusable way. Scripts and basic HTML provide ways to complete jobs in hours rather than days or months.

In Summary...

This chapter introduced the basic technologies that provide the inner workings of the Internet, which are TCP/IP and HTML. Web designers should have at least some notion of how these technologies work, even if they have no plans to become network administrators or programmers. All practitioners need to know the fundamentals of their medium.

The next chapter explains how to install and configure a Web server.

Installing and Configuring a Web Server

Learning new techniques to design fabulous Web pages doesn't do you much good if you don't have a Web server that delivers your work to others. In most cases, your Internet service provider or information technology department provides and manages a Web server, and you won't have to concern yourself greatly about it. Occasionally, though, you might need to set up or configure your own server, or at least know enough about the process so that you can communicate effectively with the people who do the work.

A second reason for setting up your own Web server is the need for an offline test and development environment. When you create a new Web or roll new features into an existing one, you probably don't want Web visitors browsing your half-finished work. Instead, you'd most likely prefer visitors to keep browsing the existing Web until the new or revised one is fully tested and ready for deployment.

For information about deciding how many Web servers you need, and where, refer to "Planning Your Web Environment" on page 62.

Your IT department or, less likely, your ISP can provide a development server for just this reason. If they don't—or if you have highly specific needs—once again it's time to set up your own Web server.

Although this chapter isn't a comprehensive guide to managing Web servers, it provides enough information for most Web designers to set up a Web server and configure it for the type of development they have in mind. For more detailed information, consult your product documentation or a book that describes your Web server specifically.

1049

Choosing and Configuring Your Web Server

Microsoft's flagship Web server—and the one that supports FrontPage the best—is Internet Information Services 5 (IIS). The combination of IIS 5 and SharePoint Team Services from Microsoft provides full support for every FrontPage 2002 feature. Therefore, if at all possible, you should stipulate this environment from your ISP or IT department.

> **tip**   New releases of Microsoft Web servers don't necessarily appear simultaneously with releases of FrontPage, nor of the various Microsoft Windows operating systems. This book deals primarily with IIS 5, which is part of Windows 2000. If a newer version exists when you start your installation, by all means use it.

Other choices are, of course, possible and completely workable. The FrontPage Server Extensions are available for servers running Windows NT 4 with IIS 4, and for various platforms running Netscape or Apache Web server software. Nevertheless, and particularly if you're starting from scratch, you might as well have the most compatible and up-to-date environment possible, and that's IIS running on Windows 2000.

> **on the web**   For up-to-date news about availability of the FrontPage Server Extensions for various platforms, browse *http://www.microsoft.com/frontpage,* click FrontPage Server Extensions, and then click List Of Supported Platforms.

In almost every case, it makes sense for your production and test Web servers to be as similar as possible. Otherwise, what works in test might not work in production, and vice versa. The more dissimilar the servers, the greater this problem might be. If you're going to run your development Web server on your own computer, this argues strongly for using Windows 2000 Professional as your desktop operating system and Windows 2000 Server as your production Web server operating system.

Keep in mind that the FrontPage Server Extensions 2002 no longer support personal Web servers running on the Windows 9X family of operating systems. If this is your current environment, your options are as follows:

- Upgrade to Windows 2000.

- Use a disk-based Web. This is an excellent choice if you don't plan to develop or test any Web pages that require server-based processing; that is, if you don't plan to use features such as the following:

■ Save Results (saving the content of an HTML form as a file, sending it as mail, or adding it to a database)

■ Discussion Webs

■ Web Search

■ Hit Counter

● Obtain, install, and run Microsoft Personal Web Server and the FrontPage 2000 Server Extensions on your Windows 9X system. This was a popular option in the past—especially among new Web designers—but it's no longer recommended. As the features and capabilities of Web servers have grown, the inherent limitations of the Windows 9X operating system have simply become too much of a barrier.

Running the Server Extensions on Windows 9X

If you absolutely *must* run Personal Web Server and the FrontPage 2000 Server Extensions on a Windows 9X computer, here are the high-level steps:

1 Install Personal Web Server:

■ For Windows 95 and Windows 98, locate the Windows NT Option pack on Microsoft's Web site and run the setup program provided.

■ For Windows 98 SE, run */add-ons/pws/setup.exe* from the Windows SE CD.

■ For Windows Me, you're out of luck. There's no Personal Web Server for this operating system.

2 Don't install the FrontPage Server Extensions included with the download files or the Windows 98 SE CD.

3 Download and install the latest version of the FrontPage 2000 Server Extensions from *http://www.microsoft.com/frontpage*.

4 If you plan to use databases in your Web pages, download and install the latest version of the Microsoft Data Access Components (MDAC) from *http://www.microsoft.com/data/*.

Even if you get this working, keep in mind that it isn't a recommended configuration. For one thing, the FrontPage 2000 Server Extensions don't support all the features of FrontPage 2002. For another, downloading and integrating any collection of software—some of it more than four years old—is fraught with peril. In the long run, an operating system upgrade probably remains your best choice. The cost of fully capable computers with Windows 2000 preinstalled is dropping every day.

Installing IIS on Windows 2000

The flagship of Microsoft's Web server line is IIS. This is an extremely powerful, commercial-grade Web server suitable for a wide range of production environments.

If you want your FrontPage environment or your server environment to be 100 percent Microsoft, IIS should be your production Web server. The various Web servers tend to leapfrog one another in terms of features and performance, but IIS is perennially near the top. IIS's large installed base ensures a wide variety of third-party add-ons, and Microsoft is a leader in bringing new technologies to its server. Finally, IIS ships at no extra charge with every copy of Windows 2000.

When you install IIS on Windows 2000 Professional, it does have some restrictions:

- There's no support for virtual servers.

- You can't selectively grant or deny access based on a Web visitor's IP address.

- You can't control total bandwidth allocated to Internet services.

- Licensing prohibits more than 10 different IP addresses from connecting to a Windows 2000 Professional Web server in any 10-minute period.

> **note** If Web services running on Windows 2000 seem attractive, consider that not all FrontPage designers need their own copy of Windows 2000 Professional running a Web server. It's perfectly acceptable—and frequently desirable—to set up one Windows 2000 Web server per small workgroup, especially in collaborative environments.

These restrictions conform to Windows 2000 Professional's pricing and positioning as a single-user desktop operating system. Windows 2000 Professional's machine-to-machine connectivity is licensed for use in small workgroups, and not for use as a production Web server.

> **on the web** For more information about installing, configuring, and managing Windows 2000 in general or IIS in particular, refer to the product documentation, Microsoft's Web site at *http://www.microsoft.com,* or books dedicated to these topics.

Before installing IIS, first remove any other Web servers by using the Add/Remove Programs options in the Windows Control Panel. If you want to preserve your existing content, be sure to note the existing software's HTTP root folder.

At this point, it's also a good idea to check your computer's name. Any spaces, punctuation, or special characters are sure to become a nuisance and now is the time to remove them. Right-click My Computer, choose Properties from the shortcut menu, and then click the Network Identification tab shown in the background of Figure 37-1. Click Properties to display the Identification Changes dialog box, shown in the foreground of Figure 37-1.

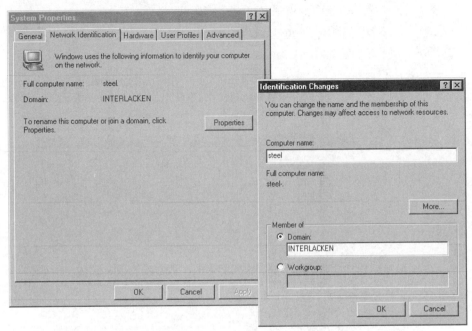

Figure 37-1. Available from the System Properties dialog box, the Identification Changes dialog box shows the computer's name. Remove any spaces, punctuation, or special characters before installing Web server software.

caution Configuring a Web server usually doesn't add the computer's name to DNS, and therefore doesn't make it available by name to other computers on the same network. If this presents a problem, either get your computer's name and IP addresses defined in DNS or update the hosts file on each computer that needs to access yours.

You can install IIS when you first install Windows 2000, but it's often better to bypass this option and install IIS later. There are two reasons for this:

- During initial setup, the only drive letter available is the system drive. Installing IIS after initial setup provides more flexibility in drive assignment (assuming, of course, that you manage disk space by allocating drives to specific applications).

- The version of IIS contained on the Windows 2000 setup CD might not be current. New releases of IIS appear more frequently than new releases of operating systems.

Here's the procedure for installing IIS 5 on Windows 2000:

1 If Windows 2000 is already running on your computer:

    a Choose Settings from the Start menu.

    b Choose Control Panel.

    c Double-click Add/Remove Programs.

    d When the Add/Remove Programs dialog box appears, click Add/Remove Windows Components. This displays the Windows Component Wizard shown in Figure 37-2.

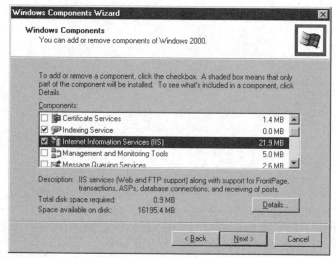

Figure 37-2. To install IIS on Windows 2000, choose Internet Information Services during setup or later in Add/Remove Programs.

2 If you're installing Windows 2000 for the first time, watch for a dialog box that looks much like the one shown in Figure 37-2. (If you miss it, you can always start over at step 1 later.)

3 In the Components list, select Internet Information Services (IIS), and then click Details. This displays the Internet Information Services (IIS) dialog box shown in Figure 37-3. (The figure is actually a composite modified to show all the subcomponents at once.) Select the options you want to install as follows:

    ■ **Common Files.** Always select this option. Otherwise, many of the other options won't work.

    ■ **Documentation.** Select this option unless disk space is incredibly scarce. Having documentation available will significantly improve your personal and professional life.

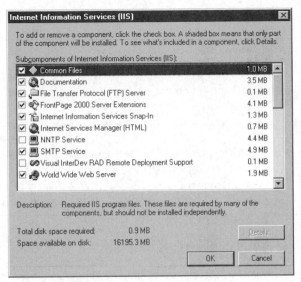

Figure 37-3. The IIS choice in Figure 37-2 includes these sub-components.

■ **File Transfer Protocol (FTP) Server.** Select this option if you or anyone else will need connectivity to the server by FTP.

■ **FrontPage 2000 Server Extensions.** Because the FrontPage 2000 Server Extensions are obsolete, don't select this option. Instead, install SharePoint Team Services or the FrontPage Server Extensions 2002 later.

For more information about installing the FrontPage Server Extensions 2002 , refer to Chapter 38, "Understanding the FrontPage Server Extensions."

■ **Internet Information Services Snap-In.** Always select this option. Without it, the dialog boxes for administering the Web server won't be available.

■ **Internet Services Manager (HTML).** Select this option to support remote Web server administration using HTML forms. (This option is available on Windows 2000 Server but not on Windows 2000 Professional.)

■ **NNTP Service.** Select this option to install an Internet News server. (Configuration of this service involves agreements with other sites to initiate and receive news feeds, and is clearly beyond the scope of this book. It's available on Windows 2000 Server but not on Windows 2000 Professional.)

■ **SMTP Service.** Select this option to install an SMTP mail server. This service is suitable for sending mail and for transferring mail to and from other servers, but not for delivering mail to individual users.

That would require a Post Office Protocol (POP) server or an Internet Message Access Protocol (IMAP) server, neither of which Windows 2000 includes.

You must install this service if you plan to use Collaboration Data Objects (CDO) described in Chapter 32.

For more information about the use of CDO, refer to "Sending Custom E-Mail" on page 912.

- **Visual Interdev RAD Remote Deployment Support.** Select this option to install a DLL that developers using Visual InterDev can use to remotely register Component Object Model (COM) objects or set up Microsoft Transaction Server (MTS) packages on the server. The need for this option is relatively rare.

  Clearing the FrontPage 2000 Server Extensions (as recommended earlier) also clears this option. Always install the version of this option that matches the version of the FrontPage Server Extensions that you install.

- **World Wide Web Server.** Always select this option. This is the Web server itself.

4 Click OK to return to the Windows Components Wizard dialog box shown in Figure 37-2. Make sure the Indexing Service option is selected, and then click Next.

5 The setup program prompts you for various file locations, such as the root folder for the Web server, for the FTP server, and so forth. You'll probably want to keep the suggested path names but change the drive letters. There are three reasons for this:

- It keeps the IIS programs and content areas off the Windows 2000 system drive, which you might someday need to delete and recreate.

- It isolates data files from software areas.

- It segregates applications with possible rapid disk growth from others that would be adversely affected.

When setup ends, you should be able to browse the local server by opening Internet Explorer and entering the URL *http://127.1*. If that doesn't work:

1 Choose Programs from the Start menu.

2 Choose Administrative Tools. You might have to right-click the Windows taskbar and select the Advanced tab's Display Administrative Tools check box to access this menu.

3 Choose Internet Services Manager. This displays the Internet Services Manager application shown in Figure 37-4.

4 The local computer name should appear in the left pane under the heading Internet Information Services. If it doesn't, setup was incomplete. Try running setup again.

5 If the local computer name does appear, click it and review the list of services in the right pane of the Internet Information Services window. If any service has a State column entry other than Running, right-click its line and choose Start from the shortcut menu.

6 If you receive an error message, browse *http://search.microsoft.com*, enter the error code or most significant portion of the message, and search for that exact phrase.

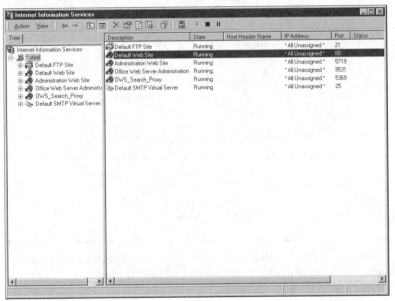

Figure 37-4. Internet Services Manager is a snap-in module for Microsoft Management Console.

Configuring IIS on Windows 2000

To configure IIS on either Windows 2000 Professional or Server, you'll need to open Internet Services Manager, a utility that's installed with IIS. To open this program, Choose Programs from the Start menu, choose Administrative Tools, and choose Internet Services Manager.

This displays the window shown in Figure 37-4. As usual, clicking a plus icon expands an item, and clicking a minus icon collapses one. In the figure, the items Internet Information Services and *steel* are both expanded. (*Steel* is the server's computer name.)

> **note** The application shown in Figure 37-4 is actually Microsoft Management Console, a general-purpose interface for managing Windows 2000 services. The capability to administer individual services comes from so-called snap-in modules, each of which appears as a first-level item under Console Root. To administer listed services running on other machines, right-click the service name and choose Connect from the shortcut menu.

You can configure IIS settings at each of the following three levels. Settings established at more general levels also apply to more specific ones, unless overridden:

- **The entire computer.** Under Internet Information Services, right-click the name of the computer you want to configure, and then choose Properties from the shortcut menu.

- **An individual Web server.** Under the computer name, right-click the Web server or other service you want to configure, and then choose Properties from the shortcut menu.

- **An individual folder.** Under the Web server name, right-click the folder you want to configure, and then choose Properties from the shortcut menu.

The Properties dialog box for all three levels is essentially the same. You should expect, however, that some tabs will be present or absent depending on the level. Similarly, some options will be enabled or dimmed.

> **tip** To create a new virtual directory, right-click the folder's parent location, choose New from the shortcut menu, and then choose Virtual Directory.

Configuring Master Properties

The *<computer-name>* Properties dialog box shown in Figure 37-5 appears only if you choose Properties for an entire computer. If you chose Properties for a particular Web server or folder, skip ahead to the section "Configuring Site and Folder Level Options."

The *<computer-name>* Properties dialog box provides an entry for configuring defaults that apply to all IIS services on the computer. Here are the options you can choose:

- **Master Properties.** This list box itemizes services available for configuration. The choice to configure the IIS Web server is, of course, WWW Service. To proceed with configuration, click the Edit button.

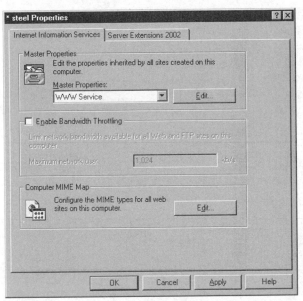

Figure 37-5. This is the IIS Properties dialog box for a computer named *Steel*.

● **Enable Bandwidth Throttling.** This check box, if selected, sets a maximum on the amount of bandwidth Internet services can consume.

● **Computer MIME Map.** This option configures the assignment of MIME types to filename extensions. Click Edit to display the dialog box shown in Figure 36-2.

> For information about the Server Extensions tab in this and subsequent dialog boxes in this chapter, refer to Chapter 38, "Understanding the FrontPage Server Extensions."

Configuring Site and Folder Level Options

There are two ways to reach the multi-tabbed dialog box that appears in Figure 37-6 on the next page:

● Select WWW Service in the Master Properties list of the <computer-name> Properties dialog box, and then click Edit.

● Click the plus icon for the computer name, right-click the entry for Default Web Site, a virtual server, or a folder, and then choose Properties from the shortcut menu.

Various options will be available or unavailable depending on the context, but here's a rundown of the complete set:

● **Web Site Identification.** Controls the server's worded and network identities:

■ **Description.** Gives the IIS server a name that serves as documentation and appears in various configuration dialog boxes.

1059

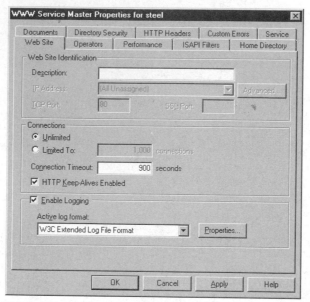

Figure 37-6. The Web Site tab configures the most general options for a default or virtual server.

■ **IP Address.** Specifies the IP address a virtual server should respond to. Recall that for virtual servers, the computer responds to more than one IP address and uses a different server configuration accordingly.

■ **TCP Port.** Specifies the port number on which the server will operate.

■ **SSL Port.** Specifies the port number on which the server will accept SSL transmissions.

● **Connections.** Sets limits on the number and duration of network connections:

■ **Unlimited.** Sets no maximum on the number of simultaneous connections the server will try to accommodate.

■ **Limited To.** Controls the number of simultaneous connections the server will allow. In extremely busy environments, it might be better to turn away some connections than to provide substandard service to everyone who connects. Browsers will usually retry refused connections.

■ **Connection Timeout.** Specifies the number of seconds the server will wait for network responses.

■ **HTTP Keep-Alives Enabled.** If selected, permits browsers to request multiple files over the same TCP/IP connection. This is beneficial for both browsers and servers, because opening a new connection for each file consumes more resources.

● **Enable Logging.** If selected, the Web server saves the details of every request it receives. The server writes one log record per request. You must enable logging if you want FrontPage's Usage reports to contain data:

For more information about FrontPage Usage reports, refer to "Viewing Usage Reports" on page 444.

■ **Active Log Format.** Selects a file format for the log files. The format most suitable for FrontPage Usage reporting (and the default) is W3C Extended Log File Format.

■ **Properties.** Displays the Extended Logging Properties dialog box shown in Figure 37-7.

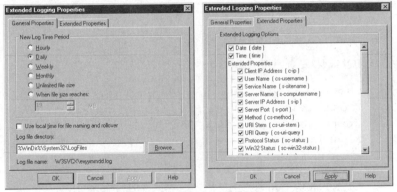

Figure 37-7. This two-tabbed dialog box configures IIS log file settings.

As shown in the figure, the Extended Logging Properties dialog box has two tabs: General Properties and Extended Properties. To receive the full benefit of FrontPage Usage reporting, you must configure both of these tabs correctly. Here's how to configure the General Properties tab:

● **New Log Time Period.** Choose how often you want the logging process to stop writing to the current log file and start writing to a new one. The default selection (and usually the best one) is Daily.

● **Use Local Time For File Naming And Rollover.** Select this check box if you want IIS to start writing a new log file at midnight, local time. Clear it if you want to start a new log file when it's midnight in Greenwich, England.

● **Log File Directory.** Specify the folder where log files should reside. The default is *%WinDir%\System32\LogFiles*, where *%WinDir%* is usually *C:\WINNT*. On a production server where log files are large, it's best to choose a different location that isn't on the system drive. That way, unexpectedly large volumes of log records won't jeopardize the system by filling up the system drive.

● **Log File Name.** This read-only field shows the pattern IIS will use when naming log files. The letters *yy* means a two- digit year, *mm* means a two-digit month, and so forth.

The Extended Properties tab controls which items of information IIS includes in each log record. You can choose whatever combination of items you want, but to gain the full benefit of all FrontPage Usage reports, you must select at least the following items:

Date	Time
Client IP Address	User Name
Method	URI Stem
Protocol Status	Bytes Sent
User Agent	Referrer

Authorizing Web Server Operators

The Operators tab, shown in Figure 37-8, appears only on Windows 2000 Server. It controls who can administer the current IIS installation or virtual server. Click Add to display the normal Windows 2000 Select Users Or Groups dialog box, which, in this context, selects additional operators. To remove an Operator entry, first select it, and then click Remove.

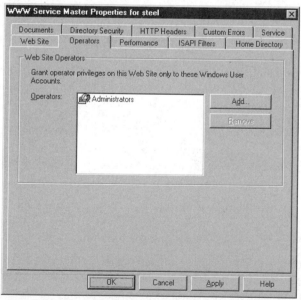

Figure 37-8. The Operators tab controls which users and groups can administer the current Web server.

Configuring Performance Settings

The Performance tab appears in Figure 37-9. The slider in the Performance Tuning frame indirectly controls the amount of memory IIS allocates to the current site. The more hits you tell IIS to expect, the more memory it allocates to the current server (at the expense, of course, of other processes on the same computer).

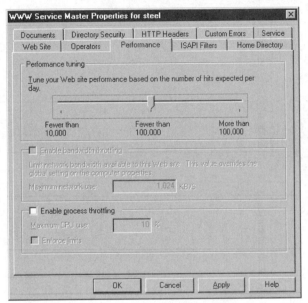

Figure 37-9. The Performance tab provides controls that optimize Web server performance.

The Enable Bandwidth Throttling check box, if selected, sets a maximum on the amount of bandwidth Internet services can consume. This setting repeats at various levels to control bandwidth allowed at each level.

The Enable Process Throttling check box, if selected, limits the percentage of CPU time the server can use for out-of-process applications. Specify the CPU percentage in the text box titled Maximum CPU Use. Any process that exceeds the given limit then generates a message in the log file. If you also select the check box titled Enforce Limits, IIS slows down the process when its reaches 150 percent of its quota, and terminates it when it reaches 200 percent.

Configuring ISAPI Filters

Figure 37-10 on the next page shows the ISAPI Filters tab. An ISAPI filter is installed as part of the Web server, taking action based on requests, responses, and other events to which it's programmed to respond. Basically, it modifies or extends the Web server's actions.

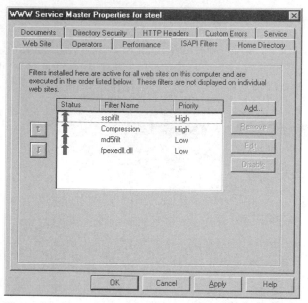

Figure 37-10. ISAPI filters are programs that hook into the Web server and modify its behavior.

You can add, remove, or modify ISAPI filter definitions—or make them unavailable—by using the buttons provided, but doing so is extremely unusual. Most ISAPI filters are components of larger software packages installed and removed by setup programs. However, if you suspect a certain filter is causing a problem, you might want to temporarily make it unavailable.

If looking at the figure makes you wonder about the file *fpexedll.dll,* yes, this is part of the FrontPage Server Extensions. It provides backward compatibility with Microsoft FrontPage for Windows, version 1.1, and Microsoft FrontPage for the Macintosh, version 1. These versions of FrontPage submit requests for the *shtml.exe, author.exe,* and *admin.exe* programs instead of the *shtml.dll, author.dll,* and *admin.dll* programs that more recent versions of FrontPage use. *Fpexedll.dll* examines every incoming HTTP request and converts any requests for those EXE files to requests for the corresponding DLL files.

Configuring Home Directory Settings

The Home Directory tab, shown in Figure 37-11, controls the location and other options for a server's HTTP root directory. The first option, at the top of the tab, controls where the server's content should come from (that is, the location of the server's HTTP Root).

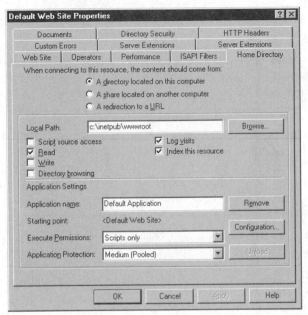

Figure 37-11. The Home Directory tab controls the starting point for Web pages and other files in a Web server.

The options include the following:

- **A Directory Located On This Computer.** By far, this is the most common option. This indicates how the root URL (a URL consisting of a single forward slash) corresponds to a location in the server's local file system:

  - **Local Path.** Specifies the drive letter and physical path to the desired physical location.

  - **Browse.** Displays a Browse For Folder dialog box for choosing the proper location.

- **A Share Located On Another Computer.** Means the Web server will deliver content physically located on another computer and accessed by file sharing. When you select this option:

  - **Local Path.** Changes to a Network Directory box, where you should enter a \\<server>\<sharename> path to the desired file server.

  - **Browse.** Changes to a Connect As button. Click this button to specify a user name and password that allows access to the specified files.

- **A Redirection To A URL.** Means that instead of delivering content, the server redirects any requests to another server. This can be a temporary redirection to another server, a temporary redirection to a subordinate folder, or a permanent redirection. You can specify exact URLs for these redirections or build them symbolically from components of the incoming URL.

This option is most useful after you've moved content to another location or server.

> **note** When notified of a permanent redirection, some browsers update stored locations (such as those on a Favorites menu).

The remaining options apply only if you chose A Directory Located On This Computer or A Share Located On Another Computer:

- **Script Source Access.** Select this check box if you select either the Read or the Write check boxes just below, and you want to give Web visitors the ability to remotely read and write scripts (such as Active Server Pages).

- **Read.** Select this check box to allow Web visitors to read files in the given server or folder.

- **Write.** Select this check box to allow Web visitors to write files in the given server or folder.

- **Directory Browsing.** Select this check box to specify what happens when a Web visitor submits a GET request with no file name, and no default document exists. If the check box is selected, the Web visitor gets a clickable list of files and folders that *do* exist. If the check box is cleared, the Web visitor gets an Access Denied error.

- **Log Visits.** Select this check box to extend a log file by one record for each request the server receives.

- **Index This Resource.** Select this check box if you want Microsoft Indexing Service to maintain a full text index of documents in the directory tree starting at this location.

- **Application Settings.** Select these options to control the settings for a Web *application*. An application starts at a specified Web folder and includes all folders within it, except folders and subfolders defined as part of *another* application. All files within an application space share certain executable program settings and certain kinds of state data. The settings include the following:

  - **Application Name.** Specifies the application's identity in words. If this option is blank, a new application doesn't start at the current folder location.

  - **Starting Point.** Specifies the folder containing the files and folders that constitute the application.

  - **Remove.** Converts an application to an ordinary folder. That is, it cancels a folder's configuration as an application root.

- **Configuration.** Displays an editable list associating filename extensions with programs that process them. For example, this list usually associates the extension *.asp* with the ASP interpreter.

- **Unload.** Stops an application and removes all programs and sessions from memory.

  This button is only available on the properties dialog box for the folder where the application starts. In addition, it's unavailable whenever there are no open sessions. Clicking the button therefore makes it unavailable.

  The application will automatically restart the next time a Web visitor requests an executable program or page (such as an ASP page). However, the Unload button won't become available until you redisplay the dialog box.

- **Execute Permissions.** Controls the way Web visitors can access the folder. Read means Web visitors can retrieve Web pages and other files in the ordinary way. Execute means Web visitors can launch executable programs residing in the directory. Scripts means Web visitors can run Web pages that contain server-side scripting.

- **Application Protection.** Controls the process in which applications run:

  - **Low.** The applications will run in the same process as the Web server itself. This usually produces the best response time and consumes the least system resources, but it maximizes the risk that an errant application could crash the server.

  - **Medium.** The application runs in a process separate from the Web server itself, but shared with other applications. This provides a tradeoff between the other two options.

  - **High.** The application runs in its own process. This minimizes the risk that an errant application could affect the Web server or another process, but consumes the most system resources.

Configuring Document Options

Figure 37-12 on the next page illustrates the Documents tab. The Enable Default Document check box controls whether IIS will look for a certain file name when someone submits a URL without one. This situation occurs when, for example, a visitor submits a URL such as *http://www.microsoft.com/*. If Enable Default Document is selected, the server switches to the directory specified in the URL and then searches for the given default document names in the order specified. Use the Add and Remove buttons to insert and delete file names from the list. Use the Up and Down buttons to change a selected name's position.

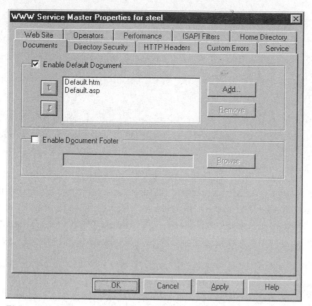

Figure 37-12. The Documents tab configures two optional settings: the default document name and a document footer.

Select the Enable Document Footer check box if you want the Web server to append a specified file to every Web page it delivers. This is useful for adding page footers to every page within a certain tree. Use the Browse button to locate the footer file.

InsideOut

The Enable Document Footer option would be much more useful if it were configurable by filename extension. As it is, after you enable document footers, IIS appends the footer file to *every* file it delivers. This includes picture files, frames pages, frame targets, and so forth. This lack of discrimination makes the Enable Document Footer feature considerably less useful than it might first appear.

Configuring Directory Security

The Directory Security tab, shown in Figure 37-13, controls three security settings:

- **Anonymous Access and Authentication Control.** Controls the use of logon accounts required for accessing Web pages.

- **IP Address and Domain Name Restrictions.** Configures rules that restrict access based on the Web visitor's IP address. For example, you can restrict all or part of a Web server to Web visitors with IP addresses belonging to a given enterprise.

Figure 37-13. The Directory Security tab configures the login account used for anonymous access, the keys used for secured communications, and access restrictions based on the Web visitor's IP address.

● **Secure Communications.** Manages the digital certificates (electronic credentials) used for secure communication over networks such as the Internet.

User-level control of Web access works like this: When a visitor first accesses an IIS site, IIS tries to access the requested file name using a so-called *anonymous* account. This is a user account, typically named IUSR_<computername>, that has no privileges other than accessing unrestricted Web content. If the Windows NT File System (NTFS) is coded so the anonymous account has access, the Web server delivers the content. If NTFS permissions *don't* grant access to the anonymous account, the Web server sends an Access Denied status code.

> **tip** Always use the NTFS file system on every drive of any computer used for Web access. Using the FAT file system, which has no built-in security, is just too risky.

When the Web visitor's browser gets the Access Denied status code, it prompts the visitor for another user name and password. Then, when the visitor presses the Enter key, it transmits those values along with the original request.

If the submitted user name is the name of a valid Windows 2000 logon account, and if the submitted password is correct, the Web server tries using that account to access the requested file. If NTFS grants access, the Web server delivers the page. In any other case, the Web server again transmits the Access Denied status code.

After a Web visitor gets a user name and password to work, that visitor's browser transmits those values on *every* subsequent request to the same server. This continues until access again fails (presumably because permissions on another area of Web content are different) or until the visitor terminates the browser program.

Figure 37-14 shows the dialog box that results from clicking the Edit button for Anonymous Access And Authentication Control in Figure 37-13. This dialog box controls four more options:

- **Anonymous Access.** If selected, instructs IIS to determine whether the Anonymous account has access to a file before prompting the visitor for a user name and password. If the anonymous account has access to the requested file, no user name/password prompting occurs. If the anonymous account doesn't have access, IIS prompts the visitor for a user name/password combination that does.

  The Edit button selects the anonymous account.

- **Basic Authentication.** If selected, instructs IIS to accept unencrypted passwords from visitors. Unencrypted passwords are a security risk because others on the network can capture, decipher, and use them without proper authority. Unfortunately, this is the only authentication scheme many Web browsers support.

  The Edit button identifies the Windows 2000 Domain, if any, that IIS will use for authenticating user name/password combinations.

- **Digest Authentication For Windows Domain Servers.** If selected, activates a feature that work much like basic authentication except that the Web server and browser establish credentials to transmit the password securely. Digest authentication is supported only by Internet Explorer 5 or later and IIS 5 or later, and only for domains with a Windows 2000 domain controller.

Figure 37-14. This dialog box controls the use of Windows 2000 user accounts for secure Web page access.

● **Integrated Windows Authentication.** If selected, indicates that IIS should verify passwords using a highly secure process also used for network logons to a Windows 2000 Server. Internet Explorer is the only browser that supports this option.

> **note** If Basic Authentication and Integrated Windows Authentication are both available, IIS will use Windows 2000 Challenge/Response if possible and Basic Authentication otherwise.

Configuring HTTP Headers

Figure 37-15 shows the HTTP Headers tab, which controls different kinds of information delivered with your Web pages.

Figure 37-15. HTTP headers transmit informational data about your Web pages.

> For more information about HTTP headers, refer to "Hypertext Transfer Protocol—A Simple Concept" on page 1033.

Options on this tab include:

● **Enable Content Expiration.** This option, if selected, controls content caching on the Web visitor's browser. This pertains only to files received from your site, and only from within the directory tree where you define the setting. There are three possible approaches:

   ■ **Expire Immediately.** The browser shouldn't cache the content at all.

▓ **Expire After.** The browser shouldn't cache the content longer than the specified interval.

▓ **Expire On.** The browser shouldn't cache content beyond the specified date and time.

● **Custom HTTP Headers.** These are strings you must type in. Use the Add, Edit, and Remove buttons to modify the list.

● **Content Rating.** Displays a dialog box where you can rate your site's content in terms of Violence, Sex, Nudity, and Language. Web visitors can then set their browsers to accept or exclude pages based on these settings. These settings can assure your visitors there's nothing objectionable about your site or, if your site contains potentially objectionable content, possibly lessen your liability.

● **MIME Map.** Displays a list of filename extensions and corresponding MIME types that override those set at the computer level (that is, those set in the Properties dialog box shown in Figure 37-5).

Customizing Error Displays

The Custom Errors tab, which appears in Figure 37-16, controls the format of standard error messages your visitors receive. Basically, there's a Web page for each standard error. It's usually better to click Edit Properties and specify a different page than to modify the default error message pages.

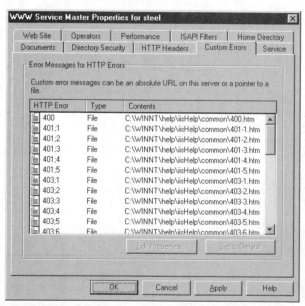

Figure 37-16. This tab specifies the Web page the server will send in the event of each standard error.

Configuring Service Settings

The Service tab, shown in Figure 37-17, specifies the IIS 5 Web server that the IIS 3 Internet Service Manager can remotely access, and also controls HTTP compression.

Figure 37-17. This tab specifies the one IIS 5 Web server that IIS 3's Internet Service Manager can remotely access. It also controls HTTP compression.

The following options appear on the Service tab:

- **IIS 3.0 Administration.** Permits the Internet Service Manager supplied with IIS 3 to administer an IIS 5 server on a limited basis. Because IIS 5's configuration is so much more flexible than IIS 3's, the IIS administration tools can administer only one designated server—the default server or one virtual server. Use the Default Web Site list to select this server.

- **HTTP Compression.** Controls whether or not IIS compresses files before transmitting them to the browser. This speeds up transmission time but consumes CPU time at both the Web server and the browser. Internet Explorer versions 5 and later support compression. IIS won't compress data it delivers to browsers that lack compression support:

    - **Compress Application Files.** Select this check box if you want IIS to compress files that are likely to be different every time a visitor request them (Active Server Pages, for example). Note that for such files, IIS must perform the compression every time it delivers the page.

Chapter 37

■ **Compress Static Files.** Select this check box if you want IIS to compress files with unchanging content: that is, files with extensions such as *.htm* and *.css*.

■ **Temporary Folder.** Specify the location of a folder where IIS can cache copies of any static files it compresses.

■ **Maximum Temporary Folder Size.** Select Unlimited if you want IIS to consume compressed file cache space without limit. This saves the overhead of managing the cache. (In theory, at least, the size of the cache should never exceed the combined size of all your content files.) Alternatively, select Limited To and specify a size in megabytes if you want to place a limit on the amount of compressed file cache space IIS can consume.

Creating a Virtual Folder

As originally defined, a virtual folder is one that appears—from the viewpoint of a Web visitor—to be within a Web server's HTTP root, but in fact resides elsewhere. More recently, Web servers have used virtual directory configuration areas to store settings that pertain to folders that reside within the HTTP root as well.

For more background information about virtual folders, refer to "Virtual Folders" on page 1037.

Here's the procedure for creating a new virtual folder in IIS:

1 Open Internet Services Manager, and display the top-level entry for the Web server you want to contain the virtual folder.

2 Right-click the Web server entry, choose New from the shortcut menu, and then choose Virtual Directory.

3 When the Virtual Directory Creation Wizard appears, bypass the entry panel by clicking Next.

4 When the Virtual Directory Alias panel appears, type the virtual folder's alias (that is, its path as Web visitors will see it) into the box titled Alias. Click Next.

5 When the Web Site Content Directory panel appears, supply the physical path to the folder that contains the desired files. You can do this by typing into the Directory box or by clicking the Browse button and using the resulting Browse For Folder dialog box. When you're done, click Next.

6 When the Access Permissions panel appears, select or clear the appropriate check boxes. Table 37-1 explains the function of each check box.

7 Click Next, and then click Finish to complete the wizard.

Table 37-1. **Permission Settings for New Virtual Folders and Servers**

Setting	Effect (if selected)
Read	Permits file access by visitors.
Run Scripts (Such As ASP)	Permits execution of server-side scripts that reside within the virtual directory.
Execute (Such As ISAPI Applications Or CGI)	Permits execution of binary programs that reside within the virtual directory. (This is somewhat riskier than letting scripts run, because the script interpreter limits the extent of damage an errant script can do.)
Write	Permits file update by visitors.
Browse	Permits directory browsing within the virtual folder. (That is, the Web server sends the Web visitor a clickable list of files when the visitor request a URL that lacks a file name and the folder doesn't contain a file with the default document name.)

Creating a Virtual Server

Virtual servers provide a way to run many Web servers on a single computer. Each Web server has its own IP address and its own HTTP root. Because each virtual server has its own IP address, it can also have its own DNS name.

> **note** Virtual servers are available only on Windows 2000 Server, and not on Windows 2000 Professional.

The first step in creating a virtual server is to give the computer an additional IP address. Typically, you would get this address from your ISP, your IT department, or whoever provides your network connection. Be sure to ask for the *subnet mask* as well.

> **note** A subnet mask is a series of numbers that indicates which portion of an IP address identifies the local network and which portion identifies a particular host on that network. Physically, a subnet mask looks like an IP address. 255.255.255.0 is a typical subnet mask.

To activate the new address:

1 Right-click My Network Places, and select Properties from the shortcut menu.

2 When the Network And Dial-Up Connections window appears, right-click Local Area Connection and select Properties from the shortcut menu.

3 When the Local Area Connection Properties dialog box appears, double-click Internet Protocol (TCP/IP).

4 When the Internet Protocol (TCP/IP) Properties dialog box appears, click Advanced.

5 When the Advanced TCP/IP Settings dialog box shown in Figure 37-18 appears, review the IP addresses listed in the IP Addresses list box. Your computer is already responding to these addresses. You have the following options:

  ▪ To add an address, click Add and enter the new IP address and subnet mask.

  ▪ To change an address, select it and click Edit.

  ▪ To delete an address, select it and click Remove.

6 Click OK repeatedly to close all dialog boxes and save your changes.

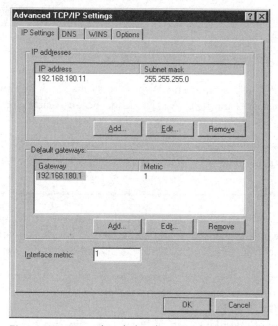

Figure 37-18. This dialog box configures a single network card to respond to multiple IP addresses.

The second step in creating a virtual server involves configuring IIS so it associates the correct HTTP root with the requests sent to the new IP address. Here's the procedure for doing this:

1 Open Internet Services Manager. Under Internet Information Services, right-click the entry for your computer.

1076

Troubleshooting

Add button in the Advanced TCP/IP Settings dialog box is unavailable

If the Obtain An IP Address Automatically option is selected on the Internet Protocol (TCP/IP) Properties dialog box, the Add button in the Advanced TCP/IP Settings dialog box will be unavailable. You can't configure a single network adapter to receive one IP Address automatically—that is, using Dynamic Host Configuration Protocol (DHCP)—and to receive others you assign by hand.

To resolve this issue, ask your Internet service provider or information technology department for a static (that is, permanently assigned) IP address. Then, in the Internet Protocol (TCP/IP) Properties dialog box:

1 Choose the Use The Following IP Address option.

2 Enter the static IP address in the IP Address field.

3 Provide values in the following fields (if necessary, ask your Internet service provider or information technology department for the pertinent values):

- Subnet Mask
- Default Gateway
- Preferred DNS Server
- Alternate DNS Server

After making these changes and clicking the Advanced button, you should find that the Add button is available.

2 Choose New from the first shortcut menu, and then choose Web Site from the second shortcut menu.

3 When the Web Site Creation Wizard appears, bypass the entry panel by clicking Next. When the Web Site Description panel appears, use the Description box to enter a brief but useful description of the new server. Click Next.

4 When the IP Address And Port Settings panel appears, configure the following options:

- **Enter The IP Address To Use For This Web Site.** Select the IP address you want the virtual server to use. All available addresses should appear in the drop-down list.

- **TCP Port This Web Site Should Use.** Specify the port number where the virtual Web server should listen. The default (and almost always the correct choice) is 80.

note Two Web servers can share the same IP address if they operate on different ports.

■ **Host Header For This Site.** This setting supports another way that two or more Web servers can share the same IP address. Beginning with Internet Explorer 3 and Netscape Navigator 2, browsers include (in the HTTP headers) the DNS name of the Web server they're trying to reach. The Web server then uses this information to deliver content from the correct HTTP root.

If you want to use this technique, enter the Web server's DNS name in this dialog box. In practice, however, this technique is less than 100 percent reliable and has never caught on. Therefore, in almost every case you can leave this option blank.

■ **SSL Port This Web Site Should Use.** Specify the port number where the virtual Web server should listen for incoming requests that use Secure Sockets Layer (SSL). The default (and almost always the correct choice) is 443.

Click Next to continue.

5 When the Web Site Home Directory panel appears, enter the HTTP root's drive letter and path in the text box titled Path. Alternatively, click the Browse button and use the resulting Browse For Folder dialog box to locate the folder.

6 Select the check box titled Allow Anonymous Access To This Web Site if you want Web visitors to visit your site freely. Clear the check box to require entry of a Windows 2000 user name and password. When you're done, click Next.

7 When the Web Site Access Permissions panel appears, select or clear the appropriate check boxes. Table 37-1 explains the function of each check box.

8 Click Next, and then click Finish to complete the Wizard.

You should now be able to browse the new Web site (assuming it has a home page or some other content) by typing *http://<ip-address>/* into the Location field of your browser, where *<ip-address>* is the IP address you chose in step 4.

To set up a DNS name that refers to the new server's IP address, contact your ISP or IT department.

To add the FrontPage Server Extensions to the new server:

1 Display the Server Administration Web page described in Chapter 38.

2 Locate the new virtual server in the Virtual Servers section of the page.

3 Click Extend.

> For more information about the Server Administration Web page, refer to "Administering Server-Level Settings" on page 1090.

Adding a Catalog to Indexing Service

Creating a new virtual Web server doesn't add it to Microsoft Indexing Service. As a result, neither the FrontPage Web Search feature nor the SharePoint Team Services shared document search feature might work as expected. To recover from this situation, perform the procedure described in the Troubleshooting sidebar titled, "SharePoint team Web site document search displays the message, 'Service Is Not Running,'" in Chapter 35.

Using a Non-Microsoft Web Server

The FrontPage Server Extensions are designed to minimize differences among Web servers. Assuming that these extensions (described in the next chapter) are available for the target server, and the server administrator has installed them, Web page designers shouldn't have to concern themselves greatly about which Web server is in use. For programmers and administrators, however, the differences aren't nearly as transparent.

Regardless of the type of Web server in use, designers will need to learn the default document name. This name is *default.htm* on most Microsoft servers and *index.html* on most others, though local configurations can vary in either case.

Security is another area where no two servers tend to be alike. Web designers, Web administrators, and system administrators will need to learn how security works on each server—target and development—and must control access on each machine appropriately.

Each Web server tends to provide a slightly different environment for running programmed elements such as CGI programs, ISAPI programs, server-side includes, and server-side scripts. Different versions of such tools are usually required for each different Web server, and few are available for all. This variance also affects programs you or others at your site might write; in general, without modification they won't be portable from one type of server to another.

To learn about the availability of FrontPage extensions for non-Microsoft Web servers, refer to "Obtaining the FrontPage Server Extensions" page 1085.

If the FrontPage Server Extensions aren't available for the target Web server or aren't installed, designers will have to publish Webs manually or using the Web Publishing Wizard. In addition, browse-time services provided by the extensions obviously won't be available—services such as Web Search, Save Results, and server-side form-field validation.

If the FrontPage Server Extensions on a server aren't up to date, you'll get various errors when designing and publishing. The best solution is to upgrade the extensions. If that isn't possible, do as much work as possible on a server that has up-to-date extensions, and then publish the results to the out-of-date server later. Before using any browse-time features, test them on the outdated server to determine whether they work as expected.

The more active services you expect from your Web server, the more difficult mixed server environments will be. If at all possible, use the same server or at least the same family of servers for development, testing, and production.

Other Windows Web Servers

All Web servers must, by definition, implement the Hypertext Transfer Protocol similarly. This means that virtually all Web servers deliver simple Web pages the same way, transparently to Web designers.

As just stated, differences are more pronounced with respect to executables, such as CGI, ISAPI, and server-side scripts. Before using any of these facilities, verify that your target Web server supports them.

Web Servers on Non-Microsoft Operating Systems

All the cautions mentioned in the previous section also apply to Web servers operating in a non-Windows environment. In addition, such servers raise issues involving non-Windows file systems.

UNIX file systems are usually case-sensitive, limited to 32 characters per file name or folder name, and subject to different restrictions on file-name characters. This means, among other things, that a URL for *Index.html* will not retrieve a file named *index.html;* instead, the server will return a Not Found message. The best policy, therefore, is to limit file names and folder names, both in the file system and in URLs, to lowercase letters and numbers only.

Some executables will run on more than one Windows Web server, but virtually none will run on both Windows and non-Windows systems. Most executables are completely nonportable between Windows and UNIX, even on the same hardware. If Windows-based designers need to invoke UNIX-based server-side programs, they'll have to work carefully from the documentation and, in the best of circumstances, test their results in an environment closely resembling production.

In Summary...

This chapter explained the basics of installing and configuring a Web server. It centered on IIS for Windows 2000 because that's Microsoft's premier Web server and also the Web server that works best with FrontPage.

The next chapter explains how to obtain, install, and administer SharePoint Team Services and the FrontPage Server Extensions.

Understanding the FrontPage Server Extensions

Microsoft FrontPage lives intimately on the Web. Not only can it create and manage Web content on your local disk; it can also function as a Web-based, client/server authoring system. In this second mode, FrontPage has processing components on both Web clients and Web servers, and these components communicate via Web protocols.

In client/server mode, the FrontPage desktop software acts as the client, and the FrontPage Server Extensions, running on your Web server, provide the complementary server processes. The FrontPage Server Extensions also provide the software for certain FrontPage components that run on the Web server when visitors access your site.

This chapter will first describe the extensions in a bit more detail, then explain how to obtain and install them. If your use of FrontPage involves only page creation and someone else administers your Web servers, you can safely skip all but the first section. However, if you manage Web servers for others—even a personal Web server for yourself—this chapter will get you started with the server side of FrontPage processing.

Understanding Disk-Based Webs

From one perspective, a FrontPage-based Web is any collection of HTML pages and support files that FrontPage administers as a unit. A Web begins at a certain folder, either on your disk or on a Web server, and includes all files within that folder and any subfolders. After you declare such an area to be a Web,

FrontPage starts managing that area as a single body of content.

Itself a denizen of the Web, FrontPage requires the presence of a Web server to deliver its full complement of features. There might be cases, however, when a Web server isn't available—not even a personal Web server operating on your own computer. Some possible reasons include the following:

- You find configuring your own Web server impractical.

- Your computer isn't on a TCP/IP network and has no IP address.

- You have access to a Web server, but for some reason FrontPage Server Extensions can't be installed. The extensions might not be available for the particular server and platform, for example.

- You notice that performance is inadequate when you're running a personal Web server.

Fortunately, FrontPage can provide most of its features in a completely serverless environment called a *disk-based Web*. Instead of having a Web server read and write files on the server's local disk, FrontPage simply reads and writes the files directly, using either your computer's local hard disk or space on a network file server.

> **tip** If two Web pages belong to the same body of content and share the same administrative control, put them in the same Web. If they're significantly different in terms of content or control, put them in separate Webs.

You can create a disk-based Web in a location where HTML files already exist, but FrontPage will "webify" that location by adding its own folders and files. To keep your original location clean, first copy it to a different location and then convert the copy into a Web. You can create one Web inside another, but the two Webs become separate bodies of content. No file or folder can belong to more than one Web.

Before FrontPage converts any folder to a disk-based Web, it displays the confirmation prompt shown in Figure 38-1.

Figure 38-1. This dialog box prompts for confirmation before FrontPage converts an ordinary disk folder to a disk-based Web.

You can publish a disk-based Web to another disk-based Web or to a real Web server. Likewise, you can publish a server-based Web to a disk-based Web. Simply specify the correct location, whether Web server or disk, when you open the source Web and also when you specify the target Web.

> **For more information about Web publishing, refer to Chapter 13, "Publishing Your FrontPage-Based Web."**

A disk-based Web has no way to run CGI or ISAPI programs. Such programs provide dynamic services, at either authoring time or browse time. They're designed to run in a Web server environment, and can't run without one. Because of this, the following FrontPage features won't work on a disk-based Web:

- Confirmation Field component
- Discussion Group component
- Save Results component
- Database Results component
- Registration component
- Search component
- SharePoint team Web sites
- Server-side scripts (ASP)
- Any other user-written, shareware, or commercial server-side programs

Using a disk-based Web doesn't prevent you from creating Web pages using these features; it prevents you only from running or testing them. Still, this is a significant list of features to lose. In addition to these restrictions, disk-based Webs have no security features at all; anyone with permission to read the disk-based Web's file area has access.

Despite their restrictions, disk-based Webs are adequate for anyone who doesn't plan to use the components already listed. If ordinary Web pages, perhaps enhanced with browser scripts, are all you plan to create, disk-based Webs are perfectly adequate. If you need more, you can always advance to a server-based Web.

Understanding Server-Based Webs

The primary disadvantage of server-based Webs is their complexity. Most users of desktop software aren't experienced Web server administrators, nor do they aspire to be. For people in this situation, disk-based Webs often provide a workable solution.

If you decide the restrictions of a disk-based Web are unacceptable, server-based Webs provide the answer. With a server-based Web, all your Web files physically reside on a Web server equipped with the FrontPage Server Extensions. This environment supports all FrontPage features for authoring, browse-time processing, and site management.

Server-based Webs are client-server environments. The client is the FrontPage desktop software, the server is the Web server running the FrontPage Server Extensions, and the two communicate entirely by HTTP. When the client needs to read files from the server, it does so just like a browser. When the client needs to upload files or send commands, it transmits the data to CGI or ISAPI programs on the server, just as browsers submit HTML forms. The server-based programs then update the requested files or settings.

A server-based Web can reside anywhere a Web server can reside: on your own computer, on another computer in your office or workgroup, on a corporate intranet server, or anywhere on the Internet. If you can browse a server's Web pages, you can author its Webs (subject, of course, to logon security).

The FrontPage Server Extensions contain the software that makes server-based Webs possible. The process of enabling server-based Webs is therefore the process of installing and configuring the server extensions.

Understanding the Server Extensions' Functions

The FrontPage Server Extensions provide four kinds of services:

- **Browse-Time Services.** Features such as text search and server-side form field validation obviously require programs that run on the server—not just when the developer creates or uploads the page, but every time a Web visitor submits a request. The FrontPage Server Extensions provide this programming in a standard way.

- **File and Folder Access.** When you open a page in FrontPage, it can retrieve any necessary files not only by reading a local file system, but also by opening an HTTP connection over the network. This pertains to the data files for the task list, Navigation view, and text indexes as well.

  At some point, however, the needs of FrontPage exceed the capabilities of standard Web servers. FrontPage needs to create, replace, rename, move, copy, and delete files on the server based on commands received from the client—that is, from FrontPage. The FrontPage Server Extensions provide the server-side software for these client-server functions.

  Compared to local file access or traditional file sharing, using Web protocols for file handling might initially seem awkward. Consider, however, that many Web developers lack facilities for local file sharing but do have Web connectivity. In this environment, using Web protocols and server extensions indeed makes sense:

- **Security Services.** The ability of Web developers to add, update, delete, and reorganize files and folders carries with it the necessity to differentiate between authorized and unauthorized users. The FrontPage Server Extensions not only provide and configure these services, but also provide network interfaces for configuring security via the FrontPage client.

- **Background Services.** The FrontPage Server Extensions also provide a number of content services that run in the background on the server. Choosing Recalculate Hyperlinks from FrontPage's Tools menu, for example, brings up the dialog box shown in Figure 38-2, advising the Web author that FrontPage is about to launch a server-side process.

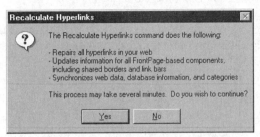

Figure 38-2. FrontPage clients can initiate server-side processes installed by FrontPage Server Extensions.

Despite running with different Web servers and on different operating systems, each implementation of the FrontPage Server Extensions provides the same services and application protocols. FrontPage and other clients can therefore use the FrontPage Server Extensions in a platform-independent way.

Obtaining the FrontPage Server Extensions

There are three ways to obtain and install the FrontPage Server Extensions. The method you use depends on your Web server's operating system and software:

- **Delivered with Microsoft Office.** The initial version of SharePoint Team Services resides in a folder name /sharrept on the Office XP CD.

  Beginning with this release, Microsoft is promoting the use of SharePoint Team Services—rather than just the FrontPage Server Extensions—on Web servers that host FrontPage-based Webs. Installing SharePoint Team Services is tantamount to installing the FrontPage Server Extensions plus additional applications.

For more information about SharePoint Team Services, refer to Chapter 35, "Using SharePoint Team Web Sites."

● **Delivered with Web Server Software.** Some Web servers include FrontPage Server Extensions on their distribution disks. Check your product documentation for availability and instructions.

Note that versions of the server extensions delivered with IIS for Microsoft Windows NT 4 and with Windows 2000 are older than the version released with Office XP. Avoid installing these old versions and install the new version instead.

● **Downloaded from Microsoft.** Versions of the FrontPage Server Extensions for many platforms, including UNIX, are available from Microsoft's Web site at *http://msdn.microsoft.com/workshop/languages/fp/*.

New versions of the server extensions (and, presumably, SharePoint Team Services) tend to appear spontaneously in response to bugs, security alerts, and releases of other products. Therefore, it's always best to check Microsoft's Web site for the latest version. Browse *http://www.microsoft.com/frontpage/* and look for information about server extensions.

Neither the FrontPage Server Extensions 2002 nor SharePoint Team Services are available for Microsoft Windows 95 or Microsoft Windows 98. If you're running a personal Web server on either of these platforms, you have the following options:

● Upgrade to Microsoft Windows 2000.

● Run an older version of the FrontPage Server Extensions (for example, the Microsoft FrontPage 2000 extensions), and expect certain new features of FrontPage 2002 not to work.

No personal Web servers are available for Windows Me. Lack of FrontPage Server Extensions 2002 for this platform is therefore a non-issue.

Installing the FrontPage Server Extensions

The procedure for installing the FrontPage Server Extensions varies somewhat, depending on the Web server, the operating system, and the Server Extensions version. In general, though, there are four steps:

1 Install the server's operating system and the Web server software.

This chapter assumes that this work is already done and tested. That is, the hardware is complete, the operating system is stable, and the Web server is delivering pages and performing other functions normally.

2 Install the SharePoint Team Services or FrontPage Server Extensions software.

In prior releases of Office, installation of the Office desktop software and installation of the FrontPage Server Extensions were integrated. If the target machine had a Web server installed, running Office Setup would copy the

Chapter 38

FrontPage Server Extensions onto the computer and, coincidentally, perform step 3 on the default Web server.

In Office XP, this is no longer true. The SharePoint Team Services or FrontPage Server Extensions setup is a stand-alone program you can run before or after—and with or without—the Office XP desktop programs.

To install SharePoint Team Services from the Office XP CD, run *sharept**setupse.exe.*

In the following cases, obtain the FrontPage extensions as described in the earlier section "Obtaining the FrontPage Server Extensions," and then run the accompanying setup program:

- Machines not running Windows.

- Machines running Web servers FrontPage Setup doesn't detect.

3 Convert any desired real or virtual Web servers to Webs.

Installing the server extensions software and creating Webs are two separate but related operations:

- Installing the server extensions provides a set of installation and administration utilities, as well as a master source of software for individual Webs. This task is step 2.

- Creating a Web means copying several programs into a Web server's file space, initializing various configuration files, and indexing any existing content. This is step 3, the current step.

---

caution   If the Web server has a large body of existing content, indexing it can take a long time.

Most Web server software allows one computer, responding to multiple IP addresses, to deliver different content for each of those addresses. Each such arrangement is called a *virtual server*. For each such server, you are perfectly free to install the FrontPage Server Extensions or not.

In virtual server environments, there's usually one server—called the *default server*—that responds to any IP address not associated with a specific virtual server. Installing the FrontPage Server Extensions on such a computer usually converts the default server to a Web (that is, it performs step 2 for the whole server and step 3 for the default Web server). For any remaining virtual servers, you'll need to install the FrontPage Server Extensions by issuing a command.

4 Create subwebs within the root Webs from step 3.

When you first install the FrontPage Server Extensions on a virtual Web server, FrontPage considers that server to be one large body of content— one Web—called the root Web. Very seldom, however, is this appropriate. Most virtual Web servers contain multiple bodies of content, each with its own set of designers and administrators. The solution is to segregate each body of content into its own folder, and then designate those folders as Webs in their own right. Because these Webs remain physically subordinate to the root Web, they're often called *subwebs*.

The root Web is so called because it begins at the Web server's HTTP root directory (that is, a URL consisting of a single forward slash: /). All other Webs on that server are subwebs that reside within the root Web or within other Webs, nested to any level.

In earlier versions of FrontPage, all subwebs had to reside in the root folder of the root Web. This is no longer the case; you can now define subwebs at any point in the server's directory tree. You can also nest one subweb inside another with no restriction (other than path length) on the level of nesting. Creating a subweb requires the parent administrator account and password.

If you installed your own Web server, you chose its root Web administrator name and password during the installation. If you're using a shared or centralized Web server, the server's administrator probably controls the root Web and performs whatever tasks require the root Web password.

If the server supports multiple groups or customers, it's usually best to create a separate Web for each one. If one physical server supports multiple virtual Web servers, the virtual servers can be FrontPage-extended or not in any combination. In addition, the system administrator can delegate administration of each virtual server to its owner.

FrontPage Server Extensions Administration Tools

Each major version of the FrontPage Server Extensions seems to use a different approach for administration:

- Microsoft FrontPage 98 and earlier used a stand-alone program called FrontPage Server Administrator to configure options that affected an entire Web server. The FrontPage desktop software configured security settings applicable to individual Webs.

- FrontPage 2000 administered the server extensions using a Snap-In for Microsoft Management Console (MMC). This provided a graphical interface for administering the server extensions, but it ran only on Windows operating systems, and it couldn't administer Server Extensions on a remote computer. Despite some overlap with MMC, the desktop software retained its features for configuring security settings for each Web. This release also included an optional set of Web pages for administering the server extensions remotely.

FrontPage 2002 essentially does away with both the MMC snap-in and the security-setting features of the desktop software. In their place, it provides an enhanced set of Web pages that can configure Webs from anywhere in the world (subject, of course, to logon security). The FrontPage desktop software still contains menu commands for Server Extensions configuration (choose Server from the Tools menu), but these commands simply start your browser and tell it to display the corresponding Web pages. There's still an MMC Snap-In for the FrontPage Server Extensions 2002, but it also simply starts the browser and displays the necessary Web page.

> **note** If you open a FrontPage 2000 or earlier server-based Web in FrontPage 2002, the FrontPage 2000–style dialog boxes that control security will still appear. However, this is for backward compatibility only.

The tools inside the FrontPage desktop software deal mostly with configuration and administration of existing Webs, with creation of subwebs, and, of course, with creation of content. You can't install the server extensions or add them to a virtual server using the FrontPage client.

Microsoft also provides two programs that can administer either SharePoint Team Services or the FrontPage Server Extensions 2002 from the command line:

● The **owsadm.exe** program runs from the command line not only on Windows but also on various UNIX operating systems. This can be useful if you want to perform FrontPage operations on a timed basis or if you just prefer working at the command line. However, this utility administers server extensions only on the local computer. Installing either SharePoint Team Services or the FrontPage Server Extensions 2002 installs owsadm.exe as well.

● The **owsrmadm.exe** program also runs from the command line but administers the FrontPage Server Extensions on a remote computer. It can administer server extensions running on any operating system—even UNIX—but the program itself runs only on Windows. Installing either SharePoint Team Services or the FrontPage Server Extensions 2002 installs owsrmadm.exe as well.

> For more information about using the command line administration utilities, refer to "Command-line administration" in SharePoint Team Services Help.

The rest of this chapter deals exclusively with administering SharePoint Team Services or the FrontPage Server Extensions 2002 with Web pages. For documentation on administering older versions of the server extensions, download the appropriate Server Extensions Resource Kit. Browse *http://www.microsoft.com/frontpage* and look for information about server extensions.

newfeature!
Administering Server-Level Settings

The Server Administration page, which is shown in Figure 38-3, provides the most all-encompassing level of administration for SharePoint Team Services and the FrontPage Server Extensions. This page controls settings that affect all Web servers operating on the current computer. The URL varies depending on the operating system.

● On Windows 2000 Professional and Windows NT Workstation, the URL shown below is likely to be correct and you're likely to have adequate security permissions for running it.

> *http://<servername>/_SharePoint*

● On Windows 2000 Server and Windows NT Server, the Server Administration page has this URL

> *http://<servername>:<admin-port>/fpadmdll.dll?page=fpadmin.htm*

where <admin-port> signifies the port number of the computer's Administration Web Server.

The following procedure describes another way to display the Server Administration page:

1 Start Internet Services Manager. The path to this program is Start, Programs, Administrative Tools, Internet Services Manager.

2 Under heading the Internet Information Services, right-click the computer name and then click Properties.

3 Click the Settings button the Server Extensions 2002 tab.

4 When the Set Installation Defaults page appears, click Administration link in the top left corner.

You'll know you've found the correct URL (and permissions) when the Server Administration page shown in Figure 38-3 appears in your browser. This Web page provides the following links:

● **Set List Of Available Rights.** Click this link to display a Set List Of Available Rights page that displays or modifies the rights available on the server. If you clear the box for a user right listed on this page, that right won't be available on any Web. The next section in this chapter, "Administering User Rights," explains how to use this page.

● **Set Installation Defaults.** Click this link to display the Set Installation Defaults page. The section "Administering SharePoint Team Services Installation Defaults" later in this chapter explains how to use this page.

● **Reset User Password.** Click this link to change a user's password. The section "Administering User Passwords" later in this chapter explains how to use this page.

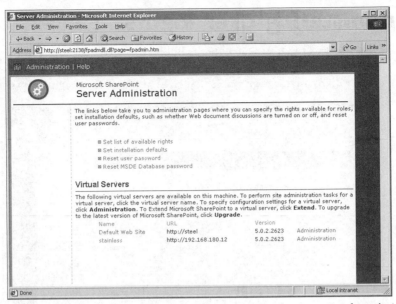

Figure 38-3. This Web page provides the top-level entry point for administering SharePoint Team Services.

● **Reset MSDE Database Password.** Click this link to change the password for accessing the MSDE that services SharePoint team Web sites. The section "Resetting the MSDE Database Password" later in this chapter explains how to use this page.

● **Virtual Servers.** The links in this part of the Security Administration page select individual virtual servers for administration:

■ **Name.** Click any link in this column to display the Administration page for the given virtual server. The section "Administering SharePoint Team Services Web Settings" later in this chapter explains how to use this page.

■ **Extend.** Click this link to add SharePoint Team Services or the FrontPage Server Extensions to the given virtual server. (Note that of this and the next two choices, only one will appear.)

■ **Upgrade.** Click this link to upgrade SharePoint Team Services or the FrontPage Server Extensions to the latest version available on the current computer.

■ **Administration.** Click this link to display the Virtual Server Administration page for the given server. The section "Administering SharePoint Team Services Virtual Server Settings" later in this chapter explains how to use this page.

Administering User Rights

Click the Set List Of Available Rights link in the Server Administration page to display the Set List Of Available Rights page shown in Figures 38-4 and 38-5. Selecting the box for any Right on this page makes that right available for assignment (in later Web

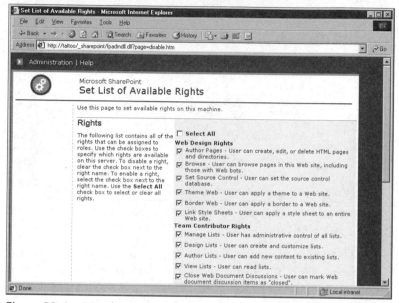

Figure 38-4. Use this Web page to enable or disable the listed rights for the entire computer.

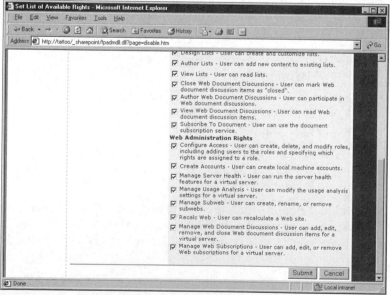

Figure 38-5. This is the bottom half of the Web page that begins in Figure 38-4.

pages) to specific users and groups. Clearing the box for any Right means no one can grant that Right to any user or group.

Here are the rights for this page:

- **Web Design Rights.** These rights control the creation, modification, and deletion of Web pages.

- **Team Contributor Rights.** These rights control the creation, modification, and deletion of lists (including document libraries and discussion groups).

- **Web Administration Rights.** These rights control the creation, modification, and deletion of any aspect of a Web.

Notice that this Web page doesn't assign individuals to these roles; it only permits or restricts capabilities on an overall basis.

> For more information about assigning individuals to roles, refer to "Managing Users" later in this chapter.

Understanding Rights and Roles

The twin concepts of rights and roles are a very useful addition to FrontPage 2002:

- A *right* denotes permission to perform a specific task in FrontPage. An administrator can either grant or revoke rights on the basis of roles assigned to individual users or groups.

  For example, one of the rights listed in Figure 38-4 is "Theme Web - User Can Apply A Theme To A Web Site." A user who has this right in a given Web can establish a new default theme for that Web and thereby replace any and all formatting already in place.

- A *role* is a group of rights settings that you can assign by name to individual users or groups.

  In the case of the "Theme Web - User Can Apply A Theme To A Web Site," right, for example, you might grant it to Administrators and Advanced Authors but not to Authors, Contributors, or Browsers. This would stop Authors and Contributors, who are presumably less knowledgeable than Administrators and Advanced authors, from making a widespread, irreversible change. Browsers are usually anonymous visitors who shouldn't change the Web at all.

You can use the roles that come with FrontPage, delete them, or add more. After you have a set of roles that match your working environment, it's a snap to assign the correct combination of rights to new users: You simply assign them the corresponding roles.

1093

Chapter 38

Administering Installation Defaults

Click the Set Installation Defaults link in the Server Administration page to display the Set Installation Defaults page shown in Figures 38-6 and 38-7 on the facing page and Figure 38-8 on page 1096. Here are the settings and what they control:

> **note** If you installed only the FrontPage Server Extensions 2002 on a computer, its Administration pages will naturally omit the sections that pertain only to SharePoint team Web sites.

- **Database Settings (SharePoint Team Services Only).** This group of settings selects the database server SharePoint Team Services uses for Web discussions, subscriptions, and lists:

  - **Database Server Name.** Specify the name of the computer where the database management system (DBMS) software is running. The DBMS must be Microsoft SQL Server or its subset, the Microsoft Data Engine (MSDE.)

  - **Database Administrator User Name.** Enter the user name SharePoint Team Services should use for accessing SQL Server or a copy of MSDE running on another computer.

  - **Database Administrator Password.** Enter the password SharePoint Team Services should use for accessing SQL Server or MSDE.

  - **Use Local MSDE Database Server.** Select this check box if SharePoint Team Services should use a copy of MSDE running on the local computer. No administrator user name or password is required if this option is in effect.

- **Web Document Discussions (SharePoint Team Services Only).** This group of settings controls use of the Web Discussions feature:

  - **Web Discussions Are.** Select On to permit Web discussions and Off to prohibit them.

  - **Allow Web Discussions On.** Specify the location of documents that the given database server will support for Web discussions:

    - **Documents Located Anywhere On The Web.** Permits use of the given database for discussing documents that reside anywhere.

    - **Documents Located On This Server Only.** Permits use of the given database for discussing documents that reside on the local server, but not for documents that reside elsewhere.

  - **Automatically Delete Stored Discussions After.** Select this check box and specify a number of days if you want SharePoint Team Services to automatically delete Web discussions based on age.

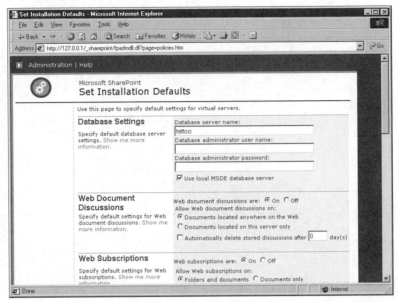

Figure 38-6. This Web page sets defaults for all virtual Web servers on a machine.

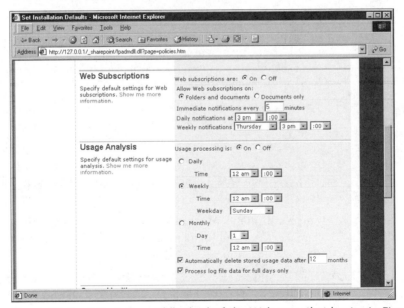

Figure 38-7. This is the middle third of the Web page that begins in Figure 38-6.

● **Web Subscriptions (SharePoint Team Services Only).** This group of settings controls use of the Web Subscriptions feature:

　■ **Web Subscriptions Are.** Click On to permit Web subscriptions and Off to prohibit them.

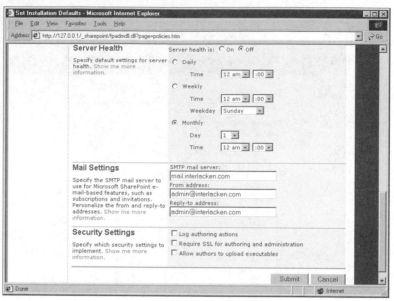

Figure 38-8. This is the bottom third of the Web page that begins in Figure 38-6.

- **Allow Web Subscriptions On.** Specify the permissible scope of change notification subscriptions:

  - **Folders And Documents.** Select this option if SharePoint team Web site members can sign up to receive notifications when any document in a given folder changes, or when a specific document changes.

  - **Documents Only.** Select this option if SharePoint team Web site members can sign up for change notifications only when a specific document changes.

- **Immediate Notifications Every.** Specify how often SharePoint Team Services should send any accumulated mail to subscribers who requested notification within a few minutes of any change.

- **Daily Notifications At.** Specify the time of day when SharePoint Team Services should send mail to subscribers who requested daily change notification.

- **Weekly Notifications.** Specify the day of the week and the time of day when SharePoint Team Services should send mail to subscribers who requested weekly change notification.

- **Usage Analysis.** This group of settings controls use of the FrontPage Usage Analysis feature:

  - **Usage Analysis Is.** If you want to activate analysis of Web server activity, select On. Select Off to suppress it.

■ **Daily.** If you want to collect usage statistics once a day, select this option and specify the time of day when usage analysis should run.

■ **Weekly.** If you want to collect usage statistics once a week, select this option and specify the day of the week and the time of day when usage analysis should run.

■ **Monthly.** If you want to collect usage statistics once a month, select this option and specify the day of the month and the time of day when usage analysis should run.

For more information about the FrontPage Usage Analysis feature, refer to "Viewing Usage Reports" on page 444.

---

note Web servers create log files that contain one record for each request they receive from a Web visitor. This is too much data for FrontPage to scan and analyze every time a designer displays a Usage report, so the FrontPage Server Extensions run a process called Usage Analysis that creates summary files every day, week, or month. This has two implications: First, be sure to keep your Web server logs at least as long as the usage analysis frequency. Second, the data designers see in Usage reports is up to date only as of the last usage analysis.

■ **Automatically Delete Stored Usage Data After.** If you want the FrontPage Server Extensions to delete summarized usage data that exceeds a certain age, select this check box. If you do select the box, you must also specify the maximum amount of time that SharePoint Team Services should retain summarized data. If you specify 12 months, for example, your Usage reports will never report more than a year of history.

■ **Process Log Files For Full Days Only.** If you want to exclude partial days of activity from your Usage reports, select this check box. Selecting the box means that all days reported or summarized in Usage reports reflect full 24-hour periods. Clearing the box means that Usage reports might contain partial days (for example, the partial day between midnight and the time that Usage Analysis runs).

● **Server Health.** This group of settings schedules a job that performs consistency checks on all Webs on a server. The job either reports problems to a designated administrator or takes programmed corrective measures:

■ **Server Health Is.** If you want to activate scheduled Server Health checking, select On. Select Off to suppress it.

■ **Daily.** If you want to check Server Health once a day, select this option and specify the time of day when the check should occur.

■ **Weekly.** If you want to check Server Health once a week, select this option and specify the day of the week and the time of day when the check should occur.

■ **Monthly.** If you want to check Server Health once a month, select this option and specify the day of the month and the time of day when the check should occur.

> For more information about server health features, refer to "Administering Virtual Server Settings" later in this chapter.

● **Mail Settings.** This group of settings controls how the FrontPage Server Extensions send electronic mail:

■ **SMTP Mail Server.** Specify the network name of the Simple Mail Transport Protocol (SMTP) mail server that the FrontPage Server Extensions should use for sending mail.

■ **From Address.** Specify the e-mail address that should appear as the sender of all change notifications.

■ **Reply-To Address.** Specify the destination of mail created when subscribers respond to a change notification by using their mail program's Reply button.

These settings affect almost every sort of mail that the FrontPage Server Extensions send—including, for example, SharePoint team Web site change notifications, reports from Usage analyses, results from Server Health analyses, and the e-mail features of the Save Results component. Some of these applications override the From Address and Reply-To Address settings. However, none of them override (and all of them require) a valid SMTP Mail Server entry.

● **Security Settings.** These settings control certain security settings that pertain to Web designers:

■ **Log Authoring Actions.** If you want to record information about addition, change, and deletion of Web content, select this check box. A log of changes appears in a file named *author.log* that's located in the root Web's *_vti_log* folder.

■ **Require SSL For Authoring And Administration.** If you want all designers to use Secure Sockets Layer (SSL) security when modifying Webs, select this check box.

■ **Allow Authors To Upload Executables.** If Web designers can upload files to executable folders, select this check box. Clear the box to stop designers from uploading files to executable folders, even if the files themselves aren't an executable type.

Troubleshooting

SharePoint Team Services reports server not configured to send e-mail messages

If you try to configure a SharePoint Team Services feature that sends e-mail, the Web page shown in Figure 38-9 might appear. This occurs because the SMTP Mail Server field just mentioned is blank. To resolve the situation, click the Change Configuration Settings page, and enter the name of a valid SMTP mail server.

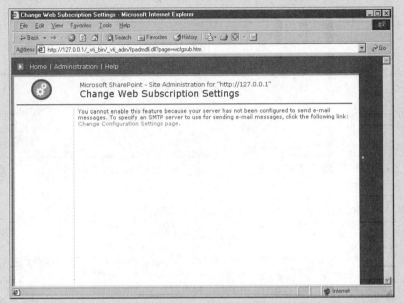

Figure 38-9. If this Web page appears, you've tried to enable a mail-related feature without specifying a mail server. This would leave the mail with nowhere to go.

Lack of a valid SMTP mail server name is a leading cause of failure when the Save Results component fails to send e-mail, even when the FrontPage desktop software is properly configured. The solution is to configure a valid SMTP server name as described in this section.

Resetting User Passwords

Click the Reset User Password link in the Server Administration page to display the Reset User Password page shown in Figure 38-10 on the next page. This page contains the following form fields:

- **Virtual Server.** Select the server where the user account resides.

- **Web Name.** Enter the name of the Web where the user account resides.

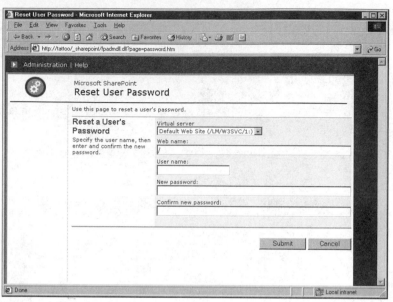

Figure 38-10. This Web page updates a user password on the local machine.

- **User Name.** Enter the name of the user account.

- **New Password.** Enter the new password.

- **Confirm New Password.** Enter the new password again. The contents of this field and the previous one must be equal.

This Web page pertains primarily to server-based Webs that don't use Microsoft Web servers. Such Webs have their own user account subsystem.

Server-based Webs running on IIS use accounts in the Windows 2000 Active Directory or Windows NT user account database for authenticating Web visitors as well.

> **on the web**   For information about changing Windows NT passwords over the Web, browse *http://search.microsoft.com/* and then search for Microsoft Knowledge Base article Q184619, "How to Change Windows NT Account Passwords Using Microsoft Internet Information Server (IIS) 4.0."

Resetting the MSDE Database Password

Click the Reset MSDE Database Password link in the Server Administration page to display the Reset MSDE Password page shown in Figure 38-11. For this page:

- If you're using MSDE, this page changes the password for your collaboration database.

● If you're using Microsoft SQL Server, you must use the SQL Server database administration tools to change the database password.

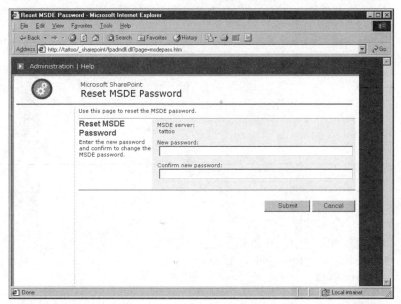

Figure 38-11. Use this Web page to change the password for the local MSDE database server.

> **note** If SQL Server was installed on your server before you installed SharePoint Team Services, or if you installed only the FrontPage Server Extensions, you might not see this option.

This page contains the following form fields:

● **New Password.** Type your new password.

● **Confirm New Password.** Type the new password again. The contents of this field and the previous one must be equal.

Administering Web Settings

Click the name of any virtual server listed in the Name column of the Server Administration page to display the Administration page shown in Figures 38-12, 38-13, and 38-14 on the next two pages. The Administration page controls settings that apply to the entire virtual server, as well as settings that apply to the root Web.

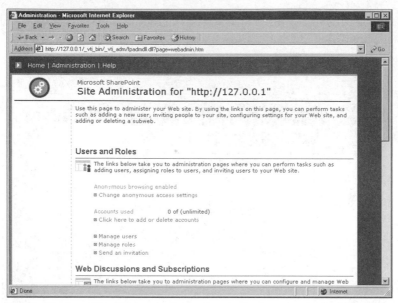

Figure 38-12. This Web page provides the highest level of administration for a virtual server or Web.

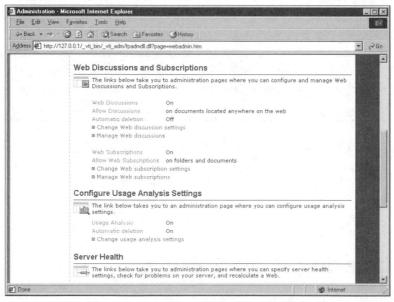

Figure 38-13. This is the middle portion of the Web page that begins in Figure 38-12.

You can also display the Administration page for subwebs. There are at least two ways to do this:

● Display the Administration page for the subweb's parent Web, scroll to the bottom, and click the subweb you want from the Subweb Name column.

> **note** Most computer operating systems (including Windows) can respond to more than
> one IP address, regardless of the number of network cards installed. Furthermore,
> most Web server software can associate a different HTTP root with each IP Address.
> This makes it possible for a single computer to host multiple Web sites, each with its
> own DNS name and IP address, without conflict. Each of these multiple sites is called
> a virtual server. For more information about virtual servers, refer to "Virtual Servers"
> on page 1038.

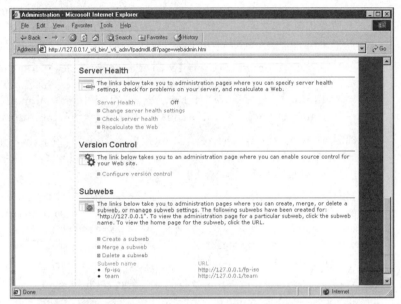

Figure 38-14. This Is the bottom portion of the Web page that begins in Figure 38-12.

- Use the FrontPage desktop software to open the subweb, choose Server
  from the Tools menu, and then choose Administration Home.

The Administration page for subwebs contains fewer options than the Administration
page for a virtual server and root Web. With regard to the following options:

- All options appear in the Administration Page for a root Web.

- All options appear in the Administration Page for subwebs unless excluded
  as follows:

  - Options marked (Root Only) are absent in the Administration Page
    for subwebs. Setting these options for the root Web applies them to
    the entire server.

  - Options marked (Unique Only) appear only in the Administration
    Page of subwebs that don't inherit permission from their parent
    Webs. However, these options always appear in the Administration
    Page for a root Web.

1103

Here are the possible options:

- **Users And Roles.** This group of options provides functions that manage user accounts pertaining to a virtual server:

  - **Change Anonymous Access Settings (Unique Only).** Click this link to display a Change Anonymous Access page that provides these choices:

    - **Anonymous Access Is.** Select On to permit anonymous access. This means that Web visitors access the virtual server without supplying a predefined username and password. Select Off to exclude non-authenticated visitors from the server. You can override this default for individual Webs.

    - **Assign Anonymous Users To The Following Role.** Choose the level of privilege that anonymous users will have. This can be Browser, Contributor, Author, Advanced Author, or Administrator. The default, and usually the only safe choice, is Browser.

  - **Click Here To Add Or Delete Accounts (Root Only).** Click this link to display a Manage Virtual Server Accounts page that adds or deletes user accounts for the current virtual server.

    This Web page pertains primarily to server-based Webs that don't use Microsoft Web servers. Such Webs have their own user account subsystem. On a Windows NT or Windows 2000 system, you can use this page only for creating local system accounts, and only if you have system-level privileges to do so.

  - **Manage Users (Unique Only).** Click this link to display a User Management page for adding users, removing users, or changing roles assigned to existing users. The section "Managing SharePoint Team Services Users" later in this chapter explains how to use this page.

  - **Manage Roles (Unique Only).** Click this link to display a Role Management page for modifying the list of roles you can assign to users. The section "Managing SharePoint Team Services Roles" later in this chapter explains how to use this page.

  - **Send An Invitation (Unique Only).** Click this link to run a wizard that gives team members access to a SharePoint team Web site and sends them e-mail. The e-mail describes the team Web site and invites them to participate. The same function is available on the Site Settings page described earlier in this chapter.

- **Web Discussions And Subscriptions (Root Only, SharePoint Team Services Only).** This group of options manages Web discussions and subscriptions:

  - **Change Web Discussion Settings.** Click this link to enable or disable Web discussions on the current server. The resulting page controls the

1104

same settings as the Web Document Discussions portion of the Set Installation Defaults page described earlier in this chapter.

- ▦ **Manage Web Discussions.** Click this link to display a list of Web discussions in progress and delete those which are no longer useful.

- ▦ **Change Web Subscription Settings.** Click this link to display a page that controls use of the Web Subscriptions feature. This page controls the same settings as the Web Subscriptions portion of the Set Installation Defaults page described earlier in this chapter.

- ▦ **Manage Web Subscriptions.** Click this link to display a list of Web subscriptions in progress and delete those which are no longer useful.

- ● **Configure Usage Analysis Settings (Root Only).** This section of the Administration page controls collection of usage data for a virtual server or Web:

  - ▦ **Change Usage Analysis Settings.** Click this link to display a page that controls the same settings as the Usage Analysis portion of the Set Installation Defaults page described earlier in this chapter.

- ● **Server Health.** The links below this heading run commands that check and, if required, correct common problems at the virtual server or Web level:

  - ▦ **Change Server Health Settings (Root Only).** Click this link to display a page that controls the same settings as the Server Health portion of the Set Installation Defaults page described earlier in this chapter.

  - ▦ **Check Server Health (Root Only).** Click this link to display a page that initiates any or all of six consistency checks on the current virtual server. The section "Checking Server Health" later in this chapter explains how to use this page.

  - ▦ **Recalculate The Web.** Click this link to display a page that initiates a Recalculate Hyperlinks operation on the current virtual server or Web. This performs exactly the same function as opening the Web and choosing Recalculate Hyperlinks from the Tools menu.

- ● **Version Control.** This section of the Administration page controls use of the Check-In/Checkout feature on the current Web:

  - ▦ **Configure Version Control.** Click this link to display a page that turns source code version control on or off for the current virtual server or Web. This performs exactly the same function as opening the Web in FrontPage, choosing Web Settings from the Tools menu, and then selecting or clearing the Use Document Check-In And Check-Out check box.

- **Subwebs.** This section of the Administration page creates and deletes subwebs:

  - **Create A Subweb.** Click this link to display a page that creates a new subweb on the current virtual server. The section "Creating A Subweb" later in this chapter explains how to use this page.

  - **Merge A Subweb.** Click this link to display a page that converts a subweb to an ordinary folder within its parent Web. This is equivalent to opening the parent Web in the FrontPage desktop software, right-clicking the subweb, and choosing Convert To Folder.

  - **Delete A Subweb.** Click this link to display a page that deletes a subweb and all its content from the server.

  - **Subweb Name.** Click the name of any listed subweb to display the administration page for that subweb.

  - **URL.** Click the URL of any listed subweb to display its home page.

In the FrontPage desktop software, you can choose Server from the Tools menu and then choose Permissions to display the Permissions Administration page shown in Figure 38-15. The links on this page work the same as the corresponding links in the Users And Roles area described earlier in this section.

Figure 38-15. This Web page controls user-level access to a FrontPage-based Web.

Managing Users

The User Management page shown in Figure 38-16 assigns roles (that is, sets of capabilities) to users of a Web. To display this page, click the Manage Users link on the Administration page shown in Figure 38-12. The page displays the following links:

● **Add A User.** Click this link to display the Configure Web User page shown in Figure 38-17 on the next page.

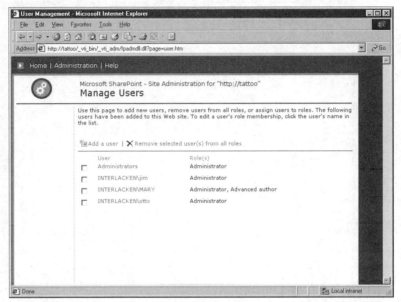

Figure 38-16. Use this page to grant, remove, and control user access to a Web.

● **Remove Selected User(s) From All Roles.** Click this link to remove all rights from one or more users. To designate the users this will affect, select their check boxes in the list of users that appears in the center of the page.

● **User.** Click the name of any user to display an Edit User Role Membership page that greatly resembles the Configure Web User page shown in Figure 38-17.

Here's the procedure for adding a new user:

1 Click the Add A User link on the User Management page. This displays the Configure Web User page shown in Figure 38-17.

2 To create a new user account and give it access to the current Web, select Add A New User With The Following Information and then supply the following data:

■ **User Name.** Enter the name that will identify the new account.

■ **Password.** Enter the password that will authenticate use of the new account.

■ **Confirm Password.** Type the new password again. The contents of this field and the previous one must be equal.

On server-based Webs that don't use a Microsoft Web server, this feature creates user accounts in each Web's local user account subsystem.

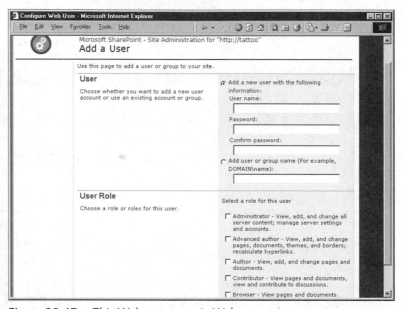

Figure 38-17. This Web page grants Web access to a new user.

On server-based Webs that run on IIS, this feature creates a local system account.

3 To provide an existing user account or group with access to the current Web, select Add User Or Group Name and type the account name (user or group) into the accompanying text box.

To specify a user or group in a Windows NT or Windows 2000 domain, prefix the account name with the domain name and a backslash.

4 In the area titled Select A Role For This User, select each role that applies to the user or group. As listed on the page, each role conveys a different set of privileges. If you assign multiple roles to the same person, that person can perform a given operation if any of those roles permits it.

5 Click the Add User button when finished.

Here's the procedure for changing the role assigned to an existing user:

1 Find the link for the user account you want to modify in the User Management page's User column, and then click it. This will display an Edit User

Role Membership page that greatly resembles the Configure Web User page shown in Figure 38-17. However, the User field won't be editable.

2 In the area titled Select A Role For This User, select or clear the check box for each role that applies to the user or group, and then click Submit.

Managing Roles

The Role Management page shown in Figure 38-18 maintains the list of roles (that is, collections of rights) you can assign to users of a Web. To display this page, click the Manage Roles link on the Administration page shown in Figure 38-12.

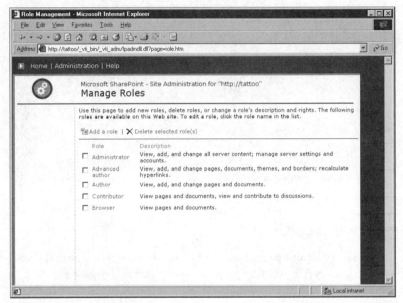

Figure 38-18. This Web page creates, modifies, and deletes roles for a FrontPage-based Web. Roles are groups of rights you can assign to individual users or groups.

The page displays the following links:

- **Add A Role.** Click this link to display the Add A New Role page shown in Figure 38-19 on the next page. Then configure the following options:

    - **Role Name.** Enter a name that will identify the new role.

    - **Description.** Enter a one-line description of the new role.

    - **Rights.** Select the check box that precedes each right that persons assigned to this role should have.

- **Delete Selected Roles.** Click this link to remove one or more roles from the current Web. To designate the roles this will affect, select the check boxes that precede their names in the Role column.

● **Role.** Click any role name in this column to modify the description list of rights assigned to that role. This displays an Edit Web Role page that resembles Figure 38-18 (except that the role name isn't editable).

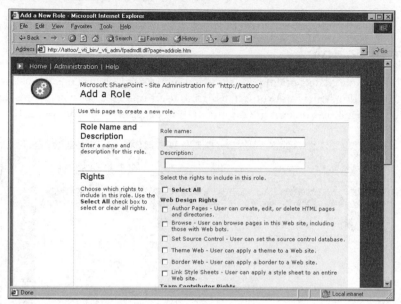

Figure 38-19. This Web page creates a new role and assigns it any combination of rights you select.

Checking Server Health

The Check Server Health page shown in Figure 38-20 controls several processes that help to keep your server running properly. To display this page, click the Server Health link on the Administration page shown in Figure 38-14.

The Server Health Check can detect and repair the current Web in any of these ways:

● **Synchronize Database (SharePoint Team Services Only).** Select the Repair check box to ensure that the information in the collaboration database matches the information in the SharePoint team Web site file system.

● **Reapply File Security Settings.** Select the Repair check box to update a Web's file security settings so they agree with policies in effect for that Web.

● **Verify Existence Of Webs.** Select the Detect check box, the Repair check box, or both to ensure that all subwebs are present. Detection means sending mail to report an error condition. Repair means taking the following actions:

  ■ If the parent Web contains the configuration for a subweb that isn't physically present, the Repair function deletes the configuration.

  ■ If the parent Web doesn't contain the configuration for a subweb, but the folder is physically present and configured internally as a

Web, the Repair function converts the partially configured subweb to an ordinary folder.

● **Check Roles Configuration.** Select the Detect check box, the Repair check box, or both to ensure that user role settings can be enforced.

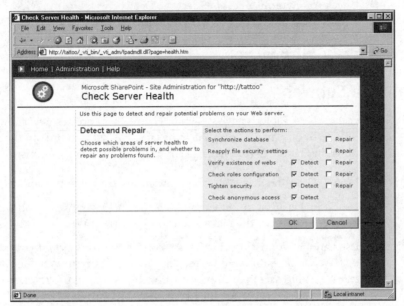

Figure 38-20. Use this Web page to detect and correct consistency errors within a Web.

Troubleshooting

Repair function converts subweb on remote storage to ordinary folder

If a subweb physically exists on a remote file server that's temporarily unavailable, the Server Health Check will report the folder as missing, the Repair function will delete the subweb configuration, and the subweb will appear as an ordinary folder when connectivity to the file server resumes. This leads to two pieces of advice:

● Don't use the Repair function to repair a subweb that's missing because of lost connectivity to another server. Doing so will cause the subweb to lose security settings and its identity as a subweb.

In other words, in the Check Server Health section, make sure the Repair check box for the Verify Existence Of Webs option is cleared if the server contains subwebs that are actually virtual directories physically residing on another server.

● If you've already used the Repair function, use the FrontPage desktop software to reestablish the folder as a subweb.

- **Tighten Security.** Select the Detect check box, the Repair check box, or both to ensure that all the necessary FrontPage Server Extensions and SharePoint team Web site files and directories are present, and that only users with the proper permissions have access to them.

- **Check Anonymous Access.** Select the Detect check box to review the anonymous user access rights for the FrontPage-based Web or SharePoint team Web site, and for all subwebs to ensure that anonymous users don't have the right to modify any content.

Creating a Subweb

The Create A New Subweb page shown in Figure 38-21 creates new subwebs within the current Web. To display this page, click the Create A Subweb link on the Administration page shown in Figure 38-14. The page controls the following options:

- **Name.** Enter the new Web's folder location, relative to the current Web.

- **Use Same Permissions As Parent Web.** Select this option if you want the new Web to inherit the permissions of the current Web.

- **Use Unique Permissions For This Web.** Select this option if you want the new Web to have different permissions than the current Web. Be sure to enter an existing user account name (probably yours) in the Administrator box so that someone can open the new subweb and fully configure its security.

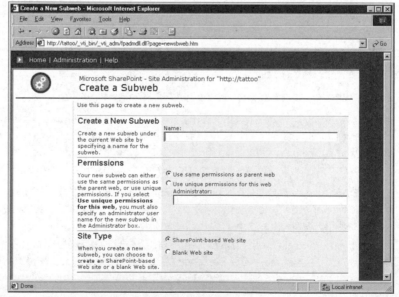

Figure 38-21. By using this Web page, you can create a new FrontPage-based Web without launching the FrontPage desktop software.

- **SharePoint-Based Web Site.** Select this option to create a SharePoint team Web site. This produces the same results as using the FrontPage desktop software to create a new Web using the SharePoint-based Team Web Site template.

- **Blank Web Site.** Select this option to create a subweb that contains no initial content. This produces the same results as using the FrontPage desktop software to create a new Web using the Empty Web template.

Administering Virtual Server Settings

Click the Administration link for any virtual server listed on the Server Administration page (Figure 38-3) to display the Virtual Server Administration page shown in Figure 38-22. This page provides the following links:

- **Uninstall SharePoint Team Services.** Click this link to display a page that removes SharePoint Team Services (and therefore the FrontPage Server Extensions) from the current virtual server.

- **Upgrade Virtual Server With SharePoint.** Click this link to display a page that upgrades the SharePoint Team Services software on the current virtual server.

> **note** When you install a new release of the FrontPage Server Extensions or SharePoint Team Services on a Web server, all existing virtual servers continue to use the old version until you upgrade them. This decreases the risk and impact of installing a new release.

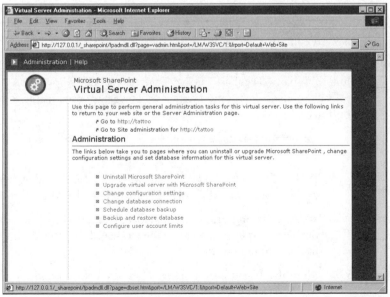

Figure 38-22. Use this Web page to form the listed tasks for a virtual server.

Chapter 38

●   **Change Configuration Settings.** Click this link to display a General Settings page that controls authoring, mail settings, performance tuning, client scripting, and security settings. The section "Changing Configuration Settings" later in this chapter explains how to use this page.

●   **Change Database Connection (SharePoint Team Services Only).** Click this link to display a Database Connection Settings page that specifies the database server, database name, and other settings related to the current virtual server's collaboration database. This page contains the following options:

■   **Database Server Name.** Specify the name of the computer where the database management system software is running. The DBMS must be Microsoft SQL Server or its subset, MSDE.

■   **Database Name.** Specify the name of the database, as known to SQL Server or MSDE.

■   **Database Administrator User Name.** Enter the user name SharePoint Team Services should use for accessing SQL Server or a copy of MSDE running on another computer.

■   **Database Administrator Password.** Enter the password SharePoint Team Services should use for accessing SQL Server or MSDE.

■   **Use Local MSDE Database Server.** Select this check box if SharePoint Team Services should use a copy of MSDE running on the local computer. No administrator user name or password is required if this option is in effect.

This option is most likely to be useful after backing up an existing database and restoring it on another database server. Specifying a nonexistent or incorrectly structured database will severely harm or completely break a SharePoint team Web site.

●   **Schedule Database Backup (SharePoint Team Services Only).** Click this link to display a Database Backup page that specifies how often and when to back up the collaboration database. This page contains the following options:

■   **Automatic Database Backups Are.** Click On to schedule automatic database backups and Off to decline them.

■   **Daily.** If you want to take database backups once a day, select this option and specify the time of day when the backup should occur.

■   **Weekly.** If you want to take database backups once a week, select this option and specify the day of the week and the time of day when the backup should occur.

■   **Monthly.** If you want to take database backups once a month, select this option and specify the day of the month and the time of day when the backup should occur.

1114

- **Backup And Restore Database (SharePoint Team Services Only).** Click this link to display a Database Backup Restore Operation page that immediately runs a database backup or restore. This page contains two form fields and two buttons:

    - **Backup Path And Filename.** Specify the full path and file name where you want the database backup file to reside.

    - **Backup.** Click this button to initiate the database backup.

    - **Restore Path And Filename.** Specify the full path and file name where an existing database backup file resides.

    - **Restore.** Click this button to initiate the database restoration.

- **Configure User Account Limits.** Click this link to display a User Account Limits page that limits the number of user accounts on the local server. This page contains the following options:

    - **Maximum Number Of User Accounts.** Enter the largest number of user accounts you want the server to accommodate. After the server reaches this limit, it won't create additional accounts unless you delete some accounts or raise the limit.

    - **Unlimited Number Of User Accounts.** Select this check box if you want no limit on the number of user accounts.

Changing Configuration Settings

The General Settings page shown in Figures 38-23 and 38-24 on the next page configures a number of miscellaneous settings for the current virtual server. To display this page, click the Change Configurations Settings link on the Virtual Server Administration page shown in Figure 38-22. The page displays the following form fields:

- **Enable Authoring.** Select this check box to permit FrontPage and other programs that update files through SharePoint Team Services to change the current Web. Clear the check box to secure the Web from changes.

- **Mail Settings.** This group of settings controls how the FrontPage Server Extensions send mail:

    - **SMTP Mail Server.** Specify the network name of the SMTP mail server to use for sending mail.

    - **From Address.** Specify the e-mail address that will, unless overridden, appear as the sender of all mail.

    - **Reply-To Address.** Specify the destination e-mail address that will, unless overridden, receive to any replies to mail that the virtual server sends. (When someone receives mail from the virtual server and clicks the Reply button in his or her e-mail program, the address you specify here will, unless overridden, appear in the To field.)

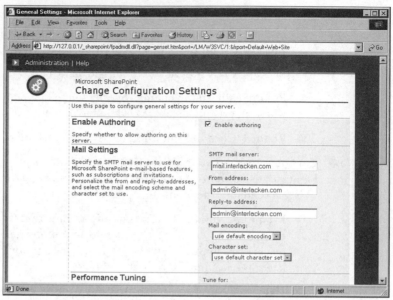

Figure 38-23. This Web page controls a variety of virtual server settings that don't fit anywhere else.

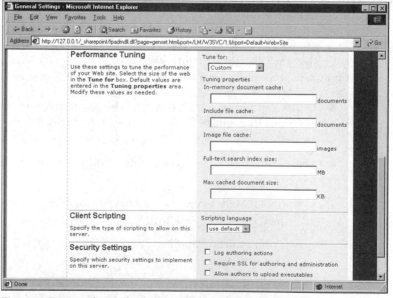

Figure 38-24. This is the bottom half of the Web page that begins in Figure 38-23.

- **Mail Encoding.** Specify the mail-encoding scheme to use for messages. The default is 8-bit encoding, which is very common. However, if your Web visitors require some other encoding scheme, you can specify it here.

- **Character Set.** Specify the set of characters used in e-mail messages. Each character set corresponds to the alphabet of a particular language.

● **Performance Tuning.** This group of settings optimizes the performance of the Web server. Unless your server is very heavily loaded, you probably don't need to worry about these settings:

- **Tune For.** Select one of the listed performance modes, depending on average daily volumes. This will enter default values in the next four settings.

- **In-Memory Document Cache.** Specify the number of documents whose property information, such as link maps and Web parameters, the FrontPage Server Extensions will keep in memory. If the setting is 4096, for example, the FrontPage Server Extensions will keep property information in memory for the 4,096 most recently accessed documents.

- **Include File Cache.** Specify the number of documents that the FrontPage Server Extensions will keep in memory for inclusion in other files. There might be header, footer, and copyright files widely included in a site's regular Web pages.

- **Image File Cache.** Specify the number of images (such as graphic files and photos) that the FrontPage Server Extensions will keep in memory for rapid delivery to visitors.

- **Full-Text Search Index Size.** Specify the maximum size of a FrontPage full-text search index. If this isn't sufficient to index all files in a Web, some files won't be indexed. However, this setting doesn't affect text indexes used by Microsoft Indexing Service.

- **Max Cached Document Size.** Specify the maximum size of a document that the FrontPage Server Extensions should store in memory. This applies to any files that might be stored in a cache.

● **Client Scripting.** This setting selects the language FrontPage will use when creating scripts that run on the browser:

- **Scripting Language.** Select the scripting language FrontPage will use when creating scripts that will run on the browser.

You can also modify this setting in the FrontPage desktop software. Choose Web Settings from the Tools menu, and then click the Advanced tab. Next, in the Default Scripting Language section, select a language option from the Client drop-down list.

- **Security Settings.** These settings control certain security settings that pertain to Web designers:

    - **Log Authoring Actions.** Select this check box to record information about addition, change, and deletion of Web content. A log of changes appears in a file named *author.log* that's located in the root Web's *_vti_log* folder.

    - **Require SSL For Authoring And Administration.** Select this check box if you want all designers to use SSL security when modifying Webs.

    - **Allow Authors To Upload Executables.** Select this check box if Web designers can upload files to executable folders. Clear the check box to stop designers from uploading files to executable folders, even if the files themselves aren't an executable type.

In Summary...

This chapter explained the functions of SharePoint Team Services and the FrontPage Server Extensions, how to install them, and how to administer them. Insofar as possible, all such administration now occurs through Web pages.

FrontPage is a remarkably full-featured program, yet it's simple to use. It provides total flexibility to create whatever kind of Web page your mind (and the state of the art) can conceive, all the while neatly automating the dreary tasks of coding HTML and managing Webs. This book is intended to help you get the most out of your software, your imagination, and all your creative pursuits. Good luck with your site.

Index to Troubleshooting Topics

Index to Troubleshooting Topics

T

W

Index

Page numbers with the prefix BC refer to bonus chapters available on the Companion CD. To find the pages beginning with BC listed in this index, choose the pdf format of the Bonus Content located on the Inside Out CD.

About the Author

Jim Buyens has been professionally involved with the World Wide Web since its inception, including roles as a server administrator, Web master, content developer, and system architect. He's currently developing Web-based business systems for AG Communications Systems, a provider of advanced telecommunications equipment.

Jim received a Bachelor of Science degree in Computer Science from Purdue University in 1971 and a Master of Business Administration from Arizona State University in 1992. When not enhancing the Web or writing books, he enjoys traveling and attending professional sports events—especially NHL hockey. He resides with his family in Phoenix.

Other books by Jim Buyens include:

- *Web Database Development Step by Step*, June 2000, Microsoft Press
- *Running Microsoft FrontPage 2000*, June 1999, Microsoft Press
- *Stupid Web Tricks*, July 1998, Microsoft Press
- *Running Microsoft FrontPage 98*, October 1997, Microsoft Press
- *Building Net Sites with Windows NT—An Internet Services Handbook*, July 1996, Addison-Wesley Developers Press

Contacting the Author

Hearing from happy readers is always a welcome and pleasant experience, and hearing from the less-than-satisfied is important as well. Please note that I can respond only if you write in English. My e-mail address is

buyensj@interlacken.com

I'm most interested in your impressions of this book: what you liked or disliked about it, what questions it did or didn't answer, what you found superfluous and what you'd like to see added in the next edition. I'll post errors, omissions, corrections, and frequently-asked questions on my Web site at

http://www.interlacken.com/fp2002/

I can accept enhancement requests only for this book, and *not* for the Microsoft software. To suggest product enhancements, send e-mail to:

mswish@microsoft.com

or browse the Web page at

http://register.microsoft.com/regsys/custom/wishwizard.asp

Please understand that I'm just one person and I can't provide technical support or debugging assistance, even for readers. Please try other channels, including the Microsoft Search page at

http://search.microsoft.com/

If you're getting an error message or error number, try searching for that exact phrase or number. If this produces too many hits, try searching within the results for the word *FrontPage*. If you're having trouble with a specific feature or component, try searching for the name of the component and again, if that produces too many hits, searching for *FrontPage* within those results.

If all else fails, please write. While I can't promise to answer each message, I'll try to provide at least a useful suggestion. Even when I can't answer your e-mail messages directly, I find it instructive to learn what problems users like you are experiencing—and therefore how I can make this and future books more useful to everyone.

The manuscript for this book was prepared and galleyed using Microsoft Word 2000. Pages were composed by Online Training Solutions, Inc. (OTSI) using Adobe PageMaker 6.52 for Windows, with text in Minion and display type in Syntax. Composed pages were delivered to the printer as electronic prepress files.

coverdesigner
GIRVIN/Strategic Branding & Design

interiorgraphicdesigner
James D. Kramer

coverillustration
Daman Studio

OTSIteam
Jan Bednarczuk
R.J. Cadranell
Liz Clark
Joyce Cox
Nancy Depper
Michelle Kenoyer
Gabrielle Nonast
Joan Preppernau
Martin Stillion

contactOTSIat
E-mail: joanp@otsiweb.com
Web site: *www.otsiweb.com*

Work smarter
as you experience
Office XP
inside out!

You know your way around the Office suite. Now dig into Microsoft Office XP applications and *really* put your PC to work! These supremely organized references pack hundreds of timesaving solutions, trouble-shooting tips and tricks, and handy workarounds in concise, fast-answer format. All of this comprehensive information goes deep into the nooks and crannies of each Office application and accessory. Discover the best and fastest ways to perform everyday tasks, and challenge yourself to new levels of Office mastery with INSIDE OUT titles!

- **MICROSOFT® OFFICE XP INSIDE OUT**
- **MICROSOFT WORD VERSION 2002 INSIDE OUT**
- **MICROSOFT EXCEL VERSION 2002 INSIDE OUT**
- **MICROSOFT OUTLOOK® VERSION 2002 INSIDE OUT**
- **MICROSOFT ACCESS VERSION 2002 INSIDE OUT**
- **MICROSOFT FRONTPAGE® VERSION 2002 INSIDE OUT**
- **MICROSOFT VISIO® VERSION 2002 INSIDE OUT**

Microsoft®

mspress.microsoft.com

Get a **Free**
*e-mail newsletter, updates,
special offers, links to related books,
and more when you*

register on line!

Register your Microsoft Press® title on our Web site and you'll get a FREE subscription to our e-mail newsletter, *Microsoft Press Book Connections.* You'll find out about newly released and upcoming books and learning tools, online events, software downloads, special offers and coupons for Microsoft Press customers, and information about major Microsoft® product releases. You can also read useful additional information about all the titles we publish, such as detailed book descriptions, tables of contents and indexes, sample chapters, links to related books and book series, author biographies, and reviews by other customers.

Registration is easy. Just visit this Web page and fill in your information:

http://mspress.microsoft.com/register

Microsoft®

Proof of Purchase

Use this page as proof of purchase if participating in a promotion or rebate offer on this title. Proof of purchase must be used in conjunction with other proof(s) of payment such as your dated sales receipt—see offer details.

Microsoft® FrontPage® Version 2002 Inside Out
0-7356-1284-6

CUSTOMER NAME

Microsoft Press, PO Box 97017, Redmond, WA 98073-9830

MICROSOFT LICENSE AGREEMENT

(Book Companion CD)

IMPORTANT-READ CAREFULLY: This Microsoft End-User License Agreement ("EULA") is a legal agreement between you (either an individual or an entity) and Microsoft Corporation for the Microsoft product identified above, which includes computer software and may include associated media, printed materials, and "on-line" or electronic documentation ("SOFT-WARE PRODUCT"). Any component included within the SOFTWARE PRODUCT that is accompanied by a separate End-User License Agreement shall be governed by such agreement and not the terms set forth below. By installing, copying, or otherwise using the SOFTWARE PRODUCT, you agree to be bound by the terms of this EULA. If you do not agree to the terms of this EULA, you are not authorized to install, copy, or otherwise use the SOFTWARE PRODUCT; you may, however, return the SOFTWARE PRODUCT, along with all printed materials and other items that form a part of the Microsoft product that includes the SOFTWARE PRODUCT, to the place you obtained them for a full refund. Microsoft makes no warranties or representations, offers no support services or help, and you assume sole responsibility regarding installation and use of third-party licensed software on the accompanying CD.

SOFTWARE PRODUCT LICENSE

The SOFTWARE PRODUCT is protected by United States copyright laws and international copyright treaties, as well as other intellectual property laws and treaties. The SOFTWARE PRODUCT is licensed, not sold.

1. GRANT OF LICENSE. This EULA grants you the following rights:

a. Software Product. You may install and use one copy of the SOFTWARE PRODUCT on a single computer. The primary user of the computer on which the SOFTWARE PRODUCT is installed may make a second copy for his or her exclusive use on a portable computer.

b. Storage/Network Use. You may also store or install a copy of the SOFTWARE PRODUCT on a storage device, such as a network server, used only to install or run the SOFTWARE PRODUCT on your other computers over an internal network; however, you must acquire and dedicate a license for each separate computer on which the SOFTWARE PRODUCT is installed or run from the storage device. A license for the SOFTWARE PRODUCT may not be shared or used concurrently on different computers.

c. License Pak. If you have acquired this EULA in a Microsoft License Pak, you may make the number of additional copies of the computer software portion of the SOFTWARE PRODUCT authorized on the printed copy of this EULA, and you may use each copy in the manner specified above. You are also entitled to make a corresponding number of secondary copies for portable computer use as specified above.

d. Sample Code. Solely with respect to portions, if any, of the SOFTWARE PRODUCT that are identified within the SOFTWARE PRODUCT as sample code (the "SAMPLE CODE"):

i. Use and Modification. Microsoft grants you the right to use and modify the source code version of the SAMPLE CODE, provided you comply with subsection (d)(iii) below. You may not distribute the SAMPLE CODE, or any modified version of the SAMPLE CODE, in source code form.

ii. Redistributable Files. Provided you comply with subsection (d)(iii) below, Microsoft grants you a nonexclusive, royalty-free right to reproduce and distribute the object code version of the SAMPLE CODE and of any modified SAMPLE CODE, other than SAMPLE CODE (or any modified version thereof) designated as not redistributable in the Readme file that forms a part of the SOFTWARE PRODUCT (the "Non-Redistributable Sample Code"). All SAMPLE CODE other than the Non-Redistributable Sample Code is collectively referred to as the "REDISTRIBUTABLES."

iii. Redistribution Requirements. If you redistribute the REDISTRIBUTABLES, you agree to: (i) distribute the REDISTRIBUTABLES in object code form only in conjunction with and as a part of your software application product; (ii) not use Microsoft's name, logo, or trademarks to market your software application product; (iii) include a valid copyright notice on your software application product; (iv) indemnify, hold harmless, and defend Microsoft from and against any claims or lawsuits, including attorney's fees, that arise or result from the use or distribution of your software application product; and (v) not permit further distribution of the REDISTRIBUTABLES by your end user. Contact Microsoft for the applicable royalties due and other licensing terms for all other uses and/or distribution of the REDISTRIBUTABLES.

2. DESCRIPTION OF OTHER RIGHTS AND LIMITATIONS.

- **Limitations on Reverse Engineering, Decompilation, and Disassembly.** You may not reverse engineer, decompile, or disassemble the SOFTWARE PRODUCT, except and only to the extent that such activity is expressly permitted by applicable law notwithstanding this limitation.

- **Separation of Components.** The SOFTWARE PRODUCT is licensed as a single product. Its component parts may not be separated for use on more than one computer.

- **Rental.** You may not rent, lease, or lend the SOFTWARE PRODUCT.

- **Support Services.** Microsoft may, but is not obligated to, provide you with support services related to the SOFTWARE PRODUCT ("Support Services"). Use of Support Services is governed by the Microsoft policies and programs described in the user manual, in "on-line" documentation, and/or in other Microsoft-provided materials. Any supplemental software code provided to you as part of the Support Services shall be considered part of the SOFTWARE PRODUCT and subject to the terms and conditions of this EULA. With respect to technical information you provide to Microsoft as part of the Support Services, Microsoft may use such information for its business purposes, including for product support and development. Microsoft will not utilize such technical information in a form that personally identifies you.

- **Software Transfer.** You may permanently transfer all of your rights under this EULA, provided you retain no copies, you transfer all of the SOFTWARE PRODUCT (including all component parts, the media and printed materials, any upgrades, this EULA, and, if applicable, the Certificate of Authenticity), and the recipient agrees to the terms of this EULA.

- **Termination.** Without prejudice to any other rights, Microsoft may terminate this EULA if you fail to comply with the terms and conditions of this EULA. In such event, you must destroy all copies of the SOFTWARE PRODUCT and all of its component parts.

3. **COPYRIGHT.** All title and copyrights in and to the SOFTWARE PRODUCT (including but not limited to any images, photographs, animations, video, audio, music, text, SAMPLE CODE, REDISTRIBUTABLES, and "applets" incorporated into the SOFTWARE PRODUCT) and any copies of the SOFTWARE PRODUCT are owned by Microsoft or its suppliers. The SOFTWARE PRODUCT is protected by copyright laws and international treaty provisions. Therefore, you must treat the SOFTWARE PRODUCT like any other copyrighted material except that you may install the SOFTWARE PRODUCT on a single computer provided you keep the original solely for backup or archival purposes. You may not copy the printed materials accompanying the SOFTWARE PRODUCT.

4. **U.S. GOVERNMENT RESTRICTED RIGHTS.** The SOFTWARE PRODUCT and documentation are provided with RESTRICTED RIGHTS. Use, duplication, or disclosure by the Government is subject to restrictions as set forth in subparagraph (c)(1)(ii) of the Rights in Technical Data and Computer Software clause at DFARS 252.227-7013 or subparagraphs (c)(1) and (2) of the Commercial Computer Software-Restricted Rights at 48 CFR 52.227-19, as applicable. Manufacturer is Microsoft Corporation/One Microsoft Way/Redmond, WA 98052-6399.

5. **EXPORT RESTRICTIONS.** You agree that you will not export or re-export the SOFTWARE PRODUCT, any part thereof, or any process or service that is the direct product of the SOFTWARE PRODUCT (the foregoing collectively referred to as the "Restricted Components"), to any country, person, entity, or end user subject to U.S. export restrictions. You specifically agree not to export or re-export any of the Restricted Components (i) to any country to which the U.S. has embargoed or restricted the export of goods or services, which currently include, but are not necessarily limited to, Cuba, Iran, Iraq, Libya, North Korea, Sudan, and Syria, or to any national of any such country, wherever located, who intends to transmit or transport the Restricted Components back to such country; (ii) to any end user who you know or have reason to know will utilize the Restricted Components in the design, development, or production of nuclear, chemical, or biological weapons; or (iii) to any end user who has been prohibited from participating in U.S. export transactions by any federal agency of the U.S. government. You warrant and represent that neither the BXA nor any other U.S. federal agency has suspended, revoked, or denied your export privileges.

DISCLAIMER OF WARRANTY

NO WARRANTIES OR CONDITIONS. MICROSOFT EXPRESSLY DISCLAIMS ANY WARRANTY OR CONDITION FOR THE SOFTWARE PRODUCT. THE SOFTWARE PRODUCT AND ANY RELATED DOCUMENTATION IS PROVIDED "AS IS" WITHOUT WARRANTY OR CONDITION OF ANY KIND, EITHER EXPRESS OR IMPLIED, INCLUDING, WITHOUT LIMITATION, THE IMPLIED WARRANTIES OF MERCHANTABILITY, FITNESS FOR A PARTICULAR PURPOSE, OR NONINFRINGEMENT. THE ENTIRE RISK ARISING OUT OF USE OR PERFORMANCE OF THE SOFTWARE PRODUCT REMAINS WITH YOU.

LIMITATION OF LIABILITY. TO THE MAXIMUM EXTENT PERMITTED BY APPLICABLE LAW, IN NO EVENT SHALL MICROSOFT OR ITS SUPPLIERS BE LIABLE FOR ANY SPECIAL, INCIDENTAL, INDIRECT, OR CONSEQUENTIAL DAMAGES WHATSOEVER (INCLUDING, WITHOUT LIMITATION, DAMAGES FOR LOSS OF BUSINESS PROFITS, BUSINESS INTERRUPTION, LOSS OF BUSINESS INFORMATION, OR ANY OTHER PECUNIARY LOSS) ARISING OUT OF THE USE OF OR INABILITY TO USE THE SOFTWARE PRODUCT OR THE PROVISION OF OR FAILURE TO PROVIDE SUPPORT SERVICES, EVEN IF MICROSOFT HAS BEEN ADVISED OF THE POSSIBILITY OF SUCH DAMAGES. IN ANY CASE, MICROSOFT'S ENTIRE LIABILITY UNDER ANY PROVISION OF THIS EULA SHALL BE LIMITED TO THE GREATER OF THE AMOUNT ACTUALLY PAID BY YOU FOR THE SOFTWARE PRODUCT OR US$5.00; PROVIDED, HOWEVER, IF YOU HAVE ENTERED INTO A MICROSOFT SUPPORT SERVICES AGREEMENT, MICROSOFT'S ENTIRE LIABILITY REGARDING SUPPORT SERVICES SHALL BE GOVERNED BY THE TERMS OF THAT AGREEMENT. BECAUSE SOME STATES AND JURISDICTIONS DO NOT ALLOW THE EXCLUSION OR LIMITATION OF LIABILITY, THE ABOVE LIMITATION MAY NOT APPLY TO YOU.

MISCELLANEOUS

This EULA is governed by the laws of the State of Washington USA, except and only to the extent that applicable law mandates governing law of a different jurisdiction.

Should you have any questions concerning this EULA, or if you desire to contact Microsoft for any reason, please contact the Microsoft subsidiary serving your country, or write: Microsoft Sales Information Center/One Microsoft Way/ Redmond, WA 98052-6399.

PN 097-0002296